KU-220-692

Contents

Acknowledgements

O
ur aim in this project has been to develop a text that introduces students to the rich and diverse nature of critical criminology, as well as engage them with thought-provoking research that links academic analysis to criminal justice policy and practice. One of our intentions is for students to see the value of sociological and criminological writing and to get a sense that a social critique also offers practical alternatives to injustice. In our quest to do this, we are indebted to the authors in this book for their insightful contributions, their inspiring research and knowledge and their devotion to their disciplines and to social justice work.

We wish to thank many people for their direct encouragement and assistance with this book. We have benefited tremendously from the diverse and thought-inspiring faculty, sessionals, and other colleagues at or affiliated with the University of Saskatchewan. We have been influenced and inspired by their insights, research, and many conversations. We are also indebted to the hundreds of students who are impassioned by a search for justice, who have shared themselves with us in the classroom, and whose wisdom and enthusiasm are part of this book. We also wish to acknowledge and thank all those who used our first edition in their classrooms and to those who made invaluable comments towards this new edition.

Thank you to Joanne Butler, Keely Kinar, and Harpreet Aulakh, who assisted in the development of the first edition of the book, and to Glenn Andre and Marg Gauley for their professional work on this new edition. Also, thanks Katie and Marilyn Jutras for their photographic work of the cover art, Rob Carey for his assistance in selecting the cover art, and especially to the artist, Crystal Kishayinew, for her powerful rendering which heartens our work. We gratefully acknowledge SCYAP (Saskatoon Community Youth Arts Programming) dedicated to arts-skill acquisition for at risk youth and community revitalization—who worked with the artists who produced the front covers for both editions of this book—Chris Moffat and Crystal Kishayinew. Our gratitude to the University of Saskatchewan, Office of Research Services Publication Fund, and to the skills and dedication of the staff in the Department of Sociology, University of Saskatchewan.

We are deeply indebted to everyone at Fernwood Publishing for their work and support for the initial edition, for their tireless efforts in working with us on improving our collection, and more generally, for their commitment to providing a Canadian publishing context in which social justice is paramount. We thank Wayne Antony, in particular, for his thorough editing, for his skills as a sociologist, and his creative mindfulness, and to Errol Sharpe for his vision and dedication. Special thanks to Tim Dunn for his copy edit of the manuscript, to Beverley Rach for coordinating production, to Debbie Mathers for typing the final manuscript, and to Brenda Conroy for design and layout as well as proofreading the final book pages.

Lastly, we thank our friends and families for providing the context in which we feel both inspired and fulfiled, especially: to *Rob, Ben and Andrew* — from Carolyn; to *Wendy, Nathan and Matthew* — from Bernard.

Finally we thank each other for a continuing productive, memorable, and important collaboration.

Contributors

Shahid Alvi

Shahid Alvi is a professor of criminology in the Faculty of Criminology, Justice, and Policy Studies, University of Ontario Institute of Technology, Oshawa, Ontario, where he teaches criminology, youth crime, research methods, and introductory sociology. He is the author or co-author of numerous journal articles, and four books including the recently released *Deviance and Crime*. He is currently researching violence against immigrant women, crime and social exclusion, inner-city crime, and homelessness.

Sandra Bell

Sandra Bell is an associate professor in the Department of Sociology and Criminology at Saint Mary's University, Halifax. She is the author of *Young Offenders and Juvenile Justice*. She teaches graduate and undergraduate courses in youth crime and justice, and her current research interests are in the area of youth justice reform in Canada and Scotland and girls and women in the justice system.

Helen Boritch

Helen Boritch is an associate professor of sociology at the University of Alberta. Her research interests focus on women and crime and Canadian criminal justice history. She is the author of *Fallen Women: Female Crime and Criminal Justice in Canada*.

Carolyn Brooks

Carolyn Brooks is an instructor of sociology and researcher at the University of Saskatchewan. She is the co-editor of the first edition of *Marginality and Condemnation*. Her publications and research focus on globalization and punishment, theoretical criminology, intimate partner violence, photovoice methods, and Indigenous peoples' health.

Vanessa Chopyk

Vanessa Chopyk is an analyst with the Royal Canadian Mounted Police. She completed her M.A. in sociology at the University of Manitoba. Her thesis research focused on the issue of gender differentials in sentencing for violent crime.

Elizabeth Comack

Elizabeth Comack is a professor of sociology at the University of Manitoba, where she teaches the sociology of law and feminist criminology. Her publications include *Locating Law* (as editor), *Criminalizing Women* (co-edited with Gillian Balfour), *The Power to Criminalize* (with Gillian Balfour), and *Women in Trouble*.

Helen Cote

Helen Cote is a member of the Anisinābē people and of the Cote First Nation. She has completed an MA in sociology at the University of Saskatchewan and is the director of her reserve's youth centre. She is being encouraged to run for the position of chief.

Willem de Lint

Willem de Lint is associate professor of criminology and head of the Department of Sociology and Anthropology at the University of Windsor. He teaches security and regulation, crime and exclusion, policing, and social exclusion and the state. His recent work and publications are in public-order policing, border security, and post-9/11 policing and security models.

Lauren Eisler

Lauren Eisler is an assistant professor and program coordinator for the criminology program at Wilfrid Laurier University. Her work focuses on the relationship between institutional control of disadvantaged youth and the public construction of youth culture as criminogenic.

Karlene Faith

Karlene Faith is professor emerita in criminology at Simon Fraser University in British Columbia. She is also a community activist and prisoners' rights advocate. Her publications include: *Unruly Women*; *The Long Prison Journey of Leslie Van Houten*; and *13 Women: Parables from Prison*.

Kearney Healy

Kearney Healy, a lawyer, works for the Saskatchewan Legal Aid Commission, Saskatoon Office. For several years his work has focused mainly on young people. As a volunteer, he has helped build a forty-eight-townhouse housing co-op, enabled people to obtain telephone service, and drafted a proposed law that would allow children sexually abused by pimps and johns to sue them (with the guidance of the young women involved in the cases, street outreach workers, and several professors of law).

Carl E. James

Carl E. James teaches in the Faculty of Education and in the graduate program in sociology at York University, Toronto. His research interests include identification and racialization in Canada's multicultural context; educational and occupational access and equity; and the nature of sports in the educational outcomes of minority students. His publications include: *Race in Play*; *Possibilities and Limitations*; and *Seeing Ourselves*.

Yasmin Jiwani

Yasmin Jiwani is associate professor in the Department of Communication Studies, Concordia University, Montreal. She previously worked at the FREDA Centre for Research on Violence Against Women in Vancouver, where she was critically engaged in research and advocacy focusing on the intersecting influences of race, class, and gender. She is the author of *Discourses of Denial* and editor of *Girlhood*.

Patricia Monture

Patricia Monture is a citizen of the Mohawk Nation, Grand River Territory (near Brantford, Ontario). She is a mother, sister, and auntie. Trisha was educated as a lawyer in Ontario and has taught in Canadian law schools. She teaches in the Department of Sociology at the University of Saskatchewan, in the Aboriginal Justice and Criminology Program. Professor Monture has published several books and numerous journal articles. Her interests include the advancement of Aboriginal justice at the community level, federal corrections, the rights of Aboriginal women, constitutional issues, and issues of theory and philosophy.

Donald Morin

Donald Morin is a law student at the University of Saskatchewan. He has served time in both federal penitentiaries and provincial jails.

Janet Mosher

Janet Mosher is an associate professor at Osgoode Hall Law School, York University, and a former director of Osgoode's Intensive Program in Poverty Law at Parkdale Community Legal Services. She is a co-author of *Walking on Eggshells* and co-editor of *Disorderly People*.

Christian Pasiak

Christian Pasiak is currently completing his MA at the University of Windsor. His research explores private and public partnerships used to regulate cyber-security and access control in New Zealand. He is also interested in how discourses of "security" and "trust" are constructed for the "virtual" realm.

Les Samuelson

Les Samuelson is an associate professor, Sociology Department, University of Saskatchewan, Saskatoon. His primary subject is criminology, with areas of concentration including Aboriginal peoples and justice, criminal justice policy and administration, and comparative research on Aboriginal peoples and policing/corrections in Canada, Australia, and New Zealand. His fourth edition, with Wayne Antony (eds.), of *Power and Resistance* was released in April 2007.

Bernard Schissel

Bernard Schissel is a professor of sociology at the University of Saskatchewan. In general, his research focuses on the marginal position that children and youth occupy in western democracies and how such institutions as law, education, medicine, the political economy, and the military exploit children and youth in subtle, politically acceptable, and publicly endorsed ways. His current books are *Still Blaming Children* and *The Legacy of School for Aboriginal People*.

Wendy Schissel

Wendy Schissel is the dean of humanities and distance learning at Mt. Hood Community College in Gresham, Oregon, and an adjunct professor in the College of Graduate Studies and Research at the University of Saskatchewan. She holds an interdisciplinary doctorate in Canadian poetry and painting, and her research interests are in the areas of Canadian literature, gender studies, and the study of children and youth. She is editor of the book *Home/Bodies*.

Laureen Snider

Laureen Snider is a professor of sociology at Queen's University, Kingston, Ontario. She has studied corporations for twenty-five years and written extensively on corporate crime, law, and punishment. Her recent work has centred on the deregulation and decriminalization of laws prohibiting corporate crime, the removal of sanctions, and the disappearance of enforcement officials. Her books include *Bad Business* and *Corporate Crime* (co-edited with Frank Pearce).

Rob White

Rob White is professor of sociology at the University of Tasmania. He has published extensively in the areas of juvenile justice, youth studies, and criminology. Among his recent publications are *Youth & Society* (with Johanna Wyn), *Juvenile Justice* (with Chris Cunneen), *Crime & Society* (with Daphne Habibis), *Australian Youth Subcultures*, and *Controversies in Environmental Sociology*.

Linda Wood

Linda Wood is a PhD candidate in the Department of Community Health Sciences, University of Manitoba. Her PhD dissertation explores the structural and behavioural dimensions of a healthy lifestyle. Her master's thesis research examined the impact of Winnipeg's zero-tolerance policy on the criminal justice response to domestic violence. She teaches research methods in the Department of Sociology, University of Manitoba.

Scot Wortley

Scot Wortley is an associate professor at the Centre of Criminology, University of Toronto. His research projects include studies of remand, conviction, and sentencing outcomes in Toronto-area criminal courts; racial differences in police stopping and searching practices; and the depiction of racial minorities in the Toronto-area print media; among several other concerns.

Introduction

Bernard Schissel and Carolyn Brooks

This book is an overview of the rich and diverse nature of criminology and the thought-provoking research that often links academic analysis to criminal justice policy and practice. It examines theoretical approaches to explaining crime, public construction of crime (through media and law), the historical and contemporary shape of crime and punishment, and future directions of theory and crime control. Many of the chapters and the main arguments developed throughout are shaped by critical criminology; they examine how some individuals and groups come to be defined as "criminals" — as immoral or abnormal or simply "bad" — and conclude that this stigma is often not because of what they have done but because of who they are and where they fit into Canada's social and economic system.

Many traditional criminology books concentrate on philosophies and studies that focus on the characteristics, origins, and effects of abnormal or non-conventional behaviour. We do not take that orthodox approach to crime here. Our focus, on the contrary, is primarily on the connections between socio-economic and political power and social control. We look at how the morals, values, and welfare of socio-economic elites are translated into the morality of the law and how power generates privilege through the courts. We critique conventional criminology as a "scientific discipline" — as a force that is an integral part of a particular worldview. Working within the boundaries of that worldview, the law exonerates and legitimates the powerful and indicts the poor for their poverty. We explore, in essence, the politics of morality and the morality of crime control.

Our approach, broadly framed, argues that it is difficult to define acceptable behavioural norms and appropriate penalties for violations of those norms. Definitions of and prohibitions for crime change over time and across social groups and societies, with little consensus around just what criminal behaviour is or even what constitutes criminal behaviour. As a result, our critical criminology is informed, in part, by historical studies that track changing modes of crime control. Historically, definitions of deviance and crime have been based on explanations ranging from sin to sickness to questionable lifestyle — explanations coinciding with the influences of religion, science, and the law. In our approach we assume that laws and norms are not necessarily unchangeable or correct, or even shared by most people. In effect, people in positions of power construct codes of conduct and, generally, they use them to control the behaviours and cultures of people who are on the social and economic margins, outside the mainstream, or somehow disadvantaged. The sensitivity and objectivity that criminologists struggle to maintain in studying deviance must be based on the realization that research in the areas of crime and deviance, however important, can be misused and misrepresented to the detriment of certain people. For, as several writers here point out, today the definitions and control of crime are connected to the workings of global capitalism, which, in most respects, are creating an ever-increasing global underclass of marginalized people. For example, of the largest one hundred economies in the world fifty-one are not countries but transnational corporations; and *they employ less than 1 percent of the world's workforce* (see chapter 13). Their mandate is to reduce reliance on labour, which is often the most costly (or uncontrollable) factor of production; and ultimately they work to secure more and more of the world's resources while driving a greater proportion of the world's population into poverty.

In the months following the horrendous events of September 11, 2001, as the discourse of terrorism unfolded, the focus of public debate and policy clearly shifted to security and its corollary, crime. This is crime specifically as perpetrated by "the other" — individuals or groups that operate outside the norm — and explained as the cultural or religious pathology of those groups. We are now loathe to consider terrorism in the context of international corporate exploitation. Importantly, the same discourse of crime that occurs in a global context happens, as well, in a local context. Crime, in the public eye, is about bad people, from bad places, doing bad things. The reaction to crime, much like the reaction to terrorism, is about finding and punishing. Much like the discourse of terrorism, the political talk is rarely about the geopolitical or socio-economic conditions under which crime occurs. It is relatively easy to see how the monopolization of the world's wealth by fewer and fewer people creates the root conditions of terrorism. It should be equally easy to envision how growing marginalization and impoverishment create the conditions under which poor people end up in jail. Ironically, as a society we focus on evil people doing evil things to innocent people. We rarely take a more "relativist orientation."

This relativist orientation — that what constitutes virtuous or evil behaviour is relative to time, place, culture, class, gender, and age, among other factors — stands in contrast to absolutist thinking, exemplified by consensus theories, which assumes that crime and deviance are essentially norm-violating behaviour and that norms of conduct are agreed upon and are, by definition, correct. The consensus theorist focuses on identifying the offender and recommending either punishment or rehabilitation. Social policy-makers, most of them absolutist in their thinking, assume that the basic problem facing society is the rule-breaker, either as an individual or a group. They advocate policies that will either deter or dissuade a violator.

The system of justice and punishment in our society is based on the rather conventional assumption that the law is correct both because it reflects the will of the majority and because the practice of law (jurisprudence) is an objective, impartial mechanism for protecting the rights of all citizens. Interestingly, the philosophy that frames such consensus approaches is the same one that frames the way in which we think about science and its ability to detect and treat deviance. As we consider the origins of modern science, we find that our conventional understanding of crime and punishment has, embedded in it, a strong forensic element, which assumes that the commission of crime represents a pathology, either social or biological, that can be diagnosed and treated. For example, forensic psychiatrists now use a well-established method of detecting psychopathology (the psychopathy checklist) to determine and treat what they define as psychopaths or dangerous offenders. The implications for law are that psychiatrists get to decide what constitutes the traits of a psychopath and who gets defined as dangerous.

A critical counterargument might be that this mode of definition is, in part, a political act, for in the end the traits that constitute psychopathology are much the same traits that also appear in a modern, large business — aggression, self-indulgence, lack of empathy. Then, too, most of the individuals who end up in forensic psychiatric facilities, and who get defined as dangerous, come from the lower strata of society. This is not to say that they are not a danger to themselves or others; it is to say that their identification has much to do with where they come from, how they dress, or how articulate they are, and less to do with the actual science of identification. The science of criminology, then, becomes largely a political mechanism that often works to define and "morally evaluate" the activities of only certain kinds of people, to the exclusion of others.

It is, then, the abuse of power and the inequality inherent in the Canadian criminal justice system that inspire critical criminology. The critical perspective in criminology and that of crime causation is based on Marxist frameworks and focus attention on the political, social, and economic structures of capitalism. A criminal is not necessarily immoral, but is, rather, often someone who is disadvantaged socially or economically, or even perhaps physically. That disadvantage becomes another person's advantage as the supposed deviant is detected, defined, condemned, and punished, not for bad behaviour necessarily, but for occupying a low, stigmatized position in the socio-economic hierarchy. The person's poverty in itself becomes a crime, and in the end the crime control system identifies and punishes poverty as the only immorality. Jails are full of poor people. The critical criminological position identifies imprisonment as a political act — an act that constructs and reconstructs the criminal in the eyes of the world.

The critical social analyst is thus impassioned to discover changes that, ultimately, can help the people who are most oppressed by discriminatory justice. This critical passion goes hand in hand with a desire to help bring fundamental change to the system of crime control. We hope that the readers of this text will be similarly impassioned by a sense that there are concrete social justice alternatives to the "crime problem." For this reason, we believe that courses in crime and delinquency, and books that are pertinent to a profound and sensitive understanding of oppression and crime, must incorporate literature that investigates the roles of the "actors of crime" in more depth than is usual in conventional courses. The various analysts here examine crime and punishment as the embodiment of ideological institutions that operate within a larger structural context. To that end, the discussions address the role of poverty and inequality not only in criminal conduct, but also in how we define and punish bad conduct. This general theoretical and methodological focus must necessarily deal with the inequities of race, class, gender, age, and geography in Canadian criminal justice.

By offering an analysis of the often prejudicial treatment of women, youth, and men of marginalized racial and class backgrounds in the criminal justice system, we hope to demonstrate the importance of a critical understanding of crime. Such discussions are most poignant and relevant when they include the promise of alternative, restorative justice and community models of social justice. Using current critical theory we also aim to provide a thought-provoking pedagogical study that demonstrates how criminology links up not only with social and criminal policy but also with possible alternatives to the punitive treatment of offenders.

The book as a whole explores the diversity and importance of critical perspectives in criminology, but we do not ignore mainstream, traditional inquiry. Part I, "Explaining Crime," begins with a discussion of the theoretical underpinnings of the debates in criminology and the sociology of crime and justice. Chapter 1 presents the conventional, consensus-based theories of crime as a point of departure for the following discussions. Chapter 2 then builds a critical orientation through a survey of current and former critical theories. Chapter 3 provides a survey of the theories that form a paradigm labelled Pluralist Theory. This chapter describes how a theoretical and pragmatic accommodation can occur between the apparently polarized theories of consensus and conflict. Chapter 4 provides an important contemporary dimension to criminology; it includes an historical overview of the development of feminist theory in crime and justice and shows how the incorporation of feminist and gender issues have made a significant contribution to crime and justice theory and policy.

Whatever theoretical perspective we choose to study crime and justice, a primary, unforgettable factor is that some rules are just while others are unfair; some rules are applied without prejudice while others discriminate against the underprivileged; and certain types of crime are more prevalent amongst certain categories of people than others.

The chapters that follow Part I bring to life critical theoretical perspectives by linking them to the analysis of and explanations for crime and delinquency within Canadian communities. They suggest how different subgroups in the society come to terms with being the victims or the agents of social control. In Part II, "The Public Construction of Crime," the contributions examine the mechanisms through which we come to see certain types of people as criminal. The chapters focus, in large part, on the connections between corporate interests, the media, and politics as they investigate the construction of crime stories in the public consciousness. The authors consider the popular cultures and political mechanisms through which marginalized or relatively powerless people come to be indicted less for their crimes and more for their place in society.

In Part III, "The Historical Shape and Form of Crime," the chapters focus on the historical connections between oppression and crime. The debates centre largely on how certain people become condemned for their criminality at certain times in history and how the condemnation is tied to the social and economic conditions of those times. The authors argue, ultimately, that the definition and control of crime are, in large part, connected to managing the people most damaged by industrial development and colonialism. The historical studies presented in this part of the book are a counter to typical traditional histories that describe — almost empirically — temporal changes without presenting a social analysis. These chapters help us understand how the political and economic forces of a particular time period contribute not only to the creation of criminal behaviour but also, and more importantly, to the definition of crime and the extent of crime control.

Part IV, "The Contemporary Shape and Form of Crime," extends the discussion into the present. The authors outline the forces that historically have relegated certain people to the margins of society and then condemned them for acts related to that marginality; and they suggest that today those same forces are allowing corporate crime to flourish at the expense of criminalized women, children in the sex trade, Third World citizens, and so on. This section reveals much about how our common conceptions of crime are based on contemporary stereotypes of how people should act and how a typical criminal looks and behaves.

Part V, "The Contemporary Shape and Form of Punishment," examines the complex nature of punishment in modern society. The process of punishment often begins with the police and, in a surprisingly small number of cases, ends with jail. Discretion occurs at all levels of the justice system, and the chapters here document how the punishment meted out relates to conditions of privilege and power. Indeed, as we will come to see, punishment has little to do with the commission of crime, and much to do with the degree of discretion that occurs at various levels of the system: when crime is defined, when the police decide to arrest, when the courts decide to indict, when the judges and juries decide to punish, and when the prison institution takes on the management of inmates. The authors explore punishment as a range of discriminatory practices in the criminal justice system. An important theme throughout is the overrepresentation of and discrimination against Aboriginal peoples in the criminal justice system.

Part VI, "Changing Responses to Crime," brings us to the crux of critical criminological investigation: the connections between theory and research and the creation of policy for an emancipatory criminal justice. Its introduction reiterates the competing theories of crime to show the complexities of criminology, both critical and consensus, and to point to the ambiguities and contradictions embedded in all theories. Our intent is not to confuse or overwhelm students of criminology with these ambiguities and contradictions, but to suggest the importance of a nuanced understanding of crime. The section's chapters take this same approach. They are optimistic in their understanding of the policies and practices that address the concerns of critical social analysis, but they are also somewhat cautious in their optimism regarding social change, especially with respect to the ability of law reform — and all new methods of justice — to fundamentally redress the inequities in our social world. Fittingly, the final chapter, a letter from youth court, provides a compelling challenge for all of us not to lose sight of the direct and specific needs of those involved in the justice system — not to let theorizing distract us from actually helping the varied individuals who come into conflict with the law.

By focusing on explaining crime as well as treating it, the book as a whole brings together broader issues of "criminality" as related primarily to inequality in Canadian society. The book is designed around the discussion of specific crimes placed within a structural context — a context that includes the socio-economic and cultural forces that produce not just unconventional behaviour but also biases in crime control. The substantive chapters following Part I are more specific in their content than are most discussions in introductions to criminology. They contain both theoretical and substantive issues and illustrate the best that social research offers; and they remind us that social analysis is at its very best when it is circumscribed by a sound theoretical position. We believe that discussing specifics will allow readers to "sink their teeth" into both the sociological problems that underlie what we call crime and the immorality (and consequent societal devastation) of the differential and discriminatory treatment practised within Canada's criminal justice system.

Many of the chapters are based on composites of several theories. They employ a type of theory raiding, which is also a compelling component of contemporary research, especially as framed in what has come to be known as a postmodern perspective: that the world is complex and multidimensional, and that many of the issues that arise (in our case) in the study of crime and justice are best explained by drawing on knowledge of an array of related theories. This complexity, though perhaps daunting, can help us avoid the trap of theoretical nihilism (that nothing works); when certain parts of a theory appear to be untenable, the social analyst can proceed not by rejecting or redrafting the theory, but by augmenting it with other insights. This rethinking of the use of theory can allow researchers to be social advocates and to shape social policies that are both just and practical.

Our intent is to introduce readers to the critical analysis of crime by presenting a concrete critique of the current and past treatment of offenders in Canada. Most importantly, we hope readers will share our passion — a passion developed in a long quest to have criminology recognize and support tangible alternatives in restorative justice and community development. Much of that passion emerges from investigations informed, again, by postmodern sensibilities, which remind us of the individual biographies and stories of offenders and their experiences with the Canadian criminal justice system. Those biographies and stories, we hope, will supplement the more common structural, statistical, and impersonal accounts of oppression and discrimination. We hope too that readers will discover the richness of a critical perspective that builds on the necessary, solid alternatives to a system that now treats people with contempt, anger, and vengeance.

Part I

Explaining Crime
Theoretical Approaches

W̲e begin Part I by examining the general explanations — the theories, perspectives, paradigms — about "crime" as offered by criminologists.

An understanding or explanation of crime cannot focus merely on rule-breakers, on people violating laws. While the causes of violations and the individual motivations that lie behind those violations are important, they are not the only aspects of crime that call for explication: far from it. Whatever their approach, all explanations of crime must, in one way or another, explicitly or by assumption, address a number of key issues. All theories must consider how and why rules — laws — are made. Do the laws created by politicians and legislators reflect the actual harms inflicted by various forms of anti-social behaviour? Do laws reflect what all, or even most of us believe are harmful behaviours that need to be controlled? Once laws and rules are made, they are meant to be enforced; to understand the full process of crime we must consider the actions of police, prosecutors, and judges; and criminologists must ask questions about their work. Do these agents of crime control apply laws fairly? Is justice impartial?

Other areas of interest for criminologists include issues related to the sanctions applied to people convicted of violating laws. We not only need to know whether or not the "punishments" meted out are fair to individuals, befitting their behaviour, but we also need to consider the effectiveness of particular punishments, or even punishment itself, in achieving the goals of justice. In other words, all theories have policy implications that must be openly and squarely discussed, and not all theories adequately answer the questions that need to be asked.

Chapter 1 provides an overview of "traditional/consensus" criminological theories — the classical schools, and the biological, functionalist, social control, and interactive approaches — and examines their contributions to the discipline of criminology as well as their policy implications. Other chapters throughout the book implicitly or explicitly critique these theories by focusing on the relative failure of the consensus paradigm to acknowledge the substantive inequalities of class, race, and gender. They also consider that paradigm's failure to understand the social construction of crime categories as they relate to systemic discrimination in the application of criminal law.

Consensus theories tend to focus on individuals and their relation to social organization in an attempt to understand the nature of rule-breaking (its form, causes, and consequences) rather than engaging with how society produces marginalized or criminalized people and/or considering laws and other control mechanisms that privilege some and discriminate against others. Traditional theories, then, are part of mainstream ideology and, as a result, contribute to the labelling of offenders, the depoliticization of inequality and discrimination, and conditions that enhance crime rather than decrease it. By searching for the "cause" of someone's criminal activity, these theories have only asked why offenders have not upheld their responsibilities to the community, and not whether the community has upheld its responsibility to the offenders. For example, conventional wisdom would suggest that jails are populated primarily by poor people because the poor commit most crimes. A critical approach would contend, in contradiction, that when the state constructs the Criminal Code, it does so either deliberately or inadvertently in a way that primarily targets the activities of poor people. In addition, when the state applies the rules of law, it does so to the disadvantage of those who cannot "afford justice."

The critical paradigm, described in chapter 2 and applied throughout the book, is an antidote to conventional consensus criminological theory. The theories making up the critical paradigm offer uncommon but profound insights into understanding criminal behaviour and the moral and practical contradictions in the criminal justice system. We know that in the absence of such an understanding we will continue to condemn and punish those already condemned by society.

Chapter 2 also provides a theoretical foundation for what follows, outlining the theories of Marxism (instrumentalist and structuralist), critical race theory, abolitionism, peacemaking, postmodernism, poststructuralism, governmentality, and feminism. The discussions focus on how various theories understand crime not necessarily as the result of bad people behaving badly, but rather as a condition rooted in politics, in the inequalities of power in our society. Critical theories explore, in general, how the mechanisms for both defining and controlling the criminal — the lawmakers, courts, jails, law reformers — tend to differentiate people on the bases of socio-economic characteristics. Such theories, as a result, provide explanations of justice and punishment that account for a basic contradiction: while the systems of policing, courtroom justice, and corrections are based on principles of equality and fairness, they exist in a socio-economic context of inequality and unfairness. In these "paradigms of injustice," equal and fair treatment of criminal behaviour is a fiction — but it is a fiction that has provided many believers with a good deal of influence in defining the connections between evil or badness and being poor or otherwise marginalized. Importantly, many of the critical theories support restorative justice and preventative approaches, although acknowledging that such policy approaches are impotent as long as injustice and inequality in class, race, age, gender, and geography flourish.

Chapter 3 provides a description of those theories that blend consensus and conflict theories in an attempt to bridge the philosophical and practical gap between those theories that advocate for law and order and those that advocate for human rights. Several theories bring the critical and conventional orientations together in an attempt to understand how power operates in concert with individual human motivations and personal conditions. These bridging paradigms are provocative. They are not easily categorized as consensus or critical, and in the end they may both apologize for the status quo and advocate for it. Such "apologist theories" may be just another version of orthodox status quo criminology.

In general, pluralistic conflict theorists suggest that crime results from the use and abuse of power, from inequality. Pluralists, however, see conflict and accommodation as stemming from more than economic inequality. Max Weber gave the name "status groups" to groups that gain power and privilege because of wealth, status, political power, or occupational authority. On the bases of power and inequality, privileged groups try to influence the content and application of our systems of laws. The drama that is played out is one of constant struggle for influence.

As you will see, some of the theories in this chapter overlap somewhat with the theories provided in chapters 1 and 2. This overlap is intentional as it provokes the reader to think of applied social theory in a more complex way than is suggested in the first two chapters. While the dichotomous paradigm of consensus-conflict is an important heuristic device for understanding the social world, it is somewhat lacking at the applied level. In the end, the world is not built on complete consensus or enduring conflict.

Chapter 4 is a new and welcome addition to this second edition of Marginality and Condemnation. Elizabeth Comack provides a comprehensive overview of feminist theories and their application to crime and justice. The author takes us through the theoretical paradigms presented in the first three chapters but provides a gender framework and critique. We see how criminology has been largely constructed from a patriarchal paradigm that was about men, with women interjected when convenient. Clearly, women (and the larger issue of gender) historically have been an afterthought in criminology until recently. As the author describes, the new gender, feminist paradigm of criminology does more than just add women to the mix; in their various incarnations, feminist criminology and gender theory sees gender as a fundamental reality in issues of crime and justice. In effect, these theories have opened our eyes to the reality that men and women may inhabit different worlds of crime and victimization and that a blanket paradigm of crime and justice is both inappropriate and doubly victimizing to women. The author takes us through the historical development of feminist criminology and she shows clearly how criminology has evolved and will continue to evolve to better understand how issues of gender, class, race, and other social traits form the complexity that is the social world and that crime and justice theory and policy must evolve to incorporate the nuanced world that feminist criminology has helped us understand.

1

Orthodox Criminology
The Limits of Consensus Theories of Crime

Bernard Schissel

KEY FACTS

> Prison populations are increasing worldwide with the highest rate of incarceration in the United States.

> Law enforcement agencies compare DNA evidence gathered in crimes that have no suspect to DNA files stored in CODIS (Combined DNA Index System — a joint Canada/U.S. DNA forensic databank). If a match is made between a sample and a stored profile, CODIS can identify a suspect.

> In Canada, the percentage of prisoners with mental illnesses doubled in the last ten years; in 2007, 20 percent of offenders in prisons in Canada had a mental illness in need of treatment.

> The majority of homeless youth in Canada come from families that are economically strained and which exhibit, as a consequence, dysfunctional parenting styles.

> The Psychopathy Checklist (PCL) is a clinical rating scale of twenty items based on characteristics such as superficial charm, grandiosity, need for stimulation, pathological lying, conning and manipulating, lack of remorse, callousness, poor behavioural controls, impulsivity, irresponsibility, and failure to accept responsibility for one's own actions. The PCL is used to predict criminal reoffending and the likelihood of rehabilitation.

> Low school grades, school failure, and school drop-out are associated with the experiences of child abuse and/or victimization, poor health and low self-esteem, and ultimately with adolescent involvement in the criminal justice system.

Sources: Hare 1998; DNA Canada 2006.

Acts that society defines as criminal or deviant change over time and place. For example, until several decades ago vagrancy was considered a criminal act. If someone was found on the street without money or any visible means of support, that person could be arrested under vagrancy laws. Today vagrancy is not a grievance offence, although some urban governments in Canada are attempting to outlaw panhandling. Similarly, Canada once had an active trade in opium, which was even available in over-the-counter medicines such as children's cough syrup. Then, in 1908, the Canadian government introduced a criminal law prohibiting its importation, manufacture, and sale, a move largely based on racial prejudice against Asian immigrants rather than on any accepted scientific rationale. Since then opium (especially in the form of heroin) has been an illegal substance. The penalties for possession are often severe, including incarceration. Prior to 1983 in Canada, a husband could not be charged for raping his wife. With the sexual assault legislation of 1983 this became no longer the case; in the eyes of the law, there is no immunity for offenders based on the relationship between offender and victim.

As we observe these changing laws and the changing definitions of crime, we are left with a number of fundamental questions. Why do laws and the definitions of crime change? Are there certain immutable acts that we consider universally criminal? Or is all crime "relative"? What do these changes reflect about the relationship between power and control?

The traditional and contemporary consensus theories of criminology, which form a large part of criminological work in North America, rarely discuss structural power — power that exists through the economy, politics, and other forms of privilege. Instead, they assume that morality and the rules proscribing behaviour are natural, universal, and unchanging. The general social policy response to such a belief system is that the individual rule-breaker can be changed into a law-abiding citizen or can be dissuaded from committing crimes. The criminal justice system in a world based on consensus assumes that bad behaviour can be identified and corrected or punished, a philosophical approach that tends to psychologize crime as something living within the individual.

> Research based on traditional and consensus theories is widely used in the academic community, government, and other social policy organizations. These theories are strongly supported as the basis of the "science of criminology."

The types of research based on traditional and consensus theories remain widely used today, not only in the academic community but also in government and other social policy organizations. As betokens their popularity, the theories are highly touted, and financially backed, as the basis of the "science of criminology." Indeed, their very popularity stems, in part, from their claim to scientific support — that empirical and objective research methodologies will uncover the "facts" of crime — and, in part, from the belief that they are intuitively logical: good people do good things and bad people do bad things. But the theories are also popular because they focus on a certain type of crime that is largely individual and highly visible because it occurs "on the street." Because of that focus, they appeal to people in positions of power and influence. The theories tend to isolate and condemn those who are relatively powerless and thus unable to object to, much less oppose, the cultural definitions of crime. Statistics show, for instance, that most of those in jail in the United States are poor, visible minority males, people who are poorly educated and minimally employed, many of them convicted of drug offences. In Canada, we lock up more young offenders per capita than we do adults. This is a somewhat odd finding, given that in terms of loss of life and loss of property, corporate crime and corporate wrongdoing cause much greater damage than do individual crimes.

Classical Theory and the Modern Extensions

The classical period embraced the scientific principles that started with Francis Bacon (1561–1626) and formed the philosophical framework for the Enlightenment. Prior to this historical period, knowledge was religion-based: bad behaviour was the result of the devil at work, and heretics and criminals were exterminated in the belief that the devil could be literally burned out of existence. The only morality was that defined by "God," and to understand the world believers needed only to discover what God wanted. During the Enlightenment, when knowledge came to be based upon the principles of science and objectivity, matters of immorality became objective and observable. Crime, while still envisioned as something absolute, was now understood as a result of natural tendencies towards hedonism or of human tendencies towards self-preservation. These "classical" approaches to criminology formed what amounted to the first modern approaches.

Beccaria and Bentham and Classical Criminology

Classical theorists envisioned crime as the result of rational, calculated decisions by human beings, who are by nature predisposed to maximize pleasure and minimize pain. Several principles guide this perspective: (a) people are basically hedonistic; (b) people have free will; (c) people form a social contract with society (by birthright) whereby they agree to forgo selfish pursuits to partake of and foster the greater good of the society; and (d) punishment is an appropriate form of social control because it changes the pleasure-pain calculus, thus keeping criminals and crime under control. The Italian Enlightenment philosopher Cesare Beccaria (1738–94), who cautioned that punishment was only justified if it deterred hedonistic pursuits, articulated these principles in the late eighteenth century. He believed, furthermore, that punishment, as a means of social control, had to be minimized — that there should be just enough punishment to prevent further crime. In a very "enlightened way," classical theorists such as Beccaria abhorred punishment, especially execution, and recommended the prison as the appropriate form of minimal punishment.

> Classical theorists envisioned crime as the result of rational, calculated decisions by human beings, who are by nature predisposed to maximize pleasure and minimize pain.

Jeremy Bentham (1748–1832), whose work provided the blueprint for the modern prison system, again used the calculus of pleasure and pain as the starting point for social reform. Bentham used mathematical models to understand and evaluate the compelling nature of crime and the deterrent effect of punishment. He argued that money and other societal resources should be used in proportion to the degree of seriousness of the crime. Like Beccaria, he maintained that punishment should never exceed the degree necessary to prevent unacceptable behaviour.

Bentham's major contribution to modern systems of justice was his principle of the panopticon. For classical theorists, prison was an ideal form of punishment: the length of sentence could be determined in days and years proportionate to the seriousness of the crime. A state could also use the prison as a place in which the prisoner could re-evaluate the social contract and embrace a new belief in the value of conformity. The panopticon architecture was based on a circular design in which prison officials occupy a central observation tower surrounded by cells situated in a circular pattern around the tower and opening into the centre. The panopticon allowed prison officials to watch over inmates and staff without being seen. Both inmates and staff would conduct themselves properly — conforming to the rules — because of the certainty of being seen. They would be unlikely to go astray because of the high probability of detection. The panopticon became the architectural plan for many prison systems throughout the world. Ironically, social philosophers such as Michel Foucault (1979) used the concept of the panopticon in a metaphorical way to represent the omnipresent forces of social control in modern society.

Modern Classical Theory

Modern classical, or neo-classical, theories extended the approaches of Beccaria and Bentham to include some of the principles of law that we see in present-day society. For example, the justice system today takes mitigating circumstances into account when judging "culpability" for criminal action. If someone commits a criminal act in self-defence, we no longer assume that person is a criminal, simply by virtue of the act. When we calculate punishment, we now consider the record of the offender and adjust the punishment on this basis. While classical theory decried all forms of unequal punishment as unjust and unnecessary, neo-classical thought maintains that free will is not uniform and that the law must account for disparities in the will to commit criminal or deviant acts. For example, the law now acknowledges that some violators may suffer from insanity or that some criminal acts occur under duress. Violators are not seen as having free will in such cases.

The basis of neo-classical theory is that it is better to prevent crime than to punish it and that punishment is unsavoury no matter how it is administered. The modern extension of this philosophy is variously subsumed under Deterrence Theory (containment theory) or Rationality Theory. In effect, deterrence theory is one branch of social-control theory that studies the various types of positive and negative sanctions that encourage normal behaviour and discourage or deter abnormal behaviour. People who commit deviant acts, then, not only lose social rewards such as job promotion and peer respect but may also suffer fines or imprisonment. Deterrence Theory attempts to assess the effectiveness of official, state-administered punishment in inhibiting (a) the individual violator (specific deterrence) and (b) the general public (general deterrence) from engaging in a targeted act. Individuals, aware that they can be punished, take this information into account when they consciously choose to commit or refrain from deviant activity. One of the basic premises of our system of law and punishment is the principle of deterrence and cost-benefit. Of course, we need to ask why in certain instances we punish more than necessary — why drug users are put in prison rather than dealt with through medical facilities, for instance — and why certain categories of individuals are targeted for more severe forms of punishment (either formal or informal) than others, even when the deviant acts committed are similar.

> Deterrence theory attempts to assess the effectiveness of official, state-administered punishment in inhibiting individual violators and he general public from engaging in a targeted act.

The interest in neo-classical criminology increased in the early 1970s in North America and Europe with a rapidly growing body of literature that focused on criminals as rational actors. James Q. Wilson, a conservative U.S. political scientist, in a popular book entitled *Thinking about Crime* (1975), argued against the position that crime was a function of poverty and lack of privilege that could be changed or corrected by investing in government programs. He, and others like him, described the typical criminal as basically wicked and untamed by convention. His argument was that the primary purpose of the justice system was to make sure that anti-social individuals face the consequences of their actions. The state's mandate, then, is to deter through harsh punishment and to incapacitate through imprisonment. Some two decades later Wilson turned his conservative criminology into the study of and advocacy for biosocial research, which explained aggressiveness and criminality on the bases of the innate hormonal composition of the individual (Wilson 1975). His later position was related to his earlier arguments that crime tendencies are part of individual makeup.

Although neo-classical theory approaches to crime and punishment seem to have an intuitive logic — punishment should deter bad behaviour — they do leave unanswered some fundamental socio-legal questions. For example, the decision to offend may not be the result of a rational choice. Also, the distribution of crime is unequal across social groups — the bulk of offending rests among those with low incomes. Laws are written by powerful people and tend to give privilege to those in positions of power and authority.

Biological and Psychological Positivism: The Pathology of Criminality

Classical theory does not — and cannot — explain certain types of deviant or abnormal behaviour. Acts that seem to stem from truly evil sources, such as the crimes of serial killers or child molesters, defy logical social explanations. Rather than using criminological theory, we tend to explain such behaviours by invoking medical concepts of pathology or sickness. Biological or genetic explanations for human actions have persisted for hundreds of years, and while notions about discovering and treating biological sources of behaviour have changed, the basic premises remain: deviant behaviour is a condition lodged within the individual. Some people follow deviant paths not for rational reasons but because of a disease or defect of the body or mind.

> Biological or genetic explanations for human actions have persisted for hundreds of years; their basic premise remains unchanged: deviant behaviour is a condition lodged within the individual.

These theories advocate correcting the mal-condition and use a medical model of cure or rehabilitation. They are based on a positivist model of understanding the world — a model founded on principles of science and evidence-gathering to uncover the secrets of both the natural and social worlds. This line of thought explains crime by studying the biology and/or the psychology of the individual and linking the differences between people to biological or psychological factors.

The Lombrosan Legacy and Social Darwinism

The earliest biological theories linked evil or abnormal behaviour with the idea of human evolution, making the assumption that evil humans were evolutionarily regressive or atavistic. The English natural historian and geologist Charles Darwin (1809–82) laid the groundwork for this theorizing, and his followers applied his concept of "survival of the fittest" in nature to the interpretation and management of human existence. Social Darwinists maintained that the marginalized and the unacceptable were less fit than the more privileged people in the society. For them, the criminals and deviants were proliferating because society was interfering with natural selection by artificially sustaining less fit and less deserving people.

Cesare Lombroso (1836–1909), an Italian physician working in the late nineteenth century, argued that criminal behaviour was a symptom of a lower position on the evolutionary scale. Based on a comparison of a sample of inmates and Italian soldiers, Lombroso found that, relative to the soldiers, inmates were characterized by physical aberrations, such as high cheekbones, protruding foreheads, eye defects, poor teeth, and malformed arms and legs. Deviants, he argued, could thus be distinguished from normal people because of their atavistic body characteristics. His logic had obvious and fundamental flaws: just being in prison, for instance, can have marked effects on the physical body; and the physiological traits identified in inmates may well be socially stigmatized traits that prevented the individuals involved from leading normal, productive lives and eventually landed them in jail. Poverty and malnutrition, moreover, can produce both physical abnormalities and the need to engage in criminal activity. Lombroso's faulty logic and poor research design, coupled with future research that failed to support his findings, discredited these particular types of biotheories, and his work is only of historical interest today. But the implications of his work and the connections to Social Darwinism have led to altered, and still flourishing, versions of the biological approach.

Contemporary Biosocial Research

The work of William Sheldon (1949) is one of the most noteworthy extensions of biological theories. Working in the 1940s, Sheldon attempted to link body type to criminal and deviant behaviour. He argued that certain body types — the ectomorph, who is skinny and fragile, the mesomorph, who is muscular, stocky, and athletic, and the endomorph, who is soft, round, and fat — each have associated temperaments and behaviours. Sheldon found an excessively high percentage of criminals, especially juvenile gang members, to be mesomorphs, which led him to argue for a cause and effect relationship between physiology and behaviour. Again, the argument shows a dubious logic because rather than being a matter of cause and effect, it may well be that mesomorphs are more likely to be recruited to delinquent gangs or that judges see strong athletic boys as more of a threat than other types. Like Lombroso's theories, Sheldon's theory was based on weak supporting evidence.

The findings of later research that deviants were more characterized by genetic abnormalities than were non-deviants created excitement in the medical and crime-control communities. With the discovery of Klinefelter's syndrome (men with an XYY genetic makeup instead of the "normal" XY) in males who were aggressive, large (excessively tall) body types, and had mental deficiencies, researchers concluded that the extra Y chromosome was the genetic marker for violent criminality (Shah and Roth 1974). Once again, subsequent evidence has suggested that faulty research and causal logic underpinned these studies. Even if we accept the association between chromosome composition and deviant tendencies, this finding does not suggest how or why the abnormality leads to crime. It could be that the physical difference isolates individuals and restricts them from conventional society. If XYY individuals have lower mental capacities, for example, it may be that they find it impossible to engage in conventional social and economic activities and are "driven" into the world of crime. The stigmatizing effects of an intolerant world may force deviant behaviour.

Despite the flaws in earlier biostudies, biological research has gained a new life in recent decades. Current sociobiological research on alcoholism concentrates on identifying the neurological or genetic traits of individuals with high-risk propensities to alcoholism (Pollock et al. 1986; Goodwin 1986). Recent studies comparing identical and non-identical twins, also show an interest in biological phenomena. The basic research question in these studies is the degree to which twins of different types share criminal or deviant tendencies (Mednick and Volavka 1980). The general findings suggest a greater similarity in deviant behaviour for identical compared to non-identical twins. As well, recent work on male predispositions to violence attempts to link evolutionary concepts, such as reproductive competition — which is characteristic of our lower primate ancestors — and status competition with homicidal behaviour in male gangs, again based on a "survival of the fittest logic" (Wilson and Daly 1985). As practised, this popular evolutionary approach is strongly class-biased and sexist. When we strip away the language and the logic, such approaches are, arguably, amusing and fictitious.

The premise of one evolutionary approach, "cheater theory," is that in society there is a subpopulation of men who have evolved with genes that predispose them to low parental involvement:

> Sexually aggressive, they use their cunning to gain sexual conquests with as many females as possible. Because females would not willingly choose them as mates, they use stealth to gain sexual access, including such tactics as mimicking the behaviour of more stable males. They use devious and illegal means to acquire resources they need for sexual domination. Their deceptive reproductive tactics spill over into other endeavours, where their talent for irresponsible, opportunistic behaviour supports their anti-social activities. Deception in reproductive strategies is thus linked to a deceitful lifestyle.
>
> Psychologist Byron Roth notes that cheater males may be especially attractive to those younger, less intelligent women who begin having children at an early age. State-sponsored welfare, claims Roth, removes the need for potential mates to have the resources needed to be stable providers and family caretakers. With the state meeting their financial needs, these less-intelligent women are attracted to men who are physically attractive and flamboyant. Their fleeting courtship process produces children with low IQs, aggressive personalities, and little chance of proper socialization in father-absent families. Because the criminal justice system treats them leniently, argues Roth, sexually irresponsible men are free to prey on young girls. Over time, their offspring will supply an ever-expanding supply of cheaters who are both anti-social and sexually aggressive. (Siegel and McCormick 1999: 157)

This remarkable passage illustrates how, despite its seemingly absurd premise, such a theory works to draw on the public's trust of science to make its heavily laden biological assumptions legitimate. Most importantly, biosocial theories like this one condemn people for their "lack of intelligence," their lower-class (welfare) origins, their regressive evolutionary conduct, their inability to maintain a mother–father nuclear family (a subtle way of blaming single mothers for deviant children), and their dependence on the state. All of these features are linked to biological (animal-like) traits. Interestingly, "cheater theory" also engages in politics by blaming the state, in part, for being too lenient on predatory males. While these kinds of theories are blatant in their attacks on class, gender, race, and culture, and while their logic appears to be somewhat absurd, they are powerful tools for advocating a certain position: that bad people are out there, that they are unlike you and me, and that their biology, their psychology, and their environment combine to make them monsters. Such theories have considerable ideological power. The potency of scientific approaches to crime appears to be on the increase, and the overall orientation will no doubt continue to gain credibility as the Human Genome Project comes to fruition.

The Human Genome Project began in 1990 and was completed in 2003. It is funded by the U.S. departments of energy and health, which committed billions of dollars to a project that would fundamentally alter how we view human wellness and human potential. The purpose of the project is to identify and map all of the 20,000–25,000 genes in the human DNA and eventually to turn the massive database over to the private sector. It provides a gateway not only to understand the complete genetic makeup of a person, but also to alter the genetic code either before or after birth to "correct" genetic anomalies. The implications for medicine, including cancer, are astounding. Gene therapy has the potential to eliminate cancer, generate new organs and blood vessels, detect genetic diseases at the embryonic stage, and even alter the genetic code that causes cells to age. Similarly, for forensic science, gene-mapping carries the almost foolproof potential for identifying suspects using evidence from crime scenes, absolving those wrongly accused, establishing paternity, and tracking criminals based on their DNA identity.

In relation to crime and punishment, however, contemporary genetic research has a dark side. The discovery of a genetic basis for various disorders raises the possibility of identifying genes connected to criminal behaviour. The implications of this development are staggering. We will have the potential of giving someone, at a very early age, a DNA-based identity that has a moral definition attached to it. If we have the ability to detect and prove that a person has a genetic predisposition to crime, will we create a new taxonomy that will link genetic makeup to criminality? The fundamental legal question will be whether the person with the genetic flaw had a guilty mind (*mens rea*) when he or she committed the act. At present the law is premised on crime as a product of deliberate wrongdoing. Will crime-control agencies (including medicine and the law) become more proactive as they try to alter the "criminal design" of those we detect as genetically impaired (Hodgson 2000)? Will genetic engineering become part of crime control once the technology to alter genetic makeup becomes practical?

While biological studies are compelling and persistent, they have gained little favour in sociological research, for two reasons. First, the research has failed to control for psychological and social factors that interact with biology. Second, the implications of such research appear to be frightening. For instance, potential policy implications affecting genetic engineering and selective abortions of defective foetuses involve a kind of tampering with human life that would be carried out with scientific fervour but without moral ballast. At the end of the day, however, the most important issue that frames these debates is who gets to say what is a good and bad gene/organism/person, just as critical legal scholars ask who gets to decide what is moral and immoral.

Psychological Theories

Like biological theories, psychological explanations of deviant behaviour adopt a scientific approach and focus on the causes of crime as originating within the individual. Psychological theories argue, though, that character and personality are acquired traits and not just inherited. For example, the psychoanalytical theories of Sigmund Freud (1856–1939) concentrated on the improper development of conscience. Freud maintained that personality is comprised of the id, the ego, and the superego. The id, the mostly animalistic part of the personality that leads us to aggressive, self-destructive, and anti-social tendencies, stands in conflict with the ego (the social self) and the superego (the conscience). Criminals or deviants, then, are those whose ego and superego are poorly developed, and they are thus inadequately equipped to hold the id in check. For Freud this impairment starts at the earliest stages of infant development and is influenced by the degree and type of parental training.

As an extension of Freudian psychoanalysis, the frustration-aggression hypothesis (Berkowitz 1969) suggests that frustration, a result of unmet needs, leads to aggressive behaviour that may be manifested in anti-social or self-destructive behaviour. Albert Bandura and Richard H. Walters (1963) use such an explanation

> Like biological theories, psychological explanations of deviant behaviour find the causes of crime within the individual, but argue that character and personality are acquired traits.

of aggression in their theory of social learning. They suggest that people come to behave aggressively through a process called modelling: when individuals who observe the deviant/criminal behaviour of others being rewarded are prone to internalize the rewarded behaviour as acceptable. Much of this research focuses on the influence that violence on television has on deviant behaviour. Simply put, if the viewer is exposed to depictions of crime and deviance that are socially acceptable, then that person may become insensitive to the crime and deviance and may no longer see acts of violence as negative.

The types of vicarious conditioning discussed by social-learning theorists are fundamental to the theory of behaviourism. Beginning with the work of B.F. Skinner (1953), behaviourism assumed that behaviour was instilled through reward and punishment and that, because behaviour is learned, bad behaviour can be unlearned. H.J. Eysenck (1977) argued that immoral behaviour is the result of improper conditioning; children never learn to associate fear and pain with bad conduct. Eysenck considered this conditioned fear as the basis of conscience. In this general arena of psychological research stressing the effect of fear and punishment on moral development, the theory of cognitive development focused on how moral development coincides with stages of psychological and physical maturity. For psychologists such as Jean Piaget (1932) and Lawrence Kohlberg (1969), the individual is the source of "badness," and, as in psychoanalytic theories, deviants are characterized by deficits in moral reasoning. These deficits occur at certain stages of psychic development, and redirecting the individual through the appropriate stages of development can rectify deviant tendencies.

Psychological theories have maintained their appeal in the study and control of crime primarily because the emphasis on the individual permits the development of a treatment program based on psychotherapy. Therapies such as behaviour modification are still used in prison to establish conformist behaviour. The main criticism of psychological theories, however, is that they ignore the relative nature of crime: definitions and reactions to criminal behaviour depend on social power and social context. As well, psychological theories ignore major forms of criminal behaviour, including violations committed by organizations (corporate crime), political crimes, and certain types of rational individual crimes such as credit-card fraud. Lastly, they study deviant and criminal acts "out of context" — they isolate the individual primarily as an independent organism.

The psychopathy checklist, a tool developed by Robert Hare and colleagues (Hare 1998) illustrates this approach. The development of the psychopathy checklist was considered to be a significant improvement over earlier methods of evaluating psychopathy, primarily because it uses objective information taken from official personal records and is based on a carefully structured interview. Because it is a psychometric instrument, it has stood the scrutiny of scientific testing over time. However, many of the characteristics that the instrument isolates are based on issues such as a high sense of self-worth, tendency to boredom, pathological lying, lack of remorse, impulsiveness, and callousness. These traits, while not attractive, are common to many people in highly competitive occupations in which aggressiveness and self-interest are admired characteristics. In the end, the psychopathy checklist allowed the psychiatric profession to expand its mandate into the non-criminal world. As Steve Keyes (2001) points out,

> There are many psychopaths in society that we know virtually nothing about. These are the psychopaths who don't necessarily commit homicide, commit serious violence, or even come to the attention of the police. They may be successful businessmen, successful politicians, successful academics, successful priests;

they exist in all areas of society. There is a growing awareness that psychopathic behaviour is around us in all walks of life. There are telltale signs in road rage incidents and in the violence that surrounds sport. But it's in the cut and thrust of the business world, an arena where traditionally ruthlessness verges on a virtue that it's becoming increasingly worrying. (Keyes 2001: 1)

This brief passage illustrates a phenomenon common in the psychiatric profession: that psychiatry is in a constant search to expand its purview and its patient base (Szasz 1970). Most importantly, it illustrates how definitions of crime and criminality are constructed to the benefit of those in the practice of crime detection. Theorists and practitioners tend to have little regard for the context in which people act and little regard for the unfairness of labelling a person as potentially criminal on the bases of assessment instruments that do not account for factors such as culture, race, class, gender, or age. They are, like other mechanisms of biological and psychological assessment, vehicles through which highly educated, well-heeled individuals and professions define morality and themselves on their own terms.

Consensus Theories and the Sociology of Crime

Sociological theories that are based on a consensus model make prior assumptions about social behaviour. The basic assumptions are that the rules and norms by which we conduct ourselves are shared and, therefore, correct. Morality is a given. The basic problem facing society then is that certain people fail to conform. For example, there is a largely indisputable argument that a person who kills someone in an act of vengeance does not belong in mainstream society. We also believe that someone who steals from someone also breaks the law — even if the thief is in need of food, clothing, or shelter. These two examples are almost polar opposites with respect to the gravity of the offence and the motives for committing crime. Yet both are considered criminal violations, and very often both result in time in prison for the offenders. Both acts violate norms of conduct that prohibit murder and stealing despite the motives.

Functionalism, Anomie, and Strain

Structural-functionalist theories can be traced to the work of Emile Durkheim (1858–1917), a French thinker known as one of the founders of modern sociology. For Durkheim and subsequent functionalists, the basic determinant of abnormality is a lack of social cohesion; societies with low levels of social cohesion are typified by high rates of crime and deviance. When societies change rapidly, people are less likely to experience integration and regulation, and such societies will, as a consequence, experience high rates of unconventional behaviour. The psychological state experienced by people in such societies is called *anomie* or normlessness. Anomie exists when very few values and norms are shared and, thus, formal mechanisms of social control fail. For example, in his book, *The Dispossessed*, Geoffrey York (1992) describes how the rapid industrialization of Canada's Northern areas and the expropriation of Aboriginal lands and communities in the 1950s and 1960s resulted in the erosion of Aboriginal communities. The rapid change — the influx of money and Southern culture, alcohol and drugs, geographical displacement, new forms of exchange — resulted in a blurring of cultural values and expectations. The end result was that many communities that had previously experienced almost negligible violence and rates of substance abuse became characterized by overwhelming substance abuse, family violence, and sexual abuse. Structural functionalists would suggest that the problems resulted from the lack of integration of local people into the community and the lack of regulation. The citizens are anomic — they lack shared values and commitments.[1]

Durkheim also suggested that because criminal and deviant behaviours are endemic to all societies, they have a positive or functional role to play in the stability of the society. He and his functionalist successors argued that deviance and crime serve to establish the boundaries of morality. They strengthen community and group ties through the presence of a common enemy (criminals and deviants), provide opportunities for the release of tension determined by rigid social norms, and provide alternative norms that could engender adaptability to new values. Two classical studies that illustrate the positive functions of crime are Kingsley Davis's (1937) study of prostitution and Kai Erikson's (1966) study of puritan society. Davis views prostitution as functioning as a safety valve, protecting the family by providing a sexual outlet for men who might otherwise choose to abandon their spouses for different sexual experiences. Erikson argues that public deviancy and public displays of shame and punishment provide cohesiveness by redefining morality and illustrating the consequences of violating the moral code.

> Anomie, Strain, or Blocked Opportunity Theory proposes that the discrepancy between life goals and the means of achieving them leads some people to find non-legitimate ways of circumventing blocked opportunity.

Robert Merton (1938) drew upon the Durkheimian paradigm by studying the social and economic forces that influence relatively vulnerable people. This contemporary body of research, labelled Anomie, Strain or Blocked Opportunity Theory, proposes that anomic societies do not provide adequate acceptable avenues for people to achieve conventional life goals. The discrepancy between goals and the actual means of achieving those goals creates strain, and this strain, in turn, leads some people to find various non-legitimate ways of circumventing blocked opportunity. Merton categorized five types of responses to the strain of blocked opportunity: conformity, innovation, ritualism, retreatism, and rebellion. Conformity is the only non-deviant response. Innovation involves the acceptance of shared goals but not the acceptance of the legitimate means of achieving them. For example, an unsuccessful student may cheat on an exam, or a corporate executive may decide to defraud his company or the shareholders. Most types of criminal behaviour fall into the category of innovation. Ritualism identifies activity wherein the means are accepted and the goals are rejected or altered. For example, Merton considered individuals to be deviant if they simply show up for work but do not accomplish as much as they should be able to or are expected to. This type of goal de-escalation, considered somewhat harmless, has received little attention in research on crime. Retreatism, as a response to blocked opportunity, has received more attention. Retreatists reject the goals and the means of achieving them by "dropping out" of society. Mental illness, substance abuse, and compulsive gambling may all be forms of retreatist behaviour and are highly visible in studies on social control and crime, despite the likelihood of being primarily victimless activities. Lastly, rebellion signifies a form of deviance much like retreatism in that it rejects the goals and means. Rebellion, however, constitutes behaviour that advocates new forms of achievement. Merton might argue that political rebellion, for example, is born of blocked opportunity, and that actions such as revolutionary activity on university campuses in response to funding cuts or political protests of First Nations peoples in North America typify forms of rebellion in response to lack of opportunity.

Merton's theory explained the class-based nature of crime by positing that lower-class individuals most frequently innovate in response to blocked opportunity because they are less likely than their higher-class counterparts to be socialized against the use of illegitimate means of pursuing success. Higher-class individuals, on the other hand, because they are socialized to conformity, are reluctant to break the law and tend to reduce their aspirations (ritualism) if they suffer the strain of blocked opportunity. In the end, the propensity for criminal behaviour is highest amongst the lower classes, in large part, because they suffer the greatest levels of blocked opportunity and adapt by engaging in illegitimate opportunities.

Various subsequent theories provided nuance to the general theory of Strain/Blocked Opportunity. Albert Cohen (1955) modified Merton's theory by suggesting that lower-class delinquency is a sub-cultural adaptation to the predominance of middle-class culture in society. His theory of Status Frustration proposed that the place in which middle-class cultural values are most predominant and influential is education and that lower-class youths often do not meet the standards of attitude and achievement that are demanded of them. The frustration that results for lower-class youths is manifested in considerable frustration as they struggle to achieve in an essentially foreign culture. This status frustration results in a cultural adaptation in which lower-class youths form their own system of hierarchy and achievement that is based on criteria of success antithetical to middle-class values. The resulting cultural norms, in the words of Cohen, include "non-utilitarian, malicious, and negativistic" values, performed out of the pursuit of status and not out of need. Clearly, present-day public opinion about youth gangs would incorporate a sense that such gangs are typified by non-utilitarian and violent pursuits.

> Albert Cohen modified Merton's theory by suggesting that lower-class delinquency is a sub-cultural adaptation to the predominance of middle-class culture in society.

Cloward and Ohlin (1960) provide a further extension to Merton's Theory by positing the theory of Differential Illegitimate Opportunity, the essence of which is that many lower-class people are denied access to both legitimate and illegitimate opportunities. Simply put, not all lower-class individuals who suffer a discrepancy between "ends" and "means" know how to commit crime. Those who do commit crime obviously have been in a position to learn the skills of criminality and are able to survive in the criminal subculture; those who do not commit crime live in what Cloward and Ohlin describe as conflict subcultures and become "double failures." They neither partake of criminal activity nor violence-based status attainment activities, and as a result, "retreat" into the world of drugs and alcohol. In the end, Cloward and Ohlin provide a more complex framework for understanding the world of those who are denied access to legitimate means to attain the goals of a middle-class world.

Despite the intuitive logic embedded in the functionalist theories of anomie and strain, they, like most of the theories in this chapter, are biased in favour of middle-class values and structures. It is arguable that lower-class people are no more deviant than people from the middle and upper classes, especially when we consider issues of white collar and organizational crime. The theories are based on interpreting official crimes rates and we will see throughout this book that official crime rates most often measure the extent and the nature of crime and punishment and not necessarily the amount of crime committed. By dwelling on the crimes of the lower classes, the theories tend to mask the wide range of crimes committed by well-heeled members of the society, which are often ignored by mechanisms of social control. Further, the theories tend to depict lower-class cultures as characterized by frustration and misery, and this is certainly open to question. As a related issue, blocked opportunity can occur at all levels of class and status; feelings of deprivation are relative to group and class expectations. For example, business people who have all the resources they need to lead the affluent lifestyle often struggle for more in the "game" of making money. Their personal sense of frustration and social angst should fit within the paradigm of blocked opportunity although the theories ignore high status crime. Lastly, the notion of value consensus — that all people share a set of common values, especially in relation to material success — is questionable. In highly complex societies like Canada in which difference and plurality are the cornerstones of the society, to contend that everyone aspires to the same goals is naïve and culturally insensitive.

Social-Control Theory

Deterrence Theory, and its parent, Social-control Theory, are typically functionalist in their assumption that norms are generally shared, and, as a result, the appropriate areas of study are the mechanisms that compel some people to violate norms and others to resist the temptations to deviate. Unlike most other consensus theories, however, social-control theory assumes that norm violations are attractive and that most people are motivated to engage in criminal or deviant behaviour. Simply put, we humans are rational, self-interested beings, and we will thus choose to violate society's norms if there is an advantage in doing so. This theory concentrates on the legal, social, and personal reasons behind why so few people engage in illegal or criminal behaviour, given that such behaviour can be highly advantageous.

> Deterrence theory and social-control theory assume that norms are generally shared, and they study the mechanisms that compel some people to violate norms and others not to deviate.

Early control theorists were concerned with the influences that prevented an individual from engaging in crime given the "classical" criminology assumption that crime is rational and an easy and attractive means to an end. The answer to this dilemma for social-control, Containment Theory (Nye 1958; Reckless 1973) rested with the concepts of inner and outer control. Inner control addresses the notions of guilt and remorse that result when people who adhere to and believe in the rules and norms of the society violate those rules. People who consciously choose to deviate, then, do so because they lack moral socialization; they lack conscience. The psychopathology of a serial killer, for example, may result from a complete lack of morality or conscience — the psychopath is neither moral nor immoral, but rather amoral in the sense of not being able to empathize with or even understand the trauma or pain of a victim. Outer control involves the sanctions that discourage anti-social and criminal behaviour. Quite clearly, the most common and accepted form of sanction for criminal behaviour is the use of prison — and, ultimately, capital punishment in some jurisdictions — to discourage criminal behaviour. As mentioned in the introduction to this chapter, the notion of outer control, encapsulated in Deterrence Theory, is the cornerstone of our criminal control system. Although we pose prisons as places of "correction," the predominant public thinking on prison is that it is a place of punishment and deterrence, a place in which the pain and suffering of criminal sanction becomes known to both the criminal and the general public.

For some social-control theorists, deviant behaviour is not so much controlled by fear of punishment as by an internal logic or "morality," the "natural" result of internalizing the rules and norms shared and valued by most people in society. The acceptance of such rules controls behaviour because people experience guilt and remorse as a matter of course when they act in a deviant manner. Crime results from a lack of moral socialization, a lack of conscience. Psychopaths represent the typical anomaly: they have no morality or conscience; they are not immoral, but rather amoral.

Travis Hirschi's Social Bonding Theory (1969) focused on morality and inner control. Hirschi's interest was in the degree of bonding to conventional society as a general determinant of inner control and moral conduct. He introduced the dimensions of attachment, involvement, commitment, and belief as components of bonding — as they relate to family, education, and peer group. His theoretical model suggests that bonding is made up of attitudes and behaviours. Bonding involves both inner control, tapping the strength of conscience or morality, and outer control, the degree to which individuals respond to social pressure and proscription. The model defines attachment as an attraction to parents, school, and peers. Commitment involves an attitude of aspiring to conventional goals in occupation and education. Involvement means participation in conventional goal-oriented activities. The belief component involves attitudes towards moral values, which are generated by society as a whole — in essence, as a measure of morality or conscience. For Hirschi, the greater the bond between an individual and society — attached to school, committed to a good job, involved with family, believing in social values — the less likely is that individual to engage in criminal or deviant behaviour.

More recent incarnations of Hirschi's work have tried to link the conservative tendencies of control theory to obvious differences in power in society. Power-Control Theory focuses on how families reproduce power differences between gender and class. For power-control theorists, children are more likely to be deviant if their parents are less involved in their lives. Patriarchal family practices and structures influence how boys and girls approach risk-taking behaviour. Patriarchal, traditional families tend to produce boys who are aggressive and goal-oriented (and risk-takers) and girls who are passive and aspire to domestic life (non risk-takers). More modern, egalitarian families tend to produce girls who are relatively high risk-takers and have, according to the theory, a greater propensity to engage in deviant behaviour. The theory, then, attempts to explain how the relationships of power, social class, and parental influence can lead to the creation of deviant children (Hagan, Simpson, and Gillis 1995). (See chapter 3 for a more in-depth overview of Power-Control Theory).

One of the attractive qualities of social-control theories is that they are open to empirical verification. Empirical (survey research) on youth crime often shows that how attached a young person is to family, school, and the community, among others, is indeed correlated with levels of criminal involvement. On the other hand, the general theoretical framework is suspect in that it fails to question how power operates for some and against others in institutions like education and the law. It also fails to question the efficacy of such institutions — do schools provide conventional space for only certain kinds of students to succeed? Schools are, in fact, middle-class establishments that are highly rigid and mostly unable to adapt to non-middle-class students who might require different methods of education, different methods for evaluating success and different priorities regarding life skills versus routine, formal knowledge. In fact, a failure to become attached and involved in education might be a failure of education and not of the individual or culture. Lastly, control theory simply cannot explain high-status criminality or why society comes to see crime only as a street activity and not an organizational activity.

Social Disorganization, Socio-cultural Theory, and Human Ecology

Socio-cultural theories of crime and deviance focus on the context in which individuals learn criminal behaviour and how they learn it. Cultures and subcultures are targeted as the "transmitters" of deviant values. Beginning with work in the sociology department at the University of Chicago in the 1930s (The Chicago School), a substantial body of research has focused on the relationships between environmental or spatial patterns and deviant cultures. This body of research was based on a natural science paradigm that focused on plants and animals and their relationships to one another and to the physical world around them. The central premise was that like the natural world, human groups, based on race, class, and other group identifiers, affect one another's daily lives and that these groups are affected by the physical urban environment. Shaw and McKay (1969) were the foundational proponents of this "ecological" paradigm which contended that certain areas of cities had disproportionately high crime rates and that crime declined as one moved outward (concentric zone theory). This geographical approach coincided very well with the average citizen's commonsense perception of the location of crime in urban areas, and in fact, these largely socio-cultural theories arose in response to the "objective" study of deviant and criminal groups in time and space. Urban settlement patterns were shown to be associated with pockets of crime. Shaw and McKay observed, for example, that inner-city urban areas inhabited by the poor, by recent immigrants, and by visible minorities had relatively high rates of non-conformity. Their work, which came to be known as Disorganization Theory, rested on the assumption that geographic and cultural pockets of crime, which they described as transitional zones, were highly disorganized and lacked the community infrastructure that was needed in functional societies. The more functional societies were situated far from the core of the city, at the suburban edges. In fact, Disorganization Theory draws on Durkheimian functionalism in its contention that such high crime communities often have a transient population which results in disruptions of the social order.

> Socio-cultural theories of crime and deviance focus on the context in which individuals learn criminal behaviour and how they learn it. Cultures and subcultures are targeted as the "transmitters" of deviant values.

While ecological theories of crime shift the attention on criminality away from the individual to the society and address geographic patterning of crime, they are flawed with respect to the nature and permanence of inner-city communities. In fact, many inner-core, marginal communities are highly organized despite socio-economic disadvantage. Furthermore, to assume that the values of a delinquent or criminal group are the values of a community is highly contentious. Most importantly, the theories fail to take into account how power is wielded throughout the society and how disadvantage in one sector of the society fosters advantage for other sectors. This is a critique that is fundamental to all of the theories in this chapter and is central to the critical focus of this book.

Cultural Transmission Theory was a natural extension to theories of social disorganization as it extended the paradigm to suggest that crime is indeed concentrated in identifiable urban areas, such as the inner city. For this theory, not only is abnormal behaviour a part of the culture of certain urban areas, but also unconventional values, attributed primarily to inner-city subcultures, are passed on from generation to generation. Walter Miller (1958), for example, said that the propensity to be involved in delinquent (gang-related) behaviour is relatively high in lower-class areas and that a delinquent subculture which exists in such communities passes on the tradition of crime and delin-quency to future generations. Values such as toughness, trouble, smartness, fatalism, and autonomy were, for Miller, the traits that made lower-class boys and men more likely to be involved in crime than their higher-class counterparts. Miller's theories, like many of the functionalist theories in this chapter, make several basic assumptions that are highly suspect, the most important of those is the suggestion that lower-class communities have different sets of values than wealthier communities. In fact, lower-class youths, including those who are involved in the justice system, often share values with the greater society and have aspirations that are much like those of their more advantaged counterparts (Eisler 2004).

Differential Association Theory was influenced by social-disorganization and cultural-transmission theo-ries to explain the mechanisms through which values become part of certain subcultures and how and why crime is transmitted from one generation to the next. This more micro-level (socio-psychological) approach to crime and environment focused on the person-to-person dynamics of becoming criminal. Edwin Sutherland (1939), for example, argued that people learned deviant behaviour in close association with intimates and friends. Deviant behaviour is probable if an individual is exposed to a relatively high number of deviant influences. This theory focuses on the process of socialization into crime and concentrates on the learning and evaluating of moral and immoral definitions of what constitutes values such as masculinity, bravery, honour, and loyalty in a deviant subculture. In the end, differential association theory argued that some communities have pro-social norms and some have anti-social or pro-criminal norms and that such norms are transmitted from generation to generation, a paradigm that came to be know as Cultural Transmission Theory.

> Cultural transmission theo-ry suggests that crime is con-centrated in identifiable urban areas and that unconventional values, attributed primarily to inner-city subcultures, are passed on from generation to generation.

For example, street drug-trafficking is common in many inner cities in North America due to the drug-trafficking culture, which, because of the need to escape police scrutiny, is transient out of necessity. Drug dealers move in and out of communities and not only cause the social pathology of the drug trade but also raise fear and anger among the citizens. According to disorganization theory, such disruptions ultimately contribute to unstable cultural values and poorly defined mechanisms of inner and outer control. Community members, especially the young, may decide out of desperation or necessity to partake in the criminal lifestyle and will become socialized to the anti-social norms and values of life in the drug trade. Their exposure to drug dealers and customers orients them to what an outsider would consider a criminal culture. Their reasons for becoming part of the drug culture, however, are complex, having little to do with a criminal orientation and much to do with fitting in and learning to become part of the "deviant" community. According to this group of socio-cultural theories, the socially disorganized community, most likely located in the inner city, passes on the drug trade from generation to generation.

While it is difficult to reject the notion that criminal behaviour is learned in concert with others, the core of the theory is suspect for several reasons. The primary flaw is that like many other functionalist theories, it does not focus on how non-cultural fac-tors like economic disparity and inequalities in power across communities influences street crime. And, like many other orthodox theories, it does not address high-status crimes, especially how high status people become involved in criminality despite their conventional associations and "non-criminogenic" communities.

Summary

Consensus theories of crime are based on several presumptions: our morality and the rules that control immoral behaviour are natural, universal, and unchanging; through "correction" and punishment the individual rule-breaker can be changed into a law-abiding citizen; and the criminal justice system can identify and deal with criminal behaviour. In the end, though, conventional explorations of crime ignore fundamental issues. They leave out the relationships between social and political power and the construction or definition of abnormal behaviour. They also disregard the relationship between socio-political power and the official control of crime. Power is a type of currency or wealth, and its ownership makes certain peoples privileged over others. Those who have power are more able than those without power to define what constitutes immoral behaviour, and they are more able to influence the lawmakers. Their definitions of badness and goodness and the methods of justice and punishment become legitimate. Justice and punishment, then, comprise a social institution that becomes essential to social control and justice, and punishment can be applied in discriminatory and preferential ways.

> Consensus theories of crime presume that morality and the rules that control immoral behaviour are universal, and that "correction" and punishment can change rule-breakers into law-abiding citizens.

DISCUSSION QUESTIONS

1. What are the basic presumptions of a consensus model of crime and justice?

2. How do scientific approaches to crime and deviance — typified by the Human Genome Project — support conventional or consensus views of crime and justice?

3. How is classical criminology incorporated into our justice system? Describe the principles involved in a classical, deterrence model of justice and punishment and discuss whether these principles are valid in modern society.

4. How do theories of human ecology incorporate the theory of differential association?

5. Why is it so easy for society and its members to adopt and endorse a consensus model of crime, justice, and punishment?

GLOSSARY OF TERMS

Anomie: a social condition that comes about when formal mechanisms of social control break down and, consequently, people's shared values and norms disappear. When this state exists, people lack guidelines for behaviour and experience a high degree of confusion about basic social norms. In this uncertain and frustrating atmosphere, some people respond in criminal and deviant ways.

Consensus Theory: a general body of theories based on the overarching assumption that morality and the rules that proscribe behaviour are natural, universal, and unchanging. Crimes are behaviours that are repugnant to all elements of the society.

Classical Theory: based on the view that it is better to prevent crime than to punish it and that punishment, although necessary to deter criminal behaviour, is unsavoury no matter how it is administered. Various types of negative sanctions discourage or deter criminal behaviour.

Differential Association Theory argues that people learn deviant behaviour in close association with intimates and friends. Deviant behaviour is probable if an individual is exposed to a relatively high number of deviant influences.

Human Genome Project: an international genetics program funded primarily by the u.s. departments of energy and health and dedicated to identifying and mapping all of the human genes that constitute an individual human being.

Social Control Theory makes the presumption that individuals will engage in crime unless they have the moral compass (inner control) to avoid criminal behaviour or if they are deterred from committing crime due to fear of being punished (outer control).

Socio-Cultural Theories: focus, in the field of crime and deviance, on the context in which and the processes by which individuals learn criminal behaviour. Cultures and subcultures are targeted as the "transmitters" of deviant values.

Strain or Blocked Opportunity Theory proposes that anomic societies do not provide adequate acceptable avenues for people to achieve conventional life goals. The discrepancy between goals and the actual means of achieving those goals creates strain, and this strain, in turn, leads some people to find various non-legitimate ways of circumventing blocked opportunity.

Status Frustration Theory: proposes that Lower class youths often do not meet the standards of attitude and achievement that are demanded by middle class culture. status frustration results in a cultural adaptation in which lower class youths form their own system of hierarchy and achievement that is based on criteria of success antithetical to middle class values.

SUGGESTED READINGS

Einstadter, Werner, and Stuart Henry. 1995. *Criminological Theory: An Analysis of Its Underlying Assumptions*. Fort Worth, TX: Harcourt Brace College Publishers.

Vold, George, and Thomas Bernard. 1998. *Theoretical Criminology*. New York: Oxford University Press.

White, Rob, and Fiona Haines. 2000. *Crime and Criminology*. Melbourne: Oxford University Press

Williams, Frank P., and Marilyn D. McShane (eds.). 1993. *Criminological Theory: Selected Classical Readings*. Cincinnati, OH: Anderson Publishing Co.

NOTE

1. There are, of course, other ways of viewing the history of the development of Northern Canada, and York, himself, would not share the structural-functionalist theoretical understanding. His work focuses much more on economic oppression and marginality (1992: 29–30).

REFERENCES

Bandura, A., and R.H. Walters. 1963. *Social Learning and Personality Development*. New York: Holt, Rinehart and Winston.

Berkowitz, L. 1969. *Roots of Aggression: A Re-Examination of the Frustration-Aggression Hypothesis*. New York: Atherton Press.

Cloward, R., and L. Ohlin. 1960. *Delinquency and Opportunity*. New York: Free Press.

Cohen, Albert. 1955. *Delinquent Boys: The Culture of the Gang*. New York: Free Press.

Davis, Kingsley. 1937. "The Sociology of Prostitution." *American Sociological Review* 2: 744–55.

(DNA) Canada. 2006. National DNA Data Bank. Available at <http://www.nddb-bndg.org/main_e.htm> accessed July 2007

Durkheim, Emile. 1964. *Suicide*. (Originally published in 1897.) Glencoe, IL: Free Press.

Eisler, Lauren. 2004. "Youth in Custody: A Foucauldian Analysis of Norm Internalization." Saskatoon, SK: University of Saskatchewan Doctoral Thesis.

Erikson, Kai. 1966. *Wayward Puritans: A Study in the Sociology Of Deviance*. New York: John Wiley.

Eysenck, H.J. 1977. *Crime and Personality*. London: Routledge and Kegan Paul

Foucault, Michel. 1979. *Discipline and Punish: The Birth of the Prison*. New York: Vintage Books.

Goodwin, Donald W. 1986. "Studies of Familial Alcoholism: A Growth Industry." In Donald W. Goodwin, Katherin Teilman Van Dusen, and Sarnoff A. Mednick (eds.), *Longitudinal Research in Alcoholism*. Boston: Kluwer Academic Publishing Group.

Hagan, John, John Simpson, and A.R. Gillis. 1995. "A Power-Control Theory of Gender and Delinquency." In Robert Silverman and James Creechan (eds.), *Canadian Delinquency*. Scarborough, ON: Prentice-Hall.

Hare, R.D. 1998. "The PCL-R Assessment of Psychopathy: Some Issues and Concerns." *Legal and Criminal Psychology* 3: 101–22.

Hirschi, Travis. 1969. *Causes Of Delinquency*. Los Angeles: University of California Press

Hodgson, D. 2000. "Guilty Mind of Guilty Brain? Criminal Responsibility in the Age of Neuroscience." *Australia Law Journal* 74: 661.

Keyes, Steve. 2001. "Are You Working with an Industrial Psychopath?" Available at <http://www.ignite-me.com/articles_viewcategory.cfm?ArticleCategoryID=13> accessed January 18, 2007.

Kohlberg, Lawrence. 1969 "Stage and Sequence: The Cognitive-Developmental Approach." In David A. Goslin (ed.), *Handbook of Socialization Theory and Research*. Chicago: Rand McNally.

Lombroso, Cesare. 1911. *Crime: Its Causes and Remedies*. Boston: Little, Brown.

Mednick, S.A., and J. Volavka. 1980. "Biology and Crime." In N. Morris and N. Tonry (eds.), *Crime and Justice: An Annual Review of Research*. Chicago: University of Chicago Press.

Merton, Robert K. 1938 "Social Structure and Anomie." *American Sociological Review* 3: 672–82.

Miller, Walter. 1958. "Lower Class Culture as a Generating Milieu of Gang Delinquency." *Journal of Social Issues*. 14.

Nye, F.I. 1958. *Family Relationships and Delinquent Behaviour*. New York: John Wiley.

Piaget, Jean. 1932. *The Moral Judgement of the Child*. New York: Harcourt.

Pollock, V.E., T.W. Teasdale, W.F. Gabrielli and J. Knop. 1986 "Subjective and Objective Measures of Response to Alcohol among Young Men at Risk for Alcoholism." *Journal of Studies on Alcohol* 47: 297–304.

Reckless, W.C. 1973. *The Crime Problem*. Third edition. New York: Appleton Century Crofts.

Shah, Saleem A., and Loren H. Roth. 1974. "Biological and Psychophysiological Factors in Criminology." In Danial Glaser (ed.), *Handbook of Criminology*. Chicago: Rand McNally.

Shaw, C., and H.D. McKay. 1969. *Juvenile Delinquency and Urban Areas*. Chicago: The University of Chicago Press.

Sheldon, William. 1949. *Varieties of Delinquent Youth: An Introduction to Constitutional Psychiatry*. New York: Harper and Row.

Siegel, Larry, and Chris McCormick. 1999. *Criminology in Canada: Theories, Patterns and Typologies*. Toronto: ITP Nelson.

Skinner, B.F. 1953. *Science and Human Behaviour*. New York: MacMillan.

Sutherland, Edwin. 1939. *Criminology*. Philadelphia: J.B. Lippincott.

Szasz, Thomas. 1970. *The Manufacture of Madness: A Comparative Study of the Inquisition and the Mental Health Movement*. New York: Harper and Row.

Wilson, James Q. 1975. *Thinking About Crime*. New York: Vintage Books.

Wilson, Margo, and Martin Daly. 1985. "Competitiveness, Risk Taking, and Violence: The Young Male Syndrome." *Ethology and Sociobiology* 6: 59–73.

York, Geoffrey. 1992. T*he Dispossessed: Life and Death in Native Canada*. Toronto: Little Brown and Company.

2

The Emergence of Pluralist Theories in Criminology

Lauren Eisler

KEY FACTS

> In 1999/2000, 60 percent of the 57,000 convicted offenders in Canada, between 18 and 25, had one or more previous convictions in either youth or adult criminal court. Seventy-two percent of those had multiple prior convictions.

> Males are more likely to be recidivists and to commit crime — 62 percent of males had prior convictions in 1999/2000 compared to 48 percent of female offenders.

> Young offenders often pick up the "tricks of their trade" within detention centres and correctional facilities.

> Trauma within families is statistically connected to trouble with the legal system. Disadvantage within family life is related to relatively high levels of arrest and incarceration. "In effect, we punish many young people for the disadvantages they are born into; ones over which they have almost no control."

> A study by the Federation of Saskatchewan Indian Nations (FSIN) showed that Aboriginal youth join gangs for acceptance and belonging, for money, power, and security, and for excitement, because they feel disenfranchised and unattached to family, school, and community. Some, especially those who have served time in custody, are forced to join gangs.

> The Seattle Social Development Project reported that learning disabilities, negative perceptions by authority figures, labelling, limited school success, and weak attachments to school are associated with gang membership.

Sources: Thomas, Hurley and Grimes 1999/2000; Winslow and Zhang 2006; Schissel 2006: 121; FSIN 2003; Hill et al. 1999.

Pluralist theories emerged during the second half of the twenty-first century in an attempt to bridge the gap between conventional and critical perspectives around the issue of power. Conventional theories are based on two fundamental notions of society. First is the notion that a majority of members of society agree on what is morally right and wrong. And second, that the myriad of elements within society, including social institutions like schools, churches, business, and government agencies, work cooperatively towards a common vision of the greater good. Pluralist theories, in an attempt to bridge the considerable gap between conventional and critical theories, posit that power is held by a variety of groups that compete with each other for social dominance. Since no one group or class is able to dominate all other groups, a plurality of competing interest groups and political parties is seen to characterize democratic societies. Within this view, conflict is based upon the competitive interactions between different types of groups that are jockeying for power. From this perspective, conflict, compromise, and accommodation result from the plural nature of society itself.

Key features of a pluralist paradigm include the premise that social power is decentralized, fragmented, and widely dispersed, and originates from a multiplicity of sources. This decentralization of power naturally occurs because society is comprised of many diverse groups that have dissimilar and often competing interests and struggle for control over resources. Pluralist theories and theorists posit that the variances found within society include dif-

> Pluralist theories try to bridge the gap between conventional and critical theories by positing that various groups share power and compete with each other for social dominance.

ferences in age, gender, sexual orientation, class, and/or ethnicity, and that they often provide the foundation for naturally occurring diversity. Such differences may unite individuals who have common interests that naturally set them apart from other groups in society. This multiplicity allows for a broadening of the variables to be considered when examining how and why conflict occurs within modern society — a fundamental way that pluralist theories attempt to bridge the divide between conventional and conflict explanations of delinquency and crime. It is also important to note that a pluralist perspective recognizes that some groups hold more power than others and, therefore, may have greater opportunity to set the agenda and exert control over the access to and distribution of resources. It is also a fundamental premise of pluralist theorists that power balances are in a constant state of flux between these competing groups and that no one social group dominates society over the long term.

An important point within this perspective is that while various social groups have different and often competing values, beliefs, and interests, there is agreement on the usefulness of law as a value-neutral and formal means of dispute resolution. According to Schmalleger (2003: 74):

> from a pluralist perspective, the law, rather than reflecting common values, exists as a peace-keeping tool that allows officials and agencies within the government to settle disputes effectively between individuals and among groups. It also assumes that whatever settlement is reached will be acceptable to all parties because of their agreement on the fundamental role of law in dispute settlement.

In summation, pluralist theories essentially argue that conflict is a natural occurrence in societies characterized by multiplicity and its potential for competitiveness. However, this perspective also entails consensus on the role of law as a value-neutral mediator of the inevitable disputes that arise in modern pluralist societies.

> Pluralist theories argue that conflict is a natural occurrence in societies comprised of different groups who hold often competing beliefs.

Thorsten Sellin (1938), one of the first theorists to incorporate a pluralist perspective, focused on the impact of cultural diversity in modern, industrial society. Sellin argued that law reflected the values and interests held by the dominant cultural or ethnic group within that society. Criminal law defines what we may refer to as crime norms — those behaviours deemed socially inappropriate — and clearly establishes punishments considered acceptable by the dominant group. The conduct norms of other social groups reflect their values and belief systems and may contradict or come into conflict with the established crime norms. As a result, the everyday behaviours of individual members of competing and less powerful social groups may be defined as deviant and/or criminal. Sellin (1938) posited that as society became more heterogeneous, the probability of conflict between social, cultural, or ethnic groups would increase. This in turn would cause an increase in behaviours deemed deviant or criminal.

George Vold (1958) expanded upon Sellin's concepts when he suggested that instead of trying to explain crime as individual law violations, we needed to consider its social nature. Vold draws attention to crime as the by-product of group struggle and conflict. Competition arises as different groups struggle to maintain or increase the strength of their position in society concerning the control of resources — employment, money, education. The most successful group achieves the authority to create and pass legislation that limits the fulfilment of minority group needs. Vold thus furthers the pluralist contention that deviance and crime result from conflict and competition among groups struggling for social dominance, not from individual pathologies.

> Pluralists contend that deviance and crime stem from conflict and competition between groups struggling for social dominance, not from individual pathologies.

Ralf Dahrendorf further developed the analysis of power relations within society by shifting the focus from those who control the economics of society to those who control the social institutions present in modern society. Dahrendorf argued that in order to understand power one needs to focus on the competition for institutional authority (Liska 1987). Institutional authority is the power embedded in the structural relations found within specific societies that is often not directly related to the ownership of productive forces. Instead, power is located in the social institutions that govern everyday life. Authority is vested within groups that control central positions within educational, governmental, and religious institutions (Liska 1987).

Austin Turk builds on Dahrendorf's analysis and turns the focus to legal conflict and criminalization when he explores the conditions under which certain types of social, behavioural, and cultural conflicts are redefined and reclassified into legal conflicts and the conditions under which people who violate the law become criminalized. In essence, "under what circumstances are laws enforced?" (Liska 1987: 178). For Turk, the law, far from being a neutral arbitrator of disputes is in fact a mechanism for the expression of power and influence (1969).

The 1930s also saw the emergence of a new way of examining the nature of deviant and/or criminal behaviour. Radical shifts in criminological thought occurred when the Chicago School of Sociology began to challenge the Lombrosian idea that some individuals were born criminals. This, combined with an emergence of critical assessment of social institutions — including government — established to control crime, influenced the emergence of this new school of thought. The idea of individual pathologies as an explanation for deviance and criminal behaviours began to lose support during the 1930s, and a new understanding of conflict as social reaction emerged.

Theories of Interaction

By 1938 a new theoretical perspective known as Symbolic Interactionism emerged. In contrast to structural theories, which focused both on the characteristics of the deviant and the social structure that leads to deviance, interactionist explanations focus on the relationship between individuals and groups when defining and labelling certain acts as deviant (Rubington and Weinburg 1987). Interactionist theories challenge the structural argument that social consensus on norms and values ensures that deviant behaviour is easily recognized and that the punishment of deviant acts or actors is a necessary and functional reaffirmation of social norms and values. Instead, interactionist theories argue that all members and groups within a society use symbols, and place meanings on these symbols, through communication, and that labels of deviance are best understood as symbols that identify and marginalize those so labelled. Because people act on the basis of these socially constructed definitions and labels of individuals and/or groups, the reaction of those labelled and those who create and implement the label are important (Rubington and Weinburg 1987).

Symbolic interactionism was greatly influenced by the work of George Herbert Mead and Charles Horton Cooley, and focused on individual levels of interaction. Cooley is best known for his concept of the looking-glass self (Schur 1971). He postulated that our understanding of ourselves is, in essence, a reflection of our perception of how others perceive and react to us. Mead further develops this concept by drawing attention to the interaction between an emerging self and the perceptions of others' reactions to that self. According to Adler and Laufer (1993), Mead's concept of the "I and Me" represented attempts to describe the way in which the individual both affects and is affected by the social environment through the process of interpretation" (Adler and Laufer 1993: 4).

Labelling Theory

Frank Tannenbaum's theoretical model (1938) known as the "dramatization of evil," has its roots in the work of Mead and Cooley and began to emerge in the mid- to late 1930s. Tannenbaum expanded the work of these two theorists by concentrating on what occurs after an individual is caught and identified as having engaged in a criminal act (Brown, Esbensen and Geis 2004). The term "dramatization of evil" refers to this process of social reaction to illegal behaviour and changes the focus from what is happening inside the individual who engages in criminal behaviour to what is occurring in the environment of the individual that creates the need for deviant behaviour (Summer 1994). The causes of criminality, according to Tannenbaum, lie in society's inability to accept deviation from the socially constructed concepts of "normal." This concept of "normal" is the passing of judgments on the habits and ways of life of different groups. From this perspective, individuals or groups that engage in what is defined as deviant or criminal activity challenge the dominant groups' habits, values, and beliefs. Those who challenge the dominant norms are excluded and branded "deviant" to ensure that the status quo is not threatened. The challenge, therefore, is to explore how a particular group ends up in conflict with mainstream society and how the individual is drawn into a criminal group.

> Interactionist theories argue that those who challenge dominant norms are branded "deviant" to protect the status quo; they explore how groups conflict with mainstream society and how individuals are drawn into criminal groups.

Edwin Lemert continued to explore the results of labelling in his 1951 work "Social Pathology" in which he set out to show that deviance was the result of interactions between individuals and the social reactions to their behaviours. Lemert also used this work to outline his concept of primary and secondary deviance. For Lemert, primary deviance occurred when the individual engaged in actions that violate social norms but in which the individual does not view him or herself as engaging in a deviant role. In other words, the deviations "are rationalized or otherwise dealt with as functions of a socially acceptable role" (Lemert 1951: 75). In contrast, for Lemert, secondary deviance occurs:

> When a person begins to employ his deviant behaviour or a role based upon it

as a means of defense, attack, or adjustment to the overt and covert problems created by the consequent societal reaction to him, his deviation is secondary. Objective evidences of this change will be found in the symbolic appurtenances of the new role, in clothes, speech, posture, and mannerisms, which in some cases heighten social visibility, and which in some cases serve as symbolic cues to professionalism. (1951: 76)

At this juncture, the individual undergoes a shift in self-identity and begins to internalize the deviant role. This internalization of the deviant self-identification is reinforced by the negative labels, which, in turn, are reinforced by the individual's continued engagement in deviant activities. Lemert also posited that the adoption of the deviant label occurred over time and, for the most part, a single occurrence of deviant behaviour was not likely to generate a severe enough social reaction for secondary deviance to occur. Instead, for Lemert, there were stages to the development of secondary deviance, and he provides an example showing how negative social reactions can move the individual from primary to secondary deviation:

As an illustration of this sequence the behaviour of an errant schoolboy can be cited. For one reason or another, let us say excessive energy, the schoolboy engages in a classroom prank. He is penalized for it by the teacher. Later, due to clumsiness, he creates another disturbance and, again he is reprimanded. Then, as sometimes happens, the boy is blamed for something he did not do. When the teacher used the tag "bad boy" or "mischief maker" or other invidious terms, hostility and resentment are excited in the boy, and he may feel that he is blocked in playing the role expected of him. Thereafter, there may be a strong temptation to assume his role in the class as defined by the teacher particularly when he discovers that there are rewards as well as penalties from such a role. (1951: 77)

To summarize, once an individual is labelled deviant, society will view and react to the individual based on the label. This encourages the individual to accept the label and continue in the deviant role. Such acceptance leads to a change in the individual's self-concept and results in secondary deviance. For Lemert, "deviance is established in social roles and is perpetuated by the very forces directed to its elimination or control (1967: v).

The work of Edwin Lemert brings into focus the role of societal reactions in the creation and adoption of labels for and on the individual. According to Lemert (1974), the term "societal reaction" refers to the process by which societies respond to deviant behaviours, and includes informal reactions and formal reactions through agents of social control (i.e., police, courts, corrections). He claims

> Once individuals are labelled deviant, society stereotypes them, which encourages them to continue in the deviant role. This change in self-concept results in secondary deviance.

that the term "societal reaction" is a "very general term summarizing both the expressive reaction of others... and the action directed to its control" (1967: 41–42). While societal reaction may not be a causal factor in primary deviation, once the labelling takes place the deviant behaviour is encouraged and perpetuated through a self-fulfilling prophecy.

Howard Becker continued to explore and expand on labelling theory in his 1963 work "Outsiders: Studies in the Sociology of Deviance." Becker argued that deviance was not a naturally occurring phenomenon but was socially constructed to reflect the interests, beliefs, values, and norms of those in positions of power. For Becker, what was important to study was not the individual acts of deviance but how rules, as the reflection of social norms held by the majority of society, were enforced both formally and informally. Becker argued that enforced rules were applied differentially to individuals and groups and that these rules tended to facilitate favourable consequences for those who implement the label.

Becker also contributed to the development of labelling theory through the creation of a number of terms. One term — "outsiders" — is used to describe rule-breakers who are labelled and who internalize and accept the label and come to view themselves as different, or outside mainstream society (Becker 1963). Becker also builds on Lemert's (1951) work on primary and secondary deviance through his exploration of how an individual comes to accept deviance as his or her "master status." Master status refers to the primary role by which an individual internalizes and defines him or herself. For Becker, primary deviance, as defined by Lemert, is the first step in the adoption of a master status and may be taken intentionally or unintentionally. The process of being caught and labelled as deviant acts as a stepping stone to secondary deviance. If individuals accept the label "deviant" as a master status, they become outsiders and either reject or are denied opportunities to succeed in a socially acceptable manner. Once this occurs, the individual moves into secondary deviance and turns to illegitimate means to succeed or survive. The final step in this transformation occurs when the rule-breaker enters or joins a deviant subculture. This affiliation provides the individual with support and allows them to rationalize and justify their behaviour and activity.

Becker (1963) also explores how rules are created and enforced within society. He examines how individuals in positions of power and authority make rules, and he uses the term "moral entrepreneur" to describe them. For Becker, a moral entrepreneur is a person who takes the lead role in crusading for a rule or rules to deal with a perceived social evil. The creation, implementation, and enforcement of the rule occur when the moral entrepreneur brings the rule infraction to the attention of the general public. According to Becker (1963), the success of each new moral crusade creates a new group of outsiders and new responsibilities for enforcement agencies. Therefore, according to Becker, it is less important to study the behaviour of the individual than to examine how and why rules are created and enforced and who becomes an outsider in the process.

> According to Becker, it is less important to study individual behaviour than to study how and why rules are created and enforced and who becomes an outsider in the process.

John Braithwaite, in his 1989 work "Crime, Shame, and Reintegration," sets out to explore the process of social control that he calls "shaming." Braithwaite begins by defining two forms of shaming: reintegrative and disintegrative. When reintegrative shaming is utilized, the individual is brought back into society after making amends for deviant or criminal behaviours. Just the opposite occurs when disintegrative shaming is employed. In this case the offender is permanently shunned by mainstream society. Braithwaite, in keeping with labelling theory claims, argues that disintegrative shaming creates a special class of outcasts who are prevented from reconnecting with society and are forced to re-engage in criminal activities to survive. He also argues that reintegrative shaming is possible when social rituals of forgiveness take place but that there are few such rituals available to the deviant. Instead there is an overabundance of disintegrative ceremonies used to confer deviant status on individuals, through formal agents of social control, such as the criminal justice system, as well as through informal social sanctions.

Labelling theories have helped to explain how internalizing socially constructed labels may increase the likelihood of criminal behaviours among individuals in society. However, labelling theories tend to be deterministic and view individuals as passive entities who are led to behave in predictable ways through the simple acceptance of the label. They also fail to explore how crime is socially constructed and how justice is applied.

Phenomenology and Ethnomethodology

Phenomenological theory emerged in the 1960s with the work of Alfred Schutz and posits that reality is a socially constructed and shared phenomenon. People act on the meaning that events and others have for them. Schutz suggested that subjective experience is a shared reality that draws upon a common stock of knowledge comprised of typifications and formulas for accomplishing particular tasks, and also utilizes common-sense understanding and theories shared by members of a group. Through the processes of socialization, these typifications and understandings are internalized by members of society (Berger and Luckmann 1967).

> Phenomenological theory emerged in the 1960s with the work of Alfred Schutz and posits that reality is a socially constructed and shared phenomenon

Although the primary focus of ethnomethodology differs from that of phenomenology, both are centred on describing the emergence of order from the shared experience of members of particular societies (Zimmerman and Wieder 1970: 286–90). This focus on order as a practical accomplishment of the everyday interaction of members of a group produces ethnomethodology's distinctive perspective on deviance. Simply put, deviance in and of itself is not a concern for ethnomethodological analysis. Deviance, as a social construct, is viewed as an organizing concept that emerges through social interactions. These ongoing constructions produce a sense of order within the world of everyday life. Within the context of these interactional constructions, which distinguish the normal and ordinary from the abnormal and strange, ethnomethodological interest is raised.

> Ethnomethodology and phenomenology are both centred on describing the emergence of order out of the shared experience of members of particular societies.

For the ethnomethodologist, there is no shared set of understanding and meaning that members of a society attach to the world around them. There is no shared sense of deviance that can be called upon to order the strange and unusual behaviours of others. What members of a group share are methods for making sense. Schutz's common stock of knowledge is re-conceptualized as a shared set of interpretive procedures — in essence, these are "making-sense activities," which are invoked and employed continually in human interactions. These procedures allow members to produce practical accounts of specific individuals engaged in specific activities in the context of specific situations. Deviance and deviants emerge as particular designations that provide practical understandings of everyday situations. By constructing a sense that particular people and specific behaviours are "outside" the norm, members produce a shared understanding of the reality of the norm.

The construction of deviance is always from a particular point of view. The meaning of being a criminal is not contained within the act one commits but emerges from the context through which one's act is interpreted.

Through this process organizations emerge as definers and controllers of deviance;

individuals come to be "understood" as deviant, and they often come to see themselves as deviant. The important component here is what we typically fail to see, or at least forget: that it is through our "work" that reality and our sense of self is constructed. These accounts develop a natural, taken-for-granted character that shapes the social response which, in turn, generates new contexts — and the process continues (Phofl 1994).

> For ethnomethodologists the meaning of being a criminal is contained not within the act one commits but the context through which one's act is interpreted.

Once we arrive at a particular account (explanation) of a situation or person, we reflexively reconstruct our understanding of the process so that our decision or definition appear to us as normal, natural, and "real."

> The power of these constructions when they are couched in an assumption of deviant behaviour can be so overwhelming as to shape an actor's identity and lead to his or her immersion within a world of deviance. The former identity, at best, receives the accent of mere appearance... what he is now is what, "after all, he was all along." (Garfinkel 1965: 422)

The construction of the deviant is a process that occurs at several levels. At the interpersonal level the construction of deviance allows individuals to examine and define behaviours as problematic, and to use these definitions as a measuring tool to examine and compare their own behaviours. At a formal level the identification and control of activities and individuals labelled deviant become a practical activity embedded within the routines of organizational life (Sudnow 1965). Therefore, accounts of deviance provided by official agencies of social control (crime rates, prevalence of illicit drug use, etc.) are not viewed by the ethnomethodologist as the reality of deviant behaviour "but as indicators and reflections or organizational properties and routines" (Liska and Messner 1999: 154).

Ethnomethodology suggests that definitions of deviance and the deviant are socially constructed and given meaning within situational context of everyday life. This perspective forms a foundation for understanding how deviant labels and categories are created and applied through the social processes of interpretation, typification, and negotiation. As Liska and Messner state:

> The qualities and attributes of a particular individual become lost or distorted as she or he is located within the context of a particular category of deviance. His or her behaviour, and identity, comes to represent the category of deviance, and the category of deviance, in turn, becomes an explanation for the behaviour or identity in question. (1999: 173)

Like labelling theories, however, ethnomethodology fails to explain how laws are constructed and differently applied to individual members of society.

Integrated Theories

Integrated theories began to appear in the 1940s but gained strength and credibility during the 1970s. Criminologists began to combine existing theories to explore the causes of crime more fully. Traditional theories did not adequately account for the myriad of variations in crime rates, including differences in gender, race, social class, and criminal activity. This new perspective recognized that there may be multiple issues involved in trying to determine the causes of crime. According to Brown, Esbensen, and Geis (2004), another reason for increased interest in integrated theories is the development of more sophisticated statistical methods in the social sciences during the 1950s. They argue that

> Integrated theories began to appear in the 1940s but gained strength and credibility during the 1970s. Criminologists began to combine existing theories to better explore the causes of crime.

> Early theories were usually limited to the examination of relationships between two variables, the connect, for example, between social class and crime. On occasion a third, or controlling variable, would be introduced to see if there were different patterns of association. This did not permit criminologists to talk about causes of crime, only correlates. (429)

The most common attempts at integration have involved social control and social learning theories. Less common has been the integration of social control and strain theories, and even less common have been attempts to integrate all three of the major perspectives. Still other attempts at integration have included the labelling approach, social disorganization, conflict, and deterrence theories.

Clifford Shaw and Henry McKay (1942) provided an early attempt at integrating social disorganization and social learning theories. They posit that the organization and physical structure of the community were of major importance in affecting behaviour and interaction patterns. It was the diversity of values and behaviours in communities, however, that was instrumental in exposing youth to deviant alternatives.

Cloward and Ohlin's differential association theory (1960) incorporates elements of traditional strain theory with social learning theory. Societal goals can be attained through the use of legitimate or illegitimate means, depending in part on a person's access to different opportunity structures. According to strain theory, when legitimate opportunities for success are unavailable and illegitimate means are present, a criminal subculture may develop. Cloward and Ohlin merge this perspective with a fundamental element of social learning theory when they posit that delinquency is a learned behaviour requiring social support and confirmation. Exposure to strain alone will not cause delinquent behaviours, but strain combined with exposure to delinquent subcultures and the presence of illegitimate opportunity may cause an individual to turn to illegitimate means of goal attainment.

Elliott, Ageton, and Canter (1979) combine elements of strain, social learning, and social control theories to create a theoretical model that "avoids the class bias inherent in traditional perspectives and takes into account multiple causal paths to sustained patterns of delinquent behaviour" (3). They argue that it is not only possible but preferable to be able to identify individuals who are engaged in habitual criminal activity through the examination of early socialization experiences as resulting in weak or strong bonds (Brown, Esbesnson, and Geis 2004). The behavioural patterns developed through early socialization processes are challenged as children enter early adolescence. They begin to experience an increased exposure to social institutions — school, work, athletics — and situations that may either challenge or support the early socialization outcomes. The peer group also begins to take on a more significant role in the life of the adolescent, and the types of peer groups the youth associates with likewise support or challenge. Thus, there is no dominant theory to explain why some youth move towards delinquency while others avoid such behaviours. A combination of explanations is needed to do justice to the complexity of such behaviours.

Colvin and Pauly (1983) challenge traditional theories of juvenile delinquency for focusing too heavily upon micro-sociological levels of explanations. These theories focus on behaviours or conditions that tend to occur prior to delinquent behaviours, but they do not attempt to address how these variables are distributed in social systems. In order to address this theoretical weakness, Colvin and Pauly develop a structural-Marxist theory that integrates elements of social control theory and maintains that capitalism, and its accompanying social relations to the means of production, produce different attitudes and responses to authority. Based upon the type of social control found within the workplace, workers develop respect and comply with the power structures, or they develop hostility and alienation. The stronger and more coercive the control, the greater the levels of alienation and resistance. Workplace experiences are recreated in the home and affect children's socialization experiences within the family, school, and peer groups.

Power-control theory by Hagan, Simpson, and Gillis may be viewed as an attempt to incorporate gender into social control theories of crime and deviance. The basic premise resembles other social control theories in assuming that delinquency and criminality are forms of risk-taking behaviour. The goal of this theory, however, is to explore sex differences in delinquency and criminality by examining the influence of variations in parenting styles on delinquent behaviours of young males and females (Hagan et al. 1979; Hagan et al. 1990). In particular, power-control theory posits that parental control and youth attitudes towards risk-taking behaviours are affected by family relations. Two distinctive ideal-family types are considered. First there is the patriarchal family, in which the husband is employed in a position of authority and the wife in not employed outside the home. The second ideal type is the egalitarian family, in which both husband and wife are employed in authority positions outside the home. Power-control theory argues that in the patriarchal family a traditional division of labour will exist. Fathers, and more importantly, mothers are expected to control their daughters more than their sons. Daughters will be socialized to concentrate on domestic labour, while sons will be socialized to prepare for their eventual participation in the outside workforce. In an egalitarian family type, both sons and daughters will experience the same types of parental control. "In other words, in egalitarian families, as mothers gain power relative to husbands, daughters gain power relative to sons" (Hagan et al. 1987: 792). Based on these assumptions, Hagan et al. predict that "patriarchal families will be characterized by large gender differences in common delinquent behaviours, while egalitarian families will be characterized by smaller gender differences in delinquency" (1987: 793).

> Power control theory explores sex differences in delinquency and criminality by examining the influence of variations in parenting styles on delinquent behaviours of young males and females

Left realism is a relatively new orientation in criminology developed in Britain in the 1980s during the era of Thatcherism. Lea and Young (1984) argue that there were four fundamental reasons for the development of Left realist criminology. These were (1) the crisis of causality, represented by increasing crime rates; (2) the crisis of penality, represented by the failure of the prison system and methods of rehabilitation; (3) the growing public awareness of crimes that had been invisible and the effects on the victims; and (4) an increasingly critical public that demanded efficiency and accountability from the criminal justice system and agents of social control.

Left realist theorists argued that there was a need to "take crime seriously," which meant that while they acknowledged the structural conditions that exist within society and contribute to the unequal distribution of advantage and resources, they felt that short-term policies needed to be developed and implemented to protect those most at risk of criminal victimization and condemnation. They also argued that most crime was intra-class located — committed against others in the same class. But they also noted that those who suffered the most from any crime were those who were economically and socially marginalized. This acknowledgement brings into consideration the impact of crime and gender, and of race and class, and may be the most important contribution of the theory. Left realists also acknowledged and drew attention to the impact that crime and the fear of crime has

> Left realists argued that most crime was committed against others in the same class and that those who suffered the most from crime were the economically and socially marginalized.

on victims and argued that risk statistics should be replaced by impact statistics (Lea and Young 1994).

Left realists were also highly critical of traditional approaches to criminology that focused on either structural conditions (Marxist theories) or the individual in society (functionalist theories) as causal explanations for crime. They argued that crime must be examined within its social context. With this in mind, Left-realist criminologists posited that crime occurs at the intersections of the "square of crime." The square of crime includes the victim, the offender, the state (formal social control), and the public (informal social control), and all these elements must be considered when examining issues of crime.

The fundamental points of Left realism include the need to examine crime in its "natural state." By this, they mean that one must examine the form of the crime, its social context, and location, and its trajectory through time and space (Lea and Young 1994). The form of crime includes two dyads: the victim and the offender, and the state and the public. In this sense, Left realists were the first to consider the role of public opinion within the study of criminology. They also argue for the principle of multi-causality. It is not enough to look for structural explanations of crime, nor can one simply concentrate on the role of the individual. Instead, we need to examine a number of elements that contribute to the occurrence of crime if we hope to develop comprehensive anti-crime strategies. Left realists also acknowledge that crime occurs within specific contexts and that findings cannot be generalized. As well, they draw upon social surveys to collect information that can be used to develop a clearer understanding of the issues. They argue that victimization surveys are also important because one should consider the fear of victimization as well as the impact of crime on victims. They are, however, suspicious of crime statistics, which do not necessarily reveal the true nature of crime. They argue that the "dark side of crime" remains unexplored through the use of crime statistics.

Left-realist criminology has successfully drawn attention to the complicated relationships among victim, offender, state, and public in its analysis of crime and victimization. The use of social surveys, focus on the multiple causal factors for criminal behaviour, and incorporation of the voices of victims of crime opened new doors of exploration, including abuse against women, the elderly, and the young.

> Integrative theories provide a more complete exploration of variances between race, gender, and class in relationship to both crime and social responses to crime and offer detailed analyses of causal variables and criminal behaviour.

In summation, integrative theories, while present in the work of theorists in the 1940s, gained strength and credibility in the 1970s and 1980s as theorists began to challenge traditional one-dimensional theories of crime and punishment.

Integrative theorists continue to push the boundaries of explanation when examining issues of crime, criminal behaviour, and justice. These theories have pursued a more complex and complete exploration of variances between race, gender, and class in relationship to both crime and social responses to crime, and have offered more detailed and complex analyses of causal variables and criminal behaviour.

Postmodernism and Postmodern Theories

Postmodern theories, which emerged from European intellectual endeavours during the twenty-first century, are highly critical of traditional theories that use scientific methods to discover universal truths and explanations for social phenomena. Postmodernists argue that universal truths, or grand theories, do not exist and that there is a need for the recognition and acceptance of multiple, and often competing, truths. Michel Foucault ("The Birth of the Clinic," 1975, "Discipline and Punish," 1979, and "The History of Sexuality," 1980b) offers what may be considered a postmodern analysis of the ability of individuals to offer resistance and instigate social change.[1] Foucault claimed that the determining characteristic of modern society has been the expansion of domination over both human and non-human nature. Despite the promise of progress, the development of science and scientific discourse operates as a form of social control over both the actions and body of the individual. Indeed, according to Foucault, scientific discourse, with its promise of universal truths, objectivity, and rational organization, replaced religion as the bearer of authority and control in modern society. Schissel argues that Foucault

> extends the theme that as we become more "civilized" and knowledgeable, we increase our ability to define, detect, and control an increasing number of marginalized (deviantized) individuals. In effect, Foucault argues that we are creating an increasing number of "docile bodies" through scientific knowledge-based disciplines, such as criminology, that continually define and redefine unacceptable behaviour and enforce discipline. (in Schissel and Brooks 2002: 26)

The concept of power is central to the work of Foucault, who argued that power is not a binary force to be administered from the top down, or from the dominant to the repressed. Nor does power exist explicitly in social institutions such as medicine or education, or in rules or laws. Instead, power exists in the everyday transactions between social institutions and individuals. It is "the multiplicity of force relations immanent in the sphere in which they operate and which constitutes their own organizations" (Foucault cited in Fillingham 1993: 140). This means that power relations are not static but rather in a continual state of flux, being redefined and reinvented through the interactions of individuals and patterns of power within social institutions. For Foucault the existence of power relations

> For Foucault, power exists in the everyday transactions between social institutions and individuals, as "the multiplicity of force relations immanent in the sphere in which they operate and which constitutes their own organizations."

> depends on a multiplicity of points of resistance: these play the role of adversary, target, support, or handle the power relations... They [resistance] are the odd term in relations of power; they are inscribed in the latter as an irreducible opposite. Hence they too are distributed in irregular fashion: the points, knots, or

> focuses of resistance are spread over time and space at varying densities, at times mobilizing groups or individuals in a definitive way, inflaming certain points or the body, certain moments in life, certain types of behaviour. (1980a: 96)

Or, as Garland (1997) explains:

> The chains of interaction along with power flows are made up of a dense entanglement of freedoms and coercions, choices and constraints, the exercise of "voluntary choice" is itself entangled in calculations of interest, patterns of habits, and emotions of love, fear and obligation. (197)

Therefore, any analysis of power relations within society cannot be reduced to the study of a series of institutions but must be considered as rooted in the system of social networks.

Within his power/knowledge paradigm, Foucault conceptualized bio-power as a system of non-physical forces created and implemented in order to exert power and control over individual bodies. Bio-power consists of two elements: disciplinary technology and regularizing technologies. Disciplinary technology is aimed at the individual and is used to monitor movements, gestures, and locations. Foucault (1979) cited Bentham's panopticon as an example of disciplinary technology at its best. The structure of the panopticon, with its central observation tower and cells with open fronts facing the tower, ensured that prisoners could be under constant surveillance without ever being sure when, and if, they were being watched. This uncertainty resulted in prisoners learning to monitor their own actions and the creation of what Foucault termed the "docile body" — individuals who participated in self-surveillance and modified their behaviours accordingly. For Foucault, the function of the panoptic prison is

> to arrange things so that the surveillance is permanent in its effects…that the perfection of power should tend to render its actual exercise unnecessary; that this architectural apparatus should be a machine for creating and sustaining a power relation independent of the person who exercises it; in short, that the inmates should be caught up in a power situation of which they are themselves the bearers. (1979: 201)

The individual subject continues to be the focal point of concern, as the "target of power and knowledge techniques and the locus upon which docility is based" (Disano 2003).

Regularizing technologies incorporate technologies of normalization and confession, are aimed at the "species," and rely on examination instead of force to achieve control under the guise of welfare and compassion. Here we see the development of techniques such as actuarial tables and census taking in order to gather information about various factions of society. Technologies of normalization involve the creation and presentation of social reality by experts. Here, individuals are encouraged to believe that they can gain a deeper understanding of themselves with the help of experts. The individual can both know and become known through this process and can learn to effect changes. It is here that we see the development of experts who hold specific knowledge over a particular element of the body and utilize this knowledge as power over the individual. Language is created and utilized by the expert as a means of exerting power and control over the individual.

According to Sawicki, "Foucault claims that deviance is controlled and norms are established through the very process of identifying the deviant as such, then observing it, further classifying it, monitoring and treating it." (1991: 39). Normalizing technologies establish common definitions of goals and procedures that become accepted examples of how a well-ordered domain of human activity should be organized.

In conjunction with technologies of normalization, Foucault explores what he refers to as the "technologies of the confessional." The technologies of the confessional have their roots in the nineteenth-century medical examination in which, as in other forms of confession, individuals exposed to authorities their deepest sexual fantasies and hidden practices. Equally important, and closely related to normalization, was the idea that individuals were convinced that through their participation in the confession it was possible to gain greater self-knowledge (Rabinow 1984). Foucault saw the confession, especially about sexuality, as a central component in the expanding technologies for the discipline and control of bodies, populations, and society itself. From this perspective, the individual equals a body of knowledge, both to him/herself and to others. Disciplinary and regularizing technologies are tied to scientific discourse in the technologies of the self, and work towards the creation of the "docile body."

> Foucault saw the confession, especially about sexuality, as a central component in the expanding technologies for the discipline and control of bodies, populations, and society itself.

Foucault's work has been criticized for its perceived neglect of the state and for its tendency to characterize individuals as "docile bodies" instead of active subjects (Garland 1997). Foucault's work on governmentality addressed both these issues. His 1982 essay, "The Subject and Power," presented a re-conceptualized concept of power that stressed the fundamental role of the active subject as the entity through which power is exercised. Here governmental power constructs individuals who are capable of choice and action, shapes them as active subjects, and seeks to align their choices with the objectives of governing authority (Garland 1997). Within this context, government is not the suppression of individual subjectivity but rather the cultivation of that subjectivity in specific forms, aligned to specific governmental aims. Subjects of government are to be seen as participating in the process over which they exert no control.

It is important to note that while Foucault's analysis of government does not focus primarily on a substantive or institutional account of the "state," it does, at times adopt this broad perspective. However, for the most part Foucault focuses on particular practices of governing that are located in a variety of sites. This emphasis on practices, together with an extended conception of "governmental authorities" (one that embraces, families, churches, professional, experts, and all the many powers that engage in what Garland (1997) refers to as the "conduct of conduct") dissolves any rigid line of demarcation between the private and the public, or between state and civil society. So while the state is without doubt a point from which emerges a variety of projects of government, and a location from which numerous private powers derive support for their authority, it is by no means the focus of all governmental activity. For Foucault, then, power is much more insidious and surrounds the individual with an invisible web of constraints from which they are powerless to escape. In fact, through the technologies of normalizing, the individual becomes a willing participant in subjectification.

> For Foucault, power surrounds the individual with an invisible web of inescapable constraints. The technologies of normalizing make individuals willing participants in their own subjectification.

There have been criticisms of Foucault's work, and the postmodernist/poststruc-turalist perspective in general, for ignoring issues of class, gender, and race. As Schissel states:

> and Foucault's writing as a whole tends to ignore the larger, structural sources of power, instead focusing on how power operates at the individual level. For example, if we, as Foucault did, want to study how new prisoners come to un-derstand and conform to the rule and demands of prisons, we may certainly uncover the formal and informal mechanisms of social control. The prisoner code, the discretion of the guards, the diagnoses of social workers, and the prison rules all create an identified and disciplined prisoner. But as we study this "microphysics of power" we could easily ignore the larger structural issues that brought mostly marginalized people into prison — issues such as poverty, exploitation, discriminatory policing, and prejudicial legal treatment. (in Schis-sel and Brooks 2002: 26)

However, this body of work has made significant contributions to the study of the con-nections between power, knowledge, and social control, and we are encouraged to study the ulterior motives found within language and knowledge systems that are created and controlled by a privileged few (Schissel 2002).

Conclusion

Pluralist theories have not been without criticism for their perceived failure to acknowl-edge power structures that operate within societies to limit choices for individual be-haviours. There appears to be an inherent assumption in pluralist theories that groups within society have equal opportunities to influence change and to gain power and dominance in society. Critics of this theoretical perspective would argue that while pluralist theories acknowledge conflict between social groups competing for social dominance, they fail to explore how social structures and institutions develop and work to maintain power imbalances within society that tip the scales in favour of certain individuals or groups. Pluralist theories are also accused of being unconcerned with, or unable to explain, how different groups are processed through the criminal justice system or why laws are applied in different ways to different groups. According to Brooks, there is a need to focus on issues such as patriarchy, capitalism, and coloniza-tion to begin to understand how structural inequalities may impede a group's ability to compete for social power and dominance (2002).

> Pluralist theories have been criticized for not ac-knowledging power structures that limit individual choices.

However, pluralist theories have attempted to bridge the gap between conventional and critical theories in order to develop and further our understanding of how power operates in tandem with human motivation and personal conditions. Conflict is not nec-essarily based on economic conditions but instead on the competitive interactions between different types of groups that jockey for power and control over resources. Pluralist theories have contributed to the development of criminology as a discipline by arguing that the vari-ances found within society include differences in age,

> Pluralist theories have con-tributed to criminology by ar-guing that the variances within society include differences in age, gender, sexual orientation, class, and race.

gender, sexual orientation, class, and race. In this way, pluralist theories, including labelling theories, ethnomethodology theories, integrated theories, and postmodern/post-structuralist theories, have encouraged criminological research and researchers to look beyond a single-cause exploration of criminal behaviour to a multi-variable exploration of deviance, crime, and criminality.

DISCUSSION QUESTIONS

1. How do structural pluralist theories attempt to our advance our understanding of deviance, crime, and criminality? How well do they succeed?

2. What role do negative social reactions play in the formation of secondary deviance?

3. What key insights does labelling theory provide to illuminate our understanding of deviance?

4. What is distinctive about the ethnomethodological approach to deviance that distinguishes it from other interactive and structural approaches?

5. Compare the different integrated theories detailed in the chapter.

6. What is central to Foucault's perspective on deviance and criminality that distinguishes it from "modern" approaches?

GLOSSARY OF TERMS

Bio-Power: a term developed by Michel Foucault that describes modern societies as characterized by systems of non-physical forces created and implemented in order to exert power and control over individual bodies. Bio-power consists of two elements: disciplinary technology and regularizing technologies. Disciplinary technology is aimed at the individual and is used to monitor movements, gestures, and locations.

Labelling Theory: sometimes called societal reaction theory, labelling theory is an extension of symbolic interactionism. Labelling theory entails analysis of social processes involved in the social attribution of positive or (more usually) negative characteristics to acts, individuals, or groups. It asks not only "who gets labelled" but "who does the labelling."

Moral Entrepreneur: a term used by Howard Becker to describe people who take the lead role in crusading for a rule or rules to deal with a perceived social evil. The creation, implementation, and enforcement of the rule occur when the moral entrepreneur brings the rule infraction to the attention of the general public. Becker argues that the success of each new moral crusade creates a new group of outsiders and new responsibilities for enforcement agencies.

Outsiders: a term used by Howard Becker to describe rule-breakers who are labelled and who internalize and accept the label and come to view themselves as different, or outside mainstream society

Pluralist Theories: a theoretical approach that attempts to bridge the gap between conventional and critical theories by positing that power is dispersed among variety of groups that compete with each other for social dominance. Since no one group or class is able to dominate all other groups, a "plurality" of competing interest groups and political parties is seen to characterize democratic societies. For pluralists, conflict is a natural occurrence in societies comprised of many different groups with different and often competing values and beliefs. This perspective also holds that there is consensus on the role of law as a value-neutral mediator of the inevitable disputes that arise in modern pluralist societies.

Power-Control Theory: an attempt by Hagan and associates to expand pluralist theory by incorporating gender and family type into social control theories of crime and deviance.

Primary Deviance: according to Edwin Lemert, primary deviance occurs when the individual engages in actions that violate social norms but does not view him or herself as engaging in a deviant role. Rather, such deviations are rationalized or otherwise dealt with as functions of a socially acceptable role.

Secondary Deviance: Edwin Lemert argues that when a person begins to employ his deviant behaviour or a role based upon it as a means of defence, attack, or adjustment to the overt and covert problems created by the consequent societal reaction to him, his deviation is secondary. In other words, secondary deviance involves a shift in self-identity in which an individual begins to internalize the deviant role. This internal-

ization of the deviant self-identification is reinforced by the negative labels, which in turn are reinforced by the individual's continued engagement in deviant activities.

Societal Reaction Theory: refers to the process by which societies respond to deviant behaviours. It includes informal reactions and formal reactions through agents of social control (i.e., police, courts, corrections).

Strain Theory: argues that societal goals can be attained through the use of legitimate or illegitimate means, depending in part on a person's access to different opportunity structures. According to strain theory, when legitimate opportunities for success are blocked or otherwise unavailable, and illegitimate means are present, a criminal subculture may develop.

Symbolic Interactionism: a theoretical approach that focuses on the relationship between individuals and groups in the defining and labelling of certain acts as deviant, rather than focusing on social structural conditions. Interactionist theories argue that all members and groups within a society use symbols and place meanings on these symbols through the communication process. They maintain that deviant labels can best be understood as symbols that identify and marginalize those who are labelled as deviant. Since people act on the basis of these socially constructed definitions and labels of individuals and/or groups, the reaction of those labelled and those who create and implement the label are important.

SUGGESTED READINGS

Becker, H. 1963. *Outsiders: Studies in the Sociology of Deviance*. New York: Free Press.
Braithwaite, J. 1989. *Crime, Shame and Reintegration*. Cambridge: Cambridge University Press.
Foucault, M. 1979. *Discipline and Punish: The Birth of the Prison*. New York: Vintage Books.
Garfinkel, H. 1967. *Studies in Ethnomethodology*. Englewood Cliffs, NJ: Prentice- Hall.

Lemert, E.M. 1967. *Human Deviance: Social Problems and Social Control.* Englewood Cliffs, NJ: Prentice Hall.

Schur, E.M. 1971. *Labeling Deviant Behavior: Its Sociological Implications.* New York: Harper & Row.

Shaw, C., and H.D. McKay. 1942. *Juvenile Delinquency and Urban Areas.* Chicago: University of Chicago Press.

Tannenbaum, F. 1938. *Crime and the Community.* Boston: Ginn.

NOTE

1. It is important to note that Michel Foucault has been considered many different things to many different people. His work may be considered as critical, functional, or postmodern, depending on who is discussing his work and depending on what piece of work is being analyzed.

REFERENCES

Adler, F., and W.S. Laufer (eds.). 199). *New Directions in Criminological Theory.* New Brunswick: Transaction Publishers.

Becker, H. 1963. *Outsiders: Studies in the Sociology of Deviance.* New York: Free Press.

Berger, P. and T. Luckmann. 1967. *The Social Construction of Reality,* Garden City, New York: Anchor Books.

Braithwaite, J. 1989. *Crime, Shame and Reintegration.* Cambridge: Cambridge University Press.

Brooks, C. 2002. "New Directions in Critical Criminology." In Bernard Schissel and Carolyn Brooks (eds.), *Marginality and Condemnation: An Introduction to Critical Criminology.* Nova Scotia: Fernwood Publishing.

Brown, S.E., F. Esbensen, and G. Geis. 2004. *Criminology: Explaining Crime and its Context.* Cincinnati: Anderson Publishing.

Cloward, R., and L. Ohlin. 1960. *Delinquency and Opportunity: A Theory of Delinquent Gangs.* New York: Free Press.

Colvin, M., and J. Pauley. 1983. "A Critique of Criminology: Towards an Integrated Structural-Marxist Theory of Delinquency Production." *American Journal of Sociology* 89, 513–51.

Dahrendorf, R. 1959. *Class and Class Conflict in an Industrial Society.* London: Routledge & Kegan Paul.

Disano, J.M. 2003. "Beyond our Borders: A Foucauldian Analysis of 'At-Risk' Youth." Unpublished Thesis. University of Saskatchewan.

Elliott, D., S. Agrton, and R. Cantor. 1979. "An Integrated Theoretical Perspective on Delinquent Behavior." *Journal of Research on Crime and Delinquency* 16: 3–27.

Fillingham, L.A. 1993. *Foucault for Beginners.* New York: Writers and Readers Publishing Inc.

Foucault, M. 1969. *Madness and Civilization.* New York: Mentor.

_____. 1975. *The Birth of the Clinic: An Archeology of Medical Perception.* New York: Vintage Books.

_____. 1979. *Discipline and Punish: The Birth of the Prison.* New York: Vintage Books.

_____. 1980a. *Power/Knowledge: Selected Interviews and Other Writings 1972–1977.* New York: Pantheon Books.

_____. 1980b. *The History of Sexuality, Vol. 1: An Introduction.* New York: Vintage Books.

Garfinkel, H. 1965. Conditions of Successful Degradation Ceremonies. *American Journal of Sociology* 61: 420–24.

_____. 1967. *Studies in Ethnomethodology.* Englewood Cliffs, NJ: Prentice- Hall.

Garland, David. 1997. *Punishment and Modern Society: A Study in Social Theory.* Chicago: University of Chicago Press.

Hagan, J., A.R. Gillis, and J. Simpson. 1979. The Sexual Stratification of Social Control: A Gender-

Based Perspective on Crime and Deviance. British Journal of Sociology, 30, 25–38.
_____. 1990. Clarifying and Extending Power-Control Theory. *American Journal of Sociology* 95, 4, (January) 1024–37.

Hagan, J., and B. McCarthy. 1987. *Mean Streets: Youth Crime and Homelessness.* Cambridge, UK: Cambridge University Press.

Lea, J., and J. Young. 1984. *What Can Be Done About Law and Order?* New York: Penguin.

Lemert, E.M. 1951. *Social Pathology: Systemic Approaches to the Study of Sociopathic Behavior.* New York: McGraw- Hill.

_____. 1967. *Human Deviance: Social Problems and Social Control.* Englewood Cliffs, NJ: Prentice Hall.

_____. 1974. Beyond Mead: The Societal Reaction to Deviance. *Social Problems* 21 (4), 457–68.

Liska, A. 1987. *Perspectives on Deviance.* Second edition. Englewood Cliffs, NJ: Prentice-Hall.

Liska, A., and S. Messner. 1999. *Perspectives on Deviance.* Third edition. Englewood Cliffs, NJ: Prentice Hall.

Phofl, S. 1994. *Images of Deviance and Social Control: A Sociological History.* Second edition. New York: McGraw Hill Inc.

Rabinow, P. 1984. *The Foucault Reader.* Pantheon Books: New York.

Rubington, E., and Martin S. Weinburg. 1987. *Deviance: The Interactionist Perspective.* New York: Macmillan Publishing Company

Sawicki, J. 1991. Disciplining Foucault: Feminism, Power, and the Body. New York: Routledge.

Schissel, B. 2002. "Orthodox Criminology: The Limits of Consensus Theories of Crime." In Bernard Schissel and Carolyn Brooks (eds.), *Marginality and Condemnation: An Introduction to Critical Criminology.* Nova Scotia: Fernwood Publishing.

Schissel, B., and C. Brooks (eds.). 2002. *Marginality and Condemnation: An Introduction to Critical Criminology.* Nova Scotia: Fernwood Publishing.

Schmalleger, F. 2003. *Criminology Today: An Introduction.* Third edition. Upper Saddle River, NJ: Prentice-Hall.

Schur, E.M. 1971. *Labeling Deviant Behavior: Its Sociological Implications.* New York: Harper & Row.

Sellin. T. 1938. *Culture and Conflict in Crime.* New York: Social Science Research Council.

Shaw, C., and H.D. McKay. 1942. *Juvenile Delinquency and Urban Areas.* Chicago: University of Chicago Press.

Sudnow, D. 1965. "Abnormal Crimes." *Social Problems* 12, Winter: 255–76.

Tannenbaum, F. 1938. *Crime and the Community.* Boston: Ginn.

Thomas, M., H. Hurley, and C. Grimes. 1999/2000. "Pilot Analysis of Recidivism Among Convicted Youth and Young Adults." *Juristat* 22 (9).

Turk. A. 1969. *Crime and Legal Order.* Chicago: Rand McNally.

Vold. G. 1958. *Theoretical Criminology.* New York: Oxford University Press.

Winslow, Robert, and Sheldon Zhang. 2006. *Criminology: A Global Perspective.* Toronto: Pearson Publications.

Zimmerman, D.H., and D.L. Wieder. 1970. "Ethnomethodology and the Problem of Order: Comment on Dentin." In Jack Douglas (ed.), *Understanding Everyday Life.* Chicago: Aldine Publishing.

Critical Criminology
Rejecting Short-term Solutions to Crime

Carolyn Brooks

3

KEY FACTS

> Contrary to public perceptions, crime rates in Canada have been falling since the early 1990s.

> Approximately 75 percent of 18-year-old male African Americans will be in jail at least once before they are thirty-five.

> It is estimated that 90 percent of adult Aboriginal men in Canada have been in prison at least once.

> More blacks than whites are imprisoned and executed. Nils Christie states: "it is an ironic situation... Slavery was abolished... The African Americans were free to move. So they do — and end in prisons."

> For the same "crime," poor people are more likely arrested. Once arrested, the poor are more likely to be charged, convicted, and serve time in prison — with longer prison sentences — than the middle or upper classes.

> In one study of 180 white 15- to 17-year-old males from diverse socio-economic backgrounds it was found that "virtually all respondents reported having committed not one but a variety of different offences... those from the middle classes constituted 55 percent of the group, [yet admitted to] 67 percent of the instances of breaking and entering, 70 percent... of property destruction, and an astounding 87 percent of all the armed robberies."

> In the U.S., white offenders who kill white people are two times less likely to receive a death sentence than black offenders who kill whites. Black offenders are four times more likely to get a death sentence for killing white people than black offenders who kill black people.

Sources: Statistics Canada, cited in Balfour 2006; Christie 2000; Frideres and Gadacz 2001; Reiman 2007.

How often I think neither I know, nor any (one) knows, aught of them, May-be seeming to me what they are (as doubtless they indeed but seem) as from my present point of view, and might prove (as of course they would) nought of what they appear, or nought anyhow, from entirely changed points of view.
— Walt Whitman, "Calamus," *Leaves of Grass* (1965)

From the time of the discipline's emergence in the late 1960s and early 1970s, the advocates of critical criminology have based their approach on an intensive critique not just of mainstream criminology, but also of the state institutions that surround the discipline — institutions such as law, media, schools, and the criminal justice system. Critical criminology sprang from Marxist theory and the protest movements of its early years but has since broadened to include analyses from feminism, left realism, peacemaking, postmodernism, and more. As Don Gibbons (1994: 60) points out, "A sizable body of theorizing, in the broad sense, has accumulated in recent years and can be identified as critical criminology." Many of these perspectives draw on a common theory and methodology, but as Gibbons argues, "This work does not form a coherent whole, that is, a shared body of broad propositions or generalizations and supporting evidence. Indeed, critical criminology is an intellectual posture around which a variety of criminological endeavors have been pursued."

Not surprisingly, those postures and endeavours offer a diversity of solutions to problems of crime, from arguments for redefining what constitutes "crime," to proposals for the abolition of prisons; from challenging the state institutions that frame public understanding of crime and political responses, to calls for restorative justice or transformative justice. In general, though, the critical perspectives do have commonalities. They share a desire to look not at individual flaws as a means of explaining criminal behaviour, but at societal problems that create, breed, and sustain criminals. Critical criminology rejects tougher laws and incarceration as short-term solutions and instead advocates fundamental socio-economic and cultural change — complete structural transformation. Critical theories bring into view decisions around what acts are called "crimes" and the ways in which different groups of people are processed differently through the criminal justice system. For example, the justice system tends to define poor people and "street" crimes (theft, assault and homicide, trafficking offences, aggressive panhandling) as "criminal" and punishes these offences more readily than it does the "suite" crimes of corporations and the elite (environmental pollution, exploitation of human and natural resources, formation of illegal monopolies, illegal use of child labour, unsafe work conditions), even though the corporate and elite actions may well cause greater human suffering and devastation. From the perspective of critical criminology, power and the inequalities of class, race, and gender play a central role in any understanding of crime and criminal justice.

> Critical criminology offers diverse solutions to problems of crime: from redefining "crime" to abolishing prisons; from challenging the state institutions to calling for restorative justice or transformative justice.

The "Boom" of Critical Criminology

Emerging partially in response to the labelling and social interactionist perspectives, the critical perspective grew mostly out of the political protests of the post-war period. Following the Second World War, struggles for social equality intensified, largely because of rising expectations. Blacks in the United States, for example, gained the sense that they could now venture into typically white domains. Although the wages of Blacks saw a significant increase between 1939 and 1947, the "modest gains in the post-war years were soon reversed as white males reassumed their positions in the peacetime economy" (Pfohl 1985: 335). The continuing inequality fuelled the anger that led to the civil rights protests of the 1960s. Glaring police brutality and obvious injustice also spurred violent protests and rioting in the Black ghettos.

This same political energy was felt within U.S. prisons, which were disproportionately filled with Black inmates. Prisoners began to see themselves as victims of racism, interpreting their confinement as part of the political manipulation of an oppressive state (Cleaver 1968). The prisoners began to educate themselves and organize to challenge the criminal justice system. The response by prison administrators and parole boards was harsh. Many of those who participated in or supported the struggle died, including "over forty inmates and guards slaughtered by state police in quelling the rebellion at New York's Attica State Prison" (Pfohl 1985: 336). In part, prisoners and their supporters became feared. Their rebellion risked uncovering that they were more than just "individual bad guys" and symbolized what was wrong with the unequal, racist, and class-based economy.

> Critical crimi/ gists began to/ the real sources oɩ nal activity as the lack or secure jobs, victimization, racism, and classism.

The struggles behind bars, as well as the police brutality and general struggles of Blacks in the United States, gave impetus to nascent critical criminological perspectives. Critical criminologists began to identify the lack of secure jobs, victimization, racism, and classism as the real sources of criminal activity. They saw prisons as a means of ensuring that the political hierarchy remained unchallenged and a way to hide the injustices facing marginalized people.

Marxist Criminology

Marxism and Crime Causation: Induced Selfishness and Greed

We shall show that, as a consequence of the present [capitalist economic system], man [sic] has become very egoistic and hence more capable of crime than if the environment had developed the germs of altruism.
—Bonger 1969: 40–41, cited in Akers 1997: 168

Even though Karl Marx (1818–83) wrote very little about criminal justice and crime, the critical perspective in criminology and its formations of crime causation are based on Marxist frameworks: they focus attention on the political, social, and economic structures of capitalism. Marxists argue that the fundamental inequality in capitalist society, with a small percentage of haves and a majority of have-nots, gives rise to individualistic and competitive struggles for material gains. Crime is partly a rational response to the competitive and individualistic struggle for material wealth in a society that encourages conflict — between rich and poor or among the ranks of the wealthy or the poor themselves. Thus, for Marxist criminologists poverty is not the only factor that causes crime; the alienating and exploitative nature of capitalism itself also leads to crime. In other words, the link between poverty and crime is not only that those in dire need are driven to anti-social acts, but is also related to the influence of a consumer culture that perpetuates an ideology of individualism and competition. Similarly, violent crime arises out of the brutal conditions that many poor people are forced to live in. "It is not that man behaves as an animal because of his 'nature' [under capitalism]: it is that he is not fundamentally allowed by virtue of the social arrangements of capitalism to do otherwise" (Taylor, Walton, and Young 1975, quoted in Bohm 1997: 125). Capitalist society is *criminogenic*, that is, fundamentally structured to encourage all members of the society to take up anti-social behaviour. Capitalist institutions foster greed, selfishness, and unlimited desires. Results are all that count. Even the well-off are encouraged

> Not only does poverty drive people to anti-social acts; the influence of a consumer culture also perpetuates an ideology of individualism and competition.

to find ways to acquire more material goods. Obviously, in such a scheme many people will lose out.

Willem Bonger (1876–1940), a Dutch criminologist, was the first to apply Marxism to criminology. Bonger argued that the profit motive inherent in capitalism induces greed and selfishness, creating what he called egoistic tendencies. He suggested that under different conditions an environment of "altruistic tendencies" could just as easily have developed. But under capitalism everyone was necessarily subjected to the workings of greed and egoism. With the law controlled by the ruling class, the actions most likely to be defined as "crime" are those of the working class, and given the inequality characteristic of capitalist societies the most obvious crimes will occur among marginalized people.

Although Bonger's theory of crime received little acceptance in its day, during the boom period of Marxist theory in the 1970s a similar explanation was to surface again. Ian Taylor, Paul Walton, and Jock Young (1973, 1975) argued that crime was a logical response to the oppression and exploitation of working-class marginalized people under capitalism. Crimes of accommodation (individual crimes) they argued, are signs of survival in the class struggle. Individual crimes, such as theft, organized crime, and prostitution, are often a means of survival in the competitive capitalist system, with the aim of achieving material wealth or status. The authors also point to crimes of rebellion, which are responses to the inequality of the capitalist system. Such crimes are political acts against an often oppressive state. Richard Quinney (1980) added that violent crimes are accommodation crimes by individuals in response to the brutality of capitalism. Others pointed out that ruling-class crimes, corporate crimes, or crimes of domination and repression (for example, environmental pollution, marketing of defective products, illegal and unsafe working environments) are also a result of capitalism — acts by capitalists protecting economic privilege and domination (Quinney 1980; Lynch and Groves 1986).

Radical Marxist criminologists challenge the traditional definition of criminal behaviour as conduct that violates a criminal code. Marxist criminologists see this view as serving the interests of the elite, because for Marxists the real crime is behaviour that violates human rights, including some actions that violate criminal codes, such as murder or robbery. Tony Platt (1975), for example, argues that behaviour infringing on the rights to decent shelter, food, human dignity, and self-determination is in fact criminal. This means racism, classism, sexism, human exploitation, and the infliction of human misery and deprivation can be defined as crime.

Marxism and the Criminal Justice System as Ideology

Just 'cause they're poor and m'norities,
It's them the p'lice mistrust —
And then you think they're Sons of Sam,
And make a great big fuss!
— from a song inspired by working with offenders, in Morris 2000: 99

Marxism does not focus as much on crime causation as consensus theories do. It is more concerned with the role of criminal justice as a means of controlling marginalized people in society. The criminal justice system functions in part as an idea that society must fear the poor and marginalized as the dangerous class. North American prisons are highly overpopulated by poor, Native, and Black people. This reality is presented in the media and by criminal justice officials as evidence that certain classes and races are to be feared. For the Marxist theorist, however, this state of affairs signifies the workings of a classist and racist system. That poor, marginalized people fill our jails does not mean that they are the people who cause the most harm to society, or that they are the most pathological, or that they above all others lack social conscience. On the contrary, dispossessed people are as generous and loyal as anyone else — especially to each other (see, for example, Schissel 1997). What their overrepresentation in the criminal justice system means is that the law works to define the behaviour of the marginalized as criminal and to weed out the rich at every step of the way (Morris 2000; Reiman 1998, 2007; Mathiesen 1974).

> The overrepresentation of poor and racialized people in the criminal justice system means that the law defines the behaviour of the marginalized as criminal and excuses the rich.

Weeding-out of the rich begins long before law enforcement starts. Defining "crime" is a creative act in itself — subjective, political, and based on decisions made by state-appointed officials. For example, Canadians are six times more likely to die from unsafe working conditions on the job than to be murdered on the street (see Gordon and Coneybeer 1999). On-the-job death rates are thirty times higher than the homicide rates in Canada and the United States. Yet the state does not define employer negligence as murder. Jeffrey Reiman (2007: 85) graphically demonstrates that workers may be safer in the underworld than the workworld:

> Lest we falter in the struggle against crime, the FBI includes in its annual *Uniform Crime Reports* several "crime clocks," which illustrate graphically the extent of the criminal menace. For 2003, the crime clock shows a murder occurring every 31.8 minutes. If a similar clock were constructed for occupational deaths… this clock would show [for the workforce] an occupational death about every 10 minutes! In other words, in about the time it takes for two murders on the crime clock, more than six workers have died *just from trying to make a living*.

Not only has criminal law failed to emphasize dangerous corporate actions as "criminal," but governments are also deregulating corporate misbehaviour. In this edition Laureen Snider demonstrates these contradictions in the current legal system. Many of the activities of corporations and the elite pose grave threats to our community and individual well-being, much more so than those of the "typical" street criminals; yet the individuals and organizations responsible are not dealt with through our criminal justice system. In fact, these individuals may be promoted for contributing to increased corporate profit by reducing expenditures on workers or environment safety.

> Many activities of corporations and the elite pose much graver threats to our well-being than do "typical" street criminals; yet they escape our criminal justice system. They may even be promoted for contributing to corporate profit.

Two variants of neo-Marxism — instrumentalist Marxism and structuralist Marxism — try to explain these contradictions. Beginning with a similar starting point in political economy, both theories argue that state institutions, including the law and criminal justice, protect the long-term interests of the capitalist class. The two variants differ only in the particulars of this process.

Instrumentalist Marxism: In Bed with the Elite

Instrumentalist Marxists argue that the elite class is directly involved in the activity of the state, including the criminal justice system (Miliband 1969; Quinney 1974). From this perspective, society's elite controls not only the economy, but also all state institutions, including law, criminal justice, and education. The criminal justice system — the law, courts, police and criminal justice, and definitions of "crime" — contains mechanisms to ensure the power of the dominant class. The elite and the rich have the power to impose morality on the rest of society, often in the form of what they define as illegal or criminal behaviour; and what they consider criminal are actions that could threaten the status quo or interfere with the quest for profit.

Instrumentalists say that the people who work in the system are directly supporting their own class. Those in government and justice decision-making positions have class backgrounds, education, financial goals, and attitudes that are similar to the corporate elite (Miliband 1969; Quinney 1974). Because the government and business elites are part of the dominant class, when they violate the law the state seldom enforces laws against them. Some instrumentalists even say that the elite class is immune from criminal sanction of any kind (Chambliss 1975; Quinney 1975). Whether or not the poor commit more crimes than the rich is not the question; the fact is that the poor are arrested more and punished more (Chambliss 1975; Quinney 1975; Pearce 1976; Goff and Reasons 1978). This perspective sensitizes us to the class bias in the workings of criminal justice.

> Because the government and business elites are part of the dominant class, when they violate the law the state seldom enforces laws against them.

When we combine the instrumentalist investigation of the state and law with crime causation, what emerges is a story of manipulation and social control. The Marxist position (shared by instrumentalists) maintains that crime occurs as a result of class conflict. The working class is alienated from and develops hostility for the system that encloses them and prevents them from shaping or fully participating in the social order, or even benefiting from the fruits of their labour. Eventually they find this situation intolerable and they take action, often minor acts of rebellion; sometimes more serious acts. Those acts become defined as criminal, and the capitalist system, in its formation of law, creates a scapegoat. The working class and marginalized are blamed for the problems of the system they are rebelling against. Their defined pathology and criminality deflect attention away from the structural injustices and the makeup of the system itself.

The most obvious difficulty with instrumentalist Marxism is that it cannot account for the legal and legislative limits on the elite class, such as human rights legislation, health and safety legislation, and employment standards. For that reason, many neo-Marxists have instead adopted the structuralist Marxist position.

Structuralist Marxism

Structuralist Marxists emphasize that although state institutions, including the criminal justice system, benefit the elite class, to appear fair and just these institutions must still maintain a degree of relative autonomy from all classes (Althusser 1971; Poulantzas 1973; Balbus 1977; Chambliss and Seidman 1982; Quinney 1980). They argue that the state has two main functions: accumulation and legitimation. The accumulation function requires that the state ensure that appropriate conditions are in place for generating wealth and profit. The legitimation functions ensure that most citizens believe that the state is fair and just and has the loyalty of its citizens (O'Connor 1973). Thus the state may work in the short-term interests of working-class and marginalized people as long as it does not interfere with the hierarchy of power relations. At times, then, the organized resistance of the working class creates political movements that force the law to work in the interests of all people. This theory helps to explain why the law and the state can transcend the particular interests of capitalists.

A structuralist position extends the instrumentalist position that law and the criminal justice system are coercive to include a more in-depth discussion of ideology. The criminal justice system functions as an ideological tool, maintaining the status quo over the long term and helping to maintain the domination of the elite class. Structuralist Marxists see this as hegemony, a concept initially introduced by Antonio Gramsci (1971). It is the process by which the elite try to make their ideas, knowledge, and values appear to be legitimate or natural — as something that everyone in society should want for themselves and their communities. Gramsci (1971) examines the creation of hegemonic ideologies that perpetuate capitalist order. He writes that those with power in capitalist societies rule not only through the state's legal apparatuses, but also by educating the "consent of the governed." This refers to the state's ability to control ideological production and secure hegemonic powers. This universalization of ruling-class ideas takes place in the law, criminal justice system, and media, and it partly explains why many working-class and marginalized people support tougher crime control laws.

Hegemony and the Media: A Structuralist Marxist Critique

The criminal justice system and media function as powerful tools to manipulate most of the population into believing that it is the poor and marginalized that must be feared as the dangerous class (Reiman 2007; Clarke 2000; Schissel 1997, 2007). Critical criminology appropriates the tasks of cultural analysis, attempting to penetrate the ideologies that mask interests of capitalist exploitation "that deflect attention away from capitalist society's real interests, naked oppressions and structural inequalities" (Pavlich 2000: 51). This approach emerges in several writings, including Hall et al. 1978; Ratner and McMullan 1985, and contemporary research on the media, law and criminal justice, including Schissel 1997, 2007; Wortley 2002; Faith 1993, 2002; Reiman 1998, 2001, 2007).

> Critical criminology tries to penetrate the ideologies "that deflect attention away from capitalist society's real interests, naked oppressions and structural inequalities."

A very influential radical criminological writing that draws on Gramsci's ideas of ideological hegemony is Hall et al. in *Policing the Crisis* (1978). Hall attempts to apply neo-Marxist analysis to mugging and moral panics in England in the 1970s. He examines the connections between the media, ideological production, and the elite, without which media may be interpreted as acting in isolation from economic and political roots. Hall suggests that moral panic is created by ruling elites to divert attention from political and economic problems. The British industrial state in England in the 1970s was in social and fiscal distress; stirring up a moral panic over mugging and street crime deflected attention from British capitalism (rising unemployment and poverty). In a destabilized society, blaming a scapegoat or "folk devil" creates the illusion of providing political solutions, thus deflecting attention from severe political, economic, and ideological crisis. Constructing an ideologically driven moral panic drawing on stereotypes of black men and a dangerous "soft" criminal justice system, helped the British state secure the consent of those it governed.

Bernard Schissel (1997) similarly writes that the state encourages moral panic at times of hegemonic crisis to secure the consent of the governed. His focus is on youth in Canada. He argues that most kids inside Canadian youth facilities are marginalized youth, forced to live on the fringes of society, and that they are often there for relatively minor crimes. Most sensationalistic media articles focus on the violent acts of the youth, creating a myth that violent youth crime is out of control, unpredictable, and committed by pathological or nihilistic children (a whole generation of them). Typical headlines are, "Killer Girls" (*Alberta Report*, July 31, 1995), "Junior Gone Wild: An Aging Do-Your-Own-Thing Generation Lashes Out at Its Savage Offspring" (*Alberta Report*, May 9, 1994), and "Teen Violence: Murder, Mayhem Have their Roots in Boredom" (*Calgary Herald*, April 18, 1995). These headlines suggest a generation gone wild, yet the stories themselves are about rare isolated incidences of violent crime. Schissel (1997) explains that articles about teens who murder seldom refer to the rare occurrence of the acts; instead they provide testimonial to the "naturalness of youth violence." Articles about youth violence focus on gang membership, individual pathology or wickedness, family pathology, single parenting, and poverty. These overgeneralized, stereotypical, and inaccurate descriptions of youth criminals give media consumers the impression that an entire class of people, those who live on the margins, is out of control. They create a false sense of fear regarding poor and marginalized youth and their families. The misinformation and sensationalistic view of criminality — which is not supported by statistics from government and police — help to shape public opinion and demands for harsher measures against all young offenders. The result of fearmongering and stereotyping young offenders is probably to increase crime.

This critical criminological literature on hegemony and the media is also powerful in its depiction of gender and race (see, for example, Scott Wortley 2007). For example, the majority of women in conflict with the law are not a danger to society. They are generally young, Aboriginal, have no job experience, low education and have been emotionally, physically or sexually abused (Faith 1993; Comack 1996; Boritch 2002, 1997; Adelberg and Currie 1993; DeKeseredy 2000). In Canada, most women's crimes are property offences. Yet as Karlene Faith's work (1993, 2002) demonstrates, decades of films have portrayed the female "villain" as a nihilistic and pathological "lesbian butch predatory killer maniac" — a complete contrast to the real woman in conflict. The films of the 1990s amplify the woman offender as a super-bitch killer beauty — beautiful on the outside but "evil" by nature. These films present inaccurate descriptions of women in prison, yet they shape an ideology that forms public opinion.

Critical media research consistently finds that violent crimes are dramatically over-represented on fictional crime shows as well as on TV news programs. As has been well documented, "if it bleeds it leads" (Matusow, January, 1988: 102; cited in Reiman 1998: 62). Debra Seaqgal (cited In Reiman 2007: 175) states:

> By the time our 9 million viewers flip on their tubes, we've reduced fifty or sixty hours of mundane and compromising video into short, action-packed segments of tantalizing, crack-filled, dope-dealing, junkie-busting cop culture. How easily we downplay the pathos of the suspect; how cleverly we breeze past the complexities that cast doubt on the very system that has produced the criminal activity in the first place.

Hegemony and Prison: A Structuralist Marxist Critique

Prison is part of the same hegemonic control mechanism, hiding capitalist inequalities and reinforcing the poor as criminal, according to the early works of Thomas Mathiesen and Ian Taylor and current writing by John McMurtry, Nils Christie, and Jeffrey Reiman. This position is also argued by infamous prisoners such as George Jackson.

George Jackson (1970), a prisoner and activist, writes that the idea that prisons contain "dangerous people" is a complex political act. Jackson, subject to racism and struggling to get a job, was arrested for a $70 theft, imprisoned, and, while incarcerated, labelled dangerous. He argues that this process makes scapegoats out of individuals, depoliticizing inequalities such as classism and racism in the larger social structure. Mathiesen (1974) similarly argued that the ideological function of prison is to blame individuals for acts that are stimulated by capitalism's economic and social inequality. Taylor (1981) adds that prison's high walls and towers reinforce the image of the criminal as dangerous and (dichotomously) different from the "respectable, conforming" population.

> Prison reproduces the imagery of the criminal as dangerous and (dichotomously) different from the "respectable, conforming" population by the very presence of high walls and towers.

More contemporary criticisms of the prison and the criminal justice system reiterate these earlier themes, as well as enlarging the idea that defining "crime" is a creative act; this draws into question corporate crime versus street crime. Critical theorists write that although poor people are overrepresented in prisons, this is not because they are committing the greatest social injustices or lack a conscience. Rather the poor are overrepresented in the criminal justice system because we weed out the actions of the rich at every step in the criminal system, including what we define as "criminal." We ensure that the individual in prison is going to be a member of the lowest social status (Reiman 2001; Schissel 1997; Morris 2000). This has two results. First, it creates an image of the "typical criminal" — one who is involved in one-on-one harm, is usually young, lower-class, and a member of a racial minority (Reiman 2001). Second, associating criminal behaviour with the individual has the powerful effect of undercutting efforts (class struggles) to address divisions between the rich and the poor and systemic abuses of human rights, which Marxist criminologists see as responsible for crime (Snider 1999; Currie 1998; Reiman 2001). The resultant ideological message is that the poor are defective morally and therefore that poverty and crime is their own fault — not a symptom of economic or social injustice (Reiman 1998: 152). Research and writing by Marxists criminologists question the extent to which definitions of crime and the processes of criminal justice protect the interest of the most powerful economic class. Their studies demonstrate how actions that are not defined as criminal (corporate crime) often cause the most social harm (see, for example, Snider 2002; Reiman,2001; Gordon and Coneybeer 1999).

Hegemony and the Official Version of the Law: A Structuralist Marxist Critique

Key to how effectively the law and the criminal justice system manipulate the public is the so-called Official Version of the Law. This dominant discourse posits that the law is fair, just, and equal for everyone. Elizabeth Comack (1999: 21–22) asks us to remember the image of the young "maiden" who holds the scales to dispense justice — demonstrating the supposed "impartiality," "neutrality," and "objectivity" of the legal system to date:

A "maiden" is a virginal young (white?) woman — presumably untouched, untainted, or uncorrupted. That she is blindfolded suggests she is not swayed or influenced by the characteristics of those who stand before her — she sees no class, no race, no gender distinctions. The scales she is holding connote the measured and precise nature of the decisions produced. But the Official Version of Law is reflected in elements other than the symbol of the blindfolded maiden. In both its form and its method, law asserts its claim to be impartial, neutral, and objective.

This claim to objectivity and neutrality makes the law a powerful ideological tool. The law tells us that everyone — rich and marginalized alike — is subject to its rule and that everyone is treated alike. Anatole France's famous quotation is instructive: "The law in all its majestic impartiality forbids both rich and poor alike to sleep under bridges, to beg in the streets and to steal bread" (France, quoted in Hunt 1976: 184). The problem is that when we are substantially unequal in a society, formal equality before the law is a moot point.

> "The law in all its majestic impartiality forbids both rich and poor alike to sleep under bridges, to beg in the streets and to steal bread" (France, quoted in Hunt 1976: 184).

Structuralists are criticized for emphasizing "the system" to the detriment of the individuals involved in daily struggles. Ronald Hinch (1992), for example, argues that structuralists lack an understanding of the real people who live with and create the social order and laws. As Comack (1999: 42) says, "While instrumentalism was criticized for its overemphasis on capitalist class input into, and control over, the state, it could be argued that the structuralist account went too far in the other direction: it is the constraints and limitations of the structure — not human agency — that determine the direction of society."

Marxist Criminology: Policy and Reform

The policy implications of Marxist criminology, including instrumentalism and structuralism, are obvious. First, it challenges what is defined as crime. The position argues that victimless offences must be decriminalized, and violations of real human rights (through racism, classism, sexism, human exploitation, the infliction of human misery, and more) must be defined and controlled as criminal. In other words, the consequences of uncontrolled pollution and the destruction of species, or the consumption of non-renewable resources (by-products of corporate activity), are, from this perspective, more criminal than the activities of the aggressive panhandler or squeegee kid, both of whom may now, in Ontario, receive a $500 fine or incarceration for activities so obviously connected to their poverty.

This perspective comes under severe attack, however, because no reform of existing institutions could eradicate the problem of crime without a movement towards a socialist economy and system of justice. As David Gordon (1976: 206, quoted in Bohm 1997: 127) states:

> First, capitalism depends quite substantially on the preservation of the conditions of competition and inequality. Those conditions… will tend to lead almost inevitably to relatively pervasive criminal behaviour; without those conditions, the capitalist system would scarcely work at all. Second, as many have argued, the general presence of racism in this country, though capitalists may not in fact have created it, tends to support and maintain the

power of the capitalists as a class by providing cheap labour and dividing the working class.

In the end, Marxist criminology argues that since conditions under capitalism create crime, the solution is socialism (see, for example, Quinney 1980; Bonger 1916; Lynch and Groves 1986), seemingly an unlikely prospect in today's modern, global world.

Critical race theory, abolitionism and peacemaking criminology draw on the Marxist understanding of the link between inequalities and "criminality." Critical race theorists recognize multiple oppressions and make central the socially constructed reality of "race" and racism. Abolitionists and peacemaking criminologists draw attention to the harm and violence against humanity evident in the criminal justice system and call for peaceful resolutions, including an eventual abolition of prisons and other crime control measures.

Critical Race Theory: A Culture of Racism and Inequality

Our Aboriginal youth want what all other young persons in Canada want — hope.
—Ms. Jamie Gallant, Youth and Labour Market Intern, Congress of Aboriginal Peoples

Marxist criminologists have documented the "whiteness" and "maleness" of the criminal justice system. This is well established. Critical race theorists posit that racial minorities are not equally served by the law because of their race and that the condition is structural, not simply a product of jurists' individual racism. "Critical race theorists have demonstrated that law is structurally racist: the racialization of crime, criminalization of race, and/or the discriminatory sentencing and lack of serious legal response to attacks on the persons and property of minority citizens, are structural" (Schur 2002; cited in Hudson 2006).

> Critical race theorists posit that racial minorities are not equally served by the law because of their race, and that this is structural, not a product of jurists' individual racism.

Critical race theorists teach that the social construction of "race" creates segments of the population who are subordinate. Jaccoud and Brassard (2003: 143), for example, write that the marginalization of Aboriginal people in an urban environment begins in childhood and is rooted in the consequence of colonization — poverty, violence, alcohol, homelessness, reliance on shelters and food banks. Statistics Canada (2003) notes that Aboriginal peoples continue to suffer disenfranchisement. Aboriginal peoples continue to lack adequate housing and child-care facilities; their likelihood of finishing school is less than the national average — 48 percent of Aboriginal youth do not complete secondary school. The effects of racism include much shorter life expectancy and lower educational levels and employment rates (Statistics Canada 2003). The present generation of Aboriginal youth are very vulnerable to poverty, social alienation, racism, high suicide rates (estimated to be five to six times higher for Aboriginal youth), and criminal activity (Assembly of First Nations Proceedings, June 2002).

Critical race theory identifies lower levels of education; high unemployment; dysfunctional families and low levels of support; high levels of substance abuse; lack of housing; experience of racism, poverty, loss, alienation, and isolation as pressure points for criminal activity. There is no direct correlation between incarceration, crimes committed, and these legacies — factors of discrimination within the criminal justice system are also a central explanatory factor. Aboriginal people are over-policed, less likely to receive bail, more likely to be charged with multiple offences, spend less preparation time for trials with lawyers, and spend more time in pre-trial detention (Manitoba Justice Inquiry; cited in Waldrum 1997). Green and Healey (2003) concur with regards specifically to Aboriginal youth:

> the causes of Aboriginal over-representation are wide-ranging and complex… and include: the poor socio-economic circumstances of many Aboriginals… the level of policing in Aboriginal communities, the "snowball": effect of a prior criminal record, a greater likelihood of an Aboriginal accused being denied bail, and the lack of sentencing alternatives available…

Mary Ellen Turpel/Aki-kwe writes that Canada has violated the international human rights standards with its treatment of Aboriginal people. The overrepresentation of Aboriginal peoples and youth is one legacy of European colonialism, and the oppression, cultural destruction and dislocation of Indigenous people can only be understood in this social, political, and economic context (Samuelson 2000). Critical Marxist criminology and critical race theorists assert that addressing these deeper structural issues is key to reducing Aboriginal peoples' involvement in criminal activities.

> The overrepresentation of Aboriginal peoples is a legacy of European colonialism's oppression, cultural destruction, and dislocation of Indigenous people and can only be understood in this context.

Criminal activity, trouble in school, family violence, inequality, racism, and poverty are indicators of misery and signs of serious problems in the status quo. Criminalization of race and poverty contributes to the social construction of ethnic minorities and marginalized youth as "the other," and misrepresents the social problems of race and class discrimination as individual pathologies.

Green (2005) argues that the process of privilege and subsequent racism is normalized and therefore not visible. This creates anger against those who are privileged and at the same time deny that their privilege is a result of racism. Lawrence (2004: 39) defines the practice of racism and colonialism as "extreme discursive warfare," existent in media, legislation, and government. The language of the media normalizes the white model, reinforcing racist assumptions. When Aboriginal people are written about, stereotypes are reproduced as the social pathologies of those who participate in violence, gangs, and crime. This is paralleled by stories of criminal involvement focusing on harsh events and decontextualizing the individual, familial, social, and political realities that largely account for Aboriginal peoples' overrepresentation in prison populations.

Critical race theory defines the construction of "identity" as key to understanding how Aboriginal people are "othered" (Hudson 2006). Narratives that define the otherness are necessary to the self-identity of the "western subject's idea of himself" (Hudson 2006: 33). The criminal justice system and the law do not take racialized harm seriously (Hudson 2006; Comack and Balfour 2004). Criminal activity among Aboriginal people and Aboriginal youth is seen as linked to the material consequences of racism, yet the youth are defined in the law, media, and many government reports as a racialized "other," obviating the need to deal with the material consequences of racism. High rates of social pathology disturb the public but are not put into political and social context. The statistics used in media and government reports seldom have accompanying theoretical and political analyses, which may explain why certain groups and communities systematically suffer from unaddressed social problems.

Abolitionism and Peacemaking Criminology: "Punishment and Repression Never Solve Problems"

There are guards and officials who find pleasure
To see your mind and manhood wilt with pressure.
But if your mind and beliefs remain strong,
You will surely overcome all inflicted wrong.
— The poetry of an inmate named Mike, in Morris 2000: 89

The founders of abolitionism in criminology are Thomas Mathiesen and Nils Christie (both Norwegians) in the 1970s, as well as the Dutch scholars Louk Hulsman and Herman Bianchi. Drawing on the labelling, Marxist, and left-realist approaches, the abolitionist perspective declares that the criminal justice system (more often referred to as the "criminal (in)justice system"), not only fails morally but also fails to meet its own stated objectives. Abolitionists advocate against a state that inflicts pain under the guise of reducing criminal activity; they seek the abolition of prisons, capital punishment, slavery, racism, sexism, and classism. The abolitionist struggles take many faces, yet the essential philosophy is always the same — that punishment and repression never solve problems.

Peacemaking has its roots in Marxist criminology, abolitionism, ideals of transformative and restorative justice, and religious traditions (Pepinsky 1991). Like abolitionism, peacemaking criminology seeks to uncover the violent and warlike characteristics of the criminal justice system. The peacemaking criminologists argue fervently that we cannot eradicate violence or human suffering with more human suffering and more violence: "Crime is suffering and crime can only therefore be eliminated by ending suffering" (Pepinsky and Quinney 1991). The criminal justice system is a failure because it perpetuates the same violence that it seeks to eliminate. As such, the peacemaking adherents endorse humanistic and restorative principles both at the level of dealing with the offender and in the larger society.

Like Marxists, prison abolitionists and peacemaking criminologists point out that prisons are really warehouses for the poor. Many of the people who fall into the criminal justice system are victims first of classism, racism, and sexism, and only by addressing the issue of an unequal society will we effectively respond to crime. In other words, rather than acting for social and economic justice, society hides the problems of the economy by focusing on people labelled "bad." The blame for social problems falls on certain races and classes, letting larger structural inequities off the hook.

Claire Culhane (1991), for example, a prison abolitionist, said Canada is in breach of the International Convention on the Rights of the Child. Throughout the country there are children whose mental, physical, moral, and spiritual development is impaired because of their standard of living. But rather than dealing with this national crisis, the government cuts social programs designed to assist the poor and increases spending on criminal justice. Culhane points

> Abolitionists and peacemaking criminologists point out that prisons are really warehouses for the poor.

to the contradictions involved in waiting until the laws are broken to deal with poverty and then putting our poor in jails. She asserts that at least 1 percent of the billion dollars that Canada spends on police, courts, and prison should instead go into social programs to help the poor get off the treadmill.

Abolitionists and peacemaking criminologists have exposed the dysfunctional and dangerous features of the criminal (in)justice system. The criminal law symbolizes values gone wrong in our society — especially the lack of concern for crime victims, inequities in criminal trials, and the unethical treatment of our disenfranchised, whom we throw into cages. The theorists and activists have documented the physical and psychological problems of imprisonment and demonstrated the abuses in the system: for example, solitary confinement, forced transfer, inadequate health care, overcrowding, and excessive sentences.

Abolitionists and peacemakers declare that prisons foster recidivism because of their stigmatization and social exclusion. They argue for a less stigmatizing and more inclusive mechanism of social control. When punishment is needed, we should use only a minimum level of isolation. For abolitionists, crime is no different than other social problems, and the responses to crime should spring from within the community in which the crime was committed. They call for measures of restorative and transformative justice as well as the abolishment (dismantling) of the prison system. They advocate models of participatory justice in which offenders and victims must redefine their conflicts and their needs for healing (Culhane 1991; Morris 2000). Examples of participatory justice include mediation, reconciliation, alternative dispute resolution, sentencing circles, and other non-penal measures to create safety within our society. For many peacemaking criminologists this means addressing not simply the semblance of conflict but its essence. Nils Christie (1977) argues, for example, that individuals must take ownership of their own conflicts rather than give them away to the state as we do presently. Within our criminal justice model, the state provides a decision, voice, and resolution. The offenders have no power to speak on their own behalf or to decide on the best means of resolution. The state decides what kind of punishment and compensation (if any) will be handed out to the offender and victim, respectively. Christie argues that our conflicts are an important part of being human and that through human interaction we must deal with the essence of the problems and conflicts, digging below the surface. As it is now, only legally pertinent parts of a conflict — those deemed important by the courts — are allowed into the courtroom. The criminal justice system thus blocks out key elements of life experience, excluding the people involved from full participation. The result is what Christie (1977) calls double victimization, which is doubly damaging because the person involved is denied the right to complete participation in an important symbolic event. The criminal justice system is, in essence, engaged in appropriating conflict because the political, economic, and legal systems are designed to offer little chance for the participation and influence of either victims or offenders.

However, these theorists also insist that restorative measures will fail unless the system addresses the roots of injustice. In this regard the true emphasis of abolitionism and peacemaking criminology is transformative justice, which insists that we cannot solve the problem of crime or rebuilding communities unless we challenge the true impact of capitalist inequalities, globalization, patriarchy, and colonialization.

Some critics argue that abolitionism and peacemaking offer no concrete solutions (Braithwaite 1989), mainly because prison abolitionists not only call for the implementation of restorative measures, but also demand the eventual closure of all prisons. As a critical criminological approach, then, it may be more utopian than realistic. Don Gibbons (1994) asserts that peacemaking criminologists offer little that is new, nor do they show how to achieve the large-scale structural changes necessary in a movement working for non-violence and peace.

Postmodernism and poststructuralism provide a critique of the modern conceptions of "truth," and argue that "crime," "crime control," and criminology are modernist ideas, which lay claim to a scientific truth that is philosophically problematic. Governmentality theory (as a critical theory in criminology) demonstrates the multiplicity of social controls, and, many argue, deepens the postmodern analysis.

Poststructuralism and Postmodernism

Only themselves understand themselves and the like of themselves,
as souls only understand souls.
— Whitman 1965

Poststructuralism and postmodernism are critical of all of the previous theories, which are all modernist. With its beginning in the Enlightenment, modernism is characterized by the use of the scientific method to uncover certain truths. Postmodernism points to a number of assumptions characteristic of modernism. For one thing, modernists believe in the possibility of human progress and emancipation through uncovering "truths" about human behaviour by means of science. Carol Smart states that modernism entails a search for "meta-narratives," or grand theories (Smart 1990: 194; Comack 2000: 62). Postmodernists and poststructuralists argue that we must abandon the modernist search for some kind of universal "truth" and instead accept the existence of a number of often competing truths.

Although postmodernism and poststructuralism take inspiration from Marxism, they ultimately reject it. Reaching beyond neo-Marxism, these theories investigate the dominant modes of expression (dominant discourse/accepted truths) in a society. Postmodernism and poststructuralism are critical theories; like the Marxist notion of hegemony, they view dominant discourses as being linked to the major powerholders in society. They assert that these discourses attempt to create a public that conforms to the visions of the prevailing political economy. Discourse theorists point out, for example, how, from the fifteenth century on, people were compelled to believe in a dominant discourse that insisted on hard work as the source of success and goodness. They also assert that emancipatory discourse cannot provide alternatives to the status quo; the dominant discourses of our day, they argue, have marginalized and silenced such alternative views.

The methodology of discourse theories involves highlighting discourses and deconstructing them. Deconstruction is a "method of analysis that takes apart socially constructed categories in order to determine the makeup of a particular world view" (Ristock and Pennell, quoted in Comack 1999a: 62). This process entails not only demonstrating how communication is formed but also how the dominant powerholders of the political economy are supported by the discourse.

Poststructuralism

Poststructuralists (such as Michel Foucault, Pierre Bourdieu, and Mikhail Bakhtin) reject the mainstream assumption that discourses are constructed simply as a means for communication. They assert that communication and language are tools of social control that create conformity. Language is constructed according to the needs of the powerful. As Bernard Schissel (1997) points out, poststructuralism uncovers the motives that lie behind the language and systems of knowledge that belong to the privileged.

Foucault (1977), for example, draws attention to the power and oppression of language, especially the language created by criminal justice and academic professionals under the guise of scientific objectivity. In this light, definitions of criminal behaviour are created as discourse according to the privileged — those with the power to control the knowledge. Mainstream discourse about crime in general is restricted to individual explanations and pathology, with almost no consideration of structural inequalities or the suffering of people on the margins. For example, an article in *Alberta Report* (July 31, 1995: 1) states: "Girls, it used to be said, were made of sugar and spice. Not anymore. The latest crop of teenage girls can be as violent, malicious and downright evil as the boys." The voices of experts back up these claims with professional knowledge and jargon. As Schissel (1997) emphasizes with regards to youth:

> This contemporary medical/psychological discourse of goodness and badness sets youth crime in a context of orthodox criminology: individuals gone wrong, either inherently or culturally. The underlying ideological position is that society is structured correctly and that individuals who offend are individually or socially pathological and identifiable. (1997: 105)

The dominant discourse is a powerful tool of social control precisely because it hides structural and societal problems and is written under the guise of expert knowledge and "scientific" objectivity.

Postmodernism

The theories of postmodernism and poststructuralism often come from the same authors, in similar writings. In fact, some critics argue that there is no difference between the two theories. Postmodernists analyzing crime and criminal justice focus on the position of the privileged in the creation of theories of crime and law (see, for example, Ferrell 1993; Henry and Milovanovic 1991; Pfohl and Gordon 1986). Like poststructuralists, postmodernists argue that we must abandon any search for "truth" and deconstruct the discourses of our day that lay claim to this knowledge. Many postmodernists are cynical about the world, seeing people as caught in consumeristic images representing a "hyperreal fantasy" in our ways of knowing. They seek to overturn the "dominant narratives" often characteristic of middle-class, white, male-dominant claims to information (Smart 1995).

Left theorists have often tried to speak for the oppressed; postmodernists allow the oppressed to speak for themselves.

Once discourse is deconstructed, the goal of postmodernism is to highlight less linear ways of thinking (see, for example, Smart 1990; Denzin 1990; Einstadter and Henry 1995). Here, postmodernists say that the redefinition of our truths must come from the words of those who experience oppression. Left theorists have often tried to speak for the oppressed; postmodernists allow the oppressed to speak for themselves. Postmodernists aim at including biographies, stories, and personal experiences of crime and involvement with the criminal justice system (Smart 1990). An excellent example is the work of criminologists, historians, and others that incorporate the opinions of individuals who have been in conflict with the law (see, for instance, Sangster 2002). Comack, for instance, gives voice to many women's different experiences, as in the following passage:

> Some people are violent, some people take it out in other ways, but that was my only way to release it. It was like, it's almost orgasmic, you know, you'd write the cheques, and you'd get home and you'd go through all these things and it's like "there's so much there. I have all these new things to keep my mind off of. I don't have to deal with the old issues." And so you do it. And it becomes an escape. You don't know what else to do... I've tried other things like drugs. All it did was give me track marks, 'cause I was using drugs intravenously. And... what more can you do? (Comack 1996: 86)

This perspective helps lay the ground for a postmodern legality challenging traditional definitions of crime and criminal justice. The practice supports and develops forms of dispute resolution that empower minority groups to define their own problems (Einstadter and Henry 1995). Postmodernism embraces the same forms of restorative justice and transformative justice that seek to have the offender, victim, and community come to their own resolutions. It therefore supports the movement towards sentencing circles, family group conferencing, mediation, and other practices that give the conflict back to those directly involved. In the end, restorative justice is based on believing the stories (accounts) of the oppressed.

Governmentality and Risk Theories: The Crisis of Critical Criminology and the Demise of Grand Narratives

Critical criminology has been identified as in crisis since the end of the 1980s, especially because of the judgmental critique. "Whether one wanted to blame 'the end of history,' the demise of grand narratives of progress and emancipation, the bankruptcy of socialism or the victory of individualistic consumerism, the project of critical criminology does not really seem to fit any more in the post-1984 world," write van Swaaningen and Taylor (1994: 183). There is no question that the power of radical challenges of the structures of justice are powerful. However, this level of critique privileges "authoritative judgment" above other discursive techniques, and times have changed, raising "important questions for the plight of such criticism in truth regimes that problematise the authority of expert or critical judgment" (Lyotard 1984; cited in Pavlich 2000: 60). Let's examine the specifics.

Zygmunt Bauman (1995) defines postmodernity as the declining role of the state and the recognition that the market manages the co-ordination of society. Citizens follow rules not because we are citizens of the state but because of the seductive promise of consumerism. Pettigrew (1996) describes this as a process of regulation that is based on envy, self-interest, competitions, consumerism and endless production. What feeds the new global market, therefore, is the abstraction, not human need. A shift in thinking embracing neo-liberal ideas accompanies these institutional changes. Citizens are viewed as autonomous individuals responsible for their own actions and fate. Economic opportunity is recast as individual responsibility, not connected to social structural conditions.

Under these conditions, individuals are responsible for their own successes as well as their failures, leading to the importance of understanding the analysis of a risk society. A number of provisions have arisen to deal with managing risk (Rose 2000; Ericson, Barry, and Doyle 2000), most beyond the confines of the state and state institutions (rendering an analysis of state institutions not irrelevant but only a small piece in a large puzzle). The power of the state is decentred (Garland 1997), with diverse risk-management strategies within "a black hole" of new market conditions controlling consumer identities (Bauman 1997).

Let's examine what this means in relation to crime control. In postmodern times, the state is no longer responsible for our protection; increasingly, managing our risks is considered our own responsibility. Managing risk includes buying better security systems, alarms, insurance; living in gated communities; and more. Important to note here is that very few of society's have-nots can afford these risk-management measures — again leaving the poor more susceptible to crime.

The promise of critical and radical criminology can be assessed under this new terrain of risk management and extended forms of governmentality (Pavlich 2000). Although it is important to outline the state's role in managing the fallout of global market changes (for example in containing the most desperate and most vulnerable sections of the population: see chapter 13) and in reinforcing its authority by imposing tougher sentencing legislation (White 2002: 388), this is only one means of upholding the postmodern social terrain and must be understood as such. The grammar of authoritative judgment is not capable of challenging fragmented, state-imposed, risk-based, diverse political technologies directed at new images of deviance and crime. Attention must be paid to the changing epistemological horizons where "judgmental grammar" no longer can thrive (Bauman 1997; Lyotard 1984; Vattimo 1997) and to recovering a critique that does not serve the technocratic demands of "advanced liberal" governmentalities dominant today (Osborne 1996; Rose 1996). Further, the diversity acknowledged within literature on governmentality — the fractured social identities of postmodern conditions and life choices (in class, race, gender, age, sexual orientations) — nullifies the meta-narrative towards emancipation. Can we realistically say there is a universal vision broad enough to address all of the oppressions of our time? Yet this is often what radical criminology assumes (Butler 1992). Derrida points out that "nothing seems to be less outdated than the classical emancipatory idea" (1992: 28).

This critique also applies to the movement within critical criminology to keep discussions relevant to existing crime control — a movement that looks like a renegotiation of radical thinking with a pragmatism that seeks real solutions — often technocratic solutions, aligning themselves with correctional criminologists. This is especially relevant to critical criminologists who may blur boundaries between socialist pragmatism and "administrative" criminology. There is an acceptance of these neo-liberal agendas as well as neo-conservative solutions to the crime problem. Contemporary critical and radical criminologists' work often advocates (although cautiously) for restorative and communitarian justice (as we see throughout the book), such as family group conferences, sentencing circles, alternative models of education, and community policing. As Pavlich (2000: 67) argues, "what strikes one in these debates is not so much the acceptance of several neo-conservative and neo-liberal foundations (which are there), but the sheer absence of any attempt to think beyond the ambit of techno-administrative rationales." Debates over restorative justice, zero tolerance, and police-community relations are all part of a struggle that is political and part of a regulatory practice — the responsibilization of citizens. Thus, governmentality theorists recognize a blend of Keynesian and neo-liberal strategies, both acting as social control in risk-based society, and criminology that supports this as simply a distraction. Rock (1994) argues that radical criminology remains vulnerable to administrative pressures to be co-opted by a wider institutional demand for a "normal science." The question becomes whether a radical criminology can embrace a technocratic logic that assumes the necessity of the reality it is are also trying to critique. Pavlich (2000) argues that critical criminology must continue to challenge administrative criminology and discourse in a way that does not support the advanced neo-liberal governmentalities. If critical criminology supports crime control measures (even restorative and progressive looking measures), then it becomes part of social control and simply engages in a debate over existing policy. Governmentality theory argues that the role of criminology should remain at the level of understanding new forms of governmentality and continue to critique. This critique may include the question of why criminology has shifted to become more administrative in our global world.

The spirit of the Marxist critique remains relevant — but needs to be expanded to understand modern times. Human beings are rendered knowable, shapeable, and incapable of freedom within governmentality forces. Although governmentality recognizes diverse and decentred forms of social control, each of these can be examined, not with the intent of developing technical solutions to things such as the crime problem, but with the spirit of a critique that acknowledges human potential loss:

> A lesson to be drawn from critical thinking is this: the needed revisions to a grammar of (modern) judgmental critique cannot be achieved by accepting the dictates of a postmodern performance-based knowledge-producing ethos. Perhaps, an alternative grammar of critique could seek legitimacy by contesting this ethos, and developing alternative strategies to question the realties encompassing contemporary political subjects. (Pavlich 2000: 74)

Derrida (1994) calls for critical and radical texts to include the Marxist emphasis on change and escaping life limits. Governmental critiques can continue to embrace the spirit of Marxism and concepts of justice and democracy as promises that are ongoing — not endpoints that are achievable (Pavlich 2000). There cannot be an emancipatory goal, but we may embrace ongoing critique.

Conclusion

> *I saw a beggar leaning on his wooden crutch*
> *He said to me, "You must not ask for so much."*
> *And a pretty woman leaning in her darkened door,*
> *She cried to me, "Hey, why not ask for more?"*
> — Leonard Cohen, "Bird on the Wire," 1968

The sociological imagination (Mills 1959) must feed critical criminology — that is, the sociological imagination that understands the links between individual life chances and larger structural and historical forces. The critical perspectives ask not only whether individuals have maintained their responsibility to the community, but also whether the community has maintained its responsibility to individuals. The approach does not focus on individual flaws; rather, it questions societal structures and the role of those structures in breeding and sustaining criminals. Inequality and disenfranchisement, abuse and victimization, classism, racism, and sexism produce criminal and anti-social behaviour. The approach looks at both criminal behaviour and the workings of the criminal justice system at the structural level. The issue in all critical criminology is whether it is a criminal justice system or an (in)justice system. Critical criminology raises questions about what is defined as criminal and how laws are enforced to work in the interests of powerful groups (men, professional, and capitalist classes). It also questions how society responds to criminal behaviour. Does the criminal justice system help to reduce crime and recidivism, or does it instead work to reinforce criminogenic conditions? Jeffrey Reiman, for me, provides a clear answer. The current criminal justice system, he says, is the best model for the creation of crime that anyone could possibly think of: the system labels someone as an "offender," expects criminal tendencies from that individual, fails to deal with social issues that create criminogenic conditions, lowers self-esteem, criminalizes victimless and consensual acts, lumps disenfranchised individuals together in demeaning conditions, and in general creates a breeding ground for dangerous and criminal behaviour.

Critical criminology rejects short-term solutions and "get-tougher" law-and-order responses to crime. The diverse proposals share a philosophy of healing, rebuilding, restoring, and transforming — a movement away from punishment. The diversity is often found in the extent to which critical theorists are willing to embrace short-term restorative measures. Peacemaking, abolitionism, left realism, postmodernism all call for restorative and transformative justice for offenders as well as the need to restructure society towards less violence and more justice. Each position continues to support the argument of Stanley Cohen (1985: 135): "It still makes sense today that mutual aid, good neighbourliness and real community are preferable to the solutions of bureaucracies, professionals and the centralized state."

Yet many neo-Marxist theorists remain extremely cautious about these community solutions. Their position is that restorative programs are often co-opted by the state to further control marginalized people. Some suggest that the projects could have a net widening effect, that judges could use restorative measures such as mediation, community services, and restitution for "offenders" who might otherwise have been let go. Furthermore, restorative measures do not address the root causes of injustice. By implementing reforms that appear to be more humanitarian, measures that could actually alleviate suffering may well be forgotten. Neo-Marxism tends to demand a redefinition of what we define as criminal behaviour as well as a wake-up call for true equality (and, for many, socialism). Further, theories of structural Marxism and governmentality demonstrate how restorative measures fit within a neo-liberal ideology and thereby continue to control consumers to accept the status quo (and their own responsibilization to be consumers and law-abiding citizens) and to critique those who cannot succeed within this paradigm as "unfit" or compel them to become responsibilized (which may be through restorative justice or correctional paradigms). Either way, the global and numerous inequalities and social control measures remain unchallenged.

Transformative justice and the other long-term solutions of critical criminology are often criticized as being unattainable and, for recent governmentality theorists, no longer applicable in a world of complex and multiple social controls. For example, postmodernism is criticized for simply raising nagging theoretical questions about discourse. Even one of the leading peacemaking criminologists, Hal Pepinsky (1992), admitted that peacemaking strategies will not be replacing "law-and-order" initiatives any time soon. Some critics see abolitionism as seeking an idealist utopia. Some declare that the best critical criminology can offer is a rethinking of conservative political responses. The hope is that an enlightening of individual beliefs may then travel to the larger community through grassroots organizations. Police, media, public, politicians, and criminologists may also be alerted by critical insights into the contradictions in our legal system, the benefits of healing and peace and the idea that things do not have to be the way they are. Still, many neo-Marxists claim that long-term structural changes can only be made slowly through law and other measures. This means we must continue to challenge globalization, the growing inequalities between the rich and the poor, downsizing, the dismantling of the social welfare system, the increased funding of the criminal justice system, the destruction of the environment in the pursuit of more profit, the deregulation of corporate crime, and structural racism.

DISCUSSION QUESTIONS

1. You have been invited to a prison abolition conference in Toronto to hear a presentation by a prison abolitionist and peacemaking criminologist entitled If Prison is the Answer, then What is the Question? In preparing for your trip you research the central assumptions of both perspectives on prison and develop a preliminary idea of what will be presented. What do you find?

2. Describe the difference between consensus theories that attempt to explain criminal behaviour as an event and critical criminological theories that examine the role of power in the creation and maintenance of "criminality."

3. Define hegemony and explain the structuralist Marxist position that the media, prison, and law are hegemonic institutions.

4. Marxist criminologists assert that although the poor and racial minorities are the people who fill prisons, this does not mean that they are the most dangerous or lacking in social consciousness. Rather, the overrepresentation means that the actions of the marginalized are defined as criminal and the rich are weeded out at each step of the criminal justice process. Explain.

5. Postmodernism, poststructuralism, and governmentality theories are said to both provide a critique and/or an extension of Marxist-based criminology. Explain.

6. Anatole France quips: "The law in all its majestic impartiality forbids the rich and poor alike to sleep under bridges, to beg in the street and steal bread." Explain this statement with reference to the structural Marxist position that one role of state institutions is to ensure social harmony and the loyalty of dominated classes.

GLOSSARY OF TERMS

Abolitionism: organizes against prison, capital punishment, slavery, racism, classism, and sexism. Abolitionist struggles maintain that (severe) punishment never solves problems.

Critical Race Theory: a progressive movement that views race as a social construction and law as sustaining white supremacy.

Governmentality: theorists who have become disenchanted with Marxist-informed criminology have re-conceptualized Michel Foucault's notion of governance. Governmentality theorists have broken from the modernist conceptions of power/knowledge in favour of a multiplicity of governance, including "practices," "discourses," "ideologies," and "techniques" that inform governance strategies. Governance includes the responsibilization of ourselves and minimization of risk. This means that crime control and "criminality" is no longer about state control but includes our ability to buy additional security in our homes, secure employment/insurance, and live in certain neighbourhoods (even gated communities).

Instrumental Marxism: argues that the criminal justice system and definitions of crime ensure the power of the dominant class. This class has such inordinate influence on legal definitions of criminality that what is defined as criminal is often action that only threatens the status quo.

Marxist Criminology: focuses on the fundamental class inequalities in capitalist society. In this theory, crime is in part a rational response to individualistic struggles for material wealth arising in an unequal society. The primary focus, however, is on how the criminal justice system acts as a means of controlling marginalized people.

Modernism: a culture committed to inventing social structures that are dynamic and believed to bring about continued improvements in human existence, including science's alleged ability to discover truths about human behaviour.

Official Version of the Law: a method through which the legal world defines itself, to the effect that the law is a neutral, impartial, and objective system designed for the resolving of social conflict.

Peacemaking: seeks to uncover the warlike characteristics of the criminal justice system, prison and punishment. Peacemakers maintain we can end crime and suffering only by eliminating suffering.

Postmodernism: offers that we must reject the search for universal truth and knowledge. These theories point out that dominant discourses reflect the interests of the powerful and tend to silence alternative views and voices. In criminological analysis, these alternative voices are most often marginalized and labelled "criminal."

Structural Marxism: argues that the criminal justice system and the "official version of the law" through claims to objectivity and neutrality legitimate capitalism. The law tells us that rich and marginalized are to be treated alike — but because our society is substantially unequal, such formal equality before the law perpetuates marginalization and class inequality.

SUGGESTED READINGS

Davis, Angela. 2003. *Are Prisons Obsolete?* Seven Stories Press Open Media Series.

Foucault, Michel. 1977. *Discipline and Punish: The Birth of the Prison.* New York: Pantheon.

Pepinsky, Harold E., and Richard Quinney (eds.). 1991. *Criminology as Peacemaking.* Bloomington: Indiana University Press.

Taylor, Ian, Paul Walton, and Jock Young. 1975. *Critical Criminology.* Boston: Routledge and Kegan Paul.

Young, Jock, and Roger Matthews (eds.). 2003. *The New Politics of Crime and Punishment.* Cullompton, Devon: Willan Publishing.

James, Matthew Thomas. 2005. *The New Abolitionists: (Neo)slave Narratives and Contemporary Prison Writings*. Suny Press.

REFERENCES

Adelberg, Ellen, and Claudia Currie (eds.). 1993. *In Conflict with the Law: Women and the Canadian Justice System*. Vancouver: Press Gang Publishers.

Akers, Ronald L. 1997. *Criminological Theories: Introduction and Evaluation*. Second edition. Los Angeles: Roxbury.

Alberta Report. 1994. "Junior Gone Wild." May 9.

_____. 1995. "Killer Girls." July 31.

Althusser, L. 1971. *Lenin and Philosophy and Other Essays*. New York: New Left Books.

Assembly of First Nations. 2002. *Proceedings*. June 11. Matthew Coon Come, National Chief. Available at <http://www.turtleisland.org/news/absenyouth2.htm> accessed Feb. 1, 2006

Balbus, I. 1977. "Commodity Form and Legal Form: An Essay on the 'Relative Autonomy' of the Law." *Law and Society Review* 11: 571–88.

Balfour, G. 2006. "Introduction." In G. Balfour and E. Comack (eds.), *Criminalizing Women: Gender and (In)Justice in Neoliberal Tines*. Halifax: Fernwood Publishing.

Bauman, Z. 1995. "From Welfare State into Prison." Unpublished paper for the International Conference on Prison Growth, Oslo. April.

_____. 1997. *Postmodernity and Its Discontents*. New York: New York University Press.

Bohm, Robert M. 1997. *A Primer on Crime and Delinquency*. Wadsworth Publishing Company: An International Thomson Publishing Company.

Bonger, Willem. 1916. *Criminology and Economic Conditions*. Boston: Little, Brown.

_____. 1969. *Criminology and Economic Conditions*. Boston: Little, Brown.

Boritch, Helen. 1997. *Fallen Women*. Toronto: ITP Nelson.

_____. 2002. "Women in Prison in Canada." In B. Schissel and C. Brooks (eds.), *Marginality and Condemnation: An Introduction to Critical Criminology*. Halifax: Fernwood Publishing.

Braithwaite, J. 1989. *Crime, Shame and Reintegration*. New York: Cambridge University Press.

Burtch, Brian, and N. Larsen (eds.). 1999. *Law in Society: Canadian Readings*. Toronto: Harcourt Brace Canada.

Butler, J. 1992. "Feminism and the Question of "Postmodernism." In J. Butler and J.W. Scott (eds.), *Feminist Theorize the Political*. London: Routledge.

Calgary Herald. 1995. "Teen Violence." April 18.

Chambliss, William J. 1975. "A Sociological Analysis of the Law of Vagrancy." In W. Carson and P. Wiles (eds.), *The Sociology of Crime and Delinquency in Britain*, Volume 1. Oxford, UK: Martin Robertson.

Chambliss, W.J., and R.B. Seidman. 1982. *Law and Order, and Power*. Second edition. Reading, MA: Addison Wesley Publishing.

Christie, Nils. 1977. "Conflicts as Property." *The British Journal of Criminology* January.

_____. 1993. *Crime Control as Industry*. New York: Routledge.

_____. 2000. *Crime Control as Industry*. Third edition. New York: Routledge.

Clarke, J. 2000. "Serve the Rich and Punish the Poor." In Gordon West and Ruth Morris (eds.), *The Case for Penal Abolition*. Toronto: Canadian Scholars Press.

Cohen, Leonard. 1994. "There is a War." *Cohen Live*. Stranger Music (BMI).

Cohen, Stanley. 1985. *Visions of Social Control*. Cambridge: Polity Press.

Comack, Elizabeth. 1996. *Women in Trouble*. Halifax: Fernwood Publishing.

_____. (ed.). 1999. *Locating Law: Race/Class/Gender Connections*. Halifax: Fernwood Publishing.

_____. 2000. "The Prisoning of Women: Meeting Women's Needs." In K. Hannah-Moffat and M. Shaw (eds.), *An Ideal Prison? Critical Essays on Women's Imprisonment in Canada*. Halifax:

Fernwood Publishing.

Comack, Elizabeth, and Gillian Balfour. 2004. *The Power to Criminalize: Violence, Inequality, and the Law*. Halifax: Fernwood Publishing.

Culhane, Claire. 1991. "Prison Abolition." In L. Samuelson and B. Schissel (eds.) *Criminal Justice: Sentencing Issues and Reform*. Toronto: Garamond Press.

Curran, Daniel J., and Claire M. Renzetti. 1994. *Theories of Crime*. Boston: Allyn and Bacon.

Currie, Dawn. 1998. "The Criminalization of Violence Against Women: Feminist Demands and Patriarchal Accommodation." In Kevin Bonnycastle and George Rigakos (eds.), *Unsettling Truths: Battered Women, Policy, Politics, and Contemporary Research in Canada*. Vancouver: Collective Press.

DeKeseredy, Walter S. 2000. *Women, Crime and the Canadian Criminal Justice System*. Cincinnati: Anderson Publishing Company.

Denzin, N. 1990. "Presidential Address on the Sociological Imagination Revisited." *The Sociological Quarterly* 31 (1).

Derrida, J. 1992. "Force of Law: The "Mystical Foundation of Authority." In D. Cornell, M. Rosenfeld, and D.G. Carlson (eds.), *Deconstruction and the Possibility of Justice*. New York: Routledge.

Einstadter, Werner, and Stuart Henry. 1995. *Criminological Theory: An Analysis of Its Underlying Assumptions*. Fort Worth, TX: Harcourt Brace.

Ericson, R., D. Barry, and A. Doyle. 2000. "The Moral Hazards of Neo-liberalism: Lessons from the Private Insurance Industry." *Economy and Society* 29: 532–58.

Faith, K. 1993. *Unruly Women: The Politics of Confinement and Resistance*. Vancouver: Press Gang Publishers.

_____. 2002. "The Social Construction of 'Dangerous' Girls and Women." In B. Schissel and C. Brooks (eds.), *Marginality and Condemnation: An Introduction to Critical Criminology*. Halifax: Fernwood Publishing.

Ferrell, Jeff. 1993. *Crimes of Style: Urban Graffiti and the Politics of Criminality*. New York: Garland.

Foucault, Michel. 1977. *Discipline and Punish: The Birth of the Prison*. New York: Pantheon.

_____. 1980. *The History of Sexuality: An Introduction*. New York: Vintage Books.

Frideres, James S., and Rene Gadacz. 2001. *Aboriginal People in Canada: Contemporary Conflicts*. Toronto: Prentice Hall.

Garland, D. 1997. "Governmentality and the Problem of Crime: Foucault, Criminology, Sociology." *Theoretical Criminology* 1: 173–214.

Gavigan, Shelly A.M. 1999. "Poverty Law, Theory and Practice: The Place of Class and Gender in Access to Justice." In Elizabeth Comack (ed.), *Locating Law: Race/Class/Gender Connections*. Halifax: Fernwood Publishing.

Gibbons, Don C. 1994. *Talking About Crime and Criminals: Problems and Issues in Theory Development in Criminology*. Englewood Cliffs, NJ: Prentice Hall.

Goff, C., and C. Reasons. 1978. *Corporate Crime in Canada*. Scarborough, ON: Prentice-Hall.

Gordon, David. 1976. "Class and the Economics of Crime." In W.J. Chambliss and M. Mankoff (eds.), *Whose Law, What Order?* New York: Wiley.

Gordon, Robert, and Ian Coneybeer. 1999. "Corporate Crime." In Nick Larson and B. Burtch (eds.), *Law in Society: Canadian Readings*. Toronto: Harcourt Brace Canada.

Gramsci, A. 1971. *Selections from the Prison Notebooks of Antonio Gramsci*. New York: International Publishers.

Green, Joyce. 2005. "Self-determination, Citizenship, and Federalism: Indigenous and Canadian Palimpsest." In Michael Murphy (ed.), *State of the Federation: Reconfiguring Aboriginal-State Relations*. Instituted of Intergovernmental Relations, School of Policy Studies, Queen's University. McGill-Queen's University Press.

Green, Ross Gordon, and Kearney Healey. 2003. *Tough on Kids: Rethinking Approaches to Youth Justice*. Saskatoon: Purich Publishing.

Hall, S., C. Critcher, T. Jefferson, J. Clarke, and B. Roberts. 1978. *Policing the Crisis: Mugging, the State, and law and Order*. London: Macmillan.

Henry, Stuart, and Dragan Milovanovic. 1991. "Constitutive Criminology: The Maturation of Critical Theory." *Criminology* 29.

Hinch, R. 1992. "Conflict and Marxist Theories." In R. Linden (ed.), *Criminology: A Canadian Perspective*. Toronto: Harcourt Brace Jovanovich, Canada.

Hudson, Barbara. 2006. "Beyond White Man's Justice: Race, Gender and Justice in late Modernity." *Theoretical Criminology* 10 (1): 29–47.

Hunt, Alan. 1976. "Law, State and Class Struggle." *Marxism Today* 20 (6).

Jaccoud, Mylene, and Renee Brassard. 2003. "The Marginalization of Aboriginal Women in Montreal." In David Newhouse and Evelyn Peters (eds.), *Not Strangers in These Parts: Urban Aboriginal Peoples*. Ottawa: Policy Research Initiative.

Jackson, George. 1970. *Soledad Brother: The Prison Letters of George Jackson. Introduction by Jean Genet*. New York: Coward-McCann.

Lawrence, Bonita. 2004. *"Real" Indians and Others: Mixed-blood Urban Native Peoples and Nationhood*. Vancouver: UBC Press.

Lynch, M., and Groves, W. 1986. *A Primer in Radical Criminology*. New York: Harrow and Heston.

_____. 1989. *A Primer in Radical Criminology*. Second edition. New York: Harrow and Heston.

Lyotard, J.F. 1984. *The Postmodern Condition: A Report on Knowledge*. Minneapolis: University of Minnesota Press.

Manitoba Aboriginal Justice Inquiry. 1991. V.1. *The Justice System and Aboriginal People*. Winnipeg: Queen's Printer.

Mathiesen, T. 1974. *The Politics of Abolition: Essays in Political Action Theory*. London: Martin Robertson.

_____. 1990. *Prison on Trial*. London: Sage Publications.

McCormick, Christopher Ray. 1995. *Constructing Danger: The Mis/representation of Crime in the News*. Halifax, NS: Fernwood Publishing.

McMullan, John L. 1992. *Beyond the Limits of the Law: Corporate Crime and Law and Order*. Halifax, NS: Fernwood Publishing.

McMurtry, J. 1998. *Unequal Freedoms, The Global Market as an Ethical System*. Toronto: Garamond Press.

Miliband, R. 1969. *The State in Capitalist Society: The Analysis of the Western System of Power*. London: Quartet.

Mills, C. Wright. 1959. *The Sociological Imagination*. New York: Oxford University Press.

Morris, Ruth. 2000. *Stories of Transformative Justice*. Toronto: Canadian Scholars' Press.

O'Connor, J. 1973. *The Fiscal Crisis of the State*. New York: St. Martin's Press.

Osborne, P. (ed.). 1996. *A Critical Sense: Interviews with Intellectuals*. London: Routledge.

Panitch, Leo (ed.). 1977. *The Canadian State: Political Economy and Political Power*. Toronto: University of Toronto Press.

Pavlich, George. 2000. *Critique and Radical Discourses on Crime*. Burlington, Great Britain: Dartmouth Publishing Company Ltd.

Pearce, F. 1976. *Crimes of the Powerful: Marxism, Crime and Deviance*. London: Pluto Press.

Pepinsky, Harold. 1991. *The Geometry of Violence and Democracy*. Bloomington: Indiana University Press.

_____. 1992. "Abolishing Prisons." In M. Schwartz, L. Travis, and T. Clear (eds.), *Corrections: An Issues Approach*. Third edition. Cincinnati: Anderson.

Pepinsky, Harold E., and Richard Quinney (eds.). 1991. *Criminology as Peacemaking*. Bloomington: Indiana University Press.

Pettigrew, P. 1996. "Notes from Speech to a Conference on 'Accelerating Rural Development in Africa.'" Airlie, Virginia, September 23.

Pfohl, Stephen. 1985. *Images of Deviance and Social Control: A Sociological History*. New York: McGraw-Hill.

Pfohl, Stephen, and Avery Gordon. 1986. "Criminological Displacements: A Sociological Deconstruction." *Social Problems* 33.

Platt, Tony. 1975. "Prospects for a Radical Criminology in the USA." In I. Taylor, P. Walton, and J. Young (eds.), *Critical Criminology*. Boston: Routledge and Kegan Paul.

Poulantzas, N. 1973. *Political Power and Social Class*. Atlantic Fields, NJ: Humanities Press.

Quinney, Richard. 1974. *Critique of Legal Order: Crime Control in Capitalist Society*. Boston: Little, Brown.

_____. 1975. "Crime Control in Capitalist Society: A Critical Philosophy." In I. Taylor, P. Walton, and J. Young (eds.), *Critical Criminology*. London: Routledge and Kegan Paul.

_____. 1980. *Class, State and Crime*. New York: Longman.

_____. 1991. *Criminology as Peacemaking*. Bloomington: Indiana University Press.

Ratner, R.S., and J.L. McMullan. 1985. "Social Control and the Rise of the 'Exceptional State' in Britain, the United States, and Canada." In T. Fleming (ed.), *The New Criminologies in Canada: State, Crime, and Control*. Toronto: Oxford University Press.

Regush, N. 1991. "Health and Welfare's National Disgrace." *Saturday Night*. April.

Reiman, Jeffrey. 1998. *The Rich Get Richer and the Poor Get Prison: Ideology, Class and Criminal Justice*. Boston: Allyn and Bacon.

_____. 1999. "The Rich (Still) Get Richer: Understanding Ideology, Outrage and Economic Bias." *The Critical Criminologist* 9 (2).

_____. 2001. *The Rich Get Richer and the Poor Get Prison: Ideology, Class and Criminal Justice*. Boston: Allyn and Bacon.

_____. 2007. *The Rich Get Richer and the Poor Get Prison: Ideology, Class and Criminal Justice*. Boston: Pearson Press.

Rock, P. 1994. *History of Criminology*. Aldershot: Dartmouth Publishing Company.

Rose, N. 1996. "Governing 'Advanced' Liberal Democracies." In A. Barry, T. Osborne and N. Rose (eds.), *Foucault and Political Reason: Liberalism, Neo-liberalism, and Rationalities of Government*. Chicago: University of Chicago Press.

Samuelson, Les. 2000. "Indigenized Urban 'Community' Policing in Canada and Australia: A Comparative Study of Aboriginal Perspectives." *Police Practice and Research* 2 (4).

Sangster, Joan. 2002. *Girl Trouble: Female Delinquency in English Canada*. Toronto: Between the Lines.

Schissel, Bernard. 1997. *Blaming Children: Youth Crime, Moral Panics and the Politics of Hate*. Second edition. Halifax: Fernwood Publishing.

_____. 2006. *Still Blaming Children: Youth Conduct and the Politics of Child Hating*. Halifax: Fernwood Publishing.

Smart, Carol. 1990. "Feminist Approaches to Criminology or Postmodern Woman Meets Atavistic Man." In L. Gelshthorpe and A. Morris (eds.), *Feminist Perspectives in Criminology*. Bristol, England: Open University Press.

_____. 1995. *Law, Crime and Sexuality: Essays in Feminism*. London: Thousand Oaks: Sage Publications.

Snider, Laureen. 1999. "Relocating Law: Making Corporate Crime Disappear." In Elizabeth Comack (ed.), *Locating Law: Race/Class/Gender Connections*. Halifax: Fernwood Publishing.

_____. 2002. "The Sociology of Corporate Crime: An Obituary." *Theoretical Criminology* 4 (2).

Standing Senate Committee on Aboriginal Peoples. 2003. "Urban Aboriginal Youth: An Action Plan for Change." October. Available at <http://www.turtleisland.org/news/absenyouth.htm> accessed July 2007.

Statistics Canada. 2003. "Aboriginal Peoples Survey: Well-Being of the Non-reserve Aboriginal Population." *The Daily*. September 24. Available at <http://www.statcan.ca/Daily/English/030924/d030924b.htm> accessed July 2007.

Taylor, I. 1981. *Law and Order: Arguments for Socialism*. London: Macmillan.

_____. 1983. *Crime, Capitalism and Community: Three Essays in Socialist Criminology*. Toronto: Butterworths.

_____. 1999. *Crime in Context: A Critical Criminology of Market Societies*. Boulder: Westview.

Taylor, I., P. Walton, and J. Young. 1973. *The New Criminology: For a Social Theory of Deviance*. New York: Harper and Row.

_____. 1975. *Critical Criminology.* Boston: Routledge and Kegan Paul.

Van Swaaningen, R., and I. Taylor. 1994. "Rethinking Critical Criminology: A Panel Discussion." *Crime Law and Social Change.* 21: 183–90.

Vattimo, G. 1997. *Beyond Interpretation: The Meaning of Hermeneutics for Philosophy.* London: Polity Press.

Vold, George B. 1986. *Theoretical Criminology.* Third edition. New York: Oxford University Press.

Waldram, James B. 1997. *The Way of the Pipe.* Peterborough: Broadview Press.

West, W. Gordon, and Ruth Morris (eds.). 2000. *The Case For Penal Abolition.* Toronto: Canadian Scholars' Press Inc.

White, R. 2002. "Restorative Justice and Social Inequality." In B. Schissel and C. Brooks. *Marginality and Condemnation: An Introduction to Critical Criminology.* Halifax: Fernwood Publishing.

Whitman, Walt. 1965. *Leaves of Grass.* New York: Norton New York

Wortley, Scott. 2002. "The Depiction of Race and Crime in the Toronto Print Media." In B. Schissel and C. Brooks (eds.), *Marginality and Condemnation: An Introduction to Critical Criminology.* Halifax: Fernwood Publishing.

4 The Sex Question in Criminology

Elizabeth Comack

KEY FACTS

> Women were not considered "legal persons" in law until 1929 in Canada — and only after a group of first-wave feminists appealed to the Privy Council in Britain to overturn a Canadian Supreme Court decision.

> It was illegal to disseminate information about birth control in Canada until 1969.

> It was not until 1982 that the first woman — Madame Justice Bertha Wilson — was appointed to the Supreme Court of Canada.

> In 2003 men represented 84 percent of adults charged with violent crime, 78 percent of adults charged with property crime, 87 percent of adults charged with impaired driving offences, and 88 percent of adults charged with cannabis offences.

> Consistent with previous years, in 2005 nine in ten persons accused of homicide and three-quarters of homicide victims were male.

> While Aboriginal peoples are overrepresented in the criminal justice system relative to their numbers in the general population, the overrepresentation of Aboriginal women is even more acute than it is for Aboriginal men.

> It costs $150,867 a year to incarcerate a female inmate (in a multi-level security facility) and $71,640 to incarcerate a male inmate (in a medium security facility) in Canada.

Sources: Wallace 2004; Dauvergne and Li 2005; Finn et al. 1999; Correctional Service Canada 2005.

Even a cursory look at crime statistics tells us that males make up the vast majority of persons who come into conflict with the law and an even greater proportion of those who are sent to prison. In 2003, for example, 81 percent of adults charged with Criminal Code offences in Canada were men (Statistics Canada 2004). In 2003/04 men represented 94 percent of admissions to federal custody, 90 percent of provincial/territorial sentenced admissions, and 89 percent of remand admissions in Canada (Beattie 2005). Criminologists have long known this correlation between sex and crime. Yet until recently the maleness of their subject matter has escaped close scrutiny. It was the feminist critique of criminology that put the "sex question" front and centre on the criminological agenda. Initially, this critique took the form of documenting the invisibility of women in criminological accounts, but it soon broadened to include a more concerted focus on the discipline's ability to explain male patterns of criminal activity. As a result, the past decade has seen a veritable explosion of work in the area of men, masculinity, and crime.

The purpose of this chapter is to explore the sex question — or the placement of men and women — in criminological theorizing. As Judith Allen (1990: 21) has noted, the capacity to explain the correlation between sex and crime and the sexed character of many criminal activities could be considered "a litmus test for the viability of the discipline." As we will discover, theorists more often than not have premised their work on some notion of "difference," both between men and between women and men. While some theorists have located the sources of this difference in *sex* (the physical and sexual differences between males and females), others have located its sources in *gender* (the cultural constructions of man and woman). Still others have argued that we need to abandon this sex/gender distinction altogether and focus on *sexed bodies* (the meanings that different sexes carry at the cultural level).

Mainstream Criminology: Biology as Destiny?

Early criminologists understood "difference" as rooted in biology. Cesare Lombroso's (1912) biological determinist approach, for instance, sought to uncover those constitutional predisposing factors that drove some men to criminality. In the process, a clear demarcation was made between the criminal male and the law abiding male. In sharp contrast to his opposite, criminal man was pathological — "an atavistic being who reproduces in his person the ferocious instincts of primary humanity and the inferior animals" (Lombroso, cited in Wolfgang 1972). While Lombroso posited clear differences between criminal versus non-criminal men, he also saw women as being "naturally" different from men. Following his evolutionary premise that criminals were a biological throwback to an earlier, more primitive form of man, Lombroso reasoned that women had lower crime rates than men because of their natural inferiority; women simply had not progressed as far along the evolutionary continuum and so could not degenerate as far. Given that women were relatively "primitive," the criminals among them would not be highly visible. As well, Lombroso held that women were by nature deceitful, vengeful, and jealous, but these negative traits were supposedly neutralized by their maternal instinct, piety, and inherent weakness, thereby producing greater conformity in women.

> Early criminologists understood "difference" as rooted in biology.

As more sociologically-informed work emerged throughout the twentieth century, the search for the causes of crime — criminology's leitmotif — broadened to include factors in the social environment that produced criminality. These factors were variously located in terms of anomie (Merton 1938), differential associations (Sutherland 1949), subcultures (Cohen 1955), and illegitimate opportunity structures (Cloward and Ohlin 1960). Although endeavouring to distance themselves from the biologically based formulations of their predecessors, these more sociologically oriented criminologists continued the focus on the individual offender and the distinction made between the offending (criminal) man and the non-offending (conformist) man. Biology also surfaced in their efforts to account for the sex differentials in criminal activity. In this regard, one theorist to have a profound influence on criminological theorizing in the mid-twentieth century was sociologist Talcott Parsons.

In the 1940s Parsons coined the term "sex roles," which Allen (1990: 27) describes for us as "socially ascribed behaviours, attributes and capacities assigned to be appropriate for each sex." Parsons saw women and men playing two different roles in the family that help to integrate the overall social system: an *expressive* role that involves integration and an *instrumental* role that involves goal attainment. According to Parsons, women's biological capacity to reproduce naturally disposed them to the expressive role of child rearing in the private domain of the family, while men were considered better suited to the instrumental role of providing financial support by performing work outside the home:

> In our opinion the fundamental explanation of the allocation of the roles between the biological sexes lies in the fact that the bearing and early rearing of children established a strong presumptive primacy of the mother to the small child and this in turn establishes a presumption that the man who is exempted from these biological functions should specialize in the alternative instrumental direction. (Parsons and Bales 1955: 23)

In turn, Parsons maintained that the family unit prepared children for adequate participation in society by socializing them into their appropriate sex roles: masculine (instrumental) for males and feminine (expressive) for females. While boys were raised to be assertive, competitive, and achievement-oriented, girls were expected to be passive, nurturing, and compliant.

Parsons, then, located the differences between men and women in relation to the social roles they occupied in society. However, these roles — and the resulting forms of masculinity and femininity attached to them — had a distinctly biological basis. In Parsonian terms, it was "functional" for women to be confined to the home as their reproductive capacities and inherent nature (the maternal instinct) made them better suited to the roles of mother-hood and acting as the emotional mainstay to their husbands. Similarly, men's more assertive, outgoing, and independent nature made them better suited to the rough and tumble of the work world in the public sphere and the provision of economic support for their wives and children.

> In Parsonian terms, it was "functional" for women to stay at home as their inherent nature made them better suited to motherhood and being the emotional mainstay of their husbands.

This particular conception of "difference" between men and women found its way into mainstream criminological theorizing. Edwin Sutherland's differential association theory, for instance, was intended as a general, non-sex-specific theory of crime that focused on the learning and transmission of criminal patterns of behaviour. As Ngaire Naffine (1987: 30) notes, Sutherland's first mention of females comes late in his work, where he comments on the fact that the male crime rate is "greatly in excess" of the crime rate for females: "sex status is of greater statistical significance in differentiating criminals from non-criminals than other traits" (Sutherland and Cressey 1966: 138). Sutherland accounts for this discrepancy in terms of the differential socialization of boys and girls: "From infancy, girls are taught that they must be nice, while boys are taught that they must be rough and tough" (Sutherland and Cressey 1966: 142). According to Sutherland, females are more conforming than males because they are supervised more closely in the home and positively schooled in anti-criminal behaviour patterns.

Similarly, Albert Cohen's (1955) subcultural theory of delinquency drew heavily on the Parsonian conception of sex roles and their corresponding traits of masculinity and femininity. The delinquency of lower-class boys, according to Cohen, represented not only a reaction to the demands of the middle-class value system, but also an effort to distance themselves from the feminine persona represented by their mothers:

> Because his mother is the object of the feminine identification which he feels is the threat to his status as a male, he tends to react negativistically to those conduct norms which have been associated with mother and therefore have

> acquired feminine significance. Since mother has been the principal agent of indoctrination of "good," respectable behaviour, "goodness" comes to symbolize femininity, and engaging in "bad" behaviour acquires the function of denying his femininity and therefore asserting his masculinity. This is the motivation to juvenile delinquency. (Cohen 1955: 164)

Delinquency, then, is represented in Cohen's theory as a means by which boys can assert their masculinity; it is a male solution to a male problem. On the other hand, destined to become wives and mothers, girls were preoccupied with establishing relationships with the opposite sex. According to Cohen (1955: 142, 147) while "boys collect stamps," "girls collect boys." Given their domestication, the delinquency of girls was less frequent than that of boys, and when it did occur was most likely to involve sexual promiscuity. Even so, Cohen (1955: 46) claimed that males' illicit heterosexual relations were "richer" and "more varied" than that of females.

These explanations for the sex differentials in crime that draw upon sex role theory have been critiqued from a number of angles. Allen (1990: 28) has commented that in relying on differential socialization, Sutherland failed to consider *why* it is the case that females are treated differently than males. In other words, his remarks may describe, but they do not explain. Naffine (1987: 31) observes that Sutherland effectively transforms females into the anomaly or exception to his supposedly general theory of crime; "he describes as general what he later reveals to be limited to the male case." In a similar fashion, Cohen's subcultural theory basically amounts to the tautological or circular claim that "men commit crimes because crime is masculine and women do not because crime is masculine" (Allen 1990: 32). Even more problematic than these critiques, however, is that Parsonian functionalism had the political effect of reaffirming a particular sexual division of labour — and the relations of power between men and women that flowed from it — as "functional" for society. This rationalization for women's inequality came under heavy criticism with the advent of the second wave of the women's movement in the 1970s.

Feminist Criminology: From Sex to Gender

Intent on challenging the functionalist assumption that women "naturally" belonged in the home and were "naturally" inferior to men, second-wave feminists shifted the discourse from sex to gender in their theorizing. While sex was used to describe the sexual and physical differences between men and women, gender was understood as a cultural construction; it referenced the socially produced differences that arose from the ways in which boys and girls were socialized and the limited nature of the social roles assigned to men and women. This shift had the political effect of drawing attention to the power relations between men and women, thereby enabling an interrogation of the social basis of women's inequality in society. For feminists, in other words, the problem was not rooted in women's biology (sex) but in the way in which femininity and the roles assigned to women in a patriarchal or male-dominated society had been socially constructed (gender).

In criminology, this feminist attention to gender led to a far-reaching critique of the discipline. According to feminist criminologists (see, for example, Smart 1976; Naffine 1987; Gelsthorpe and Morris 1988; Daly and Chesney-Lind 1988; Comack 1992), mainstream theories were really "malestream" as they were decidedly premised on the criminal as male, with females positioned as an afterthought. Despite the use of generic terms

— such as "criminal," "defendant," or "delinquent" — criminology has historically been about men. More often than not, mainstream criminologists simply gave no consideration to women. Robert Merton's (1938) anomie theory, for example, was offered as a general theory explaining crime in relation to the strain that results from the disjunction between culture goals (like monetary success) and institutionalized means (education, jobs). While Merton's theory reflected a sensitivity to the class inequalities that exist in society, the same could not be said of his awareness of gender inequalities. If lower class individuals were more likely to engage in crime because of a lack of access to the institutionalized means for achieving monetary success, then it follows that women — who as a group experience a similar lack of access — should also be found to commit their share of crime as a consequence of this strain. But the statistics tell us that this is not the case.

> For feminists, the problem was not rooted in women's biology (sex) but in how the roles assigned to women in a male-dominated society had been socially constructed (gender).

Travis Hirschi's (1969) control theory was likewise characterized by a neglect of the female. While other criminologists focused their attention on explaining deviance, Hirschi turned the tables and set out to explain conformity. Since women appear to be more conformist than men (given, for example, their underrepresentation in crime statistics), it would have made sense for Hirschi to treat women as central to his analysis. Nevertheless, despite having collected data on females, he simply set these data aside and — like his colleagues — concentrated on males.

When women did come into view in criminological theories, they were understood in relation to a male standard or measuring rod, and typically judged to be lacking. Naffine (1987: 12), for instance, notes that Cohen's subcultural theory is premised on a male-centred conception of American society. Cohen singles out values such as ambition, autonomy, individualism, achievement, rationality, and emotional restraint as constituting "the American way of life." In effect, what he describes are those traits associated with the male role. Women, who are described by Cohen as "inactive, unambitious, uncreative, and lazy," are simply relegated to the sidelines. Feminist criminologists, then, took issue with the sexism of criminological theories — socially undesirable characteristics were attributed to women and assumed to be intrinsic characteristics of their sex.

> When women did come into view in criminological theories, they were understood in relation to a male standard or measuring rod, and typically judged to be lacking.

As a consequence of this feminist critique, increasing attention was devoted to the sex question in criminology throughout the 1970s and 1980s. Why are women less likely than men to be involved in crime? What explains the sex differences in rates of arrest and in the variable types of criminal activity between men and women? Numerous studies were conducted to address these questions (see, for example, Scutt 1979; Kruttschnitt 1980–81, 1982; Steffensmeier and Kramer 1982; Zingraff and Thomson 1984; Daly 1987, 1989). The main issue that guided this research was one of chivalry: were women being treated more leniently by the criminal justice system than men? The results, however, were mixed. Research that supported this chivalry hypothesis indicated that when it does exist, chivalry benefits some women more than others — in particular, the few white, middle-class or upper-class women who come into conflict with the law. It also appears to apply only to those female suspects who behave according to a stereotypical female script, that is, "crying, pleading for release for the sake of their children, claiming men have led them astray" (Rafter and Natalazia 1981: 92). In this regard, Nicole Rafter and

Elena Natalizia argued that chivalrous behaviour should be seen as a means of preserving women's subordinate position in society, not as a benign effort to treat women with some special kindness. Naffine (1997: 36), however, pointed to a larger problem with this research. By turning on the question of whether women were treated in the same way as men, or differently, the chivalry thesis (and its rebuttal) took men to be the norm: "Men were thus granted the status of universal subjects, the population of people with whom the rest of the world (women) were compared."

Another variation on the sex question that attracted considerable attention in the 1970s and 1980s was the women's liberation thesis. This thesis posited that women's involvement in crime would come to resemble men's more closely as differences between men and women were diminished by women's greater participation and equality in society. As reflected in the work of Rita Simon (1975) and Freda Adler (1975), the women's liberation thesis suggested that changes in women's gender roles would be reflected in their rates of criminal involvement. Simon argued that the increased employment opportunities that accompanied the women's movement would also bring an increase in opportunities to commit crime (such as embezzlement from employers). Adler linked the apparent increase in women's crime statistics to the influence of the women's movement and suggested that a "new female criminal" was emerging: women were becoming more violent and aggressive, just like their male counterparts.

The women's liberation thesis "captured the imagination of the media and practitioners" (Morris and Gelsthorpe 1981: 53 cited in Gavigan 1993: 221). While law-enforcement officials were quick to confirm its tenets, charging that the women's movement was responsible for triggering a massive crime wave, the media had a heyday with its claims, featuring headlines such as "Lib takes the lid off the gun moll" (*Toronto Star* 15 May 1975, cited in Gavigan 1993: 222). Nevertheless, representations of emancipated women running amok in the streets and workplaces did not hold up to closer scrutiny (see, for example, Chesney-Lind 1978; Weiss 1976; Steffensmeier 1980; Naffine 1987; Gavigan 1993). Carol Smart (1976), for one, noted that the women's liberation thesis was premised on a "statistical illusion" in that the supposed increases in women's crime were being reported as percentages. Given the small base number of women charged with criminal offences, it did not take much of a change to show a large percentage increase. Holly Johnson and Karen Rodgers (1993: 104) provided an example of this problem using Canadian data. Between 1970 and 1991, charges against women for homicide increased by 45 percent, but that figure reflected a real increase of only fifteen women charged with that offence. As well, while the women's movement was primarily geared toward privileged white women, poor women and women of colour were most likely to appear in police and prison data. These women were not inclined to think of themselves as "liberated" and — far from considering themselves as feminists — were quite conventional in their ideas and beliefs about women's role in society. For many feminist criminologists, the main difficulty with the women's liberation thesis — similar to the chivalry thesis — was that it posed a question that took males to be the norm: were women becoming more liberated and thus more like men, even in their involvement in crime?

Given the difficulties encountered in efforts to explain the sex differentials in crime — in particular, the tendency to take men as the standard or measuring rod — many feminist criminologists saw the need to "bracket" these issues for the time being in order to understand better the social worlds of women and girls (Daly and Chesney-Lind 1988: 121). Maureen Cain (1990) took this suggestion further. She noted that while feminist criminologists needed to understand women's experiences, existing criminological theory offered no tools for doing this. Therefore, feminists needed to transgress the traditional boundaries of criminology, to start from outside the confines of criminological discourse. In carrying out this project, feminist criminologists drew inspiration from the violence against women movement.

Transgressing Criminology: The Issue of Male Violence Against Women

At the same time as feminists were fashioning their critiques of criminology, the women's movement in Canada and other Western countries was breaking the silence around the issue of male violence against women. This violence was understood as a manifestation of patriarchy — the systemic and individual power that men exercise over women (Brownmiller 1975; Kelly 1988) — and various reports and surveys revealed it to be a widespread and pervasive phenomenon. The Canadian Advisory Council on the Status of Women (CACSW), for instance, estimated that one in every five Canadian women will be sexually assaulted at some point in her life, and one in every seventeen will be a victim of forced sexual intercourse. In 1981 CACSW released a report, *Wife Battering in Canada: The Vicious Circle* (MacLeod 1980), which estimated that, every year, one in ten Canadian women who is married or in a relationship with a live-in partner is battered. In 1993, Statistics Canada released the findings of the Violence Against Women (VAW) Survey. The first survey of its kind anywhere in the world, the VAW Survey included responses from 12,300 women (see Johnson 1996). Using definitions of physical and sexual assault consistent with the Canadian Criminal Code, the survey found that one-half (51 percent) of Canadian women had experienced at least one incident of physical or sexual violence since the age of sixteen. The survey also found that 29 percent of ever-married women had been assaulted by a spouse.

The violence against women movement had a number of implications for the work of feminist criminologists. For one, the movement allowed feminists to break away from the confines of mainstream criminology, which had been complicit in the social silencing around the issue of male violence against women. Official statistics suggested that crimes like rape were relatively infrequent in their occurrence. Victim surveys — which asked respondents whether they had been victimized by crime — indicated that the group most at risk of victimization was young men, not women. Most mainstream criminologists took these data sources at face value. They seldom questioned whether (and why) acts like rape might be underreported, undercharged, or underprosecuted, or the extent to which victim surveys had been constructed in ways that excluded the behaviours women feared most. When criminologists did turn their attention to crimes like rape, the focus was on the small group of men who had been convicted and incarcerated for the offence, and these men were typically understood as an abnormal and pathological group. Much of traditional criminology also tended to mirror widely held cultural myths and misconceptions about male violence against women (such as women "ask for it" by their dress or behaviour; see Morris 1987; Busby 2006). In these terms, the issue of violence against women pointed to significant knowledge gaps in mainstream criminology and encouraged a host of studies by feminist criminologists intent on rectifying this omission (see Dobash and Dobash 1979; Klein 1982; Stanko 1985; Gunn and Minch 1988; Kelly 1988).

For another, in pointing to the widespread and pervasive nature of male violence against women, the movement raised the issue of the impact that experiences of violence have had on women who come into conflict with the law. Several quantitative studies in the 1990s began to expose the extent of abuse experienced by women caught up in the criminal justice system. In interviewing women serving federal sentences, Margaret Shaw and her colleagues (1991) found that 68 percent had been physically abused as children or adults, and 53 percent were sexually abused at some point in their lives. Among Aboriginal women, the figures were considerably higher: 90 percent said that they had been physically abused, and 61 percent reported sexual abuse (Shaw et al. 1991: vii, 31). Another study of women in a provincial jail (Comack 1993) found that 78 percent of the women admitted over a six-year period reported histories of physical and sexual abuse.

Influenced by these findings, as well as Cain's call to transgress the boundaries of criminology and discover more about the lives of women who come into conflict with the law, feminist criminologists began to engage in qualitative research.

Women in Trouble

One of the primary tasks of feminist scholarship has been to produce knowledge that is "women-centred"; knowledge that is about and for women. This has involved placing women as knowers at the centre of the inquiry in order to produce better understandings of women and the world (Naffine 1997: 46). In criminology, this undertaking took the form of interviewing women who were caught up in the criminal justice system to find out more about their lives. Central to much of this research were the links between women's victimization and their criminal involvement.

In the United States, Mary Gilfus (1992) conducted life-history interviews with twenty incarcerated women to understand their entry into street crime. Most of these women had grown up with violence, and violence was a common feature in their relationships with men. Repeated victimization experiences, drug addiction, involvement in the sex trade, relationships with men involved in street crime, and the demands of mothering: these themes marked the women's transitions from childhood to adulthood.

> One of the primary tasks of feminist scholarship has been to produce knowledge that is "women-centred"; knowledge that is about and for women.

Beth Richie's (1996) study focused on African-American battered women in prison. Richie (1996: 4) developed a theory of "gender entrapment" to explain the "contradictions and complications of the lives of African-American battered women who commit crimes." Gender entrapment involves understanding the connections between violence against women in their intimate relationships, culturally constructed gender-identity development, and women's participation in illegal activities. In these terms, Black women were "trapped" in criminal activity in the same way that they were trapped in abusive relationships.

Working in Canada, Ellen Adelberg and Claudia Currie (1987) reported on the lives of seven women convicted of indictable offences and sentenced to federal terms of imprisonment. Regularly occurring themes in these women's lives included "poverty, child and wife battering, sexual assault, women's conditioning to accept positions of submissiveness and dependency upon men," which led Adelberg and Currie to conclude: "The problems suffered by women offenders are similar to the problems suffered by many women in our society, only perhaps more acutely" (Adelberg and Currie 1987: 68, 98).

My own work, *Women in Trouble* (Comack 1996), was built around the stories of twenty-four incarcerated women. The women's stories revealed complex connections between a woman's law violations and her history of abuse. Sometimes the connections are direct, as in the case of women sent to prison for resisting their abusers. Janice, for instance, was serving a sentence for manslaughter. She talked about how the offence occurred at a party:

> I was at a party, and this guy, older guy, came, came on to me. He tried telling me, "Why don't you go to bed with me. I'm getting some money, you know." And I said, "No." And then he started hitting me. And then he raped me. And then [pause] I lost it. Like, I just, I went, I got very angry and I snapped. And I started hitting him. I threw a coffee table on top of his head and then I stabbed him. (Janice, cited in Comack 1996: 96)

Sometimes the connections only become discernible after a woman's law violations are located in the context of her struggle to cope with the abuse and its effects. Merideth, for example, had a long history of abuse that began with her father sexually assaulting her as a young child, and the abuse extended to several violent relationships with the men in her life. She was imprisoned for bouncing cheques — she said she was writing the cheques to purchase "new things to keep her mind off the abuse":

> I've never had any kind of conflict with the law. [long pause] When I started dealing with all these different things, then I started having problems. And then I took it out in the form of fraud. (Merideth, cited in Comack 1996: 86)

Sometimes the connections are even more entangled, as in the case of women who end up on the street, where abuse and law violation become enmeshed in their ongoing, everyday struggle to survive. Another woman in prison, Brenda, described her life on the street:

> Street life is a, it's a power game, you know? Street life? You have to show you're tough. You have to beat up this broad or you have to shank this person, or, you know, you're always carrying guns, you always have blow on you, you always have drugs on you, and you're always working the streets with the pimps and the bikers, you know? That, that alone, you know, it has so much fucking abuse, it has more abuse than what you were brought up with!... I find living on the street I went through more abuse than I did at home. (Brenda, cited in Comack 1996: 105–106)

Overall, these efforts to draw out the connections between women's victimization experiences and their lawbreaking activities had the benefit of locating law violations by women in a broader social context characterized by inequalities of class, race, and gender.

In contrast to the women's liberation thesis, feminist criminologists have suggested that any increases in women's involvement in crime are more directly connected to the feminization of poverty than to women's emancipation. In recent decades, poverty has increasingly taken on a "female face" — especially in terms of the number of single-parent families headed by women (Gavigan 1999; Little 2003; Chunn and Gavigan 2006; Mosher 2006). As more and more women are confronted with the task of making ends meet under dire circumstances, it is argued, the link between poverty and women's lawbreaking becomes more obvious.

Locating women's involvement in crime in its broader social context also means attending to racial inequalities. For instance, Aboriginal people in Canada are disproportionately represented in crime statistics, but the overrepresentation of Aboriginal women in Canadian prisons is even greater than that of Aboriginal men. Aboriginal women are incarcerated for more violent crimes

> In contrast to the women's liberation thesis, feminist criminologists have suggested that increases in women's involvement in crime are more directly connected to the feminization of poverty than to women's emancipation.

than are non-Aboriginal women; and alcohol has played a role in the offences of twice as many Aboriginal women in prison as it has for Aboriginal men (La Prairie 1993; Statistics Canada 2001). To make sense of these patterns involves acknowledging how the historical forces that have shaped Aboriginal experience — colonization, economic and political marginalization, and forced dependency on the state — have culminated in a situation in which violence and drugging and drinking have reached epidemic proportions in many Aboriginal communities (Royal Commission on Aboriginal Peoples 1996). As the Supreme Court of Canada has acknowledged, "Many Aboriginal people are victims of systemic and direct discrimination, many suffer the legacy of dislocation, and many are substantially affected by poor social and economic conditions" (*R. v. Gladue* 1999: 20).

Attention to gender inequality — and its interconnections with race and class — has assisted in explaining some forms of prostitution or sex-trade work (Brock 1998; Phoenix 1999). According to Johnson and Rodgers (1993: 101), women's involvement in prostitution is a reflection of their subordinate social and economic position in society: "Prostitution thrives in a society which values women more for their sexuality than for their skilled labour, and which puts women in a class of commodity to be bought and sold. Research has shown one of the major causes of prostitution to be the economic plight of women, particularly young, poorly educated women who have limited *legitimate* employment records."

In learning more about the lives of women and the "miles of problems" (Comack 1996: 134) that brought them into conflict with the law — problems with drugs and alcohol use, histories of violence and abuse, lack of education and job skills, and struggles to provide and care for their children — feminist criminologists took pains to distance their work from formulations that located the source of women's problems in individual pathologies or personality disturbances. Instead, the structured inequalities in society that contour and constrain the lives of women provided the backdrop for understanding women's involvement in crime. As British criminologist Pat Carlen (1988: 14) phrased it, "Women set about making their lives within conditions that have certainly not been of their own choosing."

The feminist critique of mainstream criminology and the effort to draw attention to the gendered nature of women's lives soon led to a call to "gender" crime more broadly. Women, it was held, were not the only ones with a gender; men's lives too needed to be understood in gendered terms. In this regard, while mainstream criminology had been characterized by its neglect of the female, critics pointed out that the discipline's aptitude for explaining male patterns of criminal activity was just as troublesome. As Elizabeth Gosz (1987: 6 cited in Allen 1990: 39) framed it, there was a need to question "what is it about men, not as working class, not as migrant, not as underprivileged individual, but *as men* that induces them to commit crime?" During the 1990s, various criminologists responded to this challenge by initiating studies of men, masculinity, and crime.

Men, Masculinity, and Crime

One criminologist to take up this project was James Messerschmidt. In his book, *Masculinities and Crime: A Critique and Reconceptualization of Theory*, Messerschmidt directly addressed the sex question in criminology by posing the question: "Why do men engage in more and different types of crime than women and in differing amounts and forms amongst themselves?" (Messerschmidt 1993: 77). In the course of framing his answer to this question, he offered a number of criticisms of sex role theory, which can be summarized as follows:

- Sex role theory presumes "natural" traits in men and women, for instance, men are "naturally" aggressive and women are "naturally" compliant or passive. As Janet Katz and William Chambliss have noted, however, "An individual learns to be aggressive in the same manner that he or she learns to inhibit aggression. One is not a natural state, and the other culturally imposed; both are within our biological potential" (Katz and Chambliss 1991: 270, cited in Messerschmidt 1993: 25).
- "Sex" is itself a cultural construction. Assuming that there are only two sexes — male and female — is a culturally specific move. Messerschmidt cites a number of examples of cultures where sex is not assigned on the basis of genitalia (as is the practice in Western cultures) but social activities, and where more than two dichotomous sexes are recognized.
- In concentrating on the differences *between* men and women, sex role theory ignores variability not only across but also *within* cultures, for example, in terms of the variations in the construction of masculinity among boys and men.
- Sex role theory tends to reduce individuals' capacities for action; it is the sex roles into which we are socialized that are "determining." In this respect, sex role theory "obscures the work that is involved in producing gender in everyday activities" (West and Zimmerman 1987: 127, cited in Messerschmidt 1993: 28).
- Sex role theory fails to situate sex roles within a structural explanation of their origin. Its referent is more biology and the focus is more on gender differences than on gender relations (and the tensions, conflicts, and power dynamics attendant to these relations). It also neglects power relations *between* men.

In his endeavour to move criminological theorizing beyond the limitations of sex role theory, as well as to contribute to a "feminist theory of gendered crime" (1993: 62), Messerschmidt has designed a theory that situates men's involvement in crime in the context of "doing" masculinity.

"Doing" Masculinity

In developing his theory, Messerschmidt adopts sociologist Anthony Giddens' (1976) concept of "structured action" to resolve an issue that continues to haunt social thinkers: how to theorize the seeming disconnect between social structures (such as capitalism, patriarchy, and colonialism) and individual agency (the location and wilful activity of individuals within those structures). Following Giddens, Messerschmidt conceptualizes the relation between structure and action as reciprocal: "as we engage in social action, we simultaneously help create the social structures that facilitate/limit social practice" (1993: 62). Moreover, rather than conceptualizing structures of inequality as separate yet interconnected (as many feminist theorists have done), Messerschmidt suggests that divisions of labour based on class, gender, and race are *simultaneously* produced in the everyday interactions of social actors (1993: 64).

Following on the work of ethnomethodologists Candace West and Don Zimmerman (1987; see also Fenstermaker, West, and Zimmerman 1991), gender is viewed as a "situated accomplishment." While sex is the social identification of individuals as man or woman, gender is the accomplishment of that identification in social interaction: "we coordinate our activities to 'do' gender in situational ways" (1993: 79). In the process, individuals realize that their behaviour is accountable to others and, as such, "they construct their actions in relation to how they might be interpreted by others in the particular social context in which they occur" (1993: 79). In a culture that believes there are but two sexes — male and female — this accountability will involve living up to the gender ideals that have been tied to each sex; that is, behaving "as a man" or "as a woman" would in a given social situation. Moreover, because we accomplish masculinity and femininity in specific social situations (although not necessarily in circumstances of our own choosing), these are never static or finished products.

From the work of R.W. Connell (1987, 1995, 2000) Messerschmidt borrows the concept of "hegemonic masculinity." Connell was interested in theorizing how a particular gender order — a "historically constructed pattern of power relations between men and women and definitions of femininity and masculinity" (Connell 1987: 98–99) — comes to be reproduced in society. He suggested that male dominance in the gender order is achieved by the ascendancy of a particular idealized form of masculinity that is culturally glorified, honoured, and exalted. Hegemonic masculinity references not just a set of role expectations or an identity; it is a "pattern of practice" (Connell and Messerschmidt 2005: 832). Different from a male sex role, this cultural ideal may not correspond with the actual personalities of the majority of men, and may well not be "normal" in a statistical sense as only a minority of men may enact it. In these terms, exemplars such as sports heroes, movie stars, and even fantasy figures (such as Rambo or the Terminator) offer representations of masculinity that come to be normative in the sense that they embody "the currently most honored way of being a man" and require all other men to position themselves in relation to these representations (Connell and Messerschmidt 2005: 832).

Hegemonic masculinity is constructed in relation to women and what Connell (1987: 188) refers to as "emphasized femininity"; a femininity organized as an adaptation to men's power and emphasizing compliance, nurturance, and empathy as womanly virtues. As well, because men will "do" masculinity according to the social situation in which they find themselves, different types of masculinity — complicit, subordinated, and oppositional — exist in relation to the hegemonic form. For example, while hegemonic masculinity valorizes heterosexuality, a key form of subordinated masculinity is homosexuality. In these terms, it makes more sense to speak of masculinity in the plural — as *masculinities*.

Messerschmidt argues that it is in the process of "doing" masculinity that men simultaneously construct forms of criminality. He explains: "Because types of criminality are possible only when particular social conditions present themselves, when other masculine resources are unavailable, particular types of crime can provide an alternative resource for accomplishing gender and, therefore, affirming a particular type of masculinity" (1993: 84).

Messerschmidt subsequently put his theory to work to understand varieties of youth crime, street crime, corporate crime, sexual harassment in the workplace, wife beating, and rape (Messerschmidt 1993) as well as the lynching of Black men in the American South in the late nineteenth century, the life of Malcom X, violence among working-class girls in gangs, and the decision to launch the space shuttle *Challenger* in 1986 (Messerschmidt 1997). Key to his analysis is the thesis that gendered power is central to understanding why men commit more crimes and more serious crimes than women: crime is one practice in which and through which men's power over women can be established, and the different types of crime men may commit are determined by the power relations among them (1993: 84).

> Messerschmidt argues that it is in the process of "doing" masculinity that men simultaneously construct forms of criminality.

Messerschmidt's theorizing, then, marked an important advance in thinking about the relation between men and crime. As an antidote to sex role theory and its limitations, his formulation called attention to the ways in which men's crime is connected to broader structural features and power relations and tied to culturally dominant and contested constructions of what it means to be a male in modern industrialized societies. As Kathleen Daly (1997: 37) has noted, rather than seeing crime as an attribute of a person, this "doing gender" approach has the benefit of putting the focus on "how situations and social practices produce qualities and identities associated with membership in particular social categories." Nevertheless, Messerschmidt's work — especially his use of the concept of "hegemonic masculinity" — has been subject to criticism by other criminologists interested in the sex question in criminology.

Masculine Subjectivity: The Case of Mike Tyson

Tony Jefferson (1994, 1996a, 1996b), for one, notes that pressures on men to live up to the "patriarchal masculine ideal," to be a "man's man," can create considerable feelings of insecurity and vulnerability. He cites the example of falling in love: "Here the need for and dependence on another is posed most starkly, in direct contradiction to the notions of self-sufficiency and independence central to hegemonic masculinity. It is almost as if to succeed in love one has to fail as a man" (1994: 12). This recognition of the difficulties men may experience in relating to dominant models of masculinity, according to Jefferson, points to the need for a theory of masculine subjectivity, one capable of connecting social and psychic processes.

Jefferson demonstrates his point through an analysis of the biography of Mike Tyson, who transformed himself "first from a pudgy, passive, lisping schoolboy — the butt of local bullies — to a feared neighbourhood bully and thief, and then to a boxing prodigy who went on to become the youngest-ever [at the age of 20] world heavy-weight champion" (Jefferson 1996b: 153). He argues that Tyson cannot be explained solely by reference to his structural location as a poor Black boy from the American ghetto, and aims to show "how subjectivity can be both a product of various social discourses, and of unique personal biography" (Jefferson (1996b: 158).

Jefferson understands Tyson's transformation as connected to his adoption of the "tough guy" discourse, wherein toughness connotes "one's ability to survive on the streets" as well as "the ability to meet and resist physical challenges" (1996b: 160). Identifying with a "bad boy" image enabled Tyson to socially succeed in the world of boxing, with its "hypermasculine ethos." But Tyson's identification with boxing was not just about winning, money, or power, it was also a way of suppressing feelings of powerlessness and anxiety. In relation to a statement made by Tyson before the 1982 Junior Olympics that, "I'm 'Mike Tyson,' everyone likes me now," Jefferson suggests:

> Tyson desperately wanted it to be true that 'everyone,' but especially those close to him, liked him as a person; but the response of 'everyone' close to him, in teaching him to control and surmount this fear in the ring, only convinced

him that the 'truth' of his identity lay only in the boxing ring, as the 'compleat destroyer.' Then, and possibly only then, in the act of destroying another man, the psychic anxiety underpinning the feared passivity could be (if temporarily) assuaged, and the delight of all those close to him, and his fans, could be 'good enough' testimony of love. (Jefferson 1996b: 164)

While boxing may have provided a socially acceptable (and decidedly masculine) venue for Tyson to resolve his contradictory feelings (passive quitter/compleat destroyer; gentle/vicious; needy/needing no one), things were far less straightforward outside the ring. As Jefferson notes, Tyson was particularly ill-equipped to deal with the fame and fortune that accompanies heavyweight championships, and his troubles eventually extended to include a conviction and six-year prison sentence for rape.

Jefferson's work has the advantage of highlighting the complex and variable nature of men's experiences and emotions. Men (as with women) can be assertive or timid, hateful or loving, confident or unsure. While not denying the social costs of men's actions (violence against women being one prominent example), it bears remembering that men too have their troubles and uncertainties. His insights also showcase the kinds of pressures, contradictions, and tensions that boys and men encounter in their struggles to live up to the "patriarchal masculine ideal." Without an appreciation of this complexity, we are confined to a view of men as "always already empowered" (Collier 1998: 295).

Critiquing the "Masculinity Turn"

Richard Collier (1996, 1998, 2004) has taken Messerschmidt to task for his tendency to over-emphasize the negative or undesirable traits associated with "doing" masculinity. Messerschmidt, for instance, tells us that hegemonic masculinity "emphasizes practices toward authority, control, competitive individualism, independence, aggressiveness, and the capacity for violence." As Collier (1998: 22) notes, what men are not seen as "doing" is a masculinity that might in any sense be interpreted as positive. In these terms, understanding masculinity primarily in relation to a set of negative traits could easily lead to a kind of essentialist position that views "real men" as inherently oppressive, dominating, and violent. It may well be, for instance, that for some boys and men (especially those marginalized by their race and class position), a search for independence constitutes a positive trait that emanates from their desire to escape the oppressive conditions of their existence. It is important, therefore, to resist demonizing *all* men simply *because* they are men. This means being continually mindful of the particular social contexts in which boys and men find themselves as they endeavour to "accomplish" masculinity.

Criminologists have also been critical of Messerschmidt's use of hegemonic masculinity to explain the causes of crime. John Hood-Williams (2001: 43) makes the point that crime is a highly generalized notion "which puts together disparate practices and invites us to treat them as if they were similar." Men are seen as "doing" masculinity through engaging in such varied practices as the rape of women, property theft, corporate crime, violence toward other men, and even football hooliganism. As Collier notes, "To account for such diversity in terms of men 'accomplishing' a gender identity is asking a great deal of the concept of masculinity" (Collier 2004: 292).

In addition to these concerns, there are other difficulties encountered with Messerschmidt's treatment of the category "crime." In his 1993 book, he makes the following statement three times in the space of two pages: "Crime is a resource that may be summoned when men lack other resources to accomplish gender" (Messerschmidt 1993: 84-

85). Here he seems to be suggesting that crime is like the default button on your computer — an option taken when other resources are inoperable. In the process, Messerschmidt sets up a dualism whereby law-abiding behaviour is taken to be the norm while criminal behaviour is the exception. Such a dualism operates to obscure the similarities between so-called "law abiding" and "criminal" behaviours — especially in relation to "doing" masculinity. In short, what actually constitutes "crime" is never made problematic in Messerschmidt's theorizing. Even in his later works (Messerschmidt 1997, 2004), he entertains no theoretical discussion of crime as a category of analysis, but only situates it as a "resource" for enacting gender.

Collier (1998) locates Messerschmidt's work as a key component of what he calls "the masculinity turn" in criminology, the recent body of work that explores the relationship between men and crime by means of an explicit foregrounding of the concept of masculinity. Skeptical of this turn, Collier (2004: 297) maintains that, "it is open to question, ultimately, just how adequate the concept of masculinity is when seeking to explain, understand, or otherwise account for the crimes of men." Instead of "gendering crime," he argues, what is required is a "sexing of the criminal."

Sexed Bodies and the Issue of "Embodiment"

As Messerschmidt (1993) pointed out in his critique of sex role theory, "sex" is actually a cultural construction. Assuming that there are only two sexes — male and female — is a culturally specific move. To make a distinction between sex and gender, then, as feminist philosopher Judith Butler (1990) has argued, does nothing but reproduce as gender (man/woman) the assumption of a prediscursive sexual difference (male/female). In other words, "the distinction between sex and gender turns out to be no distinction at all" since the use of the term "gender" commonly refers to "sex," that is, the cultural meanings ascribed to bodies sexed as male or female (Butler 1990: 7). For Butler, gender is merely a "performance" of the cultural significance of sex. Theorists who adopt a "sexed bodies" approach (Daly 1997), therefore, have argued that we need to begin with the concept of sex; it is sex — more specifically, the "sexed body" — and not gender that should be the focus of our investigation.

To focus on bodies as "sexed" does not signal a return to the kind of biologically based formulations found in earlier criminological theories. Instead, it represents an effort to transcend the sex-gender distinction altogether. The aim is to showcase how our bodies are more than just markers of difference (as male or female). In these terms, *embodiment* is considered central to our sense of self; it is our way of "being in the world" and therefore an essential part of our subjectivity or identity. Feminist theorists such as Iris Marion Young (1990) and Moira Gatens (1996) have pointed out that the way we experience our bodies is not direct or unmediated; how we experience our bodies as male or female is a reflection of both our personal histories and the culturally shared notions of certain bodily forms. For instance, Young suggests that many of the ways in which females relate to their bodies comes from the experience of living in a patriarchal society where women are continually under threat (especially in terms of their sexual safety) and constantly exposed to the male gaze (whereby women come to see themselves and their bodies as they think men see them). In these terms, femininity and masculinity are ways of living in differently shaped bodies and our identities as women and men are formed as ways of giving significance to different bodily forms.

Despite Collier's harsh verdict as to the limits of "masculinity" as a theoretically useful concept, Messerschmidt has gone on to revise his theorizing on masculinity and crime in his later writing, especially in relation to this issue of "embodiment." In his most recent book, *Flesh and Blood: Adolescent Gender Diversity and Violence* (2004), he proposes to "bring the body back in" to criminology — not by "sexing the criminal" but by "embodying gender"; that is, by concentrating on embodiment as a lived aspect of gender, on the way in which our bodies constrain and facilitate social action and therefore mediate and influence social practices. As Connell (1995: 52) has noted, masculinity involves "a certain feel to the skin, certain muscular shapes and tensions, certain postures and ways of moving, certain possibilities of sex." In these terms, the physical sense of "maleness" is central to the social interpretation of gender.

Messerschmidt's revised theory, then, conceptualizes "doing gender" as both mindful and physical: "the body is a participant in the shaping and generating of social practice. Consequently, it is impossible to consider human agency — and therefore crime and violence — without taking gendered embodiment into account" (Messerschmidt 2004: 49). Utilizing case studies of two white working-class boys and two white working-class girls involved in assaultive violence, Messerschmidt (2004) applies his revised theory of gendered embodiment to understand how motivations for violence (and non-violence) emerge in three different sites — the home, the school, and the street — in the life histories of these youth. In the process, he is able to show "how gender difference is not simply constructed between boys and girls (as most criminologists contend), but it is also prominent among boys and among girls as well as individually *across* the three settings" (Messerschmidt 2004: 131).

Gender Matters

Attention to the "sex question" in criminology has generated a corpus of thought-provoking literature. Earlier formulations of mainstream criminologists that rested on biologically based notions of "difference" between men and women — and women's "natural" inferiority to men — have been challenged by feminist criminologists intent on developing distinctly women-centred theory and research that exposes how the gendered nature of women's lives in a patriarchal society affects both their risk of victimization at the hands of violent men and their involvement in crime. Responding to the call to "gender" crime more broadly, criminologists initiated a "masculinity turn" that sought to understand the connections between men, masculinity, and crime. One realization that has emerged from this corpus of literature is that *gender matters*. Criminologists can no longer afford to ignore the ways in which the gendered nature of women's and men's lives brings them into conflict with the law. Addressing the tendency of mainstream criminologists to neglect women in their theories, Lorraine Gelsthorpe and Allison Morris have noted:

> Criminologists can no longer afford to ignore the ways in which the gendered nature of women's and men's lives brings them into conflict with the law.

> Theories are weak if they do not apply to half of the potential criminal population; women, after all, experience the same deprivations, family structures, and so on that men do. Theories of crime should be able to take account of *both* men's

and women's behaviour and to highlight those factors which operate differently on men and women. Whether or not a particular theory helps us to understand women's crime is of *fundamental*, not marginal importance for criminology. (Gelsthorpe and Morris 1988: 103; emphasis added)

This attention to the sex question in criminology has had the benefit of drawing attention to how gender matters in another way: in terms of how the criminal justice system responds to those who are caught in its reach. In this respect — and as various chapters in this book will testify — masculinity and femininity are cultural constructions that not only give contour to the lives of men and women, they also infuse the ways in which law operates to categorize and criminalize particular behaviours and particular individuals. For instance, to the extent that aggression comes to be understood as "masculine" behaviour, criminal justice actors (police officers, defence lawyers, Crown prosecutors, and judges) will come to define violence by men as "normal" or expected and violence by women as an anomaly, a breach of expected gender scripts (see, for example, Comack and Balfour 2004: ch 3).

But while it is important to address the gendered experiences of men and women and the particular ways in which criminal justice processes may work to "gender" crime, it is also the case that other factors — race and class in particular — have a bearing on people's lives. To the extent that approaches such as "doing" gender or "sexed bodies" take gender/sex as a priority in their theorizing, then these other factors are given secondary status. The challenge, then, is to fashion an approach that recognizes the importance of gender in the construction of identities or subjectivities as well as how gender practices inform and constrain people's lives while at the same time not losing sight of these other important factors.

Theorizing is never a static process. Theories are continually subject to revision and reformulation as their creators endeavour to respond to critiques from their colleagues and — just as significant — to the changing and dynamic nature of the social world that they are trying to understand (see, for example Connell and Messerschmidt 2005). In this regard, the effort to grapple with the "sex question" is sure to be an ongoing — and vital — project in criminology.

DISCUSSION QUESTIONS

1. Why do you think mainstream criminology traditionally ignored or neglected to consider women?

2. What are some of the limitations of relying upon "sex roles" to answer the sex question in criminology?

3. In what ways do you see "hegemonic masculinity" operating in our culture? What about "emphasized femininity"?

4. Why should gender matter for criminologists?

GLOSSARY OF TERMS

Biological Determinism: the belief that human behaviour is fundamentally directed by innate, inborn, or "essential" factors.

Embodiment: connotes the idea that the body is an entity that both derives meaning from and gives meaning to social and cultural processes.

Emphasized Femininity: refers to a cultural ideal that is celebrated for women (for instance, that women should be nurturing, passive, sociable, receptive to male desire). Because it is constructed in a subordinated relation to hegemonic masculinity, women's adherence to this ideal reinforces male power and privilege.

Gender: cultural constructions of what it means to be a man or woman.

Hegemonic Masculinity: a concept used to refer to the ways in which culturally idealized forms of masculinity (for example, risk taking, aggression, independence, competitiveness) become dominant in society. These forms set out "scripts" for males that are acted out differently depending upon the social situations and social locations (class and race) of the participants.

Patriarchy: a system of male domination; a structure and an ideology that privileges men over women.

Sex: the physical and sexual differences that are thought to exist between males and females.

The Sex Question in Criminology: focuses on the placement of men and women in criminological theorizing, especially in terms of the ability of the discipline to explain both male and female patterns of criminal activity.

Sexed Bodies: refers to the meanings that different sexes carry at the cultural level. Rather than assuming a dualism between "sex" and "gender," the sexed bodies approach views the differences that are thought to exist between the sexes (male and female) as culturally inscribed.

SUGGESTED READINGS

Balfour, Gillian, and Elizabeth Comack (eds.). 2006. *Criminalizing Women: Gender and (In)justice in Neo-liberal Times.* Halifax: Fernwood Publishing.

Barker, Gary T. 2005. *Dying to be Men: Youth, Masculinity and Social Exclusion.* London: Routledge.

Collier, Richard. 1998. *Masculinities, Crime and Criminology: Men, Heterosexuality and the Criminal(ised) Other.* London: Sage.

Messerschmidt, James. 2004. *Flesh and Blood: Adolescent Gender Diversity and Violence.* Maryland: Rowman and Littlefield.

Naffine, Ngaire. 1997. *Feminism and Criminology.* Sydney: Allen and Unwin.

REFERENCES

Adelberg, Ellen, and Claudia Currie. 1987. "In Their Own Words: Seven Women's Stories." In E. Adelberg and C. Currie (eds.), *Too Few to Count: Canadian Women in Conflict with the Law.* Vancouver: Press Gang.

Adler, Freda. 1975. *Sisters in Crime.* New York: McGraw-Hill.

Allen, Judith. 1990. "'The Wild Ones'" The Disavowal of Men in Criminology." In R. Graycar (ed.), *Dissenting Opinions: Feminist Explorations in Law and Society.* Sydney: Allen and Unwin.

Beattie, Karen. 2005. "Adult Correctional Services in Canada, 2003/04." *Juristat* 25, 8.

Brock, Deborah. 1998. *Making Work, Making Trouble: Prostitution as a Social Problem.* Toronto:

University of Toronto Press.

Brownmiller, Susan. 1975. *Against Our Will: Men, Women and Rape.* New York: Bantam Books.

Busby, Karen. 2006. "'Not a Victim Until a Conviction Is Entered': Sexual Violence Prosecutions and Legal Truth." In E. Comack (ed.), *Locating Law: Essays on the Race/Class/Gender Connections.* Second edition. Halifax: Fernwood Publishing.

Butler, Judith. 1990. *Gender Trouble: Feminism and the Subversion of Identity.* New York: Routledge.

Cain, Maureen. 1990. "Towards Transgression: New Directions in Feminist Criminology." *International Journal of the Sociology of Law* 18: 1–18.

Carlen, Pat. 1988. *Women, Crime and Poverty.* Milton Keynes: Open University Press.

Chesney-Lind, Meda. 1978. "Chivalry Re-Examined." In Lee Bowker (ed.), *Women, Crime and the Criminal Justice System.* Lexington, MA: Lexington Books.

Chunn, Dorothy E., and Shelley A.M. Gavigan. 2006. "From Welfare Fraud to Welfare As Fraud: The Criminalization of Poverty." In G. Balfour and E. Comack (eds.), *Criminalizing Women: Gender and (In)justice in Neo-Liberal Times.* Halifax: Fernwood Publishing.

Cloward, Richard, and Lloyd Ohlin. 1960. *Delinquency and Opportunity: A Theory of Delinquency Gangs.* New York: Free Press.

Cohen, Albert. 1955. *Delinquent Boys: The Culture of the Gang.* New York: Free Press.

Collier, Richard. 1996. "'Just (More) Boys Own Stories'? Gender, Sex and the 'Masculinity Turn' in Criminology." *Social & Legal Studies* 5, 2: 271–78.

_____. 1998. *Masculinities, Crime and Criminology: Men, Heterosexuality and the Criminal(ised) Other.* London: Sage.

_____. 2004. "Masculinities and Crime: Rethinking the 'Man Question'?" In C. Sumner (ed.), *The Blackwell Companion to Criminology.* Oxford: Blackwell Publishing.

Comack, Elizabeth. 1992. "Women and Crime." In R. Linden (general editor), *Criminology: A Canadian Perspective.* Second edition. Toronto: Harcourt Brace Jovanovich.

_____. 1993. "Women Offenders' Experiences with Physical and Sexual Abuse: A Preliminary Report." Criminology Research Centre, University of Manitoba.

_____. 1996. *Women in Trouble: Connecting Women's Law Violations to Their Histories of Abuse.* Halifax: Fernwood Publishing.

Comack, Elizabeth, and Gillian Balfour. 2004. *The Power to Criminalize: Violence, Inequality and the Law.* Halifax: Fernwood Publishing.

Connell, R.W. 1987. *Gender and Power.* Cambridge: Polity Press.

_____. 1995. *Masculinities.* Cambridge: Polity Press.

_____. 2000. *The Men and the Boys.* Berkley: University of California Press.

Connell, R.W., and James Messerschmidt. 2005. "Hegemonic Masculinity: Rethinking the Concept." *Gender & Society* 19, 6: 829–59.

Correctional Service Canada. 2005. "Basic Facts About the Correctional Service of Canada. Available at <www.csc-scc.gc.ca> accessed July 6, 2005.

Daly, Kathleen. 1987. "Discrimination in the Criminal Courts: Family, Gender, and the Problem of Equal Treatment." *Social Forces* 66, 1: 152–75.

_____. 1989. "Rethinking Judicial Paternalism: Gender, Work–Family Relations, and Sentencing." *Gender and Society* 3, 1: 9–36.

_____. 1997. "Different Ways of Conceptualizing Sex/Gender in Feminist Theory and Their Implications for Criminology." *Theoretical Criminology* 1, 1: 25–51.

Daly, Kathleen, and Meda Chesney-Lind. 1988. "Feminism and Criminology." *Justice Quarterly* 5, 4: 101–43.

Dauvergne, Mia, and Geoffrey Li. 2005. "Homicide in Canada, 2005." *Juristat* 26, 6.

Dobash, R. Emerson, and Russell Dobash. 1979. *Violence Against Wives: A Case Against Patriarchy.* New York: Free Press.

Fenstermaker, Sarah, Candace West, and Don Zimmerman. 1991. "Gender Inequality: New Conceptual Terrain." In Rae Lesser Blumberg (ed.), *Gender, Family and Economy.* Newbury Park, CA: Sage.

Finn, A., S. Trevethan, G. Carriere, and M. Kowalski. 1999. "Female Inmates, Aboriginal Inmates, and Inmates Serving Life Sentences: A One Day Snapshot." *Juristat* 19, 5.

Gatens, Moira. 1996. *Imaginary Bodies: Ethics, Power and Corporeality*. London and New York: Routledge.

Gavigan, Shelley A.M. 1993. "Women's Crime: New Perspectives and Old Theories." In E. Adelberg and C. Currie (eds.), *In Conflict with the Law: Women and the Canadian Justice System*. Vancouver: Press Gang.

_____. 1999. "Poverty Law, Theory and Practice: The Place of Class and Gender in Access to Justice." In E. Comack (ed.), *Locating Law: Race/Class/Gender Connections*. Halifax: Fernwood.

Gelsthorpe, Lorraine, and Allison Morris. 1988. "Feminism and Criminology in Britain." *British Journal of Criminology* 23: 93–110.

Giddens, Anthony. 1976. *New Rules of the Sociological Method*. London: Hutchinson.

Gilfus, Mary. 1992. "From Victims to Survivors to Offenders: Women's Routes of Entry and Immersion into Street Crime." *Women and Criminal Justice* 4, 1: 63–89.

Gunn, Rita, and Candace Minch. 1988. *Sexual Assault: The Dilemma of Disclosure, The Question of Conviction*. Winnipeg: University of Manitoba Press.

Hirschi, Travis. 1969. *Causes of Delinquency*. Berkeley: University of California Press.

Hood-Williams, John. 2001. "Gender, Masculinities and Crime: From Structures to Psyches." *Theoretical Criminology* 5 (1): 37-60.

Jefferson, Tony. 1994. "Theorising Masculine Subjectivity." In Tim Newburn and Elizabeth A. Stanko (eds.), *Just Boys Doing Business? Men, Masculinities and Crime*. London and New York: Routledge.

_____. 1996a. "Introduction to Masculinities, Social Relations and Crime." Special issue of *The British Journal of Criminology* 36, 3: 337–47.

_____. 1996b. "From 'Little Fairy Boy' to 'The Compleat Destroyer': Subjectivity and Transformation in the Biography of Mike Tyson." In Mairtin Mac an Ghaill (ed.), *Understanding Masculinities*. Buckingham: Open University Press.

Johnson, Holly. 1996. *Dangerous Domains*. Toronto: Nelson.

Johnson, Holly, and Karen Rodgers. 1993. "A Statistical Overview of Women in Crime in Canada." In Ellen Adelberg and Claudia Currie (eds.), *In Conflict with the Law: Women and the Canadian Justice System*. Vancouver: Press Gang.

Kelly, Liz. 1988. *Surviving Sexual Violence*. Minneapolis: University of Minnesota Press.

Klein, Dorie. 1982. "The Dark Side of Marriage: Battered Wives and the Domination of Women." In N. Rafter and E. Stanko (eds.), *Judge, Lawyer, Victim, Thief: Women, Gender Roles and Criminal Justice*. Boston: Northeastern University Press.

Kruttschnitt, Candace. 1980–81. "Social Status and Sentences of Female Offenders." *Law and Society Review* 15, 2: 247–65.

_____. 1982. "Women, Crime and Dependency." *Criminology* 195: 495–513.

LaPrairie, Carol. 1993. "Aboriginal Women and Crime in Canada: Identifying the Issues." In Ellen Adelberg and Claudia Currie (eds.), *In Conflict with the Law: Women and the Canadian Justice System*. Vancouver: Press Gang.

Little, Margaret. 2003. "The Leaner, Meaner Welfare Machine: The Ontario Conservative Government's Ideological and Material Attack on Single Mothers." In D. Brock (ed.), *Making Normal: Social Regulation in Canada*. Scarborough: Nelson Thompson Learning.

Lombroso, Cesare. 1912. *Crime: Its Causes and Remedies*. Boston: Little, Brown, and Company.

MacLeod, Linda. 1980. *Wife Battering in Canada: The Vicious Circle*. Ottawa: Canadian Advisory Council on the Status of Women.

Merton, Robert. 1938. "Social Structure and Anomie." *American Sociological Review* 3: 672–82.

Messerschmidt, James. 1993. *Masculinities and Crime: Critique and Reconceptualization of Theory*. Lanham, MD: Rowman and Littlefield.

_____. 1997. *Crime as Structured Action: Gender, Race, Class, and Crime in the Making*. Thousand Oaks, CA: Sage.

_____. 2004. *Flesh and Blood: Adolescent Gender Diversity and Violence*. Lanham, MD: Rowman and Littlefield.

Morris, Allison. 1987. *Women, Crime and Criminal Justice.* Oxford: Basil Blackwell.

Mosher, Janet E. 2006. "The Construction of 'Welfare Fraud' and the Wielding of the State's Iron Fist." In E. Comack (ed.), *Locating Law: Race/Class/Gender/Sexuality Connections.* Second edition. Halifax: Fernwood Publishing.

Naffine, Ngaire. 1987. *Female Crime: The Construction of Women in Criminology.* Sydney: Allen and Unwin.

_____. 1997. *Feminism and Criminology.* Sydney: Allen and Unwin.

Parsons, Talcott, and Robert Bales. 1955. *Family, Socialization and Interaction Process.* Glencoe, IL: Free Press.

Phoenix, Joanna. 1999. *Making Sense of Prostitution.* New York: Palgrave.

R. v. Gladue. 1999. 1 S.C.R. No. 699.

Raftner, Nicole H., and Elena M. Natalazia. 1981. "Marxist Feminism: Implications for Criminal Justice." *Crime and Delinquency* 27 (January): 81–98.

Ritchie, Beth. 1996. *Compelled to Crime: The Gender Entrapment of Battered Black Women.* New York: Routledge.

Royal Commission on Aboriginal Peoples. 1996. *Report of the Royal Commission on Aboriginal Peoples.* Ottawa: Department of Indian and Northern Affairs.

Scutt, Jocelyn. 1979. "The Myth of the 'Chivalry Factor' in Female Crime." *Australian Journal of Social Issues* 14, 1: 3–20.

Shaw, Margaret, Karen Rogers, Johannes Blanchette, Tina Hattem, Lee Seto Thomas, and Lada Tamarack. 1991. *Survey of Federally Sentenced Women: Report on the Task Force on Federally Sentenced Women: The Prison Survey.* Ottawa: Ministry of the Solicitor General of Canada. User Report No. 1991-4.

Simon, Rita. 1975. *Women and Crime.* Lexington, MA: D.C. Heath.

Smart, Carol. 1976. *Women, Crime and Criminology: A Feminist Critique.* London: Routledge and Kegan Paul.

Stanko, Elizabeth. 1985. *Intimate Intrusions: Women's Experience of Male Violence.* London: Routledge and Kegan Paul.

Statistics Canada. 2001. *Aboriginal Peoples in Canada.* Ottawa: Centre for Justice Statistics Profile Series. Catalogue no. 85F0033MIE. Available at <http://www.statcan.ca/english/research/85F0033MIE/85F0033MIE2001001.pdf> accessed July 2, 2007.

_____. 2004. *Canadian Crime Statistics 2003.* Ottawa: Canadian Centre for Justice Statistics. Catalogue no. 85-205.

Steffensmeier, Darryl. 1980. "Sex Differences in Patterns of Adult Crime, 1965–1977." *Social Forces* 58, 4 (June): 1080–09.

Steffensmeier, Darryl, and J. Kramer. 1982. "Sex-based Differences in the Sentencing of Adult Criminal Defendants." *Sociology and Social Research* 663: 289–304.

Sutherland, Edwin. 1949. *Principles of Criminology.* Fourth edition. Philadelphia: Lippincott.

Sutherland, Edwin, and Donald Cressey. 1966. *Principles of Criminology.* Philadelphia: Lippincott.

Wallace. 2004. "Crime Statistics in Canada, 2003." *Juristat* 24, 6.

Weiss. Joseph. 1976. "Liberation and Crime: The Invention of the New Female Criminal." *Crime and Social Justice* 6 (Fall–Winter): 17–27.

West, Candace, and Don Zimmerman. 1987. " Doing Gender." *Gender & Society* 1, 2: 125–51.

Wolfgang, Marvin E. 1972. "Cesare Lombroso." In H. Mannheim (ed.), *Pioneers in Criminology.* Montclair, NJ: Patterson Smith.

Young, Iris Marion. 1990. "Throwing Like a Girl." In I.M. Young (ed.), *Throwing Like a Girl and Other Essays in Feminist Philosophy and Social Theory.* Bloomington: Indiana University Press.

Zingraff, M., and R. Thomson. 1984. "Differential Sentencing of Women and Men in the U.S.A." *International Journal of the Sociology of Law* 12: 401–13.

Part II

The Public Construction of Crime

A fundamental issue in criminology is the question of how the general public comes to see crime from a particular vantage point. In our society the conventional or usual vantage point rests in a collective belief system that tends to see people who break the law as being not just "bad" but also usually "evil or immoral" — people whose behaviour has to be strictly controlled. In addition, that vantage point tends to attach certain social characteristics to the definition of evil or criminal; by design the social context defines what is considered immoral. In other words, when people observe bad behaviour from this vantage point, either directly or vicariously with the aid of certain media, the observing eye focuses not necessarily on the bad behaviour but on the race, class, age, or gender of the violator — which can all be part of the "package of criminality."

This particular understanding of crime and punishment — that crime is about bad people doing bad things — is the framework for conventional criminological theory. As a result, social control theory focuses on external and internal control. To make sure that people conform to social norms, we work with either their individual sense of conscience or their fear of punishment. Similarly, social disorganization and differential association theorists focus on the criminogenic cultures that produce the values and norms of criminality in its members — values and norms that run contrary to the norms of greater society. The psychological theories, such as social learning theory and cognitive development theory, assume that we can change individuals to conform to already established moral rules. Even the biological and genetic theories assume that the physical body can be altered to repair the genetic damage that causes crime, again without questioning whether the targeted norms and values are correct or not. These theories all assume that public values, beliefs, and norms are, for the most part, consensual and therefore correct.

From the public's vantage point, crime is about street criminals, about those individuals who consciously choose to break into homes, or who rob a 7-11 store, or murder someone in drunken rage. Criminals are not like us; they are, in the eyes of the world, poor, relatively young, mostly male, mostly visible minorities, ethnically and socially. The public perception of the evil criminal is also part of the public's perception that crime is increasing, that society is more dangerous now than in the past, and that tougher "lock-em-up" crime control measures are the order of the day for dealing with rampant criminality. Almost all political campaigns in Canada and the United States are based, in part, on a "get tough" approach to crime, which is in turn based on the presumption that crime is increasing and that more and more people are "getting away with murder."

The logic of the get-tough position is based on the principle of deterrence: if you punish sufficiently (or just threaten to punish sufficiently) people will be discouraged from breaking the law.

The question, again, is how the public comes to see crime this way: primarily as an ever-increasing phenomenon and as perpetrated by the most marginalized segments in society. Although crime rates do fluctuate, they are not always on the increase, as the public seems to believe and some politicians emphasize. Indeed, in recent years violent crime rates have gone down in Canada and the United States; and the crimes that damage the public the most are those committed by high status offenders who rarely get caught or whose actions are rarely deemed to be dangerous or criminal.

In important ways, consensus-based criminologists ignore the public construction of crime. When they do examine the political consequences of the widespread beliefs about "criminals out of control" — that these beliefs and attitudes back up the calls by politicians and crime bureaucrats for tougher criminal justice policies and practices — they often simply gloss over the inaccuracies and rarely question the sources of beliefs. Most people do not have much direct personal experience with "crime." Most Canadians get their information about crime and criminals from the media, which, in turn, get their information from crime bureaucrats, the police, and academics. Given this source of information, questions about the accuracy of media reporting of crime should be high on the research agenda. Most conventional criminologists seem, by default, to assume that media reporting is by and large a fair representation of the actual crime in our communities.

The chapters that follow are aimed at providing insights into the origins of public misinformation about crime. They focus on the media and on official statistics, and they explore the politics of using information in a partial or biased way. They reveal that media accounts are biased constructions of crime, and that official statistics count only those who get caught (people who are easily identifiable and easy to convict). They point to how, at times, politicians use crime policy to promote themselves in election battles.

Scott Wortley's chapter, "Misrepresentation or Reality: The Depiction of Race and Crime in Toronto's Print Media," shows that in news coverage and content, much depends on the race of the offender and the victim. Quite clearly, the media's orientation towards crime is not entirely objective or based in journalistic integrity. Toronto's press is more likely to present Black people as criminal offenders than as crime victims; it is more likely to portray Black offenders as being involved in violence and drug trafficking. As crime victims, Black people receive much less news coverage than do their white counterparts. Wortley's analysis of the content of news stories also suggests that stories of white offenders tend to focus on individual pathology, while stories of Black offenders focus on the pathology of the Black culture or Black community. His work focuses attention on how the news media, which operate ostensibly on the basis of objective, journalistic integrity, have tremendous latitude in how they present "factual" accounts. As a result, the media exert considerable influence in the condemnation of race through crime stories.

In "The Social Construction of 'Dangerous' Girls and Women," Karlene Faith and Yasmin Jiwani explore the world of popular images of violent girls and women by taking up several high-profile cases that have captured the public's imagination. Looking at the history of the condemnation of women, they place this history in the context of the development of "scientific knowledge" about women and badness. Their historical review ends in the present with an overview of current studies of female violence, most of which draw on conventional (conservative) understandings of femininity and masculinity. They then investigate three high-profile cases: Leslie Van Houten, in California; Karla Homolka, in Ontario; and Kelly Ellard, in British Columbia. These cases show how the media construct images of immoral girls and women that are consonant with the views of those in power. In the end the authors discuss how the media draw on orthodox gender stereotypes to create powerful images of "bad women." The creation of such images is, in itself, an ideological or political act. Faith and Jiwani argue that the media, by condemning women for their "out of character" behaviour, reinforce a sexist normative, and moral order.

Sandra Bell, in "Girls in Trouble," finds that the popular media tend to depict girls who are involved in violence as particularly evil, and she examines some of the mechanisms the media use to do this. In doing so she points out the contradictions between the public panic about increasing female violence and the statistics, which generally do not bear out this finding. She shows us how statistics are manipulated to present a picture of increasingly violent girls. She also demonstrates that, contrary to public opinion, the justice system tends to treat female offenders more harshly than their male counterparts. In exploring the inadequacy of the youth justice and social services systems for girls, she illustrates how, in many ways, the justice system further damages girls who are disadvantaged by the world they live in. Overall, Sandra Bell's work, like the other chapters in this section, reveals that crime control, in many ways, condemns those already condemned to the margins of the society.

5

Misrepresentation or Reality?
The Depiction of Race and Crime in the Toronto Print Media

Scot Wortley

KEY FACTS

> North American, European, and Australian research has found that at least nine out of ten people list the media as their most important source of information regarding crime, policing the courts and corrections.

> Black people are depicted in about 16 percent of all news photos, they represent only 2 percent of the photos associated with both politics and business and 0 percent of the characters depicted in science stories.

> Although homicide is by far the most common crime to appear in local newspaper coverage, homicides actually represented only 0.03 percent of all crimes reported by the Toronto police in 1998.

> Compared to whites, Blacks are more likely to be depicted as criminal offenders than as crime victims. In addition, racial minority crime victims tend to receive significantly less news coverage than white victims do.

> One study of over one hundred U.S. cities found that increases in the Black population, accompanied with media coverage of minority crime, are much stronger predictors of police budget increases than are both the official crime rate and overall population growth.

> Researchers in the United States suggest that before the average American child completes elementary school they will have witnessed more than 8,000 televised murders.

Sources: Reiman 2007; Tremblay 1999; Jackson 1989.

In April 1994, Arnold Minors, a member of Toronto's Police Services Board, was harshly critical of the Canadian news media at a dinner for Black business leaders. Commenting on the extensive coverage of a recent interracial homicide, Minors charged that the entire West Indian community "should not be criminalized for the actions of a few." The Toronto press, he argued, was reinforcing an image of Blacks "as malevolent by presenting people of colour almost exclusively in the context of crime and social deprivation" (DiManno 1994c: A8). Not surprisingly, editorial writers denied the allegations, making the standard response that reporters and editors work to provide "objective" coverage of important news stories (Editorial 1994: 10).

The accusations made by Minors are by no means new. In Toronto Black West Indians have long complained that the local news media provide a biased, stereotypical portrayal of their community (Ginzberg 1995; Fleras 1994; Henry and Bjornson 1999; Henry and Tator 2000). Indeed, my own research — both quantitative and qualitative — into the Toronto print media reveals that reports tend to depict people of Black, West Indian descent in a narrow range of social roles: as criminals, entertainers, or athletes. Racial minority crime victims receive significantly less news coverage than their white counterparts, and while white crime is almost always attributed to individual pathology or immorality, Black crime is frequently blamed on Black or Caribbean cultural origins.

> The Toronto print media tends to depict people of Black, West Indian descent in a narrow range of social roles: as criminals, entertainers, or athletes.

Previous Research on Race and Crime in the Media

Most of us rely heavily on the mass media for information about crime, law, and criminal justice. Indeed, North American, European, and Australian research has found that at least nine out of ten people list the media as their most important source of information regarding crime, policing, the courts, and corrections (Graber 1980; Knowles 1982; Canadian Sentencing Commission 1987; Ericson, Baranek, and Chan 1991; Rome and Chermak 1994). Not surprisingly, then, research also suggests that media coverage greatly influences public opinion about crime-related issues (Roberts 1992; Henry and Tator 2000). The influence of media coverage shows up in different ways. For example, although very few Canadians have actually visited a criminal court or a prison, the majority have strong opinions about these institutions (Moore 1985). Similarly, the general public appears to grossly overestimate the level of violent crime in society, a tendency that would seem to be directly related to the overrepresentation of violent crimes in media coverage (Liska and Baccaglini 1990; Marsh 1991; Chermak 1994). Although official crime figures declined significantly throughout the 1990s, most people continued to believe that criminal activity was on the rise (Gartner and Doob 1994; Roberts and Grossman 1990; Sacco 2000). The media, then, undoubtedly have a strong effect on public perceptions of racial minorities in general — and the relationship between race and crime in particular. Numerous studies suggest that the mass media typically depict Blacks and other racial minority groups negatively either as criminals or as people plagued by numerous social problems (Martindale 1990; Barlow 1998; Henry and Tator 2000). Still, most of the research suffers from serious sampling problems (see discussion in Rome and Chermak 1994). For example, Effie Ginzberg's (1995) study of the Toronto print media produced many examples of racially biased reporting, but it focused only on a small, non-random sample of news items. Furthermore, all of the stories Ginzberg selected for analysis depicted minorities in a negative light. In other words, the research made no effort to estimate either the proportion of items that involved minority people in relation to all news items or the ratio of "negative" to "positive" stories. Furthermore, Ginzberg did not explicitly examine how minorities were depicted in comparison to the white majority. Such weaknesses characterize a great deal of the qualitative work on this topic (see Barlow 1998; Mann and Zatz 1998). Although qualitative deconstructions of selected news items can be an excellent method of documenting the finer details of news reporting — including the use of racialized language, images, and narratives — such research cannot be easily generalized or used to draw accurate conclusions about the media coverage of different racial groups.

> Although official crime figures declined significantly throughout the 1990s, most people continued to believe that criminal activity was on the rise.

Recently a number of quantitative investigations have attempted to address these shortcomings. For example, a study of over three thousand stories appearing in the Boston press reveals striking differences in how racial minorities are depicted by the African American and mainstream (white-owned) press. In the white media, 85 percent of the stories about Boston's Black community dealt with crime, poverty, or family dissolution. By contrast, along with some crime coverage, stories in the Black press often focused on positive topics, including entrepreneurial breakthroughs, high academic achievement, and successful campaigns to remedy poor living conditions (Johnson 1990). Frances Henry and Marnie Bjornson's (1999) examination of Canadian newspapers yielded similar results. They found that almost half of their sample of 2,622 stories depicting Jamaicans fell into either the sports or entertainment categories. An additional 40 percent dealt with social problems such as crime, poverty, and deportation. Only 2 percent of all stories involving Jamaicans could be classified as "positive." Henry and Bjornson (1999: iii) conclude that, in the Toronto press, Jamaicans "are quite clearly constructed as a problem people."

Although these findings are compelling, they are also somewhat limited. Most importantly, both the Boston and Toronto study do not include any adequate comparison group. While Henry and Bjornson can estimate the percentage of Jamaican stories that fall into the crime category, they cannot provide the corresponding figures for whites, Asians, or people from other racial backgrounds. However, a number of U.S. studies — with an exclusive focus on crime news — provide more detailed racial comparisons, with mixed results. While some of those studies found an overrepresentation of older, white, higher-status offenders in news accounts as compared with arrest statistics (Graber 1980; Roshier 1981), others reported an overrepresentation of lower-status offenders and racial minorities (Gans 1979; Sheley and Ashkins 1984; Smith 1984; Barlow, Barlow, and Stojkovic 1995; Barlow 1998). A consistent finding is that, in general, racial minority crime victims receive significantly less media coverage than their white counterparts (see Damphousse, Chermak, and Gilliam 1999; Sorenson, Manz, and Berk 1998; Brownstein 1995). In addition, research indicates that the media are especially likely to provide extensive coverage to crimes that involve white victims and non-white offenders (Deepe-Keever, Martindale, and Weston 1997). Thus, it appears that the media are much more likely to portray racial minorities as criminal offenders than as people who suffer from criminal activity (Romer, Jamieson, and deCoteau 1998). Unfortunately, by focusing on crime stories in isolation, these studies do not provide a complete picture of how the mainstream news media depict different racial groups.

A detailed media investigation that does not focus on a particular type of story (such as "crime") or a particular racial group (Blacks) would seem, then, the best way of determining the magnitude of racial differences in news coverage. Previous research strategies have not adequately addressed a number of important research questions:

1) Compared to census statistics, are Blacks and other racial minorities underrepresented or overrepresented in the print media?
2) Are Blacks and other racial minorities overrepresented in crime news? Are Blacks and other minorities more likely to be depicted as criminal offenders or crime victims?
3) Do crimes involving Black and other racial minority victims receive as much newspaper coverage as crimes involving white victims?
4) Do crime news narratives differ by the race or ethnic background of victims and offenders?

To answer these questions, I first provide a content analysis of all news stories appearing in Toronto's two daily newspapers — the *Toronto Star* and the *Toronto Sun* — from

June 16 to August 4, 1997. Both papers are read by more than one million people on an average day.[1] During the seven week period I recorded the basic characteristics of each story. Variables included: 1) type of story (politics, business, crime, sports, for example); 2) location of the story (did the events take place locally, regionally, or in another country?); 3) headline size (in inches); 4) the page number where the story appears; 5) the amount of space devoted to the story (in square inches); 6) the number of photographs (if any) connected with the story; 7) the size of photographs; 8) basic descriptions of photographs; 9) the age and gender of the main characters depicted in the story; and 10) the race and/or ethnic background of the main characters depicted in each story. The final sample included 8,457 separate news items.

I also collected detailed information on each crime story that appeared in both the *Sun* and the *Star* from July 2 to September 3, 1998. I added these stories to the crime stories collected during the 1997 study period in order to increase the size of our crime-story database, producing a total of 1,932 crime stories examined. In addition to the other variables, for each crime story I collected information on: 1) the type of crime depicted; 2) the number of victims and offenders; 3) the gender and age of victims and offenders; 4) the race, ethnicity and/or immigration status of victims and offenders; 5) the nature of the relationship between victims and offenders (family, friends, strangers); and 6) the status of each case (an arrest, a continuing investigation, a sentencing, for example).

Still, although we can use this type of quantitative data to identify general trends, it cannot capture important details of story language and narrative. Thus, in the second part of my analysis, I provide a qualitative deconstruction of stories that reflect the issue of race and crime in the Toronto area. At the heart of this analysis is a comparison of the newspaper coverage of two high-profile, interracial homicides: one involving a white victim and Black offender, the other involving a Black victim and a white assailant.

Race and Type of News Story

How are people from different racial backgrounds depicted in the print media? Here I was specifically interested in the portrayal of Black people, particularly those of West Indian descent. The majority of Toronto's Black community, over 80 percent, are either immigrants from the West Indies or report that their parents are from the Caribbean region. Additionally, almost all immigrants from the West Indies report a Black racial identity (see Ornstein 2000). Thus, in Toronto, "Black" racial background has come to represent people who have cultural roots in the Caribbean (see Henry and Bjornson 1999). Other racial groups identified in my analysis include the "white" or European majority, "Asians" (people of Chinese, Vietnamese, Korean, Japanese, or Filipino ancestry), and "other" racial groups (such as Aboriginals, South Asians, and Latinos).[2]

The main texts of news articles rarely identify the racial and/or ethnic identities of the people appearing in them (Rome and Chermak 1994). Indeed, photographs are by far the most common method of communicating race. In my study, over three-quarters of all news photos (76 percent) depict white characters, 16 percent depict Black characters, 4 percent depict Asians, and another 4 percent depict people from "other" racial backgrounds (see Table 5-1).

Given that Black people represent only 9.6 percent of Toronto's total population (see Ornstein 2000), it appears that Blacks are overrepresented in local media coverage, which is not necessarily a positive development for the West Indian community. Indeed, a sizable negative press coverage can reinforce stereotypes and contribute to racial discrimination. Bad press can be much worse than no press at all.

In my research, I identified ten different types of news stories: 1) *politics*: local, na-

Table 5-1:   Story Type, by the Racial Background of the Central Character(s)
Depicted in Newspaper Photographs

	Black	White	Asian	Other	Total	N
Politics	2.0%	84.5%	10.8%	2.7%	100%	437
Crime	21.6%	69.2%	5.7%	3.5%	100%	403
Criminal justice	9.6%	81.7%	0.0%	8.6%	100%	93
Sports	27.8%	65.6%	1.3%	5.3%	100%	1644
Entertainment	13.4%	83.7%	2.4%	0.6%	100%	619
Human interest	7.6%	85.1%	3.4%	3.9%	100%	726
Business	2.1%	93.7%	3.4%	0.6%	100%	331
War/upheaval	4.6%	63.1%	13.8%	18.4%	100%	152
Accident/disaster	7.1%	82.3%	5.7%	5.0%	100%	141
Science/medicine	0.0%	91.6%	4.8%	3.6%	100%	83
Total	15.6%	76.4%	3.8%	4.2%	100%	4630

tional, and international subjects (including articles on all major government issues); 2) *crime*: coverage of specific cases of alleged wrongdoing or criminal offenders (including recent criminal events, continuing criminal investigations, arrests, and criminal trials; 3) *criminal justice*: coverage of aggregate crime statistics, changes to criminal law, policing, corrections, crime prevention strategies; 4) *sports*: including baseball, football, hockey, basketball and all other sports-related activities; 5) *entertainment*: including the theatre, movies, music, television, dance; 6) *human interest*: articles related to various aspects of lifestyle, recreation, and community life (community and cultural activities, travel, food and nutrition, health, religion, personal accomplishments); 7) *business*: reports on the economy, corporate activity, the stock market; 8) *war/upheaval*: coverage of war, political uprisings, rebel activity, terrorism, riots; 9) *accidents/disasters*: natural disasters, famine, car accidents, fires; and 10) *science/medicine*: discoveries, medical developments, leaders of the scientific community.

Although, as we found, Black people are depicted in about 16 percent of all news photos, they represent only 2 percent of the photos associated with both politics and business and 0 percent of the characters depicted in science stories (see Table 5-1). By contrast, Blacks are greatly overrepresented in crime stories (22 percent) and articles related to entertainment (13 percent) and sports (28 percent). Thus, while Black people account for less than one-tenth of Toronto's population, they represent almost one-fourth of the characters depicted in both crime and sports stories. Interestingly, other racial minority groups appear to be underrepresented in crime stories. For example, while Asians represent about 15 percent of Toronto's population, they amount to only 6 percent of the people depicted in crime stories.

White people (60 percent of Toronto's population) represent the majority of characters depicted in all types of news story. However, whites are clearly overrepresented in stories dealing with politics, criminal justice, entertainment, human interest, and accidents/disasters and heavily overrepresented in stories in the business (93.7 percent) and science/medicine (91.6 percent) categories. While white people appear to be overrepresented in news stories dealing with power and social accomplishment (politics, business, science, for instance), Blacks are overrepresented in stories dealing with crime, entertainment, and sports.

The data also indicate that the print media depicts Black people in a limited number of social roles (see Table 5-2). Indeed, almost two-thirds of the news photos containing Black subjects are related to sports stories alone. An additional 12 percent of the photos of Black people are associated with crime stories and 11 percent are related to entertainment news. Thus, nine out of ten appearances of Black people have to do with sports, crime, or entertainment. By contrast, a mere 1 percent of Black photo appearances are associated with political stories. Similarly, very few stories (1 percent) depicting Black people have to do with business, criminal justice, or accidents/disasters. Finally, Blacks are not represented in any of the stories dealing with issues of science or medicine. The data suggest that the Toronto media portray whites in a much wider variety of social roles (Table 5-2). While sports, crime, and entertainment may represent the majority of stories for both white and Black people, Blacks are virtually invisible in all other types of news stories.

> White people appear to be overrepresented in news stories about power and social accomplishment, while Blacks are overrepresented in stories dealing with crime, entertainment, and sports.

The narrow range of news stories in which Black people are present is particularly striking when I remove sports and entertainment stories from the data set and focus exclusively on "serious" news coverage (see Table 5-3), where Black people are depicted in only 8 percent of the stories. Further analysis reveals that almost half of the serious news stories that include Black people are crime-related — a much higher proportion than the corresponding figures for whites, Asians, or people from other racial minority groups. An additional one-third of the serious news stories depicting Blacks fall into the "human interest" category. By contrast, Black people are rarely, if at all, depicted in stories

Table 5-2: The Racial Background of the Central Character(s) Appearing in Newspaper Photographs, by Story Type

	Black	White	Asian	Other	Total
Politics	1.2%	10.4%	26.5%	6.3%	9.4%
Crime	12.0%	7.9%	13.0%	7.3%	8.7%
Criminal justice	1.2%	2.1%	0.0%	4.1%	2.0%
Sports	63.1%	30.5%	12.4%	45.3%	35.5%
Entertainment	11.5%	14.6%	8.5%	2.1%	13.4%
Human interest	7.6%	17.5%	14.1%	14.4%	16.1%
Business	1.0%	8.8%	6.8%	1.0%	7.1%
War/upheaval	1.0%	2.7%	11.9%	14.4%	3.3%
Accident/disaster	1.4%	3.3%	4.5%	3.6%	3.1%
Science/medicine	0.0%	2.2%	2.2%	1.5%	1.4%
Total	100.0%	100.0%	100.0%	100.0%	100.0%
Sample size	723	3,536	177	194	4,630

Table 5-3:   The Racial Background of the Central Character(s) Appearing in Newspaper Photographs, by Type of "Serious" News Story*

	Black	White	Asian	Other	Total
Politics	4.9%	19.0%	33.6%	18.5%	18.5%
Crime	47.3%	14.4%	16.4%	17.0%	17.0%
Criminal justice	4.9%	3.9%	0.0%	3.9%	3.9%
Human Interest	29.9%	31.9%	17.9%	30.7%	31.5%
Business	3.8%	16.0%	8.6%	2.0%	14.0%
War/upheaval	3.8%	4.9%	15.0%	27.5%	6.4%
Accident/disaster	5.4%	5.4%	5.7%	6.9%	5.9%
Science/medicine	0.0%	3.9%	2.9%	2.9%	2.7%
Total	100.0%	100.0%	100.0%	100.0%	100.0%
Sample Size	185	1,940	140	102	2,367

* Data on "serious" news stories do not include items related to either sports or entertainment.

that highlight their contributions to the areas of politics, business, criminal justice, and science and medicine. These findings are consistent with previous U.S. and Canadian research (see Henry and Bjornson 1999; Johnson 1990).

Types of Crime

I divided my crime stories into seven distinct categories: 1) *homicide*: such as murder or manslaughter; 2) *violent theft*: robbery, mugging, and any other property crime that involves the use of physical force; 3) *sex crimes*: including rape, sexual assault, and child molestation; 4) *other violence*: all other forms of non-lethal violence, including attempted murder, aggravated assault, and domestic assault; 5) *street crimes*: including a variety of other common property and vice crimes, such as car theft, prostitution, drug trafficking, and vandalism; 6) *white-collar crime*: including embezzlement, fraud, tax evasion, and insider trading; and 7) *traffic-related violations*: including drunk driving, leaving the scene of an accident, and dangerous driving.[3]

Almost one-third of all the crime stories collected during the study period were homicide-related. Although homicide is by far the most common crime to appear in local newspaper coverage, homicides actually represented only 0.03 of 1 percent of all crimes reported by the Toronto police in 1998 (Tremblay 1999).[4] In other words, while one out of every three crimes reported by these newspapers is a homicide, homicides represent just twenty-eight out of every hundred thousand crimes known to the authorities. The actual figure is much lower given that more than half (53 percent) of all the homicides that appeared in the Toronto press during the study period took place outside of the Toronto area. Indeed, while 14 percent of the homicides covered by the Toronto press took place in other Canadian jurisdictions, one-fourth (24 percent) actually took place in the United States, and an additional 14 percent took place in other foreign nations. It appears that when local homicides are not available, the Toronto media focuses on murders that have taken place in other areas of the world.

While one-third of all crime coverage relates to homicide, an additional 16 percent involves violent theft, 15 percent involves "other" violence, and 11 percent involves sex crimes. Thus, although violent crime represented only 14 percent of all criminal offences reported by the Toronto police in 1998 (see Tremblay 1999), about three-quarters (74 percent) of all the crime news that I documented involved some form of violent behaviour. Furthermore, an additional 17 percent of all crime stories involved other forms of common street crime, such as prostitution, drug trafficking, and car theft. Thus, nine out of every ten crime stories (91 percent) documented involved either violence or other street crime. By contrast, very few stories — only 6 percent — involved white-collar or corporate crime (for similar results see Marsh 1991; Roberts 1992; Altheide 1997; Baer and Chambliss 1997). Given these results, it is not at all surprising that the general public grossly overestimates the extent of violent crime in Canadian society (Liska and Baccaglini 1990).

The Race of Criminal Offenders

In studying the news articles I based almost two-thirds (59 percent) of all racial identifications on accompanying photographs. The details of the race of an offender, or alleged offender, rarely appear in the text of stories. However, descriptions of recent crimes in which the suspect is still at large often do include racial identifiers:

> One of the suspects is black, in his late teens to early 20s, 5-foot-8 with short black hair. He was wearing a blue jacket with white stripes. A second suspect is black, in his late teens, 5-foot-8 to 5-foot-10 with black hair. He was wearing a dark sweat shirt and black jeans. (Crime Stoppers 1998: 26)[5]

The majority of articles (65 percent) did not identify the race of offenders. The stories that did identify racial characteristics revealed that about one-half (54 percent) of all the offenders were white, 22 percent were Black, 9 percent were Asian, and 16 percent came from other racial minority groups (see Table 5-4).

Clearly, Black people are overrepresented among the criminal offenders depicted by the two Toronto newspapers. People of Afro-Caribbean descent represent only 10 percent of Toronto's population but 22 percent of all criminal offenders appearing in the *Sun* and the *Star* over the study period. They are particularly likely to be depicted in news associated with street crime and violence. While Blacks represent only 14 percent of homicide offenders, they are almost 40 percent of those offenders involved with violent theft, 30 percent of the offenders associated with "other" violence, 49 percent of the offenders associated with street crime, and 23 percent of the offenders depicted in association with traffic-related crimes. By contrast, Blacks are not overrepresented among sex offenders (9 percent) and are underrepresented among those who commit white-collar crimes (5 percent). White people are underrepresented among the offenders depicted in most crime categories, but they do represent over 70 percent of sex offenders and 75 percent of offenders associated with white-collar crimes. People of Asian descent are underrepresented among the offenders from each crime category.

Over one-third of the Black offenders (34 percent) identified in our analysis are depicted in the violent theft/robbery category and an additional 16 percent are associated with other types of non-lethal violence (see Table 5-5). Thus, about half of all the Black offenders (50 percent) included in my media analysis are depicted in these two crime

Table 5-4:   Type of Crime, by the Racial Background of Offender(s)

	Black	White	Asian	Other	Total	Sample Size
Homicide	14.2%	59.5%	8.2%	18.1%	100%	232
Violent theft/ robbery	38.8%	39.5%	10.9%	10.9%	100%	129
Sex crimes	9.5%	70.3%	8.1%	12.1%	100%	74
Other violence	30.4%	38.0%	10.1%	21.5%	100%	79
Street crimes	49.5%	26.2%	6.5%	17.8%	100%	107
White-collar crimes	5.0%	75.0%	10.0%	10.0%	100%	40
Traffic offences	22.7%	63.6%	4.5%	9.1%	100%	22
Total	21.8%	53.9%	8.6%	15.7%	100%	683

Table 5-5:   Racial Background of Offenders by Type of Crime

	Black	White	Asian	Other	Total
Homicide	22.1%	37.5%	32.2%	39.3%	34.0%
Violent theft/robbery	33.6%	13.9%	23.7%	13.1%	18.9%
Sex crimes	4.7%	14.1%	10.2%	8.4%	10.8%
Other violence	16.1%	8.2%	13.6%	15.9%	11.6%
Street crimes	18.8%	14.4%	11.9%	17.8%	15.7%
White-collar crimes	1.3%	8.2%	6.8%	3.7%	5.9%
Traffic offences	3.4%	3.8%	1.7%	1.9%	3.2%
Total	100%	100%	100%	100%	100%
Sample size	149	368	59	107	683

Table 5-6:   Type of Crime, by the Racial Background of Crime Victim(s)

	Black	White	Asian	Other	Total	Sample Size
Homicide	22.4%	51.0%	6.7%	20.0%	100%	210
Violent theft/robbery	17.9%	53.6%	21.4%	7.1%	100%	28
Sex crimes	0.0%	50.0%	0.0%	50.0%	100%	16
Other violence	9.3%	66.7%	5.6%	18.5%	100%	54
Street crimes	5.6%	44.4%	11.1%	38.9%	100%	18
White-collar crimes	0.0%	50.0%	0.0%	50.0%	100%	4
Traffic offences	11.1%	33.3%	33.3%	22.2%	100%	9
Total	17.4%	52.8%	8.3%	21.5%	100%	339

categories alone, compared to only 22 percent of white offenders. By contrast, 37 percent of the white offenders described in my sample are associated with homicide, compared to only 22 percent of Black offenders. White offenders are also more likely than Black offenders to be depicted in association with both sex crimes and white-collar offences.

In my sample of crime stories, both violent theft/robbery and other violent crimes are much more likely to involve the victimization of strangers. Homicides, sex offences, and white-collar crimes are much more likely to involve victims and offenders who have had a previous relationship. Thus, it appears that the media are much more likely to portray Black offenders as being involved in predatory street crimes against strangers, while associating whites with crimes against people that they know. It could be argued that the general public views "stranger crimes" as being more serious. Because they are both unpredictable and seemingly unprovoked, these crimes are more likely to produce fear and calls for tougher law enforcement and criminal sentencing.

The Race of Crime Victims

I was able to identify the racial background of crime victims in only 17 percent of the crime stories. Apparently, the media are much more likely to communicate the race of criminal offenders than the race of crime victims. Furthermore, unlike information on offenders, information on the race of crime victims is not evenly distributed across crime types. Indeed, while I was able to identify the race of 34 percent of all murder victims, I could only identify the racial background of less than 10 percent of the victims of violent theft/robbery, sex crimes, street crimes and white-collar crimes. This may be due to the protection of the identity of victims of some crimes, such as sexual assault. Furthermore, many street crimes, such as drug trafficking, are considered "victimless." For a number of violent thefts and white-collar crimes (bank robbery, corporate embezzlement, tax evasion, for example), the victims are actually institutions rather than individual people with identifiable racial characteristics.

Black people made up about 17 percent of all the crime victims (see Table 5-6). Thus, although the media overrepresent Black or West Indian people among both victims and offenders, they are somewhat more likely to depict them as criminal offenders (22 percent) than as crime victims (17 percent). This discrepancy is more pronounced for some crime categories than others. For example, although Blacks represent 39 percent of robbery offenders, they make up only 18 percent of robbery victims. Similarly, Blacks are 30 percent of "other" violent offenders, but only 9 percent of the victims of this type of crime. Blacks also represent half (49 percent) of those depicted as the offenders involved in street crime, but only 6 percent of street-crime victims. Finally, although Black people represent about 10 percent of the sex offenders appearing in the two Toronto papers, not a single sex-crime victim was Black. The data further reveal that Black people are rarely depicted as the victims of crimes other than homicide (see Table 5-7).

Indeed, 80 percent of the Black victims depicted in the Toronto newspapers were murder victims, compared to 60 percent of white victims, 50 percent of Asian victims, and 57 percent of the victims of other racial minority groups. Unless they are killed, Blacks rarely appear in the media as crime victims. It may be that the "minor" victimization experiences of whites are considered more newsworthy than the "minor" victimization experiences of Blacks or West Indians.

How the media present a crime is almost as important as whether they report on it

Table 5-7:   The Racial Background of Crime Victims, by Type of Crime

	Black	White	Asian	Other	Total
Homicide	79.7%	59.8%	50.0%	57.5%	61.9%
Violent theft/robbery	8.5%	8.4%	21.4%	2.7%	8.3%
Sex crimes	0.0%	4.5%	0.0%	11.0%	4.7%
Other violence	8.5%	20.1%	10.7%	13.7%	15.9%
Street crimes	1.7%	4.5%	7.1%	9.6%	5.3%
White-collar crimes	0.0%	1.1%	0.0%	2.7%	1.2%
Traffic offences	1.7%	1.7%	10.7%	2.7%	2.7%
Total	100%	100%	100%	100%	100%
Sample size	59	179	28	73	339

at all (see Rome and Chermak 1994; Damphousse, Chermak, and Gilliam 1999; Sorenson, Manz, and Berk 1998; Pritchard 1985). I measured the relative "importance" or "newsworthiness" of crime stories based on four factors: 1) whether or not the story appeared on the front page of the paper; 2) whether or not the story appeared on the first five pages of the paper; 3) the size of the story headline; and 4) the amount of space the story took up in the newspaper. Judged by these criteria, crimes committed against Black and other racial minorities receive less "priority" news coverage than crimes committed against whites. For example, over 20 percent of the murder cases with white victims were presented on the front page of either the *Star* or the *Sun*. By contrast, stories involving only 7 percent of Black and 4 percent of Asian murder victims appeared on the front page. Similarly, 35 percent of white murder victims appeared on the first five pages of the paper, compared to 26 percent of Black victims and only 7 percent of Asian victims. In the headline size and space allocation, the same racial pattern occurs.[6] Together, these findings strongly suggest that the Toronto print media consider crimes involving white victims to be more important than crimes involving Black and other racial minority victims.

Still, all of these stark statistics do not convey how crime stories present and discuss different racialized groups. Numbers tell us little about the language and narratives that further distinguish the coverage of criminal events.

The Coverage of Interracial Homicide: Moral Panic or Isolated Tragedy?

In the 1990s, about four years apart, two interracial homicides took place in the Toronto area: one involved a white victim and a Black offender, the other a Black victim and a white offender. The homicide involving the white victim and Black offender received extensive news coverage; the Toronto news media constructed it as a major social crisis. Indeed, the news coverage of this crime arguably created a "moral panic" over West Indian crime. In contrast, the homicide involving the Black victim and the white offender received relatively little media coverage. The press depicted it as an isolated tragedy rather than a significant social problem.

> The homicide involving the white victim and Black offender was extensively reported while the murder of a Black person by a white offender was depicted as just an isolated tragedy.

The "Just Desserts" Murder

Shortly before midnight on April 5, 1994, three young Black men burst through the doors of an upscale, midtown Toronto café called Just Desserts and held twenty patrons and staff at gunpoint. The assailants demanded money and jewellery. After encountering resistance, one of the gunmen pulled the trigger of a sawed-off shotgun, mortally wounding a young white woman, Georgina (Vivi) Leimonis. The assailants escaped in a waiting car driven by a fourth suspect (Hall and Stancu 1994; Stewart 1994a).

The "Just Desserts" incident received saturation coverage in the local media. The shooting was front-page news in both the *Toronto Star* and *Toronto Sun* on nine of the next fourteen days. During this two-week period, the *Star* ran forty-one and the *Sun* thirty-five stories and editorials on the shooting. Radio and television news coverage of the event was also extensive. Most Torontonians were probably aware of this crime and the news narratives that surrounded it.

The term "news narratives" refers to the "stories" told to the public through various media sources. These "stories" usually consist of plots that have beginnings and endings and easily identified central characters. As Ronald Jacobs (1996: 1240–46) notes, news narratives also appear in comic, romantic, and tragic forms (see also Alexander and Smith 1993: 156). Social scientists increasingly recognize the importance of narrative analysis for investigating issues of social action and identity. Given that most of us rely on the media for our knowledge about and understanding of the world we live in, the narrative in a news story is at least as important as how often a story appears (Darnton 1975; Schudson 1982; Jacobs 1996). In this case, the narratives introduced by the Toronto media clearly depict the shooting as a social crisis and an encounter between the sacred and the profane.

> The term "news narratives" refers to the "stories" told to the public through various media sources; they usually consist of plots with beginnings and endings and easily identified central characters.

Toronto, a city of about four million people, has never experienced more than a hundred homicides in a year. Indeed, over the past two decades homicide rates have declined almost by half. Furthermore, compared to U.S. cities, "stranger" homicides are relatively uncommon. Nonetheless, the Just Desserts shooting provoked headlines of "Urban Terrorism" (*Toronto Star* 1994a). The press proclaimed that the crime was committed "In Cold Blood" (*Toronto Star* 1994b) and that the suspects had showed "No Mercy" to their victims (Stewart 1994a). The Just Desserts incident was also said to show that criminals were "Getting More Vicious" (Stewart 1994a) and that a new type of criminal activity, involving the "Lowest of the Low," was sweeping the city (Lamberti 1994). Commentators further urged that "Toronto the Good" had lost its innocence and was experiencing an urban violence previously associated with U.S. cities (Blatchford 1994b, 1994c; Zerbisias 1994). The chief of police remarked, "In the 10 years I was in the homicide squad, I certainly have not seen anything quite as horrible as this" (Lamberti 1994). Echoing these sentiments, one police sergeant warned that violent crime had increased so dramatically in Toronto that "wherever you have people gathered together with money in their pockets, they are liable to get knocked off " (Mascoll 1994a).

The media depictions of the victim and villains of this social crisis were sharply drawn. As a result, the spectre of interracial violence pervaded coverage. For example, the front page of both the April 7 *Star* and *Sun* featured high-quality photos of the young, attractive, white, female victim and grainy security-camera photographs of the young,

Black, male suspects. These photos were repeated on the April 8 front page of the *Sun* and on page 6 of the *Star*. Four days later the police released the name and earlier arrest photo of a suspect: a Caribbean Canadian immigrant, Lawrence "the Brownman" Brown. A photo of Brown, depicting a sullen, angry-looking Black man with unruly dreadlocks, appeared on the front page of the *Sun*, alongside a funeral photo of the white victim's father grieving over the open casket of his daughter. Photos of Brown appeared in the *Sun* for the next four days, twice on the front page, usually with a photo of the white female victim. Brown's photo also appeared on the front page of the *Star* on four consecutive days.

Brown surrendered to the police on April 14, and the on following day both the *Star* and the *Sun* published front-page photos of his first court appearance. Stories in both papers stressed the profane nature of this event. Both papers noted that Brown appeared cocky and that he smirked at the crowd (Robertson 1994; Wilkes and Small 1994). The front-page *Star* picture featured the handcuffed Brown smiling while being escorted from court. Such coverage openly supported the claim, made by several news narratives, that the Just Desserts shooting represented the classic confrontation of "Good vs. Evil" (Blatchford 1994a).

Although the press focused a great deal of attention on the pain and suffering of the murder victim and her family (Small 1994; Burnett 1994a, 1994b; Christopoulos 1994a), early narratives of the shooting also clearly indicate that Vivi Leimonis was not the only perceived victim of the Just Desserts shooting. Indeed, the incident was taken to symbolize a more general threat to Canada's tradition of middle-class, peaceable society. Typical of much of the narrative tone was the approach of Christie Blatchford, one of the city's most popular newspaper columnists. Blatchford (1994b) argued that the Just Desserts shooting was a landmark event:

> Going out for a piece of apple crumble pie and a coffee after the ball game, to a nice little cafe in a chi-chi mid-town neighbourhood, can now cost you your life. The touching innocence of this excursion, and the unthinkable price a young woman named Georgina Leimonis paid for it at Just Desserts on Tuesday night, may be what sets this shooting apart from all the rest and why it has become an instant benchmark, one of the dreadful defining moments by which a city measures its descent into New York style fear and loathing.

Not only Vivi Leimonis, then, but all "decent citizens" of Toronto were portrayed as the victims of this crime. Blatchford (1994c) later lamented, "It's not the end of the world, and there will always be much to like about Toronto. But changed it is, and a city's safety and self-confidence, like a woman's virginity, is lost only once and is never retrieved."

Similarly, the press identified the city's reported problem of "Black crime" as the villain. Much of the media attention focused on how the suspects were Black, Caribbean immigrants to Canada. The chief of police was one of the first to point fingers at the immigrant community when he commented, "Our culture is not accustomed to this type of savagery" (Lamberti 1994). Several editorials argued that violent crimes were largely the result of "two decades of choosing too many of the wrong immigrants" (Blatchford 1994b) and that the government should therefore "turf out crooked aliens" (Macdonald 1994). The police union president urged the deportation of illegal immigrants and the dissemination of race-crime statistics, which are not routinely collected in Canada (Smyth 1994; Barber 1994; Gangley 1994). Even the funeral for the shooting victim was not immune from the racial conflict that pervaded the shooting. While giving the eulogy, the head of the Greek Orthodox Church in Canada endorsed the use of race-crime-nationality statistics to limit immigration to Canada from selected countries (Blatchford 1994c; Wilkes and Small 1994). Perhaps *Toronto Sun* columnist Raynier Maharaj best captured the anti-Black sentiment:

> Unfortunately, these days most of the murderers seem to be Black... Given the society we live in, racial conflict is often the result when there is Black-on-white crime... Are we a society of racists? Certainly not. It's just that white Canadians are understandably fed up with people they see as outsiders coming into their country and beating and killing them. (Maharaj 1994: 11)

Media narratives also portrayed Torontonians as united in their sympathy for the victim's family and their outrage towards the robbery suspects. Special attention was paid to a visit that a large number of citizens made to the murder scene in the days immediately following the killing; they went to leave flowers and notes of condolence and to express their concern over what was happening to their city (Lem 1994a). The press also gave extensive coverage to the victim's funeral, attended by over three thousand people (Wilkes and Small 1994), most of them strangers, who were "moved to tears" by the tragic nature of the event (Christopoulos 1994b).

As the news narratives suggest, once the details of the Just Desserts shooting were set out, and public reaction had been established, a number of public figures attempted to claim the "hero" role in the tragedy. Immediately following the shooting, the press placed special emphasis on the police manhunt and the "heroic" efforts of individual police officers who "worked around the clock" in their efforts to identify and apprehend the suspects (Mascoll 1994b; Conroy 1994; Stewart 1994b, 1994c; Stewart and Hann 1994; Tyler 1994). The chief of police used the opportunity to argue for increased police funding so that the police force would be in a better position to fight the scourge of violent crime in the future (Gangley 1994; Lamberti 1994). Politicians and citizen groups also stepped forward to call for tougher sentences for violent offenders (McCarty 1994; Edwards 1994), stricter gun control legislation (Moon 1994; Durkan 1994; Harder and Fife 1994; Coutts 1994; Lem 1994b; Brent 1994), and a return to the death penalty (*Toronto Sun* 1994; Luyk 1994). Finally, the Canadian minister of immigration responded to the race-crime-immigration debate with promises to "get tough" on criminals and to "plug immigration loopholes" (Thompson 1994; Sarick 1994; Campion-Smith 1994). These responses served to assure the public that the authorities were treating the Just Desserts incident seriously and that they would soon be taking action to decrease the risk of violent victimization.

Most of the news coverage of the Just Desserts shooting portrayed the event as both a major tragedy and a national threat. The white victim came to symbolize Toronto's innocence, while the Black West Indian suspects came to represent a foreign, outside threat to Canadian principles of law and order. Nonetheless, this dominant theme was not the only narrative to emerge. A competing narrative held that the media and the police were blaming all Black people for the actions of a few and that the negative portrayal of the Black community would eventually be used to justify further discrimination (DiManno 1994a, 1994b; Robertson 1994; Moodie 1994; Desir 1994; Armstrong 1994). This narrative did not receive front-page coverage until more than five weeks after the shooting (Campbell 1994). The second narrative was also tempered because several minority observers had already gone on record to argue that the Black community should take some of the responsibility for the causes of and solutions to Black crime (Maharaj 1994; Foster 1994a, 1994b).

> Most of the reporting of the Just Desserts shooting suggested a major tragedy. The white victim symbolized Toronto's innocence, while the Black West Indian suspects represented a foreign threat to Canadian principles of law and order.

Media coverage of this shooting created a crisis around issues of immigration and crime that eventually divided the Toronto community along racial lines (Henry and Bjornson 1999). However, as our second case reveals, not all interracial crimes receive such extensive media coverage or are elevated to the level of "moral panic."

The Christine Ricketts Murder

At 3:40 a.m. on March 6, 1998, the body of Christine Ricketts, a young African Canadian woman, was found in the stairwell of a high-rise apartment building in suburban Toronto. She had been sexually assaulted and strangled to death. Ricketts, a thirty-one-year-old single mother of two young daughters, had been working in the building as a canvasser for the *Toronto Star*. On March 16, both the *Star* and the *Sun* reported that the police had arrested Adrian Clive Paul, a white man, charging him for the Ricketts murder. The papers later reported that Paul had recently been released from prison on early parole after serving only part of a sentence for a previous sexual assault conviction. He was living with his mother in the apartment building in which Ricketts had been working.

In many important ways, the Just Desserts killing and the Ricketts murder are similar. Both cases involve young female victims and male offenders. Both murders are "stranger" crimes: the victims did not know their assailants before the crimes took place. Both murders took place in public spaces: Leimonis was killed while patronizing a café, and Ricketts was killed while performing her job as a door-to-door canvasser. Both cases involved an intensive police investigation: the offenders in both cases were not apprehended until more than a week after the murder. Both cases are interracial crimes. Finally, in both cases, loved ones were left behind to mourn and go on with their lives. Vivi Leimonis left behind her family and fiancé, while Christine Ricketts left behind her family and two young children. At least on the surface, both cases appear equally tragic and deserving of something close to an equal amount of press coverage.

In the saturation coverage of the Just Desserts shooting, the *Star* and the *Sun* ran a total of seventy-six stories and editorials directly related to the case in the two weeks following the murder. In contrast, the papers published only seventeen stories — and not a single editorial — on the Ricketts murder. With respect to sheer volume, then, the Just Desserts case received four times more coverage than the Ricketts case. Furthermore, while the Leimonis murder made the front page on seventeen separate occasions over the fourteen-day period following the crime (nine times for the *Sun* and eight times for the *Star*), the Ricketts case made the front page on only two occasions (once for the *Star* and once for the *Sun*). Moreover, on several occasions, the Just Desserts killing was the lead story for both papers and came with large headlines and photographs dominating the front page. On the two occasions that the Ricketts murder did make the front page, it was only a secondary story with a small headline and no photographs.

Clearly, the two Toronto papers saw the Ricketts murder as being far less important than the Just Desserts shooting. When the Leimonis murder was first reported it was the lead story, making the front pages of both the *Star* and the *Sun*. The Ricketts murder was first reported in the *Sun* on page 4 (Christopoulos 1998). The *Sun* reserved its front page that day (March 6) for a big story about a young (white) heart transplant patient and two smaller stories about the debut of a professional hockey player (also white) and a Black male who had, a day earlier, publicly apologized for paralyzing an innocent bystander during a shooting incident. Although the Ricketts murder did make the front page of the *Star*, coverage consisted only of a small (quarter-inch) headline and an extremely brief (single-column, nine-line) story. Of the five stories appearing on the front page of the *Star* on March 6, the Ricketts murder was by far the smallest and least prominent. The full story of the crime did not appear until the second section of the paper. This coverage, nonetheless, was extensive and included photos of the victim, the apartment, and the stairwell where the body was found (Rankin and Ebden 1998: B1).

> Clearly, the two Toronto papers saw the Ricketts murder as being far less important than the Just Desserts shooting.

Significantly, on the day of the Ricketts murder both the *Star* and the *Sun* gave much more prominent coverage to the story of Tyrone Edwards, the Black male who had accidentally shot an innocent bystander, leaving her paralyzed (Drummie 1998; Vincent 1998), and had recently been acquitted in the "gang related" shooting death of another Black male named Elrick Christian. The shooting had taken place two years earlier during the popular West Indian street festival, Caribana. For example, in the *Sun* the Caribana shooting was reported on the same page (4) as the Ricketts murder. However, the Edwards case takes up the top 75 percent of the page, while the Ricketts murder is allocated to the bottom 25 percent. The headline and photos accompanying the Edwards case are much larger. The *Star* reported the full story of the Caribana shooting on the front page, with a large headline and photos of both Edwards and Cecily Malcolm, the woman paralyzed in the shooting. The front-page coverage of this story is about ten times greater than the front-page coverage given the Ricketts murder. Much of the March 6, 1998, coverage focused on how Edwards had been subject to a "reign of terror" by Jamaican posse (gang) members and had fired a gun in self-defence during the Caribana "showdown" (Drummie 1998: 4). In both the *Star* and *Sun* reports, Edwards apologized for his part in the shooting and lamented about the problems of violence and gangs in the Black community (Drummie 1998: 4; Vincent 1998: 1). Thus, even on the day that a young Black woman was found brutally murdered, the press gave more attention to a previous case — about two years old — that more clearly highlighted the association between Black males, West Indian social events, and violence.

The coverage of the funerals also reveals the relative importance of the two murder victims in the eyes of newspaper decision-makers. The Leimonis funeral (April 12, 1994) dominated front-page headlines for both the *Star* and the *Sun*. The *Sun's* front page, for example, featured a huge headline that screamed "How Can They Live with What They Have Done?" and a dramatic photograph of the victim's father grieving over an open casket. Juxtaposed to this funeral photograph was a mug shot of a sullen, dreadlocked Lawrence Brown, the Black suspect wanted for the shooting. The funeral headlines also conveyed to the public that the Leimonis murder should be seen as a community tragedy that touched the lives of all Torontonians: "Loving Memory: Community Offers Bouquets of Tears for Young Woman" (Lem 1994a). By contrast, the Ricketts funeral (March 15, 1998) did not receive front-page coverage, but was relegated to small stories on page 4 of both papers. These stories came with rather unremarkable headlines that suggested that Ricketts' death was a loss for the family rather than a community tragedy: "Murder Victim's Family Bids Goodbye" (Mascoll 1998) and "I Hope You Like It in Heaven" (Granatstein 1998a).

News coverage of the Just Desserts shooting and the Ricketts murder also varied dramatically on the day that the police apprehended the offenders. The arrest of the Just Desserts suspects had dominated the front pages of both the *Star* and the *Sun* (and included large photos of the Black suspect and the white victim). The arrest of Ricketts's murderer appeared in the *Sun* only on page 8 (Kingstone 1998). Significantly, on that day, March 16, 1998, the *Sun's* front page showed a worried-looking cab driver, the victim of an armed robbery, with the huge headline "Cabby's Ride of Terror." On page 5, where the full story of the robbery appears, the suspects are described as males, "two Black and one white" (Magnish 1998: 5). A related headline on the same page proclaims, "Taxi Drivers Live in Constant Fear" (Granatstein 1998b: 5). The *Sun's* editors apparently decided that the robbery of a cab driver by two Black suspects was far more important or newsworthy than the arrest of a white man, following a police manhunt, for the brutal murder of a Black female. The *Toronto Star's* coverage of the arrest of Ricketts' killer was just as subdued, even though Christine Ricketts was a *Star* employee. The paper did not report on the arrest until its second section that day (Brown 1998: B1). It reserved its front page for stories about the Canadian curling championship, allegations of sexual harassment against U.S. President Bill Clinton, violence in Rwanda, and Quebec politics.

> The news narratives differed dramatically; the Ricketts stories contained little moralistic discourse or fear-mongering; the Just Desserts headlines cried out with a sense of shock and fear.

Besides big differences in the amount and priority of news coverage, the news narratives also differed dramatically. The media portrayed the Just Desserts shooting as a major social crisis, attributing much of a supposed increase in urban crime to the activities of Black immigrants who frequently preyed on white Canadian-born citizens. In contrast, the narratives surrounding the Ricketts case contained little moralistic discourse or fear-mongering. The Just Desserts headlines cried out with a sense of shock and fear: "Urban Terrorism," "In Cold Blood," "The Lowest of the Low," "Good vs. Evil," "No Mercy: Crooks Getting More Vicious," "Horror of a Bloody Night," "Gun City: Just How Cheap Has Life Become?" and "Armed and Dangerous." The Ricketts murder headlines were more factual, morally neutral, and unsensational: "Young Mother Slain," "Door-to-Door Sales Rep Slain in Highrise," and "Man Charged in Slaying of Canvasser." Even after an arrest was made, the narratives remained seemingly objective and devoid of moral overtones:

> A man has been charged in the slaying of Christine Ricketts, whose strangled body was found in an apartment stairwell. Toronto police made the arrest around 7:45 pm yesterday, said Toronto police sergeant Mike Boothby. Ricketts, a contract employee for the Star, was last seen about 4:45 pm March 4 in the lobby of 5 Brookbanks Dr. near York Mills Road and the Don Valley Parkway. She was selling Star subscriptions when she vanished. Her body was found at 3:40 am the next day in a fifth floor stairwell of the building. An autopsy revealed that the mother of two had died of asphyxiation. Adrian Clive Paul, 33, of Dovercourt Crt. in North York is charged with first degree murder. He will appear at the Metro North Courts at 10 am today. (Brown 1998: B1)

Such coverage was typical for this case. Thus, while newspaper columnists, the police, and politicians all had something to say about the causes and consequences of the Just Desserts shooting, the "expert opinion" was silent when it came to the Ricketts murder.

There was not a single editorial designed to express the collective outrage of the Toronto community, there were no stories questioning the humanity of the white suspect, there were no calls for tougher criminal sentencing (even though the man arrested for the murder was on parole for another crime at the time of the murder), and there were no blatant calls for increased police budgets. Most importantly, there was no mention of the interracial nature of the crime. The coverage did not mention that Ricketts was Black and the offender white (that information could only be derived from news photographs). Thus, compared to the Just Desserts case, the Ricketts murder, although tragic, was depicted as an isolated incident that was not related to wider social problems or crime trends. Furthermore, while Black West Indian culture was depicted as being at least partially responsible for the shooting of Vivi Leimonis, the white offender in the Ricketts case was viewed as an individual offender and not at all representative of his racial group.[7]

The newspaper coverage of homicide victims does not always, of course, match the patterns established by these details of the Leimonis and Ricketts murders.[8] Some white murder victims have received much less coverage than that given to Leimonis, and some Black victims have undoubtedly received more coverage than did Ricketts. Still, the great disparity in media coverage given these two murders does seem to fit a general pattern. Indeed, numerous U.S. examples illustrate the same type of racially biased coverage (Rome 1998: 90). Furthermore, this analysis of newspaper crime reporting leaves several disturbing questions: 1) why did the Leimonis murder receive so much more coverage than the Ricketts murder? 2) why did the Just Desserts shooting result in a moral panic, while the Ricketts case produced little concern among politicians, the police, and the general public? and 3) would the newspaper coverage of the Ricketts murder have been more extensive, and the public outcry greater, if the victim had been a white, hardworking, mother of two — and the killer a Black male, with a previous record for sexual assault, who had recently been released from prison on parole?

> Would the coverage of the Ricketts murder have been more extensive if the victim had been a white mother of two and the killer a Black male recently released from prison on parole?

Explaining Media Crime Coverage

Several findings concerning how the Canadian media depict people of Black West Indian descent require explanation. First of all, Black people actually appear to be slightly overrepresented in total news coverage, but compared to whites, Blacks are depicted in a narrow range of story types. Indeed, about 90 percent of the stories involving Black subjects fall into sports, crime, or entertainment categories. Furthermore, almost half of the "serious" news stories (all stories excluding sports and entertainment) involving Blacks are related to criminal activity. Blacks are also much more likely to be associated with certain types of crimes (such as robbery and street crime) than are their counterparts from other racial groups. Compared to whites, Blacks are more likely to be depicted as criminal offenders than as crime victims. In addition, racial minority crime victims tend to receive significantly less news coverage than white victims do. Finally, while news narratives commonly attribute white crime to individual pathology, Black crime is frequently attributed to racially specific cultural influences.

How can we account for the manner in which people of Black Caribbean descent are portrayed by Toronto newspapers? There are at least three possible explanations: 1) the "news as reality" perspective; 2) the "news as business" perspective; and 3) the conflict perspective.

The "news as reality" perspective holds that media organizations simply report or communicate the "truth" to their consumers. According to this position, if Blacks are underrepresented or overrepresented in certain types of news stories, this representation simply reflects social reality. This explanation may have some legitimacy. For instance, Black people are dramatically overrepresented in sports stories and dramatically under-represented with respect to politics. In reality, a large proportion of the athletes on Toronto's professional baseball and football teams (two sports that received a great deal of coverage during the study period) are Black. Thus, Blacks may be overrepresented in sports stories because, in reality, they represent a high proportion of high-profile athletes. By contrast, most political stories depict white people. This racial disparity, however, probably reflects the fact that very few major political figures in Canada are Black. Indeed, the majority of political stories during the study period dealt with four specific figures: Toronto's mayor (Mel Lastman); the premier of Ontario (Mike Harris); the prime minister (Jean Chrétien); and the president of the United States (Bill Clinton). All are white males. Thus, it could be argued that with respect to both sports and politics, racial disparities in news coverage only mirror racial disparities in the wider society. Can the same be said about crime news?

Do the print media's stories reflect the true nature of criminal offences in the Toronto area? Do Black people, as news coverage suggests, actually represent 22 percent of all criminal offenders in Toronto, 39 percent of those who engage in robbery, and 49 percent of those people who engage in common street crime? Conversely, are the media — or the police, who provide the media with information about crime (Rome and Chermak 1994) — more likely to select or focus on offences that involve Black offenders? Since Canada does not collect or release official statistics on the race or ethnicity of criminal offenders (Wortley 1999), it is impossible to determine whether or not the media provide a reasonably accurate picture of the relationship between race and crime.[9] Black people, however, are overrepresented in the types of crimes that are more likely to involve both media and police discretion. For example, according to police statistics, only 76 homicides occurred in Toronto during 1998. In contrast, there were 5,669 recorded robberies (Tremblay 1999). While most if not all murders committed in Toronto receive at least some media coverage, only a fraction of robberies make the daily news.

The "news as reality" perspective simply cannot adequately explain why only a small percentage of all crimes makes the news. It also cannot explain why certain types of crime (homicide) receive extensive coverage while other types of crime (white-collar crime, corporate crime) receive relatively little media attention. Furthermore, the "reality" explanation cannot account for how crimes involving white victims tend to receive considerably more attention than crimes involving Black or other racial minority victims. How can this perspective, for example, account for the extensive coverage of the Just Desserts shooting compared to the Ricketts murder? Is there an objective criteria that would determine that the Leimonis killing was at least four times more tragic than the Ricketts case? A news editor at a public forum once commented that the Just Desserts case received more coverage than the Ricketts case because it was so uncommon. He argued that while robbery-homicides are extremely rare, sexual assault killings "happen almost every day." An analysis of official crime statistics, however, reveals that "stranger" sexual assault killings are actually more uncommon than murders that take place during robberies. Clearly, the selection of crime news and the narratives that accompany crime stories involve a much more complicated process of subjective decision-making by both reporters and editors.

News organizations, like any other business, are motivated by profit (Altheide 1997; Ericson, Baranek, and Chan 1991). Newspaper editors are interested in covering stories that they believe will increase circulation and thus increase both sales and advertising revenue. This may explain why almost half of all the news stories in my study fall into the sports, entertainment, and crime categories. These types of stories may dominate total news coverage because they are popular with readers and thus sell newspapers.[10] This economic argument may also explain why crime coverage often focuses on violent crime rather than white-collar offences. Market research may reveal that the coverage of crimes such as homicide, armed or violent robbery, and drug-dealing sells more papers than does the coverage of corporate criminality and corruption. The "news as business" perspective may also partially explain why crimes involving white victims generally receive more coverage than do crimes involving racial minority victims. If the majority of newspaper readers are white, and white readers respond more strongly to stories about white victimization, newspapers may highlight crime stories that involve white victims in order to increase circulation. In fact, this appears to be how the *Toronto Sun* explained their extensive coverage of the Just Desserts case. In response to charges that their coverage of the Leimonis murder was racially biased, the *Sun* editors argues:

> We did not give blanket coverage to this story because the alleged assailant was Black... This crime struck at the heart of Metro not for reasons of race, but of class, and the simple economic reality that most of our readers (as is the case with all of our competitors) are middle class. When a crime is committed which underscores that anyone can be shot and killed while they sit at a table eating dessert in a nice little restaurant in a quiet part of town, that, for the Sun, is news. (*Toronto Sun* 1994: 10)

Although the *Sun* editors cite the element of class rather than race, they basically admit that in their coverage of the Just Desserts case they were only responding to the needs and concerns of their "middle-class" (primarily white) audience. By default, they are also admitting that crimes against lower-class people (and racial minorities), who do not represent the majority of their readership, are of less concern. Crimes against racial minorities, as in the Ricketts murder, just don't have the same marketability as crimes against white, middle-class people, and thus they receive significantly less coverage.

The economic motivation of news organizations cannot be discounted when we seek an explanation for how the news media depict different racial groups. However, the "conflict" perspective holds that we must also consider the possibility that powerful social groups, who often have direct access to the media, control and shape the information disseminated to the public (Quinney 1970; Randall 1987; Van Dijk 1993). As Jean Van Dijk (1991:124) states:

> The news media do not passively describe or record news events in the world, but actively (re)construct them, mostly on the basis of many types of source discourses. Corporate interests, news values, institutional routines, professional ideologies and news schema formats play an important role in this transformation. These factors favour preferential access of powerful persons, institutions and nations to the media, more stories about these powerful elites, special fo-

cus on negative, conflictual or dramatic events and generally a white, Western, male and middle class perspective on news events... These properties of news processing tend to lead to a reproduction and legitimation of the ideology of political, socio-economic and cultural elites.

Law enforcement is one powerful interest group that has a particularly strong impact on the reporting of crime news (Sacco 2000; Rome and Chermak 1994; Chermak 1994; Ericson 1991; Ericson, Baranek, and Chan 1989). The police are a primary news filter and thus have the power to decide what crimes and crime details will be presented to the media. The police also provide "expert opinion" about crime to the media and thus increase the legitimacy or credibility of crime reporting.

The police are by no means an unbiased source of crime information. They have a strong interest in crime and criminal justice stories that will promote their own interests, improve their image, and increase public support. The police understandably appreciate stories that portray the members of their profession in a positive light: as courageous crime fighters or the protectors of society. Conversely, police organizations tend to downplay or dismiss stories that depict police incompetence and/or corruption. These tendencies might partially explain the differences in the coverage of the two cases I studied. While the police openly expressed their disgust and concern regarding the Just Desserts murder and provided the media with daily updates about how the case was proceeding, they were "usually tight-lipped" (as the press put it) when it came to releasing details about the Ricketts murder (Kingstone 1998: 5). One possible reason for the police caution regarding the Ricketts case was a breakdown in police surveillance during the investigation. During this lapse, another racial minority woman was strangled to death and the man eventually arrested for the Ricketts murder became the prime suspect in that case as well (Blatchford 1998: 7). The police may have wanted to downplay the Ricketts case because some of the details would not have made them "look good."

Can police interests help explain the depiction of race and crime in the media? Some scholars suggest that the depiction of Black crime, particularly when it involves the victimization of whites, increases both white fear of crime and support for the police (see Mann and Zatz 1998). Indeed, one study of over one hundred U.S. cities found that increases in the Black population, accompanied with media coverage of minority crime, are much stronger predictors of police budget increases than are both the official crime rate and overall population growth (Jackson 1989). Others suggest that media depictions of drug use and trafficking in racial minority neighbourhoods were used to justify the War on Drugs — a policy that greatly increased law enforcement budgets and police powers (Banks 1997; Tonry 1995). The police may well use cases like the Just Desserts shooting as a platform to create moral panic over crime and as an opportunity to call for greater police resources (Fishman 1998).

Politicians, particularly conservative politicians, have also played into media depictions of minority crime to further their electoral ambitions and gain support for policy initiatives. Much has been written about how Republican presidential candidate George Bush, for example, used a crime spree by an African American parolee (Willie Horton) to paint his Democratic counterpart (Michael Dukakis) as "soft on crime." By associating Dukakis with rampant Black criminality, Bush was able to overcome an early deficit in the polls and defeat the Democrats in

> Police may well use cases like the Just Desserts shooting as a platform to create moral panic over crime and as an opportunity to call for greater police resources.

the 1988 election (Culverson 1998). Other studies have suggested that Ronald Reagan used images of Black criminality, welfare fraud, and "reverse discrimination" (caused by affirmative action programs) to garner support for his neo-liberal economic and social policies (Barlow 1998).

In Canada, analysis suggests that the Ontario Conservative Party incorporated images of immigrant crime and welfare abuse in its 1994 election campaign. Combined with a sustained media attack on employment equity programs, the Conservatives were able to gain the support of the non-urban, largely white electorate and easily defeat the ruling social-democratic party.[11] Others have argued that the extensive media coverage of the Just Desserts shooting and the murder of Todd Baylis (a police officer killed in the line of duty by a Black Jamaican immigrant) galvanized support for regressive changes to Canada's immigration and deportation laws (Henry and Tator 2000).[12]

News organizations themselves may also have a vested interest in promoting a particular view of the social world. First of all, the people who control major media corporations, as part of society's ruling economic elite, are interested in producing news and news discourses that support the status quo and thereby contribute to the reproduction of wealth. In other words, the media have a specific interest in covering the news in a manner that will maintain current power relations and prevent or impede radical structural change.[13] In the case of depictions of race and crime, this interest leads to a focus on common street crime, in which disadvantaged people are more likely to be involved, and from there to the overrepresentation of racial minorities; and it means rarely focusing on the criminality of white elites, including white-collar, corporate, military, and political crime, which causes much more damage to society.[14]

News narratives generally focus on microlevel explanations for crime problems. Thus the news media largely portrays crime as stemming from either individual pathology/immorality or from the cultural dictates of specific subgroups (including racial minorities). By contrast, crime causation is rarely explained in terms of structural conditions such as poverty, inequality, unemployment, alienation, or systemic racism (Welch, Fenwich, and Roberts 1998; Ericson, Baranek, and Chan 1991, 1995). Furthermore, media discussions about how to prevent crime tend to focus almost exclusively on increasing the efficiency and punitiveness of the criminal justice system, rather than on more structural solutions such as job creation and economic reform. As such, the media are more likely to rely on criminal justice sources for "expert" opinion about crime and its solutions than on academics or researchers who frequently provide a critical analysis (Welch, Fenwich, and Roberts 1998).

> Crime causation is rarely explained in terms of structural conditions such as poverty, inequality, unemployment, alienation, or systemic racism.

Finally, a number of scholars note that it is not only the "ruling class" who benefit from media depictions of minority crime and social problems, but also the entire white majority — because the images serve to justify racial inequality and white privilege. As Laura Fishman (1998: 119) notes: "Although images of Black criminality evoke fear ... these constructed monsters also reassure whites of their self-worth and superior moral standing.... In turn, the more self-righteous whites become, the easier it is for them to justify the domination and exploitation of Blacks." Adeno Addis (1993: 526) reiterates this argument:

> The picture portrayed of African Americans by the media is one that enables the majority to hold a largely virtuous picture of itself and its institutions. The

invention of the African American as the problem allows the majority simultaneously to acknowledge the predicament of African Americans and to absolve itself and its institutions from responsibility for that state of affairs.

Thus, in Canada, as in the United States, negative media images of Blacks, Aboriginals, and other racial minorities can become a means of justifying the continued exclusion of these groups from various social, economic and political arenas.

All of this is to show that explaining the nature of news coverage is a complex task. Debate continues to rage between news organizations and media critics over the factors that truly shape the coverage of crime and the stories involving racial minorities. However, in addition to outlining the boundaries of this debate, I must also consider the *implications* of the mainstream media's depictions of Blacks and other racial minorities. The media play a vital role in constructing social reality — particularly with respect to phenomena that most of us do not ordinarily encounter in day-to-day life. As with crime, most people, from whatever social or ethnic group, rely on the media for their information about minority groups. But given that the mainstream news media tend to depict Blacks in a narrow range of social roles — as athletes, entertainers, and criminal offenders — and this is the only type of information that whites receive about Blacks, the news media will thus have a strong impact on the formation and maintenance of racial stereotypes. Media coverage could account for the fact that about two-thirds of Toronto residents believe that there is a relationship between a Black West Indian racial background and criminal activity (Henry, Hastings, and Freer 1996). Such stereotypes, in turn, most likely contribute to racial discrimination in education, employment, housing, treatment by the criminal justice system, and all other areas of social existence.

> Media coverage could account for two-thirds of Toronto residents believing in a relationship between Black West Indian racial background and criminal activity. Such stereotypes contribute to racial discrimination in all areas of social existence.

In addition, media coverage of minorities also has an impact on the minority community itself. Many critics have argued that mainstream images of racial minorities can have a negative effect on how minorities view their worth as human beings. For example, in an important series of studies, Kenneth Clark discovered that by the age of seven, many Black children have internalized the media's view of Black people as being less intelligent, less moral, and less physically attractive than whites (Clark 1964; see also Goodstein 1997).

At the same time, many minority people clearly do resist and reject these negative images of themselves (Grier and Cobb 1980; Wilson 1994; Dyson 1996). For many of these people, negative media coverage of racial minorities only reinforces the belief that racism is a major problem in modern society and confirms that they do not participate fully in our social institutions (Wortley, Macmillan, and Hagan 1997). This disillusionment is strengthened because most Black people do not "see themselves" in the mainstream press. They do not see or read about the majority of the Black population who work hard at "normal" occupations or struggle with the burden of poverty without breaking the law. They see only images of Black professional athletes, entertainers, or criminals — the types of people who play little or no part in their daily lives. The isolating effect of such media coverage, and the alienation it causes, are nicely captured by Patricia Raybon (1989: 11), an African American journalist, when she states:

This is who I am not. I am not a crack addict. I am not a welfare mother. I am not illiterate. I am not a prostitute. I have never been in jail. My children are not in gangs. My husband does not beat me. My home is not a tenement. None of these things defines who I am, nor do they describe the other Black people I've known and worked with and loved and friended over these 40 years of my life. Nor does it describe most of Black America, period. Yet in the eyes of the American news media, this is what Black America is: poor, criminal, addicted and dysfunctional.

Indeed, as my research into the Just Desserts and Ricketts cases, along with previous research, strongly suggests, the North American press often distorts the image of West Indian Blacks and other racial minorities. Furthermore, negative media depictions have a profound impact on the formation of racial stereotypes among the white majority and on how racial minorities see both themselves and the social world around them. How can this situation be changed? How can we ensure that the news media provide a more balanced, realistic portrayal of minority communities? Those adhering to the conflict perspective maintain that, as long as the mainstream press is controlled by the ruling elite, negative coverage of powerless groups is not likely to change. More optimistic critics maintain that the coverage of racial minority groups will only change once the workforce of major news organizations becomes more racially diverse. The hiring of minority reporters and editors, they argue, should lead to a more balanced depiction of racial minority groups (Addis 1993; Johnson 1991). Others maintain that intense racial diversity training is needed for all people working in the news media. The argument is that all reporters and editors need to become more sensitive to the potential impact of their reporting on race relations (Rome and Chermak 1994; Ehrlich 1988). For my part, I believe that the academic community could play a valuable role in such diversity training by continuing to do research on the portrayal of minority groups by the media, and by revealing the impact of such depictions on racial attitudes and beliefs. Research can be used to highlight the importance of portraying racial minorities in all walks of life, not only with respect to crime, poverty, and social deprivation. As one news editor laments, the need for a more balanced media portrayal of minorities is great:

> Negative media depictions have a profound impact on the formation of racial stereotypes among the white majority and on how racial minorities see both themselves and the social world around them.

> Every time we say that the vicious acts of some ghetto criminal were only to be expected and extenuate them by suggesting that they are probably the norm in that put-upon world, we are doing a disservice to the very people we should be most trying to help and whom we have the greatest reason to admire. The real stories of guts and virtue are the stories of those millions of people trapped in the poverty swamp who are resisting the temptations all around them and who are struggling mightily and honourably to do right and do well with little available to them.... I think our reflexive habit of projecting the crimes and defaults of the few onto the many, of universalizing and even, in some cases, romanticizing the worst elements of ghetto pathology is self-indulgent, cruel and, yes, racist. (Greenfield 1989: 86)

DISCUSSION QUESTIONS

1.   What interest groups might benefit from the negative portrayal of Blacks and other minorities in the Canadian news media?

2.   What is a moral panic? How do the news media contribute to the creation of moral panics?

3.   How does negative media coverage have an impact on Black people and other racial minority groups?

4.   What changes could lead to a more balanced or accurate portrayal of racial minorities in the media?

5.   Why does crime make up such a large proportion of total news coverage? Why do the news media focus on violence and street crimes rather than white-collar offences?

GLOSSARY OF TERMS

Moral Panic: strong, widespread fear — the level of which is out of proportion to the threat that exists — among the public that evil is occurring, that certain enemies of society are trying to harm some or all of us.

News Narratives: the "stories" told to the public through various media sources. These "stories" usually consist of plots that have beginnings and endings and easily identified central characters.

News as Reality Perspective: holds that media organizations simply report or communicate the "truth" to their consumers.

News as Business Perspective: the idea that because news organizations, like any other business, are motivated by profit, newspaper editors are primarily interested in covering stories that they believe will increase both sales and advertising revenue.

News as Conflict Perspective: holds that we must consider the possibility that powerful social groups, who often have direct access to the media, control and shape the information that is disseminated to the public.

SUGGESTED READINGS

Addis, Adeno. 1993. "Hell Man, They Did Invent Us: The Mass Media, Law and African Americans." *Buffalo Law Review* 41: 523–625.

Baer, Justin, and William Chambliss. 1997. "Generating Fear: The Politics of Crime Reporting." *Crime, Law and Social Change* 27: 87–107.

Barlow, Melissa. 1998. "Race and the Problem of Crime in *Time* and *Newsweek* Cover Stories." *Social Justice* 25: 149–83.

Chermak, Steven. 1994. "Body Count News: How Crime Is Presented in the News Media." *Justice Quarterly* 11: 561–82.

Ericson, Richard, Patricia Baranek, and Janet Chan. 1991. *Representing Order: Crime, Law and Justice in the News Media*. Toronto: University of Toronto Press.

Henry, Frances, and Carol Tator. 2000. *Racist Discourse in Canada's English Print Media*. Toronto: Canadian Race Relations Foundation.

Welch, Michael, Melissa Fenwich and Meredith Roberts. 1998. "State Managers, Intellectuals and the Media: A Content Analysis of Ideology in Experts' Quotes in Feature Newspaper Articles on Crime." *Justice Quarterly* 15: 219–41.

NOTES

The research presented in this paper was supported by a research grant from the School of Graduate Studies, University of Toronto. I would like to thank both Erin Pancer and Winnie Finklestein for their devoted research assistance on this project.

1. I decided not to collect information on the *Globe and Mail* for three reasons: the paper markets itself as a national newspaper, not a local daily; it has a much smaller circulation (only about three hundred thousand daily readers in the Toronto area) and, perhaps most importantly, I simply did not have the research funds needed for the inclusion of a third news source. The *National Post* was not in circulation during the study period.

2. Aboriginals, South Asians, Latinos and people of Middle-Eastern descent seldom appeared in the Toronto media coverage during the study period (less than forty cases for each group). I thus collapsed these groups into the "other" category in order to simplify the analysis.

3. The stories in this final category usually involved traffic-related fatalities or serious injuries that resulted in criminal charges.

4. In 1998 the Toronto police reported 268,282 Criminal Code violations (excluding traffic offences). Out of this more than a quarter-million documented criminal events, only seventy-six could be classified as homicide (Tremblay 1999).

5. The argument is that such descriptions serve to warn the public and help the police make arrests. However, many argue that such descriptions are far too vague to serve any real criminal justice purpose. Indeed, the description of a Black teen "5-foot-8 with short black hair" could realistically apply to a large proportion of the innocent Black youth living in the Toronto region. Such descriptions do, however, communicate to the public that a Black person has committed a violent crime.

6. Many other factors besides the race of the victim can account for the extent of coverage given a particular crime story: for example, the type of crime, nature of the offender-victim relationship, and the age and gender of the victim. Furthermore, the existence of other big news stories on any given day can reduce the amount of coverage given specific criminal events. I plan to explore these relationships in future analyses.

7. These findings are consistent with other media analysis holding that Black culture is often depicted as being responsible for Black crime, while white crime is seen as resulting from individual pathology (Rome 1998; Oliver 1998).

8. I do not want to suggest that Black victims never receive priority coverage in Toronto newspapers. Indeed, in several recent murder cases Black victims did receive extensive front-page exposure. For example, the murders of the Ottey sisters (two middle-class, African Canadian teenagers found stabbed to death in their suburban home) dominated headlines for several days. However, such highly-publicized murders are almost always those committed by Black male offenders, thus perpetuating the stereotype of the violent Black male.

9. Official crime statistics are highly suspect because they reflect only crimes that are known to or reported to the police. For that reason official crime statistics do not necessarily provide an accurate depiction of the relationship between race and crime (for a critique of race-crime statistics, see Wortley 1999). However, as it stands, we cannot even compare media depictions of race and crime with official statistics in order to determine if the media images are at least in line with official numbers.

10. It may also explain why newspapers like the *Globe and Mail*, which focus more on politics and business, have a much smaller circulation than papers like the *Sun* and the *Star*, which focus more on crime, sports, and entertainment.

11. A major message of the "Common Sense Revolution" campaign seemed to be that immigrants cause problems. First of all, their criminal activity threatens the safety of "good" Canadians.

Second, their abuse of the welfare system increases taxes and takes money out of the pockets of hardworking people. Finally, despite their supposed criminality and welfare abuses, employment equity threatened to help such immigrants take employment away from more deserving (white) Ontario residents.

12. A recent study by Valentino (1999) underscores the potential role of racialized images of crime in the political arena. During an experiment, subjects were asked to read various news stories and then provide an evaluation of U.S. President Bill Clinton. As predicted, President Clinton's support suffered when subjects were exposed to stories about violent crime. However, his support was lowest among those respondents who were exposed to crime stories that involved racial minority suspects.

13. At the microlevel it could be argued that the newspapers had an interest in downplaying the murder of Christine Ricketts because she was a newspaper canvasser who was murdered while doing her job. In other words, the industry did not want to produce fear among other canvassers or dissuade people from seeking this type of employment.

14. For example, in the United States, estimates place the cost of street crime at about $4 billion per year, while the damage caused by white-collar offences approaches $200 billion per year (Albrecht, Wernz, and Williams 1995; Mokhiber and Wheat 1995).

REFERENCES

Addis, Adeno. 1993. "Hell Man, They Did Invent Us: The Mass Media, Law and African Americans." *Buffalo Law Review* 41: 523–625.

Albrecht, Steve, G.W. Wernz, and T.L. Williams. 1995. *Fraud: Bringing Light to the Dark Side of Business*. Burr Ridge, IL: Irwin.

Alexander, Jeffrey, and Philip Smith. 1993. "The Discourse of American Civil Society: A New Proposal for Cultural Studies." *Theory and Society* 22: 151–207.

Altheide, David. 1997. "The News Media, the Problem Frame and the Production of Fear." *Sociological Quarterly* 38: 647–68.

Armstrong, Lin. 1994. "Crime: Let's See the Big Picture." *Toronto Sun* (April 20): 11.

Baer, Justin, and William Chambliss. 1997. "Generating Fear: The Politics of Crime reporting." *Crime, Law and Social Change* 27: 87–107.

Banks, Rae. 1997. "Race, Representation and the Drug Policy Agenda." In Cedric Herring (ed.), *African Americans and the Public Agenda*. California: Sage.

Barber, John. 1994. "The Threat of Violence Hits Home." *Globe and Mail* (April 8): A9.

Barlow, Melissa. 1998. "Race and the Problem of Crime in Time and Newsweek Cover Stories." *Social Justice* 25: 149–83.

Barlow, Melissa, David Barlow, and Stan Stojkovic. 1995. "Economic Conditions and Ideologies of Crime in the Media: A Content Analysis of Crime News." *Crime and Delinquency* 41: 3–19.

Blatchford, Christie. 1994a. "Good Vs. Evil." *Toronto Sun* (April 7): 5
_____.1994b. "Innocence Lost." *Toronto Sun* (April 7): 16.
_____.1994c. "The Day Toronto Changed." *Toronto Sun* (April 8): 5.
_____.1994d. "What Have We Built?" *Toronto Sun* (April 12): 5.
_____. 1998. "Police Blow Surveillance?" *Toronto Sun* (March 18): 7.

Brent, Bob. 1994. "Metro Police Services Board Calls for Tougher Gun Laws." *Toronto Star* (April 8): A6.

Brown, Josh. 1998. "Man Charged in Slaying of Canvasser." *Toronto Star* (March 16): B1.

Brownstein, Henry. 1995. "The Media and the Construction of Random Drug Violence." In Jeff Ferrell and Clinton Sanders (eds.), *Cultural Criminology*. Boston: Northeastern University Press.

Burnett, Thane. 1994a. "Quiet Life Shattered: Murder Victim 'Such a Nice, Happy Girl.'" *Toronto Sun* (April 7): 5.
_____.1994b. "She is Among the Saints." *Toronto Sun* (April 12): 4.

Campbell, Dennis. 1994. "Young, Black and Male." *Toronto Star* (May 15): A1.

Campion-Smith, Bruce. 1994. "Marchi Plans to Get Tough on Criminals." *Toronto Star* (May 1): A1.

Canadian Sentencing Commission. 1987. *Sentencing Reform: A Canadian Approach*. Ottawa: Ministry of Supply and Services Canada.

Chermak, Steven. 1994. "Body Count News: How Crime is Presented in the News Media." *Justice Quarterly* 11: 561–82.

Christopoulos, George. 1994a. "Mom's Tears: Dreams End at Daughter's Funeral." *Toronto Sun* (April 9): 4.

_____. 1994b. "Goodbye: Thousands Moved to Tears at Vivi's Funeral." *Toronto Sun* (April 12): 14.

_____.1998. "Door-to-Door Sales Rep Slain in Highrise." *Toronto Sun* (March 8): 4.

Clark, Kenneth. 1964. *Prejudice and Your Child*. Boston: Beacon.

Conroy, Pat. 1994. "Alert for 3 in Cafe Killing." *Toronto Star* (April 10): A1.

Coutts, Jane. 1994. "Tonks Sidetracked in Anti-Crime Bid: Focus on Councillor's Gun-Amnesty Move Takes Away From Call for Joint Action." *Globe and Mail* (April 19): A10.

Crime Stoppers. 1998. "Nightclub Killers Hunted." *Toronto Sun* (July 6): 26.

Culverson, Donald. 1998. "Stereotyping by Politicians: The Welfare Queen and Willie Horton." In Coramae Richey Mann and Marjorie Zatz (eds.), *Images of Color, Images of Crime*. Los Angeles: Roxbury: 109–26.

Damphousse, Kelly, Steven Chermak, and Jay Gilliam. 1999. "Evaluating the Newsworthiness of African-American Homicide Victims." Paper presented at the Annual Meeting of the American Society of Criminology, Toronto (November).

Darnton, Robert. 1975. "Writing News and Telling Stories." *Daedalus* 104: 175–94.

Deepe-Keever, B., Carolyn Martindale, and Mary Weston. 1997. *U.S. News Coverage of Racial Minorities: A Sourcebook, 1934–1996*. Westport, CT: Greenwood Press.

Desir, Finbar. 1994. "Young Blacks Wear a Stranger's Guilt on Their Faces." *Toronto Star* (April 11): A7.

DiManno, Rosie. 1994a. "Bishop's Polemic on Crime Wrong at ViVi's Funeral." *Toronto Star* (April 12): A6.

_____.1994b. "Police Union Boss Has Right to Make an Ass Out of Himself." *Toronto Star* (April 29): A7.

_____.1994c. "Sharing Guilt 'Appalling,' Blacks Told." *Toronto Star* (April 18): A6.

Drummie, Gretchen. 1998. "Caribana Shooter Grieves." *Toronto Sun* (March 8): 4.

Durkan, Sean. 1994. "Minister Supports Gun Ban." *Toronto Sun* (April 12): 15.

Dyson, M. 1996. *Between God and Gangsta Rap: Bearing Witness to Black Culture*. New York: Oxford University Press.

Edwards, Peter. 1994. "Group Protesting Crime Wants Tougher Prison Terms." *Toronto Star* (April 25): A8.

Ehrlich, H. 1988. "Mixed Media Messages." *Forum* 3: 1–5.

Ericson, Richard. 1991. "Mass Media, Crime, Law and Justice." *British Journal of Sociology* 40: 219–49.

Ericson, Richard, Patricia Baranek and Janet Chan. 1989. *Negotiating Control: A Study of News Sources*. Toronto: University of Toronto Press.

_____.1991. *Representing Order: Crime, Law and Justice in the News Media*. Toronto: University of Toronto Press.

Fishman, Laura. 1998. "The Black Bogeyman and White Self-Righteousness." In Coramae Richey Mann and Marjorie Zatz (eds.), *Images of Color, Images of Crime*. Los Angeles: Roxbury: 109–26.

Fleras, Augie. 1994. "Media and Minorities in a Post-Multicultural Society: Overview and Appraisal." In J. Berry and J. LaPonce (eds.), *Ethnicity and Culture in Canada: The Research Landscape*. Toronto: University of Toronto Press.

Foster, Cecil. 1994a. "Solution Lies in African Canadian Community." *Toronto Star* (April 10): A6.

_____. 1994b. "Black Heroes vs. Black Criminals." *Toronto Star* (April 25): A11.

Gangley, Ciaran. 1994. "200 Protest Violence." *Toronto Sun* (April 10): 11.

Gans, Herbert. 1979. *Deciding What's News*. New York: Pantheon.

Gartner, Rosemary, and Anthony Doob. 1994. "Trends in Criminal Victimization in 1988–1993." *Juristat* 14 (13). Ottawa: Canadian Centre for Justice Statistics.

Ginzberg, Effie. 1995. *Power Without Responsibility: The Press We Don't Deserve*. Toronto: Urban Alliance on Race Relations.

Goodstein, Renee. 1997. "Racial and Ethnic Identity: Their Relationship and Their Contribution to Self-Esteem." *Journal of Black Psychology* 23: 275–92.

Graber, Doris. 1980. *Crime News and the Public*. New York: Praeger.

Granatstein, Rob. 1998a. "I Hope You Like it in Heaven." *Toronto Sun* (March 15): 4.

_____.1998b. "Taxi Drivers Live in Constant Fear." *Toronto Sun* (March 15): 5.

Greenfield, M. 1989. "Other Victims in the Park." *Newsweek* (May 15): 86.

Grier, H., and P. Cobb. 1980. *Black Rage*. New York: Basic Books.

Hall, Joseph, and Henry Stancu. 1994. "Four Sought After Woman Dies in 'Crash' Robbery," *Toronto Star* (April 7): A1.

Harder, Jeff, and Robert Fife. 1994. "United Against Guns." *Toronto Sun* (April 14): 7.

Henry, Frances. 1999. *The Racialization of Crime in Toronto's Print Media: A Research Project*. Toronto: School of Journalism, Ryerson Polytechnic University.

Henry, Frances, P. Hastings, and B. Freer. 1996. "Perceptions of Race and Crime in Ontario: Empirical Evidence from Toronto and the Durham Region." *Canadian Journal of Criminology* 38: 469–77.

Henry, Frances, and Carol Tator. 2000. *Racist Discourse in Canada's English Print Media*. Toronto: Canadian Race Relations Foundation.

Jackson, Pamela. 1989. *Minority Group Threat, Crime and Policing: Social Context and Social Control*. New York: Praeger.

Jacobs, Ronald. 1996. "Civil Society and Crisis: Culture, Discourse, and the Rodney King Beating." *American Journal of Sociology* 101: 1238–72.

Johnson, K. 1990. "Media Images of Boston's Black Community." In W. Reed (ed.), *Racial Stereotyping: The Role of the Media*. Boston: University of Massachusetts Press.

_____.1991. "Objective News and Other Myths: The Poisoning of Young Black Minds." *Journal of Negro Education* 60: 401–30.

Kingstone, Jonathan. 1998. "Man, 33, Charged in Mom's Murder." *Toronto Sun* (March 16): 8.

Knowles, Jeffrey. 1982. *Ohio Citizens' Attitudes Concerning Crime and Criminal Justice*. Third Edition. Columbus: Governor's Office and Criminal Justice Services.

Lamberti, Rob. 1994. "Lowest of the Low: Chief McCormick Blasts New Criminal Attitude." *Toronto Sun* (April 7): 18.

Lem, Sharon. 1994a. "Loving Memory: Community Offers Bouquets of Tears for Slain Woman." *Toronto Sun* (April 18): 18.

_____.1994b. "Gun Laws Targeted." *Toronto Sun* (April 25): 5.

Liska, Allen, and William Baccaglini. 1990. "Feeling Safe by Comparison: Crime in the Newspapers." *Social Problems* 37: 360–74.

Luyk, Joe. 1994. "Bring Back the Death Penalty." *Toronto Star* (April 12): A16.

MacDonald, Bob. 1994. "Turf Out Crooked Aliens." *Toronto Sun* (May 1): 14.

Magnish, Scot. 1998. "Give Bank Card or Die, Cabby Told." *Toronto Sun* (March 16): 5.

Maharaj, Raynier. 1994. "Crime Crosses All Barriers." *Toronto Sun* (April 15): 13.

Mann, Coramae Richey, and Marjorie Zatz. 1998. *Images of Color, Images of Crime*. Los Angeles: Roxbury.

Marsh, H. 1991. "A Comparative Analysis of Crime Coverage in Newspapers in the United States and Other Countries from 1960 to 1989: A Review of the Literature." *Journal of Criminal Justice* 19: 67–79.

Martindale, C. 1990. "Coverage of Black Americans in Four Major Newspapers: 1950–1989." *Newspaper Research Journal* 11: 96–112.

Mascoll, Philip. 1994a. "More Brutality in Crimes, Chief Says." *Toronto Star* (April 7): A6.

_____.1994b. "Cafe Killers Linked to Another Robbery: Wallet and Shell Found as Tips Flood in to Police." *Toronto Star* (April 8): A1.

_____.1998. "Murder Victim's Family Bids Goodbye." *Toronto Star* (March 15): A4.

McCarty, Shawn. 1994. "Rock Promises Tougher Sentences for Young Offenders." *Toronto Star* (April 9): A4.

Mokhiber, Russel, and Andrew Wheat. 1995. "Shameless: 1995's 10 Worst Corporations." *Multinational Monitor* (December): 9–16.

Moodie, Andrew. 1994. "Forget About Colour of Criminals." *Toronto Star* (April 16): B3.

Moon, Peter. 1994. "Clamour Over Legislation Called an Overreaction." *Globe and Mail* (April 12): A5.

Moore, Robert. 1985. "Reflections of Canadians on the Law and the Legal System." In Dale Gibson and Janet Baldwin (eds.), *Law in A Cynical Society: Opinion and Law in the 1980s*. Calgary: Carswell.

Oliver, William. 1998. "Reflections on Black Manhood." In Coramae Richey Mann and Marjorie Zatz (eds.), *Images of Color, Images of Crime*. Los Angeles: Roxbury: 81–85.

Ornstein, Michael. 2000. *Ethno-Racial Inequality in the City of Toronto: An Analysis of the 1996 Census*. Toronto: Centre for Excellence for Research on Immigration and Settlement.

Pritchard, David. 1985. "Race, Homicide and Newspapers." *Journalism Quarterly* 62: 500–507.

Quinney, R. 1970. *The Social Reality of Crime*. Boston: Little, Brown and Company.

Randall, D. 1987. "The Portrayal of Business Malfeasance in the Elite and General Public Media." *Social Science Quarterly* 68: 281–92.

Rankin, Jim, and Theresa Ebden. 1998. "Canvasser Found Slain in Stairwell." *Toronto Star* (March 8): B1.

Raybon, Patricia. 1989. "A Case of Severe Bias." *Newsweek* (October 2): 11.

Reiman, Jeffrey. 2007. *The Rich Get Richer and the Poor Get Prison: Ideology, Class and Criminal Justice*. Boston: Allyn and Bacon.

Roberts, Julian. 1992. "Public Opinion, Crime and Criminal Justice." In Michael Tonry (ed.), *Crime and Justice: A Review of Research* Volume 17. Chicago: University of Chicago Press.

Roberts, Julian, and Michelle Grossman. 1990. "Crime Prevention and Public Opinion." *Canadian Journal of Criminology* 32: 75–90.

Robertson, Ian. 1994. "Remand for Brown: Accused Killer in Court Smirking and Smiling." *Toronto Sun* (April 15): 4.

Rome, Dennis. 1998. "Stereotyping by the Media: Murders, Rapists and Drug Addicts." In Coramae Richey Mann and Marjorie Zatz (eds.), *Images of Color, Images of Crime*. Los Angeles: Roxbury: 85–96.

Rome, Dennis, and Steven Chermak. 1994. "Race in Crime Stories." In James Hendricks and Bryan Byers (eds.), *Multicultural Perspectives in Criminal Justice and Criminology*. Springfield: Charles Thomas.

Romer, D., K. Jamieson, and N. deCoteau. 1998. "The Treatment of Persons of Color in Local Television News: Ethnic Blame Discourse or Realistic Group Conflict." *Communication Research* 25: 286–305.

Roshier, Bob. 1981. "The Selection of Crime News by the Press." In Stanley Cohen and Jock Young (eds.), *The Manufacture of News: Social Problems, Deviance and the Mass Media*. Beverly Hills: Sage.

Sacco, Vincent. 2000. "Media Constructions of Crime." In Robert Silverman, James Teevan, and Vincent Sacco (eds.), *Crime in Canadian Society* Sixth Edition. Toronto: Harcourt-Brace.

Sarick, Lila. 1994. "System Failed Us, Marchi Concludes." *Globe and Mail* (April 28): A1.

Schudson, Michael. 1982. "The Politics of Narrative Form: The Emergence of News Conventions in Print and Television." *Daedalus* III (Fall).

Sheley, Joseph, and Cindy Ashkins. 1984. "Crime, Crime News and Crime Views." In Ray Surette (ed.), *Justice and the Media: Issues and Research*. Springfield: Charles Thomas.

Small, Peter. 1994. "'Please Give Yourself Up' Says Brother of the Victim." *Toronto Star* (April

8): A1.

Smith, Susan. 1984. "Crime in the News." *British Journal of Criminology* 24: 289–95.

Smyth, Julie. 1994. "Search For Shooting Suspect Widens: OPP Given Descriptions, Names as Protesters Call for Action." *Globe and Mail* (April 11): A2.

Sorenson, Susan, Julie Peterson Manz, and Richard Berk. 1998. "News Media Coverage and the Epidemiology of Homicide." *American Journal of Public Health* 88: 1510–14.

Stewart, Mark. 1994a. "No Mercy: Crooks Getting More Vicious." *Toronto Sun* (April 7): 4.

_____. 1994b. "Dragnet: Cops Pull out all Stops to Catch Killers." *Toronto Sun* (April 8): 4.

_____. 1994c. "Cops Sift Tips: Police Optimistic They'll Nail Just Desserts Killers." *Toronto Sun* (April 10): 5.

Stewart, Mark, and Kevin Hann. 1994. "Arrest: Suspect Surrenders in Just Desserts Murder." *Toronto Sun* (April 14): 4.

Thompson, Allan. 1994. "Allowing Suspect to Stay Was Mistake, Marchi says." *Toronto Star* (April 28): A4.

Tonry, Michael. 1995. *Malign Neglect: Race, Crime and Punishment in America*. New York: Oxford University Press.

Toronto Star. 1994a. "Urban Terrorism Blamed in Cafe Killing." (April 7): A1.

_____. 1994b. "In Cold Blood: Has it Come to this in Metro?" (April 7): 1.

_____. 1994c. "Color Classification for Crime Statistics." (April 16): B2.

_____. 1994. "Readers Demand Death Penalty." (April 8): 18.

Tremblay, Silvain. 1999. "Crime Statistics in Canada, 1998." *Juristat* 19 (9). Ottawa: Canadian Centre for Justice Statistics.

Tyler, Tracey. 1994. "Suspects Arrested in ViVi Slaying: Man Sought by Police Surrenders." *Toronto Star* (April 14): A1.

Valentino, Nicholas. 1999. "Crime News and the Priming of Racial Attitudes During Evaluations of the President." *Public Opinion Quarterly* 63: 293–320.

Van Dijk, Teun. 1991. *Racism and the Press*. New York: Routledge.

_____. 1993. *Elite Discourse and Racism*. California: Sage.

Vincent, Donvan. 1998. "Man in Caribana Case Seeks Forgiveness." *Toronto Star* (March 8): A1.

Welch, Michael, Melissa Fenwich and Meredith Roberts. 1998. "State Managers, Intellectuals and the Media: A Content Analysis of Ideology in Experts' Quotes in Feature Newspaper Articles on Crime." *Justice Quarterly* 15: 219–41.

Wilkes, Jim, and Peter Small. 1994. "3,500 Mourn Woman Killed at Cafe." *Toronto Star* (April 12): A6.

Wilson, A. 1994. *Black-on-Black Violence: The Psychodynamics of Black Self-Annihilation in the Service of White Domination*. New York: Afrikon World Infosystems.

Wortley, Scot. 1999. "A Northern Taboo: Research on Race, Crime and Criminal Justice in Canada." *Canadian Journal of Criminology* 41 (2): 261–74.

Wortley, Scot, Ross Macmillan, and John Hagan. 1997. "Just Des(s)erts: The Racial Polarization of Perceptions of Criminal Injustice." *Law and Society Review* 31: 637–76.

Zerbisias, Antonia. 1994. "Let's Not Bury Our City With ViVi." *Toronto Star* (April 8): A21.

6

The Social Construction of "Dangerous" Girls and Women

Karlene Faith and Yasmin Jiwani

KEY FACTS

> Women have been charged with approximately 10 to 15 percent of all violent crimes since the beginning of record-keeping.

> While the media continued to falsely report a rising degree of violence by girls and women, the actual rates of violence, and rates of most other crimes (by both men and women), were on the decline through the 1990s and continue to decline.

> In 2000, about 18 percent of the 357 federally sentenced women incarcerated in Canada were classified as "maximum," and they were disproportionately Aboriginal women.

> Only two women in Canada, Marlene Moore and Lisa Neve, have been designated dangerous offenders. Critics observe that men require much more serious criminal histories, usually involving rape and/or murder, before being designated a dangerous offender.

> A study of sixty televised crime and legal dramas found that fictional stories on crime and homicide focus on individual and psychological episodes in characters lives. There is little effort made to examine social institutions or the nature of the society.

> Canadian newspaper industries are increasingly monopolized by major media corporations: CanWest Global, Shaw Communications, Rogers Media, and Bell Canada own and control a significant portion of Canadian media. CanWest Global, for example, owns twenty-six daily Canadian newspapers (and the corresponding television stations in the same locations) and 50 percent of the *National Post*.

Sources: Reiman 2007; Fabianic 1997; Brownlee 2005.

Most criminalized women do not come from middle-class families. The crimes committed by women tend to be the result of poverty, privation, and past experiences of abuse. When women kill, their victims are most often family members, particularly abusive spouses (Boritch 1997: 219–20), and these women cannot readily be characterized as "violent." Rather, these criminalized women are the "underclass," generally not the stuff of which big news is made.

Instead the news focuses on another class: the "dangerous" woman, a figure who appears regularly on our newspaper pages and television screens. Intensive media attention targets in particular women who commit crimes of fatal violence against strangers. Print and television journalists and traditionalist criminologists are mutually reinforcing in their attention to sensational, anomalous violent offences by girls and women. Indeed, popular and academic theories of girls' and women's "dangerousness" in this regard abound. The general effect is to place disproportionate attention in the least representative cases of the women who come into contact with the criminal justice system — and to draw generalizing conclusions from those atypical cases. The dangerous, violent women become the ones whose media images extend in the public imagination to all "criminal" women. The result is the skewing of the public's perception of girls and women convicted of illegal behaviour.

> Print and television journalists and traditionalist criminologists are mutually reinforcing in their attention to sensational, anomalous violent offences by girls and women.

The decontextualized nature of news reporting results in misrepresentations of social reality. A one-year study (1992–1993) of Saturday news stories in five regional papers concerning crime by women found that more than 50 percent of the stories focused on the issue of women committing serious violence. Such crimes represent less than 0.5 percent of all charges laid against women for violent crimes (Boritch 1997: 16). (Most violence-related charges are for common assault.) The majority of the articles, aside from those that dealt with Karla Homolka, were stories about women who had killed their spouse or a child (Gordon, Faith and Currie 1995). This press coverage is a serious overrepresentation of violent crimes by women. There was not a single article in any of the papers on shoplifting, which is the predominant crime committed by both men and women. Ultimately, this phenomenon prompts fear, outcry, more aggressive prosecution of girls and women, harsher punishments for all women convicted of crime, and a backlash against feminist and womanist movements.

Prison is a junction in which social inequities converge. In Canada it is primarily Aboriginal people and Blacks who are overrepresented in jails and prisons and this is because of structured racism. But media accounts of crimes by girls or women seldom acknowledge structural factors. Focusing on uncommon crimes of violence, the accounts individualize and pathologize the accused (see Appendix) with little or no reference to social context. The accounts tend not to stress another fact: that recidivism among women who have served sentences for murder is extremely rare (which is also the case for men).

In the following pages, as examples of media-saturated crimes involving girls or women, we discuss three cases: Leslie Van Houten, who was involved in one of the 1969 "Manson murders" in California; Karla Homolka, who in the early 1990s assisted Paul Bernardo in the sexual-torture killings of three young women, including her own sister, in Ontario; and Kelly Ellard, convicted of the brutal 1997 murder of classmate Reena Virk, in British Columbia. In each instance, the offender was a pretty, middle-class white girl, which not only distinguishes her from most criminalized women but also exacerbates the horror of the white majority — because, after all, "she's one of us." In other words, people seem to expect violent behaviour from people who are "not like themselves," people who are different. They do not expect it from themselves or their own. As it seems to go: when "we" (whoever "we" is) commit behaviour that shocks "our own kind," we are appalled, unlike when "they" misbehave, to which "we" respond with "Well, what can you expect?"

The three young women in our cases exuded danger because they broke gender codes in the most extreme ways possible. Their crimes are not comprehensible to the white middle class that bred them. Although the crimes seemed senseless, all three cases are indicative of power abuses — either because of having social power or reacting to others who have it.

The stigma of dangerousness, as applied selectively to individuals and to entire marginalized populations, is rooted in tradition. We begin, then, by setting the historical context in which the social divisions of "us" (good) and "them" (bad) became firmly entrenched in Western societies.

The Construction of "Dangerous Classes" in Western History

According to the Christian Bible, the first woman on Earth, Eve, committed the first human sin by eating an apple from the tree of knowledge, thus losing her innocence. She exacerbated her sin by seducing Adam; the snake signified the sexualized evil that now contaminated God's first human creatures. Women were by nature either evil or saints: whores or madonnas. It was about their sex. The dangers of women's sexuality is a recurrent theme in religion and in the history of theoretical criminology (Lombroso and Ferrero 1895; Pollak 1950). The theme reflects attitudes that feminists generally refer to as misogyny. The evil of women as sexual beings has also been a dominant theme in modern Western practices of criminal (in)justice.

The witchhunts of the fifteenth to eighteenth centuries are a conspicuous example of traditional fears of women, and of the uses of the church, law, and public hysteria to construct the idea of a dangerous woman (Klaits 1985; Marwick 1975; Trevor-Roper 1975; McFarlane 1970; Parrinder 1963). The Bible declared that witches, as allies of Satan, were to be killed (Exodus 22: 18). The churches conducted the witchhunts, generating rumours, distrust, accusations, and social panic. They turned suspects over to the state for trial in a court of law followed by execution (burned at the stake; drowned in boiling oil; hanged; beheaded). About 15 percent of the executed witches were men; often they had the choice of testifying against their wives or being themselves convicted of witchcraft (Wilson 1993).

> The witchhunts of the fifteenth to eighteenth centuries are a conspicuous example of traditional fears of women and how church, law, and public hysteria construct the idea of a dangerous woman.

Understanding that the best defence is a good offence, a woman afraid of being accused would lay blame on a neighbour for causing a misfortune: a miscarriage, illness or death, a cow drying up or a chicken that stopped laying, a storm damaging the barn, or some other calamity. The accused were charged with fornicating with the Devil, as his servant. Since witches committed havoc unseen by mortal eyes, no witnesses were necessary. Married women, rich as well as poor, and mothers together with their daughters were executed indiscriminately. Disproportionate numbers of single women and widows were executed — women without men, women who by choice or circumstance lived independently of men's supervision. If they kept small, domesticated animals as companions, as many did, they were de facto suspects. These were women who did not satisfy gender-role expectations, and they were thus perceived as dangerous women. As many as nine million women and girls may have been executed over three centuries, contributing to one of Europe's greatest holocausts (Ehrenreich and English 1973).

Women were censored and silenced in all realms of public life, and it was up to the men to keep their wives in line. For one thing they would not tolerate abusive language (Sharpe 1984). In accordance with Blackstone's British legal commentaries in the eighteenth century, men had a responsibility to discipline women, with the caveat that the stick the man used to beat his wife should not be thicker than his own thumb (from whence tradition came the expression "rule of thumb"). When women scolded, both men and women were breaching gender codes. It was a crime for women to nag their husbands or harangue others in public. The punishment for this crime was public humiliation of both the woman and the man. The harshest punishments fell on women, who were often whipped, confined in a pillory in the town square, dunked in water, or forced to wear a brank, also known as a "scold's bridle" — a helmet with a mouthpiece with small metal spikes inserted into the woman's mouth; if she attempted to speak, it would cut into her tongue (Underdown 1985: 123). Men were humiliated in noisy public rituals, subject to intensive ridicule for failing at manhood.

The formal tradition of criminology, the study of crime and punishment, commenced in nineteenth-century Europe in concert with the Industrial Revolution and the emergence of modern capitalism. In England, masses of people migrated to the newly urbanized centres, particularly London, where the lure of factory jobs supplanted agrarian culture (Thompson 1963). The promise of urban comforts, however, was not fulfiled for many of these unskilled migrants, and high unemployment produced rashes of what we now call street crime. These crimes, primarily related to the theft or destruction of property, were indicative of class divisions that separated the emerging capitalist class from people who were relegated to bare-survival wages or no paid work at all. The more affluent members of society, a distinct minority of the population, correctly perceived the antipathy of the unruly masses upon whose labour they depended for their affluence. Thus was born the political notion of "the dangerous classes."

The writings of Karl Marx were unequivocally focused on the work and social conditions of working-class men, whom he identified as the proletariat who would ultimately overthrow the capitalist class and establish communal, profit-sharing, worker-owned industry. He failed to recognize the significance of the chronically unemployed, the lowly riff-raff, whom he labelled the lumpenproletariat. In his estimation, they were social pariahs and parasites who contributed nothing to society. In his glib dismissal of the least resourceful victims of capitalism, Marx, in effect, was colluding with the bourgeois notion of the dangerous classes.

Women who failed to find legitimate employment, however dubious the benefits of such labour, often found themselves in brothels or working as street prostitutes and petty thieves. In Marx's terms, they, too, were relegated to the despised lumpenproletariat. More seriously, they were stigmatized as the dangerous carriers of sin and disease, which justified England's *Contagious Diseases Acts* (1860–83). This Act gave police the power to stop any woman on the street and send her off for an invasive medical examination. By the late nineteenth century the nuclear family, with parents and children living as an insulated unit and the patriarchal father at the head, had replaced the extended family in which women had held more decision-making power. This familial arrangement was "naturalized" through social ritual and legal regulation, effectively domesticating middle-class Western women. Rather than being described by male authors as evil, they were now idealized as the heart of the family, virtue personified. Their "natural" compliance and nurturing ways would earn them the protection of their husbands and, by their example and adherence to Christian teachings, instill morality in their children. As Kathleen Kendall (1999: 111) puts it, "Convict women were perceived as either more morally corrupt than criminal men because they violated natural law, or as innocent victims of circumstance."

Canada's first separate jail for women, Toronto's Mercer Reformatory, which opened in 1880, was built on the premise that women and men require different approaches to confinement (Strange 1985–86). Incarcerated women were perceived as being more rowdy than the men, requiring strict discipline to develop good work habits, self-control over passions, and a cessation of drunken or violent behaviours (Goff 1999: 165). With its emphasis on instruction in the domestic arts and religion, the reformation of imprisoned women in Canada was inspired by the work of Elizabeth Fry in England. Her goal was to reform women who, upon release, could attract a husband and manage a household, and who would give up drinking, prostituting, gambling, yelling, and cursing. With sufficient religious and domestic instruction, and with discipline and patience, she believed, these rebellious, ill-kempt, mean-tempered women would metamorphose into quiet, respectable homemakers.

Like women in jail, women at large required instruction in the arts of compliance and subordination — the need for which contradicted the ideology of women's natural submission to men (Faith 1993a). In European criminal courts, men could be held responsible for crimes committed by their wives, because women (notwithstanding their "natural" evil) were now thought to be "naturally" passive, and therefore incapable of conceiving and carrying out a crime. If a middle-class woman became unruly, that behaviour was blamed on the father or husband. These attitudes culminated in the Victorian age.

When ill-paid workers engaged in strikes and protests against those who exploited their labour, they were perceived not only as a threat to the smooth running of a profit-driven market economy but also as a danger to the safety and comfort of those upon whom they were dependent for their meagre livelihoods. Women were often active as "Luddites," weavers who smashed mechanical looms in protest against losing jobs to technology (Thompson 1963: 216–19). They protested food prices and scarcities and chased after the middleman, taking the grain from him and paying him a fair market price (Stevenson 1979). Women who aggressively and collectively protested on the streets and in the factories were de facto dangerous because they were behaving like men.

Cesare Lombroso (with his son-in-law, William Ferrero) was the first "scholar" to write about women who broke the law (1895). The "father of criminology," he formally established the myth that, when out of (men's) control, women at large were more vicious, dangerous, and monstrous than any man. In 1950 criminologist Otto Pollak published a speculative essay on "female criminality" in which he asserted that women were more deceptive than men, due to having both to hide their monthly period and to fake orgasm. Biology thus equips women with the skill of deception. He speculated that nurses and caretakers often kill the ill or elderly with poison, but get away with it.

Men have taken a great deal of effort over the centuries to teach women to stay in their place, and to restrict their opportunities for immoral or illegal behaviour. In this postmodern age, gender-bending is commonplace, and gendered hierarchies are legally challenged, often successfully, everywhere in the Western world. Women themselves are now in social-control positions, as policy-makers, practitioners, and professionals in every field. And yet, half a century later, Pollak's concerns with women's dangerousness, apparently based on fear of women's sex, have by no means abated in society (Hudson 1989), despite and consistent with the preponderance of male sexual violence.

The Twentieth Century

The popularization of psychology in the mid-twentieth century caused a shift from generalizing women as inherently bad to seeing them as inherently mad. In the 1950s new pharmaceutical industries promoted mood-changing and tranquilizing pills specifically targeted for depressed housewives and prisoners. Women were more likely to be sent to a mental hospital than to a prison. Because the numbers of women in the criminal justice system were so low, relative to men, and because men dominated the academic world, very little was published that shed any light on women in the system. When they weren't fictionalized as masculine and violent, they were seen, as by the Gluecks in the 1930s, as a pathetic but dangerous class who transmitted sexual diseases and bred inferior offspring (Glueck and Glueck 1934/1965). "Bad seed" theories have proliferated in Western history, literature, and entertainment: the simple idea that some people are born bad — supernaturally cursed or genetically unfortunate.

> The popularization of psychology in the mid-twentieth century caused a shift from generalizing women as inherently bad to inherently mad. In the 1950s mood-changing and tranquillizing pills were targeted for depressed housewives and prisoners.

Beginning in the late 1960s, the interdisciplinary field of criminology came under the strong influence of critical sociologists and historians, some of whom were examining criminal justice systems as implicated in widespread social injustice and material disparity. Others, particularly feminist scholars, began to rectify the absence of women in the criminology literature (Heidensohn 1968; Bertrand 1969; Klein 1973). By the end of the 1970s, an abundance of new research had produced a rapidly growing literature in the areas of women, crime, and punishment. Two of the most prominent books, Freda Adler's *Sisters in Crime* (1975) and Carol Smart's *Women, Crime and Criminology: A Feminist Critique* (1976), were to have significant international influence on the direction of new scholarship. By the 1980s, gender was an exponentially expanding area in criminological research, as well as in every other discipline.

Adler's work stimulated a shift from thinking of criminalized women as monstrous, pathetic, and/or pathological to thinking of women as independent agents, in a process of "gender convergence" with men in society as a consequence of the "freedoms" gained by the women's movement. These new freedoms, as Adler saw it, included women's increased opportunities to break the law. This "liberation thesis" was unsupportable, but the media were unrelenting in associating a fictional rise in violent crime by women with the women's movement. In fact, women have been charged with approximately 10–15 percent of all violent crimes since the beginning of record-keeping, but to make their point the media offered skewed percentage increases. For example, if one jurisdiction had zero murders by women in 1974, but two murders by women the following year, the homicide rate for women would increase by 200 percent, as a blip. The press would headline the percentage increase but omit the low base numbers in their reports. When in the following year there were again zero murders by women, the press did not issue headlines declaring that women's homicide rate had decreased by 200 percent. Women killing people is far more titillating and newsworthy than women behaving themselves.

Adler (1975) was strenuously criticized for suggesting that women's liberation would result in increased crimes by women, and Smart (1976) demonstrated otherwise. Women's theft rates did go up in the late 1970s, but the robberies were not committed by women who had been influenced by women's liberation, nor by serious crooks. They were primarily the work of young single mothers who were experiencing the "feminization of poverty." They bore no resemblance to news reporters' fictionalized versions of wild, violent women running amok, as was propagated through the 1970s and again in the 1990s (Chesney-Lind 1997). At all periods of history, when women have organized for women's rights, they have met with fierce resistance from men and women who represent the status quo. In exploiting Adler's study, the media played directly into the hands of male supremacists. However, Adler's work as a sociologist also invited challenges from feminist scholars, and much research was catalyzed by her theory.

While the media continued to falsely report a rising degree of violence by girls and women, the actual rates of violence, and rates of most other crimes (by both men and women), were on the decline through the 1990s (CCJS 1999: 188–226), and continue to decline (Alvi 2000: 56–57). Marge Reitsma-Street (1999) thoroughly examined the data, arguing that it conclusively proved that over the past twenty years charges for murder and attempted murder by girls had been constant and infrequent. The work of Walter DeKeseredy and his colleagues (1997) demonstrates that when girls and women are violent they are most commonly defending themselves or fighting back, with a man initiating the violence. Assault rates have gone up for girls in some locations, but this has less to do with more violence by girls than with social responses to those behaviours (DeKeseredy 2000: 45-46; Pate 1999: 39; Schramm 1998), including official reporting and prosecution. The kind of schoolyard bullying or scuffles with parents that would formerly have been resolved privately has now, with "zero tolerance," become a matter for criminal justice.

In 1998 the Canadian journalist Patricia Pearson revived and capitalized on the recurrent myth of women's dangerousness. Recycling an old theory, Pearson asserted that the feminist movement bears some responsibility in this (fictional) crime wave by violent women. Her basic argument, which is much like Pollak's earlier theory, is that our "politically correct" society is in denial about female aggression; in the feminist tradition of identifying girls' and women's victimizations and systemic powerlessness, feminists rob women of the need to accept responsibility and to be accountable for their actions, such as husband-beating (Pearson 1998: 30). Feminists, in Pearson's critique, have failed to recognize women as "rational" decision-makers with personal agency, who commit aggressive and/or violent crime as a calculated individual choice. The news media again, predictably, exploited the provocation that women's liberation was making excuses for violence by women.

Meda Chesney-Lind (1999: 114) points out, though, that feminists do not campaign for the right to be violent. She criticizes Pearson's "conflation of aggression and violence" and her false assertions of increases in women's serious crime. As Chesney-Lind (1999: 116) notes, "Troublesome facts rarely disrupt Pearson's flow." Given that men commit up to 90 percent of violent aggression, rather than vie for equality in this area it would make more sense, as Chesney-Lind observes, to focus on theorizing about the "consistent, powerful sex difference" in men's and women's crime rates. Moreover, Pearson "minimizes and dismisses women's victimization and its clear connection to women's violence, and then argues that such violence should be punished without regard to gender" (Chesney-Lind 1999: 117–18).

Chesney-Lind (1997) uncovers how the media and criminal justice tend to label a group of girls a "gang" if they are not white. Bernard Schissel (1997: 51) refers to the exaggerated press coverage accorded to youth gangs as hate crimes perpetrated by the media. Journalists quote academics who haven't studied gangs but offer expert opinions (DeKeseredy 2000: 55). Media reports about gangs take on a tone of moral panic even though, as Sandra Bell (1999: 157–63) observes, most so-called youth gangs are involved neither in violent crime nor in claiming turf. In support, Bell cites Karen Joe and Chesney-Lind (1993), who found that girl gangs are primarily social support groups for marginalized girls.

Critical scholars recognize how the media skew reality by focusing on statistically insignificant but culturally sensational crimes, such as school shootings or a girl beating another girl to death. Contrived imagery of a rising tide of delinquency sets up destructive misrepresentations about young people and crime (Alvi 2000: 15–18; Bell 1999: 84–85; Schissel 1997). Shahid Alvi (2000: 18) reports that 94 percent of Toronto newspaper stories on youth crime involve violence, even though most crimes by youth, such as theft, are non-violent (Bell 1999: 80). Girls are rarely aggressors in these stories, and they more often appear as victims.

> Critical scholars recognize how the media skew reality by focusing on statistically insignificant but culturally sensational crimes. Contrived imagery of a rising tide of delinquency creates destructive misconceptions about young people and crime.

A study of girl violence in Western Canada (Artz 1998) was based on interviews with just six adolescent girls who were involved in assaultive behaviours. The media colluded with the author's emphasis of girl-on-girl violence as signifying a rising trend, with the attendant theme of family dysfunction. In a study of girl's "dope gangs" in Detroit (Taylor 1993), the author emphasizes the factor of violence as an element in the drug use, but does not suggest that girl gangs signify a trend. Certainly the evidence is lacking for establishing a trend of violent girl gangs in Canada, but the media insist on it with an explicit anti-feminist stance. For example, in *Alberta Report,* under the headline "Killer Girls," the author states: "The latest crop of teenage girls can be as violent, malicious and downright evil as the boys. In fact, they're leading the explosion in youth crime. It's an unexpected by-product of the feminist push for equality" (quoted in DeKeseredy 2000: 38). By contrast, the Detroit study includes an analysis of poverty, racism, and criminal (in)justice, and a discussion of a steady stream of resourceless Black girls who are processed through the system unheard and unseen, as if they were dangerous (Taylor 1993).

In establishing various levels of security, Correctional Services of Canada (CSC) classifies prisoners: those who are not deemed a risk (for escape, or to cause harm to others) are classified minimum or medium security; maximum security is reserved for those perceived as a threat to the good order of the institution, whatever their crime. In 2000, about 18 percent of the 357 federally sentenced women incarcerated in Canada were classified as "maximum," and they were disproportionately Aboriginal women. Through the 1990s women labelled "maximum" were sent to men's psychiatric prisons around Canada, where they were placed in solitary and drugged. In committing millions of dollars to new segregation buildings at four women's prisons, CSC is implying that these units are needed for the safety of the public (Hayman 2000). In fact, very few women are criminally "dangerous," or even perceived to be. The women so labelled would be more accurately generalized as "uncooperative" with the prison regime.

Even more restricted than prisoners labelled "maximum security" have been those officially declared by the court as a "dangerous offender." Following from the *Habitual Offenders Act* of 1947 and the *Criminal Sexual-Psychopath Act* of 1948, the dangerous offender designation was first proposed by the Ouimet Committee, a 1969 government commission for prison reform. The commission reasoned that the distinction, and tight control over those so labelled, would encourage communities to be more accepting of the vast majority of prisoners and those newly released, who pose no threat. The designation, which came into force in 1977, is based on these criteria:

- Pattern of unrestrained behaviour;
- Pattern of aggressive behaviour with indifference as to the consequences;
- Behaviour of such a brutal nature that ordinary standards of restraint won't control it. (Criminal Code, Part XXIV, Section 753)

Only two women in Canada, Marlene Moore and Lisa Neve, have been designated dangerous offenders. Critics observe that men require much more serious criminal histories, usually involving rape and/or murder, before being designated a dangerous offender, and that Moore and Neve were victims of a double standard. Neither of them had killed anyone, but the net-widening law permits use of the designation with just one violent offence, which can be assault, as in the case of both Neve and Moore. Both were chronically abused, in trouble from a young age, and in and out of prison from their teens. Marlene Moore robbed a woman on the street at knifepoint. Lisa Neve, who worked in the sex trade, assaulted a co-worker with a knife, and issued threats. Moore, after spending much of her life in prison, committed suicide at the Prison for Women in 1988 at age twenty-eight (Kershaw and Lasovich 1991). After five years with the label, Neve's super-maximum dangerous offender classification was overturned in 1999, when she was twenty-six, and she was immediately released from prison. By all accounts, she has been "reformed."

Facing the Contradictions

For half a century, from *Caged* in 1950 to the prison-porn flicks of the 1990s, Hollywood movies set in women's prisons have consistently presented a pat set of stereotypes: evil, masculine women, both prisoners and matrons, presented as violent lesbians, often as women of colour; the sweet, innocent, blonde white girl who is imprisoned due to a mistake, often wrongly convicted for a crime committed by her boyfriend; the psychotic criminal who goes berserk; the super-sexy bad girls who cheerfully do the dirty work for a controlling, sadistic dominatrix. The most common stereotypes are devil women; lesbians as villains; teenage predators and super-bitch killer beauties (Faith 1993a, 1993b; Birch 1993).

The fictions of Hollywood rarely coincide with the truths of women's lives. It is neither monsters nor pathetic victims who get locked up. Rather, upon first entering a woman's prison, one is struck both by the diversity of the women, in terms of age, appearance, and demeanour, and by their ordinariness and approachability. The same "types" of women one finds in prison would be found in an urban department store. They do not look dangerous, and indeed few are. Certainly women of colour are vastly overrepresented (Monture-Angus 2000a; Gilbert 1999; Neugebauer-Visano 1996), and the white women are not middle class. Race, class, and gender are both distinct and conjoined, each dynamically influencing the other in criminal justice processes.

Women on death row are not usually conventionally feminine in appearance (Farr 2000). An exception was the softly appealing Karla Faye Tucker, who was executed in Texas in 2000 after winning the hearts of Christians throughout the United States through national television interviews. Tucker was not a feminine woman when she was sentenced; she was softened by her conversion to Christianity, following the crime. Women with masculine characteristics are not more likely to kill than feminine women. They are, however, perceived as more dangerous, and if convicted they are more likely than feminine women to receive the death penalty, especially if they are lesbians and most especially if they are women of colour (Farr 2000).

The closer a woman is to the ideals of femininity, the more shocking it is when she violently betrays her gender role. Because the offence defies "common sense," particularly when the victims are strangers, the accused are often dismissed as pathological (see Appendix). But pathology suggests that the crime is the outcome of a deranged mind, a sick individual detached from society at large.

The three very feminine women who make up our case studies are far from the stereotypical monsters of film, psychiatry, or criminology, although the seriousness of their crimes rivals any of the monster stories. In addition to the headline murders in which they were implicated, they continue to attract media attention because they were attractive, white, middle-class young women at the time of their crimes. All are currently in prison. We focus on these sensational cases even while critiquing sensationalism.

> The three women in our case studies are far from the monsters of film, psychiatry, or criminology... they still attract media attention as attractive, white, middle-class young women at the time of their crimes.

We do not see these women as presented by the media, but as women whose life experiences prior to their crimes were not unlike those of other women of their cultures and generations. They are not aliens but rather signifiers of the times and places in which they lived.

Leslie Van Houten[1]

On August 9 and 10, 1969, in affluent neighbourhoods in Los Angeles County, two sets of murders were orchestrated by a cult guru who had spent most of his life in prison. Four men and three women were killed, and the name Charles Manson entered the lexicon of American popular culture, signifying an end to the idealism of the 1960s. Manson, in his mid-thirties, and three young women aged nineteen to twenty-one were arrested in late 1969. In July 1971 they were sentenced to death and transported to state prisons to await execution. The media were unrelenting in the attention given to the case until spring 1972, when the U.S. Supreme Court declared the death penalty unconstitutional and their sentences were amended to life in prison.

Manson had about twenty-five followers (aged thirteen to early twenties), any of whom would have been happy to have been selected for these murder missions. Most of these disciples had been extremely feminine young women when he met them — on streets, in parks, in hippie pads in San Francisco. Each of them, all white and most of them middle class, had been successfully socialized to be attractive, soft and feminine in appearance and demeanour. They were all skilled in the domestic arts, and they honoured men's hierarchical privilege in the social order. They excelled in submissiveness.

In the beginning Manson presented himself as a gentle man with spiritual wisdom and no fear. Through the use of drugs, especially LSD, and intensive, unrelenting mind-control games, his followers became convinced that he had supernatural powers. They revered him as the reincarnation of Jesus Christ. At a time when millions of young people throughout North America were rebelling against the hypocrisies and barbarities of the establishment, and seeking enlightenment from Eastern religions, these young people were convinced of Manson's higher authority. He looked up to Aboriginal peoples, he opposed the war in Vietnam, he preached peace and love. He had magical qualities. He played his guitar and sang self-penned songs with social commentary. Wild animals weren't afraid of him. Even rattlesnakes let him pet them. He washed the feet of his disciples, just as Christ had done. His followers were ready to follow him anywhere, which turned out to be "Helter Skelter." This was Manson's vision of the world in chaos, with himself, a white man, at the helm of a new revolution that would give the power back to the Black man and rain terror on "Whitie" for centuries of abuse against transported, enslaved Africans and their descendants. Manson, an undisguised sexist, recruited young trophy women to serve him and his male friends in every respect. His plan to start a race war was patronizingly racist; and his selection of victims was based on straightforward class antagonism against materialist consumer "piggies."

On August 9, 1969, Manson selected four of his followers, "Tex" and three of "the girls," and sent them out to start the revolution. (On this first night he didn't send Leslie, who stayed home at the communal ranch to take care of the family's babies.) He targeted a home formerly the residence of a music producer who had failed to satisfy Manson's ambition for a rock 'n' roll career. Unbeknownst to Manson, the house had been leased to a film director who was then away. At home were his pregnant wife, an actor, and several of her friends. Five people were mercilessly killed, and messages taken from lyrics in Beatles songs were left in blood on the walls. Manson himself didn't attend the killing; he just told his followers what to do and they obeyed. He was the general, and they were his soldiers.

When the crew reported back to Manson, he was displeased with their "messy" job. On the following night, August 10, he went along with a somewhat changed crew to make sure things were properly set up. Again, Tex was chosen to commit the murders along with two girls, Pat and Leslie. Like most of the other girls, Leslie had a wholesome upbringing. She sang in the church choir as a teen, and was a smart, popular, classic beauty, a homecoming princess, active in the community and just generally a well-admired middle-class Southern California girl. She had joined up with Manson in September 1968. In the spirit of the times, a period of great social upheaval and protest against universal injustices, Leslie was looking for answers to life's big questions, and she thought Manson had them. He promised to help her kill her ego. As his disciple, she gave up her name, her birthday, and every facet of her former self. She was just nineteen.

This second night, Manson chose a house at random, though significantly in another affluent neighbourhood and next door to a house where he had once partied as an aspiring rock 'n' roller. He and Tex went in first and tied up the occupants, Leno and Rosemary LaBianca, parents and owners of successful retail businesses. Manson then left the house, telling Pat and Leslie to go in and do whatever Tex told them to do. Manson himself drove to what he mistakenly thought was a Black neighbourhood, where, in a gas station restroom, he left the wallet he'd stolen from Mr. LaBianca. He expected Black men would be blamed for the crime, and that Black men would then rise up in a race war. The "family" would live in a hole in the desert, staying young and healthy somehow, until the war ended and they would surface as the ally of the victorious Blacks. Anything he said sounded like prophecy to those who believed in him, and they were prepared to do his bidding at any cost. Yet, in the LaBianca home, Leslie was unable to perform as a good soldier. She recoiled at the prospect of killing, and backed off into another room when the murders started. After Tex had already killed Leno Bianca, and had struck the fatal blow to Rosemary after Pat was unsuccessful, he then insisted that Leslie also come into the room and stab the by-now dead woman, which she did, fourteen to sixteen times in a brutal act of frenzy. She later described to a parole board that she both felt like a wild animal with its prey and was filled with fury at herself for having not lived up to Manson's faith in her.

As he was to later testify, and contrary to the women's boastful testimony at trial, later refuted, it was Tex Watson who dealt the death blow to all seven of the victims of Manson's forays into Helter Skelter. (Watson was tried separately, and continues to serve life in a California state prison.) All three of the women had proven inadequate to the task.

Like any good girl would be, each was terrified at the murders. Each resisted, and each proved incompetent as murderers, even while trying to act the good soldier. As young women, they had no training for violence. It was not so much a matter of conscience that bothered Leslie afterward but rather frustration and disappointment at her inability to perform as instructed, and her failure to meet their leader's expectations.

The press routinely demonizes people who have been criminalized, and with Manson this practice did not require much journalistic imagination. He presented himself as both a deity and Satan. (He was once booked in jail as Jesus Christ, Saviour and Lord.) As the mastermind conspirator, he was sentenced to death along with the three women who took credit for the killings on the two nights. During trial, on his instruction, they all shaved their heads, carved Xs into their foreheads, and taunted the judge. The press characterized the women as pathologically evil, and they did appear to be serving Satan. Compounding the theatrics were the numerous "Manson girls" who lived on the sidewalk outside the L.A. court building for almost two years in solidarity. They too shaved their heads and wore long cloaks that reinforced the witchy impressions.

In 1972, when the death penalty was rescinded throughout the United States (until 1976), Leslie and the others were still housed on death row in the California women's state prison. They continued to live in their six-by-nine-foot cells for four more years, when they were gradually transferred to the main prison. By 1974, five years after the trial, Leslie had completely shed her attachment to Manson. She was racked with remorse, and expressed her guilt with anorexia. In 1976 her case was separated from that of her co-defendants. Because she was not in her right mind at the time of the crime, had never killed anyone, had been the victim of cult conditioning, and, most relevantly, had never had a proper defence (her lawyer had drowned on a camping trip during the trial), her previous sentence (death, converted to life in prison) was overturned and she was granted a new trial. In this 1977 trial the jury was deadlocked as to her guilt, so a third trial was scheduled.

For six months prior to and during the third trial, Leslie was permitted to leave the county jail on bail, having now served over eight years, much of it in solitary. While on bail she worked as a legal secretary when not in court, and she was able to reunite with family and old friends. She lived a normal life and the media was respectful of her privacy. Reporters were startled to discover the change in her, from the 1971 clone of Satan to the calm young woman of 1977 who showed humility, remorse, compassion, integrity, and a grounded intelligence. This time she was convicted for robbery-murder (the wallet, some coins), rather than first-degree murder, and she was returned to state prison. She is still there, at the age of fifty-seven, in 2006.

The public first saw the rehabilitated Leslie in 1976 when she was interviewed on ABC television by Barbara Walters. She did not disclaim responsibility for the crimes, and said she was as guilty as if she had taken the victims' lives. Her guilt was for following Manson, giving him her power. With that interview, the public began to see "the Manson girls" as individuals, not as robots who all used the same voice — saying the same words, using the same mannerisms — when they were under Manson's control. Subsequent interviews with Leslie by Larry King and Diane Sawyer further erased the monstrous images that had accompanied the first seven years of reportage on the case.

Over twenty-five years ago, while in her early twenties, Leslie returned to her "self" with help from therapists, family, friends, teachers, and sympathetic prison staff. She would have to live with the nightmare of the torment she helped cause and the enduring grief of the victims' family and her own. Permanently humbled, she lives as healthfully as anyone can while incarcerated, and she became a model prisoner who engages in service to her prison community and beyond. By day she works full-time at prison jobs, which rotate every several years, in the hospital, school, administrative and chaplain's offices. In her spare time she reads onto tape for the blind; makes quilts for the homeless; teaches English to women for whom it isn't a first language; and organizes talent for the annual AA dinner show. When she entered the prison, there were six hundred women there. Now there are two thousand. Younger women who come in learn from Leslie how to survive prison with grace. She's the oldtimer who doesn't complain. The parole board has turned her down in fifteen hearings, often reluctantly, it seems; they encourage her to remain hopeful that "one day soon" she'll be released.

> The death penalty may have been a less painful punishment than serving a life sentence with a deeply injured conscience and no hope of making restitution.

The death penalty may have been a less painful punishment than living out a life sentence with a deeply injured conscience and no hope for making restitution. Life sentences commonly do not exceed twenty-five years, especially for someone like Leslie with an unblemished prison record and who poses no threat of violence or escape. If she is soon released her nightmares will accompany her, and getting out after almost forty years would not be getting off easy.

Karla Homolka

Normally, in making a release decision, the Canadian National Parole Board conducts a risk assessment, considering the applicant's criminal history, alcohol or drug use, violence on record, psychological state, information from experts, and, sometimes, victims of the crimes. Those convicted of first-degree murder must generally serve a minimum of twenty-five years. In the case of Karla Homolka, whom many consider dangerous, a deal was made in 1993 in which she was granted a maximum twelve-year sentence on manslaughter charges. In exchange she offered information about her husband, but without revealing the extent of her own role.

The story of Karla Homolka and Paul Bernardo erupted on the media landscape in February 1993 with Bernardo's arrest on charges of murder and sexual assault. The murder charges stemmed from the discovery of the cement-encased body-parts of fourteen-year-old Leslie Mahaffy and the abused body of fifteen-year-old Kristen French. Both young women had been kidnapped, raped, and tortured. Bernardo and Homolka were also implicated and subsequently charged with the murder of Homolka's younger sister, Tamylynn. It was subsequently discovered that Bernardo had routinely engaged in sexual assault between 1983 and 1993. He was charged with two counts of first-degree murder and forty-three counts of sexual assault. The extent to which Homolka was a willing accomplice in committing the murders was then a matter of conjecture. Bernardo's lawyers argued that she was actively involved, as "home movie" tapes later demonstrated. While the actions of both Bernardo and Homolka were equally brutal, the media spotlight and public attention were focused on and continue to dwell on Homolka.

The 1992–93 survey of print media on issues dealing with women and the criminal justice system yielded a preponderance of stories dealing with Homolka (Gordon, Faith, and Currie 1995). A total of 136 women and crime articles appeared in the Saturday editions of five urban Canadian newspapers. Twenty-one of these articles focused on Karla Homolka, all of them published between May and July. Eight articles, more than a third, were in the *Toronto Star*, given the provincial interest in the case, but for three months

Homolka stories dominated the media nationwide.

Despite a court-ordered publication ban, there were more stories published on the Homolka and Bernardo case than on any other criminal case that year. The media tended to focus their initial coverage not on details of the crimes but rather on the freedom of the press and the public's right to know (Gordon, Faith, and Currie 1995; McCormick 1995). The publication ban itself incited speculation and rumours about the case, as well as a proliferation of Web sites and Internet news discussion groups (Regan Shade 1994). The cloud of secrecy intensified speculation when Bernardo's own lawyer argued against the ban (Walker 1994). In 1995 Homolka again dominated the airwaves and print media with her testimony at Bernardo's trial.

> While the actions of both Paul Bernando and Karla Homolka were equally brutal, the media spotlight and public attention were focused on and continue to dwell on Homolka.

Initially Homolka's media representation alternated between heartless killer and victim slave. As with most media coverage, the tendency was to confine the figure or issue in easily understandable binary oppositions (bad versus good; savage versus civilized) (Hartley 1982). Yet this binary framing tended to collapse from the sheer velocity of the vacillations between competing representations. The oppositions relayed in news accounts were so extreme that the story became an exceptionally bizarre case of inconsistencies. For instance, a *Globe and Mail* article begins with a description of Homolka's "Barbie" image, describing her as "a stunning 23-year-old veterinarian's assistant… long blonde hair and blue eyes… peaches and cream complexion… wouldn't hurt a fly." The same article refers to Bernardo as "26… accountant… tall… charming… handsome enough to melt a young girl's heart. But behind the Ken and Barbie masks lurked the face of grotesque evil" (quoted in its entirety in McCormick 1995: 186).

Crime reporting is also based on the element of sensationalism, and much depends on how far a story departs from conventional standards and encapsulates an extreme (McCormick 1995). Homolka's crimes were unusual in the extreme. They were committed by a woman. They were taken as being crimes against humanity because they involved the torture and murder of adolescent women, one of whom was her sister. The pleasant, clean-cut news-photo images of Homolka and Bernardo were incompatible with the standard idea of sex murderers. The cognitive dissonance created by the juxtaposition of the stories with the photographs served to draw in readers who would not normally seek out stories about sex and violence. The sensationalism was supported by the unusualness of having a woman challenged and convicted of pornographic murders and by the offenders' disarmingly wholesome profiles.

Each time she appeared in the public arena, the media scrutinized and communicated Homolka's behaviour to fit into a conception of her as either cold psychopath or battered woman. At no time did the media engage in a critical analysis of the many women who are battered, murdered, raped, and mutilated throughout the world on any given day, or of the reality that most homicides are committed by men. Rather the media focus on the unusual event or situation, and especially one that becomes a "continuing story," with new developments day by day or from time to time (Connell 1980; Hartley 1982). In the case of Homolka, the continuity was ensured for a period of at least two years — until 1995, when she was called to testify at Bernardo's trial. Homolka's plea bargain, resulting in the twelve-year sentence on the lesser charge of manslaughter, generated intense and negative public reaction, which, in itself, became a media story. More than three hundred thousand signatures were collected on a petition opposing the Crown's settlement and the lenient sentence (Boritch 1997: 3).

This intense reaction can be explained in terms of the contradictory identification that Homolka evoked — as a daughter and sister, and as tormentor and killer. Not only did she symbolize the deepest betrayal of trust among women by killing those of her own kind, but she also offered a symbol of daughter, sister, or wife. She epitomized the potentiality of an evil that society seeks to constrain through the rationale of law and order, which gains its legitimacy at least partially through the media.

An additional but highly critical factor underpinning the moral outrage ignited by this case sprang from the identities and repre-

> The media interpreted Karla Homolka's behaviour as a psychopath or a battered woman. There was no critical analysis of the women worldwide who are battered, murdered, raped, and mutilated every day, or the fact that men commit most homicides.

sentations of the victims. The young women tortured, raped, and murdered were not "deserving" victims. They were not on the streets. They came from good homes. They were innocent, pretty, white schoolgirls whose parents were solid citizens. In contrast, Homolka and Bernardo represented the fractured identities of individuals who were not what they purported to be.

Crime reporting is incident-driven and decontextualized (Gordon, Faith, and Currie 1995; Schissel 1997). It is the lack of an overall social context that gives news stories their poignancy and dramatic flavour; the stories reveal the extremes of human behaviour without placing those extremes in context. Over a time the repeated stories and their common themes communicate a sense that the issue — whatever it is — is pervasive and increasing in intensity. The prevailing "new filter" — the means by which some details get into stories and others are left out — becomes entrenched, suggesting that the issue has always been problematic (Hall et al. 1978; Hall 1990). The most common example of this kind of entrenchment can be seen in news coverage of ethno-racial groups that are often presented as problematic immigrant groups who will not assimilate (Jiwani 1993).

From the start of the Homolka-Bernardo case, the media drew on entrenched filters to make sense of the story. For example, in one of the early articles published by the *Globe and Mail* the reporter notes, "The striking blonde is the daughter of Czechoslovakian refugees..." (Sept. 28, 1993: 24–25). That this bit of information was considered pertinent suggests the reporter's search for potential explanations that would resonate with the public imagination and make "common sense."

As the case unfolded in media reports, part of the "common sense" explanations included the rationale that Homolka was either devoid of a moral conscience or under Bernardo's power. During her trial, the coverage described her as "stone-faced" amidst the "gasps of horror" that greeted her testimony (*Globe and Mail* Sept. 28, 1993). She provided "chilling testimony" (Warwick 1995). Reporters who listened to the audio tracks of four Homolka–assisted rapes by Bernardo underlined the horror of the murder-rapes. As a means of conveying unprintable words, one reporter explained, "The words were the same as those uttered on most X-rated movies — expletives and crude instructions to perform sexual acts" (Galloway 1995). Reporters noted that "a stunned silence took over the courtroom" during the playing of an audio tape of a drug-induced rape. According to one reporter, "The scant dialogue was enough to send an eerie chill through the courtroom. For several moments after the tape stopped, nobody said anything" (Legall 1995).

The press alternately depicted Homolka as the devil's accomplice and a battered woman, helping to justify her short sentence and ensure Bernardo's conviction (Blackwell 1995a). By her own testimony, Homolka said she acquiesced and did everything she could to please Bernardo until she left him on January 5, 1993. She testified, "He treated me like a princess, like I was the only girl in the world" (Brown 1995), but said she feared for her life. Headlines communicated the press's skepticism of the use of the battered woman's syndrome to describe Homolka's actions by using such terms as "robo-victim defence" (Verburg 1995), despite photographic evidence of severe physical abuse (Blackwell 1995a).

These competing points of view accelerated as her testimony continued from late May to July 14, 1995, in what was described as "one of the longest and most dramatic appearances to take place in a Canadian courtroom" (Makin 1995b). Reports described Homolka as an extremely cold, manipulative, and possibly insane personality who has "a truly sick, twisted side" (Stepan 2000), and they used testimony from experts to legitimize this perspective. The media representation was bolstered by the very backlash it helped to foment. From most media perspectives, Karla Homolka personified evil — a kind of evil that the justice system cannot rehabilitate. The system is "soft" and thus allows for the likes of Karla Homolka to escape without retribution (Wente 1999).

On the victimization-criminalization continuum, where does Homolka stand on the level of guilt? The only agency permitted her is that of complicity in a series of heinous crimes with her apparently psychopathic husband/abuser. Neither of them were aberrant in their observed everyday behaviours. As presented by the media, Bernardo and Homolka were oversocialized to the worst extremes of their respective gender possibilities. It would seem that Homolka's femininity was her nemesis. Her feminine passivity and fear led to her inability to resist Bernardo's sex, violence, and death games. Her external femininity also caused uneasiness, because her media-transmitted image of attractive, pleasant normality disrupts conventional notions of women who can be trusted not to hurt people. Paradoxically, her crimes were also consistent with her image: she was acting out the extreme end of the compliant femininity continuum — absolute obedience.

Once placed in the centre of the media spotlight, Homolka and Bernardo were mutually but separately challenged to recreate themselves through the lens of innocence; they had to be reconstructed, based on who they were — or who they appeared to be — before the violence — the previously undisclosed but now fully discussed identities based on the media-constructed reality of two incomplete human beings, sufficiently banal to be all the more terrifying. They appear to be inflicted with the "shallow personality syndrome," which is endemic to a materialistic, individualistic, image-obsessed society. They invite armchair psychologizing. In her demeanour, Homolka retains a superficial quality, that of a "material girl" gone berserk.

Given the limits on and biases in media coverage, the rest of us are backed up against the limits of the personal/political dialectic — the contradictions inherent in trying to understand crime at a societal level but believing that explanations for certain types of crime must come from within the individual — forced to retreat with the conservatives, from the search for internal logic to the paradigm of pathology. Given the conflicting details of the crimes, it would be difficult to formulate a reading of the case that goes beyond the boundaries of the mainstream print and television coverage, which vacillates so strongly between Karla the Monster and Karla the Victim. The relatively restrictive Canadian approach to criminal trials, even one as sensational as this, is a far cry from the circus of the simultaneous O.J. Simpson trial in Los Angeles. We can only speculate from our global knowledge of femicide, ritual rape, wife battering, and sex slavery that there is much more to the story than the newspapers and television stations are telling us, or than what Homolka and Bernardo themselves know, but aren't telling us — yet.

In 2005, after serving twelve years in federal prison, Karla Homolka was released in accordance with the deal she made prior to the court's knowledge of the extent of her involvement in the rapes and murders. Her release was not renegotiated despite protest from the public and the legal community. In 2006 Karla is now living as anonymously as possible somewhere in the province of Quebec.

Kelly Marie Ellard

On November 14, 1997, seven girls (aged fourteen to sixteen years) and one sixteen-year-old boy brutally attacked Reena Virk, a young girl of South Asian origin, in a suburb of Victoria, B.C. As Reena left the scene of the beating to make her way home, she was followed by two members of the group — Kelly Ellard and Warren Glowatski. Kelly called out to her to ask if she was okay. Reena told them to leave her alone and staggered across the road. They followed her to the other side of a park, near a body of water. According to Glowatski's testimony, Kelly asked Reena to remove her jacket and shoes. Kelly then proceeded to beat her up again, smashing her head against a tree trunk to the point where Reena was rendered unconscious. Ellard and Glowatski dragged the unconscious body to the water, where Kelly hit Reena in the throat again and forcibly drowned her. According to Glowatski in his trial, Ellard stood in the water with her foot over Reena's head and smoked a cigarette. Neither Ellard, nor Glowatski, had met Virk until that night.

The discovery of Reena's body eight days later and the subsequent arrest of the teens involved in the initial attack resulted in intense media scrutiny and publicity. Both nationally and internationally, Reena Virk's murder came to symbolize the increasing violence of girls and young women, despite statistical evidence to the contrary.

The early media coverage advanced a "liberation thesis" to explain the murder, dwelling on the violence as an outcome of girls achieving gender equality. Reena, as a victim, was explained in terms of her inability to "fit" into her peer culture. She was described as being overweight, tall for her age, and plain in her looks. The news media failed to mention her South Asian origin or reflect on how her racial difference contributed to not fitting into the school culture (Jiwani 1999). She was not exotic enough in her difference to fit, nor was she acceptable according to the dominant, normative standards of her peer group or her family.

In March 2000, Kelly Marie Ellard was tried for the murder of Reena Virk. Media speculation about Ellard's role in the murder had continued throughout the two-year period prior to her trial. From January to April 21, more than a hundred local and national radio and television newscasts and press articles focused on the Virk murder. This sustained and, at times, heavy coverage appeared to be motivated by a desire to advance explanations of the crime that made "common sense." That desire to make sense emanated from the same cognitive dissonance that had occurred in the cases of Karla Homolka and Leslie Van Houten. Like them, Ellard came from a middle-class, white family. Although her parents were divorced, she appeared to have a close relationship with her family, which motivated one judge to rule that she could stay at home rather than be incarcerated in a youth detention centre. Her appearance did not fit her crime. As one columnist opined, "How do you match the sweet-looking teenage girl who doesn't stand five feet in her platform shoes, who's a little heavy in the hips, who speaks tremulously on the stand, with the image of an accused killer...?" (McMartin 2000).

From the beginning of the trial, the press presented Ellard as a normal-looking teenager "with straight black hair cut just above the shoulders," wearing "a gray sweater and black pants" (Stonebanks 2000). However, these descriptions were juxtaposed with photographs that portrayed Ellard with a smug expression, downcast eyes, and a hint of a smile. The pictures communicated an image of an individual cognizant of more than she was willing to reveal.

The coverage of the Ellard trial was influenced by a number of external factors. Reporters attending the trial had followed the story from its inception two years earlier. Hence they were privy to details revealed in the testimonies presented at the previous trial of Warren Glowatski, the co-accused, and the hearings of the other young women who were involved in the beating. It was not uncommon to see reporters gather outside the courtroom to verify what they had heard and identify common themes of relevancy for their particular articles and newscasts. Additionally, reporters were cautioned by the outcomes of a preceding event in which one newspaper was severely chastised by a particular judge for revealing details of a trial prior to the jury going out for deliberation. In the Ellard trial, the presiding judge, Madam Justice Morrison, had decreed that the jury would not be sequestered for the length of the trial. This meant that journalists could not report on anything other than what witnesses stated in their testimonies. The reportage was thus extremely factual and rarely included the same level of descriptive discourse that appeared in the Homolka case. Nonetheless, reporters used terms such as "chilling," "gang-murder," "savage," "cold-blooded killing" and "calculated" to describe both Ellard and the murder. They borrowed most of these words directly from testimony provided by witnesses.

> Reporters used terms such as "chilling," "gang-murder," "savage," "cold-blooded killing," and "calculated" to describe both Ellard and the murder. They borrowed most of these words from testimony provided by witnesses.

From the testimonies, the media constructed an image of Ellard as a cold-blooded killer who had deliberately murdered Virk. They portrayed her as being the most aggressive and leading the assault. She was also described as having bragged about the murder to her friends. Throughout the trial, Ellard's composure, as reported, vacillated from being tearful to being calm, depending on who took the witness stand. Between the sessions in court, she was often seen, and captured on camera, laughing and joking with her family and defence counsel.

Some thirty witnesses were called to testify at the trial over a three-week period. The Crown maintained that Ellard had committed the crime to ensure that Reena would not "rat" on the members of the group who had beaten her up. The defence strategy was to portray Ellard as a helpless victim of a conspiracy organized by the co-accused, Warren Glowatski. Ellard and members of her family were the key witnesses for the defence. Together they wove a picture of middle-class normalcy and concern. Ellard was composed on the stand. She spoke softly and denied any involvement. She identified Glowatski and two other young women as having committed the murder. According to news reports, Ellard cried when asked to recount why she had delivered the first blow to Reena Virk. She replied, "I guess I was being like them, victimizing her" (Moore 2000a).

While the media coverage was contained and cautious throughout the trial, once the jury went into deliberation the press focused on the information presented in the *voir dires* — information not accepted as evidence by the judge or seen by the jury. The media pointed to the inconsistencies between Ellard's statements to the police and the testimonies presented by the various Crown witnesses. Despite this, the tenor of the articles was not as damning as the coverage that came after the verdict was announced.

The jury's verdict was a conviction for second-degree murder. Justice Morrison set the eligibility for parole at five years.

The news media used stock theories to account for Ellard's criminal behaviour. In some instances they identified teen group loyalty as the main motive underpinning Ellard's actions, as well as those of Glowatski, who refused to testify as a Crown witness against Ellard (Teahen 2000). Other accounts drew on previous psychological assessments to demonstrate Ellard's pathological character, her inability to assume responsibility, and her lack of internalized social values (Hall 2000; see Appendix). Other news items focused on the need for increased law and order to control the increasingly violent actions of teens. This last point was underscored by Crown counsel, who stated to reporters, "I hope it will spur parents particularly to do whatever they can to make sure they know where their children are so that a little more control can be taken of the situation" (Canadian Press, March 31, 2000). Some of the coverage utilized the previous frame of girl violence, alleging that most of the girls involved in the attack on Virk had criminal records (Moore 2000b).

These same theories appear in letters to the editors. In an anonymous letter (April 4, 2000) printed in the *Province* (Vancouver), the author addresses "Killer Kelly Ellard" stating, "Perhaps we don't want to know how an attractive young woman like yourself, 15 at the time, could murder a younger school mate with a cruelty we've always preferred to believe was reserved for the vilest of villains — nearly always adult males." The author ends the letter by stating, "We'll just write you off as a whacky weirdo with a rotten childhood whose hatred of herself and the world is etched in her eyes. What else can we do? Except keep our fingers crossed that if the social network should fail, the jury system will prevail."

> Significantly absent from stories about Reena Virk was her marginalized social status. The issue of race and racism was either ignored or presented in terms of her inability to fit.

Significantly absent in the range of explanations put forward by the media was Reena Virk's marginalized positioning vis-à-vis those who had beaten and killed her. The issue of race and racism was either absent from the media discourse or presented in terms of her inability to fit. Rarely did the media question why she could not fit, and what she might have been attempting to fit into. Even though both Ellard and Glowatski are white, and both were convicted of killing a young South Asian girl, the issue of racism only surfaced when Justice Morrison stated in her sentencing, "Whatever the motive for this crime, it was not racism" (Ivens 2000). Justice Morrison went on to portray Ellard as someone who had shown remorse as well as the potential for rehabilitation. She spoke at length about Ellard's love for animals and the positive references she had seen in the twenty-nine letters she had received from Ellard's friends and family.

Although the media work in concert with other dominant/elite institutions in society to legitimize perspectives that are consonant with the views of those in power (Hall et al. 1978; Hall 1980; van Dijk 1993), the relationship between the media and dominant institutions is not a direct one. Rather, in putting forward competing explanations, the media favour the explanations that make "common sense," and "common sense" perspectives often work in support of the dominant ideology. In this particular case, Justice Morrison underlined Ellard's presumed innocence and thereby contributed to the media's more muted condemnation of the murder. The coverage is starkly different from that of the Homolka case. It colludes with dominant "common sense" definitions of racism as extremist behaviours confined to the actions of hate groups, or as overtly racial slurs and insults. Within the landscape of "multicultural" Canada, these dominant definitions do not include systemic and invisible forms of everyday racism.

If the crime were to be recast — if a South Asian girl murdered a white girl or, more dramatically, an Aboriginal boy murdered a white girl — the denial and erasure of racism in the Ellard case would become apparent. Public outrage would have been intense, and the crime would probably not have elicited the same light sentence of five years.[2] Given the omission of the factor of racism and, with it, a profound denial of the unequal and hierarchical nature of society, we can only see the media as being complicit in presenting an image of a democratic society in which all members are equally vulnerable to victimization and equally accountable in the eyes of the law.

Media and Dangerous Girls and Women

When they occurred, these three cases incited considerable media coverage and public scrutiny. At the root of the public fascination and extensive coverage was that all three cases ruptured stereotypical notions of appropriate gender behaviour.

In numerous respects, these three women and their crimes have distinct commonalities. All three were involved in uniquely horrific murders. These were exceptional crimes in that the victims were also girls/women and primarily strangers. Van Houten and Homolka, and perhaps Ellard as well, explicitly committed their crimes in seeking a man's approval. None of them was a feminist. In the aftermath, all of them seemed unaffected by the consequences of their crimes, the immense pain caused by their actions. They were all from balanced, middle-class homes, which sets them apart from the majority of criminalized women. (This did not benefit Van Houten, who was declassed through her association with the outcast Manson.) According to contemporary, white femininity standards, all are good-looking with likeable personalities, which may well have been factors in the lenient deal/sentencing of Homolka and Ellard. (It didn't help Van Houten, who was originally sentenced to death.) None of them suffered from disabilities or was in any way stigmatized as "other" prior to their crimes. They all "fitted in." Thus their behaviours were regarded as radical aberrations of gender expectations. In short, they were marked as dangerous women.

Van Houten, along with twenty-five or so other young people, was a straightforward victim of brainwashing by a cult guru. Her decisive crime was in surrendering her power to him. Her reasons were of a spiritual nature; she was seeking truths and believed he had them. Although Homolka was similarly entranced by Bernardo, her motives weren't at all spiritual. Van Houten's crime occurred at the peak of a massive social movement that had disrupted traditional capitalist values. By contrast, Homolka's crimes, and Ellard's, occurred during a period of conformity, consumerism, and materialism. Whereas Van Houten rejected the consumer society, Homolka embraced it. According to the accounts, she was interested in the surface appearance of things.

The perception of dangerousness in each of these cases was heightened and exaggerated by intense media coverage. The coverage served to re-entrench the proverbial notion that women are as dangerous as men, and that an increasing proclivity to violence among women is a result of their liberation from patriarchal control. Certainly some women such as Homolka and/or Ellard can be readily perceived as dangerous, but men are ten times more likely to kill someone. The fear of "criminal women," as a generalized, stereotyped group, is irrational. However, the hardware invested in locking up women — the bars, fences, lasers, electronic locks, cameras, guards, and walls — are all signals to the public that these unseen women are dangerous. In a prison, every real or contrived crisis or emergency that gathers media interest is a means for correctional workers to express to the public the dangers of their occupations, and to be granted better wages, working conditions, and "danger pay."

Theories of female criminality and dangerousness have evolved from essentialist notions regarding women's innate nature. The dangerousness of women, after all, can be traced back to Biblical times and Eve. Notions of women's inherent dangerousness have also existed in other cultural milieus, in part as a result of colonization and the spread of the Judeo-Christian and Islamic traditions.[3] Contradictory representations in this historical tradition clearly cohere around the notions of women as virgins or vamps, madonnas or whores.

The placing of some women on a pedestal of purity and innocence (representing woman as virginal) often comes at the expense of non-white, sexualized women in low-income households. To be effective, one representation is contrasted with another that is its opposite. We know that not all women are pure, innocent, or chaste. We do not understand quite as well how social class, race, age, sexuality, and ablebodyness influence a girl's or woman's vulnerability to violence as victim and/or perpetrator. The three cases demonstrate the need to complicate the analysis — to begin to consider interlocking forms of oppression (Razack 1998) and relations of power that have an impact upon and among women who are in different places in the social hierarchy. Media monopolies are gendered, race-based, and class-based. They are controlled by white, upper-class men. Media explanations for women's criminality borrow from an androcentric historical tradition and reflect the views of those who control them. From this perspective, women's "inherent proclivity" to criminality tends to be confined to the sexualized, racialized, and low-income classes. Women who break the mould are most newsworthy.

The three cases illustrate the media's strategic use of isolated examples of female criminals to establish a generalized female proclivity to crime. These cases were headlined simply because such cases are rare — that is what makes them sensational. The horrors of the crimes committed by Leslie Van Houten, Karla Homolka, and Kelly Marie Ellard are used to underscore how women in general are capable of committing violent crimes and becoming "like men." By this logic, women do not deserve any special consideration on the grounds of gender inequality; their criminality becomes a result of their achieving gender-parity. The media's decontextualized and case-specific reportage lends itself well to this kind of explanation.

> Media monopolies are controlled by white, upper-class men; from this perspective, women's "inherent proclivity" to criminality tends to be confined to the sexualized, racialized, and low-income classes.

Pathology occurs at extreme ends of a continuum of social values and behaviours. We are socialized for pathological behaviours as surely as we are socialized for acceptable behaviours. In focusing on these women's transgressions, the media reinforce the normative social and moral order. They imply the rewards that accrue if women stay "in their place." However few and far between are these cases of horrific violence by girls and women, their actions ignite the fears engendered by Adler's work in the 1970s and Pearson's book in the 1990s. Women who engage in "senseless violence" are demonized and, if they excite the media, permanently stigmatized. Their identities are lost to processing by the state: the literal replacement of a person's name with a number, and the social death and invisibility of living behind bars. Their identities are reduced to their crimes.

Gayle Horii, a woman who served a life sentence in Canada, writes of that experience:

> I realized that probably less than five minutes of my life dictated my punishment, but it need not wipe out the woman I was for forty-two years previous to my particular madness, nor dictate how I live the remainder of my life. Because of the crime I committed, it may be difficult to accept my assertions that I should be granted human rights and that I could still maintain decent values. It is a most abstract conundrum, to wrap one's mind around the fact that a killer and/or prisoner could also be a good person. (Horii 2000: 104)

Appendix

Summary of Psychopathology Checklist as developed by Dr. Robert D. Hare. *Without Conscience: The Disturbing World of the Psychopaths among Us.* New York: Pocket Books, 1993, pp. 3–34

1. Glib and superficial
2. Egocentric and grandiose
3. Lack of remorse or guilt
4. Lack of empathy
5. Deceitful and manipulative
6. Shallow emotions
7. Impulsive
8. Poor behavioural controls
9. Need for excitement
10. Lack of responsibility
11. Early behavioural problems
12. Adult anti-social behaviours

Note: Everyone has some of the above characteristics. Others, the psychopaths, have strong constellations of many of these characteristics. Most of Hare's examples of psychopaths are men, which is consistent with the infrequency of women's crimes of violence.

DISCUSSION QUESTIONS

1. In what ways can the media be seen as an arm of the criminal justice system?

2. What are some of the social or policy effects of the media focus on murders by girls?

3. How do you explain the erasure of racism in the murder of Reena Virk and in the trial of the defendant Kelly Ellard?

4. Cite reasons why Leslie Van Houten should be released from prison or reasons why she should not be released. Include a discussion of whether there should be limits to punishment.

5. If Karla Homolka were to be retried, and you were the presiding judge, what would be your sentencing decision? (Consider options outside of conventional punishments.)

6. Explain the social construction of "dangerousness" as it affects women who are criminalized.

GLOSSARY OF TERMS

Backlash: negative reaction that thwarts someone's intentions.

Biblical Constructions: ways of seeing the world that are formed from the traditions and lore of early Christianity as documented in the Bible, including patriarchal and hierarchical social relations.

Common Sense: also known as "conventional wisdom"; the unexamined cultural beliefs, attitudes, and opinions held as truths by a majority of a specific group within a specific time period.

Criminalized Women: those who, through discriminatory social processes and law enforcement, are selected for the prosecution of illegal behaviours, convicted and imprisoned, and thereafter labelled and stigmatized as a member of the criminal class.

Dangerousness: a presumed propensity for causing physical harm to others.

Dangerous Offender: a designation that came into effect in 1977, based on patterns of unrestrained behaviour, aggressive behaviour and behaviour deemed "brutal" in nature. Those designated as "dangerous offenders" are sentenced to indeterminate sentences that have no set warrant expiry date.

Girl-on-Girl Violence: an occasion on which one girl assaults another, or a group of girls assaults one or more other girls.

Liberation Thesis: criminologists in the 1970s predicted wrongly that the women's liberation movement would cause women to commit a higher rate of violent crime.

Luddites: members of a nineteenth-century movement in Great Britain that protested the replacement of human labour with machines. The term Luddite comes from Ned Lud, a feeble-minded man who smashed two frames belonging to a Leicestershire employer, and was adopted by a group of workers in England who between 1811 and 1816 smashed new labour-saving textile machinery in protest against reduced wages and the unemployment attributed to that machinery's introduction.

Pop Psychology: commonplace formulations of "truths" about human behaviours, feelings, and thoughts based on the superficialities of popular culture and commonly reflecting a disinterest in or lack of access to scholarly research. For example, over the last two decades there has been an increase in the publication of "psychology" books for laypeople to satisfy a growth in interest in understanding personal behaviour and the lives of those around them. These are the books you find in the psychology section in book stores on issues such as multiple intelligence, personality typologies and emotional intelligence. Most materials of this nature are written by psychologists, adding at least a veneer of respectability.

SUGGESTED READINGS

Adelberg, Ellen, and Claudia Currie (eds.). 1993. *In Conflict with the Law: Women in the Canadian Justice System.* Vancouver: Press Gang.

Arbour, The Honourable Louise. 1996. *Commission of Inquiry into Certain Events at the Prison for Women in Kingston.* Ottawa: Solicitor General of Canada.

Cook, Sandy, and Susanne Davies (eds.). 1999. *Harsh Punishments: International Experiences of Women's Imprisonment.* Boston: Northeastern Press.

DeKeseredy, Walter S. 2000. *Women, Crime and the Canadian Criminal Justice System.* Cincinnati, OH: Anderson Publishing Co.

Faith, Karlene. 1993. *Unruly Women: The Politics of Confinement and Resistance.* Vancouver: Press Gang.

Hannah-Moffat, Kelly, and Margaret Shaw (eds.). 2000. *An Ideal Prison? Critical Essays on Women's Imprisonment in Canada.* Halifax: Fernwood Publishing.

Kershaw, Anne, and Mary Lasovitch. 1991. *Rock-a-Bye Baby: A Death Behind Bars.* Toronto: McClelland & Stewart.

Weibe, Rudy, and Yvonne Johnson. 1998. *Stolen Life: The Journey of a Cree Woman.* Toronto: Alfred A. Knopf.

NOTES

1. This section is culled from *The Long Prison Journey of Leslie Van Houten* (Faith 2001).
2. By spring 2002 Kelly Ellard's case had been appealed, and she was out of prison, living at home, pending a decision. Her second trial was aborted on a technicality. In her third trial, in the summer of 2005, Kelly was convicted of second degree murder and she is now serving a life sentence in a federal prison.
3. This is not to suggest that these religions do not have their own feminist traditions, which have emerged in response to an androcentric interpretation of the respective faith and have resulted in a herstory that identifies the female aspects of a revered universal being.

REFERENCES

Adler, Freda. 1975. *Sisters in Crime: The Rise of the New Female Criminal.* New York: McGraw Hill.

Alvi, Shahid. 2000. *Youth and Canadian Criminal Justice System.* Cincinnati: Anderson.

Artz, Sibylle. 1998. *Sex, Power and the Violent School Girl.* Toronto: Trifolium.

Bell, Sandra J. 1999. *Young Offenders and Juvenile Justice.* Toronto: Nelson.

Bertrand, Marie-Andree. 1969. "Self-Image and Delinquency: A Contribution to the Study of Female Criminality and Woman's Image." *Acta Criminologica* 2.

Birch, Helen (ed.). 1993. *Moving Targets: Women, Murder and Representation.* London: Virago.

Blackwell, Tom. 1995a. "Jury faces Question of Homolka's role: Was She a Battered, Blackmailed Handmaiden to a Driven Murder or a Willing Participant in Killing?" *Vancouver Sun,* June 17.

_____. 1995b. "Homolka Ignored Teen's Plea Because She was 'Too Afraid' of her Husband." *Vancouver Sun,* June 23.

_____. 1995c. "Bernardo 'Happy' after Killing Girl on Easter Sunday." *Vancouver Sun,* June 28.

_____. 1995d. "Homolka Denies 'Obsession': Court Hears Gushing Notes on Wedding to Bernardo." *Vancouver Sun,* July 6.

_____. 1995e. "Homolka Cursed Parents, Scorned Dad's Grief." *Vancouver Sun,* July 8.

_____. 1995f. "Homolka selected French as 2nd Victim, Defence says." *Vancouver Sun,* July 13.

_____. 1995g. "Battered Women can be Forced to Help Murderers, Expert Says." *Vancouver Sun,* August 4.

_____. 1995h. "Accused 'Enjoyed' Assaulting Captive Girl." *Vancouver Sun,* August 17.

_____. 1995i. "Murder not 'Planned': Accused Says He'll Probably Get Help for 'Sexuality Problem.'" *Vancouver Sun*, June 20.

Boritch, Helen. 1997. *Fallen Women: Female Crime and Criminal Justice in Canada*. Scarborough, ON: ITP Nelson.

Brown, Barbara. 1995. "Homolka says She Watched Killing of 2 Girls in Bedroom: 'Paul Strangled Them with a Black Electrical Cord,' ex-wife tells Court." *Vancouver Sun*, June 20.

Brownlee, Jamie. 2005. *Ruling Canada: Corporate Cohesion and Democracy*. Black Point, NS: Fernwood Publishing.

Canadian Centre for Justice Statistics (CCJS). 1999. *Canadian Crime Statistics: Annual Catalogue*. Ottawa: Statistics Canada.

Canadian Press. 2000. "Teen Girl Begins Life [sic] Sentence for Killing Reena Virk." March 31.

Chesney-Lind Meda. 1997. *The Female Offender: Girls, Women and Crime*. Thousand Oaks, California: Sage.

_____ 1999. "Review: P. Pearson, When She Was Bad." *Women & Criminal Justice* 10 (4): 113–18.

Connell, Ian. 1980. "Television News and the Social Contract." In Stuart Hall, Dorothy Hobson, Andrew Lowe and Paul Willis (eds.), *Culture, Media, Language*. London, UK: Hutchinson Press and the Centre for Contemporary Cultural Studies, University of Birmingham.

DeKeseredy, Walter S. 2000. *Women, Crime and the Canadian Criminal Justice System*. Cincinnati: Anderson.

DeKeseredy, W.S., D.G. Saunders, M.D. Schwartz, and S. Alvi. 1997. "The Meanings and Motives for Women's Use of Violence in Canadian College Dating Relationships: Results from a National Survey." *Sociological Spectrum* 17.

Ehrenreich, Barbara and Deirdre English. 1973. *Witches, Midwives, and Nurses: A History of Women Healers*. Old Westbury: Feminist Press.

Fabianic, David. 1997. "Television Dramas and Homicide Causation." *Journal of Criminal Justice* 25 (3).

Faith, Karlene. 1993a. *Unruly Women: The Politics of Confinement and Resistance*. Vancouver: Press Gang Publishers.

_____. 1993b. "Media, Myths and Masculinization: Images of Women in Prison." In E. Adelberg and C. Currie (eds.), *In Conflict with the Law: Women in the Canadian Justice System*. Vancouver: Press Gang.

_____. 2001. *The Long Prison Journey of Leslie Van Houten, Life Beyond the Cult*. Boston: Northeastern University Press.

Farr, Kathryn Ann. 2000. "Defeminizing and Dehumanizing Female Murderers: Depictions of Lesbians on Death Row." *Women & Criminal Justice* 11 (1).

Galloway, Gloria. 1995. "Bernardo Jury Stoic as 'Disturbing' Videotape of Rape Played." *Vancouver Sun*, June 1.

Gilbert, Evelyn. 1999. "Crime, Sex, and Justice: African American Women in U.S. Prisons." In S. Cook and S. Davies (eds.), *Harsh Punishment: International Experiences of Women's Imprisonment*. Boston: Northeastern Press.

Glueck, Sheldon, and Eleanor Glueck. 1965 (original 1934). *Five Hundred Delinquent Women*. New York: Kraus Reprint.

Goff, Colin. 1999. *Corrections in Canada*. Cincinnati: Anderson.

Gordon, Jody, Karlene Faith, and Dawn Currie. 1995. "The Case of Karla Homolka: Crime, Media and Gender Politics." Unpublished data. President's Research Grant. School of Criminology, Simon Fraser University.

Hall, Neale. 2000. "Ellard's Nickname was Killer Kelly, Court Told." *Vancouver Sun*, April 1.

Hall, Stuart. 1980. "Race, Articulation and Societies Structured in Dominance." In Stuart Hall, (ed.), *Sociological Theories: Race and Colonialism*. Paris: UNESCO.

_____. 1990. "The Whites of Their Eyes." In M. Alvarado and J.O. Thompson (eds.), *The Media Reader*. London: British Film Institute.

Hall, Stuart, Chas Critcher, Tony Jefferson, John Clarke, and Brian Roberts. 1978. *Policing the Crisis: Mugging, the State, and Law and Order*. London: Macmillan.

Hartley, John. 1982. *Understanding News*. London & New York: Methuen.

Hayman, Stephanie. 2000. "Prison Reform and Incorporation." In K. Hannah-Moffat and M. Shaw (eds.), *An Ideal Prison? Critical Essays on Women's Imprisonment in Canada*. Halifax: Fernwood Publishing.

Heidensohn, Frances. 1968. "The Deviance of Women: A Critique and an Enquiry." *British Journal of Sociology* 19 (2).

Horii, Gayle. 2000. "Processing Humans." In K. Hannah-Moffat and M. Shaw (eds.), *An Ideal Prison? Critical Essays on Women's Imprisonment in Canada*. Halifax: Fernwood Publishing.

Hudson, Annie. 1989. "'Troublesome Girls:' Towards Alternative Definitions and Policies." In Maureen Cain (ed.), *Growing Up Good: Policing the Behaviour of Girls in Europe*. London: Sage.

Ivens, Andy. 2000. "No Apology by Killer, She got the Lightest Sentence Possible: Five Years without Parole." *The Vancouver Province*, April 21.

Jiwani, Yasmin. 1993. "By Omission and Commission: 'Race' and Representation in Canadian Television News." Unpublished doctoral dissertation, School of Communications, Simon Fraser University.

_____. 1999. "Erasing Race: The Story of Reena Virk." *Canadian Woman Studies* 19 (3).

Joe, K., and M. Chesney-Lind. 1993. "Just Every Mother's Angel." Paper presented at meetings of the American Society of Criminology. Phoenix, Arizona, October.

Kendall, Kathleen. 1999. "Beyond Grace: Criminal Lunatic Women in Victorian Canada." *Canadian Woman Studies* 19 (1&2).

Kershaw, Anne, and Mary Lasovitch. 1991. *Rock-a-Bye-Baby: A Death Behind Bars*. Toronto: McClelland & Stewart.

Klaits, Joseph. 1985. *Servants of Satan: The Age of the Witch Hunts*. Bloomington: Indiana University Press.

Klein, Dorie. 1973. "The Etiology of Female Crime: A Review of the Literature." *Issues in Criminology* 8 (2).

Legall, Paul. 1995a. "Graphic Dialogue sends Eerie Chill through Court: 200 Spectators Hear 6 Minutes of Drug-Induced Rape of Homolka Sister." *Vancouver Sun*, June 1.

_____. 1995b. "Accused Killer Wails for his Wife: Court Hears Tape Recording of Pleas for Homolka to Return." *Vancouver Sun*, June 16.

Lombroso, Cesare, and William Ferrero. 1895. *The Female Offender*. New York: Philosophical Library.

MacFarlane, Alan. 1970. *Witchcraft in Tudor and Stuart England: A Regional and Comparative Study*. New York: Harper and Row.

Makin, Kirk. 1995a. "Homolka Chose Kristen for Abduction, Lawyer says: Bernardo's Ex-Wife Keeps up Verbal Battle with Defence over her Role in Girl's Death, Tells Court her Level of Intelligence is 'Very Debatable.'" *Globe and Mail*, July 13.

_____. 1995b. "Homolka Ends Graphic Testimony." *Globe and Mail*, July 15

_____. 1995c. "Judge says Bernardo Trial Staying from Main Issue: Battered Women's Syndrome Explored in Testimony: Trial not about Whether Homolka was Abused." *Globe and Mail*, August 8.

Marwick, Max (ed.). 1975. *Witchcraft and Sorcery*. Harmondsworth, Middlesex: Penguin.

Marx, Karl. 1970–2. *Das Kapital*. Moscow: Progress.

McCormick, Chris. 1995. *Constructing Danger: The Mis/Representation of Crime in the News*. Halifax: Fernwood Publishing.

McMartin, Pete. 2000. "Shock of Virk Trial is Ordinary Appearance of Accused Teen — A Scared Little 17-year-old in Person Comes as a Surprise after Grisly Testimony and a Smug-Looking Photo." *Vancouver Sun*, March 23.

Monture-Angus, Patricia. 2000. "Aboriginal Overrepresentation in the Canadian Criminal Justice System." In David Long and Olive Patricia Dickason (eds.), *Visions of the Heart: Canadian Aboriginal Issues* 2nd edition. Toronto: Harcourt Canada.

Moore, Deme. 2000a. "Accused Teen Killer Says She Wasn't There when Virk Killed." *Canadian Press*, March 23.

_____. 2000b. "Girls who Beat Virk had Long Histories of Violence." *Canadian Press*, April 1.

Neugebauer-Visano, Robynne. 1996. "Kids, Cops, and Colour: The Social Organization of Police-Minority Youth Relations." In G.M. O'Bireck (ed.), *Not a Kid Anymore: Canadian Youth, Crime, and Subcultures*. Toronto: Nelson.

Ouimet, R. 1969. *Report of the Canadian Committee on Corrections*. Ottawa: Information Canada.

Parrinder, Geoffrey. 1963. *Witchcraft: European and African*. London: Faber & Faber.

Pate, Kim. 1999. "Young Women and Violent Offences: Myths and Realities." *Canadian Woman Studies* 19 (1&2).

Pearson, Patricia. 1998. *When She Was Bad*. Toronto: Vintage.

Razack, Sherene H. 1998. *Looking White People in the Eye: Gender, Race, and Culture in Courtrooms and Classrooms*. Toronto: University of Toronto Press.

Regan Shade, Leslie. 1994. "Desperately Seeking Karla: The Case of alt.fan.karla.homolka." Proceedings of the Canadian Association for Information Science, 22nd Annual Conference, May 25–27, McGill University, Montreal.

Reiman, Jeffrey. 2007. *The Rich Get Richer and the Poor Get Prison: Ideology, Class and Criminal Justice*. Boston: Allyn and Bacon.

Reitsma-Street, Marge. 1999. "Justice for Canadian Girls: A 1990s Update." *Canadian Journal of Criminology* 41 (3).

Schissel, Bernard. 1997. *Blaming Children: Youth Crime, Moral Panics and the Politics of Hate*. Halifax: Fernwood Publishing.

Schramm, Heather. 1998. *Young Women Who Use Violence: Myths and Facts*. Calgary: Elizabeth Fry Society of Calgary.

Sharpe. J. A. 1984. *Crime in Early Modern England, 1550–1750*. New York: Longman.

Smart, Carol. 1976. *Women, Crime and Criminology: A Feminist Critique*. London: Routledge & Kegan Paul.

Stepan, Cheryl. 2000. "Homolka Transcript Brings Tears to Court." *Calgary Herald*, April 28.

Stevenson, John. 1979. *Popular Disturbances in England, 1700–1870*. New York: Longman.

Stonebanks, Roger. 2000. "The Last Accused in Reena's Death: Families Gather to Witness Final Trial in Teen Tragedy." *Victoria Times Colonist*, March 7.

Strange, Carolyn. 1985–86. "'The Criminal and Fallen' of Their Sex: The Establishment of Canada's First Women's Prison, 1874–1901." *Canadian Journal of Women and the Law/Revue juridique "La femme et le droit"* 1 (1).

Taylor, Carl S. 1993. *Girls, Gangs, Women and Drugs*. East Lansing: Michigan State University Press.

Teahen, Kelley. 2000. "When Loyalty turns Threatening." *London Free Press*, Opinion, April 4.

Thompson, E.P. 1963. *The Making of the English Working Class*. London: Penguin.

Trevor-Roper, H.R. 1975. "The European Witch-Craze." In M. Marwick (ed.), *Witchcraft and Sorcery*. Harmondsworth, Middlesex: Penguin.

Underdown, David E. 1985. "The Taming of the Scold: The Enforcement of Patriarchal Authority in Early Modern England." In A. Fletcher and J. Stevenson (eds.), *Order and Disorder in Early Modern England*. Cambridge: Cambridge University Press.

Van Dijk, Teun. 1993. *Elite Discourse and Racism*. California: Sage Publications.

Verburg, Peter. 1995. "'Battered Wife Syndrome' on Trial: Homolka's Complicity in the Bernardo Atrocities Dealt a Heavy Blow to the 'Robo-Victim' Defence." *Western Report* 10 (22), June 26.

Walker, Robert. 1994. "Publication Ban Doing More Harm than Good, Lawyer Argues." *Montreal Gazette*, February 7.

Warwick, Liz. 1995. "Violent Women." *Ottawa Citizen*, August 1.

Wente, Margaret. 1999. "The New and Self-Improved Karla Homolka." *Globe and Mail*, November 6.

Wilson, Nanci Koser. 1993. "Taming Women and Nature: The Criminal Justice System and the Creation of Crime in Salem Village." In R. Muraskin and T. Alleman (eds.), *It's a Crime: Women and Justice*. Englewood Cliffs, NJ: Regents/Prentice Hall.

7

Crime Statistics and the "Girl Problem"

Sandra J. Bell

KEY FACTS

> Some researchers suggest that increases in youth violent crime, particularly that of girls, can be partly explained by the stricter approach to schoolyard fights and bullying in recent years, which has led educators, parents and police to label as "assaults" behaviours once viewed as unfortunate or "bad."

> Only 12.2 percent of street youth in Toronto reported their criminal victimization to the police. One of the main reasons cited for not reporting to the police was their belief that the police would not believe them.

> According to a study by the American Bar Association, stricter domestic-violence laws have contributed to a rise in the arrest rates of girls for assault because much female juvenile crime takes place in the home rather than on the street, as it does for boys. Compulsory arrest laws mean police officers are not allowed to walk away from a domestic dispute.

> In 2003, female children and youth, at every age, were assaulted more than males by a family member while male children and youth were more likely to be assaulted by persons from outside the family.

> Children who experience higher levels of punitive parenting and lower parental nurturance are also more likely to report higher frequencies of aggressive behaviour.

> Girls' violence is produced within social contexts of extreme gender inequality. How and when girls choose to adopt violent strategies, as well as when and how girls negotiate within potentially violent situations — each of these is best understood by recognizing the significance of the contextual construction of unequal power relations and gender asymmetries.

Sources: Public Health Agency of Canada 2005; Gaetz 2004; *Current Events* 2003; Aucoin 2005; Sprott, Doob and Jenkins 2001; Miller and White 2004.

There was a little girl
who had a little curl
Right in the middle of her forehead.

And when she was good
she was very very good,
But when she was bad she was HORRID.
— Henry Wadsworth Longfellow

Crime and criminology is largely about men, and youth crime and criminology is largely about boys. Until the last two decades or so, women and girls have been like Sleeping Beauty (Heidenson 1996: 1000), completely cut off and largely absent from mainstream criminology. The feminist contribution to criminology, starting in the 1970s, brought women into mainstream criminology, and interest in girls' involvement in criminal activity began about ten years ago. Meanwhile, with the introduction and implementation of the *Young Offenders Act* in 1984 came an increased attention on youth crime, an interest largely

> Women and girls have been like "Sleeping Beauty" (Heidenson 1996: 1000), completely cut off and largely absent from mainstream criminology.

fuelled by media crime reporting. By the latter part of the 1990s the Canadian public, from coast to coast, was inundated with media stories about violent girls.

Crime and criminology is also about statistics, but many people have little interest in statistics or statistical analysis. It has certainly been my experience in teaching statistics courses to criminology undergraduates, that most students dread statistics. Yet, crime statistics, as with all statistics, are critical to our understanding of crime because they often provide the weapons and evidence used to develop, support, and justify policy and program responses to crime. Indeed, the very laws that frame and govern the adult and youth justice systems are to a great extent influenced by crime statistics and how Canadians and their elected politicians respond to them. The media are also an influential player in promoting public concerns about crime and they too use statistics to make and support claims about crime and criminal activity. Court judges too are sometimes required to address crime statistics. In a sentencing hearing for a fourteen-year-old youth in Nova Scotia, a defence lawyer tried to use statistics about Canada's high rate of youth incarceration and declining youth violent-crime rates to support his recommendation for sentence. The judge rejected the argument on the grounds that he didn't believe the statistics:

> There are lies, damn lies, and statistics... I hear the statistics, but in my 22 years as a judge I've noticed just the opposite... you can quote your statistics, but all I can go by is my own experience. (Fairclough 2004: B7)

In rejecting current crime statistics, he insisted that girls are more involved in assaults, that there is more violent crime because he sees it more in his court, and that "these kinds of things have flowered..." [in recent years] (Fairclough 2004: B7).

While criminology as a discipline is concerned about understanding why people engage in particular types of criminal behaviour an equally important aspect of criminology involves the study of crime as a concept. In the 1960s, Howard Becker changed the course of criminology by insisting that there was nothing inherent in an act that made it criminal. Rather, behaviours were defined as criminal. Killing someone is not murder, for example, if it is undertaken by the state. Rather, legislation such as the Criminal Code of Canada defines the conditions under which particular behaviours will be considered to constitute murder. A case in point is the recent announcement by the federal government of proposed legislation that will make "street racing" a Criminal Code offence — a crime rather than a traffic violation (Mertl 2006: A3). Most criminologists today accept as a given that crime is a social construction, that whether we respond to behaviour as criminal is the result of complex processes of construction. In this sense, the media and statistics play a vital role in the social construction of crimes and that role is the focus of this chapter. Through a critical examination of media coverage and statistical data on "girl violence," the chapter examines the construction of girl violence as a "crisis." Through this discussion we will gain an appreciation for the power of statistics as weapons in the processes of crime construction and crime control, and an understanding of the ways the media treat girls' problems.

Girl Crime, Public Perceptions and Popular Culture

Most peoples' understanding and knowledge about youth crime comes largely from the media, and most media reporting of youth crime focuses on violent crime (Sprott 1996). Reid-MacNevin (1996, 2003) examined both Canadian newspapers and Internet coverage of youth crime (during the summer of 1996 and 2002 respectively) and found that more than half the newspaper stories and two-thirds of the Internet stories involved a focus on violent youth crime. Furthermore, this was a time when youth violent crime accounted for only 18 percent of the total volume of reported police crime (2005: 146–47). The Canadian media generally rely on Statistics Canada and their periodical "Fast Facts" press releases on the latest crime statistics as well as on the testimony of experts. These "experts" are most often police officers and other criminal justice professionals, whose testimonies are largely based on their "on the job" experience. Reid-MacNevin found that almost half the news stories on crime involved police reports and a majority promoted a "law-and-order ideology" (2005: 147). Politicians often join the fray in constructing youth crime as "out of control," particularly during elections. In concert with media portrayals of crime, their pronouncements against youth and youth crime often take the form of what Welch, Fenwick and Roberts refer to as "demagoguery" (484).

The Girl Problem

Judging by news stories in the 1990s, Canadians seemed to be facing a crisis in girl violence that peaked in the latter part of the decade. In the five year period from 1995–2000, the media told stories of "out of control" violent girls. In 1997, we were told of two fifteen-year-old girls who stabbed Helen Montgomery to death in her North Battleford, Saskatchewan, home. The girls had been living in Montgomery's home under an open-custody arrangement at the time of the murder (Cross 1998). In 1995, a fifteen-year-old Saskatchewan girl, with an eight-year-old accomplice, pled guilty to the murder and mutilation of a seven-year-old boy (Savage 1998). In London, Ontario, a thirteen-year-old girl was convicted of attempted murder in 1998 for stabbing a nine-year-old boy in a schoolyard. On the east coast, a sixteen-year-old girl was convicted for first-degree murder in adult court for the murder of sixteen-year-old Kristy Salter, who had been found on the grounds of a high school, her throat slit. The co-accused in Kristy's murder was a teenage boy (Jeffrey 1995).

Perhaps the most newspaper coverage during this period was given to the murder of Reena Virk, a fourteen-year old Southeast Asian girl. On November 22, 1997, her body was found in a tidal inlet at the Gorge waterway in Victoria, British Columbia. Drowning was given as the official cause of her death, but she had also been severely beaten before drowning and had suffered "internal injuries more common to a car accident than a teen fight" (Moore 2000a). A sixteen-year-old boy and fifteen-year-old girl were accused and subsequently convicted, in adult court, of second-degree murder in her death. In addition, six other teenage girls aged fourteen to sixteen were charged with aggravated assault and convicted in youth court for their part in Reena's final ordeal (Chisholm 1997; Joyce 2000).

Media accounts readily portray pathologized and demonized images of girls (and other minorities) by decontextualizing their behaviour and "attaching" their behaviour to ready-made labels provided by a variety of experts. In the Virk case, for example, the newspaper coverage implied a number of explanations for the girls' violence. According to the reports, some of the accused were "wannabe" gang members, and all of them had long histories of violent behaviour. One girl was said to display "all the elements of sociopathic conduct" and another to have an "omnipotent attitude." As a group, they were said to be a "criminal clique" (Moore 2000b). One girl's mother reportedly described her daughter as "a habitual troublemaker utterly lacking in remorse" (Chisholm 1997: 16).

Even Reena Virk's behaviour was scrutinized in the media, and she was both pitied and blamed for her victimization. Articles reported that she had lived in a foster home, had been sexually abused by her father, and had attempted suicide (Chisholm 1997; Purvis 1997). The same articles also reported that according to her parents, Reena had run away from home "to gain more freedom" (a view largely discredited by those who work with homeless youth — see Lundy and Totten 1997) and that she had lied about the sexual assaults, was self-conscious about her weight, and was caught in a "downward spiral of plummeting self-esteem" (Chisholm 1997: 15). In other words, according to the reports, she was the author of her own fate.

News reports of these and other equally violent events involving teenage girls not only alerted the public to a "crisis," but fuelled and reinforced the crisis with sensational newspaper headlines. The headlines — "Fury of Her Peers: A Teenager's Brutal Assault and Drowning Raise Questions in a Quiet Canadian Town" (Purvis 1997); "Bad Girls: A Brutal B.C. Murder Sounds an Alarm about Teenage Violence" (Chisholm 1997); "Killer Girls" (*Alberta Report* 1995); "Ruthless Violence Part of Girl Gang Reality" (Vincent 1995); "Teen's Torture Again Reveals Girls' Brutality" (Vincent 1998a) — generated claims that Canadian girls were out of control, and that they were far more violent now than in the past. In the words of the *Alberta Report* (1995: 1) "Girls, it used to be said, were made of sugar and spice. Not anymore." According to a *Globe and Mail* journalist, "Today experts on youth violence see some of them as a dangerous threat to society — ruthless, volatile and brutal" (Vincent 1995).

Official crime statistics seemed to support media claims and added fuel to public concerns and fodder for journalistic accounts of girls' violent behaviour. Statistics Canada (1999), for example, reported that between 1988 and 1995 youth violent crime had increased steadily, and the rate of girls' violent crime increased "twice as fast as male youth violent crime." Further it reported that after 1995, although the violent crime rate for male youth went into decline, the violent crime rate for girls continued to climb. In the 1990s, the rate of violent charges for girls increased by 127 percent (Savoie 1999: 5, 12). Facing statistics such as these, one wonders why the Nova Scotia judge would argue that the statistics are a lie as they actually seem to support his position.

Newspaper stories also used expert testimony to substantiate this apparent crisis. Readers were told that according to veteran police officers, the details of some girls' attacks on their victims were too horrifying to retell. "Believe me, you don't want to know," a police sergeant reportedly commented about one case. "It was horrifying," said the veteran of over twenty-eight years on the force. He had seen "assaults and robberies over the years," but never anything like that one (Vincent 1998a). "Law-enforcement officials," often quoted as experts on the crisis, said that girls were "more likely than boys to use firearms," and other "authorities" on girls' violence made claims that "girls are often more ruthless and aggressive than their male counterparts" (Vincent 1995). Some academics, citing police officers, also took this view:

> In an earlier day female gangs were rare, even in big cities, but such is no longer the case. By 1989, they were numerous enough in Toronto to be targeted by the police and, by the early 1990s, they were being described as a "big problem." Some police maintain that they are as capable of violence as boys and that they show no remorse for attacking people. (Carrigan 1998: 196)

At the end of the twentieth century, girl violence was an "official fact" — both official statistics from Statistics Canada and experts themselves had confirmed girl violence, that it was something we had never seen before and that it was worse than boys' violent behaviour. As we move into the twenty-first century, fears about girls' violence continue. In 2004, for example, we were informed by CTV news that "Swarming Girl Gangs a Crime Problem In Winnipeg" (CTV News, December 5, 2004). In this story, police report that there have been a number of incidents of girls "swarming" both girls and boys and robbing them of money, cellphones, and CD players and that the oldest of these girls was fourteen. Now there is a new threat posed by girls — bullying. Some of this bullying occurs on Internet chat rooms where girls are making online threats to classmates. Police are now charging youth with criminal harassment and uttering threats in cases of cyber bullying. Recently, two girls, aged fourteen and fifteen, from Odessa, Ontario, were charged with fifteen counts of threatening and one of conspiracy to commit murder for online threats made to students and teachers in their high school. Similarly in Halifax, two girls, aged thirteen and fifteen, and two boys, aged thirteen and fourteen, were charged with conspiracy to commit murder for exactly the same reasons (Arsenault 2006: A1–2). The expert cited in the Odessa story, from Florida Atlantic University, claims that "the Internet has become a weapon for some young people to bully and attack their peers" (*Chronicle Herald* 2006: A4).

A highly publicized case of this nature also comes from British Columbia. It has served as a precedent-setting case for bullying charges and conviction. In November 2000, fourteen-year-old Dawn-Marie Wesley hanged herself. She left a suicide note naming three of her friends as having bullied and threatened her such that "she believed death was her only escape." The three girls were charged with uttering threats and one was charged and convicted of criminal harassment as well as uttering threats (CBC News, March 26, 2002). The case is also discussed in a 2004 National Film Board of Canada documentary *It's a Girl's World: How Girls Use Their Power to Hurt Each Other* produced by Gerry Flahive, written and directed by Lynn Glazier. In this documentary, Glazier links the death of Dawn-Marie to the daily interactions of a friendship group of ten-year-old girls at school and on the playground — implying that suicide can be the outcome of girl type interaction — or what is referred to as "the hidden culture of aggression in girls." The *It's a Girl's World* CD cover describes this world as:

> about sharing secrets, giggling over boys and carefree fun. But lurking underneath this façade of niceness is a hidden culture of nastiness that pits one friend against another... they are motivated to use their closest relationships as weapons. (*It's a Girl's World*)

This then is the threat of the twenty-first century, and popular culture is capitalizing on the image of nasty girls. Definitions of girl violence have become more inclusive and have moved from "badness to meanness" (Chesney-Lind and Irwin 2004: 45). Where ten years ago girls' violence was perceived as "girls behaving like boys" or crossing the boundaries of "femininity," it is now more often perceived as a result of "girls being girls." The twenty-first-century discovery seems to be that girls are quite simply mean and nasty creatures. Movies such as *Mean Girls* (2004), based on Rosalind Wiseman's (2002) book *Queenbees and Wannabees,* present depictions of the horrors inflicted by "popular girls" on their class mates as "comedy" while other films, such as *Odd Girl Out* (2005), based on Rachel Simmons (2002) book of the same title, present girls' behaviour in far more sinister terms. In a recent book, *See Jane Hit* (2006), psychologist James Garbarino presents this twenty-first-century threat as a behaviour endemic to girls. More specifically, he blames "femininity" and explains that we are just now seeing this nastiness because girls have been "empowered," by advances in the status of women. Most importantly, we are only seeing the "true" nature of girls because they are also now, "unfettered." In making his argument, Garbarino offers a new twist on Longfellow's view of little girls cited at the start of the chapter.

> Where ten years ago girls' violence was perceived as "girls behaving like boys" or crossing the boundaries of "femininity," it is now more often perceived as a result of "girls being girls."

> The culture of girls is shifting away from the stifled femininity of the past toward a more egalitarian social reality in the present and the future. This is happening both at the top, where talented girls are now free and empowered to achieve in traditionally male domains... and at the bottom, among the victimized, angry, traumatized, and troubled girls who are looking for a fight and are willing to deliver the ultimate blow against anyone who gets in their way or pushes their buttons. Unless we see the trends emerging in the thinking and feeling of the new girl, the empowered girl, the unfettered girl, we shall not see her as she is. When she is good, she is very, very good. But when she is bad, she can be lethal. (Garbarino 2006: 193)

Interestingly, the book cover on *See Jane Hit* features a facial close-up of a little girl, eight to ten years old, with pinkish-white coloured skin, blue eyes, and reddish blond hair in "pigtails,"; she looks much like the popular fictional character Anne of Green Gables. Unlike Anne, this little girl has a scowl on her face, her blue eyes are squinted, and her lips are tightly pursed — she looks very nasty indeed.

> Unless we see the trends emerging in the thinking and feeling of the new girl, the empowered girl, the unfettered girl, we shall not see her as she is (Garbarino 2006).

On the surface, then, there seems good reason for concern — the media, popular culture, experts, and even Statistics Canada is telling us that girl violence is a growing problem — that while we learned in the 1990s to fear the "dangerous girl," the current message is that we now should fear even the "little girl next door." However, knowing something about the media and how they report crime leads us to take a more critical approach to these claims and question their truth value. Are girls really more violent now than in the past? Is their behaviour worse than that of boys? Is the judge quoted earlier correct in his belief that his experience is a valid measure of youth crime. Is he correct in believing that crime statistics are wrong because he is seeing more girls in his court charged with assault than ever before? Or are there other explanations for these claims. Answering these questions requires us to take a closer critical look at the media and crime reporting as well as crime statistics themselves.

Girl Crime and Media Misrepresentations

As we have seen, newspaper headlines clearly sensationalize violent criminal activity, but the articles that follow the headlines do far more. A crime is merely an event. The content of newspaper articles about these events serves to define for the reading public what is significant about the occurrence (Acland 1995). In this sense, media crime discourse in general is about what is "wrong" with our society, and it also preys on fears and insecurities about the future, because, after all, youth are the "next generation." The media readily interpret and present incidences of violent youth crime as evidence of dangerous cracks in the system and in our society (Acland 1995: 28–29).

Child and youth discourses are the "projection screens" of adult fears (Davis 1990), and as some have argued, the very concepts of childhood and youth are the products of adult desires and longings (Brown 2005: 210). The media play a critical role in defining the connections between young people, crime, and the state of society, to the extent that adult fears — about everything from unemployment to global unrest — find expression in a "lament for the lost generation" of youth (211–12). Hence, what is considered newsworthy about girl crime is not the crime but the gender of the criminal. As Batchelor (2001) points out, "nowhere is the violence of young men reported as 'boy violence'" (27). The news raises public fears that long-standing class, race, gender, and age boundaries are not only being crossed but also are being challenged, at our peril, and that they cannot be restored without strict law-and-order measures.

For example, as precursors to *Girls World* and *See Jane Hit*, a *Globe and Mail* article (Vincent 1998b) on "girl gangs" and their activities in schools warns of the negative consequences of women's struggles for gender equity. A police officer, "an expert on youth crime," says:

> We shouldn't be surprised by what's happening... What we're looking at is ladies coming of age in the 1990s, and girls are taking on a much more aggressive, violent role... These are not crimes of chance... These crimes are planned out and very methodical. (Cited in Vincent 1998b)

Another "expert" identified as a psychologist and director of youth programming concurs:

> The[se] patterns of behaviour are typical... We've got to start accepting that girls... can be every bit as aggressive, violent and bullying as the boys, and they're helping to turn schools into more violent places... We can see girls doing this in 100 other schools in this country. (Cited in Vincent 1998b)

For some critics, media accounts of crime and youth crime in particular do far more than sensationalize; they are hate literature (Schissel 1997). They target the vulnerable for condemnation — the poor, racially based gangs and groups, immigrants, mothers, and mothers who work outside the home (Schissel 1997: 51, 53). And now girls have been added to the list.

Most important, the media decontextualizes crime. Crimes are always, by the very nature of newspaper reporting, discussed out of context. A journalist provides information or details about the crime event in a manner that generates a number of emotions

— fear, moral outrage, despair, panic, and hatred — emotions all directed from readers towards the vulnerable in society (Schissel 1997: 34, 37). As such, media discourse is extremely powerful in promoting and reinforcing a sense that the only thing that can be done about girls' violence is to implement punitive repressive measures or, in Garbarino's terms, to "fetter" girls.

> Media accounts of crime and youth crime condemn the vulnerable — poor, racially based gangs, immigrants, and mothers who work outside the home (Schissel 1997: 51, 53). Now girls have been added to the list.

Misrepresented and sensationalized media portrayals of girl behaviour are not just a North American issue. Susan Batchelor (2001) talks about her research work in Scotland with girls' violent behaviour and the media's distorted response to her work. Batchelor's research indicates that women and girls in Scotland are responsible for only 7.5 percent of convictions for non-sexual crimes of violence; that only 5 percent of the 800 teenage girls she interviewed reported using physical violence towards others, and that not one of the girls reported involvement in a gang or even knowing any girl-gang members. Yet newspaper reporting of her research results consistently misrepresented and distorted her results with headlines such as "Deadly as the Males — Experts Probe Explosion of Violence by Girl Gangs" in the *Daily Record* (September 30, 2000, cited in Batchelor 2001). Furthermore, Batchelor says that her research was precipitated because of the media focus on girls' violence and because there was little actual knowledge about girls' behaviour from girls' points of view. Nonetheless, headlines in the Scottish newspaper *The Herald*, depicted the research as a response to increasing girls violence: "Concern at Girls and Violence — Study Investigates Female Aggression" (*The Herald*, October 20, 1998, cited in Batchelor 2001).

Also of interest, in confirming what others such as Schissel (1997) have indicated, is media misrepresentation of events. For example, Batchelor found that 41 percent of the girls she surveyed had been a victim of physical violence, and that most of the physical violence reported by girls (almost two-thirds) involved conflicts with siblings. This was reported in newspapers as "four out of ten [girls] has been beaten up." Similarly, as with other studies, the girls in the Scottish survey reported that verbal aggression, such as name-calling, threats and intimidation, were "often experienced as potentially *more* hurtful and damaging than physical violence." One newspaper referred to this survey with the headline "Violence is Just a Fact of Life Say Teenage Girls" (*Daily Telegraph*, October 10, 2000, cited in Batchelor 2001) and another said "Girls Fear Losing their Friends More than Rape (*Sunday Herald*, September 24, 2000, cited in Batchelor 2001). This is a hideous misinterpretation that demonizes girls, trivializes the issues that are of significance to them, and distorts and masks the realities of their victimization.

Crime Statistics

> *You start at 13 stealing cars, at 14 you rob a store, at 15 you're pregnant, at 16 you have a kid, and your whole life is over.* (Female young offender, cited in Totten 2001: 26)

While the media play a primary role in defining what is problematic about a criminal event, police and courts are the primary sources of crime statistics. For them, the production of statistics is a fairly straightforward and standardized activity. However, for the criminologist, measuring criminal activity and interpreting crime statistics is a complex and difficult task. The quality of the information gathered about crime is only as good as the tools we have at hand for measuring. While a ruler is a fairly precise instrument for measuring a person's height, we have no such instrument for measuring criminal activity. Rather, information about criminal activity comes from the police and other criminal justice agencies, mostly the courts. Sources from these agencies are referred to as *official statistics*. These agencies regularly report their statistics to Statistics Canada, which publishes them in "Fast Fact" releases and in yearly lists (*Juristat*) of general crime and court statistics for adults and youth, including adult prison admissions, remand, and community sentences that require supervision (such as probation). Statistics Canada also periodically provides special publications, also through *Juristat* on particular offences such as break and enter or drug offences. Complete homicide statistics are provided on a yearly basis. Other crime statistics come from population surveys and field research. Some surveys focus on asking people about their involvement in criminal behaviour (self-report surveys) while others ask people if they have ever been victims of crime (victimization surveys).

Police Statistics

There are important differences between these sources as measures of criminal activity. Police statistics are the most complete measure of criminal activity on a national, regional, or local basis. These statistics provide more information on actual criminal activity than court statistics, largely because not all charged youth go to court. The police practice of exercising discretion in charging youth has been formalized with extra-judicial measures provisions in the *Youth Criminal Justice Act* (YCJA). These provisions encourage police to divert cases from the courts (including those where a charge is justified) by issuing a warning or referring the youth to a community-based program such as a restorative justice program or a family conferencing session. In addition, police charges can be altered by the Crown through plea negotiations. Both factors can change the overall number of charges and the type of charges appearing in published statistics from police to court statistics. Hence, there will be far fewer crimes recorded at the court level than at the police level. So, for example, in 2003, there were 25,345 Criminal Code charges laid against girls, 30 percent of the total Criminal Code charges for youth that year. At the same time, 14,915 or 21 percent of the youth court cases for that year involved girls (Wallace 2004: 23–24; Statistics Canada 2003).

Crime statistics are reported to the Canadian Centre for Justice Statistics in Ottawa by individual police departments. Police reporting on crime was standardized in 1962 through the adoption of the Uniform Crime Reporting (UCR) system. This system limits police reporting to 132 Criminal Code offence categories and several drug and traffic offences (Creechan 1995: 99). These categories are collapsed into 30 specific categories for publication in the *Juristat*. These categories are further collapsed into three categories of "index crime" — violent, property, and other Criminal Code. More detailed information is also reported by a sample of police departments (120), the UCR2. This survey provides information on characteristics of victims, offenders, and incidents — such as sex, age, level of damage, etc. The main difference between the two types of police statistics, aside from the sample nature of the UCR2, is that UCR statistics are aggregated. This means that while we may know how many charges were laid against youth, compared to adults, we cannot match these individuals with their offences or victims. The UCR2 data, because it is recorded on the basis of incidents, does report information on individual offences.

> Official statistics are actually very limited measures of crime because they were designed as measures of the activities of the agencies rather than of crime.

While official statistics provide an overall measure of crime, they do not provide information on actual criminal activity, or detailed information about crime, as do surveys or field work. Official statistics are actually very limited measures of crime because they were designed as measures of the activities of the agencies rather than of crime. On the other hand, surveys and field research are designed for the sole purpose of gathering information about criminal activity. So, for example, following news reports about school bullying, if we want to know how many school age youth are "beating up" their peers or carrying weapons, among the thirty categories reported by police, two would apply: Assault and Offensive Weapons. For 2004, there were 29,728 incidents of assault and 3,401 incidents of offensive weapons reported by the police involving youth aged twelve to seventeen (Sauve 2005: 21). If we want corresponding statistics just for girls, we have to look at the *Juristat* report based on 2003 statistics. Here we are informed that girls are responsible for 29 percent (8,833) of the assault incidents in that year and 8 percent (261) of the incidents of offensive weapons (Wallace 2004: 23, 25). Girl information is also provided for 2002 and in this *Juristat* we find that girls were responsible for 126, or 8 percent of the offensive weapons charges and 5,276, or 31 percent of the assaults (Wallace 2003: 22, 23). Using these statistics, there is certainly support for an argument that girl assaults on their peers is decreasing (from 31 percent in 2002 to 29 percent in 2003) and that their use of weapons has not changed (8 percent for two years in a row).

What is Recorded

Drawing such a conclusion would constitute the type of "statistical lie" referred to earlier by the judge in the sentencing hearing. Interpreting statistics is a complicated matter requiring an understanding of the statistics and what they represent — and in the case of police crime statistics, how they are recorded. First, as you may have already noticed, the absolute numbers of offences for girls is considerably lower for both offences in 2002 than it is for 2003 even though their proportionate representation is roughly the same. This is because UCR reporting changed in 2003 as a result of the implementation of the YCJA. UCR police crime statistics represent all incidents of crime reported to the police where police believe there is sufficient evidence to proceed with charging an individual with an offence. This is significant with regard to measuring actual crime; it means that not all offences reported to the police will be reported in the UCR statistics, but only those that result in charges. Moreover, youth statistics are reported differently since the YCJA was implemented.

Prior to 2003, youth crime statistics represented only youth who were actually charged by the police; they did not include those known to police and not charged, even where police may have considered there was sufficient evidence to do so. Since the YCJA, the UCR statistics for youth are now reported as "number charged" as well as "number cleared otherwise." This latter category includes youth processed by means of extrajudicial measures provisions in the YCJA. It also includes cases where a complainant did not want the police to lay a charge and those where an accused was involved in a number of incidents and the police only laid charges for some of them (Wallace 2004: 4). Hence, returning to the 2003 youth statistics for assault and offensive weapons, we find that while 30,459 incidents of youth assaults were reported, only 14,731 were actually charged (Wallace 2004: 23). This figure is closer to the 2002 figure of 17,020, and the change is not nearly as dramatic as that implied by comparing the charge figure of 2002 with the 2003 figure that includes both youth charged and youth cleared otherwise. Nonetheless, even though we are told that girls are responsible for 29 percent of the incidents of assault, we still cannot apply that percentage to this reduced figure of 14,731 because this is aggregate data and we have no idea if police charged these girls at the same rate that they charged the boys.

For the purpose of police statistics, an "incident" can include more than one offence. More importantly, in these cases, UCR statistics only record the most serious offence, and violent offences always take precedence. This means that less serious offences are always underestimated. For the same reason, comparisons of changes in crime statistics over time can be misleading, particularly if police charging practices have changed. Zero-tolerance policies toward incidents of bullying, for example, in combination with extrajudicial measures that will increase the number of less serious offences "cleared otherwise," will likely result in inflated assault statistics as a proportion of total offences. Furthermore, violent incidents are recorded differently than other offences in that they are recorded by the number of victims involved in the incident — one victim and a number of offenders is counted as one incident, while one offender with multiple victims is counted as multiple incidents (Sauve 2005: 14).

> Zero-tolerance policies toward bullying, in combination with extrajudicial measures, which will increase the number of less serious offences "cleared otherwise," will likely result in inflated assault statistics as a proportion of total offences.

Changes in Categories

Statistics are also not always measuring the information we want, and categories are not always comparable over time because they themselves change as does their application by the police. As we saw earlier, because of the decision in the Dawn-Marie Wesley case, certain types of bullying are now being categorized as criminal harassment by police. Similarly, Nova Scotia has been pressuring the federal government to modify the *Youth Criminal Justice Act* so that vehicle theft and joyriding can be classified as violent offences. As well, in the assault case that we are considering it makes no sense to look at assault cases as a measure of bullying. The statistics we have looked at are for all assault cases, and assault is further categorized in the UCR data as level 1, 2 and 3, where level 1 is "common assault," the category where bullying behaviour such as pushing, shoving, and hitting is likely to be found. Level 2 is assault with a weapon, such as hitting with a stick or baseball bat, and level 3 is aggravated assault, which causes serious injury. The statistics that we looked at for boys and girls were for the total category of assaults because the 2002 and 2003 *Juristat*s on police statistics only provide gender proportions for total assaults. From this information we cannot determine how many girls were involved only in common assaults.

Furthermore, it would be hard to find out how girls' bullying or even assaultive behaviour now compares to that before the *Young Offenders Act* because the categories for reporting youth crime have changed since 1984. For example, in 1983, youth crime (or juvenile delinquency, as it was called under the *Juvenile Delinquents Act* [JDA], when statistics included children as young as seven and up to fifteen to seventeen) was categorized into seven Criminal Code offences: property, which included break and enter, theft, mischief, possession of stolen goods and "other"; violent offences; and all other Criminal Code offences. This final "other" category included twenty-five separate offence categories. What we know about boys' and girls' offences from this data is even less than we know now. All we can say from the data provided is that in 1983, 64,301 youth were charged with criminal offences and 4.8 percent (or 3,086) of these involved violent offences. Compared to boys, girls made up a small proportion of these offences, approximately 14 percent (Statistics Canada 1984: 4). Since, twenty years later, girls accounted for 26 percent of the violent charges, it certainly seems reasonable to conclude that girls are now charged more for violent offences. It also seems reasonable to conclude that the Nova Scotia judge is correct in his argument that he is now seeing more girls in his court than ever before. However, it cannot be concluded from this information that girls are necessarily behaving in more violent ways. Girls' increased proportions in violent offence categories are as likely to be created by growing public intolerance for violent behaviour and changes in police charging practices as by any change in girls' behaviour. Furthermore, some statistics can be misleading because of how they are calculated or because of the base rate used for comparisons.

> Girls' increased proportions in violent offence categories are as likely to be created by growing public intolerance for violent behaviour and changes in police charging practices as any actual change in girls' behaviour.

Changes in Denominators and Base Rates

Making statements from official statistics about changes in crime from year to year is also tricky business because some statistics are more appropriate for comparisons than others. Earlier in our discussion of assault and weapons charges, absolute numbers of youth charged or cleared were compared, and this is problematic. When the time frame being compared is large enough, such as ten years, increases or decreases in actual numbers of crimes committed and reported can change simply because the number of youth in Canada between the ages of twelve and seventeen can change. For this reason, crime statistics are also reported as a "rate" that is proportional to the number of youth in the population. Usually, the rate is calculated per 100,000 or 10,000 youth in the population. The violent crime rate for girls in 1998 was 47 per 10,000 youth in the population, this compared to 131 for boys (Savoie 1999: 5). Since that time, violent crime rates have decreased overall for youth and this is reflected in the 2003 rates of violent crime, the rate for girls was roughly 40 in 10,000, compared with boys at 112 in 10,000 — one-third the rate for boys (Wallace 2004: 23, 25).

Interestingly, while the rate of violent crime for girls is one-third that for boys, court statistics show that the proportion of girls found guilty in court, unlike that for boys, has increased between 1991 and 2000. In 1991, girls accounted for 16 percent of all guilty findings and in 2000, they accounted for 20 percent — a 25 percent increase (Sprott and Doob 2003: 75). Some observers see these increases as evidence of changes in girls' behaviour (Gabor 1999) while others suggest that the justice system is responding more harshly to girls (Reitsma-Street 1999). Sprott and Doob (2003: 75) challenge both these interpretations of the statistics by looking at *rates* of guilty findings for boys and girls in court rather than *proportions*, and their conclusion is very different. There have not been any increases in guilty findings for girls over the last ten years. Overall, rates of guilty findings for girls have remained fairly stable over this time period, 114 per 10,000 in 1991 and 113 in 2000. On the other hand, boys' rates have decreased from 575 per 10,000 in

1991 to 435 in 2000. Hence, Sprott and Doob (2003: 75) argue that the 25 percent increase in the *proportion* of girls found guilty is primarily due to decreases in the *rate* of boys found guilty. What needs explaining then is why rates for boys are decreasing and those for girls are not. This takes us back to Judge White, who seems to believe that greater numbers of girls in court prove girls are becoming more violent. If the number of boys in his court is declining, then he is likely seeing proportionately more girls — but not necessarily for the reasons that he thinks.

Base rates also emerged in a larger debate about changes in overall rates of violent crime under the *Young Offenders Act* (YOA) and once again, the issue was whether youth behaviour was changing or police charging practices were changing. This debate began with a 1992 Statistics Canada report that stated the rate of youth violent crime had increased by 117 percent between 1986 and 1992 (from 41.5 per 10,000 to 90 per 10,000) (Frank 1992). The author of the report, Jeffrey Frank argued that most of this increase was due to more charges being laid by police for minor violent offences because of changing public attitudes towards violence. He noted an increase in complaints, more police reporting and charging, and a greater willingness on the part of Crown prosecutors to prosecute minor assault cases.

Others disagreed, arguing that there was, rather, a real increase in violent youth crime over this time period. Raymond R. Corrado and Allan Markwart (1994: 351), examining rates for specific violent offences and comparing the percentage charged to those that were not, found no change in the rate of police charges for some offences but changes in common-assault charging practices. Nonetheless, they argued that even this actual change in police charging practices "can only account for approximately 20 percent of the increase in that period" (1986–92).

On the other hand, Peter J. Carrington (1995) argued that it is not useful to use police charge rates to make comparisons over time, precisely because, as Frank (1992) argued, police charging practices are susceptible to changing public attitudes and zero-tolerance policies. Rate comparisons, he maintains, should be based on offences reported to police rather than on police charges. Furthermore, he argues that percentage changes depend on the year used for a benchmark. Carrington points out that 1986 was a year with one of the lowest rates of violent offence charges and 1992 one of the highest: "Using 1986 as a baseline year for comparison of youth crime rates is like using the employment rate in the depths of a recession as a baseline for assessing annual employment rates: in comparison any other year will seem high" (Carrington 1995: 62). As far as Carrington is concerned, police-reported youth violent crime showed a real increase during the YOA years, and these increases were due to a trend towards increased police reporting of violent crime. And back to the issue raised by Sprott and Doob, perhaps the reason boys' rates have shown declines is because the base rate used for comparison is 1991, a particularly high year, which means we are back where we started. If boys' rates have declined simply because 1991 was such a high rate, then the question remains: Why have girls' rates not also declined?

Where the YOA led to more formal charging of youth in general and violent offences in particular, the exact opposite has occurred with the implementation of the YCJA. Now we are seeing a dramatic decrease in youth charged — 15 percent in the first year of the YCJA and a corresponding increase in youth "cleared otherwise" of 30 percent (Wallace 2004: 1). By the second year of the YCJA, the legislative impact had levelled off. The rate of youth charged dropped by 6 percent and the rate of youth cleared otherwise dropped by 2 percent (Sauve 2005: 1). A similar pattern occurred for assault. Assault charge rates dropped by 17 percent in 2003 and assaults cleared otherwise increased by 22 percent, while 2004 showed a levelling off. Both charges and cleared otherwise showed declines, of 1.7 and 2.8 percent respectively. The difference is that for assaults the decline for cleared otherwise was slightly higher than for those charged (Wallace 2004: 23; Sauve 2005: 21). Whether these changes will impact equally for boys and girls remains to be seen.

Girl Crime and Official Statistics

With these words of caution in mind, it is important to know what police and court statistics tell us about youth violent crime, and girl crime in particular, because these statistics often form the basis of media accounts and lobby campaigns to toughen laws and other mechanisms for controlling youth. Youth crime statistics are now available for every year from 1984, when the *Young Offender's Act* was implemented, to 2004. Police data is not reported by Statistics Canada every year for male and female youth. The most recent data for girls is 2003. The last report that offered details on girl crime from Statistics Canada using official police statistics is based on 1998 data and focuses specifically on youth violent crime (Savoie 1999).

Most crimes, whether they involve youth in general or girls in particular, are petty property offences. Official police statistics indicate that of the 78,100 youth aged twelve to seventeen years of age charged with a criminal offence in 2004, 26 percent were charged with a violent offence. The rate of youth charges for violent crime decreased by 2 percent from the previous year and has been fairly stable for the last ten years, with a slight increase in 2000 (Sauve 2005: 13, 21). Not so for girls. The rate of charges for girls' violent offences increased twice as fast as boys' over this period (127 percent vs. 65 percent, respectively) and at the end of the 1990s, violent crime accounted for a slightly greater proportion of female youth charges (23 percent) than male charges (20 percent) (Savoie 1999: 5).

Statistics such as these might well lead one to wonder how or why anyone might suggest that girls' violent behaviour is not "out of control." Again though, we are looking at "statistical lies."

Selective Presentations of Official Statistics

Girls' criminal behaviour is exaggerated through the selective use of official statistics. The statistics I have just cited, for instance, represent only a small part of the picture of female youth violent crime, and it is a picture slanted to present girls' violence in the worst possible light. Other statistics, from the same source, tell us that the rate of violent crime charges for girls, even though it has increased at a much more rapid rate than boys, is consistently much lower than that for boys. In 1998, the rate of violent crime for girls was only one-third the rate for boys (47 for every 10,000 youths vs. 131 for boys) and the same difference is apparent for 2004 with girls at 20 for every 10,000 compared to 58 for boys (see Figure 7.1). Furthermore, minor assault, or level 1 assault, which includes such behaviours as pushing, slapping, punching, and threatening, was the most frequent violent crime category for all youth, and even more so for girls. In 1998, 67 percent of girls' charges were for common assault, as compared to 46 percent for boys (Savoie 1999: 5).

A considerable portion of the increase in violent crime charges for girls between 1988 and 1998 came about because of increases in charges for common assault. When we exclude common assault, the increase in the girls' violent charge rate drops to 95 percent (versus 127 percent overall). In addition, common assault charges for girls are proportionately similar to adult female proportions, at 65 percent, and their charge rate is half the male youth rate (see Figure 7.2) (Savoie 1999: 5). As for major assault, or level 2 (assault with a weapon or causing bodily harm) and level 3 (aggravated assault) the rate for girls is eight for every ten thousand youth in 1998 and 4.5 per 10,000 in 2004. These figures are less than one-third the rate for male youth (see Figure 7.3). More importantly, as a proportion of all female youth charges, the 1998 figure is 3 percent less than it was in 1988 (Savoie 1999: 6).

Girls are also minimally represented in charges for other violent crimes. Their robbery rate increased by 176 percent from 1988 to 1998, but it was also less than one-sixth that of male youth (3 per 10,000 vs. 241 per 10,000) and remains so through to 2004 (see Figure 7.4) (Savoie 1999: 6). In addition, in 2004, only 44 female youth were charged with sexual assault, compared with 1,329 male youth. This is comparable to 1998, when only 48 female youth were charged with sexual assault compared with 1,390 male youth (see Figure 7.5) (Statistics Canada 1999: 18). Lastly, in 1998, only two girls were charged with first-degree murder and three were charged with attempted murder, compared with fifty-four male youth charged with a homicide offence and seventy-two charged with attempted murder (Statistics Canada 1999: 18). Indeed, the number of charges for these offences was higher twenty years earlier. In 1978, ten girls were charged with murder, attempted murder, or manslaughter. The years after that saw lower numbers of girls charged, except for 1992–93, when thirteen were charged (Reitsma-Street 1999: 50). In 2004, the youth homicide rate was at its second lowest point in more than thirty years, it was only slightly lower in 2001 (1.57 compared with 1.28 per 100,000, respectively). In 2004, 40 youth were accused of homicide and 3 were girls. The corresponding figures for 2001 show that of 32 youth accused, 5 were girls (Dauvergne 2005: 13, 23).

Charges for violent crimes also vary across the country and by city. The greatest increases in charge rates for girls over the ten years of 1988–98 came in the Atlantic region. Newfoundland showed an increase of 289 percent, Nova Scotia 300 percent, and New Brunswick 203 percent. Sherbrooke and Chicoutimi-Jonquière reported the highest increases in charge rates for girls (114 percent and 128 percent, respectively), while Calgary, St. Catharines-Niagara, and Sudbury reported the largest decreases (36 percent and 11 percent, respectively) (Savoie 1999: 7, 10). These findings are also significant in a larger context, because it is difficult to construct a tenable argument that 1), all girls today are somehow more violent, except in Calgary, Sudbury, and St. Catharines, and 2), that girls in Atlantic Canada are more violent than those anywhere else in the country.

False images of girls' behaviour are created not only when crime rates are viewed out of context of the larger youth-crime picture, but also when percentage increases are reported out of context. Large increases in rates and proportions can be extremely misleading if the base rate is very small. A change in the robbery rate for girls from 1.6 per 10,000 to 3 per 10,000 becomes a 176 percent increase. Batchelor found that while Scottish newspapers were reporting that "the number of violent crimes committed by girl thugs in Scotland has almost doubled in the last decade," her examination of the official statistics for the same time period showed only a 15 percent increase (or thirty-eight more convictions for violence) (2001: 27). When researchers or journalists report only percentage increases, they give the impression of "out-of-control" girls, but official crime statistics do not in themselves present that picture. Rather, that view only comes from a selective interpretation and presentation of statistics to the exclusion of others that present a less dramatic image of girls' violent behaviour.

Figure 7.1: Youth Charged with Violent Crimes, by Sex, Canada, 1988–2004 (rate per 10,000 youth)

Sources: Statistics Canada 1999 and UCR survey, 1999-2004, Centre for Justice Statistics (prepared for the author).

Figure 7.2: Youth Charged with Common Assault, by Sex, Canada, 1988–2004 (rate per 10,000 youth)

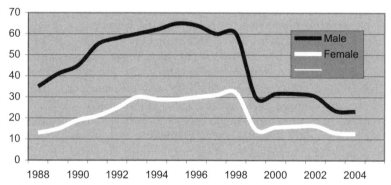

Figure 7.3: Youth Charged with Major Assault, by Sex, Canada, 1988–2004 (rate per 10,000 youth)

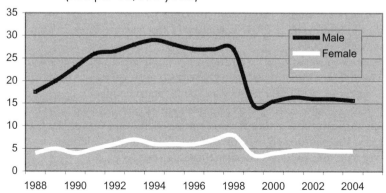

Figure 7.4: Youth Charged with Robbery, by Sex, Canada, 1988–2004 (rate per 10,000 youth)

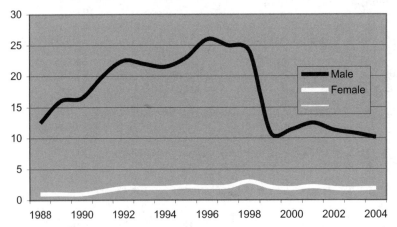

Official police statistics, then, taken as a whole, do not indicate that girls are or ever have been "a deadly threat." The increases are more likely due to increased public perceptions of certain girl behaviours as "violent," reclassification of behaviours as criminal, increased reporting of such behaviours to police, and a corresponding increased formality in criminal-justice processing rather than to changes in girls' behaviour or in the nature of their crimes (see also Doob and Sprott 1998; Stevenson et al. 1998; Bala 1997; Gartner and Doob 1994). While these first few years of the YCJA have impacted on police charging practices for minor offences and first-time offenders, they have also been accompanied by an increased hardening of attitudes toward "bullying" and subsequent criminalization. The extent to which these changes will be reflected in girls' violent-crime rates over the next few years remains to be seen. Since their rates are already low in some categories, even small changes will produce large percentage changes.

As a case in point, you may have noticed when examining Figures 7.1 through 7.6 that there is a large drop in crime rates for most offences between 1998 and 1999. This drop is almost entirely due to changes in how the statistics are recorded and reported. As mentioned earlier in the chapter, the introduction of the YCJA led to changes in Statistics Canada reporting of youth crime, creating categories of "charged" and "cleared otherwise." Because girl-violence statistics for specific offence categories are not available in the yearly *Juristat* publications, I contacted Statistics Canada to obtain girl-violence statistics to bring the figures up to 2004. The figures I received are those in Figures 7.1 through 7.6 from 1999 to 2004.

To my surprise, even statistics prior to 2003 were reported in two categories, youth "charged" and youth "not charged." Prior to the YCJA, youth crime statistics were reported in the *Juristats* in only one category as youth "apprehended" or sometimes as youth "charged." Hence, these retrospective figures cannot be compared with the 1998 statistics available through the *Juristat*. Furthermore, youth "not charged" statistics are not available by sex. I was informed that, particularly for girls, it would take "too much police time" to record these statistics because there are too few girls.

Table 7.1 shows the percentage differences between 1998 figures and the retrospective figure for 1999. This table clearly illustrates the effects of category changes and

Figure 7.5: Youth Charged with Sexual Assault, by Sex, Canada, 1988–2004 (rate per 10,000 youth)

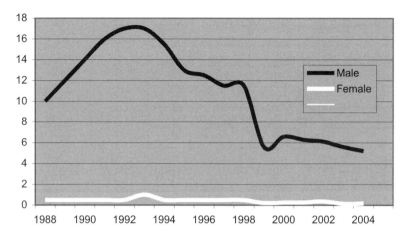

Figure 7.6: Youth Charged with Homocide, by Sex, Canada, 1988–2004 (rate per 10,000 youth)

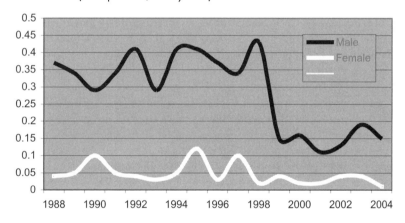

how percentage comparisons can be misleading. It is also suggestive of behavioural change. The question is whether the change is in police charging practices or girls' behaviour.

The drop in overall charges for violent offences is about half for both boys and girls (50.8 and 54.0 respectively). The change in rate for most of the specific offences follows this pattern with two exceptions — homicide and robbery. Boys' homicide rate drops by 64.3 percent while the girls' rate increases by 100 percent. This is due to the fact that homicide offences would not be processed through extrajudicial measures so we are probably looking at a real increase in numbers of offenders. Before we jump to any conclusions about girls being more violent, we must look at the actual numbers. This increase amounts to nine girls charged in 1999 compared with five in 1998. As pointed out earlier in the chapter, in 2004, only three girls were charged with homicide.

Robbery rate changes for girls are not as easy to dismiss as a potential artifact of cat-

Table 7-1: Percentage Change in Rate per 10,000 Youth "Charged" for Specific
Violent Offences, by Sex, 1998–99

	Male	Female
Common Assault	-50.2	-54.7
Major Assault	-47.5	-55.0
Robbery	-54.6	5.0
Sexual Assault	-49.1	-60.0
Homicide	-64.3	100.0
Total Violence	-50.8	-54.0

Source: Calculated from UCR statistics provided by the Canadian Centre for Justice Statistics, July,
2006 and Statistics Canada 1999, Catalogue 85-002-VPE 19(13).

egory changes or small numbers. Between 1988 and 1998, the rate of robbery charges for girls has increased and while the numbers of girls charged are low, they are high enough that calculations of percentage increases and decreases are more valid than with homicide. Since 1999, the number of girls charged with robbery has varied from a high of 540 in 2001 to a low of 461 in 2003. Hence, the fact that girls' robbery charges do not show a decrease with category changes in 1999 but rather an increase of five percent suggests two things. It may be that police have always been more likely to charge girls involved in robbery and continue to do so or it might also mean that girls are more involved in robbery than they were twenty years ago. Research on girls' involvement in robbery and police processing would be required before such conclusions could be drawn.

Similarly, a comparison of charge rates for specific offences from 1999 to 2004 indicates decreases in all categories of violent offences for both boys and girls, except for major assault. Between 1999 and 2004, the charge rate for boys increased 6.8 percent and for girls, the rate increased 25 percent. Since 1999, the number of girls charged for major assault has increased steadily from 885 to 1,138, while the number of boys charged has varied from a high of 4,062 in 2001 to a low of 3,593 in 1999. These rate increases, 6.8 and 25 percent, also hold for differences between 2002 and 2004 charge rates. Hence, for major assault, increases in charge rates are likely the effect of the YCJA, that is, a drop in the use of extrajudicial measures for more serious violent offences.

Court statistics for 2003, the first year of the YCJA, provide more information on specific offences than police statistics. These statistics indicate that girls accounted for slightly less than one-quarter (24.1 percent) of the youth going to court with a violent offence charge. In all categories, their proportional representation is less than boys but it does appear that girls are more likely than boys to be sent to court for common assault. Here they account for almost one-third of the cases (32.9 percent). Girls also account for 14 percent of the robbery cases and 23 percent of the major assault cases. With regard to the "reclassification" of bullying offences, it is interesting to note that girls made up one-quarter of the charges for "uttering threats" (23.9 percent) and one-fifth (20 percent) of the "criminal harassment" charges. This amounted to 675 and 41 girls respectively compared to 2,146 and 164 boys (Statistics Canada 2003). While it is not appropriate to use absolute numbers to discuss crime trends, it is important, when talking about "crime waves" and "youth crisis" to recognize that the numbers in question are very small.

Indeed, when there are 2,535,053 youth between the ages of twelve to seventeen in the Canadian population, approximately half of whom are girls, 716 girls representing the "worst" cases of threats and harassment hardly constitutes a "threat to society."

Indigenous and other visible minority youth are always "missing" from official statistics, except for custody and community services statistics, and girls get little mention in these statistics. While there are good reasons for not reporting crime statistics by racial categories from the point of view of misuse and exploitation by racist and white supremacist groups, potentially useful information is not available for social policy development. Custody statistics for 2003–04 indicate that while Aboriginal youth comprised about 8 percent of the youth population, they accounted for 44 percent of admissions to remand, 46 percent of the admissions to custodial institutions, and 32 percent of the admissions to probation (Reitano 2004: 2). Girls are more likely to be held in detention at younger ages and for minor offences than boys; this is particularly true for Aboriginal girls, since more than one-third of the girls admitted to detention (36 percent) are Aboriginal and girls make up 16 percent of the institutionalized Aboriginal youth population, compared with 12 percent of the non-Aboriginal youth population (Latimer and Foss 2004: 10).

Research-Based Statistics

Another way of measuring crime and delinquency is to use a survey. With this approach, people are simply asked about their involvement in criminal or delinquent behaviour (self-report), or if they have ever been victimized (victimization survey). Early versions of self-report surveys were typically administered to school population samples. The first self-report study of delinquent behaviour to have a significant impact on criminologists' thinking about delinquency was that done in the United States in the late 1950s by Nye and Short (1957: 328). Prior to this research, the only statistics available on the criminal and delinquent behaviour of young people came from official sources (i.e., courts, police, or institutions). When the self-report questionnaire was introduced, it became immediately apparent that the actual amount of criminal and delinquent behaviour by young people was much higher than had ever been reported through official statistics. In addition, self-report studies revealed a profile of people involved in crime and delinquency that was very different from that gleaned from official records. Official records tend to underrepresent the offences of middle-class youth, presenting instead a profile of delinquents and young offenders as poor, working class, and members of visible minorities.

In the mid-1990s, Statistics Canada and Human Resources Development Canada began a joint project to collect longitudinal data on children and youth — the National Longitudinal Survey of Children and Youth (NLSCY). Beginning in 1994–1995, the project began collecting information on a sample of 22,000 children up to age eleven. These children are to be interviewed every two years until they reach age twenty-five. Prior to age ten, teachers and/or parents or guardians were interviewed on behalf of the child. There are a few questions included in the survey about child and youth involvement in stealing, vandalism, and aggressive behaviours directed toward others (Dauvergne and Johnson 2001: 2; Sprott, Doob, and Jenkins 2001: 2–3). Other self-report information on crime and delinquency comes from independent non-government research, some of which is field-based, such as surveys of homeless youth.

> Official records tend to underrepresent the offences of middle-class youth, presenting instead a profile of delinquents and young offenders as poor, working class, and members of visible minorities.

Typically, results from self-report studies indicate that delinquent and criminal behaviour is far more widespread than one would ever think from looking at official statistics. According to Bortner (1988: 144), self-report measures of delinquency report estimates that range from four to ten times the amount reported by official statistics. In one American study she cites, 88 percent of the 13- to 16-year-old youth surveyed admitted to participating in at least one delinquent act during the three years prior to the study; less than 3 percent of these offences had been detected by police, while only 22 percent of the juveniles had ever had contact with police and less than 2 percent had ever gone to court (Bortner 1988: 145). Generally, these early self-report studies found much higher rates of "delinquency" than more recent studies because they asked questions about behaviours not necessarily considered "criminal" but certainly "delinquent," such as "Have you ever taken something that didn't belong to you," or, "Have you ever disobeyed your parents."

A more recently developed method of acquiring information about criminal behaviour is the victimization survey. This approach involves asking people if they have ever been victimized by the criminal behaviour of others. Although victimization data do not provide a direct measure of the nature or prevalence of youth crime, they do provide considerable information that is useful in combination with other sources. While the United States government has collected victimization data on an annual basis from a sample of the general population since 1966 and also conducts victimization surveys of high school students (Creechan 1995: 98), the Canadian government conducted its first victimization survey through the Ministry of the Solicitor General and Statistics Canada in the early 1980s. Known as the Canadian Urban Victimization Survey (CUVS), it gathered data from some 61,000 Canadians aged sixteen and over (Johnson and Lazarus 1989: 311). Since then, information collected by Statistics Canada about crime victimization has been incorporated into the federal government's General Social Survey (GSS). In this survey, which began in 1988 and is undertaken every five years, a sample of more than 10,000 Canadians over the age of fifteen are asked questions about assault, robbery, sexual assault, personal theft, break and enters to their house, theft of household property or cars, and vandalism. In 1999, questions on spousal violence were added to the GSS (Besserer and Trainor 2000: 2). In addition, some victimization data is now available for children and youth from the NLSCY. The NLSCY asks four questions about victimization. Children and youth are asked how many times someone physically attacked or assaulted them on a school bus, at school, or elsewhere, including at home (over the past twelve months). They are also asked if anyone threatened to hurt them at school, on a school bus, or elsewhere, including at home (Fitzgerald 2003: 9).

Victimization surveys focus on crimes against individuals and households and thus do not measure offences committed against businesses or corporations such as shoplifting. Nonetheless, victimization surveys do tell us something about crime trends and whether crime levels are changing, particularly violent crime. Comparisons between the four GSS survey periods (1988, 1993, 1999, 2004) show a relatively flat trend with respect to the victimization rate. Victimization rates were 24 percent for the first two periods (Gartner and Doob 1994) and increased slightly to 26 percent in 1999 and to 28 percent by 2004. These increases are primarily due to increases in household related property crimes (Gannon and Mihorean 2005: 4, 5). Interestingly, and contrary to impressions conveyed by the media, the 2004 GSS also indicates that more people feel safe from crime and satisfied with their personal safety than they did in 1999 (Gannon and Mihorean 2005: 4). In spite of their higher rates of victimization, young people are even more likely than older respondents to say they feel safe, but girls are less likely than boys to say they feel safe staying home alone at night, walking alone, or taking public transportation alone (Statistics Canada 2001: 8).

As with other victimization surveys, the 2004 GSS also confirms that official crime rates are underreported and that this varies by offence. About 34 percent of the 2004 GSS respondents reported their victimization to police, but youth are less likely to report victimization than older people (Gannon and Mihorean 2005: 13, 25). Among violent victimizations, robberies and physical assaults were reported (46 and 39 percent) more than sexual assaults (8 percent). Approximately half of the reported break and enter and motor vehicle/parts thefts (54 and 49 percent) were reported to police while 31 percent of vandalism and 29 percent of household property thefts were reported to the police (Gannon and Mihorean 2005: 12, 16).

What is particularly useful about victimization surveys, then, is that they allow us to know something about "unofficial" police clearance rates for specific offences and about which offences will be underestimated in police statistics. This rate is ascertained by comparing victimization survey results on crimes reported to police to police charges for similar offences during the same time period. These comparisons generally show that reporting and clearance rates for crimes against persons are very different from property crimes. We have seen that reporting rates for crimes against persons tend to be lower than the number of household property crimes, but clearance rates for these offences are considerably higher than for property offences. According to the 1999 GSS, where about half of the vandalism cases were not reported to the police, among those reported, only 15 percent were cleared. For household break and enters, 17 percent of the cases reported to the police were cleared. In sexual-assault cases, where about 10 percent were reported to police, a suspect was named in about two-thirds of these cases. Most homicides are reported, and police are able to name a suspect in 75 percent of the cases (Doob and Cesaroni 2004: 82).

With regard to measuring the offences that young people commit, victimization surveys are not able to give us information about an offender's age if there has not been any contact between the victim and the offender. Even if the victim saw the offender in a particular case, age is not always easily discernible. Hindelang and McDermott (1981) report that sex is the easiest characteristic for victims to recall, race is somewhat difficult, and age is the most difficult. Nonetheless, they did find that victims' accuracy rates for estimating the age of an offender was not less than 89 percent for any age group. On the other hand, Doob, Marinos, and Varma (1995) point out that if an offender is a stranger of about eighteen, victims are not likely to be able to judge whether the offender is an adult or a youth. Age is known when a victimization is reported to the police and someone is charged. In this case, the GSS indicates that, in 2004, only 15 percent of the accused in reported victimizations were young offenders (Gannon and Mihorean 2005: 24). Furthermore, Doob and Cesaroni (2004) compare the age of accused and the age of victims from the 1999 GSS and find that young people are more likely to victimize other young people and older people to victimize people their own age rather than youth.

It is sometimes suggested that girls' official crime rates are lower than boys because girls are less likely than boys to be caught and/or charged. This notion was first theoretically formalized by Otto Pollak (1950), who insisted that girls and women are as criminal as men, but less likely to be caught because they are inherently deceitful. He further maintained that girls and women are also less likely to be formally processed, because men and boys victimized by women and girls are reluctant to report these offences, and men in the criminal justice system — police, prosecutors, judges, and jurors are reluctant to prosecute women and girls — his so-called "chivalry hypothesis." While the overtly sexist and misogynous aspects of Pollak's theories can be rejected outright, ample evidence, both research-based and anecdotal, also exists to suggest that chivalry is dead (if it ever existed).

For one thing, as we have already seen in our discussion of media and popular culture representations of girls, public opinion and sentiment are not forgiving of women and girls, particularly those involved in violent crime. As well, results from victimization surveys contradict Pollak's arguments. Only 5 percent of all victimizations involve women or girls as assailants, and incidents perpetrated by women or girls are more likely to be described as a crime (rather than a threat or attempt) than those perpetrated by male assailants (Hatch and Faith 1991: 71; Johnson 1986).

Girl Crime and Research Statistics

In general, self-report surveys show that girls are considerably less involved in criminal behaviour than are boys. A self-report study in Montreal in the early 1980s indicated a 3:1 male-female ratio (Le Blanc 1983: 37). A more recent study showed the same ratio (Simourd and Andrews 1996). Both these Canadian studies, as well as studies in the United States, indicate that boys and girls engage in many of the same activities but that girls participate in criminal behaviours far less frequently than boys do (Reitsma-Street 1991; Conway 1992: 9; Chesney-Lind and Shelden 1992: 18).

Data from the NLSCY indicates that for the 1994–95 and 1996–97 survey, approximately 30 percent of the girls surveyed at age twelve or thirteen reported involvement in delinquency of a property or aggressive nature while 40 percent of the boys reported involvement in property related delinquency and 66 percent in aggressive behaviours (Sprott, Doob, and Jenkins 2001: 3). By 1998–99, 19 percent of the girls in that age group reported involvement in property crime and 10 percent in violent crime while the proportions for boys are 29 percent for both types of offences. Furthermore, the more serious the offence, the more likely boys are to be involved compared to girls. For example, boys are three times more likely than girls to report "fencing stolen goods," almost five times more likely than girls to report "carrying a stick or club as a weapon" and three times more likely to report being in a fight and "causing personal injuries" (Fitzgerald 2003: 11). The ratio of violent offending is 2.9:1 — almost three boys for every girl, and for property crime, 1.6:1. Police charges for 2001, also indicate a ratio of 3:1 (Fitzgerald 2003: 12). These figures are comparable to the first self-report studies done in Montreal in the 1980s and strongly suggest that girls' behaviour has not changed, at least with regard to violence. If there has been any change, it is that girls are slightly more involved in property crime than they were twenty years ago.

Surveys of street youth show similar patterns. Homeless youth in Toronto report a high involvement in criminal activity (notably though, 37 percent of youth reported no involvement in criminal activity) and even here on the streets, girls are less involved in criminal activity than are boys. One-third of the girls reported engaging in assaults, compared to almost one-half of the boys; 45 percent in shoplifting, compared with 58 percent of the boys; and 23 percent of the girls reported involvement in theft for the purpose of selling the items, compared with 47 percent of the male youth (Gaetz 2004: 437).

It is also worth noting that these youth crime patterns are not unique to North

America. In 1991–92, an international self-report survey of youth in eleven countries was undertaken and showed that in Europe and the United States, girls' involvement in criminal behaviour is similar to what we see in Canada. They are less involved than boys, their involvement peaks at a younger age than boys, and their involvement in property offences and vandalism is slightly less than that of boys. Importantly, girls' involvement in serious crime and violent offences is considerably less than that of boys. There is very little difference in offences such as truancy and running away (Junger-Tas, Marshall, and Ribeaud 2003: 60).

Some self-report surveys are commissioned or conducted by private groups such as the Calgary police department and various teachers' federations. All of these studies, according to Gabor (1999), show that police and school administrators "feel" there has been an increase in the frequency and seriousness of violence among youth, including girls. "Not one police official and just two percent of the educators felt that the problem was less serious than it had been a decade earlier." Apparently, close to 80 percent of those polled by Gabor (1999: 389) "felt that the problem of violence in the schools had grown."

These conclusions are highly questionable since they seem to be based on what officials "feel" is happening. It is plausible to argue that because officials "feel" youth behaviour is more violent, they are more likely to complain to police who, then, are more likely to charge youth. Sibylle Artz (1998: 198), for example, reports that evaluations of anti-violence programs in schools were accompanied by increases in reported violent behaviour two to three years after their implementation. Furthermore, results from other school self-report surveys provide a mixed view. A 1995 survey of Calgary middle and high schools noted that 31 percent of the boys and 41 percent of the girls reported having slapped, punched, or kicked someone in the last year, and 24 percent of the girls and 33 percent of the boys reported having threatened to hurt someone (Smith et al. 1995). Another Canadian survey, focusing on more serious acts of violence, found that half the boys surveyed (51.9 percent) and one-fifth (20.9 percent) of the girls reported "that they had beaten up another kid once or twice" (Artz 1998: 27). A five-year longitudinal self-report survey of Canadian school children aged ten to twelve indicated that 10 percent of girls reported "beating up another kid" and 17 percent "carrying a weapon." The corresponding figures for boys were 40 percent and 36 percent respectively (Artz, Riecken, MacIntyre, Lam, and Maczewski 1999: 10). A 1999 survey of high school students in Alberta that differentiated frequency of behaviour found that boys and girls were roughly equal in their reporting of never being involved in violence-related delinquency (54 percent for boys and 59 percent for girls) and low-level involvement (34 percent for boys and 36 percent for girls). Girls' reporting of involvement in frequent violent delinquency, four or more times in the past year, was half that of boys — 6 percent, compared with 12 percent for boys (Gomes, Bertrand, Paetsch, and Hornick 2002: 84).

Victimization Surveys and Girl Crime

Results from victimization surveys confirm the gender patterns apparent in both official and self-report surveys, but only for face-to-face crimes and not in a manner that readily separates youth from adults. Johnson's (1986) report on the 1982 Canadian victimization survey and the more recent GSS (1999, 2004) allow us to conclude that victimizations perpetrated by women and girls is increasing. Only 5 percent of all victimizations involved one or more female assailants in 1982 while the 1999 GSS reports that 18 percent of all assailants were female (Besserer and Trainor 2000: 21). However, with regard to violent victimizations, women and girls account for a small proportion. Of all the accused in victimization surveys, 12 percent were women and girls, and they were responsible for 14 percent of the reported physical assaults. For all other types of reported violence, the numbers of women and girls as assailants were too small to provide clear proportional figures. Importantly, incidents perpetrated by women and girls are more likely to be described as a crime than a threat or an attempt (32 percent vs. 49 percent for male perpetrators). (Gannon and Milhorean 2005: 24).

Victims First

Much of the violence perpetrated by girls stems from their victimization. In the words of one young offender:

> I started being assaulted, and that's how my youth charges began... I was twelve... I never knew how to fight and they [older girls in the child welfare home] would always hit me... They would always fight me, and I would start fighting back... I wasn't hitting her just to be violent, I was hitting her because I thought if I got her then maybe the other girls would leave me alone... First I got thirty days, then I got sixty days, and then I got ninety days. (Totten 2001: 37)

While girls are perpetrators of violence, albeit at a lesser rate than boys, their violence often stems from having been "beaten up" by peers. Canadian self-report research has found that school girls who report involvement in "hitting" their peers also report significantly higher amounts of victimization by their peers than do other girls (Artz 2004; Artz 1998: 46–48; Artz and Riecken 1994). Girls identified as being "very aggressive" are twice as likely as other girls to report negative relations with friends (42.6 percent vs. 22.9 percent) and that other children "say mean things to them" (18.9 percent vs. 8.7 percent). These girls are also three times more likely to report being bullied by other children (19.2 percent vs. 7.5 percent) (Sprott and Doob 2000: 130).

> Girls identified as "very aggressive" are twice as likely to report negative relations with friends and say other children "say mean things to them." These girls are also three times more likely to report being bullied by other children (Sprott and Doob 2000: 130).

Data from the GSS reports that youth between fifteen and nineteen have higher rates of victimization than any other age group in the Canadian population, and girls rates are higher than boys at 280 per 1,000 compared to 248 per 1,000 for boys. The higher rate of victimization for girls is primarily due to higher rates of sexual assault victimization among girls (111 per 1,000 compared to rates close to zero for boys) Statistics Canada 2001: 5). According to police statistics for 2003, 80 percent of the victims of sexual assaults were girls. Interestingly, strangers were implicated in only 5 percent of the sexual assaults against children and youth (Aucoin 2005: 7). Contrary to these victimization surveys and official statistics, girls surveyed in the NLSCY reported lower rates of victimization than boys — 28 percent compared to 48 percent, respectively (Fitzgerald 2003: 9, 12–13). The lower rates of victimization in the NLSCY compared to the GSS and police statistics are a result of the questions asked. The NLSCY does not ask questions about sexual assault. While rates of sexual victimization are highest for teen girls (twelve to fifteen), rates of sexual offending are highest among teen boys (Kong, Johnson, Beattie, and Cardillo 2003: 1).

Gaetz (2004) found that rates of victimization among homeless youth are as high as

82 percent overall — that is, of youth reporting at least one incidence of vandalism, break and enter, sexual assault, robbery, or assault. This compares to a rate of 40 percent for "domiciled" youth. In all categories, except for robbery, girls are victimized more than boys. Rates of assault and theft are not much different; robbery victimization rates are double for boys what they are for girls, and rates of sexual assault are three times higher for girls (Gaetz 2004: 435).

Measurement Issues

Validity and Reliability

A major issue for academics concerned with the measurement of criminal activity, be it youth or adult, is the reliability and validity of the measuring instrument. Reliability refers to whether or not we can repeat the results that we get; validity refers to whether we are measuring what we think we are measuring. Both reliability and validity can be compromised in official statistics. We have already seen how easy it is to find inconsistencies in police-based statistics that depend on what is compared and how the comparisons are made. In addition, the validity of police statistics is always an issue because crimes known to police and clearance rates are susceptible to public and political pressures, as well as to changes in policy and police administration. Similarly, court statistics are susceptible to public, institutional, and political pressures, as well as police, Crown prosecutor, and judicial behaviour.

Self-report survey results are generally accepted as reliable in that, as we have seen, researchers can get relatively comparable results from their surveys if they ask similar questions. Nonetheless, some are skeptical about self-report questionnaires because of an assumption that people will not be truthful in filling them out. This is particularly a concern with regard to young people because it is thought that they, more so than adults, may feel a sense of bravado about misdeeds and will want to elaborate and exaggerate their involvement. Adults, on the other hand, are thought to be more likely than young people to underreport their criminal activities because they fear the consequences of being caught. Hindelang, Hirschi, and Weis (1981) conducted a large survey in Seattle, Washington, throughout the years 1978 and 1979 for the purpose of testing the reliability and validity of self-report questionnaires. Their research involved surveying a sample that included high-school students and young people not in school who had police records and/or court records. Responses to the self-report questions were then cross-checked with police records, court records, school records, and parents to determine the truthfulness of responses. They found that, in general, young people do not lie about their misdeeds.

What Are We Measuring?

It is validity that is considered particularly problematic with respect to self-report questionnaires. As mentioned earlier, the issue concerns the types of questions that have been included in the survey, what they measure, and the usefulness of responses for making assessments about crime levels. The NLSCY is a case in point. In the first survey (1994–95) only very general questions were asked about frequency of "stealing at home, stealing outside the home, destroying other people's things and vandalizing." Only two questions were asked about aggressive behaviour: "getting in fights and physically attacking people" (Sprott, Doob, and Jenkins 2001: 3). The second survey (1996–97) asked far more specific questions about property offences and aggressive behaviours; for example, whether the youth had ever "stolen something from a store... from a school," "broken into a house," "threatened to beat someone up," "used a knife for an attack," or "forced sex." In all, eight questions were asked in this later survey about property type offences and nine about aggressive behaviours (2001: 3). As a result of these changes in questions, not all responses are comparable across the two surveys, and the authors of a report on the two survey results caution about interpreting the findings of the surveys.

> Readers are cautioned that it is probably not meaningful to make simple com-
> parisons across "types" of delinquency. The fact that, for example, delinquent
> acts involving property appears to be less prevalent than aggressive behaviour...
> may reflect more the nature and specificity of the two types of questions that
> were asked rather than any "real" underlying difference. (Sprott, Doob, and
> Jenkins 2001: 3)

Other validity problems stem from attempts to compare self-report or victimization surveys with police statistics or court statistics. It is often assumed that self-report questionnaires measure the true incidence or prevalence of crime and that police statistics do not. Strictly speaking, results from the two are not comparable because of the nature of police activity and the role of police in the criminal justice system. It is important to keep in mind when interpreting police statistics that they are as much a measure of police discretion to lay a charge as they are a measure of criminal activity (Doob and Cesaroni 2004: 95). Police have discretionary power in the kinds of behaviours they will charge and in their interpretation of the Criminal Code. A police officer must determine if someone's behaviour is a criminal offence in law. Some offences known to the police are determined by them to be unfounded. Police may categorize an offence as "unfounded" after investigating a complaint and determining that either no crime took place or there wasn't enough evidence of a crime for a charge to be laid. Alternatively, police may use their discretionary power and determine that an offence is not serious enough to proceed with a charge (in lieu of a charge, the officer may give the person a warning). Yet persons who have been involved in "unfounded" situations might report in a self-report questionnaire that they had committed a crime — or, in a victimization survey, that they had been victimized. In either case, it is a judgment call as to which source is valid as a "true" measure of whether a crime took place.

Comparisons of sources are also difficult because, with victimization surveys, people are likely to confuse or forget the time of occurrence since these events are usually always significant and sometimes frightening or traumatic. In addition, Bortner (1988:149) suggests that victimization surveys would give a less reliable picture of unreported crime than self-report surveys because victims are more likely to remember events that they reported to the police. In the 2004 GSS, questions on spousal violence asked how many times the respondent had been assaulted that year but only asked whether respondents had *ever* reported any of these incidents to the police. Hence, it would be impossible to know how many offences reported in the survey were actually reported to the police (Gannon and Mihorean 2005: 3).

The "Truth" About Girl Crime

Over the past ten years the media have presented Canadian girls as increasingly violent in their behaviour, and that representation has now extended to constructing the "girl next door" as mean and nasty and to be feared for her willingness to harm even her friends. As we move into the twenty-first century, it seems from these messages that girls are "unfettered" and "out of control." Official statistics suggest that girls' violence has increased as much as 200 percent during the last decade. This media construction is not confined to North America. As we have seen, newspapers in Scotland are reporting dramatic increases in official statistics, and the same is happening elsewhere in Europe and the United States. As in North America, throughout the 1980s and into the 1990s, official statistics in European countries have been indicating a sizable increase in assaults and robberies, and more assaults and theft with violence (Junger-Tas, Marshall, and Ribeaud 2003: 52).

The question to be answered by criminologists is whether these claims have any validity. Answering this question is a complex matter because the reality of girl crime, as viewed through official statistics and research, can be used to both support and refute these claims. Sorting through the complexity is simplified by a knowledge of the statistics — how they are calculated, how they are recorded, and what they are measuring. In this sense, none of the statistics will provide a "true" measure of girl crime in an absolute sense. Official statistics are sometimes thought to be a more valid measure of "serious" criminal activity because these are the ones tested by law through rules of evidence and due process. On the other hand, we know that these statistics are subject to a variety of social, political, and administrative factors that make them unreliable. Self-report statistics are reliable but their validity can be suspect if questions are not carefully worded. Self-report studies that focus on serious offences produce delinquency estimates closer to those found in official statistics (Jensen 1996).

Self-report studies are also problematic as valid measures of actual crime because many involve small samples of youth and only those in public schools. These samples will overrepresent middle-class and conforming youth and underrepresent truants, dropouts, and chronic offenders. This is the value of national surveys such as the NLSCY and surveys of homeless youth, which are not confined to school populations and include more serious offenders. In this regard, victimization surveys are considered more valid than self-report surveys because they involve larger samples. Victimization surveys, however, only include those over fifteen or sixteen and exclude offences against youth and children. Hence, all three sources of crime statistics are only estimates of criminal activity and are each measuring different events. As such, the statistics they produce are not comparable in any absolute sense (proportions, percentages, and rates will vary between them); self-report statistics will always be higher than official statistics and victimization surveys. As we have seen, though, they all provide a measure of crime patterns and trends and, in this regard, they can be compared. Junger-Tas, Marshall, and Ribeaud (2003) compared police statistics on youth violence in Europe to their self-report estimates, victimization surveys, and hospital records, and argue that statistics from these sources do not support the increases in youth violence being reported through police statistics. Their answer to the question of increasing youth violence is that, taking into account methodological problems, most of the official increases are due to "better police record keeping, increased computerization and greater willingness in the population to report these crimes." Furthermore, they maintain that the "formal social control net has tightened," more offences are being officially processed and behaviours are being redefined as "more serious," In short, Junger-Tas, Marshall, and Ribeaud conclude that "there probably has been a moderate increase in the less serious violent crimes" (2003: 52).

With this in mind, what can we now say about the question of the "girl problem" in Canada? First, the statistics are problematic in themselves because, to a great extent, girls are often "missing" from the statistics or they receive scant mention. Missing information, combined with methodological issues of measurement, makes it hard to determine trends. Nonetheless, the information we have examined, from official sources, surveys, and other research, does indicate some clear patterns. First, girls are engaged in violent behaviour and some of it is serious, but their numbers, rates, and proportions are small compared to boys. Most girls' violence, similar to that of boys, involves common assault. Girls were responsible for one-third of the Criminal Code charges in 2004, one-fifth of the court cases, and one-quarter of the violent charges going to court; one-third of these were for common assault. Self-report studies for the past twenty years have consistently shown a 3:1 ratio of violent offences — boys are three times more involved in these offences than girls. Girls' violent behaviour is also less serious and less frequent than that of boys. The most valid measure of girl violence — victimization surveys — indicate that, in the early 1990s, women and girls were responsible for 12 percent of reported victimizations and 14 percent of physical assaults. Unfortunately, we do not have recent victimization data to compare for potential increases, nor does this data separate women from girls.

It would seem then that girl violence has been misrepresented by the media and that it does not constitute the new threat of the twenty-first century. What remains to be explained is why a judge would question the validity of statistics on youth crime that now indicate youth violent crime is beginning to decline. We have seen that violent crime rates increased dramatically throughout the 1990s and have only recently begun to decline. These increases were reflected in court populations that also saw dramatic increases, particularly for violent crime. As these rates begin to decline so too do the court populations. However, because of the extrajudicial measures provisions in the YCJA, the number of violent offences going to court will increase proportionately as increasing numbers of less serious and property offences are diverted from the courts. Hence, judges will see more violent offences, proportionately, in their courts than in the past. We have also seen that the rate of violent offences in court is decreasing for male youth, thereby creating a statistical increase in the rate of girls' violent offences in court. This does not mean that more girls are behaving in violent ways. Rather, as in Europe, there is every reason to believe that, for girls, the "formal social control net has tightened."

Herein lies the significance of media misrepresentations and misogynist views of girls and their behaviour. Where ten years ago girls were demonized for behaving "like boys," they are now demonized for "being girls." Rather than acknowledging the extent to which hegemonic definitions of "femininity" frame the boundaries of girls' behaviours, choices, and priorities, they are defined as "evil," "mean," and "nasty" and criminalized as "bullies" engaged in "relational aggression." Yet much of their violence is a response to their vulnerability to violence. Without this understanding, girl violence is decontextualized; crime statistics become weapons in the processes of crime construction and crime control, and girls themselves are problematized through these media processes. When this happens, girls' issues and genuine problems are marginalized and ignored. Issues such as oppression, victimization, sexual exploitation, social injustice, gender inequality, and poverty are never addressed.

DISCUSSION QUESTIONS

1. How has media coverage of girls crime changed since the 1990s and what are the implications of this shift for social justice for girls?

2. How do official statistics misrepresent girls' crimes? Give specific examples.

3. Which source of statistics offers the most valid measure of girl crime and why?

4. Are girls more violent today than in the past? Why or why not?

5. Why is youth crime, particularly that involving girls' violent behaviour, of more public interest than other violent crimes?

GLOSSARY OF TERMS

Chivalry Hypothesis: a belief that crime rates are lower for women and girls because people, including the police, are less likely to view their behaviour as criminal. Hence, it is the belief that victims are less likely to complain to police when the assailant is a female person and/or police are less likely to charge women and girls even when there is a complainant.

Crime Rate: a statistic representing the number of crimes reported by police as a ratio of the total population. Crime rates are usually presented as per 10,000 or 100,000 population.

Decontextualize: to remove something from its context. Of concern in criminology is the misinformation promoted about crime by media stories, which by their nature decontextualize crime.

Extrajudicial Measures: created and defined by Part II of the *Youth Criminal Justice Act.* It refers to provisions that allow police to process accused young offenders by means other than through the youth or adult courts.

Hegemonic: refers to systems of power that are accepted as "natural" or "true" and that serve to reinforce the interests of the powerful and secure the disadvantage or oppression of the less powerful.

Misogyny: generally refers to a hatred of women. Beliefs, behaviours, practices, and attitudes, among many other things, are said to be misogynous when they support, promote, reinforce, or promulgate a hatred of women.

Police Discretion: the power that police have, legal and otherwise, to charge a person with a criminal offence or to decide not to charge. Under the *Youth Criminal Justice Act,* police are urged to use more discretion with the minor offences of young offenders; that is, not to charge and/or to use alternatives to formal justice processing for youth offences.

Relational Aggression: is contrasted to physical or "direct" aggression and considered to be "indirect" aggression that is expressed through personal interaction. Things such as gossip and ridicule are examples.

Reliability: in the behavioural sciences, this concept refers to the extent to which variable measurement and research findings can, and have been, repeated.

Validity: refers to the extent to which research variables have been measured in a way that is consistent with the theoretical concept or what was intended.

Zero-Tolerance Policies: curtail the use of discretion. Most commonly, they have been developed as a means of controlling violence. Many schools have implemented these policies with regard to bullying and other forms of aggressive behaviour. Zero tolerance means that every accused person is sanctioned in the same manner without exception. Many police departments also have these policies for domestic violence complaints, and police are required to lay charges.

SUGGESTED READINGS

Alder, C., and A. Worrall (eds.). 2004. *Girls' Violence: Myths and Realities*. Albany: State University of New York Press.

Brown, L.M. 2003. *Girlfighting: Betrayal and Rejection Among Girls*. New York: New York University Press.

Harris, A. (ed.). 2004. *All About the Girl: Culture, Power and Identity*. New York: Routledge.

Jiwani, Y. 2006. *Discourses of Denial: Mediations of Race, Gender, and Violence*. Vancouver: UBC Press.

Jiwani, Y., C. Steenbergen, and C. Mitchell. 2006. *Girlhood: Redefining the Limits*. Montreal: Black Rose Books.

Underwood, M.K. 2003. *Social Aggression Among Girls*. New York: Guilford Press.

REFERENCES

Acland, C. 1995. *Youth, Murder, Spectacle: The Cultural Politics of "Youth in Crisis."* Boulder: Westview Press.

Alberta Report. 1995. "Killer Girls." July 31.

Arsenault, D. 2006. "15-year-old girl fourth accused of plotting murder." *Chronicle Herald*, May 25: A1–2.

Artz, S. 1998. *Sex, Power and the Violent School Girl*. Toronto: Trifolium Books

_____. 2004. "Violence in the Schoolyard: School Girls' Use of Violence." In C. Alder and A. Worrall (eds.), *Girls' Violence: Myths and Realities*. New York: State University of New York Press.

Artz, Sibylle, and T. Riecken. 1994. "The Survey of Student Life." In *A Study of Violence Among Adolescent Female Students in a Suburban School District*. Victoria: British Columbia Ministry of Education, Education Research Unit.

Artz, S., T. Riecken, B. MacIntyre, E. Lam, and M. Maczewski. 1999. "A Community-Based Violence Prevention Project." British Columbia Health Research Foundation, Final Report, September. Vancouver, B.C. Health Research Foundation.

Aucoin, K. 2005. "Children and Youth as Victims of Violent Crime." *Juristat* 25 (1).

Bala, N. 1997. *Young Offenders Law*. Concord, ON: Irwin Law.

Batchelor, S. 2001. "The Myth of Girl Gangs." *Criminal Justice Matters* (43): 26–27.

Besserer, S., and C. Trainor. 2000. "Criminal Victimization in Canada, 1999." *Juristat* 20 (10). Ottawa: Statistics Canada, Canadian Centre for Justice Statistics.

Bortner, M. 1988. *Delinquency and Justice: An Age of Crisis*. Toronto: McGraw-Hill Ryerson.

Brown, L.M. 2003. *Girlfighting: Betrayal and Rejection Among Girls*. New York: New York University Press.

Brown, S. 2005. *Understanding Youth and Crime: Listening to Youth?* Maidenhead, Berkshire: Open University Press.

Carrigan, D. Owen. 1998. *Juvenile Delinquency in Canada: A History*. Concord, ON: Irwin.

Carrington, P. 1995. "Has Violent Youth Crime Increased: Comment on Corrado and Markwart." *Canadian Journal of Criminology* 37.

_____. 1998. *Factors Affecting Police Diversion of Young Offenders: A Statistical Analysis.* Report to the Solicitor General Canada, February.

CBC News. 2002. "B.C. Girl Convicted in School Bullying Tragedy." March 26.

Chesney-Lind, M., and K. Irwin. 2004. "From Badness to Meanness: Popular Constructions of Contemporary Girlhood." In A. Harris (ed.), *All About the Girl: Culture, Power, and Identity.* New York: Routledge

Chesney-Lind, Meda, and R.G. Shelden. 1992. *Girls, Delinquency and Juvenile Justice.* Belmont, CA: Brooks/Cole.

Chisholm, P. 1997. "Bad Girls: A Brutal BC Murder Sounds an Alarm About Teenage Violence." *Macleans* December 8.

Chronicle Herald. 2006. "Teen Girls in Ontario Charged with Conspiracy to Commit Murder." April 27: A4.

Conway, J. 1992. "Female Young Offenders, 1990–91." *Juristat* 12 (11).

Corrado, R., and A. Markwart. 1994. "The Need to Reform the YOA in Response to Violent Young Offenders: Confusion, Reality or Myth?" *Canadian Journal of Criminology* 36.

Creechan, J. 1995. "How Much Delinquency Is There?" In J. Creechan and R. Silverman, (eds.), *Canadian Delinquency.* Scarborough, ON: Prentice Hall.

Cross, B. 1998. "A Killing Lights a Prairie Fire." *Globe and Mail* February 12.

CTV News. 2004. Swarming Girl Gangs a Crime Problem in Winnipeg. December 5.

Current Events. 2002. Girl Troubles: Have Girls Gone Bad? September 5, V. 103 i1.

Dauvergne, M. 2005. "Homicide in Canada, 2004." *Juristat* 25 (6).

Dauvergne, M., and H. Johnson. 2001. "Children Witnessing Family Violence." *Juristat,* 21 (6). Ottawa: Statistics Canada, Canadian Centre for Justice Statistics.

Davis, J. 1990. *Youth and the Condition of Britain: Images of Adolescent Conflict.* London, UK: Althone Press.

Doob, A., and C. Cesaroni. 2004. *Responding to Youth Crime in Canada.* Toronto: University of Toronto Press.

Doob, A., V. Marinos, and K. Varma. 1995. *Youth Crime and the Youth Justice System in Canada: A Research Perspective.* Toronto: University of Toronto, Centre of Criminology.

Doob, A., and J. Sprott. 1998. "Is the Quality of Youth Violence Becoming More Serious?" *Canadian Journal of Criminology* 40 (2).

Fairclough, I. 2004. "Judge Bucks Stats in Teen's Sentencing." *Chronicle Herald* December 2: B7.

Frank, J. 1992. "Violent Youth Crime." *Canadian Social Trends.* Ottawa: Statistics Canada.

Gabor, T. 1999. "Trends in Youth Crime: Some Evidence Pointing to Increases in the Severity and Volume of Violence on the Part of Young People." *Canadian Journal of Criminology* 41 (3): 385–92.

Gaetz, S. 2004. "Safe Streets for Whom? Homeless Youth, Social Exclusion and Criminal Victimization." *Canadian Journal of Criminology and Criminal Justice* 46 (3) July.

Gannon, M., and G. Doherty. 2005. Criminal Victimization in Canada: 2004. *Juristat* 25 (7). Ottawa: Statistics Canada, Canadian Centre for Justice Statistics.

Garbarino, J. 2006. *See Jane Hit: Why Girls are Growing More Violent and What We Can Do About It.* New York: Penguin.

Gartner, Rosemary, and Anthony Doob. 1994. "Trends in Criminal Victimization in 1988–1993." *Juristat* 14 (13).

Gomes, J.T., L.D. Bertrand, J.J. Paetsch, and J.P. Hornick. 2003. "Self-reported Delinquency Among Alberta's Youth: Findings from a Survey of 2002 Junior and Senior High School Students." *Adolescence* 38 (149): 75–91.

Hatch, A., and K. Faith. 1991. "Female Offenders in Canada: A Statistical Profile." In R. Silverman, J. Teevan, and V. Sacco (eds.), *Crime in Canadian Society* Fourth edition. Toronto: Butterworths.

Heidenson, F. 1996. *Women and Crime,* Second edition. London: Macmillan.

Hindelang, M., T. Hirschi, and J. Weis. 1981. *Measuring Delinquency.* Beverley Hills, CA: Sage.

Hindelang, M., and J. McDermott. 1981. *Analysis of National Crime Victimization Survey Data on Study Serious Delinquent Behavior.* (Monograph 2). Washington, DC: U.S. Department of Justice, Office of Juvenile Justice and Delinquency Prevention.

It's a Girl's World: How Girls Use Their Power to Hurt Each Other. 2004. Produced by Gerry Flahive, written and directed by Lynn Glazier, National Film Board of Canada.

Jeffrey, D. 1995. "Judge Orders Adult Court Trial for 16-year-old Girl." *Chronicle-Herald* September 27.

Jensen, G.F. 1996. "Violence among American Youth: A Comparison of Survey and Agency Images of Crime over Time." Paper presented as the 48th annual meeting of the American society of Criminology, Chicago, November.

Johnson, Holly. 1986. *Women and Crime in Canada.* Ottawa: Solicitor General of Canada, Communications Group. TRS N09.

Johnson, H., and G. Lazarus. 1989. The Impact of Age on Crime Victimization Rates. *Canadian Journal of Criminology* 31: 309–18.

Joyce, G. 2000. "Friend of Accused Tells of Attack on Virk." *Chronicle Herald* March 11: D32.

Junger-Tas, J., I.H. Marshall, and D. Ribeaud. 2003. *Delinquency in an International Perspective: The International Self-Reported Delinquency Study.* Monsey, NY: Criminal Justice Press.

Kong, R., H. Johnson, S. Beattie, and A. Cardillo. 2003. "Sexual Offences in Canada." *Juristat* 23 (6).

Latimer, J., and L.C. Foss. 2004. *A One-day Snapshot of Aboriginal Youth in Custody across Canada: Phase II.* Ottawa: Department of Justice Canada. Research and Statistics Division.

Le Blanc, M. 1983. "Delinquency as an Epiphenomenon of Adolescents." In N. Corrado, M. Le Blanc, and J. Trepanier (eds.), *Current Issues in Juvenile Justice.* Toronto: Butterworths.

Lundy, C., and M. Totten. 1997. "Youth on the Fault Line." *The Social Worker* 65 (3).

Mean Girls. 2004. U.S. Director Mark Waters, Producer Lorne Michaels. Paramount Pictures

Mertl, S. 2006. "Street Racing Will be Outlawed." *Chronicle Herald* May 26: A3.

Miller, J., and N. White. 2004. "Situational Effects of Gender Inequality on Girls' Participation in Violence." In C. Alder and A. Worrall (eds.), *Girls' Violence: Myths and Realities.* New York: State University of New York Press.

Moore, Dene. 2000a. "Accused Teen Killer Says She Wasn't There when Virk Killed." Canadian Press. March 23, in *Canadian Newsdisc.* Don Mills, ON: Southam Electronic Publishing.

_____. 2000b. "Ellard Guilty in Virk's Death." *Chronicle Herald* April 1.

Nye, F., and J. Short. 1957. "Scaling Delinquent Behavior." *American Sociological Review* 22: 326–32.

Odd Girl Out. 2005. Director Tom McLoughlin, Lifetime Original Film.

Pacienza, A. 2000. "Community Mourns Slain Family." *Chronicle-Herald* July 15.

Pollak, Otto. 1950. *The Criminality of Women.* New York: Barnes.

Public Health Agency of Canada. 2005. "Aggressive Girls." Overview Paper. National Clearinghouse on Family Violence Publication. Available at <http://www.phac-aspc.gc.ca/ncfv-cnivf/familyviolence/html/nfntsaggsr_e.html> accessed July 2007.

Purvis, A. 1997. "Fury of Her Peers: A Teenager's Brutal Assault and Drowning Raise Questions in a Quiet Canadian Town." *Time* December 8.

Reid, S. 2005. "Youth Crime and the Media." In K. Campbell (ed.), *Understanding Youth Justice in Canada.* Toronto: Prentice-Hall.

Reid-MacNevin, S.A. 1996. "The Media Portrayal of Troubled Youth." Unpublished manuscript, University of Guelph.

_____. 2003. "Bad, Bad... Youth: The Media Portrayal of Youth." Paper presented at the Crime and Media Symposium, October, St. Thomas University.

Reitano, J. 2004. "Youth Custody and Community Services in Canada." *Juristat* 24 (9).

Reitsma-Street, Marge. 1991. "A Review of Female Delinquency." In A. Leschied, P. Jaffe, and W. Willis (eds.), *The Young Offenders Act: A Revolution in Canadian Juvenile Justice.* Toronto: University of Toronto Press.

_____. 1999. "Justice for Canadian Girls: A 1990s Update." *Canadian Journal of Criminology* 41 (3).

Sauve, J. 2005. "Crime Statistics in Canada, 2004." *Juristat* 25 (5).

Savage, L. 1998. "Natural Born Killers." *Globe and Mail* April 11.

Savoie, J. 1999. "Youth Violent Crime." *Juristat* 19 (13).

Schissel, Bernard. 1997. *Blaming Children: Youth Crime, Moral Panics and the Politics of Hate.* Halifax: Fernwood Publishing.

Simmons, R. 2002. *Odd Girl Out.* Orlando: Harcourt, Inc.

Simourd, L., and D. Andrews. 1996. "Correlates of Delinquency: A Look at Gender." In R. Silverman, J. Teevan, and V. Sacco (eds.), *Crime in Canadian Society.* Toronto: Harcourt Brace and Company.

Smith, R., L. Bertrand, B. Arnold, and J. Hornick. 1995. *A Study of the Level and Nature of Youth Crime and Violence in Calgary.* Calgary: Calgary Police Service.

Sprott, J. 1996. "Understanding Public Views of Youth Crime and the Youth Justice System." *Canadian Journal of Criminology* 38 (5).

Sprott, J., and A. Doob. 2000. "Bad, Sad, and Rejected: The Lives of Aggressive Children." *Canadian Journal of Criminology* 42 (2).

_____. 2003. "It's all in the Denominator: Trends in the Processing of Girls in Canada's Youth Courts." *Canadian Journal of Criminology and Criminology and Criminal Justice* (January): 73–80.

Sprott, J., A. Doob, and J. Jenkins 2001. "Problem Behaviour and Delinquency in Children and Youth." *Juristat* 21 (4)

Statistics Canada. 1984. Data from the Juvenile Courts — 1983. *Juristat* 4 (7).

_____. 1999. *Canadian Crime Statistics 1998.* Catalogue 85-002-VPE. 19 (13). Ottawa: Canadian Centre for Justice Statistics.

_____. 2001. *Children and Youth in Canada.* Canadian Centre for Justice Statistics, Profile Series.

_____. 2003. *Youth Court Survey 3309.* Catalogue # 85-002 Vol. 25 (4).

Stevenson, K., J. Tufts, D. Hendrick, and M. Kowalski. 1998. *A Profile of Youth Justice in Canada.* Ottawa: Statistics Canada.

Totten, Mark D. 2000. *Guys, Gangs, and Girlfriend Abuse.* Peterborough, ON: Broadview Press.

_____. 2001. *The Special Needs of Females in Canada's Youth Justice System: An Account of Some Young Women's Experiences and Views.* Technical report. Ottawa: Department of Justice.

Vincent, I. 1995. "Ruthless Violence Part of Girl Gang Reality." *Chronicle Herald* September 23.

_____. 1998a. "Teen's Torture Again Reveals Girls' Brutality." *Globe and Mail* January 20.

_____. 1998b. "Police Arrest Members of Girl Gang." *Globe and Mail* January 22.

Wallace, M. 2003. "Crime Statistics in Canada, 2002." *Juristat* 23 (5).

_____. 2004. "Crime Statistics in Canada, 2003." *Juristat* 24 (6).

Welch, M., M. Fenwick, and M. Roberts. 1997. "Primary Definitions of Crime and Moral Panic: A Content Analysis of Experts' Quotes in Feature Newspaper Articles on Crime." *Journal of Research in Crime and Delinquency* 34 (4): 474–94.

Wiseman, R. 2002. *Queenbees and Wannabees: Helping your Daughter Survive Cliques, Gossip, Boyfriends and Other Realities of Adolescence.* New York: Three Rivers Press.

Part III

The Historical Shape and Form of Crime

T raditional historians argue that crime and crime control change according to the socio-demographic nature of a particular time period. Their analyses tend to focus on the characteristics of criminality in a historical epoch: what types of people are in prison; the types of punishment they experience; the nature of their crimes (especially high-profile individual cases); government policies directed at criminality; and the ability of the state and its citizens to counter "crime waves." D. Owen Carrigan, in *Crime and Punishment in Canada: A History* (1991), for example, paints a historical picture of crime based on crime rates over time, historical descriptions about the age, race, and gender profile of criminals, the socio-economic conditions of the criminal class, and historical accounts of forms of punishment. Such traditional histories are descriptive; they are "constructed" histories, much like fiction. They tell us a great deal about the norms and values of the society the authors live in, but they do little to help us understand how and why certain peoples are more damaged by society and by the justice system than others. Nor does Carrigan's history reveal how laws and social control benefit some to the disadvantage of others, or how crime and justice are related to socio-economic conditions at specific points in history.

Traditional criminological histories, as primarily descriptive, then, tend to place changes in crime and punishment in an evolutionary framework premised on the assumption that society, as it develops technologically/scientifically, is becoming more civilized. As such, they suggest that our responses to crime are becoming more rational and civilized as well. This paradigm for understanding change tends not to place historical change in an analytical framework that helps explain oppression and marginalization or indicates why some people are condemned primarily for their place in the socio-economic structure.

As an antidote to traditional history, the chapters in Part III concern the history of oppression of certain peoples in Canada and reveal how historical forces shape contemporary criminal justice. They focus on how and why society inordinately condemns marginalized people and how this condemnation is tied to the politics and economics of a particular time. Most importantly, the discussions illustrate an often-forgotten issue: that people who are economically, socially, and spiritually oppressed over generations will be overrepresented in the crime-control system. Unlike traditional criminological history, these works show how, for example, the phenomenon of Aboriginal people in conflict with the law is related to continuing but changing forms of colonization, or how crime, detection, and punishment are related to the development of capitalism, specifically to the need for cheap and available labour (for example, of children and youth), or to the changing role of the state in managing and exploiting natural resources.

In chapter 8, Les Samuelson and Patricia Monture-Angus explore the historical roots of oppression in "Aboriginal People and Social Control: The State, Law, and Policing." They trace the history of Aboriginal peoples in Canada from European colonization to the establishment of Canada as a dominion through to the *Indian Act* and its modern-day incarnations. They focus primarily on the last thirty years in Canada, a time when Aboriginal people formally gained access to the Canadian democratic process while remaining overrepresented in the justice and prison systems. Several of the various federal initiatives under the Department of Indian and Northern Affairs were predicated on Aboriginal communities adopting a model of self-policing, as a way of making justice systems more accountable to and cognizant of the needs of disparate communities. But Samuelson and Monture-Angus illustrate how this "tinkering" with the justice system had essentially no effect. As they document, Aboriginal people have continued, well into the new millennium, to be overrepresented in the Canadian justice system. Indeed, "Prison has become for young Native men the manifestation of a just society, replacing the promise that high-school and post-secondary education represent for many other Canadians." Their analysis explores Canadian policy reform as accommodating the status quo, not as fundamental change. In other words, criminal justice policy can only be called progressive if it challenges issues of social injustice in the form of systemic racism and structural inequalities. They explore the urgency of changing a system that currently locks up Aboriginal people as much for their race as their conduct.

The historical situation they describe is poignantly captured in the following chapter, 9, where Helen Cote and Wendy Schissel describe how the Canadian state policy of forced residential schools for Aboriginal children has left a continuing legacy of cultural and personal damage. Cote and Schissel begin with the fundamental contention that the overrepresentation of Aboriginal people in the criminal justice system must be understood in the context of the "the transgenerational effects of the residential school experience." As they state, if legislators and judges do not have this historical understanding at their disposal, the system will continue to punish First Nations offenders more harshly than non-First Nations offenders. Cote's first-hand experiences as a victim of physical and sexual abuse in residential school bring alive the "national crime" perpetrated against First Nations people in the form of forced residential school education. Her account is both disturbing and instructive as the authors link the attack on children in residential school to the continuing overinvolvement of Aboriginal people in street crime and the exposure of generations of Aboriginal people to harsh justice.

The authors of "Damaged Children and Broken Spirits" argue not only for the need to rethink how people come to be involved in the criminal justice system but also for "an urgent need for new judicial and social policies that reject punishment in favour of individual healing and community restoration." They contend that a critical criminological study of Canadian society is incomplete if it does not acknowledge that damaged children become damaged adults and that residential schools both violated the liberties of Nations of Indigenous people and created a legacy of crime and punishment that stands as a national atrocity.

In chapter 10, "A Criminal Justice History of Children and Youth in Canada," Shahid Alvi focuses on the historical transformation of youth crime, policing, and justice in Canada. The emphasis is on how, throughout our history, Canadians have condemned children to a greater or lesser degree, and how our collective enmity towards children and youth is associated with historically specific socio-political and socio-economic circumstances — but especially with the criminal justice system. The critical criminological framework that Alvi presents reveals the connections between the development of different forms of youth justice and the place of children and youth in the political economy of Canada. His descriptions of the three major historical changes in youth justice in Canada show how, in large part, the official condemnation of "bad" children and youth alters with changes in the importance of young people to the demands of capitalism. In effect, what all of the works in Part III reveal is how the systems of justice and punishment, past and present, have contributed to the further condemnation of certain groups of people who are already disadvantaged and oppressed by society.

8

Aboriginal People and Social Control
The State, Law, and "Policing"

Les Samuelson and Patricia Monture

KEY FACTS

> Canada's Correctional investigator, Howard Sapers, in his fall 2006 report, refers to the treatment of Natives in the National justice system as "Canada's National disgrace."

> The North West Mounted Police/RCMP apprehended Indian children who ran away from residential school, and Indian adults who left reserve without a pass from the Indian agent.

> In 1927 the federal government made it illegal for Indians to raise money or to use band funds to bring land claim disputes to court.

> In 1978 three major stand-alone policing initiatives were started, the Dakota Ojibway Tribal Council Police (DOTC), the Amerindian Police Council for Quebec, and the Blood Confederacy Band Police in Southern Alberta.

> According to a UN report, Canada would be placed 48th out of 174 countries on the United Nations' human development scale, if the country were judged on the social and economic well-being of First Nations peoples. This is compared to its usual top 10 ranking (7th in the last report).

> There is a routine over-classification of Aboriginal prisoners, who are more likely than non-Aboriginal prisoners to be sent to maximum security prisons. That means Aboriginal offenders often serve their sentences away from family, community, their friends, and elders. They are sent into segregation more often, severely limiting their access to rehabilitative programs and services.

Sources: *National Post* 2007; CBC News Online 2005; CBC News Online 2006.

In January 2000 two Saskatoon police officers picked up an Aboriginal man on city streets one night and then dropped him off outside the city, forcing him to walk back to town on a freezing cold early morning. A complainant, Daryl Night, came forward after the bodies of two other Aboriginal men were found in the same area. They had gone missing the same weekend. Witnesses alleged that they saw the men in police custody on the night they disappeared. An RCMP investigation into the Saskatoon police force was then also expanded to include the death of another Aboriginal man, who died in 1990 under similar circumstances (*Star Phoenix* March 21, 2000: 1). The Crown subsequently laid criminal charges against the two Saskatoon police officers, who were both fifteen-year veterans. They were charged with unlawful confinement and assault (*Star Phoenix* April 12, 2000: 1).

These stark events in Saskatchewan clearly relate to another, larger point: that

Table 8-1: Provincial Variation in Aboriginal Sentenced Admissions to Custody, 1978–79 and 2000–01

Province/Territory	Percent Aboriginal Admissions	
	1978–79	2000–01
Saskatchewan	61%	76%
Yukon	51%	72%
Manitoba	50%	64%
Alberta	26%	39%
British Columbia	15%	20%
Ontario	9%	9%
Nova Scotia	n/a	7%
Newfoundland and Labrador	3%	7%
Quebec	1%	2%
Prince Edward Island	3%	1%
Provincial/Territorial Total	16%	19%

Data are not available for Nunavut, New Brunswick, and North West Territories.
Source: OFIFC 2003.

Aboriginal people are overrepresented in the criminal justice system. One of the most recent and well-documented analyses of the continued overrepresentation of Aboriginal people in prison is by Roberts and Melchers (2003). Their article examines provincially sentenced admissions to custody since 1978, when national statistics on ethnicity of offenders, Aboriginal and non-Aboriginal, were first published. They note that recent efforts have been made by Parliament and the Supreme Court to address Aboriginal overrepresentation in prison, the former by statutory recognition of the unique nature of Aboriginal offenders and their frequent negative life experiences, the latter by interpreting Criminal Code sentencing provisions introduced in 1996 (see R. v. Gladue). The unfortunate fact, they note, is that data comparing 1978–79 to 2000–01 show that virtually all efforts have failed, as seen in Table 8-1. Sadly, the federal Correctional Service of Canada (Canada 1999) reports that in Canada as a whole the percentage rate of Aboriginal peoples in custody is 8.5 times the rate for non-Aboriginals. In Saskatchewan the Aboriginal rate is an astounding thirty-five times the non-Aboriginal incarceration rate.

> The Crown laid criminal charges against the two Saskatoon police officers, who were both fifteen-year veterans.

Moreover, the problem can get worse. Predictions are for even higher involvement levels if we do not move to a truly post-colonial society. Correctional Service of Canada estimated that the Aboriginal federal offender prison population had a 38 percent growth rate, while the total number of non-Aboriginal prisoners is slowly declining, based on data available from the fall 2006 report by Howard Sappers, Canada's Correctional Investigator (cited in *National Post* 2007). He noted that Native people

> Data comparing 1978–79 to 2000–01 show virtually all efforts have failed to reduce Aboriginal admissions to custody.

make up fewer than 2.7 percent of the Canadian population. Sappers noted that while the federal (two-year minimum) inmate population went down 12.5 percent between 1996 and 2004, First Nations federal inmates increased by 21.7 percent — a 34 percent spread. He added that the situation is particularly critical when it comes to Aboriginal women. Their numbers increased by a staggering 74.2 percent over this period. The Harper Conservative government's attorney general, Vic Toews, has proposed Three Strikes legislation similar to a California law that sent one three-time inmate to prison for twenty-five years to life for stealing a slice of pepperoni pizza from young kids on a beach. As the Saskatoon *Star Phoenix* article of October 18, 2006 (A.10) noted, this third offender legislation will disproportionately hit Western Canadian Native peoples. Given demographic projections regarding the growth of Aboriginal populations in Canada, especially in Western Canada, this is an alarming trend.

> Between 1996 and 2004 the federal (two year and up) inmate population went down 12.5 percent, while First Nations federal inmates increased by 21.7 percent. Aboriginal women inmates went up 74 percent.

The concern about the overincarceration of Aboriginal peoples goes beyond Canada's borders. At the 1993 World Conference on Human Rights in Vienna, the chief of the Grand Council of Cree spoke on behalf of all Indigenous peoples in North America: "North American Indigenous peoples need protection under international law: because we wish to survive as peoples" (Watson 1996: 9). The spring of 1996 saw the opening session of the First Nations' International Court of Justice in Canada (FNICJ), with seven Aboriginal judges, one of them an Australian woman, assisted by a panel of elders. The FNICJ was established by a resolution of the chiefs of Ontario and the Assembly of First Nations of Great Turtle Island, or the Three Americas — North, Central, and South (Watson 1996):

> North American Indigenous peoples need protection under international law because we wish to survive as peoples.

> By establishing the First Nations' International Court of Justice, a vision was created; that the cries for justice from Indigenous peoples will now have the opportunity to be heard by a court that is freed from the conflicts of interest which arise when First Nations come before the colonisers' legal systems in pursuit of justice between First Nations and settler governments. (Watson 1996: 9)

While some may say the court's role is only symbolic, the court found "that the law ways of First Nations had been deliberately and systematically abrogated, disrespected and plundered by the colonizing powers" (Watson 1996: 9).

Why are Aboriginal people so highly involved in the criminal justice system?

> The frequent public perception of Aboriginal people as "drunks," "lazy," and "criminal" has long confused symptoms with the underlying causes of these social problems. Confusing symptoms with cause is convenient, because it allows for a one-way street of criminal justice policies and programs that address the "problem of crime" without seriously challenging the status quo of the Canadian political economy. Like most systems of domination from Roman slavery onward, this one depends on those in power developing strong ideologies and typifications that justify their control over subject populations. This was certainly true historically in Canada, and unfortunately it has re-emerged

in modern form recently. A 1997 poll of Canadians confirmed a general backlash of attitudes toward "Indians," Inuit, and Métis people. Conveniently and blindly ignoring historical and current realities, almost half of Canadians believe Aboriginals have an equal or better standard of living than the average citizen. Some 40 percent believe that Natives "have only themselves to blame for their problems." (Samuelson and Antony 1998: 242)

We argue, however, that this entanglement with the criminal justice system is a result of both the colonialist political–legal "policing" process, which was almost genocidal to Aboriginal peoples,[1] and the imposition of an adversarialist form of justice on Aboriginal people. The policing of Aboriginal peoples involved both the actions of law enforcers and the incarceration process as well as the creation of state policy and lawmaking.

1763 to 1960: The Benefits and Advantages of Understanding Colonialism

The crucial political-legal agreements shaping British-Aboriginal arrangements after the fall of New France to British control were the *Royal Proclamation of 1763* and the various treaties signed thereafter (see Manitoba Aboriginal Justice Inquiry 1991). The *Proclamation* was precipitated by a political crisis, an Aboriginal siege of Detroit by Chief Pontiac (Manitoba Aboriginal Justice Inquiry 1991: 56). The act forbade white settlement beyond a "proclamation line" and confirmed the principles on which Aboriginal–European relations would (or should) be based. Britain declared that the Crown (the British parliament, with the official endorsement of the king or queen) must formally extinguish Indian rights, that the Crown alone could undertake such obligations, and that private interests could not extinguish Aboriginal claims to land. Negotiations for the surrender of Indian title had to occur at an open assembly with the full consent of all people. Importantly, in legal terms, the *Royal Proclamation* did not establish Aboriginal rights in North America, but as the Supreme Court of Canada stated in *Guerin* v. *R.* [1984], it did assume their existence. The *Royal Proclamation* ultimately resulted in large tracts of Aboriginal land being "treatied" for "protected preserves" that would, in colonialist reality although not in principle, become "prison camps."

> The crucial political-legal agreements shaping British-Aboriginal arrangements after the fall of New France to British control were the *Royal Proclamation of 1763* and the various treaties signed thereafter.

With the arrival of large numbers of white settlers in the early nineteenth century, the colonial government pursued policies designed to restrict traditional Aboriginal lifestyles and land use. These restrictive laws and policies included outlawing Aboriginal ceremony and spiritual/religious practices. Other laws denied political participation to Aboriginal women, restricted movement "off-reserve," and imposed criminal justice jurisdiction contrary to the provisions of the *Royal Proclamation of 1763* (Purich 1986: 126–32). Early Aboriginal protests proved futile and were met with harsh repression, including the bombardment, in the late nineteenth century, of coastal villages by British warships (Frideres 1998: 4).

The *British North America Act* (BNA), passed by the British Parliament on July 1, 1867, created the Dominion of Canada, initially consisting of the provinces of Nova Scotia, New Brunswick, Quebec, and Ontario. In 1869 the Hudson's Bay Company agreed to transfer jurisdiction over Rupert's Land to the central government in Ottawa, extending Canada to the Rocky Mountains. In 1870 and 1871 Manitoba and British Columbia, respectively, became provinces of Canada. During this time of confederation, Canada continued to follow repressive legal instruments, such as the 1857 *Act for the Gradual Civilization of the Indian Tribes.*

Unlike the governments of the United States and Australia, under the BNA the federal government of Canada was granted the sole power to legislate in the field of criminal law. It quickly and forcefully stepped into this field. In 1869 the government abolished public hanging, and in 1875 it discontinued the use of the ball and chain, thus providing some improvement in justice for colonialist prisoners. The federal government also assumed authority for "Indians and lands reserved for Indians." Acting under this authority, the government enacted legislation in 1876 that is now recognized as one of the most shameful colonialist dimensions of Canadian law and society. The infamous *Indian Act* became the cornerstone of the colonial regulation and destruction of Aboriginal peoples and the appropriation of Aboriginal land. The 1876 Act "was not a new piece of legislation, but a consolidation of various existing federal and colonial statutes" (Purich 1986: 126). A seldom seen early insightful article by Gail Kellough (1980: 347) noted that the most important factor to consider when analyzing the feudal-like structure imposed upon Indians by their colonizers is their dependent status in interactions with government. For the colonizers, Aboriginal autonomy had to be destroyed, which sometimes meant crushing resistance. Kellough (1980: 347) observes that the clearest example of forced dependency is in the area of finances. Before 1913, the total cost of Indian administration was "borne primarily by revenues from Indian sources, such as the sale or lease of land." She notes that while Indians were literally paying their own way, the minister of Indian affairs had total authority — he could dispose of land and hold the finances as he saw fit. A short quote from Kellough (1980: 348) is informative:

> Between 1900 and 1930, Indians parted with their land for purposes of railway, road and town development. The National Indian Brotherhood has estimated that as much as half of the original reserve allotment across Canada has been lost through land sales made to benefit railways, oil and coal corporations, farmers and recreation developers. In many instances, the band did not know that part of their reserves were being sold. When they did, they operated from an inferior power position. Lucien M. Hanks (1950) reports how the government cut off rations on an Alberta Blackfoot reserve in order to get Indians to sell prime land desired for white settlement. This move divided the reserve between those who wanted to stop the starvation of their children and those who saw the long term implication of the sale. Eventually, the pro-selling group won and the money was put "in trust" for the Indians.

The original *Indian Act* and subsequent early amendments confined Aboriginal people to reserves. Until 1940 the federal Department of Indian Affairs, under the auspices of the *Indian Act*, decided which people could and could not leave reserves. "Surplus" land could be taken for use by non-Aboriginals. An alliance between the state and the church resulted in legislation that outlawed a variety of dances and Aboriginal ceremonies, including the potlatch. The federal franchise to vote was denied to registered

Indians until 1960. Aboriginal children were forcibly removed from their families and put in residential schools to "civilize" and "Christianize" them. Indian people were not legally citizens but, rather, "wards of the state."

Historically, the police were a central agency of colonization and key to the control of Aboriginal peoples (Samuelson 1995). Recent Canadian inquiries into the relation between Aboriginal peoples and the police confirm this role (see Manitoba Aboriginal Justice Inquiry 1991) — which also developed in other "white settler" societies. The report of the Australian Royal Commission into Aboriginal Deaths in Custody expresses this historical police function in no uncertain terms: "Police officers naturally shared all the characteristics of the society from which they were recruited, including the idea of racial superiority in relation to Aboriginal people and the idea of white superiority in general." As "members of a highly disciplined centralist organization," the officers tended to have fixed ideas, but in any case their very role inevitably led to conflict: "The policeman was the right-hand man of the authorities, the enforcer of policies of control and supervision, often the taker of children, the rounder up of those accused of violating the rights of the settlers" (Commonwealth of Australia 1994: 10).

The colonial nature of policing was indeed key to the relations between Aboriginal peoples and the state. In this early era, the distinction between policing and militarization was blurred. As the Manitoba Aboriginal Justice Inquiry (1991) noted, whenever an Indian agent felt the need for assistance in enforcing (anti-) Indian government policy, he turned to the Royal Canadian Mounted Police (or the North West Mounted Police before the formation of the RCMP). The NWMP/RCMP quickly apprehended any Indian children who ran away from residential schools, as well as Indian adults who left reserves without a pass from the Indian agent. The inquiry (Manitoba Aboriginal Justice Inquiry 1991: 593) concluded that these police forces represented interests that were rapidly destroying the Indian economy and way of life, which led to ongoing tensions between the police and Indian nations across the West.

As for the criminal justice system, Geoffrey York (1992: 157) reports that a study of capital murder cases from 1926 to 1957 found that the risk of execution for an Anglo Canadian who killed a white person was 21 percent, whereas an Indian who killed a white person in similar circumstances had a 96 percent risk of execution. During this period, memos from Indian Affairs bureaucrats recommend that Indian offenders be executed because Native people needed "special deterrence."

The 1857 *Act for the Gradual Civilization of the Indian Tribes* and the *Indian Act* of 1876 orchestrated a historical process of segregation and legalized paternalistic control. The five-year Canadian Royal Commission on Aboriginal Peoples (RCAP 1996a: 7) concluded from its research, and from previous reports, that it is essential to frame discussions of Aboriginal justice issues in the broadest historical-analytic context. Contemporary realities facing Aboriginal people in the justice system are the result of a historical relationship between Aboriginal and non-Aboriginal peoples:

> The sense of oppressiveness, the sense of illegitimacy that has come to characterize Aboriginal peoples' perception and experience of the justice system has deep historical roots… The importance of understanding this historical experience and recognizing that it is a history whose epilogue has not yet been written — and indeed cannot be written until a new relationship is forged — has been underlined by the most recent of the justice inquiries carried out from one end of the country to the other. (RCAP 1996a: 7)

Often the first contact, particularly on the prairies, between First Nations and the European view and practice of criminal justice was the Indian agent, who, as established under the *Indian Act,* was investigator, prosecutor, and judge. As Donald Purich (1986: 122–23) points out, encounters with the Indian agent were not always positive:

> The extent of the powers Indian agents had can be judged from this story, told by a Saskatchewan lawyer, recounting how he became interested in Indian issues in the 1930s. "I was contacted by some Indians to defend a friend of theirs who had been charged with theft, which had supposedly occurred on the reserve. I contacted the Indian agent who I was told was prosecuting the case. Well, he told me to forget it because the guy was guilty. I asked him how he could be so sure and he told me he was going to be the judge as well. I tell you that made me mad."

In other areas of the prairies, Aboriginal peoples' first contact was with the North West Mounted Police, created by an act of Parliament in May 1873. On July 8, 1874, three hundred NWMP officers left Fort Dufferin in Manitoba and headed to posts further west. This deployment was largely the result of disturbances in the Cypress Hills (Hildebrandt and Hubner 1994: 71). In June 1873, there was a massacre of the Assiniboine of Chief Manitupotis's camp by "wolfers" (U.S. whiskey traders) in the hills. Although charges were laid, no convictions were secured (Hildebrandt and Hubner 1994: 59–69). The arrival of the NWMP to keep the peace in the Cypress Hills would have been welcomed by the Assiniboine if not by the Cree who also lived there. That relationship at least approached something like trust and mutual respect. In their work on the Indians and the Northwest Rebellion (1885), Blair Stonechild and Bill Waiser (1997: 8–9) note that the NWMP was presented to the Indians throughout the West as the Queen's soldiers being "sent to protect them from unscrupulous American traders and the whiskey they peddled." Hudson Bay Company trader William McKay presented gifts to the Cree in 1874 as evidence of the Queen's good will. A few years later, during a treaty signing with the Indians at Fort Carlton, as Stonechild and Waiser (1997: 13) note, "The importance of having the Queen's 'warriors' present was not lost on the commissioners, for the Indians viewed them as potential allies to be befriended, rather than a hostile force called upon to intimidate them." The bands of Mistawasis and Ahtahkakoop, newly settled on their reserves, faced crisis when goods and supplies promised them under treaty arrived too late in the season to be of assistance and would have been inadequate in any event. The bands would have starved except for the rations provided by the NWMP (Stonechild and Waiser 1997: 29).

1960 to 1990s: Challenges, Obstacles, and Developments in "Policing" Aboriginal Peoples

The 1960s saw the emergence of Aboriginal demands that the Canadian state recognize the existence of their treaty and Aboriginal rights and eliminate restrictions on their political and civil rights. Pursuing these goals was no easy feat. After an Aboriginal bid to have unfulfiled land claims in British Columbia settled in 1927, the government made it illegal for Indians to raise money or to use band funds to bring land claims disputes to court. Also in 1927, an amendment to the *Indian Act* prohibited national political organizing of Indian people (Wotherspoon and Satzewich 1993: 226).

Not until 1960 were the obstacles that denied the federal vote to Indian people removed. The administratively established, but most likely illegal, pass system for movement off-reserve fell into disuse by the 1960s. The government also began dismantling the physically, emotionally, and culturally destructive compulsory residential school system for Aboriginal children.

In the autumn of 1964 federal Indian Affairs department officials initiated discussions with the Canadian Corrections Association regarding the high frequency of Indian appearances in court, committals, and jail. The report *Indians and the Law* (CAC 1967) was released in 1967, a year, it turns out, that was important for Aboriginal peoples and justice in both good and bad ways. It marked not only the publication of the first report on Indians and the law, covering many issues from policing to overincarceration, but also the first legal case under the relatively new Canadian Bill of Rights went to the Supreme Court. It found successfully for Joseph Drybones, an Indian from the Canadian Northwest Territories. The CAC report saw this legal decision as heralding Indians' ability to successfully challenge the repressive sections of the *Indian Act*. Mr. Justice William Morrow of the Northwest Territories Territorial Court ruled that certain sections of the federal *Indian Act* discriminated against Indians and were contrary to the Canadian Bill of Rights, especially those sections that dealt with the intoxication of Indians. In the ruling he allowed the appeal of Joseph Drybones against a conviction on a charge of being "unlawfully intoxicated off a reserve." Previous court decisions in the Northwest Territories had ruled that Indians suspected of intoxication had to be charged under the *Indian Act*, even though whites or Eskimos suspected of intoxication were charged under the territorial liquor ordinance. Justice Morrow ruled that these decisions were discrimination against Indians because the *Indian Act* dictated a stiffer minimum penalty than the liquor ordinance and made it illegal for an Indian to be intoxicated even in his own home. His ruling in favour of Joseph Drybones set the stage for subsequent challenges to the *Indian Act*.

Importantly for policing, the CAC report concluded that the forty-six band constables then spread across Canada should be increased, as part of a more formal Aboriginal special constable program. The Department of Indian Affairs and Northern Development (DIAND), which oversaw policing under the *Indian Act* of 1876, obtained Treasury Board approval to develop the band constable system. It wasn't until almost four years later, however, in September 1971, that the department issued "Circular 55," which stated that the objective of the band constable, over and above matters such as enforcing band bylaws, was to "supplement the senior police forces at the local level, but not supplant them" (RCAP 1996a: 83–84).

In 1973 a second, broader DIAND study, *Policing on Reserves*, focused on the employment of Aboriginal people in a comprehensive policing role and proposed an expansion and improvement of the band constable program (RCAP 1996a: 84). The task force that generated this report for DIAND examined three basic options; the first two were based on band council policing (the existing Circular 55 concept) and municipal policing, that is, contracting local municipalities for policing services. Option 3(a) proposed the establishment of autonomous Aboriginal police forces, while option 3(b) proposed the development of a special constable contingent within existing police forces. The task force concluded that option 3(b) should be made available to interested bands.

However, by the late 1970s all-Indian "stand-alone" police services also emerged for on-reserve policing. Stand-alone policing arrangements, or what have been characterized as Indian police forces, operate pursuant to a variety of federal and provincial agreements, *Indian Act* band bylaws, and provincial legislation (RCAP 1996a: 84). In 1978 three major stand-alone policing initiatives were started in Aboriginal communities in Canada. The Dakota

By the late 1970s all-Indian "stand-alone" police services also emerged for on-reserve policing.

Ojibway Tribal Council (DOTC) police force was established to deliver locally controlled police services to eight Dakota and Ojibway reserves in Manitoba. A force of twenty-five constables, the first tribal police force of its kind, was administered by a chief of police who reported to the police commission. The members of the commission included the chiefs of the participating reserves as well as representatives of the provincial justice department, the federal government, the RCMP, and the Manitoba Police Commission. The DOTC constables have peace officer status and authority to enforce all legislation and statutes, but their jurisdiction is limited, under the terms of the federal/provincial/DOTC agreement, to DOTC reserves. The force shares investigative responsibilities with the RCMP for minor Criminal Code offences, while major offences are turned over to the RCMP in accordance with a written protocol. In that same year, a similar policing project was set up in Quebec. The Amerindian Police Council was originally established to provide policing to twenty-three First Nations communities. In 1995 nine communities withdrew from the project (RCAP 1996a: 85). Also established in 1978 was the stand-alone band police for the Blood Confederacy in Southern Alberta, which now has about twenty-five First Nations constables.

By 1990 Canada had about 708 Indian constables, most employed under the special constable program with the RCMP and the Ontario Indian Special Constable Program. In May 1990 the federal government phased out the Special Constable Program on all reserves, with willing 3(b) constables becoming regular RCMP members. There had been conflict since 1978 about official positive evaluations of indigenized police. Aboriginal police, Aboriginal organizations, and academic writers all differed in their estimation of the worth and effectiveness of Indigenous policing (Haveman 1992: 115). Aboriginal police and Aboriginal organizations especially tried to expose the contradictions, problems, and limitations in an indigenized system imposed by the federal government. For these critics, such a system was part of neo-colonial pacification and control. In response, they lobbied for more autonomous Aboriginal policing. Some Aboriginal spokespeople, for example, argued that the Blood Tribal Police in Alberta should apply traditional law and not criminal law.

By the mid-1990s Canada had over eight hundred Aboriginal officers with full police status and band constables providing field-level policing (Atlantic Institute of Criminology 1996). While an important initiative, this Aboriginal constables program was nowhere near sufficient to deal with conflict between Indians and conflicts with colonialist-based paramilitary policing — such as that based on an RCMP model. Nor was it able to significantly reduce Aboriginal overincarceration, which continued unabated during the 1980s and 1990s despite concerns about the issue and the search for solutions.

In 1988 a report from the Canadian Bar Association (1988) noted that overincarcerations were so stark and appalling that the magnitude of the problem could be neither misunderstood nor interpreted away. The overrepresentation was most dramatic in the Western and Northern parts of Canada. In the Prairie region, Aboriginal people made up about 5 percent of the total population but 32 percent of the penitentiary population. The report stated:

Even more disturbing, the disproportion is growing. Thus, in 1965 some 22 percent of prisoners in Stony Mountain Penitentiary were native; in 1984 this proportion was 33 percent. It is realistic to expect that *absent radical change*, the problem will intensify due to the higher birth rate of native communities. Bad as this situation is within the federal system, in a number of the western provincial correctional systems, it is even worse. (quoted in Jackson 1992: 148; emphasis added).

A Saskatchewan study put the problem in an even more alarming way:

[In Saskatchewan] a treaty Indian boy turning 16 in 1976 had a 70 percent chance of at least one stay in prison by the age of 25 (that age range being the one with the highest risk of imprisonment). The corresponding figure for nonstatus or Metis was 34 percent. For a nonnative Saskatchewan boy the figure was 8 percent. (Jackson 1992: 148–49)

In Saskatchewan, then, prison has become for young Native men the manifestation of a just society, replacing the promise that high school and post-secondary education represent for many other Canadians. The prison has also become, for many young Native people, the contemporary equivalent of what the Indian residential school was for their parents.

Overincarceration is not only rooted in policing practices but also in the massive backlog of social and economic problems that contribute to the difficulties with the law experienced by Aboriginal people (CAC 1967). Ironically, the *Indians and the Law* report does not fully explore this explanation, even though it prefaces its recommendations for reforms in law enforcement and judicial and correctional services with an anti-colonialist admonition:

They [the CAC recommendations] are based on the assumption that substantial increases in services and expenditures will be provided by federal and provincial agencies… A considerable increase in expenditures for such services as housing, education, health, employment, counselling and placement, and recreation occurred in recent years… an even greater rate of increase is needed. Without this, the Indian and Eskimo people who are geographically dispersed, who are socially, economically and politically handicapped, and who are already burdened with apathy that has been building for a century, will deteriorate further. (Canadian Corrections Association 1967)

The specific issue of negative stereotyping of Aboriginal people by police forces came to the fore in 1990, when a royal commission report was issued on the wrongful conviction and eleven-year incarceration of Donald Marshall, a Mi'kmaq in Nova Scotia (Royal Commission on the Donald Marshall, Jr. Prosecution 1989). The Sydney police had clearly initiated Marshall's arrest and wrongful conviction, but the injustice carried on right down the line to prosecutors, lawyers, judiciary, and ultimately, in the appeal stages, the political system. In 1991 the Manitoba Aboriginal Justice Inquiry was set up in the wake of the Winnipeg police shooting of J.J. Harper, executive director of the Island Lake Tribal Council, and the brutal killing of Helen Betty Osborne, a young Aboriginal woman in The Pas, Manitoba, where police had waited sixteen years before seriously pursuing the matter. The 1990s floodgate of Aboriginal justice inquiries and recommendations for substantial post-colonial justice reform was open: from the Alberta *Justice On Trial* report (Task Force on the Criminal Justice System 1991), the dual reports of the Saskatchewan Indian and Métis justice review committees (Saskatchewan Indian Justice Review Committee 1992), and the Law Reform Commission of Canada report *Aboriginal Peoples and Criminal Justice* (Law Reform Commission of Canada 1991) to the Department of Justice Canada discussion paper "Aboriginal People and Justice Administration" (Canada, Department of Justice 1991). The massive report of the Royal Commission on Aboriginal Peoples (RCAP) was released in 1997. All of these intensive efforts, in one way or another, indicated the negative views of Aboriginal people embedded within Canadian police forces.

As the roundtable report *Aboriginal Peoples and the Justice System* (RCAP 1993a) noted, "The police have been the focus of the majority of recommendations made in these and other inquiries." The report of the Saskatchewan Indian Justice Review Committee (1992: 20) noted, "Policing is the most common point of contact between the Aboriginal community and the criminal justice system; policing is a crucial focal point for any alienation, cultural insensitivity or systemic racism which Aboriginal people might encounter in their dealings with the criminal justice system."

> Policing is the most common point of contact between the Aboriginal community and the criminal justice system.

Against the backdrop of the struggle for Aboriginal "self-determination," new policies emerged in the early to mid-1990s to deal with Aboriginal peoples and policing reform. On June 27, 1991, the minister of Indian Affairs and Northern Development and the solicitor general announced a new federal Indian policing policy. The primary focus was on establishing a new Aboriginal Policing Directorate in the Ministry of the Solicitor General, and on transferring on-reserve policing out of DIAND as of April 1992. The policy directive indicated, "Indian Bands should have access to policing services which are responsive to their special and unique policing needs and which meet acceptable standards with respect to the quality and level of service that would compare with communities with similar conditions in [their] region" (Canada, Department of Justice 1991: 5). Given that DIAND had overseen Indian on-reserve policing since 1876, under the provision of the *Indian Act*, now another dimension of the "Indian Agent" was leaving the reserve.

Unfortunately, by that time a large and growing part of the problem of Aboriginal policing and overincarceration had already moved off-reserve. In 1995 Carol LaPrairie (1995a: 13) concluded that research had for some time been identifying urban areas as the site of the most serious problems with respect to Aboriginal involvement in the correctional system. This research, she said, had only recently been acknowledged and had not yet necessarily resulted in the attention required by urban areas.

The same elements of breakdown seen in Aboriginal extended families in rural and Northern areas were now occurring, perhaps in even more exaggerated form, in urban areas, as a result of large-scale Aboriginal migration in the past few decades. "Urban poverty," one researcher stated, "like rural poverty and family breakdown, will continue to contribute to the well known vicious circle. It becomes a vicious cycle of social problem, conflict with the law, penalty, retribution, social problem" (Elliot 1989, cited in Harding 1994: 350). According to Jim Harding (1994: 18): "Urbanization and heightened disadvantage and conflict may already be reflected in a shift in urban criminalization rates for Aboriginal people" — to the point of "a near epidemic." While the incarceration of Aboriginal people was at one time said to be "fairly evenly split between rural and reserve areas, on the one hand, and urban centres, on the other," more recently the division had changed dramatically: only 15 percent of those incarcerated came from reserves; while 85 percent came from off-reserve, predominantly urban, areas (Harding 1994: 18).

The urban shift is particularly apparent in Western Canada. Saskatchewan has shown the greatest off-reserve migration of Aboriginal people. In 1966 only 14.2 percent lived off-reserve, compared to 46 percent in 1990 (Prairie Research Associates 1993). It was expected that the off-reserve figure would reach about 60 percent by 2000. As LaPrairie (1996: 64) noted, "With high off-reserve migration and permanent residency of Aboriginal people in these [marginalized] settings, inner cores of some western cities show signs of becoming entrenched Aboriginal-ghetto areas."

How have Canadian police, especially in Western Canada, responded to Aboriginal calls for reform in policing? In Canadian urban centres, certain initiatives to indigenize policing have come within the general move to community policing. As the RCAP (1993a: 35) roundtable noted, the primary police indigenization efforts have been cross-cultural training, affirmative action recruitment, and Aboriginal liaison committees or positions. In Saskatoon, for example, only two of 348 police officers were of Aboriginal ancestry in 1991; today the city has fifty-seven Aboriginal officers. These initiatives may well promote an awareness of Aboriginal issues, and they could allow for greater Aboriginal input, but they do not significantly alter the structure of police forces (RCAP 1993a: 35). Nor do these kinds of initiatives necessarily change racist attitudes and actions. The RCAP report (1996a: 42) stated that what the early task forces and studies failed to recognize, or did not want to address in any fundamental way, was that relatively limited "cultural indigenization" would do little to change socio-economic marginality, deprivation, and the general colonialist-generated condition of many Aboriginal peoples. The initiatives may ameliorate some parts of an alienating and abusive criminal justice system, but: "What indigenisation fails to do, however, is to address in any fundamental way the criminal justice problems which result from the socio-economic marginality. The real danger of an exclusively indigenised approach is that the problems may appear to be 'solved,' little more will be attempted, partly because indigenisation is a very visible activity" (RCAP 1996a: 42).

Cultural indigenization initiatives, which some critics would say are neo-colonialist, are indeed of little value for transforming abusive police-Aboriginal relations as long as a basic race-based social inequality continues to exist. The ongoing effects of social inequality are exemplified by LaPrairie's (1995b) on-the-street research, which provides important information about police treatment of relatively poor, inner-city urban Aboriginal peoples. Some 41 percent of this Canadian Aboriginal sample reported respectful or matter of fact treatment, but 18 percent reported rude treatment, 17 percent verbally abusive treatment, and 24 percent physically abusive treatment by police. Notably, LaPrairie (1995b: 64) added, "There was little difference when controlling for length of time in the city, which would suggest that policing innovations are not affecting the [urban Aboriginal] people in the sample."

> What cultural indigenization [of police] fails to do is to address in any fundamental way the criminal justice problems that result from socio-economic marginality.

One of the problems is the continuing effect of conservative policy and reform action in the area of Aboriginal peoples and policing (Samuelson 1995: 189). In an early article that tried to map out future government responses to militant Aboriginal movements, Ken Svenson (1978) identified three non-assimilationist state options. The least favoured government option has been separation or autonomy, while the most favoured options are accommodation and integration. Accommodation policies are reflected in the creation of autonomous but government-funded Aboriginal agencies and programs, such as in health care and education programs at the band level. But in the criminal justice system, integration policies have been dominant: "Government-sponsored reviews and research reveal that indigenisation is the preferred means of 'integrating' Indigenous people into the imposed system of social control" (Haveman 1992: 111).

Integrative indigenization is presented as the best means of managing the conflictual relationships between Aboriginal people and the criminal justice system. This preference has been particularly prevalent in policing, in which the RCMP military-based phase of colonial pacification was replaced by an integration model of imposed social control. Now we hire Aboriginal people to integrate into policing. While that approach can sometimes provide colonized groups with leverage for more autonomous action, its main drive is towards indigenization at the level of front-line service delivery, with co-optation at the organizational level. Aboriginal police officers working on the front line of policing are involved in a "visible activity," but that work does not substantially change the organization or operation of the adversarial system of justice imposed historically and today on Aboriginal people (Haveman 1992: 112).

In contrast, Aboriginal spokespersons have advocated the development of Indigenous legal processes and institutions (Brass 1979; Denny 1992; Monture-Angus 1995). Indigenous legal processes are generally based on conflict resolution and redressing imbalances in relationships that are spiritually, emotionally, mentally, and physically damaged. Healed relationships involve the "hurting individual," the family, the community, and the creator. Elders play an important role in healing "teaching," which is not the equivalent to "programs," whether community policing or corrections. These initiatives would link up with broader political-economic regeneration of Aboriginal communities that would ultimately reduce the social conditions that create criminal justice involvement in the first place.

A Future For Aboriginal Justice

What future trends, both challenges and venues for positive change, can we identify as Aboriginal peoples seek to move forward locally, nationally, and indeed internationally? Around the globe Indigenous peoples are actively, at times militantly, pushing for criminal and social justice reforms, against the backdrop of self-determination/self-government.

Chris Cunneen and Robert White (1995: 154) are quite in accord with the emergent Canadian perspective (RCAP 1993a, 1996a) in their review of the historical and current failures of non-Indigenous justice interventions. While referring specifically to Australian Aboriginal youth, their admonition is applicable generally: "The only credible way to break out of the destructive relationship between juvenile justice agencies and Indigenous young people is to facilitate the move to control by Aboriginal communities."

In Canada several concerns must be addressed in any real program of Aboriginal criminal and social justice reform. Importantly, voice must be given to the frequently marginalized Aboriginal people who have become such a very large part of the work of the criminal justice system. However, as RCAP (1996a) recognized, the notion of seeking substantial community input and control represents a frightening prospect for many people in the system. A true consultative process could mean a loss of power and control for both justice and government officials as well as established Aboriginal spokespeople, such as elected band councillors. This concern about loss of control, the RCAP report noted, can lead to a process termed "elite accommodation":

> In this process, bureaucrats or justice officials approach the leaders they trust and respect in an Aboriginal community and give them responsibility for developing and delivering a justice program. However well meaning these people might be, such a process rarely works... this has already occurred with a number of justice initiatives. (1996a: 171)

As the report added, a much broader consultative process is essential. It would have to reach out to the most marginal groups in the community — those whose views are most often ignored when important decisions are made. Very few policy-makers or researchers have taken the crucial step of going into Aboriginal communities, especially in urban areas, and examining community realities or ideologies beyond the level of aggregate statistics or social problems (LaPrairie 1995a, 1995b). This lack of urban input is perhaps not surprising: a central problem in the area of urban Aboriginal policing is obtaining input from a generally diverse, fractioned "community" that is often plagued by social problems (Samuelson 2001). But community input, though difficult to obtain, is key. In her research LaPrairie (1995b: XVI) found, "The majority of people thought either themselves or other natives should be responsible for making life better for native people." But "the lack of a political voice" was evident as the majority of respondents could not, or would not, identify an Aboriginal political entity that represented their interests." Policy-making, programs, and basic research, she concludes, must be directed at those whose needs are greatest.

Although a recognition of the need for appropriate justice services must underpin attempts to overcome the imposition of what is essentially a foreign mode of criminal justice, that approach alone will not ensure a different future. The severe problems, after all, arise as a direct consequence of colonialism. A recognition of the colonial underpinnings of the justice — and injustice — system must provide the basic context for any efforts at substantial change.

In evaluating the impact of either existing policing options or any "new" solutions (especially those that do not have as their focus First Nations' control of existing systems) we need above all to acknowledge, explore, and incorporate a First Nations' understanding of the problem in the exercise. Aboriginal peoples are not just culturally and linguistically diverse but also geographically diverse. Métis people are largely without distinct and legally recognized land bases (except in the province of Alberta). The differences between Northern and Southern realities are especially notable. Some First Nations citizens reside in their own rural communities (often called Indian reserves) but many more, as we have seen, now live in urban areas. First Nations communities range from small remote communities of several hundred people, sometimes without road access to larger communities with populations in the thousands, some of them located near or even within large urban centres. These diversities guarantee that a single "Aboriginal" policing option cannot provide, to all Aboriginal peoples, access to policing services that are effective, responsive, and respectful. The need, then, is for policing visions that respond to a variety of Aboriginal realities — but this standard remains largely unacknowledged by the people vested with the power to change things, both Aboriginal and non-Aboriginal. There is no choice to be made as to whether urban concerns or reserve-based options are more essential, because each stream affects the lived reality of many Aboriginal people.

Each contributes to the overrepresentation of Aboriginal people in the Canadian criminal justice system.

The policing services in urban areas are of particular concern because of the degree to which that site has remained invisible to decision-makers. Starting with the Donald Marshall Jr. inquiry in 1990, report after report laid bare what can only be described as abusive relationships between Aboriginal peoples and the police. This reporting of incidents includes the deaths of Aboriginal people in police lock-ups, suicides in prison, and deaths at the hands of police (Manitoba Aboriginal Justice Inquiry 1991: 1–2). These incidents, many of them outright crimes, highlight the severity of the problem. The inaction in this area has represented a fundamental, continuing breach of the equality provisions that, since 1982, have been part of Canada's Constitution.

Beyond constitutional equality guarantees, the task before us involves much more than simply creating a new relationship between Aboriginal peoples and the police. That approach ignores history. After all, the nature of the relationship between the police and Aboriginal people was not originally adversarial. The early, essentially co-operative, police-Aboriginal relationship was soon breached, and then repeatedly breached. The First Nations communities are well aware of the individual stories of arbitrary arrest and detention, and sometimes abuse, at the hands of the police — all of which left, over decades, an increasing rift — so much so that now, some one hundred years later, it will prove highly difficult to renew anything like a harmonious relationship.

In this new millennium it is not, then, a matter of attempting to establish methods of working together for the first time but, rather, of healing relationships that have been deeply damaged, if not destroyed. In the summer of 1996, for instance, while doing some justice work for the Thunderchild First Nation in Northwestern (really Central) Saskatchewan, officers of the local RCMP detachment were invited by the community to participate in justice committee meetings. As a means of trying to break down the barriers between the police and the community, the officers were asked to come to the meetings out of uniform. At the meeting, in his native Cree language, Elder Norman Sunchild asked the RCMP officers, "Where is your red serge and your horses?" He went on to explain, in Cree, how the red uniforms and the horses were symbols of the treaty partnership between the Cree and the RCMP. His point was clear: the relationship could not be renewed for the Cree of Treaty Six if the basic foundation of that relationship was not built on a solid understanding of treaty agreements.

Before reform attempts can be made, then, a first stage of understanding must involve a full understanding of treaty obligations. A second stage must be the recognition that Aboriginal societies are built on oral traditions, which means that the tradition, and importance, of sharing stories are vastly more complex and significant than in many non-Aboriginal societies. These obligations bind all parties.

Alternatives to standard paramilitary policing and even to the much-touted indigenized and/or community-based policing models must be found and set in place. These alternatives are most necessary where they are perhaps most difficult — in urban policing and in incarceration for offences largely committed off-reserve.

The *Royal Proclamation of 1763* provided:

> And Whereas it is just and reasonable, and essential to our Interest, and the Security of our Colonies, that the several Nations or Tribes of Indians with whom We are connected, and who live under our Protection, *should not be molested or disturbed* in the Possession of such Parts of Our Dominions and

> Territories as, not having been ceded or purchased by Us, are reserved to them, or any of them, as their Hunting Grounds. (R.S.C. 1985, App.II, No. 1, at 4-5; emphasis added)

This provision still forms part of the constitutional framework that establishes the Canadian state and as such is the "supreme law of the land," as provided for in section 52. The provision itself clearly indicates that the relationship established with Aboriginal peoples was to be reciprocal. It was not only "just and reasonable" but in the interests of the colonies to ensure that the Indigenous peoples were not to be molested or disturbed.

Following the *Royal Proclamation*, the British Crown and then the Canadian state chose to continue on a path of treaty relationships to further these reciprocal relationships. Many of the early written treaties contain justice provisions. For example, Treaty Six provides:

> They promise and engage that they will in all respects obey and abide by the law, and they will maintain peace and good order between each other, and also between themselves and other tribes of Indians, and between themselves and others of her Majesty's subjects, whether Indians or white, now inhabiting or hereafter to inhabit any part of the said ceded tracts, and that they will not molest the person or property of Her Majesty the Queen, or interfere with or trouble any person passing or travelling through the said tracts or any part thereof; and that they will aid and assist the officers of Her Majesty in bringing to justice and Punishment any Indian offending against the stipulations of this treaty, or infringing the laws in force in the country so ceded. (as quoted in Stonechild and Waiser 1997: 243)

This is the last substantive clause in the treaty; and in Cree ways, the most important things in negotiation are left to the last. The "peace and good order" clause is an entry that must be read generally; it gives rise to broad powers. It is also clear from several clauses of this treaty that the Indians did not fully extinguish their right as independent nations to be involved in matters of criminal justice. For example, certain clauses indicate: "they will maintain peace and good order between each other..."; "between themselves and others of her Majesty's subjects"; "whether Indian or whites"; and "they will aid and assist the officers of Her Majesty." The policing relations of the present and future must be based on this foundation.

The need for solutions is urgent. A growing consensus exists that the policy of the past is inadequate to deal with both the nature and the magnitude of the problem — which only confirms the great need for new policy frameworks and strategies. The new developments in "Aboriginal justice" must reflect both Aboriginal healing practices and a holistic worldview. The challenges are many, but so too are the opportunities for Aboriginal and non-Aboriginal peoples to live together under new legal systems in a post-colonial society.

DISCUSSION QUESTIONS

1. Why is it important to place the Canadian imposition of adversarial law and overincarceration of Aboriginal peoples in an international context?

2. Why is the *Royal Proclamation of 1763* a key to today's critical issues for Aboriginal

peoples and Canadian society?

3. Critically evaluate the history of the "policing" of Aboriginal peoples in Canada.

4. What are the main forms of "Aboriginal-run" policing services in Canada today?

5. Critically evaluate the adequacy of policing, punishment, and protection for Aboriginal women in Canada, historically and today.

GLOSSARY OF TERMS

Aboriginal Peoples and the Justice System: the roundtable report on Aboriginal people and justice released by the Royal Commission on Aboriginal Peoples (RCAP) (1993). The report had an important opening chapter that overviewed the previous inquiries in this area and the overall lack of much substantial change over time.

Act for the Gradual Civilization of the Indian Tribes 1857/Indian Act 1876: the Indian Acts, passed in Canada, which established Canadian law and policies for the handling of Aboriginal people — still highly contested.

Bridging the Cultural Divide: the second report from the RCAP (1996) on traditional ways of Aboriginal Justice and how such a system could be used to improve the current justice services.

British North America Act 1867: established Canada as a country in 1867.

Dakota Ojibway Tribal Council Police: one of the three all-Aboriginal band police

services established in Canada in 1978. It is still operating in Manitoba today.

Indians and the Law Report 1967: the Canadian Corrections Association report that stated the current concern with Aboriginal overincarceration in prisons.

Manitoba Aboriginal Justice Inquiry: the public inquiry into the police shootings in Winnipeg of J.J. Harper, an Aboriginal man stopped erroneously by the police, and the subsequent police cover-up, as well as the sixteen-year delay in bringing to light the beating death of Helen Betty Osbourne, a young Aboriginal woman killed in The Pas, Manitoba.

Royal Proclamation of 1763: established that Aboriginal people were sovereign and their land could only be obtained by the Crown through treaty.

Gladue Court: A Toronto court that processes Aboriginal offenders, trying to take into account Aboriginal life experiences and alternatives to incarceration.

SUGGESTED READINGS

Denis, C. 1997. *We Are Not You — First Nations and Canadian Modernity.* Peterborough: Broadview Press.

Ross, L. 1998. *Inventing the Savage: The Social Construction of Native American Criminality.* Austin: University of Texas Press.

Haveman, P. 1999. *Indigenous Peoples' Rights in Australia, Canada and New Zealand.* Auckland: Oxford University Press.

Frideres, J. 1998. *Aboriginal Peoples in Canada: Contemporary Conflicts.* Scarborough, ON:

Prentice Hall.

Hannah-Moffat, K., and M. Shaw. 2000. *An Ideal Prison? Critical Essays on Women's Imprisonment in Canada.* Halifax: Fernwood Publishing.

McCaslin, W. (ed.). 2005. *Justice as Healing: Indigenous Ways.* St. Paul: Living Justice Press.

Monture-Angus, P. 1999. *Journeying Forward: Dreaming First Nations' Independence.* Halifax: Fernwood Publishing.

Schissel, Bernard, and Terry Wotherspoon. 2003. *The Legacy of School for Aboriginal People.* Don Mills: Oxford.

NOTE

1. In this brief history we use the term Aboriginal peoples to refer to status Indian people, who are registered under the *Indian Act,* as well as non-status Indian people, who are not. Many Indian people belong to nations that signed treaties, while other nations, such as the Lubicon in Northern Alberta and the Nisga'a in British Columbia (who have only recently worked out a treaty settlement), never did sign. Also included in the broad definition of Aboriginal peoples are the Métis, of primarily Indian–French mixed ancestry, who trace their origins to Southern Manitoba but today include other people of mixed ancestry. Canada also has an Inuit population in the Far North.

REFERENCES

Atlantic Institute of Criminology. 1996. *First Nations Policing Survey — Draft Final Report.* Halifax References: Dalhousie University.

Brass, O. 1979. "Crees and Crime: A Cross-Cultural Study." Regina: University of Regina.

Canada. 1991. *Backgrounder, Indian Policing Policy.* Ottawa. Solicitor General Canada.

_____. 1999. *Aboriginal Peoples and Federal Corrections: Communications Strategy.* Ottawa: Correctional Service of Canada.

Canada, Department of Justice. 1991. *Aboriginal People and Justice Administration: A Discussion Paper.* Ottawa: Department of Justice.

Canadian Bar Association 1988. *Aboriginal Rights in Canada: An Agenda for Action.* Ottawa.

Canadian Corrections Association (CAC). 1967. *Indians and the Law.* Ottawa: Canadian Welfare Council.

CBC News Online. 2005. "Canada Ranked Low in UN Native Report." Monday, April 11. Available at <www.cbc.ca/canada/story/2005/04/11/UNNatives-050411.html> accessed July 2007.

_____. 2006. "Jail Conditions for Canadian Aboriginals a 'Disgrace': Ombudsman." Monday, October 16. Available at <www.cbc.ca/canada/story/2006/10/16/native-prisoners.html> accessed July 2007.

Commonwealth of Australia. 1994. *Implementation of Commonwealth Government Responses to the Recommendations of the Royal Commission into Aboriginal Deaths in Custody.* First Annual Report 1992–93, Volume 1.

Cunneen, C., and R. White. 1995. *Juvenile Justice: An Australian Perspective.* Melbourne: Oxford University Press.

Denny. M. 1992. "Beyond the Marshall Inquiry: An Alternative Mi'kmaq Worldview and Justice System." In J. Mannette (ed.), *Elusive Justice: Beyond the Marshall Inquiry.* Halifax: Fernwood Publishing.

Elliot, M. 1989. *Policing in the 1990s: Environmental Issues for the Prairies.* Regina: Mebas Consulting Ltd.

Frideres, J. 1998. *Native Peoples in Canada: Contemporary Conflicts* Fifth edition. Scarborough: Prentice-Hall.

Harding, J. 1994. "Policing and Aboriginal Justice." In R. Hinch (ed.), *Readings in Critical Criminol-*

ogy. Scarborough: Prentice-Hall Canada.

Haveman, P. 1992. "The Indigenization of Social Control in Canada." In R. Silverman and M. Nielsen (eds.), *Aboriginal Peoples and Canadian Criminal Justice*. Toronto: Butterworths.

Hildebrandt, Walter, and Brian Hubner. 1994. *The Cypress Hills: The Land and Its People*. Saskatoon: Purich Publishing.

Jackson, M. 1992. "In Search of the Pathways to Justice: Alternative Dispute Resolution in Aboriginal Communities." *University of British Columbia Law Review*. Special edition.

Kellough, G. 1980. "From Colonialism to Economic Imperialism: The Experience of the Canadian Indian." In J. Harp and J. Hofley (eds.), *Structured Inequality in Canada*. Scarborough: Prentice Hall.

LaPrairie, C. 1995a. "Community Justice or Just Communities? Aboriginal Communities in Search of Justice." *Canadian Journal of Criminology* 37 (4).

_____. 1995b. *Seen But Not Heard: Native People in the Inner City*. Ottawa: Department of Justice Canada.

_____. 1996. *Examining Aboriginal Corrections in Canada*. Ottawa: Solicitor General Canada.

Law Reform Commission of Canada. 1991. *Aboriginal Peoples and Criminal Justice*, Report No. 34. Ottawa: Law Reform Commission of Canada.

Manitoba Aboriginal Justice Inquiry. 1991. V.I. *The Justice System and Aboriginal People*. Winnipeg: Queen's Printer.

Monture-Angus, Patricia. 1995. *Thunder in My Soul: A Mohawk Women Speaks*. Halifax: Fernwood Publishing.

National Post. 2007. "Ombudsmen Accuses Prison System of 'Institutionalized Discrimination' Against Aboriginals." October 17. Available at <http://www.canada.com/nationalpost/news/story.html?id=110d0b8e-1932-49e5-8c60-84438d89a236&k=70661> accessed July 2007.

OFIFC (Ontario Federation of Indian Friendship Centres). 2003. "OAHAI Manual: Inmate Health." May. Available at <www.ofifc.org/oahai/acrobatfiles/inmatehealthupdate03.pdf> accessed July 2007.

Prairie Research Associates. 1993. *A Social Demographic and Economic Overview of Prairie Canada*. Winnipeg: Prairie Research Associates Inc.

Purich, Donald. 1986. *Our Land: Native Rights in Canada*. Toronto: James Lorimer.

RCAP (Royal Commission on Aboriginal Peoples). 1993. *Aboriginal Peoples and the Justice System*. Ottawa: Ministry of Supply and Services.

_____. 1996. *Bridging the Cultural Divide*. Ottawa: Ministry of Supply and Services.

Roberts, J., and R. Melchers. 2003. "The Incarceration of Aboriginal Offenders: Trends from 1978 to 2001." *Canadian Journal of Criminology and Criminal Justice* April.

Royal Commission Into Aboriginal Deaths in Custody. 1991. *National Report: Overview and Recommendations*. Canberra: Australian Government Publishing Service.

Royal Commission into the Donald Marshall, Jr. Prosecution. 1989. Halifax: Government of the Province of Nova Scotia.

Samuelson, L. 1995. "Canadian Aboriginal Justice Commissions and Australia's 'Anunga Rules': Barking Up the Wrong Tree." *Canadian Public Policy* XXI: 2: 187–211.

_____. 2001. "Indigenized Urban 'Community' Policing in Canada and Australia: A Comparative Study of Aboriginal Perceptions." *Police Practice and Research — an International Journal* 2 (4): 385–419.

Samuelson, L., and W. Antony (eds.). 1998. *Power and Resistance: Critical Thinking about Canadian Social Issues* Second edition. Halifax: Fernwood Publishing.

Saskatchewan Indian Justice Review Committee. 1992. *Report of the Saskatchewan Indian/Métis Justice Review Committee*, Saskatchewan.

Star Phoenix. 2000. "Task Force Wraps Up Night Investigation." March 21.

_____. 2006. "Three Strikes Bill Will Hit Natives." October 18: A1.

Stonechild, Blair, and Bill Waiser. 1997. *Loyal till Death: Indians and the North-West Rebellion*. Saskatoon: Fifth House.

Svenson, K. 1978. "Indian and Métis Issues in Saskatchewan to the Year 2001: The Explosive Years."

Regina: Department of Indian Affairs and Northern Development, mimeo.

Task Force on the Criminal Justice System and its Impact on the Indian and Métis People of Alberta. 1991. *Justice on Trial*. Edmonton: Task Force on the Criminal Justice System and its Impact on the Indian and Métis People of Alberta.

Watson, I. 1996. "First Nations' International Court of Justice: A Time to Begin." *Aboriginal Law Bulletin* 3 (9).

Wotherspoon, T., and V. Satzewich. 1993. *First Nations*. Scarborough: Nelson Canada.

York, G. 1990. *The Dispossessed: Life and Death in Native Canada*. Toronto: Little, Brown.

9

Damaged Children and Broken Spirits
A Residential School Survivor's Story

Helen Cote, Nīno Mīkana Ikē Ka-Pimosēt
(Woman Who Walks Two Roads), and Wendy Schissel

KEY FACTS

> There were initially 69 residential schools in Canada, and 1100 students attending them.

> At the peak of residential school systems in 1931 there were 80 schools. They were in every province and territory except New Brunswick, Prince Edward Island, and Newfoundland.

> Generations of children in residential schools experienced physical, sexual, mental, and emotional abuse.

> Residential schools were underfunded until the late 1950s and relied on the (forced) labour of students. This work is described as arduous and hindering students' development.

> It is estimated that there have been 50,000 deaths in Aboriginal residential schools in Canada because of diseases, abuse, and neglect.

> The tragic legacy of residential schools have left former students, their families, and communities continuing to deal with issues of sexual abuse, violence, and drug and alcohol abuse.

> The last federally run residential school, the Gordon Residential School in Saskatchewan, was closed in 1996.

> In 1990, Phil Fontaine called for the churches involved in residential schools to acknowledge the physical, sexual, and emotional abuse endured by their students.

> The Canadian government is proposing to spend two billion dollars to cover residential school lawsuits. These lawsuits have been filed against four major churches and Ottawa, by at least 7,000 Aboriginal peoples across Canada.

Sources: CBC News Online 2005; Annett 2007; Foot 2001.

The well-researched histories of Indian residential schools in Canada written by white academics (Miller 1996; Milloy 1999) and the many painful, personal stories told by First Nations survivors of those schools (for example, Knockwood 1992; Jaine 1993) demand to be regarded together in the context of criminology as a unique area for study and activism. There is an urgent need to learn more about the trans-generational effects of the residential school experience on First Nations involvement in the criminal justice system. This is so because First Nations offenders continue to be punished for their immediate offenses more harshly than non-First Nations offenders without accounting for the historical context in which their "criminal conduct" was born. There is, as a result, also an urgent need for new judicial and social policies that reject punishment in favour of individual healing and community restoration.

We have come to the point in Canadian history when we have finally recognized that for over one hundred years, the Canadian state, an alternatively willing and begrudging bedfellow to the christian churches, perpetrated and enabled what John S. Milloy calls "a national crime" against the First Nations:

> First Nations offenders continue to be punished for their immediate offences more harshly than other offenders without consideration for the historical context in which their "criminal conduct" was born.

> In the immediate post-Confederation period, ideology and rationale were brought together before the government in 1879 by Nicholas Flood Davin in his *Report on Industrial Schools for Indians and Half-Breeds.* This report, a manifesto for residential education, constituted the "official" justification for the concerted attack by church and state upon Aboriginal culture... The thought even before the deed, that is, before the residential school system took full physical shape across the country was violent in its intentions to "kill the Indian" in the child for the sake of Christian civilization. In that way, the system was, even as a concept, abusive. (Milloy 1999: xiv-xv)

The entire history of the Department of Indian Affairs, which administered the national system of residential schools, is overwritten with documents that attest to complaints of abuse and neglect ignored by that department and the federal government. Today, more and more First Nations inmates/survivors of those prison-like schools are coming forward to tell their stories of the neglect, deliberate malevolence and physical and sexual assault they received at the hands of their christian teachers and school administrators. Using a legal system which has ignored their torments in the past, these survivors are now mounting lawsuits against their tormentors. They are asking that the "national crime" be redressed and they are finally beginning to be heard. It is ironic that Canadians were quick to condemn the racial crimes of apartheid in South Africa, but that they resist acknowledging their own history of the crimes of apartheid inherent in the Department of Indian Affair's administration of reserves and the legal internment of First Nations children in residential schools. Even more ironic is the fact that South Africa modeled its apartheid on Canada's "Indian reserves" in the first place. A critical understanding of Canadian society is incomplete if it does not acknowledge the history and the enduring, incapacitating, trans-generational consequences of the treatment of residential schools victims and their children. Damaged children became damaged adults with broken spirits who were often unable or unwilling to return to their impoverished reserves. They moved instead to the racialized spaces of urban centres where poverty, segregation, denigration, crime and surveillance became their inheritance and where they have passed on to their children the damage they have internalized.

> The history of the Department of Indian Affairs, which administered the national system of residential schools, is overwritten with documents that attest to complaints of abuse and neglect.

Although she does not deal with residential schools in her article on the murder of Pamela George, Sherene Razack explains how "collective histories... are also geographies" (2000: 95). We can view her notion of the colonial, socially controlled, limited spaces — the geographies in which First Nations migrants to cities have found themselves — as a resurrection of the limited spaces of the reserves and the residential schools. The world that urban First Nations folks and their children inhabit is a space apart, a space in which "legal and social constructs [naturalize]... spatial relations of domination, highlighting in the process white respectability and entitlement and Aboriginal criminality" (Razack 2000: 96).

It is also a dangerous space, especially for First Nations children. Most of the child prostitutes on the streets of Saskatoon — with the highest rate of child prostitution of any city in Canada — are of First Nations descent. A study of young offenders in Regina and Saskatoon, many of whom were apprehended for their involvement in the sex trade (Schissel and Fedec 1999) found that 41.3 percent of these Aboriginal children suffered from neglect and 44.4 percent were runaways. The trauma of the sex trade manifested itself in self-destructive ways for these children that included drugs and alcohol (92.1 percent) and slashing (33.3 percent). Along with the sexual abuse, they suffered physical assault at an alarmingly high rate (41.7 percent).

Conservative legal and political responses to this knowledge have been to call for increasingly stringent controls such as those manifest in the new *Youth Criminal Justice Act*. While that kind of response inflicts even more punishment on already self-destructive youth, it is even harder on First Nations youth who, especially in Saskatchewan, are more often processed than white youth by the courts and more often incarcerated. As a colonizing nation, Canada continues, it seems, to punish First Nations children selectively.

It is important as we move to the story below to understand the legacy of residential schools in creating "deviance," historically from Euro/christian mores and even today from whiteness, with all its attendant privilege and power. The *intended* purpose of every parochial, state-supported residential school was to take away "Indian" identity. We are forced to consider, when we hear how the school years destroyed family and future, that the efforts of these schools continue today in more subtle forms of social control.

> The *intended* purpose of every parochial, state-supported residential school was to take away "Indian" identity. The efforts of these schools continue today in more subtle forms of social control.

Nīno Mīkana Ikē Ka-Pimosēt (Helen Cote) is a residential school survivor. She is a member of the Anisinābē people and of the Cote First Nations. Her story creates the space for the absent *subjects* in academic histories, court dockets and prison statistics where the painful, personal reality she describes is objectified. Even more distressing than her story is the realization that it is not unique to this residential school survivor and her family.

Nīno Mīkana Ikē Ka-Pimosēt (Helen's) Story

It is about time the dominant society, the educational institutions, the law makers and the government hear the stories of genocide which generations of First Nations experienced as children. The time is now because Canada's Aboriginal people are working on a massive healing movement. I ask that the dominant society hear us as we open up our wounds of past injustices committed against us by church and state.

I invite the reader to step into the world of First Nations children as they were forced to live in a war zone called residential schools. These schools were operated by the Roman

> I invite the reader to step into the world of First Nations children who were forced to live in a war zone called residential schools.

Catholic Church, the Anglican Church and the Presbyterian/United Church, but were encouraged and financed by the federal government of Canada. It was under government orders and assimilationist policies that First Nations children were forced to attend these schools. I was one of these children. I invite you to walk in these children's moccasins for a little while, by listening to my story. Through a narrative of my own childhood experiences in a residential school, I also hope to convey how such experiences have contributed to contemporary living problems of many Aboriginal people in Saskatchewan.

> The irony is that when I was in jail I found it more humane and more comfortable than the residential school I had been in.

For ten years the federal government of Canada and the Catholic Church imprisoned me. I was terrorized, raped and beaten. My child's body was not made for violent sexual and physical assaults. I became mentally ill at ten years old. I tried to escape my abuse and torture. Once dogs were used to apprehend me. None of us were a threat to anyone. In that residential school we lived in fear. When we left that residential school, some of us promptly killed ourselves, or drowned our sorrows in drugs and alcohol. We went away to hide from our people, being too ashamed to look at them. Some of us died with our shame, therefore leaving our shame to be lived on in our children and grand-children.

As an adult, I have been in prison for stealing food and money to eat and feed my family. There is no nice way of stealing food and money to eat. It is done with violence. The irony is when I was in jail I found it nicer and more comfortable than the residential school in which I had been. The prisons were more humane than residential school. As a child I needed my parents. Instead, I was subjected to cruel and brutal treatment by nuns and priests whom the government empowered to act in my parents' place.

My story discloses what residential school did to me and what its legacies are in the lives of my people, the Anisinābēk. I have read what has been written about my people's lives and how that experience has been viewed. I see why they use the term cultural genocide and not genocide. But I think the terminology serves to protect the history and does not really explain the true nature of actual genocide practiced against the Anisinābē people. I have come to understand how the term "cultural genocide" is used to hide a more ugly, more complete attempt to kill off my people.

> I have come to understand how the term "cultural genocide" is used to hide a more ugly, more complete attempt to kill off my people.

Life before a Roman Catholic Residential School

I was born August 31, 1949, during "birds beginning to fly season," when the leaves are beginning to have grey hair. It is a beautiful time. Everyone is preparing for the long winter, medicines are strong, there is rushing and joy in the air. How I love fall! It is a beautiful time.

The birth of the first daughter was sacred in my family. She was big medicine, since she was the one whose duty it would be to ensure the survival of the Anisinābēk tradition in the family. To celebrate the birth of a daughter after four sons, my father went to town and bought me new clothes.

My two sets of grandparents, my family and my extended family held a sacred naming ceremony. Everyone sat in a circle with the men sitting in one direction. It is a spiritual time and a time to be optimistic. We know Kici-manitō is very kind. Kici-manitō is in the animals, the plants, the earth and the elements.

One of my grandmothers had been told by the Spirit Helpers that I was "Woman who had two roads to travel." This is how I was introduced to my family during the ceremony. My Indian name guides me, directs me, and gives me strength during trying and happy times. The spirits promised to accompany, love and nourish me during my entire life. My grandmother told this dream to everyone. As they passed me around to the old men and the old women, each of them held me in their arms and gave me their gifts of love, wishes and blessings for my life to come.

As a young child I remember being in a red-flowered cradle-board hung on a tree so that I could see my parents as they worked and as the children played around me. Everyone had a smiling face for me. No one displayed harsh words or negative behaviour in front of me. We believe that Kici-manito loves everyone very much. In return we love each other and love all of Manito's living creations.

In later years, my dad explained the meaning of my name. There are two roads in life. I will choose the straight road. Furthermore, I will never stray off it. Should I ever become confused, the Spirits, through my dreams, will help me and I will know what to do, just as surely as I have a head on my shoulders. I will figure it out and will never forget my roots.

Life in a Roman Catholic Residential School: My First Day of School

Suddenly I was six years old. It was time to register me in school. My dad was unusually quiet, very quiet. He seemed to want to be by himself. The principal came for me and my older brothers. I screamed and cried as did my parents and relatives. Even today, it is difficult to relive these events. As I am writing this today, I am crying and my eyes are burning.

As we approached the school I became more excited, talking as loudly as I could. The priest turned me over to a nun, who took me upstairs to the infirmary and took my clothes off. She went to fill a bathtub with water. She was very rough, told me to shut up and called me a dirty, filthy, little Indian. My family had never told me to shut up. When I was first told to shut up, it shocked me. Where did she get all these terrible words from? She was pulling my hair and kept telling me to shut up and to stand still. I fought back. Nobody was going to treat me like dirt.

When I protested that she was hurting my head by pulling my long hair, she became more angry and pulled my hair harder. I jumped up to leave, but she knocked me down in the tub. I could never have guessed in a million years what she would do next. She began to scrub me up and down my body, separated my legs and began poking her fingers in my vagina. I was shocked and I protested more by jumping out of the tub and yelling. She slapped me in the face and pulled my hair harder, calling me a dirty little savage. "We have to clean you inside and out." She held me down under water several times while she continued to beat me. She almost drowned me. I am sure she would have if I had continued to resist her. Even today, I have nightmares about escaping from water. Such fear of water has been so terrifying for me that I have never learned how to swim.

How often or how many years she did that to me, I do not know. However, I learned to keep quiet when they yelled at me to shut up. Even though I was able to repress my fears, I felt so completely violated and helpless. I was totally shocked. Where were my parents? School became a blur. I do not know how I existed, but I did.

Ten Years Old and a Dummy

One of my clearest memories is of the day the girls' supervisor came and got me from the school playground. I was now ten years old. They put a nice dress on me, new shoes and new socks, too. I can still smell that ugly new smell of old moth balls. I still hate the smell of newness. I still rarely, if ever, wear a tailored dress.

The school principal took me in his small blue car to town to see a doctor. He was very pleasant about it. I had never seen him so pleasant to me. I became suspicious. "What does he want? Well, he is not getting anything from me without a fight, I thought. When we got to town, he drove to the hospital. We signed in and were told to go to a room one floor down. The principal told me to tell the doctor everything and then he left. The doctor was an old, soft-spoken man who asked me why I had quit talking and why I was being a bad girl. I had totally withdrawn from the world. I would not talk anymore. A slap or a punch by staff would result with me not feeling it and ignoring them. I refused to cry. I can remember the visit to the doctor, thinking, "I would not tell this White doctor anything."

The school principal took me back to the school. I do not remember any more abuse. I slowly came out of my shell, but I became very bossy and a good fighter. I feared no one and learned to defend myself whenever and wherever I had to.

Running Away

At twelve years old I thought, "I have had it and I am outta here." My family had broken up; my dad and my mom were alcoholics. You have to know at that time our parents tried to continue the family as the centre of our social, political and cultural systems. But as loved, small children were forcibly taken away, the mothers and the fathers couldn't bear it. My parents couldn't bear it. How could they look at each other with respect? They couldn't protect their own children.

Children who still had families and a home intact on the reserve went home for ten days at Easter break. Two other girls and I decided to make our break during Easter holidays. We asked if we could go for a ride on the back of the janitor's truck when he was driving children home. As he was turning into the driveway of one home on the reserve, we jumped off. Because I was the leader, I told the other girls to watch me. I jumped off head first, did a somersault and landed in the ditch. We looked to both sides. One side had a bush, the other side had a pasture. In the pasture was a bull and many cows. I told the girls that nobody would look for us in the pasture if we lay really still. We watched as the janitor looked for us in the bush before he finally drove away.

Two of us managed to stay away for three weeks. After the second week, the third girl got caught. We two girls were drinking and driving around with some boys. Our physical education instructor, found us by using his dogs. We rode in the back of his truck with the dogs watching us. He took us back to the school and into the Father's parlor, across the hall from the principal's office. He went to get the principal. However, before he left, he punched me right in the face full force with a closed fist because I would not shut up. I went flying across the room. When the principal came to the room, I told on him, the principal told me I was nothing but a drunken liar. He said that I had come to school looking all beat up. He refused to believe that the physical education teacher had punched me in the face. The girls' matron took us to have a bath and to come down afterwards.

After our bath, we went back to the second floor. A grandfather clock stood beside the principal's office. We were both by the grandfather clock. I went first to get strapped. They told me to pull my pajama bottom off and to lie on the desk. The matron held me down. The principal promised to give me only ten straps if I promised to say "I would never run away again." I told him "fuck you." He went on to give me ten more straps all over my bare bum. Each time I told him "fuck you," he gave me ten more straps.

Finally, I could feel no more pain and I became stronger. The matron was getting tired of holding me down. By now, I had no clothes on. The principal hit me with that strap all over my bum, back, ribs and legs. Still, I refused to say as they instructed me. Finally he was so tired. Both had to stop. When I looked at his face, it was all red and sweaty. I could see the fire and hate in his face. I have never seen anyone with such hatred and contempt in his or her face. He could barely talk as he sent me to bed. I could hardly move as I put on my pajamas. I am sure he broke my ribs and cut my bum. I could not cover with a blanket; it was too painful.

The next day they herded us into the girls' playroom and ordered all the students to sit on the floor. They put me on a high stool. The principal told the other children that this is what would happen to them should they ever have thoughts of running away. They shaved my head bald. The kids didn't laugh or stare at me. They just cried. That night in the dorm I looked in the mirror. I cried. However, before I cried, I looked to see if any supervisors were around. There was no way I was going to cry in front of them.

My punishment did not end there. For the next month they put me on hard labour. I washed and polished floors till late at night. I was forced to get up at 5:00 a.m. for early mass and back to work till 11:00 p.m. The only freedom from work I had was when I went to class.

Life after a Roman Catholic Residential School: Suicides, Parties, and Living on the Streets

I left residential school when I was sixteen years old. I had completed grade eight. My life became completely chaotic. I drank that whole summer until I requested that Indian Affairs find me a boarding place for September high school classes. I had no home by that time, so I just lived with my girlfriends at their homes. I did my grade nine over the next two years. I lasted three years in the city and did not complete grade ten.

After grade ten, I got pregnant. So I went to Winnipeg and then I went home to the reserve to live with my grandmother. It was there where I had a miscarriage. After that I drifted from city to reserve and lost track of time.

I finally got a clerk typist job in Yorkton with Indian Affairs, but I was so lonely. So at the end of my on-the-job training I hitch-hiked to Winnipeg with my two cousins. I lived on the streets and became a drunk. I hated being a teen-age drunk, but I did not know what other kind of life to live. I do not know why I stayed on the streets. That whole summer I drank and just lived on the streets. Sometimes I lived at my aunt's home, but most of the time I just ran around drinking. I got tired of drinking. It was hard work and I hated myself and my life.

Three Relationships Turn Sour and
I Lose Four Children to the Government

Eventually, I decided to take a two-year cosmetology course. I graduated at the head of my class. Before I finished my two-year cosmetology training, I became engaged to another residential school survivor. He was kind, understanding and very classy when he was sober. That was the man I loved and wanted to share my life with. He became dark, evil and sloppy when he was drunk and was very mean to me.

We lived with his parents and two younger brothers. A few months after my baby was born, he came home drunk and gave me a vicious beating. I was terrified for my life and the life of my baby. The next thing I knew I was on the operating room table. Somehow in the midst of all this commotion, he had thrust a big butcher knife into my face, near my left eye.

My common-law partner went to jail for six months. I went to live with my mother in Saskatoon. When he got out of jail, I remember, he took me and my baby to visit his relatives in Regina. We spent the weekend together. After that weekend I never saw him again.

Back in Saskatoon, I began an on and off relationship with another residential school survivor. I became pregnant by him. My second old man was massive, with a huge temper to match. He was just as mean as my first old man. He drank from morning till night and never worked. Once he beat me up with a clothes hanger.

On one occasion he punched me on the left side of my face and knocked me right out. He had a big blue ring on his finger. That ring went through my mouth knocking my tooth out and leaving a scar on my face. When he punched me, I was sitting against a wall. I felt the full impact of that punch before I blacked out.

He ended up doing a two-year prison sentence in a provincial prison for a robbery offense. This two-year prison sentence extended to nine years in a federal prison due to escapes and prison riots. He became one of the toughest and most dangerous criminals in Canada. My first old man and my second old man had been in St. Phillip's residential school with me. At age 23, I had two children, no husband, and no permanent career or address.

I met my third old man on the streets of Saskatoon. He later became my husband, the only man I ever legally married. He was five years younger than I was. He was fresh out of a foster home when I met him. I learned later he had gone to two residential schools and was severely abused in each of them. Although he became a womanizer, never worked, and was a chronic drunk, he was kind to me and did housework.

The most unforgiving thing he did to me was after I had a baby girl by him. He told the welfare I was an unfit mother. He and my ex-mother-in-law called social services and reported me. Social Services apprehended my children. The police broke down my back door and my front door one early morning. It must have been about 5:00 a.m. I begged them not to take my three children but no one listened to me. I had been drinking that night with my partner, my mother-in-law and her boyfriend. They gave me a beating and a black eye. So when the police and social services came, I was sporting an attractive shiner.

My partner and my ex-mother-in-law, after I sent them out, went to the police and made statements while intoxicated. Those statements were used against me in court and they were one of the main reasons my children were apprehended for life. When the court day came my ex-mother-in-law gave me $50 to pay for a lawyer, but she could not take her statement back. She tried, but police would not tear it up. She was a chronic alcoholic and could not make court days.

My partner was in jail when I went to family court and the court did not call him. I sat in that courtroom and never uttered one word. They would not allow me to speak even if I could have. What could I say? I went into shock. The lump in my throat was huge. I had become so shy and timid. They told me I was unfit, that I would never amount to anything because I came from a family of criminals. I never forgot those words and I still hear them. I cried and cried. After the judge hit the hammer on his desk, my family life was over. The social worker approached me and told me I could have one last visit with my two oldest children. My five-year-old little boy said, "I will be a big boy and I will not cry, I will take care of my sisters." I cried harder. My children were gone.

I didn't see my children after that until my oldest son was twelve years old and my daughter was ten years old. The adoption did not work out and the adoptive parents of my two oldest children allowed these two to return to me. They changed their birth certificates and they told me if I wanted social assistance I would have to re-adopt my own children. I refused.

I had another nervous breakdown when they took my children away. When you are having a mental break down you do not realize it. You just live day to day and you try to forget. I drank and drank and I left my third old man. I figured I would forget it. I could not hit the jackpot on a good man. I would live alone.

I became a full-fledged alcoholic and a drug addict. At especially rough periods in my life, I attempted suicides. When I got pregnant, I got abortions. I thought why should I bring more children into this world for the authorities to torture? That is how I rationalized my crazy life.

In the Anisinābēk culture we are forbidden to kill any living thing. I killed my own unborn children and I must answer to the Great Spirit for doing that. In total, I had three abortions, three miscarriages and five live births. The one thing that bothers me is I know that if I and my three mates had not been in residential school, we would have had a better chance to have relatively happy married lives. I could have had a big happy family with eleven children. Can you imagine eleven beautiful children to love and to care for, to grow with and to have until I die? The Great Spirit blessed me with many children. I hate what happened! I hate that! Can anyone or anything ever replace my family, so essential in the Anisinābēk culture? When we have many children, we are rich. Now I am poor and I am ashamed to be poor. I am someone to be pitied. Today I am alone with no husband and only one child at home. Can the dominant society ever understand this great loss?

The Legacy of Residential School Life in My Family

I remember when we went home on holidays. Sometimes the priest would give us rations. However, in times of no rations we had to survive on whatever we had. My brothers learned to hunt for small animals. By the time I came out of residential school there was lots of crime in my family. When we kids would be starving my brothers would go out and rob a store to feed us. We were proud of them for stealing food. Often we might have died if they had not stolen food for us to eat. Often my brothers went to jail for robbery. We never looked at them as criminals, but as people to be admired. By the time I left school, my home was broken up and my parents were full-fledged alcoholics.

I blame the residential school system for the break up of my home. My cousin said that when they were little children and they were starving, one of my oldest brothers showed up at their home. They were loaded down with big bags of chips, pop, chocolate bars and candy. Boy! Were they ever happy they could eat. My brothers had robbed a store. There was no nutritional food, only goodies. Is it any wonder we are all diabetics today after all the nutritional violence and starvation we went through? Why did the federal government have to put us in those prison schools? It ruined our health, our social lives and our political lives.

My oldest brother died in a small town in Manitoba. He was a director of the Indian friendship centre and a leader. He was the one who did ten years in prison for a murder he did not commit. He had an epileptic fit on the street and the police thought he was drunk. They threw him in the cell and that is where he died. He died in an RCMP cell. My big, handsome brother died in a deplorable and shameful ways. He must have suffered, being thrown in a cell like a dog. I do not know how you could not distinguish between the two, a drunk and someone having a seizure.

My mother was a residential school survivor. She never talked about her school days. That topic was never spoken of. My mother had thirteen children and she was a kind mother. However, she could be mean and rough if she had to be with other people. The little time we spent with her during holidays from the school, she taught us not to fight each other, but to protect each other. The happiest times were when we were very small. My mother was an excellent seamstress, cook and canner. We always had good food, good-home-made clothes and warm blankets. My mother became an alcoholic while I was in residential school.

I remember when I told her that the grade eight teacher was trying to seduce me. That teacher called me a sweetheart, would touch and fondle me. He would catch me off guard and touch me. I hated that bald-headed, big-headed man. He was not going to make a girlfriend or sex partner out of me. My mother slapped that teacher's face and pulled what little hair he had left on his head. She saw him at the post office in town and she went after him. She slapped and punched him with all of her strength. People talked about it.

My mother left my dad during the summer holidays. I remember the day so clearly. My mom told me that she was leaving to go to the city. She would go and find a job and come back for us later. I told her, "No, mom, don't go." She told me that she had thought about it long and hard; my dad was too mean to her and she had enough.

She told me she had arranged for us to be picked up by the school priest. The baby would be picked up by our uncle and my two little sisters and a brother would be picked up by my aunt. I, my sister and brother would be picked up by the school principal. I cried, begged her and hung unto her clothes so she would not leave. Nevertheless, she kept going and going. She never turned back. I watched till she disappeared into the horizon. I cried and cried. I hated those people who came and picked up my baby brother. I swore at them and called them names, saying "no, noooooo." Still, no one listened to me. My aunt and uncle came and picked up the three little ones and boy did I scream at them.

My world was falling apart in front of my eyes. I could not do a damn thing about it. My heart turned to ice. No one was ever going to hurt me again. My mom was never the same. My mom never went back to the reserve. My mom died of cirrhosis. The doctor told her to quit drinking, but she said she wanted to die. I begged her please to quit drinking and to live longer. I told her I would be a good girl, I would work hard and help pay the bills. My mom did not care anymore. She died and I was so mad. I hated her for leaving me. We could have made it. She should have never given up. I was growing up and getting stronger all the time.

I turned to my dad. He missed my mom; he missed us all. He was so pitiful. My whole family was broken up. My dad was a good man in my eyes and I loved him. I remember the first time I saw my dad beat up my mom. It was the time the priest was taking us back to the residential school. My dad was never the same. I told him that I was getting sexually abused in school. He could not do a thing about it. He had taken us away up north in the bush, but that priest always found us. My dad turned to alcohol and beat up my mom. He did not pray with his Indian ways anymore. He quit hunting and trapping. He just did not care anymore. When my mom died, he had no home and the reserve did not give him a house. He built a cardboard house in the bush. It looked like a doghouse. The welfare in town got a house built for him and that was his home until he died. Oh, that damn residential school system ruined my childhood, my family and my home!

In 1986, he told me he was not going to be around to help me in the rain dance anymore. I told him, "Old man, don't you dare talk of leaving me. I need you for a long time. Don't you go and die on me?" The next year he was gone.

This is how he died. He was drunk in town and the police picked him up. They threw him in the cells on a Friday. That night the old sergeant laughingly hosed him down with cold water because he said my father stank. They left him like that till Sunday morning. Sunday morning, they threw him out of the police station and he was dead by noon.

The chief and council tried to do something about the manner in which my dad died. My dad was 65 years old at the time of his death. The chief and council called an inquiry. But the RCMP was too powerful. They raided the band office and seized the accounting books. The RCMP laid formal criminal charges against the chief and his council. They all got charged with mismanagement of band funds. Some people did go to jail. After years and much financial costs, the chief was able to defeat the charges. The inquiry regarding my dad's death was forgotten.

My Healing Journey: The Painful Road Back to My Anisināběk Roots

I have, in spite of all these tragedies, had immeasurable unique personal and spiritual assets to be thankful for. My Anisināběk way of life is rich and flowing in my veins. The reason I am alive today is because the oppressors could not take all that away from me. I still see beauty in the world and no matter how horrible my circumstances have been, I remember how much my parents, grandparents and close relatives have loved me. That early parental care got me through many horrible times. I have had good physical health for many years, because of the loving, the traditional foods and medicines that my parents gave to me as a child.

I may never regain my former innocent self or achieve my full potential, but I have overcome some of my visible crippling behaviours such as suicidal attempts, my nervous breakdowns, my drug and alcoholic addictions. I developed many invisible crippling behaviours in that school and I may never regain my true Anisināběk human self or the wasted years. Although the state and church staff violently shook my spirit and tried to destroy my Anisināběk identity and my pride, I still know my spirit-helpers and my Indian name. This has helped me to continue with the ways of my culture.

I remember thinking in my drunken mind, after my children were taken away, "I have to stay alive, so that my children have someone to come home to." How many times have I used that sentence in my life? I have survived genocide. I am not a stupid, ugly and dirty Indian. It is not a simple exercise to say "I am a beautiful person." I have tried to say that for years and it is still difficult and hard to believe. Yet, I force myself to say it and I get mad at myself so I will believe it. Believe it!

I wanted to get my family, my home and my land back together. I knew from my father's teachings and life in my early childhood that I wanted to live a good Anisinābēk life. I wanted to return to that beautiful life. I remembered; I had not forgotten. I had to quit drinking and doing drugs. I did.

I remember when I lost my children. I had another mental breakdown, but I did not realize it was a mental breakdown. I became an alcoholic for two years. I lived on the streets of Saskatoon and slept on the riverbank. I was a stinky street person. I knew I should try to get out of there. I was hungry all the time and had only the clothes on my back. But I knew one thing in my drunken mind: I had to stay alive so my children would have someone to come home to. I had to sober up.

Life was very lonely and sometimes I tried to forget my children. It was a mind-shattering experience, but I tried to be normal. In Toronto I sometimes lived in a hostel for Indian girls. The director became a close friend of mine and she told me I needed to go see a psychiatrist. That insulted me, but when I had time to think about it I went. The psychiatrist gave me pills right away. After many visits he told me that he could not do anything for me but to give me pills so that I would not kill someone or someone would not kill me.

At this point I had been in Toronto for about two years. The advice of this psychiatrist was valuable. He told me that I should return to my own people, for they were the ones that would heal me. He said, that all he could do and all that his people know is how to do is give out pills when they do not know what to do. He said, as I understood it, that medical professionals are limited in what they know. He said,

> For me when I have my holidays each year I do not go to Europe or some exotic place. I go up North and visit an old Dene woman. I live with her for my entire holidays. I work for her: she makes me get up at 4:00 a.m. and haul water and cut wood. I do not ask her for knowledge. She gives it to me when I least expect it. She tells me about things and I learn many things. This is where I get my knowledge of the Indian way and that is why I am telling you this. I cannot give you any more medication, because you will become addicted and you will be worse off. You will only gain another addiction and compile your problems. Go home and your own people will heal you.

I thought of this advice for another year. I was a workaholic. During the week, Monday to Friday (9:00 am to 5:00 pm), I was a store manager. On weekends, Friday and Saturday (9:00 am to 5:00 pm), I worked in a beauty salon. I worked the graveyards shift at the hostel Saturday and Sunday. Sometimes I would fall off and go on a drinking binge.

Then I got a phone call from Winnipeg from a nurse. She told me someone had stabbed my third common-law partner and he was in critical condition. Memories came flooding back to my mind. I remembered he had told the police and social services that I was an unfit mother and how based on that the police had assisted social services apprehending my children. I could not forgive him for helping them remove my children.

I told the Winnipeg nurse not to call me and that I was not his wife because I had not married him. She called me a heartless woman with no feelings. I was inhuman. She told me, he called my name every day in his delirium and that I was a cold-hearted woman. I told her never to call me again. I hung up.

Well, I could have gone out and got drunk, but I did not for I remembered my mother's words, "Be kind to him or totally let him go." I told my cousin to watch the store and booked a flight to Winnipeg. I had to deal with my past, forgive him or I would die a wrinkled, bitter, ugly person.

I was clean and slim, but my mind was still bitter and hurting. I went to the hospital and he saw me. He said, "Am I dreaming or do I see my beautiful wife here?" I was angry but I asked what had happened to him. He said, "This guy cut my hand with a soft drink bottle. He was taking an old lady's beer and was going to rape her. I helped her out. I almost died." The story of helping the old woman melted my heart. I took him home to Toronto and married the guy. My Toronto friends told me I was stupid. Three days later he left me and started dating a MiKmaw woman.

I went to the bars looking for him. He told me to leave him alone. My cousins tried to help me to keep him from cheating and leaving me. I could not handle it, so I quit all my jobs and sat in the bars. When I found him, he was always with a different woman. I engaged in many fights to get him back and just enjoyed what little time he gave me. I took the crumbs, or worse, he only came home with me when I had the money. I loved him. That was my excuse for accepting his abuse. My husband went to jail for one year for stealing from an old man. He wanted to drink. I was with him when he did his crime. He literally told me to hold the bag while he went for a taxi and the police pulled up and caught me with the goods.

My friends came to court. One friend had $1000.00 to bail me out. Another friend from the hostel said she would take me on her own recognizance. I would live with her and work for her. The court asked if she would do the same for Mr. Quewezance. She said, "No," as if he were joking. The judge asked my other friend if he would use the money to bail Mr. Quewezance out. He said, "No, I came here with my pocket full of money to bail Helen out because she does not belong here. She is a good woman. That goodness has got her in trouble. She was good to this man and this is where it ended." So my new husband got one year in prison and I was let go. Thank the Great Spirit for good Anisinābēk people; they saved me from prison. They saw something in me as good.

When he got out, we left Toronto. I became pregnant and I decided to leave him for good. That leaving him was hard. I had to give up a companion and live a bachelor life. A bachelor woman is laughed at and made fun of. I would live it down somehow. I knew I had to choose. Financially providing for myself was easy. I had always done that. The nights were hard. I prayed hard. Many nights my mind would float away and it was a beautiful feeling. I would leave my body in my sleep. I remember doing that as a child in school when they were abusing me. I wondered why it was happening now. I remembered how I wanted to die when they took my kids away and how I rationalized in my drunken state that I must stay alive. I had to stay alive so my children would have a mother when they got home. I talked to my fears as though they were some living entities. My dad had told me to face my fears and to speak to them. Talk to them and pray. I did.

In the end I decided to search for my Anisinābēk identity and to use my traditional culture and spirituality to get back on the straight road. My dad told me that I would always go back on that road. I wanted a traditional Anisinābēk family. I had a beautiful baby boy. I told my husband I was leaving him forever. That little boy was all I would need to begin my new life. I would give up companionship. My baby came to me in a dream. I saw how he would look at grade three and he did look like that. In my dream, my child was begging me to be born. He was saying please do not get an abortion. I had three abortions and I was going to do that again. They refused me an abortion in Winnipeg.

My sweet little angel taught me to love again. He opened my heart and he gave me so much happiness. Oh my God, the feeling of love was unbearable. I was wondering when was it going to end? When is the white man coming to destroy that? I hid out from my husband because I heard he was looking for me and the baby. Yet I knew one thing. I was not going back to that life of drinking and drugs. Today I tell my son that it was an honor to have raised him.

I got a job and then I heard "Tēnās, your kids are looking for you." Wow, what a jolt. What was I going to do? I did not want my children to be ashamed of me? I would go to university and get a degree. Then I could help my kids. I would find out who these people were who abused me. I knew that my children would ask me hard questions about why they were in care.

I wanted to talk to an Elder and I had no one. My dad was the town drunk, so I chose my second oldest brother. He was the only sober Elder I had. He was in the Stoney Mountain penitentiary. I took tobacco and asked for advice on my goals for the future and on another matter. He told me to go back to our ceremonies. I was to take my mother's role. My mom was dead already and I had to finish off her dancing and praying. My elder brother told me not to think badly of people who abuse or have abused me. I have to have good thoughts about them. Whatever evil they did to me, they will get back. The Creator has promised us that.

I went to the reserve for a rain dance and I took part in it. I was unconfident and unsure of myself. I had so little stuff and no one to baby-sit while I danced. I bummed a ride off my boss. My dad was there and so was my auntie. They helped me and I thanked the Great Spirit for them. After the rain dance the reserve child care worker came up to me and I heard again, "Your kids are looking for you." I told her I will meet her at the office. I did. We phoned and my oldest son said, "Mom" and broke down and cried. I said "Wee-Small?" We both cried. He could not talk anymore. I sent him a plane ticket.

At the airport I saw this little twelve-year-old boy get off the plane, with rangy clothes and scabby knees and no luggage. He was poorer than I was. I thought he would have luggage, nice clothes and be civilized. He was a street kid at ten years old. I kissed him and he told me many sad stories. He had been so unhappy all his life. He ran away, was beaten and terrorized.

Once his adopted parents asked him "What do you want for Christmas? You can have anything you want." He said, "I want my mom." They told him that was one thing they could not give him. My oldest daughter came home at ten years old. My third daughter came back at eighteen years old. My fourth child, Desmond, who is now twenty-four years old is still in the system and I have not found him. Today my children have different last names. Their birth certificates have been changed and they say they are trying to find out who they are.

I knew I had to explore my past roads in life. I wanted to examine who had caused me so much pain in residential school. I would find out who these people were who abused me and so many others I had known including my common-law partners.

In the 1980s I entered University. It has been a terrible struggle because I have found it hard to face my fears head on. I came to understand through my university education that my ancestors have suffered because of no fault of their own. I quit blaming my people for my misfortunes. For example, my grandfather went to a Presbyterian school and he completed grade eight. He was sent to Regina to further his education. Then he went to World War II. My grandfather was a womanizer and alcoholic, but he was very kind and loving to us.

> I came to understand through my university education that my ancestors have suffered because of no fault of their own. I quit blaming my people for my misfortunes.

My mother was a second-generation residential school survivor. She died of cirrhosis of the liver and I was angry at her for dying. I knew she could have lived longer. At her death-bed we discussed many things including her death. At that time I made promises. I would not be an alcoholic and I would be kind to Aboriginal people. I promised to try and understand why my brothers were alcoholic and why they get in trouble with the law. She told me to forgive them because they had suffered in school.

In the areas of family and community consciousness-raising I had to deal with my own problems before I could get my family back together. My mother told me the stronger your family is the stronger our Nation will be. I realized my children would be returned to me damaged. I did not want to add to their problems by behaving in a shameful manner. My real healing journey began. I prayed to the grandfathers, I cried and asked for strengths of which I knew nothing. I knew that I had to be kind to my children even if they were difficult. My mother said, "Do not give up on them for if you give up on them they give up on themselves. *Kigi-ti māgizimiń*" she said, meaning we are all pitiful and poor, we are all creatures like the animals, no one is better than anyone.

There have been many troubling issues in my life that I have to come to terms with and reasoned out in my own mind and in my own behaviours. Yet, I still have more to learn; it never ends. In university I came to sort out my destructive behaviours in my mind by integrating my Anisinābēk cultural practices into my daily life. My mother's teachings taught me to forgive and to understand. These have become my goals in everything I do.

My university education has helped me to talk about my abuses and to understand them from a personal point of view. Today, I have completed two undergraduate honours degrees in Native Studies and Sociology and a Masters degree in Sociology. I have developed strengths from my cultural roots and integrated them with higher education so I can balance my life. I can see possibilities for my children and my community. We are all *Kigi-ti māgizimiń*.

Conclusion

The story I tell is the truth. I am telling my story to a colonial society that must change.

Let me briefly speak to two issues relating to that colonialism. First is the issue of identity. My Anisinābēk name was ignored and changed to an English name when I entered residential school. Therefore my identity was disregarded and thrown away. This is a major violation of my inherent rights as an First Nations person. I will continue to have major problems in my life if I never know "who I am" and "my purpose in life." *I need my name, Nīno Mīkana Ikē Ka-Pimosēt, acknowledged in the books and records.* When my children were taken away by social services and adopted, their names, birth dates and birth certificates were changed. This has compounded the problems for me and my children as we journey back to our roots. My children know not who they are. I told my daughter she is not the person named on her birth certificate; she is an Anisinābēk girl from the Cote First Nations. She is First Nations. When I told her this, she cried and said, "Yes, I understand, but in my heart. I have only known one set of parents and my identity is there. It's as if my Indian name is false." She says, "I try to change but I keep running back to my adopted parents and they don't want me." She cried. How can I help her except to be there when she comes to me. My son was adopted by white people and he calls his adoptive father his step dad. He tells me, "You have your own way, my adopted parents have their own way and I have my own way. Leave it at that." It is difficult for us to talk to one another about this issue of names, which is so important to me as I try to put my identity and that of my family back together. The systems of residential schools and foster homes are to blame, in large part, for my family problems, one way or another.

The second and last issue I want to address relates to the first. Our children are gifts from the creator and, no matter what they do or have done, they should be left within the arms of their own people. Children and youth do not belong in jails. The criminal justice system, especially jail, does not work for us, or for anyone for that matter. As we heal, only then can we begin to implement alternatives to punishment that will heal both the Aboriginal and non-Aboriginal people. In the final analysis, dominant society must be part of the solution; it needs to be decolonized, too.

DISCUSSION QUESTIONS

1. How have the experiences of residential school survivors become trans-generational problems for their children and grandchildren?

2. What does apartheid mean and how is it applicable in the Canadian context with regard to First Nations?

3. Should information about individual's experiences in residential school, or that of their parents, be something which courts should recognize as they seek to administer justice?

4. How do the geographies of Canadian urban spaces contribute to the criminalization of First Nations people?

5. Where does the culpability of the Canadian government and of the various christian churches end with regard to the victimization of First Nations children in residential schools?

GLOSSARY OF TERMS

Apartheid: official state policy of racial segregation enacted in Canada against First Nations by the implementation of the reserve system set up under *The Indian Act*. South Africa used Canada's reserve system as a model for its state policy of Apartheid.

Cultural Genocide: the practice of eliminat-ing the culture of a people. We argue here that the efforts of the christian churches was not to eliminate the many First Nations cultures, but rather was a racist effort to eliminate the people themselves.

Racialized Spaces: unofficial form of sys-temic racial segregation with distinctive class dimensions. The urban reserve is an area of a city that is inhabited primarily by poor First Nations peoples.

Residential School: historically, a boarding school usually run by members of a christian church. Although not all residential schools were for First Nations children, the ones referred to in this chapter were designed specifically to take Indian (the legal name for First Nations in Canada) children from their families and reserves for the purposes of assimilation through education.

Transgenerational effect: the devastating results of educational segregation and assimilation that play out as self-destructive behaviour and overrepresentation in the criminal justice system not only in the children damaged by Indian residential schools, but in their children and grandchildren.

SUGGESTED READINGS

Chrisjohn, Roland, Sherri Young, and Michael Maraun. 1997. *The Circle Game: Shadows and Substance in the Indian Residential School Experience in Canada*. Penticton: Theytus Books.

Jaine, Linda (ed.). 1993. *Residential School: The Stolen Years*. Saskatoon: Extension Press, University of Saskatchewan.

Knockwood, Isabelle. 1992. *Out of the Depths: The Experiences of Mi'kmaw Children at the Indian Residential School at Shubenacadie, Nova Scotia*. Lockeport, NS: Roseway Publishing.

Miller, J.R. 1996. *Shingwauk's Vision: A History of Native Residential Schools*. Toronto: University of Toronto Press.

Milloy, John S. 1999. *A National Crime: The Canadian Government and the Residential School System, 1879 to 1986*. Winnipeg: University of Manitoba Press.

NOTES

1. My family on my dad's side is my great great-grandfather who was Chief Gabriel Cote or Meemay (the pigeon), the flyer with a message. He had four wives and one of those wives had a son named Benjamin Cote and he had a son named George Bell Cote and then my dad Fred Steele Cote. Chief Gabriel Cote is known in history as the signatory chief for the Fort Pelly Indians, as the Anisinābē were mistakenly known. It is told that Gabriel Cote was chosen to be the speaker at the Treaty discussion in Fort Qu'Appelle as he was an excellent English and French speaker. He had been European and was raised as an Anisinābēk. Some people say he was not the hereditary chief, but a spokesperson.

2. Kici-manitō (pronounced Kici-Mantoo) is the Saulteaux name for the Great Spirit. In the seventeenth century the French Jesuits and the fur traders used the word Kici-Manitou.

3. Tēnās is my baby name from my four big brothers. My big brothers were trying to say little sibling and mispronounced it. Today I am known by this name by my family and the community.

4. We are all poor in our lives. This does not mean we are poor in materialist things like money, cars, houses, and jewelry. We are poor in our health, our lack of loyal relatives to assist us in our times of need; we are poor if we do not have the kindness value; we are poor if we are greedy and mean to people, especially to our family members; and we are poor if we cannot develop, maintain, and enhance our spirituality through our languages.

REFERENCES

Annett, Kevin. [Founder and secretary of the Truth Commission in to Genocide in Canada.] 2007. "Hidden from History: The Canadian Holocaust. The Untold Story of the History of Genocide of Aboriginal Peoples." Available at <www.hiddenfromhistory.org/residential-schools-investigation-farce.html> accessed July 2007.

CBC News Online. 2005. "Indian Residential Schools: Agreement in Principle." November 25. Available at <www.cbc.ca/news/background/aboriginals/residentialschools.html> accessed July 2007.

Foot, Richard. 2001. "Canada Readies Fund to Compensate Residential Schools Abuse Victims." *National Post* January 31.

Jaine, Linda (ed.). 1993. *Residential School: The Stolen Years.* Saskatoon: Extension Press, University of Saskatchewan.

Knockwood, Isabelle. 1992. *Out of the Depths: The Experiences of Mi'kmaw Children at the Indian Residential School at Shubenacadie, Nova Scotia.* Lockeport, NS: Roseway Publishing.

Miller, J.R. 1996. *Shingwauk's Vision: A History of Native Residential Schools.* Toronto: University of Toronto Press.

Milloy, John S. 1999. *A National Crime: The Canadian Government and the Residential School System, 1879 to 1986.* Winnipeg: University of Manitoba Press.

Razack, Sherene. 2000. "Gendered Racial Violence and Specialized Justice: The Murder of Pamela George." *Canadian Journal of Law and Society* 15 (2): 91–130.

Schissel, Bernard, and Kari Fedec. 1999. "The Selling of Innocence: The Gestalt of Danger in the Lives of Youth Prostitutes." *Canadian Journal of Criminology* 41 (1): 33–56.

10 A Criminal Justice History of Children and Youth in Canada
Taking Stock in the YCJA Era

Shahid Alvi

KEY FACTS

> Since the passage of the YCJA the youth incarceration rate has dropped dramatically from approximately 20 per 10,000 youth in 1994/5 to about 8 per 10,000 as of 2003/04 (Statistics Canada, 2005). Indeed, until passage of the YCJA, the rate of incarceration for young offenders increased by 26 percent since 1987.

> The term "adolescence" has only come into existence in the 1940s. The definition varies from culture to culture.

> In 2004, the Canadian Children's Rights Council argued that comprehensive and truthful review of the rights of Canadian children would be embarrassing to the government of Canada.

> Although very likely to be lower than the actual figure, an estimated 135,573 child maltreatment investigations were conducted in Canada in 1998. Nearly half of these cases were corroborated by the investigator.

> According to official statistics, over the past decade, both violent and property youth crime rates in Canada have declined or remained stable.

> It is estimated that more than 50 percent of youth in conflict with the law have experienced assault by a stranger, over 20 percent have experienced sexual assault, and more than 50 percent have been crime victims.

Sources: Canadian Centre for Justice Statistics 1997; Schissel, 2006.

[Many] people will continue to be convinced that juvenile crime is exceptionally high, that it was not a problem in the "good old days," and that it would not be a serious problem today if we only had the proper justice policies in effect.
—Thomas J. Bernard (1991: 39)

Some thirty years ago, Stan Cohen (1972) argued that societies periodically demonize people considered threats to dominant social values and interests. Writing about British youth culture, he contended that one of the most frequently demonized groups, subject to such "moral panics," has been youth. Moreover, he asserted that the categorization of young people as "folk devils" was due primarily to the influence of the media, whose role in modern societies had increasingly become that of shaping and defining events for the public.

Moral panics are not unique to Britain. Fuelled by a largely unsophisticated and often irresponsible media, Canadians have willingly participated in similar moral panics over youth crime, particularly over the past few decades. Indeed, during the era of the

Young Offenders Act (YOA) and prior to the enactment of the current law governing youth crime — the *Youth Criminal Justice Act* or YCJA which came into force in 2003 — many Canadians believed that youth-court sentences were too lenient, that it should be easier to try young people as adults, that sentencing should be harsher, and that disciplinary initiatives akin to those of a boot camp should prevail (Sprott 1996). More recently, politically conservative voices have been particularly shrill, with some calling for a return to the death penalty, transfers of young offenders to adult court, and prison sentences for parents of youth offenders, (Hartnagel 2004).

The new act has been hailed as a significant improvement over the YOA. As Hartnagel (2004) suggests, the YCJA came into force as a result of the Liberal government's stated commitment to "protect the public" while focusing on rehabilitation and reintegration of the offender, meaningful consequences, and alternatives to incarceration. However, it is also clear that the new act was a response to public dissatisfaction with the YOA, particularly in relation to perceived leniency in sentencing, and the need to "get tough" on offenders, all sentiments that were fuelled by the media's sensationalized accounts of brutal (but rare) homicides committed by youth (Varma and Marinos 2000; Doob and Cesaroni 2004).

Indeed, the recent history of youth criminal justice legislation (what I will call the era of the YOA) can be characterized as punitive, where activities once considered minor and dealt with outside the justice system became increasingly criminalized. During the period between the *Juvenile Delinquents Act* (which preceded the YOA) and the YOA, more youth were placed in custody, and the system favoured punishment and deterrence over leniency and rehabilitation. This "punishment ethos" is even more paradoxical given that since the mid-1990s the number of both violent and property crimes committed by youth in Canada decreased (Gannon 2006). Since the passage of the YCJA the youth incarceration rate has dropped dramatically from approximately 20 per 10,000 youth in 1994/5 to about 8 per 10,000 as of 2003/04 (Statistics Canada 2005). Indeed, until passage of the YCJA, the rate of incarceration for young offenders increased by 26 percent since 1987 (Canadian Centre for Justice Statistics 1997), which gave Canada the questionable distinction of having a youth incarceration rate four times higher than those for adults, twice that of the United States, and more than ten times higher than many countries in Europe (as cited in Bala and Anand 2004).

At the heart of this fixation on the discipline and control of youth was the assumption that young people's problems can be understood by focusing attention on the offenders' traits and the failure to make "good choices." Like the bulk of public perceptions, mainstream criminological accounts tend to downplay or altogether ignore the social basis and context of crime. By decontextualizing youth crime, contemporary approaches to youth justice in Canada have selectively ignored decades of criminological research pointing to the critical role of the social environment in the etiology of youth crime. What I would argue is that shifting historical perceptions of "youth" in Canada, particularly notions of the role and status of Canadian youth in relation to the economy, have been, and continue to be, crucially related to criminal justice responses to their transgressions.

Most Canadians would probably agree with the idea that childhood is, and always has been, a sacred time during which children are nourished, cared for, and socialized to take their place in society. As an extension of this romantic

> At the heart of this fixation on the discipline and control of youth was the assumption that young people's problems can be understood by focusing on the offenders' traits and the failure to make "good choices."

assumption, it might also seem logical to assume that throughout history Canadian laws have consistently reflected concern for the well-being of young people, although balancing that concern with the rights of society. To the contrary, I would argue that laws address-ing the wrongdoings of young offenders in Canada represent a broader problematic of integrating youth into the dominant economic and social norms governing society at any given time, and that various forces have accomplished this goal by demonizing those youth who are unable or "unwilling" to measure up. In the remainder of this chapter, I will outline a critical criminology framework that will be used as the theoretical "lens" through which developments in youth justice legislation can be viewed. I also provide, from a critical point of view, a preliminary assessment of the extent to which the new legislation can be viewed as an improvement over previous legislation.

A Critical Criminology Framework

Although there are many variants of critical criminology (see chapter 2), they possess in common an emphasis on the analysis of crime in its social and economic context, with particular concentration not only on the experiences of the underprivileged and weak but also on a commitment to transforming social structures (Schwartz 1991). Moreover, critical criminology recognizes that while individuals make decisions and to an extent choose their own behaviours, they do not necessarily make such decisions in circumstances chosen by and for themselves. In short, the social, political, and economic environment sets limits upon, and conditions, human behaviour.

Crime, from this perspective, is not an event, or a social fact, but rather has a dynamic history. This basic framework stands in opposition to the more commonly held view of crime as simply anything that people do or don't do that is against the law — a "legalistic" perspective that fails to recognize that laws and people possess a social history. Laws do not appear "out of thin air," nor do they necessarily reflect the consensus of the general public, as mainstream explanations of law would suggest. Mainstream perspectives, then, assume that laws are a product of people's shared values, impartial, and generated and managed by a "neutral" state committed to helping people resolve conflicts (Lynch and Groves 1989). A critical perspective, in contrast, recognizes that law reflects the continu-ing and historical concerns of those with power in society, such as lawmakers, economic elites, and the media. As Walter DeKeseredy and Martin Schwartz (1996) point out, a critical perspective on law highlights how, rather than emphasizing "justice for all," ours is more of a system that acts to maintain the interests and advantages of the wealthy and powerful in a society characterized by conflict rather than consensus.

Thus, if we are to understand the official legal response to youth crime in Canada, we need to examine the roles played by young people in our society, not just today but also historically. Additionally, we must pay attention to dominant expectations for young people, and to how laws have changed to reflect these different roles and perceptions.

Critical criminology also attempts to examine how systems of production and con-sumption influence the construction of people's roles and aspirations, as well as their capacities to attain those aspirations. To examine the relationship between the Canadian criminal justice system and young people, we will assess the links between young people's material position in society, changes in the laws concerning them, and the ideological motivations buttressing these laws.

Although very few in-depth accounts of youth in the criminal justice system exist in

Canada, we do have enough information to paint a general picture of the transformation of youth justice policies (Smandych 2001). The essence of this criminal justice history is that perceptions of Canadian children have varied between, on the one hand, the notion that youth are both dependent on adults and different from adults physically and cognitively, and, on the other, the idea that youth are independent and essentially similar to adults when it comes to rights and responsibilities. What is missing from purely historical accounts, however, is the connection between these perceptions and the conditioning effects of the socio-economic milieu.

> Critical criminology also attempts to examine how systems of production and consumption influence the construction of people's roles and aspirations, as well as their capacities to attain those aspirations.

The Pre-Legal Era: Canadian Children in the Nineteenth Century

The children of the early Canadian pioneers were treasured and valued by their parents and the community, and even indulged. Indeed, although the relatively unrestrained period of the fur trade provided ample opportunities for offending, commentators often cited parental overindulgence as one of the primary causes of children's wrongdoings (Bell 1999).

As far as we can tell, the majority of youth in the nineteenth century were relatively law-abiding. In the pioneer days of Canada youth crime consisted of a wide range of behaviours, from what we would today consider relatively minor offences—violations of local ordinances, nuisance offences, vandalism, brawling, swearing, or petty theft—to what were considered to be more serious violations of "moral" laws such as adultery, bigamy, rape, indecent behaviour, and prostitution (Carrigan 1998). Most of these offences would now be considered "status offences" (transgressions that did not apply to adults).

Most of the offences committed by children and youth were, then, relatively minor and inconsequential. Still, at that time, like today, the level of sanctions for committing offences seems to have depended greatly on the social characteristics of the offender. The minor quality of offences did not preclude harsh adjudication and penalties. Indeed, youth who did commit crimes and were caught by authorities were often punished severely. It was not unusual for youngsters caught violating a range of laws (including minor infractions) to be whipped, incarcerated in workhouses, detained in jail indefinitely, held in custody until their parents paid a fine, or even hanged (Carrigan 1998). In addition, children could be punished even if the authorities found only the potential for committing a crime (Schissel 1993). The justice meted out to young people in this era tended to be harsh, lacking in any semblance of due process, and applied inconsistently.

The range of punishments adopted indicates a basic disorganization in the justice system, which operated very much according to the whims of individual judges. But the early history of juvenile crime and punishment in Canada also suggests that children were viewed as little more than miniature adults. Except for the children of the upper classes, who had access to schooling and other privileges, young people were not seen as having special needs and were expected to toil alongside adults in menial, hard-labour jobs (Bala 1997). Children were assumed to have the same levels of understanding of right and wrong as adults. They were tried according to the principles of law existing in the adult courts, and they were frequently incarcerated with adults. Although the offenders came from diverse backgrounds, and all of them experienced parental neglect, the delinquents who committed the most serious offences tended to come from unemployed families, were indentured servants, or lived in slum neighbourhoods (Carrigan 1998). For the most part they were not the children of the wealthy.

The gradual influx of immigrant European children around the mid-nineteenth century exacerbated problems. These often-parentless children came to fulfil the function of serving the rich — of providing cheap labour as fieldworkers, or satisfying the needs of an emerging class of industrializing entrepreneurs, for instance. Many of the young newcomers were also considered to be "homeless waifs" or "street urchins," products of questionable backgrounds. Many youth wandered aimlessly around with no adult supervision, suffering from malnutrition, with "drunken and dissolute parents," a lack of education, and mental or emotional problems (Carrigan 1998). These poor and neglected youth, who were viewed as "problem children" (Currie 1986), tended to be blamed for the incidences of youth deviance (Schissel 1993; West 1984). Within urban centres especially, they received the bulk of attention from the criminal justice system.

> Children were assumed to have the same levels of understanding of right and wrong as adults.

While those in authority saw the behaviour of young people in conflict with the law as emanating from the failures of parents and families, not many of them would have linked family troubles to the pressures of a rapidly transforming society. As in other nations during this era, families in Canada were attempting to adapt to urbanization and industrialization. Children had to take their place in a society that was no longer agricultural and rural and in which close kinship ties were eroding. The family became smaller, more mobile, and, according to some scholars, internally mirrored the exploitative relationships characterizing capitalist economies (Alvi 1986, 2000; Barrett and McIntosh 1982; Currie 1986). On moral grounds, most people began to see family life as central to the socialization and control of children. But on practical grounds, as the economy increasingly required trained and skilled labourers, compulsory schooling came to be seen as a major player in the "proper" development of children.

Adolescence gradually became seen as a period of "innocence" in which, ostensibly, the child would delay entrance into the labour market by receiving compulsory education in the context of a nurturing family environment (Currie 1986). In the context of social reformism, which presumed the value of rehabilitation, a "child-saving movement" composed largely of middle-class women argued that the justice system of the past could not preserve this state of innocence, because that system assumed that children's and adults' behaviours were essentially the same. Only children under seven were considered to be incapable of understanding right from wrong, and while those between the ages of seven and fourteen could sometimes raise a defence of *doli incapax* (incapacity to do wrong), criminal liability essentially began at the age of seven (Bala 1997).

Developments in criminology, psychiatry, and psychology also played a part in transforming the approach to young offenders. Positivist criminology, which emphasized the role of factors beyond the control of the individual in causing crime, began to be preferred over the arguments previously advanced in the field of classical criminology. Thus, while classical criminology saw crime as a consequence of "bad decision-making," positivist criminologists argued that factors "outside" the individual were to blame.

Accordingly, people came to believe that if a child committed a crime, responsibility for that child's condition should be laid on institutions, especially the family (and, more specifically, mothers) and the school. Again, many critics believed that it was the "lower-class" family that tended to fail, and thus any reform of the justice system for children should provide alternatives that fit more closely with an emerging "middle-class" ideal of the family, one that emphasized proper care and nurturing, love, discipline, and appropriate education so that family members could rise above their lower-class situation. Essentially, the idea was that youth were vulnerable, in a stage of "innocence," and should be accorded special treatment under the general rubric of a model emphasizing the needs and welfare of the child. Those concerned began to argue that the country needed legislation to deal with these new perspectives on the role and nature of youth.

The first formal legislation enacted to address the new perspective on youth, *An Act for the More Speedy Trial and Punishment of Juvenile Offenders* (1857), was intended to accelerate the trial process for juvenile delinquents and to reduce the probability of a lengthy spell in jail before trial. The Act defined a juvenile delinquent as a person under the age of sixteen who had committed an offence. Sentencing consisted of imprisonment in a common jail or confinement in a correctional house, either with or without hard labour, and for no longer than three months, or a fine not to exceed five pounds. The accused could also be ordered to restore any stolen property or pay the equivalent compensation (Gagnon 1984: 21–22).

Quebec was the first province to add, in 1869, a sentencing provision reflecting a newfound emphasis on correction through proper schooling. While maintaining the three-month sentence, Quebec changed its legislation to abolish hard labour while including a mandatory two- to five-year term in a certified reformatory school after the jail sentence had been served.

By 1894 some basic principles regarding juvenile delinquents had become entrenched:

- Juvenile offenders were to be separated from adult offenders at all stages of the criminal justice process;
- Instead of imprisonment, juvenile delinquents were to be sent to certified industrial schools, a Children's Aid Society, or a home for neglected children, where they could be "taught to lead useful lives" (Gagnon 1984).

Approaches to youth crime in the pre-formal legal stage, then, reflected a new perception of youth as being marginally different from adults in their cognitive abilities and responsibilities. In addition the approaches reflected the shifting economic and political realities of a nascent Canadian society. Young people now represented an important source of labour, servicing the developing Canadian economy, which entailed transforming uneducated, indigent children into educated, docile workers. At the same time, these changes created another potential future of formal discipline, punishment, and control for those children who did not assimilate into the new order required by an emerging industrial capitalism.

While the burden of controlling young people's behaviour fell to families, and gradually widened to include schools, one other major social institution, the law, was in need of reform to reflect the changing role of Canadian youth.

The Juvenile Delinquents Act

By 1908 the passage of the *Act Respecting Juvenile Delinquents*, which later became the *Juvenile Delinquents Act* (JDA), represented a solidified philosophy of aid and protection for juvenile delinquents that located the causes of delinquency in the child's environment and maintained that the solution to youth crime was to have the state take the place of the (incompetent) parent. In effect, the system assumed that if parents could not do the job of controlling and properly socializing their children, the state would have to intervene as a "kindly parent" in or-

> The system assumed that if parents could not control and properly socialize their children, the state would have to intervene to protect the best interests of the child.

der to protect the best interests of the child — a principle known as *parens patriae.* The policy structure for this act was based on the welfare model, which assumed that certain people needed to be cared for in society and that their care could be administered by and through government.

The outcome of this philosophy was that judges were directed to treat children not as criminals but as "misdirected and misguided" children requiring "aid, encouragement, help and assistance" (*Juvenile Delinquents Act*, section 38). The Act contained a number of key principles:

1. A juvenile delinquent was defined as "any child who violates a provision of the Criminal Code, federal or provincial statute, municipal ordinance or by-law, or who is guilty of 'sexual immorality' or of similar vice, or who is liable for any other reason to be committed to an industrial school or reformatory" (section 21);

2. Judges were counselled to balance a courtroom approach to the juvenile delinquent that was informal, but still take seriously appropriate procedures and due process (section 17.1);

3. A child adjudged to be a juvenile delinquent would be subject to one or more dispositions, such as a suspension of the disposition, a fine not to exceed $25, probation, placement in a suitable foster home, commitment to the care of a Children's Aid Society or industrial school, or any other conditions the court deemed advisable (section 20); and

4. The legislation was based on a commitment to the therapeutic treatment of the juvenile delinquent with such treatment provided by professional social workers who were to aid families perceived to be lacking in supervisory skills (Alvi 2000).

In many ways, the JDA represented a fundamental shift away from the earliest approaches to juvenile justice, which tended to view youth and adult behaviour as being more or less the same. But although there was now a more formal Act in place to address the uniqueness of the young person, much of its humanitarian potential was undermined by vague language, minimal guarantees of due process, the inclusion of a wide range of "status" offences, and the almost random discretion of judges to invoke a range of dispositions (West 1984).

More specifically, as Nicholas Bala (1997) points out, one of the major problems with the *Juvenile Delinquents Act* was in its erratic and often biased application. Criminal justice officials such as police and judges had broad powers to interpret the child's best interests, so that there was little consistency in application across the country. Due process, such as the right to legal representation, tended to be inconsistently applied in different jurisdictions. The minimum age that defined a juvenile ranged from seven to fourteen, depending on the province. The application of the Act also saw considerable gender and class bias. For instance, female adolescents, but not males, tended to be arrested for the vague offence of "sexual immorality," and typically these girls came from socially disadvantaged backgrounds. Similarly, middle-class children were more likely to be released to their parents or subject to diversion, whereas immigrant and working-class children tended to receive more severe punishments, such as custodial sentences (see Sangster 2002).

A growing body of legal scholars, lawyers, and judges identified several other problems. For one thing (as discovered in the 1980s), many children were abused while inmates in reformatory schools. Another problem was the fundamental question of whether the best interests of the child and the accompanying notion of rehabilitation should be the only principle governing youth crime, or whether the system ought to be based on the principles of punishment and deterrence. Given claims that rehabilitation programs had failed, the principles of punishment and deterrence appeared to be of particular importance.

The provisions of the JDA were clear improvements over the random and disorganized system of the pre-legal era. But, tacitly, the principles of the Act supported the medicalization of deviant behaviour and an expansion and deepening of the net of social control over children to regulate them towards "normal" behaviour. The medicalization of deviance meant transforming problems with social causes and correlates into problems in which the causes of deviant behaviour were thought to lie in personal pathologies or individual traits that presumably could be "cured" through medical interventions such as drugs or therapy. In this framework, because delinquency is considered more of a disease than a social problem, the social and structural environment in which young people live becomes less important than the individual's supposed lack of ability to control personal actions. The JDA thus emphasized "therapeutic treatment," the important role of industrial schools and reformatories, and the expanding role of professional social-control agents such as probation officers and social workers. As Bala's summary of criticisms of the Act point out, too often it was the disadvantaged and poor who were singled out for these "treatments."

During the first half of the twentieth century, then, the *Juvenile Delinquents Act* provided the legal framework for youth in conflict with the law. By the 1960s, enough questions and issues had arisen to warrant reconsideration of the legislation (Hylton 1994). Eventually the dissatisfaction resulted in the development and implementation of new legislation, the *Young Offenders Act*.

The Young Offenders Act

While the central principle of the JDA was rehabilitation of the individual in the context of a welfare model, the *Young Offenders Act* (YOA) that replaced it represented a shift towards accountability within a "justice" framework — a set of ideas and practices emphasizing the rights of society, victims, due process and efficiency coupled with a philosophy of punishment rather than rehabilitation. Central to this perspective is the idea that crime is a matter of lack of personal accountability for actions, a view that pays little, if any, attention to the reality that the social environment plays a critical role in conditioning people's choices.

That the *Juvenile Delinquents Act* came under a major challenge in the 1960s is not surprising given that decade's reputation as a time of unprecedented economic, social, and cultural change. Although it is difficult to say that such large-scale changes were solely responsible for shifting attitudes and policies towards young offenders, it would be careless to dismiss their influence (Corrada and Markwart 1992). If we were to try and capture the tenor of the times in one word, we would probably be safe in calling this a modern "enlightenment" era. The heightened attention paid to the Vietnam War, for example, increased awareness of the problematic nature of foreign policy and the ultimately destructive nature of war. The second wave of the women's movement challenged male hegemony, and civil rights leaders such as Martin Luther King Jr. led the movement for greater racial equality. Bob Dylan, John Lennon, and other folk and rock and roll musicians sang songs about peace, love, and achieving higher consciousness through the use of drugs such as LSD, mescaline, and marijuana. An attitude of "free love" seemed to be sweeping sexual consciousness, as many young people attempted to break free from traditional social norms and customs. Many people sought new freedoms, experimented with alternative lifestyles, and started taking problems of social inequality seriously.

The 1960s spawned new concerns about the importance of equality and emancipation in all facets of life, including the law. The decade also provided people with a framework that would permit them to re-examine notions such as "immorality," "class," and "race." While many people were calling "traditional" social values into question, it was young people who seemed to be yelling the loudest. Indeed, some commentators, such as Bala (1997), have argued that the YOA was the expression of "anti-youth sentiment" and that today's youth are less likely to respect adult conventions of dress, taste, style, and attitudes, are more individualistic, and are less likely to show respect for authority. Then, as now, there also appears to have been a longing for a return to "basic values," entrenched in romantic notions of the "good old days" and an impetus towards conformity, in the context of a world that seemed more than ever to be fractured, fast-moving, and pluralistic. It did not help that youth crime was starting to increase, and that the media increasingly exploited the discourse of "bad kids" or "violent youth out of control."

> Then, as now, there also appears to have been a longing for a return to "basic values" and an impetus towards conformity in a world that seemed fractured, fast-moving, and pluralistic.

Economic change also played a part in creating the conditions for the transformation of juvenile justice. In the 1960s, a prosperous decade, many people enjoyed greater comforts and job security, and they seemed more willing to consider the plight of those less fortunate than themselves. In Canada these changing attitudes manifested themselves in several major social policy changes. For instance, a system of socialized health care, or Medicare, was initiated in the early 1960s and became a national program by the early 1970s. The federal *Unemployment Insurance Act* was reformed in 1955 and 1971, and the *Canada Pension Plan Act* was introduced in 1966. The ideas underpinning each of these important programs had to do with a philosophy of equality and help for those who had "fallen through the cracks" of an economic system whose fruits most people enjoyed. The approach was buttressed by the economic ideology of the Keynesians.[1] In the end these developments provided the backdrop for a focus on "rights and responsibilities," which was later solidified in law via the realization of the *Charter of Rights and Freedoms.*

The *Charter*, implemented in 1982, provided a new framework for interpreting the rights and responsibilities of Canadians. Among other freedoms, it guaranteed a host of legal rights including equal treatment under the law, the right to legal counsel, and the right not to be subjected to cruel and unusual punishment. Given these new rights, the JDA would most likely not have been able to withstand legal challenges under the *Charter* (Hylton 1994), but it was much earlier, within the context of an emerging "liberal" ideology and shifting economic conditions, that Canadian policy-makers began to question the Act's efficacy.

After much debate, the federal Committee on Juvenile Delinquency in Canada concluded in 1965 that the legislation had to be changed. Three separate bills followed the decision to replace the JDA, and in 1984 the *Young Offenders Act* became law.

Essentially, the YOA was a "hybrid" of the JDA and a new set of principles emphasizing the rights of society to protection from crime, the rights of accused young persons to fair, equitable, and consistent justice, and the notion that young people should be held accountable for their actions, but not in the same way as adults. Furthermore, and in keeping with the later *Charter* provisions, young people were guaranteed the same due process rights and freedoms as adults, including the opportunity to retain legal counsel paid for by the state if they were unable to afford a lawyer, the right to remain silent, and the right to consult with a parent or lawyer and to have them present when making a statement to police. In keeping with the Act's emphasis on the efficient and equitable administration of justice, Maureen McGuire (1997: xx) reminds us, "The *Young Offenders Act* provides instruction for criminal procedure and administration of dispositions relating to young persons. It is an offender management tool, not a crime prevention tool."

> The YOA was a "hybrid" of the JDA emphasizing the rights of society to protection from crime and accused young persons to fair, equitable, and consistent justice, and their distinct accountability.

The Act stresses that a young person in conflict with the law is a criminal (albeit a "special kind" of criminal) and not a misguided child (note, for instance, the different connotations of the term "juvenile delinquent" versus "young offender"). As well as the focus on the efficient and egalitarian administration of justice, the Act includes an important section that allows individuals in conflict with the law to avoid the stigmatizing and potentially harmful effects of processing in the criminal justice system. Section 4, "Alternative Measures," maintains that whenever possible young offenders should be diverted from the criminal justice system, as long as such diversion is consistent with the protection of society. Youth participating in diversion programs might engage in a variety of activities such as reconciliation and restitution to the victim, performing services for the victim, and making an apology or providing service to the community. As well, the provinces varied in their approaches to the types of offences considered to be eligible for alternative measures, with some considering all offences and others excluding the more serious crimes such as murder and manslaughter.

The assumption behind alternative measures was that when young people go through arrest, detention, court, and sentencing, the very act of being labelled a "young offender" greatly contributes to those individuals seeing themselves as young offenders. Thus, alternative measures exist to divert "suitable" individuals (those who are very young or who have committed minor offences) away from the criminal justice system so that they do not identify themselves as criminals and thus "become" criminals. In principle alternative measures would have reduced incarceration rates and reduced the stigma of being labelled a "young offender." The real question, however, was whether all young people had equal opportunities to participate in alternative measures programs, and while there is little good empirical data addressing this question, many critics suspect that equality of opportunity in this regard did not prevail (Alvi 2000). Indeed, a Royal

> The assumption behind alternative measures was that when young people go through arrest, detention, court, and sentencing, the very act of being labelled a "young offender" greatly contributes to them seeing themselves that way.

Commission study examining the experiences of Aboriginal youth offenders between the years of 1986 and 1989 found that only 11.1 percent were referred to the alternative measures program, compared with 33 percent of non-Aboriginal offenders (Pleasant-Jette 1993). Moreover, in practice, alternative measure programs were poorly realized, leaving criminal justice officials little choice but to apply formal legal sanctions to young offenders (Schissel 1997) and despite the fact that 54 percent of judges, according to one study, believed that more than half of cases coming before them could have been dealt with appropriately outside of the formal youth court system (Department of Justice Canada 2006a). According to a 1995 report summarizing cross-Canada consultations on youth justice with policy-makers, front-line workers, and young people, many communities cut funds to the pool of available programs designed to reintegrate young people. These stakeholders also complained that young people had inadequate access to counselling, training, or treatment programs, because those programs are rarely seen as legitimate components of alternative measures. Conversely, alternative measures programs often seemed to be restricted to a narrow range of options such as essay or apology writing, which did not adequately "address the unique needs and realities of many young people and which do little to address the harm done or to reintegrate the young person into the community" (National Crime Prevention Council 1995).

A key dimension of alternative measures is their emphasis on community delivery of programs (Wardell 1986). While it has been suggested that this strategy is designed to have community members more involved with their children, it could also be argued that alternative measures represent the inclusion of "the community" into an ever widening array of social-control mechanisms aimed at young people (Matthews 1979). Moreover, while the emphasis on community involvement places the burden on the public to deal with the transgressions of youth, an important shortcoming of the alternative measures section was that it relied on broad definitions of "the community" to determine the level and kind of restitution that a young person should offer. A further question is what happens if communities are asked to use their resources to make suitable dispositions, when these communities do not have access to such resources. As William Wardell (1986) suggests, the real reason behind government commitment to the principle of "non-intervention" may be cost control through devolution of responsibility.

In spirit the YOA recognized the special status and needs of wayward youth and the importance of due process, and it sought to balance these principles with the rights of victims and society at large. In practice, though, the era of the YOA witnessed a slide towards a law and order mentality, because deeper, structural problems in Canada, such as inequality, racism, sexism, and poverty, remained (and as I will argue, continue to remain) unexamined in relation to youth crime. Instead the system favoured a strategy that paid lip service to the possibilities inherent in alternative measures, overemphasized individual responsibilities and traits, and, consequently, witnessed the steady entrenchment of punishment and incarceration. The Act also reflected the social reconstruction of youth in conflict with the law as "young criminals" in a social environment characterized by fear of youth crime and mistaken public perceptions about the nature and level of youth criminality (Hogeveen and Smandych 2001). Moreover, via alternative measures, the Act implicitly constructed two categories of offenders: those who have temporarily stepped off the "up escalator," and those seen as "bad, dangerous, superpredators." Rather than providing a framework for critically examining the social forces that cause crime in the first place, by withdrawing from the welfare approach the YOA reflected a readiness to ignore and thereby reproduce those forces.

As noted earlier, in the late 1990s Canadians began to discuss the ramifications of a reform and partial reconceptualization of young offenders and the law. The legislation, the *Youth Criminal Justice Act* (YCJA), which went into effect in April of 2003, represents a cementing of strategies such as the cost-effective management of "risky children," a continued expansion in the age range that defines an "adult," and a focus on creating a justice system that provides "meaningful consequences" for youth. In theory, then, the new Act signifies a concern for the welfare of young people, coupled with the crystallization in law of a crime-control ideology.

Managing the "Risky Child": The Youth Criminal Justice Act

In a recent general election, British citizens were confronted with a crime-control slogan promoted by Prime Minister Tony Blair. In an attempt to be all things to all voters, Blair argued that his new policy reflected a philosophy of "getting tough on crime, [but also] getting tough on the causes of crime." Since then Home Secretary Jack Straw, the person responsible for law and order in Britain, argued that the country's increases in violent crime were attributable to wayward youth who have "never had it so good." In effect, he attributed the causes of crime to wealth instead of poverty and inequality (Assinder 2000).

Canadian politicians have taken similar steps to distract the public from the realities and social precursors of youth crime. Proponents of the new law maintained that the YOA was not "tough enough" on young offenders, and that we should instead create a legal framework reflecting current social values, one that "commands respect, fosters values such as accountability and responsibility... makes it clear that criminal behaviour will lead to meaningful consequences, [and that reflects the need for a] broader, more comprehensive approach to youth justice that looks beyond the justice system for solutions to youth crime" (Canada 2001). In effect, like developments in the U.K., the new YCJA is an attempt to be "all things to all people" (Barber and Doob 2004).

Central to this development is a growing reliance on the "criminology of the dangerous other" in which youth (as well as women, the poor, and particular racial/ethnic groups) are singled out as the category considered most risky and in need of control (Garland 2001).

In Ontario, for instance, Conservative Premier Mike Harris began his tenure in 1995 by waging a campaign to discipline particular categories of youth, most notably "squeegee kids," whose only "crime" appeared to be that of attempting to make a living in an economy that has consistently denied them legitimate opportunities.[2] Moreover, in the two decades prior to Harris's term in office, youth unemployment rates in Canada rose from 14 percent in 1980 to 18 percent in 1995 for those completing high school, and more and more youth were working part-time in low-paying, service-sector jobs with little chance of advancement, minimal training for more advanced jobs, and reduced or non-existent benefits (Health Canada 1999). These shifts occurred in the context of transformations in our market-based society that paradoxically rely on youth to consume goods and services but at the same time systematically exclude large segments of them from participation in worthwhile, remunerative work.

Indeed, today's youth are increasingly forced into a "prolonged state of social marginality" (Petersen and Mortimer 1994), given the rapid decline of decent work opportunities for young people — and in particular for those who come from poor or dispossessed backgrounds. At the same time, and perhaps more than ever, young people are subjected to a market orientation in which consumption is depicted as "an end in itself and as a measure of social status and human value" (Caston 1998). Thus we are now in an era in which more and more youth are experiencing relative deprivation,[3] coupled with fewer opportunities to attain the "glittering prizes" of capitalism through legitimate means (Young 1999).

Contemporary Canadian youth live in a context in which the state is attempting to control the activities of a new youthful "lumpenproletariat"[4] (Taylor 1999). Indeed, many Canadian youth must cope with extraordinarily difficult social circumstances. To take but a few examples:

- Despite assurances by Canada's federal government over seventeen years ago that they would seek to eliminate child poverty by the year 2000, today one out of every six children in Canada lives in poverty. For Canadian families, good jobs have been replaced by part-time, contractual or seasonal employment such that they constitute 37 percent of all jobs in Canada, compared to 25 percent in the mid-70s. Furthermore, despite economic growth in Canada, the gap between rich and poor families remains unchanged from a decade ago. Poverty, in turn, is associated with a host of social problems such as poor housing conditions, parental stress, street crime, an inability to learn, and malnutrition (Campaign 2000, 2005).
- Between 1952 and 2002 suicide rates for Canadian youth aged fifteen to nineteen rose five-fold from two per 100,000 to slightly over 10 per 100,000. This makes suicide the second leading cause of death for young people in Canada (BC Partners for Mental Health and Addictions Information 2006).
- Young people's use of anti-depressant drugs such as cannabis, glue, barbiturates, mescaline, and psilocybin increased significantly in the 1990s (Adlaf et al. 2000), and their use of illegal drugs remains fairly stable (Boyce 2004).
- To the best of my knowledge, there are no studies of psychiatric disorders among incarcerated youth in Canada. However, recent studies in the United States indicate that more than 70 percent of incarcerated youth suffer from at least one mental disorder, with 20 percent suffering from a "serious" mental health problem. There is no reason to believe that incarcerated Canadian youth are any different in this regard from their U.S. counterparts, and while the YCJA acknowledges the need to provide intensive rehabilitation for such youth, only empirical evaluation of this claim in the near future will help us to determine whether this has indeed been the case (Odgers, Burnette, Chauhan, Moretti, and Reppucci 2005).

Although provinces have the right to opt out of some provisions, the Act opens the way for provinces, like Ontario, to implement strategies embracing strict disciplinary incarceration, parental responsibility for youth offending, and privately run prisons for young offenders. In addition, the Act allows more young people to be tried for violent crimes in adult court (with the age limit dropped from sixteen to fourteen), and for the names of those involved in serious crime to be publicized, thereby seriously reducing the chances that such offenders might ever reintegrate into society.

Importantly, however, under the clause of "extrajudicial measures" (formerly known as alternative measures under the YOA) the Act proposes that those convicted of lesser crimes such as petty theft or vandalism should be afforded sanctions other than jail. The real question, which can only be answered empirically, is who these individuals are likely to be. One recent study determined that three factors — having no prior convictions, being charged with a property offence, and having fewer current and outstanding charges — were statistically significant predictors of being diverted from the formal criminal justice system (Moyer and Basic 2004). But we have little good data on whether diversion is an option considered for Aboriginal youth, youth of colour, or females. The implementation of extrajudicial measures may well result in a process of judicial triage for young offenders, with some individuals ("our" children) deemed suitable for diversion from the juvenile justice system and others ("other people's" children) sent straight to adult court (Bell 1999; Feld 1999).

> Implementing extrajudicial measures may create a process of judicial triage for young offenders, with some individuals ("our" children) being diverted from the juvenile justice system and others ("other people's" children) sent straight to adult court.

There is some degree of optimism, as of this writing, that extrajudicial measures are in fact being used. As the Department of Justice (2006b) states:

- There has been an increase in the use of extrajudicial measures by police, and, preliminary indications are that they appear to be using the full range of measures set out in section 6.
- In jurisdictions that have crown caution programs or pre-charge screening, crown prosecutors appear to be using cautions and encouraging the use of extrajudicial measures by police.

However, the same Department of Justice report notes that there are less encouraging signs and some issues that will warrant further investigation in coming years:

- Net widening can be defined as the use of interventions outside the Criminal Justice system that "may result in more, not less, intervention than would have occurred in the past. For example, police may be inclined to use formal cautions and referrals with youths with whom, in the past, police would have taken no further action" (Barnhorst 2004). While national figures reported by the Canadian Centre for Justice Statistics for 2003 do not indicate any significant increase in the number of youth being brought into the youth justice system, there have been instances where net widening appears to have occurred in the use of extrajudicial measures programs.
- There is not sufficient data yet available to determine the extent to which the use of extrajudicial measures, particularly extrajudicial sanctions, is proportionate to the seriousness of the offence.
- There is evidence that conditions are being attached to the use of some police referrals that are not consistent with the objectives of reform at the front end of the process.

Further, given that under the YCJA, police are now mandated to consider extrajudicial measures before starting judicial proceedings, it will be important to determine if communities have the necessary resources to address the needs of youth who should be diverted from the criminal justice system.

A paper drafted to justify the introduction of the new Act discusses the role of "community-based crime prevention" and the need to address "the social conditions associated with the root causes of delinquency" (Canada 1999). The document makes clear, though, that most serious offenders come from troubled homes characterized by violence, physical and sexual abuse, poverty, substance abuse, attachment disorders, poor housing, and the difficulties associated with neighbourhood disorganization — factors that critical criminologists have been calling attention to for decades. It is surely false piety to acknowledge the crucial role of social inequality in fostering youth crime in a society that continues lurching towards a "dystopia of exclusion" (Young 1999). An "ideal" or "utopian" society would possess several characteristics including low rates of crime, social advancement on the basis of merit, truly representative democracy, full and worthwhile employment, and a celebration of diversity. In contrast, as Jock Young (1999) argues, in the "dystopia of exclusion" many people are being ever more excluded from participating in "the good life" because of poverty, inequalities, insecurity, and other unfairness, and they are also increasingly demonized as being unworthy.

The truth is that as of yet, no government has seriously committed itself to programs and strategies that might begin to foster greater equality, such as increasing government support for at-risk families, creating a nationally funded child-care system, or providing real work opportunities, because such policies would entail a fundamental rethinking of the socio-economic system and the advantages that the current system confers on the wealthy and powerful in our society, including their children. Instead, the legislation proposes the need for better reintegration after custody via periods of community supervision, and vague notions of "meaningful consequences" aimed at rehabilitation.

Taken together, recent "reforms" of the laws governing youth crime in Canada reflect a heightened sense of the danger that disenfranchised youth represent to the social order, because these children underscore our failure as a society to deal with widening social and economic disparities. More fundamentally, the law and order mentality reflected in the legislation is a reflection of the attitude that such individuals can, and should, be thrown away or "quarantined" in prison, or controlled in other ways (Garland 2001); they are merely part of the wounded debris characterizing the "new economy."

> The Act also reflects a concern with cost-effectiveness, efficiency, and the management of offending risk, rather than disquiet with the structural conditions that encourage youth to offend.

The Act also reflects a concern with cost-effectiveness, efficiency, and the management of offending risk, rather than disquiet with the structural conditions that encourage youth to offend. In a culture of risk management, the emphasis is no longer on the nature of the processes and conditions that generate criminal opportunities and behaviours. Rather, risk management approaches assume that offenders simply exist, and that the real task is to manage away their existence and the potential harm they might cause through strategies such as "target hardening," a crime-reduction strategy aimed at reducing opportunities for offending (for example, by increasing lighting, shuttering windows, or placing padlocks on property). As well, the Act focuses on making the system as cost-effective as possible through the use of tools such as sentencing grids (frameworks used to determine the length and nature of an offender's sentence based on prior records and the seriousness of the offence) and risk assessment tools (designed to "predict" future offending or manage case dispositions or treatments).

And yet, as Pate (2006: 1) points out:

> Correctional authorities in many provinces and territories are utilizing actuarial risk assessment procedures with criminalized adults and youth within their

jurisdictions. Although there are some incredibly problematic philosophical issues and extremely challenging practical problems that have been created by attempts to adapt imperfect models of risk assessment(s) designed for adults to the circumstances of youth, there is virtually no research regarding the appropriateness of applying such approaches to youth. This is especially the case when one considers the circumstances of some of our most marginalized young people.

In effect, Canadian society has increased its commitment to managing the risk of dangerous/criminal youth while paying selective inattention to the social, political, and economic factors that create youth at risk. By itself, a risk-management strategy does nothing to address why offenders are motivated to commit offences in the first place. The attitude seems to be that it is much easier to lock up or in some way, shape or form, "process" those who break the law rather than to deal with the social and economic conditions that foster crime.

Conclusion

Although youth who have "failed" to integrate into society have to some extent always been demonized in Canada, never have our attitudes been so narrow, unsympathetic, and controlling as they are today. Concomitant with these attitudes, the current legislation reflects a return to the narrow individualism and decontextualized framework of classical criminology, with its emphasis on "rational choice" and crime control and its use of the rhetoric, but not the content of notions of social justice and reform.

Our legal orientation towards youth has been greatly influenced by perceptions of their role in the broader context of the socio-economic system. Prior to the rise of capitalism in Canada, the law, such as it was, reflected a blasé and ad hoc attitude towards children. As capitalism developed through the late nineteenth and early twentieth centuries, formal social-control strategies reflected the need for a well-socialized, compliant labour force at a time when jobs were relatively plentiful. Gradually, as the nature and availability of work changed in the context of an increasingly polarizing society, it became seemingly less practical to talk about rehabilitating and integrating young offenders and much more politically expedient to address real, but misplaced, public demands to "get tough on crime."

More recently, in the midst of deepening social inequality and fewer opportunities for youth, Canadian young offenders law reflects a further retreat from any realistic commitment to rehabilitation and significant social transformation. Contemporary Canadian youth justice policy is based on the erroneous assumption that punishment works, and that "shot in the arm" treatment programs are available, accessible, and effective. Its bankruptcy is also exposed by the system's willingness to continue to scapegoat and criminalize "dangerous" children to deflect attention from economic, political, and social crises in Canada, and the fundamentally inequitable nature of Canadian society. We must begin to develop adequate and sustainable solutions to the structural contradictions of Canadian society, because we will never solve crime with law.

> We must begin to develop adequate and sustainable solutions to the structural contradictions of Canadian society because we will never solve crime with law.

DISCUSSION QUESTIONS

1. What are some of the key differences between mainstream and critical accounts of the history of youth justice in Canada?

2. What are some similarities and differences between alternative measures and extra-judicial measures as laid out in the YCJA?

3. Why do some young people become marginalized in our society? Who do these people tend to be, and why are their social characteristics important?

4. Given the arguments presented in this chapter, should Canada have strengthened the YOA, rather than creating an entire new Act? Why or why not?

5. What are some elements of modern youth culture in your community? In what ways are these elements "criminalized" or at least seen to be expressions of deviant behaviour?

GLOSSARY OF TERMS

Dystopia of Exclusion: an "ideal" or "utopian" society would possess several characteristics, including low rates of crime, social advancement on the basis of merit, truly representative democracy, full and meaningful employment, celebration of diversity, and so on. In contrast, as Young (1999) argues, modern societies like Canada are tending toward a "dystopia of exclusion" in which many people are ever more excluded from participating in "the good life" because of poverty, inequalities, insecurity, and other unfairness, and they are also increasingly demonized as being unworthy.

Justice Framework: a set of ideas and practices emphasizing the rights of society, victims, due process, and efficiency coupled with a philosophy of punishment rather than rehabilitation. Central to this perspective is the idea that crime is a matter of lack of personal accountability for actions — a view that pays little, if any, attention to the reality that the social environment plays a critical role in conditioning people's choices.

Keynesianism: maintains that governments should actively intervene in the economy to create demand for products when capitalist economies are in a slump. Thus, by spending money on policies that put money in people's hands (like welfare, tax cuts, or unemployment insurance), consumers are able to continue spending, which in turn helps the private sector through the economic slump.

Lumpenproletariat: what Marx called the "refuse of all classes." Today the term refers to the idea that in situations of economic and social crisis in capitalist society, large numbers of impoverished masses tend to become disconnected from their class and also tend to be susceptible to reactionary ideas.

Relative Deprivation: the notion that people perceive their position in society relative to others. Thus, those who are poor might not view themselves as worse off than others if *everyone* around them is poor, but when such people live in a society where inequality is blatantly evident, and when they feel that such inequality is unfair, they are said to experience relative deprivation.

Etiology: the study of causation.

SUGGESTED READINGS

Bala, N. 1997. *Young Offenders Law*. Concord, ON: Irwin Law.

Bell, S. 1999. *Young Offenders and Juvenile Justice: A Century after the Fact*. Toronto: ITP Nelson.

Elliott Currie. 2004. *The Road to Whatever: Middle-Class Culture and the Crisis of Adolescence*. Metropolitan Books.

Doob, A.N., and C. Cesaroni. 2004. *Responding to Youth Crime in Canada*. Toronto: University of Toronto Press.

Schissel, B. 1997. *Blaming Children: Youth Crime, Moral Panics and the Politics of Hate*. Halifax: Fernwood Publishing.

Smandych, R. 2001. *Youth Justice: History, Legislation, and Reform*. Toronto: Harcourt Brace.

Taylor, Ian. 1999. *Crime in Context: A Critical Criminology of Market Societies*. Boulder, CO: Westview Press.

NOTES

1. Keynesianism maintains that governments should actively intervene in the economy to create demand for products when capitalist economies are in a slump. Thus, by spending money on policies that put money in people's hands (such as welfare or unemployment insurance), the government allows consumers to continue spending, which in turn helps the private sector through the economic slump.

2. The *Ontario Safe Streets Act* (2000) makes it a crime, punishable by a $1,000 fine or six months in jail, for people to approach a vehicle with intent to provide services, and also outlaws "aggressive panhandling."

3. Relative deprivation is the notion that people perceive their position in society relative to others. Thus, those who are poor might not view themselves as being worse off than others if everyone else around them is poor, but when such people live an a society in which inequality is blatantly evident and when they feel that such inequality is unfair, they are said to experience relative deprivation.

4. Marx called the lumpenproletariat the "refuse of all classes." Today, however, the term refers to the idea that in situations of economic and social crisis in capitalist society, large numbers of impoverished masses tend not only to become disconnected from their class but also to be susceptible to reactionary ideas.

REFERENCES

Adlaf, E.M., A. Paglia, F.J. Ivis, and A. Ialomiteanu. 2000. "Nonmedical Drug Use Among Adolescent Students: Highlights From the 1999 Ontario Student Drug Use Survey." *Canadian Medical Association Journal* 162.

Alvi, Shahid. 1986. "Realistic Crime Prevention Strategies Through Alternative Measures for Youth." In D. Currie and B.D. MacLean (eds.), *The Administration of Justice*. Saskatoon: Social Research Unit, Department of Sociology, University of Saskatchewan.

_____. 2000. *Youth and the Canadian Criminal Justice System*. Cincinnati: Anderson Press.

Assinder, N. 2000. "Crime Statistics Deal New Blow to Blair." *BBC News Online*. Available at <uk. news.yahoo.com/000718/116/adej1.html> accessed October 15, 2006.

BC Partners for Mental Health and Addictions Information (2006). *Suicide: Follow the Warning Signs*. Vancouver, BC: BC Partners for Mental Health and Addictions Information.

Bala, N. 1997. *Young Offenders Law*. Concord, Ontario: Irwin Law.

Bala, N., and S. Anand. 2004. "The First Months under the Youth Criminal Justice Act: A Survey and Analysis of Case Law." *Canadian Journal of Criminology and Criminal Justice* 46: 251–71.

Barber, J., and A.N. Doob. 2004. "An Analysis of Public Support for Severity and Proportionality in the Sentencing of Youthful Offenders." *Canadian Journal of Criminology and Criminal Justice* 46: 327–28.

Barnhorst, R. 2004. The Youth Criminal Justice Act: New Directions and Implementation Issues. *Canadian Journal of Criminology and Criminal Justice* 46: 231–50.

Barrett, M., and M. McIntosh. 1982. *The Anti-Social Family*. London: Verso.

Bell, S. 1999. *Young Offenders and Juvenile Justice: A Century After the Fact*. Toronto: ITP Nelson.

Bernard, T. 1991. *The Cycle of Juvenile Justice*. New York: Oxford University Press.

Boyce, W. 2004. *Young People in Canada: Their Health and Well-being*. Ottawa: Health Canada.

Canada, Department of Justice. 1999. "A Strategy for the Renewal of Youth Justice." Ottawa: Department of Justice.

Campaign 2000. 2005. *Decision Time for Canada: Let's Make Poverty History: 2005 Report Card on Child Poverty in Canada* Toronto: Campaign 2000.

Canada, Department of Justice. 2001. "Canada's Youth Criminal Justice Act: A New Law — A New Approach." Available at <http://canada.justice.gc.ca/Orientations/jeunes/penale/youth_en.html>.

Canadian Centre for Justice Statistics. 1997. "Justice Data Fact Finder." *Juristat* 16 (9).

Carrigan, D.O. 1998. *Juvenile Delinquency in Canada: A History*. Concord: Irwin.

Caston, R.J. 1998. *Life in a Business-Oriented Society: A Sociological Perspective*. Boston: Allyn and Bacon.

Cohen, S. 1972. *Folk Devils and Moral Panics*. London: MacGibbon and Kee.

Currie, D. 1986. "The Transformation of Juvenile Justice in Canada." In B.D. MacLean (ed.), *The Political Economy of Crime*. Toronto: Prentice-Hall.

DeKeseredy, W.S. and M.D. Schwartz. 1996. *Contemporary Criminology*. Belmont, CA: Wadsworth.

Department of Justice Canada. 2006a. "The Youth Criminal Justice Act: Summary and Background." Available at <http://www.justice.gc.ca/en/ps/yj/ycja/explan.html> accessed July 2007.

_____. 2006b. Youth Criminal Justice Act: 2005 Annual Statement. Available at <http://www.justice.gc.ca/en/ps/yj/YCJA/statement/execsum.html> accessed July 2007.

Doob, A.N., and C. Cesaroni. 2004. *Responding to Youth Crime in Canada*. Toronto: University of Toronto Press.

Feld, B C. 1999. *Bad Kids: Race and the Transformation of the Juvenile Court*. New York: Oxford University Press.

Gagnon, D. 1984. "History of the Law for Juvenile Delinquents." Ministry of the Solicitor General of Canada, Government Working Paper No. 1984-56.

Gannon, M. 2006. *Crime Statistics in Canada, 2005*. (Rep. No. 85-002-XIE, vol. 26, no. 4). Ottawa: Canadian Centre for Justice Statistics.

Garland, D. 2001. *The Culture of Control*. New York: Oxford University Press.

Hartnagel, T. 2004. "The Rhetoric of Youth Justice in Canada." *Criminal Justice* 4: 355–74.

Health Canada. 1999. "Healthy Development of Children and Youth: The Role of the Determinants of Health." Ottawa: Minister of Health.

Hogeveen, B., and R. Smandych. 2001 "Origins of the Newly Proposed Canadian Youth Criminal Justice Act: Political Discourse and the Perceived Crisis in Youth Crime in the 1990s." In R. Smandych (ed.), *Youth Justice: History, Legislation and Reform*. Toronto: Harcourt Canada.

Hylton, J.H. 1994. "Get Tough or Get Smart? Options for Canada's Youth Justice System in the Twenty-First Century." *Canadian Journal of Criminology* 36, 3.

Lynch, M.J., and W.B. Groves. 1989. *A Primer in Radical Criminology*. New York: Harrow and Heston.

Matthews, R. 1979 "Decarceration and the Fiscal Crisis." In B. Fine (ed.), *Capitalism and the Rule of Law*. London: Hutchinson.

McGuire, M. 1997. "C.19: An Act to Amend the Young Offenders Act and the Criminal Code — Getting Tougher?" *Canadian Journal of Criminology* 39, 2.

National Crime Prevention Council. 1995. *Mobilizing Political Will and Community Responsibility to Prevent Youth Crime: A Summary Report Of 30 Consultation Meetings to Explore Effective Community Responses to Youth Crime.* Ottawa, Government of Canada.

Moyer, S., and M. Basic. 2004. *Crown Decision-Making under the Youth Criminal Justice Act.* Ottawa: Youth Justice Policy, Research and Statistics Division.

Odgers, C., M. Burnette, P. Chauhan, M. Moretti, and N.D. Reppucci. 2005. "Misdiagnosing the Problem: Mental Health Profiles of Incarcerated Juveniles." *The Canadian Child and Adolescent Psychiatry Review* 14: 26–29.

Pate, K. 2006. *The Risky Business of Risk Assessment* Ottawa: Canadian Association of Elizabeth Fry Societies.

Petersen, A.C., and J.T. Mortimer. 1994. *Youth, Unemployment and Society.* Cambridge: Cambridge University Press.

Pleasant-Jette, Corinne Mount. 1993. *Creating a Climate of Confidence: Providing Services Within Aboriginal Communities.* National Round Table on Economic Issues and Resources (Royal Commission on Aboriginal Issues).

Sangster, J. 2002. *Girl Trouble: Female Delinquency in English Canada.* Toronto: Between the Lines.

Schissel, Bernard. 1993. *Social Dimensions of Canadian Youth Justice.* Toronto: Oxford University Press.

_____. 1997. *Blaming Children: Youth Crime, Moral Panics and the Politics of Hate.* Halifax: Fernwood Publishing.

_____. 2006. *Still Blaming Children: Youth Conduct and the Politics of Child Hating.* Halifax: Fernwood Publishing.

Schwartz, M.D. 1991. "The Future of Critical Criminology." In B.D. MacLean and D. Milovanovic (eds.), *New Directions in Critical Criminology.* Vancouver: Collective Press.

Smandych, R. 2001. "Accounting for Changes in Canadian Youth Justice: From the Invention to the Disappearance of Childhood." In R. Smandych (ed.), *Youth Justice: History, Legislation, and Reform.* Toronto: Harcourt Canada.

Sprott, J. 1996. "Understanding Public Views of Youth Crime and the Youth Justice System." *Canadian Journal of Criminology* 38, 5.

Statistics Canada. 2005. *Youth Correctional Services: Key Indicators* Ottawa: Statistics Canada.

Taylor, I. 1999. *Crime in Context: A Critical Criminology of Market Societies.* Boulder, CO: Westview.

Varma, K.N., and V. Marinos. 2000. How Do We Best Respond to the Problem of Youth Crime? In J. Roberts (ed.), *Criminal Justice in Canada: A Reader.* Toronto: Harcourt Brace.

Wardell, B. 1986. "The Young Offenders Act: A Report Card 1984–1986." In D. Currie and B.D. MacLean (eds.), *The Administration of Justice.* Saskatoon: Social Research Unit, University of Saskatchewan.

West, W.G. 1984. *Young Offenders and the State: A Canadian Perspective on Delinquency.* Toronto: Butterworths.

Young, J. 1999. *The Exclusive Society.* London: Sage.

Part IV

The Contemporary
Shape and Form of Crime

The consensus approaches within criminology assume that the state and criminal justice systems are democratic institutions. They presume that the morality we share and the ways in which we understand crime and punishment are a matter of collective agreement — hence, consensus. The general abhorrence of people who kill others is testament to a consensus about what constitutes murder. The consensus paradigm does not, however, question what is defined as murder or as "crime" generally, or whether certain classes or races are criminalized more often than others. For example, the killing of someone during wartime — especially someone in another country and of a different racial/ethnic background — is considered an act of courage and patriotism, with no regard to how easy, one-sided, or premeditated the killing might have been. Similarly, if the executive of a car company and various colleagues make a conscious decision to forgo safety measures to increase profits, they deliberately endanger (and perhaps ultimately murder) people. Those acts, however, are rarely considered to be acts of violence or murder. As acts that presumably do not immediately threaten the average citizen, they are somehow construed as acts of necessity or chance occurrences. That they are not part of people's fear of crime is an important consideration in understanding how average people come to understand good and evil behaviour.

As for the question of who tends to gets punished for acts of murder, as the chapters in this part of the book make clear, it is poor people, in general, who populate the prisons. The fundamental question is, then, whether the poor and disaffiliated who are so numerous in prison are there because they are truly bad, or there because of their life circumstances. Are the types of crimes they commit the crimes that preoccupy the public consciousness — drug trafficking, shoplifting, assaults, robbery, and theft? Are the poor more visible and vulnerable to police scrutiny than the average citizens because of where they live, their race or ethnicity, the way they dress, where they drink, and how they speak? Are they highly vulnerable to conviction and punishment for other reasons? Because they cannot afford private lawyers? Because they and their families cannot provide alternatives to incarceration? Because they lack a permanent address or visible means of support? Because they are stereotypic reoffenders in the eyes of the police and judicial officials? Because they cannot or do not speak the "language of justice"?

These are fundamental questions that we must ask as we attempt to understand, through a critical lens, how the law works. For, at the end of the day, the common sense and legal/philosophical justification for the justice system and the system of punishment is that they are fair and objective. In jurisprudence, all individuals have the same opportunity in court to accuse their accusers, to have access to counsel, and to have fair hearings before a judge and/or jury. The fairness of justice is based on the juridical principle that only the "facts" of the case are important in determining guilt or innocence. Extralegal considerations, such as race, class, and gender, should not, in theory, influence seemingly impartial judgments in law. They may influence judges' decisions about lenient punishment, but, ironically, the leniency that judges display usually disadvantages the poor, powerless, "address-less," recidivist offender.

In response to these fundamental questions, critical criminologists question the role of human decisions in the creation of what is defined as "crime" and who is criminalized. These social categories are shaped by human decisions, which themselves are shaped by the needs of the social system. One inescapable conclusion here is that the criminal justice system helps to create the reality that we see; it does not reflect the reality of crime. It is true that people who live on the margins of society commit certain crimes more often than other people, and this reality is the focus of conventional criminology and of political and social policy. Poor people from the inner city do have relatively higher rates of shoplifting, street-drug use, soliciting, and theft. But other considerations also must play a part: invisible theft and robbery occur at a corporate level — insider trading is theft of great magnitude; cocaine and marijuana use and alcohol abuse are very much middle-class activities, although they are rarely detected or admonished; and certain forms of prostitution serve a wealthy clientele and do not come under the purview of the police. It is relatively easy for academics, legal scholars, and social policy administrators to focus on crimes that occur on the street. That focus is an act of politics, and it is a part of an ideology suggesting that we are most likely to be harmed by "individuals" who are dispossessed in our socio-economic hierarchy. Importantly, the perpetrators of these crimes become embedded in the public consciousness as the people we need to fear the most, the people who will create the most harm to a society.

Not only does the criminal justice system help construct our morality, but it also determines who should be condemned and punished on the bases of socio-economic power. The critical criminology position, in response, focuses on the system of justice as a political body that is not impartial or unbiased. That the poor and racial minorities fill our prisons in contemporary Canadian society does not necessarily mean that they are the most likely to engage in socially harmful behaviour. On the contrary, critical criminology draws attention to how we excuse the rich at every stage of the criminal justice process, from the very definition of a criminal act to the sanctions of the police and judiciary. For example, the actions of corporations and the elite are often overlooked even when their actions pose a threat to social well-being. Yet the actions of the unemployed and poor are quite typically criminalized. They are more often incarcerated than wealthier lawbreakers, even when their behaviours are less damaging. Our definitions and understandings of violence and harm, then, are at once ideological and political. The law and criminal justice system, as well as journalistic and academic accounts of "criminality," are instruments of social control, for they stigmatize and scapegoat some of the most disenfranchised people in our society.

The title of Part IV, "The Contemporary Shape and Form of Crime," emphasizes that "crime" is not a universal concept but rather a social creation: moreover, punishment is highly discretionary and is served up not only to those who are easiest to punish but also to those who are most damaged by it. For example, fining an unemployed, penniless person living on the street makes little sense, because the punishment contributes to further impoverishment. Being sent to jail eventually stigmatizes the convicted person as an "ex-con" and takes the person out of the job market, both of which damage the chances for social advancement. The well-heeled corporate executive does not experience any similar damage to career or finances.

Laureen Snider's chapter, "But They're Not Real Criminals: Downsizing Corporate Crime," demonstrates the extent of social harm committed by corporations. She points out that the justice system does not often define harmful acts by corporations as being wrong, even though those acts may cause more death, injury, and financial ruin than does street crime. We have evidenced the deregulation of the harmful acts of corporations and socio-economic elites. For example, although the environment is in a state of severe damage, over the last decade regulatory agencies have continued to have their budgets slashed. Snider provides examples of the devastation involved: "Government downsizing and lack of enforcement have created a situation in which Canadian firms were much more likely than their U.S. counterparts to dump liquid pollutants directly into lakes and rivers rather than divert them to sewage-treatment plants." The cornerstone of this corporate counter-revolution is the "new citizen," defined by consumerism and individualistic in their pursuits. Individualized discourse pulls people away from any sense of collective responsibilities. She offers some hope that the power of corporate capitalism is becoming increasingly questioned (by activists throughout the world) and some new legislation has been passed.

Janet Mosher's chapter, "Welfare Fraudsters and Tax Evaders: The State's Selective Invocation of Criminality," shows the link between marginality and condemnation by comparing "fraud" and tax "evasion." Tax evasion costs the taxpayer dramatically more money than welfare fraud, yet is not defined by the public as fraudulent (by contrast there seems to be an acceptance of this type of evasion), or a serious social problem. If tax evasion is detected, it is often seen as a minor transgression and gains only a solicitous response from the state. By contrast, welfare fraud is depicted as a crime against "the needy" and extreme public (and private) scrutiny (including the welfare snitch line) is encouraged. Any failure to abide by the (quite extreme) rules may result in severe penalties — including imprisonment. As Mosher states: "the severity of the sentences imposed in welfare fraud cases is dramatically out of step with a sentence for infractions that occur in other administrative regimes and with other Criminal Code offences." She compares the offence of theft under 5,000 to welfare fraud of the same amount. The first offender of theft is many steps from incarceration, whereas there is serious risk of incarceration for fraud. These responses define poverty (and wealth) as being the responsibility of the individual, denying the consequences of structural inequalities. Snider and Mosher's chapters demonstrate crime control as a political project, one which "criminalizes" poverty and deregulates crimes of the more powerful in society.

Willem de Lint and Christian Pasiak's chapter discusses the social construction of ideas about crime and punishment, reviewing how "crime knowledge is produced" — but not under conditions of equality. They provide an overview of crime statistical data (overall crime rates) from a variety of sources. Official statistics such as the Uniform Crime Report, for example, show a decline in property crime and an increase in youth and violent crime. By contrast, victimization surveys show theft increasing and no increase in violent victimization. De Lint and Pasiak focus their attention on misrepresentation of crime through media, diverse criminological approaches, victimization surveys, and Uniform Crime Reports and lay bare the interplay of culture, ideology, and power (in the construction of each source). The uniform crime report data, for example, depends on what is defined as "criminal," who police charge, and the decision of the courts. Popular news stories of individual criminals, serial killers and murder draw media attention and are sought after (representing villains and victims) more than the more complicated stories of, for example, Enron and tax evasion. Drawing on examples such as the aftermath of hurricane Katrina and 9/11, de Lint and Pasiak also show the extreme perceptions of events — good versus evil (whereas most human encounters are neither "saintly nor wicked"). For example, stories of looting in New Orleans after Hurricane Katrina focuses on the "wicked heart of New Orleans" rather than "abandoned residents left to fend for themselves." Their position is that crime is stratified in power relations and the structure of society ensures differential rewards and protection from penalties.

Elizabeth Comack's chapter focuses on gender-based presumptions regarding violence and the reactions of male-dominated society to women who are violent. By deconstructing legal, academic, and journalistic theories, Comack inquires into the possibilities of gendering processes. In her research, she explores three positions on gender and violence. The first position, the focus of much of mainstream criminology, is that violence is what men do to other men; men are statistically more likely to be both offenders and victims. The second position, discussed largely within feminist analysis, focuses on male violence against women. Feminists have challenged the methodology of mainstream criminology that has failed to reliably detect the amount of victimization of women by men. Violence is gendered because it is what men do to women. A third position, developed by authors such as the journalist Patricia Pearson (1997), demands a recognition that women are violent too, and further that "women's violence is more masked and underhanded than men's violence: women kill their babies, arrange for their husbands' murders... commit serial murders." Specifically, Pearson claims that women are men's equals in violence. In her attempt to make sense of the three positions, Comack uses police incident reports to show that women, obviously, are capable of violence, but, more importantly, that there are gender differences in the use of violence. Comack's research challenges not only Pearson's claims about gender symmetry but also the "get-tough" crime approach and the patriarchal and gendered assumptions in law, journalism, and academics.

As the chapters in this part indicate, the people who are financially, socially, and politically secure are rarely a part of the equation that links certain forms of bad behaviour to crime, immorality, and punishment. Those who suffer the most from crime, those who are exploited because of their imputed criminal behaviour, and those who are most severely punished by the criminal justice system — they all live on the margins of the social and economic hierarchy. If you strip away all the rhetoric of immorality and deviance, privation and marginalization are the ultimate crimes.

11 "But They're Not Real Criminals"
Downsizing Corporate Crime

Laureen Snider

KEY FACTS

> Corporate crime causes more injury and death per year, and easily fifty times as much financial loss, as ordinary property crime does.

> Canadian anti-combines laws have been successively relaxed resulting in fewer merger investigations and narrowing of public interest to the simpler dictates of business efficiency and competitiveness.

> The fraud and bankruptcy of Enron Corporation cost investors, pensioners and employees 60 billion dollars.

> In a National White Collar Crime Centre survey in 2000, respondents were asked whether armed robbery causing injury or neglecting to recall a vehicle that results in a injury were more serious. Thirty-nine percent said the defective product was more serious; 48 percent said armed robbery was more serious.

> A small number of major corporate frauds from Tyco, Adelphia, Worldcom, Enron, "swamp the losses from all street robberies and burglaries combined."

> The National White Collar Crime Centre (2000) reports that less than one out of every ten corporate victimizations is reported to law enforcement or consumer protection agencies.

Sources: Rebovich et al. 2000; *Corporate Crime Reporter 25*, June 12, 2007.

Nowhere in criminology is the role of power and class more obvious than in the creation and enforcement of laws against corporate crime. To study corporate crime is to realize that equally harmful acts are not equally punished. Corporate crime causes more injury and death per year, and easily fifty times as much financial loss, as ordinary property crime does (Rosoff, Pontell, and Tillman 2004). For any government, criminalizing the corporation — holding it and its executives accountable for fraud, theft, negligence, injury, and death, and for the economic and social harm done — is an expensive operation. Corporate Canada can afford lawyers who will exploit every loophole. Cases drag on for years, even decades. Prosecuting business, especially big business, is fraught with political danger as well. With privatization and downsizing eliminating thousands of public sector jobs, corporations have become the only source of employment for many communities. They have powerful allies in local, national, and international media, and they contribute handsomely to political parties with corporate-friendly agendas.

If you kill someone accidentally in a car in Canada because you were going too fast or didn't get your brakes checked, you are likely to be charged with criminal negligence and to face, on conviction, a lengthy penitentiary sentence. If you kill someone accidentally in a mine because you decided safety equipment was too expensive and installing it would drive down quarterly profit statements, you are unlikely ever to be charged with an illegal act, let alone serve a day in prison. The same holds true if you put an experimental drug on the market prematurely to get a jump on the competition. If you are tremendously unlucky (and statistically atypical), and the best efforts of corporate lawyers plus the labyrinthine complexities of hierarchy fail, you may face a fine. In all likelihood its size will be bargained down to an amount totally unrelated to the profits generated by the offence, or the harm and injury it caused (Cohen 1989, 1991). You won't suffer any out-of-pocket loss, because the corporation will pay the fine and, in many cases, the company won't suffer either because the fine will be written off as a tax-deductible business expense. The cost, in other words, will be socialized: the unwary Canadian public will pay the fine through taxes. Since corporate crimes — acts that defraud, injure, and kill — are typically handled under civil or administrative law through regulatory tribunals or specialized courts, it is unlikely that you will ever have to face the degradation, stigma, and publicity signified by the criminal justice process.

If you are unlucky enough to be the victim of corporate crime — perhaps injured in the course of your job, as thousands of Canadians are every year (Association of Workers' Compensation Boards of Canada 2006; Canada 1996; Tucker 1995; Tombs 1996, 2004), or crippled by illegally dumped toxic waste or inadequately tested pesticides or unsafe food — you are in trouble. If you want to pursue the case, you will probably have to spend your own money, and a lot of it, to establish that you were injured.[1] Then you must prove that an illegal act by the company caused the injury. This is a particular challenge if, as is often the case, your illness did not manifest itself until years after exposure. The effects of breathing in asbestos fibres or getting cotton dust on your lungs or toxic chemicals on your reproductive organs characteristically do not show up for decades. If you had been victimized by an unemployed homeless individual through a typical mugging or assault, publicly funded police forces would investigate the offence, build the case, find and charge the suspect, and, in some cases, give you free counselling as well as the opportunity to present a "victim impact statement" to the court.

If you are victimized by a corporation, the police will not be interested. Stealing from employees by paying less than minimum wage, denying them overtime pay, or injuring them through dangerous working conditions may be illegal (though not necessarily), but such acts are not crimes. Give up any hope of receiving legal aid for your lawyer's fees, and be prepared for relentless attacks on your character and credibility from the company's lawyers and public relations officers. Should the company eventually decide to settle your claim, forget about recouping financial losses by selling your story to a newspaper or magazine, because you will probably have to sign a gag order as a condition of settlement. Gag orders prohibit you from talking publicly about the details of your complaint or settlement. While you may find this unfair, corporations love gag orders because they minimize adverse publicity (companies do not want it known that they are bad employers, or that their products and by-products cause injury and death). Gag orders not only prevent other victims from using your case as a precedent but also keep the public from discovering the real costs of production.

Throughout the 1980s and 90s, when criminalization was increasingly sold as the answer to every conceivable social problem, from squeegee kids to noisy parties, business became increasingly *exempt* from legal control. While other critical criminologies examined moral panics and intensified demonization of the poor, corporate crime specialists looked at deregulation, decriminalization, the disappearance of regulatory staff and enforcement capacity. The urge to criminalize, it appeared, stopped at the door of the executive suite. Jail sentences and criminal fines, ideal for the poor and powerless, somehow became ineffective and inappropriate responses to business assault, homicide, and fraud.

> Throughout the 1980s and '90s, when criminalization was increasingly sold as the answer to every conceivable social problem, from squeegee kids to noisy parties, business became increasingly *exempt* from legal control.

A cursory glance at popular culture and mass media, particularly before Enron (2001), provides many examples. Corporate executives whose negligence or greed led to fraud, injury, or death are not described as "criminals." Their offences are not found on the front pages of newspapers. They are not the subject of breathless, finger-pointing *Live at 5* reports. Indignant politicians do not thunder against the irresponsibility of these criminals. The platforms of political parties advocating mandatory prison sentences, "three strikes" laws, and zero tolerance of crime are not directed against those who dump toxic waste in Georgian Bay or market fraudulent stocks. While the media and law present every slip-up by welfare mothers or Black adolescent males as proof of bad character and evil intent, they represent those of corporate executives (much more costly, in dollars and in lives) as accidental and benign. Such offences are portrayed as the unavoidable result of complex organizations or technologies, "failures in communication," or "Acts of God" (God in this case being the "God of Free Markets"). When those excuses are used by traditional criminals — thieves who rationalize robbery by blaming the shopkeeper for price gouging, for example — criminologists label them "Techniques of Neutralization" (Sykes and Matza 1957). When corporations use similar excuses, many academics validate them and even invent new rationales to aid the cause.

It is perfectly acceptable to pay senior executives millions of dollars in salary and stock options while laying off and firing low-level employees with decades of service. It is okay to pollute the water systems of regions the size of France or to create toxic dumps, then shut down and expect government (that is, taxpayers) to clean up the mess. Forcing employees (parents) to be on call seven days a week, or making them appear and disappear on split shifts at the employer's convenience is not criticized. On the contrary, since this practice is more "efficient" — for the employer — it is portrayed as necessary or laudable in mainstream media. Underpaying employees is not only praiseworthy; with the institutionalization of contracting out — auctioning off jobs formerly performed by unionized employees to the employer who delivers the cheapest workforce — it is mandatory to avoid or at least delay plant closures and offshore outsourcing. But underpaying employees or forcing them to work long hours or split shifts has real consequences. It adds stress, impairs the ability to fulfil obligations as a spouse or parent, caregiver, citizen, or volunteer, and it is directly linked to the disintegration of civil, community, and family life. Still, the complicity of corporate Canada is never mentioned, let alone problematized, when business practices, ethics, or (the latest buzzword) "corporate social responsibility" are discussed.

> Increasing corporate power has benefited a select group: over the last twenty years the average Canadian family has experienced a dramatic decline in standard of living, while the top 5 percent have become much richer.

The increase in corporate power has been beneficial for a select group of elites. The gap between the rich and poor has become a chasm: over the last twenty years the average Canadian family has experienced a dramatic decline in standard of living, while the top 5 percent of the population have become much richer (Fudge and Cossman 2002, Statistics Canada 2004). One in six Canadians earned $10 an hour or less in 2000 (Wong 2006). The most needy people

— the unemployed, parents, those in impoverished regions — have suffered most in the race to cut the tax "burdens" of the corporate rich, as (federal) transfer payments and (un)employment insurance, and (provincial) welfare rates have been "reformed" (that is, decreased). In the process Canadian society has become ever more unequal. Taxation is changing from progressive to regressive — that is, rather than distributing money from rich to poor, modern tax systems increasingly do the reverse. Again, the United States leads the way. The poor in America now pay more in tax than they receive back from "the sum of social insurance, pensions and other public transfer payments" (Braithwaite 2005: 20). Business is the chief beneficiary. Enron, for example, paid *no* income tax from 1996–2000; Microsoft's effective tax rate was 1.8%; five Fortune 500 corporations paid no tax at all, *and* received millions in corporate welfare (tax rebates, holidays, etc.) With increased inequality, the lives of the disadvantaged and marginalized, and those living outside metropolitan areas, have become harder. Since NAFTA (the 1988 North American Free Trade Agreement) the Canadian state has lost much of its autonomy, its power to protects its citizens has been jeopardized — and with it the dream of Canada as a just society, a country that puts decency and equality above profit-maximization.

Downsizing Corporate Crime

At the structural/institutional level, downsizing, deregulation, and decriminalization have transformed the administration and enforcement of corporate crime, although the specific mixture varies widely by type of crime. Crimes of production (Naylor 2000) (also called social crimes) (Snider 1993) such as violating environmental or safety standards or hiding negative reports on a new drug, where the motive is to cut production costs, have been "reformed" quite differently from crimes of distribution — acts such as false advertising, combines or bid-rigging offences aimed at increasing revenue. And as we shall see crimes against investors such as inside trading or false financial statements are currently transitioning from deregulation and downsizing to re-criminalization and re-regulation!

Although the focus of this article is on Canada, nothing in a trade-globalized world happens in isolation. As noted above, trade agreements such as NAFTA have tied our economic (and therefore social) policies and practices ever more closely to those of the United States. This is not a partnership of equals. American political and economic elites set agendas for Canadian national and provincial governments. America's belief systems and laws must be considered; U.S. disapproval must be avoided at all costs. In the area of corporate crime, since the United States (along with Margaret Thatcher's Britain) pioneered the corporate counter-revolution and drove it throughout the 1980s and '90s through privatization, downsizing, and massive cuts in corporate income tax, America's influence has been profoundly anti-regulatory.

The intellectual knowledge claims powering this corporate counter-revolution originate in a branch of conservative economics known as neo-liberal theory (Friedman 1962; Posner 1977, 1976). In monetarist economic theory, the corporation is conceptualized as a "nexus of transacting relationships." Government therefore has no legal or moral right to "interfere." Regulatory agencies are seen as costly bureaucratic bodies that empower the "fiscally irresponsible" such as "environ-

> In the area of corporate crime, since the United States pioneered privatization, downsizing, and massive cuts in corporate income tax, America's influence has been profoundly anti-regulatory.

mentalists, compliant regulators and opportunistic politicians," thus causing "inefficient use of resources" and inhibiting "constructive innovation" (Pearce and Tombs 1998: 14–15). Canada's new wave economists of the 1980s (most of them trained in U.S. universities), have made inroads where it counts, in the public service and the senior ranks of government and business. As provincial and federal governments increasingly hired, promoted, and consulted neo-liberal advocates of deregulation, modes of thought which equate state regulation with inefficiency were institutionalized and thereby transformed from mere economic theories into "common sense," into unquestioned truth (Snider 1997; Doern and Wilks 1998a). When such beliefs are reinforced by powerful lobbyists in transnational corporate elites — who have long argued that regulation makes industry uncompetitive, drives stock values down, and discourages investment — most federal and provincial governments jumped on the anti-government, anti-regulatory bandwagon.

Financial Crimes

Competition and Combines

Competition/combines offences are anti-competitive practices designed to inflate profits by conspiring to restrict trade, mergers and monopolies, and by other methods such as predatory pricing, price discrimination, resale price maintenance, or refusal to supply retailers deemed to be selling too cheaply. Canada's *Combines Investigation Act*, passed in 1889, represents an early attempt to proscribe profitable economic practices in the name of citizen protection. Its long history typifies the weaknesses of laws restricting corporate malfeasance: the initial legislation was so flawed that no successful prosecutions against monopoly were *ever* registered; the Act never had sufficient funding or enforcement capability; and every attempt to strengthen it faced powerful business resistance (Snider 1978, 1991). In the post-war period, governments with liberal credentials attempted to reform the Act on several occasions, culminating in the 1969 *Interim Report on Competition Policy* which recommended modest reforms such as tighter controls on price-fixing, bid-rigging, and corporate conspiracies, and expanded rights of access and redress for consumers. For ten years business and the business press lobbied against it. In January 1976, the government caved in. The compromise act abandoned key sections of the 1969 bill but broadened the legislation to cover services such as real estate. It also prohibited practices such as bait and switch, bid-rigging, and pyramid selling and set higher maximum fines for false advertising (Stanbury 1977).

In 1984 the newly elected Conservative government under Prime Minister Brian Mulroney declared war on the "anti-American," "anti-business" practices of the preceding (Liberal) government. A blue-ribbon committee was appointed to revise the *Combines Investigation Act*, with representatives from the Canadian Manufacturers' Association, Chambers of Commerce, and the Grocery Products Manufacturers of Canada — the very groups that had lobbied so long and so successfully against the 1969 changes. Representatives of labour or consumer groups were excluded. (The deputy minister insisted that the Consumers' Association of Canada and "interested academics" were "also consulted.") Not surprisingly, this committee recommended abolishing the *Combines Investigation Act*. Its replacement, the *Competition Act* of 1986, had a different philosophy and three very different goals: to provide a stable and predictable climate for business, to promote competitiveness, and to enhance business prosperity (Canada, Bureau of Competition

Policy 1989). To reach these objectives the Act removed criminal sanctions from the merger/monopoly sector, offered advance approval for mergers or monopolies, and embraced a "compliance-centred" approach. With the exception of a few commentaries in the business press (largely supportive) this major policy U-turn passed into law unnoticed and unremarked (Snider 1993; Stanbury 1986–87; Canada, Bureau of Competition Policy 1989).

Not surprisingly, enforcement levels dropped. From 1986 to 1989 a total of 402 merger files were opened; most were unilaterally approved. Of these 402 files, 26 were "monitored," 7 abandoned, 9 restructured, 5 sent to the Competition Tribunal for judgment, and 2 appealed. By 1995–96 the number of mergers interrogated by government declined to 228. In 1996–97 the number increased to 319, with 23 deemed problematic enough to require follow-up. A total of 369 were slated for review in 1997–98 (Canada 1998). The business press described this modest increase — in reviews, not charges — as "a crackdown by the competition cops" (*Globe and Mail* March 30, 1998: B4). But as the numbers indicate, most mergers were rubber-stamped. Indeed, so few cases went to the Competition Tribunal that front-line staff worried about the image implications of "too many negotiated compromises" (Doern 1995a: 77).

The *Competition Act* is aptly named. It valorizes competition over citizen protection. While the 1986 Act eliminated the greatest legal impediment to successful prosecution in the old *Combines Investigation Act* — the requirement that the Crown prove a proposed monopoly represented "a detriment to the public" — it also eliminated the concept of public benefit. The argument is not that the old *Combines Act* was effective (it was not). However telling civil servants that "public interest" is no longer a criterion when evaluating corporate takeovers, that they must ask only whether the takeover promotes a "competitive economy," is a significant policy change. The obligations of business to civil society have been narrowed to the goals of efficiency and competitiveness. But the Canadian public has never been asked whether it *wants* these objectives — as opposed to full employment or job security — as the goal of government policy. And minimizing public expectations of business conduct facilitates anti-social corporate cultures and values (Jackall 1988).

Deceptive Trade Practices

The Marketing Practices Branch of the *Competition Act* monitors theft through false advertising and price misrepresentation, for example, Exxon's claims that its premium gasoline will reduce automobile maintenance costs; Listerine telling us its mouthwash kills cold-causing germs; Revlon claiming a skin-care product eliminates wrinkles; diet companies promising instant pain-free weight loss (the only part of the body lightened is the wallet). Officially this branch was not affected by the 1986 Act; its mandate, to ensure "the fair treatment of consumers," supposedly remained the same (Doern 1995a: 89), but in fact, within a decade and a half it lost most of its staff, most of its budget, and almost all of its regional offices — which once stretched from sea to sea. Staff who remained underwent compulsory "re-education," presumably to disabuse them of the quaint notion that their jobs were about sanctioning offenders. The problem of deceptive advertising was officially rethought. Despite the huge profits it generates for business, such advertising is now considered to be unintended or accidental, meriting primarily non-criminal and educational remedies. According to the Director of Investigation and Research for the Bureau of Competition Policy, "criminal sanctions may be too severe a response" and criminal prosecution would be "unsatisfactory" (Baldanza, New, and Facey 1995: 3). The criminal has become "the client."

Predictably, levels of prosecution fell here also. Charges for conspiracy, discriminatory and predatory pricing, misleading or deceptive practices, and price maintenance declined from thirty-seven in 1982–84 and thirty-six in 1984–86 to twenty-three in 1986–88, a 33 percent drop. The decrease was not due to rising business standards, or fewer consumer complaints. Only in 1995–96, after all the regional offices had been closed, did the number of annual complaints fall. Thus, while 15,130 false advertising complaints were logged in 1991–92, there were only 6,751 in 1995–96. Similarly, the branch made eighty-two follow-up inquiries in 1991–92, eight in 1995–96. A similar decline occurred in the number of cases referred to the attorney general for criminal prosecution. (The branch cannot lay criminal charges, it can only recommendation that the Department of Justice do so.) From 1991–92 to 1995–96, the number of cases recommended for charges dropped from fifty-five to seven. Prosecutions themselves declined from forty-four to seven, convictions from forty-three to fourteen (Canada 1997: 36).

In spring of 1998 a bill to decriminalize deceptive and fraudulent marketing was announced (*Globe and Mail* May 5, 1998: B3; Canada 1998: 3). The new policy stipulates that criminal charges will only be laid if the Crown can prove a company acted "knowingly or recklessly" (Canada 1999b, March 18). However this "does not represent a softening" in its "enforcement policy," the bureau insisted. (If applied to the laws against marijuana, such an approach would cut drug arrests by two-thirds — and be damned as a very significant "softening" indeed.

Delay and obfuscation continue to characterize enforcement today. When Poonam Puri (2001) examined recent enforcement records under the *Competition Act*, the *Income Tax Act* and selected others she found that historically lax patterns remained. Nor is there evidence of increased efficiency: in June 2003 a complaint was lodged by a coalition of health groups challenging the labelling of cigarettes as "mild" and "light." After three years of inaction, health officials sued the bureau to get it to finish and report its investigation. They lost. On April 14, 2006, the Federal Court said "there is no public legal duty in the [Competition] Act," and "nothing... requiring the bureau to complete an inquiry" (Galloway 2006).

The anti-combines branch, on the other hand, may be moving in the opposite direction. In 2003 Ottawa introduced *Bill C-19*, yet another amendment to the *Competition Act*. This proposed legislation grew out of a Liberal Government discussion paper aimed at "strengthening the civil provisions" of the *Competition Act* by instituting unlimited administrative monetary penalties (Canada 2003: 5). After consulting with business insiders, competition lawyers acting for business, and corporate executives, *Bill C-19* ultimately recommended fines be capped at $10 million for first offences and $15 million for subsequent offences. But in the fall of 2005, with rising public anger over price spikes in oil, the minority Liberal government proposed raising the maximum penalty for "pacts between rivals... likely to lessen competition" from $10 million to $25 million. And it suggested that the Competition Bureau be allowed to "examine an industry and interrogate businesses... even in the absence of evidence... [of] abusive behaviour" (*Globe and Mail*, November 2, 2005: B13). However *Bill C-19* covered only abuse of dominance offences and not, as the discussion paper recommended, other civil non-merger offences. In the end, it did not matter: the bill was never passed and in January 2006, the even more business-friendly Conservatives took office.

The story of competition law in the United States provides an interesting contrast. As in Canada debates over corporate crime are largely between elites — victims' groups and the discourse of closure are notably absent. (You are not a "victim" of false advertising, you are merely gullible — or so law directs you to believe.) But the relevant elites in the United States are split. One group hates monopoly more than it hates government intervention (many

> Criminality and law are not determined by the amount of damage corporate actors do, but by the balance of power between philosophically opposed economic and intellectual elites.

U.S. economists and policy elites fall into this group), and therefore favours competition law. The other hates government more than monopoly (born-again Republicans and business elites fit here) and therefore wants to abolish competition law (Doern 1996: 11–12). As famed neo-liberal economist Gary Becker argues, "It may be preferable not to regulate economic monopolies and to suffer their bad effects, rather than to regulate them and suffer the effects of political imperfections" (1958: 109).The lesson for students of corporate crime is this: criminality and law are not determined by the amount of damage corporate actors do, but by the balance of power between philosophically opposed economic and intellectual elites.[2]

Frauds against the Market

Deregulation, downsizing, and decriminalization have also characterized stock market regulation. Here again, American law is pivotal; policy there has been driven by a gut-level, libertarian distaste for government that is quintessentially American. Thus periodic ideologically based downsizing has consistently recurred despite the fact that it makes no sense from a logical perspective. It is clearly in the interests of capital as a class[3] for government to control the cowboys of capitalism — the fraud artists who sell overpriced shares in fly-by-night companies, owners who systematically "loot" company assets, mining promoters hyping non-existent gold fields. They undermine public confidence in the economic system, which in turn jeopardizes investment capital. Without steady, reliable capital to invest, business cannot grow. However this lesson is regularly forgotten. In the roaring 1990s, when stock prices soared and companies like Worldcom and Enron could do no wrong, the prime regulator of American stock markets, the Securities Exchange Commission, was virtually invisible (Fishman 1998: 41).

With the collapse of stock markets in 2000 and the ensuing crisis of investor confidence, corporate fraud suddenly became big news. The American government officially changed its tune — and its stance on stock market regulation. The *Sarbanes-Oxley Act* of 2002 put a number of stringent new requirements in place, covering corporate auditors, financial reports, corporate counsel (in-firm and outside), senior executives, financial officers, and boards of directors. Canada was quick to follow. In 2004 *Bill C-13* was passed, criminalizing insider trading for the first time, increasing maximum penalties for various types of corporate fraud, and strengthening enforcement capability through specialized police units known as Integrated Market Enforcement Teams (IMET) (Snider 2005).[4] North American governments (in particular) have launched a crackdown on stock market crime. Two decades of government-sponsored deregulation and downsizing, of minimizing the very existence of intentional, profit-maximizing fraud and of forgetting the lessons of the past, have officially ended. Or so it is said.

We should be cautious of such claims. New legislation applies to one small piece of corporate criminal activity, namely stock market/financial crime. No similar rule intensification has taken place with regard to employers' theft from employees. No (re-)criminalization of competition law, hazardous product legislation, or misleading advertising is in evidence (or even under consideration). Environmental, occupational safety, and food and drug agencies, prime victims of the deregulatory craze of the 1990s, are not being strengthened (the reverse, in many cases, as we shall see).[5] All new provisions are aimed at the protection of *investors*, not employees, communities, or pensioners. Investors still comprise a minority of all Canadians (Snider 2005), and a relatively privileged minority at that. And corporate financing of political campaigns, a major factor weakening enforcement and promoting deregulation, has not been reformed, particularly in the United States. Legislation passed in 1995 made it more difficult and more costly for investors to sue investment firms and financial advisors (Fishman 1998: 38). In the 1996 presidential election, twelve securities firms were among the top forty corporate donors, this money went exclusively to corporate-friendly candidates and parties.[6]

Today's flurry of enforcement activity may be merely the latest spike in a regulatory cycle as old as capitalism. A high-profile disaster — a food poisoning crisis in the 1860s (Carson 1970, 1980; Paulus 1974), a mine collapse or ferry accident, an Enron-type fraud or spectacular bankruptcy — typically launches the cycle. The disaster is followed by moral outrage and lofty rhetoric from politicians and community leaders, then by new legislation. The laws proposed are usually much weaker than promised, and are in some cases phrased in ways that make them unenforceable (as with Canada's 1889 anti-combines act discussed earlier). If this hurdle is surmounted and the issue is still politically salient, a flurry of well-publicized charges will follow. Once the media focus has shifted back onto crimes of the powerless (which never takes long), "normal" regulatory patterns resume. This may be "capture," "benign neglect" or, with the advent of neo-liberal doctrines and the subsequent increase in the economic and political power of business, outright deregulation. It is accompanied by downsizing regulatory agencies and, in some areas and countries, by privatizing formerly public enterprises. In the era of the sound bite, this is called "regulatory reform" (Doern and Wilks 1996, 1998; Tombs 1996; Fooks 2003).

Thus it is instructive to consider the collapse of Enron. Enron began as a natural gas pipeline, but management in the 1990s realized there was more money in energy trading (deregulated) than in transporting natural gas (regulated) (Rhodes and Paton 2002: 13). By 2001 it was the seventh largest U.S. corporation in America. In October 2001 Enron first "restated" its earnings to include debits of $525 million and debts of $1.2 billion; earnings for the previous five years were then "restated," and the company filed for bankruptcy on December 2. Four thousand employees lost their jobs and pensions, thousands of investors lost their life savings, and $70 billion in wealth vanished literally overnight (Rhodes and Paton 2002: 10). Middle- and low-level employees were hardest hit because, unlike senior executives, they could not sell their locked-in shares when Enron shares tanked (McBarnet 2005).[7]

Enron used a number of techniques to hide debts and losses and keep stock prices high. Most notable were "Special Purpose Entities," "Special Purpose Vehicles" — 4,300 of them — and "Off Balance Sheet Transactions" designed to "creatively exploit" the rules (McBarnett 2005). If the SEC had been active, and if the state of Texas had not transformed itself into one of the most corporate-friendly states in the union, many of Enron's problems could have been challenged much earlier.[8]

The collapse of Enron, while attracting the most media attention, is anything but an isolated case. The North American Securities Administrators Association has estimated that "Americans lose about $1 million an hour to securities fraud" (Fishman 1998: 41).

The most common frauds are profit overstatements where revenues are inflated or costs and debts hidden through special reserves accounts or similar devices. With regulators paying attention again, hundreds of companies have been forced to "restate" earnings. From 1997–2001 Xerox overstated revenues by $6.4 *billion* (Institute of Management Accountants 2004). Enron, Dynergy, Reliant Resources, El Paso, CMS Energy, and Duke Energy all inflated revenue by recording round-trip trades as sales. Adelphia executives fraudulently excused over $2 billion in bank loans. Sun Microsystems "wrote-down" $1.05 billion of tax reserves (Institute of Management Accountants 2004). It is estimated that North Americans lose $6 billion a year to fraudsters hyping worthless stocks and stealing an average of $6 billion a year, with million-dollar thefts a "near daily occurrence" (Fishman 1998: 40–41). Virtually all major corporations employ questionable spes and spvs and so-called "aggressive tax planning" (Braithwaite 2005: 16) to avoid tax, mislead investors, and maximize revenue. On August 30, 2005, eight accounting executives at the now dominant firm of kpmg (its chief rival Arthur Andersen was forced into bankruptcy in 2002 after criminal charges over Enron were laid), admitted helping corporations evade "billions of dollars in capital gains and income taxes by developing and marketing tax shelters and concealing them from the irs" (McClam 2005). The firm avoided criminal charges by agreeing to pay the Internal Revenue Service $456 million (U.S.) in penalties.

A recent study of administrative sanctions assessed by securities regulators in thirteen jurisdictions across Canada showed much less enforcement activity here (Condon 2003). Administrative sanctions, unlike offences proscribed by the Criminal Code or penal statutes under securities law, were still the penalties of choice, mainly because regulators can act without going through the Justice Department or external courts. Administrative sanctions are therefore the fastest sanctions available to provincial regulators. From 2000–2003, 296 cases were assessed across Canada, and 83 hearings were held (Condon 2003: 419, footnote 4). The majority of cases, 213 in all, were "resolved" with a negotiated settlement (no hearing), where no guilt is admitted, no sanctions assessed. While this may appear lax, there is in fact immense variation in the regulated population and in enforcement capacity, resources, and policy across jurisdictions.

Insider Trading

Insider trading is the latest component of financial crime to be reassessed. Insider trade occurs when those with information that is not available to the public use that information to make trades to generate profits or avoid loss. *Bill C-13* (2002) makes "improper insider trading" a criminal offence with a maximum fourteen-year prison term.[9] Maximum penalties for "market manipulation" were doubled from five to ten years. "Tipping," defined as "knowingly conveying inside information to another person with knowledge that it might be used to secure a trading advantage or illegal benefit," becomes either indictable (maximum prison term of five years) or summary (fines assessed) (Mackay and Smith 2004: 5).

A 1999 investigation of insider trading in Canada, by journalists, not regulators, revealed that "of the 28 friendly mergers or acquisitions announced between July 31, 1998, and July 31, 1999, valued at more than $150 million, the share price of almost half rose by more than 25 percent between the times the companies began talking and the night before the deal was disclosed" (*Globe and Mail* Oct. 18, 1999: B1). In many deals, shares rose by 50 percent or more, while stock prices overall, as measured by the Toronto Stock

Exchange index (and other relevant indicators) rose by 2 to 3 percent during the same period. Clearly, some inside parties were making fortunes by abusing their trust, at the expense of all "outside" investors. Until this fraud was publicized, neither the Ontario Securities Commission nor the Toronto Stock Exchange had taken any public regulatory action.[10]

Given the political complications of policy, it is impossible to predict future enforcement patterns here. Although stock market fraud poses a serious threat to investor confidence, and thus threatens to destroy exchange relationships which are the very foundation of capitalism, the religion of deregulation has historically remained strong, particularly in the world's only superpower. Financial elites and legislators in the U.S. have historically fought government regulation of business if it could not be turned to their advantage, and have championed measures to deregulate as soon as the media heat was off. Every country that trades with the U.S. must find a way to resist or accommodate this. Backlash against Sarbanes-Oxley in the U.S. is already strong, with local and state Chambers of Commerce and business media accusing the U.S. government of conducting "witch hunts that imperil the American dream." Cries that "draconian" new regulatory burdens will destroy the New York Stock Exchange are ongoing (*New York Times*, February 10, 2002: 3–1, *Globe and Mail*, June 1, 2002: F8).

Social Crimes

Occupational Health and Safety

- "Death Toll Climbs at Refinery: Two additional workers died yesterday after a fireball erupted in a 133-foot tower at a Tosco oil refinery." Three were killed in this incident at the Martinez plant (California). One died, and twenty-six other workers were injured in a fire a year earlier. The company was fined $277,000 (*San Diego Union-Tribune* Feb. 25, 1999).
- Young employees are particularly likely to die or be injured on the job. In February 1999 an eighteen-year-old student in Burlington, Ontario, died in a commercial dough mixer, the employer served three weeks in jail. Later that month a sixteen-year-old died the same way in a Toronto bakery; a nineteen-year-old Tilbury worker was killed because his machine lacked proper guards; and a twenty-year-old man from Milton was killed when he became entangled in a metal lathe (*Globe and Mail* July 19, 2000: A11).
- Five workers in a van owned by TIPS, a Toronto-based temporary staffing agency, were killed in a collision with a GO train in June of 2002. The agency, its president and a vice-president pleaded guilty to charges under the no-fault Workplace Safety and Insurance Act and paid a record $1 million fine (Perry 2003)
- In a 2004 study of safety at workplaces in the world's richest nations, Canada's rate of workplace fatalities was 7 per 100,000, tied for first place. Canada's record for reducing workplace fatalities over the last twenty years was the worst (CBC News online 2006).

The resurgent power of business is glaringly obvious when we look at offences against employees and the environment. The basic tenets of workplace health and safety law, the minimum standards that established a floor beneath which workplace conditions were not allowed to fall, took centuries of struggle and protest to achieve (Tucker 1996; Snider 1993). By the end of the 1970s most industrialized democratic countries had put in place a network of measures to protect employees from dangerous workplace conditions. Ontario's first workers' compensation laws based on no-fault were established in 1897 and 1914; the Canada Labour Safety Code went into effect in 1968, and in 1972 Saskatchewan laid the groundwork by guaranteeing workers the right to participate in health and safety committees, refuse unsafe work, and be informed about workplace hazards (CBC News online 2006). Ventilation levels, light and temperature levels in workplaces, minimum wages, maximum hours, regulations on work breaks, overtime pay, and safety equipment (guards on machines and air quality monitors) were laid out. Government inspectors, designated union officers and company safety personnel were responsible for enforcement.

Even in their 1970s heyday regulation was far from strict: it varied from province to province and sector to sector (Snider 1991). But these laws represented significant ideological progress: it was not easy to get government or industry to recognize that the most profitable business practices were often the most dangerous, or that revered, church-going "captains of industry" caused horrendous economic and social damage, and death (Bliss 1974; Carson 1980). Such knowledge had to be argued into consciousness, crystallized through language (named), documented statistically by "experts," passed into law, then monitored to ensure enforcement. These battles required decades of blood, sweat, and tears by a range of social activists — religious organizations, social workers, and labour politicians — who got leverage by questioning the morality of putting profit goals above the lives and health of employees. Newly organized unions risked members' lives and jobs with protest strikes. Although business resistance never entirely disappeared, the employees' cause was aided by studies showing that preventing accidents or adopting safer techniques was more cost-effective than compensating injured employees. And, sadly, regular workplace disasters kick-started new rounds of legislation. However while virtually every employer supported the idea of workplace safety, they hated the fact that such laws challenged their ownership rights, gave bargaining power to employees, and cut into profit levels with no corresponding benefit to the employer/owner (Carson 1980).

Throughout the 1980s, direct attacks on health and safety laws in Canada were rare, largely because private and public-sector unions were vigilant. However, with the passage of the *Regulatory Efficiency Act* of 1992, the federal government began downsizing in earnest, as did Alberta and Ontario when neo-liberal governments were elected there. This reduced the size and power of public-service unions. By 1998 deficit reduction was the goal, downsizing, decriminalization, and deregulation the means. Private-sector unions were downsized throughout the 1980s and 1990s by NAFTA, the globalization of capital, union-busting laws, and the collapse of heavy industry and manufacturing in Canada. As the president of the Canadian Auto Workers pointed out: "There are not enough inspectors [now] to monitor even 1 percent of the workplaces" (*Globe and Mail* July 19, 2000: A11).

However, it is still politically difficult to lobby publicly against health and safety regulation. In the value systems of most Canadians, life and health are more important than profit maximization. The compromise "solution" is self-regulation. When instituted in the workplace, self-regulation allows workers themselves to negotiate their working conditions. Working in teams they take responsibility for determining their pace of work and for reaching consensus on production goals, within management-determined parameters. In theory this system rewards productive employees, penalizes shirkers, facilitates flexibility in the workplace, and avoids "rigid" state regulation. It looks like a win-win-win situation: cheaper for government (fewer inspectors required), cheaper for employers (market forces promote competition, peer pressure promotes productivity), empowering for workers.

On this basis self-regulation became the new common sense. Unfortunately reality is different from theory. In real life the power differences inherent in the employee-employer contract determine the bargaining power of each. Within the workplace, low-level employees have less power than supervisors and managers. And while employees may have legislated rights to know about workplace risks, and to refuse unreasonable demands, exercising these rights can cost them their promotion chances, the goodwill of their supervisors and their job. (While employers are not allowed to fire workers for this reason, there are many ways to get rid of low-level staff.) Moreover the same neo-liberal tenets that backed self-regulation also championed cuts in social programs that reduced the ability of employees to survive without job income. Unemployment insurance, mother's allowance, pensions, and welfare cuts have made employees much more desperate for employment than employers are for workers.

The results are all too apparent in the de-coupled, outsourced transnational workplace of the new millennium. With teams setting production quotas "by consensus," the meaning of "hazard" has been redefined, resulting in more "reasonable" (employer-friendly) definitions of risk (Tombs 1996: 325; Walters et al. 1995). Dangerous conditions that would be expensive to fix, in other words, are less likely to be identified as hazards. With state regulatory agencies downsized, business may find it can afford less vigilance, especially if instituting safer conditions costs more than paying worker compensation fees to government, which is often the case. (Employers pay fees according to the number, nature, and cost of claims filed). Where state watchdogs do exist, workers who have "agreed" on safety standards are on shaky grounds if they get injured — why didn't they protest at the time?[11] Although compensation is supposed to be awarded on a no-fault basis, it is easier for employers and compensation boards to discount claims by blaming the employee. This presumably unintended effect of self-regulation has not escaped notice, nor is it lamented in corporate boardrooms.[12]

> It is still politically difficult for corporations to lobby publicly against health and safety regulations. The compromise "solution" is self-regulation. And while employees may have legislated rights to know about workplace risks, and to refuse unreasonable demands, exercising these rights can cost them their promotion chances, the good will of their supervisors, and their jobs.

More traditional crimes against employees also continue, exacerbated by contracting out and the resulting cut-throat competition to deliver the cheapest work force. For example, when TIPS, the agency involved in a van/train crash that killed five, was investigated, it was discovered that the company had also filed fake invoices claiming that the van driver was an independent operator not an employee. If accepted, the survivor benefits of the dependants of those killed would have been jeopardized — and the fees TIPS was assessed by the Workers' Compensation Board would not have increased. The company also pled guilty to underreporting its monthly payroll and submitting misleading information on the number of injuries suffered by other employees (Perry 2003). It is unlikely any of these offences would have come to light if the accident had not occurred. Robbing employees by altering automated systems that record the number of hours employees have worked is also widespread. Top managers at several major corporations in the United States — the Family Dollar discount chain, Pep Boys, an auto parts and repair chain, Taco Bell, Kinko, Wal-Mart, and Toys R Us have all been charged with "time shaving," "secretly deleting hours to cut [employees'] paychecks and fatten [employers'] bottom line (Greenhouse, *New York Times,* April 4, 2004: B1). According to experts on compensation, "the illegal doctoring of hourly employees' time records is far more prevalent than most Americans believe" (Greenhouse, *New York Times,* April 4, 2004: B1).

However, there are signs that this deregulatory cycle may also be changing. In the fall of 2003, after twenty years of promises, the Government of Canada introduced Bill *C-45,* an amendment to the Criminal Code that broadens the conditions for attributing criminal liability to organizations and their representatives. It introduces a legal duty for "all persons directing work to take reasonable steps to ensure the safety of workers and the public," and, in an effort to get tougher sentences, outlines factors judges must consider when sentencing. This bill had its origins in the Westray mine disaster of 1993, where twenty-six miners in New Glasgow, Nova Scotia died in a mine that had repeatedly been established to be unsafe (Glasbeek 2002; McMullan and Hinze 1999). The owners of the mine escaped all criminal liability.[13]

Although it is too early to predict the effects and effectiveness of this law, pundits are claiming it will revolutionize corporate criminal liability and end the lenient treatment accorded corporations in the past (Mann 2004). On April 19, 2004, the first charge under *C-45* was laid. A sixty-eight-year-old contractor associated with a small construction company was charged with one count of criminal negligence causing death after a trench collapsed at the site of a private house renovation, killing one employee (Media Release, York Regional Police, August 26, 2004).

Crimes against the Environment

Those seeking to rectify (or at least slow down) the environmental disasters associated with industrial production and mass consumerism have seen slow progress indeed. While some catastrophes have been averted — banning DDT allowed thousands of threatened bird species to recover — legions of new threats such as global warming and ozone holes have emerged, and others such as acid rain have reappeared. The result is species extinction and the destruction of entire ecosystems on such a scale that the survival of the planet is at risk. Canada and the United States have a particularly egregious environmental record. History provides a partial explanation: for three centuries the abundant, "free" natural resources of the New World gave North American industry a key competitive advantage over European countries. (The rights, claims, and lives of First Nations peoples were quickly extinguished.) And it goes deeper — the right to hunt, fish, clear forests, and plunder the natural world at will is engrained in the North American psyche. In Europe, by contrast, centuries of intensive cultivation had exterminated many species by 1600, and land-based aristocracies had ancient monopoly privileges over the use of rivers, game, and land. By the time Europe's new industrial capitalists had overcome these disadvantages, the basis for American dominance had been established.

Environmental legislation, moreover, is comparatively new, originating in the protest movements of the 1970s. Pollution Probe was formed in 1969, the Canadian Environmental Law Association in 1970, Greenpeace in 1971. Nine new statutes were passed between 1968 and 1972 and a new senior portfolio, the Ministry of the Environment was established. Several provinces followed suit (Schrecker 1989).

Laws protecting the environment and outlawing certain uses of it faced fierce industry resistance because, like laws on occupational health and safety, they increased the costs of production and threatened the ownership rights of employers. However, there are distinct differences between these two social crimes. In the area of occupational health and safety, employers and employees generally agree that large-scale resource-extracting industrial production is morally good as well as economically essential. Workers want the jobs it promises, employers want the profits. Many environmentalists and "deep" ecologists contest both the morality and the viability of this premise.

They question the hegemonic capitalist assumption that every river, tree, animal, idea, and genome must be put up for sale and argue that the goal of continuous economic growth is unsustainable and catastrophic. Nor do they think the problem is amenable to a quick technological fix.

> Canada and the United States have a particularly egregious environmental record. Employers and employees generally agree that large-scale resource-extracting industrial production is morally good as well as economically essential.

A second distinctive feature of environmental crime resides in the power of its advocates. The main pro-regulatory forces pushing occupational health and safety are employees, workers in primary and secondary industry and unions. As we have seen, all three lost power throughout the 1980s and '90s — union membership declined, resource extraction and manufacturing sectors were eclipsed by knowledge-based industries and the service sector, and with globalization employees as a class lost power to employers. Supporters of environmental regulation, on the other hand, are generally well-organized and media-savvy, with a strong upper-middle-class base and extensive financial resources. This has meant heavy resistance to downsizing, decriminalization, and deregulatory environmental agencies. While never powerful enough to reverse neo-liberal agendas, environmentalists often mobilized enough resistance to slow it down.

American conservationists, for example, have repeatedly succeeded in turning back government attempts to vitiate the Environmental Protection Agency. In 1981 newly elected President Reagan appointed an EPA head and a cabinet secretary with explicit instructions to "make the EPA more friendly to industry" (Barcott 2004). Both were forced to resign. In 1994 Republicans under Newt Gingrich came to office determined to weaken the Clean Water Act and EPA Superfund initiatives. Environmental protests forced them to back off. The present president, George Bush, has been more successful, eliminating requirements that would have forced power companies to install new pollution-control devices when plants are upgraded, and vitiating environmental rules in many other areas. But this had to be done "quietly and subtly by… regulatory changes and bureaucratic directives out of the public gaze" (Barcott 2004).

Despite Canada's dependence on pollution-producing resource-extracting industry, wilderness, wildlife, and environmental protection are key Canadian values (Schrecker 2000). As late as 1995 backbench members of the Liberal government went against their own party to demand that the 1988 *Environmental Protection Act* be strengthened, when a mandated review of the Act revealed the pitiful state of the environmental ministry. An all-party review committee pointed out that only twenty-eight investigators and thirty-one inspectors had been appointed to enforce federal environmental law throughout the entire country. Environment Canada was found to be ignoring its own policy directives requiring officials to follow a "strict compliance" policy, and practising a permissive "compliance promotion" policy instead (Canada 1995). From 1988 to 1995, 66 prosecutions were commenced, producing 51 convictions, an average of 7.2 per year. The most common "punishments" were warnings: in 1993–94, for example, 120 warnings and 3 prosecutions resulted from 1,548 inspections. Legislation setting out criteria for compulsory environmental assessments, supposedly required before development permits for major projects were issued, was passed in 1992 but not proclaimed into law until 1994. And then the legislation, the *Environmental Assessment Act* (EAA), lacked standards, penalties, and specifications for conducting public reviews. The recommendations produced after a review could be overruled by cabinet. The qualifications of the "experts" who would testify were not specified, which let companies shop for scientists willing to support industry claims. Some were reportedly selling their services to the highest bidder, or redoing reports to make them acceptable to the industrial sponsor (Nikiforuk 1997: 17). The Act, in other words, is a disaster (Nikiforuk 1997: 17).

Similarly, despite ongoing resistance, Environment Canada was continuously downsized throughout the 1990s. Budgets were cut by 30 percent in 1992–93 and in 1994–95, dropping from $705 million to $507 million. Staff numbers fell from 10,000 in 1992–93 to under 4,000 in 1994–95. The Department of Environment was reduced to a junior ministry, further weakening its clout and share of government money (*Globe and Mail* May 27, 1998: A3; July 30, 1997: A3; Aug. 19, 1997: A1).

We see in this example the importance of changing the hearts and minds of (senior) civil servants. By appointing and promoting hard-core apostles of neo-liberalism throughout the 1980s and 1990s, belief systems in the senior ranks of the federal government were transformed. By the mid-90s most senior civil servants were convinced (though they would express it in the sophisticated languages of economics and political science) that government regulation was useless, that command-and-control approaches were both inefficient and inappropriate, and that government had to step back and allow commerce and trade to create prosperity. Activists were denigrated as "special interests." "Voluntary codes," not state regulation, would produce a win-win: prosperity *and* sustainability. Well-funded business organizations such as the Business Council on National Issues (BCNI) worked ceaselessly with the chemical, forestry, and pulp and paper industries, and through media and websites, to ensure that their anti-government, anti-state messages were heard. And heard they were, by government insiders and cabinet ministers (Doern and Conway 1994; Doern 1995b; Leiss et al. 1996).

> By the mid-90s most senior civil servants were convinced that government regulation was useless and that government had to step back and allow commerce and trade to create prosperity.

Or consider the poisoned water disaster in Walkerton, Ontario, which killed seven people and injured an estimated 2,250 more in the spring of 2000 (Snider 2004). The neo-liberal Conservative government of Mike Harris, elected in 1995, was preceded by the left-leaning New Democratic Party of Bob Rae, in power from 1991 to 1995. Under the NDP Ontario's Ministry of the Environment was one of the most effective in the country. From 1987–88 to 1992–94 it prosecuted from 200 to 300 cases per year, often with spectacular success (Gallon 1996). When the Conservatives took power, 725 enforcement and investigation officials were let go. Annual charges dropped from 1,640 in 1994, to 724 in 1996. Prosecutions in some regions dropped by 74 percent; from 1995 to 1996 alone, fines were down 57 percent. The average pollution fine dropped from $3.6 million in 1992 to $1.2 million in 1997.[14] The provincial government's overall spending on the environment fell by almost two-thirds. By 2000 the ministry was employing 41 percent fewer people than it did in 1994–95 (58 percent fewer if contract and temporary job assignments are included) (*Toronto Star* July 8, 2000: K1, K3). The number of water treatment plants inspected annually declined from 75 percent in 1993–94 to 24 percent in 1998–99 and 29 percent in 1999–2000. From 1992 to 1997 the capital budget fell by 81 percent, and overall charges decreased by 50 percent (from 2,163 to 954). None of this came to public attention until the Walkerton disaster and subsequent inquiry revealed that E. coli bacteria from improperly treated water killed at least six people and injured hundreds more.

Newspaper headlines reflect the results:

- "Pollution Controls 'Terrible' Failure" (*Windsor Star*, Dec. 9, 2004: A10). A joint report by Environmental Defence and the Canadian Environmental Law Association states that in 2002, the latest year for which data are available, more than 4 billion kilograms of pollutants were released into Canada's air, soil, and water: this represents a 49 percent increase since 1995.
- "Canadian Factories Fingered in NAFTA Pollution Study" (*Globe and Mail* Oct. 7, 1998: A12). Government downsizing and lack of enforcement have created a situation in which Canadian firms were much more likely than their U.S. counterparts to dump liquid pollutants directly into lakes and rivers rather than divert them to sewage-treatment plants. The top Canadian polluter, Co-Steel Lasco Ltd. of Whitby, Ontario, a steel recycling plant, dumped more than 6,000 tonnes of zinc and zinc compounds into Lake Ontario
- "Criminal Polluters Finding Canada the Promised Land" (*Globe and Mail* March 23, 1999: A7). Federal environmental charges dropped 78 percent, from a never impressive high of forty-five charges in 1992 to eleven in 1997 and ten in 1998. Over the 1988–98 decade no one was sent to jail for breaking either the *Environmental Protection Act* or the *Fisheries Act*.
- "Deadbeat Polluters owe Millions: Guilty Parties in some of Ontario's most Outrageous Environmental Offences have yet to Pay a Penny or Spend a Minute In Jail" (Jaimet, *Ottawa Citizen* Apr. 22, 2002: A1, A10). Ontario's auditor reports that $10 million in environmental fines remain unpaid, much of which may ultimately be deemed "uncollectible."
- "Pollution Plan Leaves Experts Unimpressed" (Lalonde, *Montreal Gazette*, May 29, 2005: A2). While lead emissions are strictly regulated in the U.S., Canada has no specific regulations. Canada's environment minister, Stephane Dion, acknowledged the need for further action but stopped short of promising specific standards for lead emissions. Lead emissions result in irreversible developmental and nervous-system damage especially for those living in close proximity to smelters and other industries that release the toxic chemical into the air.

The Results of the Corporate Counter-Revolution

In recent decades an ideological revolution — a corporate counter-revolution — has succeeded in persuading key elites in Canadian society that potentially profitable corporate acts are not wrong. Therefore, although they cause many more injuries and deaths, and much greater financial loss than traditional assault and theft, they are not defined as acts that merit criminal status. The corporate counter-revolution has been strikingly effective. It has transformed the landscape and meaning of corporate crime and reshaped government, business, and law.

Corporate power increasingly defines how we think, as well as how we act. Citizens, now conceptualized as consumers or clients, have increasingly bought into worldviews relentlessly promoted by business (and conducive to profit maximization) — namely, that self-esteem and personal fulfilment, the ultimate goals in life, depend on acquiring the "right" consumer goods and presenting the "right" image. This individualistic goal pits individuals against each other and erodes civil society. One result is the increased reluctance of Canadians,

> The corporate counter-revolution has been strikingly effective. It has transformed the landscape and meaning of corporate crime and reshaped government, business, and law.

particularly the elite groups that command media and government attention, to pay taxes or, indeed, to pay for any social program from which they do not derive immediate benefit. Another is the glorification of business (seen as providing all our "stuff"), and the allied demonization of politics (seen as taking income away). This has produced electoral apathy and an increasing percentage of non-voting citizens.

However, governments have been often been eager participants in the corporate counter-revolution. Even would-be resistant social democratic and green parties have been forced to commit to government downsizing in the face of declining government revenues and high deficits — produced in large part by massive corporate tax cuts (Braithwaite 2005). Demands for individual tax cuts, spearheaded by elites through right-wing parties such as the Reform/Canadian Alliance (now Stephen Harper's Conservatives) have also won favour, not surprisingly since the average middle-class taxpayer now pays a higher share of income to government than any multinational corporation (Braithwaite 2005).[15] As a result Canadian governments, like governments throughout the Western world, have redefined their responsibilities, obligations, and capacities. This has led to spending cuts in everything from welfare rates and education (provincial responsibilities) to (un)employment benefits and fiscal policy (federal responsibilities).

Government's historic responsibility to help the marginalized and desperate has disappeared, but its obligation to punish the powerless has been reinforced — incarceration rates for crimes of individuals increased throughout the 1990s, even though crime rates were falling (Canada 2000). By decriminalizing and deregulating profitable acts that were once seen as corporate crime, by downsizing regulatory agencies and cutting regulatory staff, and by signing trade agreements that cede sovereignty to global trading blocks, provincial and federal governments have consistently surrendered the power to protect citizens from corporate excess, fraud, and abuse of power.

However, there are signs that we may be entering a new phase. The ideological, political, and economic power of corporate capitalism is increasingly questioned by activists throughout the world, albeit with little obvious success thus far. In Canada, as documented in this chapter, new laws have been passed to address stock market fraud and tighten the criminal liability of organizations. New technologies with the ability to penetrate corporate boardrooms have been developed, technological markers can now monitor insider trades as they happen and the retrievable quality of even deleted email messages has revolutionized evidence gathering. Newly vigorous investigative media have begun to publicize the trials and sentencing of high profile executives, and perfected rating systems to rank companies on corporate social responsibility. Measures are afoot to further publicize executive salaries. Using new internet-based tools as well as traditional methods, environmental and labour activists increasingly question government subservience to corporate agendas.

Specificities matter. The dynamics that shape the passage and enforcement of statutes on environmental crime are different from those shaping occupational health and safety, stock market fraud, false advertising, or competition offences. And there are differences within each category as well — problems of global warming require different treatment from pulp mill pollution; promoting dangerous pharmaceuticals cannot be handled the same way as altering the time records of workers. One conclusion, however, is obvious: countering corporate power through ideological, political, and legal struggle, inside and outside business and government, is crucial. Without intensified resistance, corporate crime will continue to be downsized and ignored.

DISCUSSION QUESTIONS

1. Laureen Snider argues that the state in the 1980s and '90s lacks both the ability and the desire to regulate the anti-social acts of corporations. Explain this position, providing examples of the disappearance of state law over corporate crime.

2. Do you agree that the state today (2006) is "cracking down" on corporate crime? What evidence is there to support this? To refute it?

3. Evidence in this chapter indicates that there has been a corporate counter-revolution, which has persuaded the Canadian public that the profitable acts of corporations are not wrong even when they cause more death and loss than traditional theft and assault. Explain how the Canadian public came to accept these ideas. What were its consequences?

4. Discuss and evaluate the evidence that criminal corporate liability is now being rethought.

5. What are the dominant types of resistance discussed in this chapter? Analyze the significance and potential of three of these.

6. Who are the main victims of financial and social corporate crime?

7. With downsizing, the Marketing Practices Branch which handles theft through false advertising, has lost most of its staff and budget. One consequence has been the redefinition of deceptive advertising from "criminal" to primarily accidental. Discuss and assess this shift, including at least three of your own examples of deceptive advertising.

8. Self-regulation is the dominant rationale under which the deregulation of health and safety standards in Canadian workplaces has occurred. 1) Explain how elites and intellectual "experts" argued for the adoption of self-regulation. 2) Discuss the problematic assumptions and consequences of this type of workplace regulation, and suggest alternatives.

GLOSSARY OF TERMS

Corporation: the legal form of organization for both capitalist and public enterprises. Private-sector corporations are typically administered by a managerial elite and financed through stock offered to the public through stock exchanges.

Decriminalization: the process of removing criminal law from a particular activity or group of activities.

Deregulation: the process of removing regulatory or administrative law from a particular activity or group of activities.

Downsizing: firing or laying off regulatory officials. When massive or ongoing, it refers to the process by which regulatory agencies are rendered incapable of realizing their mandate to enforce certain bodies of legislation.

Neo-liberalism: a body of ideas in which the rights of the individual are maximized, and those of the society, collectivity, or state are minimized or denied.

Regulatory Agency: a specialized body of officers of the state, such as inspectors, responsible for ensuring compliance with a particular statute governing a specified set of activities. For example, regulatory agencies are charged with enforcing regulations on false advertising, water safety, and stock market trades.

SUGGESTED READINGS

Glasbeek, Harry. 2002. *Wealth by Stealth.* Toronto: Between the Lines Press.

Pearce, Frank, and Steve Tombs. 1998. *Toxic Capitalism: Corporate Crime and the Chemical Industry.* Aldershot, UK: Ashgate/Dartmouth.

Snider, Laureen. 1993. *Bad Business: Corporate Crime in Canada.* Toronto: Nelson.

Comish, Shaun. 1993. *The Westray Tragedy: A Miner's Story.* Halifax: Fernwood Publishing.

Rosoff, Stephen, Henry Pontell, and Robert Tillman. 2004. *Profit Without Honor: White-Collar Crime and the Looting of America.* Third edition. Engelwood Cliffs, NJ: Prentice Hall.

Wood, S. 2006. "Voluntary Environmental Codes and Sustainability." In B. Richardson and S. Wood (eds.), *Environmental Law for Sustainability.* Oxford: Hart.

NOTES

1. If injured on the job you may, or may not, have access to workers' compensation. If you do your injuries will be assessed by medical staff, and if your case fits into their guidelines you may receive payments and/or treatment while you are deemed unable to work. Your right to sue the employer for damages is usually forfeited by this process.
2. The point here is not to praise competition laws. Economists are divided on whether government intervention to create a "true" competitive environment is good for the economy or not (Becker 1958; Doern and Wilks 1998a, 1998b). The often-idealized *laissez-faire* capitalism of the eighteenth century cannot be resuscitated. The evidence is also mixed on the issue that should be the primary criterion for policy decisions: namely, is a more competitive, less monopolistic economy better for the majority of employees, consumers, and citizens? In the post-war period some oligopolies, under union pressure, did deliver job security and decent wages to employees (Simpson 1989). That era was killed by merger manias of the 1980s. The 1990s combined an increased economic concentration with the elimination of well-paid jobs and job security, allied with short-term management, the globalization of stock markets and the pressure to report profits every quarter (Zey 1993).
3. Of course, capital-as-a-class does not have intentions. People have motives, structures do not. The acts of capital are made through the individual decisions of thousands of corporate executives, stock traders, and investors. But these individual acts are not random, they are intentionally taken to maximize share prices, profit levels, and productivity. This means that other players must be persuaded to put up risk capital, an enterprise that is collectively imperilled if trust in systems of exchange disappear.
4. The legislation came into force June 4, 2004.
5. Where downsizing and deregulation caused massive disasters, as in the poisoned water disaster

in Walkerton, Ontario, substantial "upsizing" has occurred (Snider 2004).

6. Public trust in exchange markets is pivotal to world capitalism, and the United States is known throughout the financial world for its tough enforcement practices. Some frauds have been prosecuted, and massive-appearing fines pronounced. (Fines typically amount to a small fraction of the profits amassed.) For example, the Drexel Burnham scandal ended with $650 million in fines and a ten-year prison sentence for the CEO, Mike Milken, who served four years on charges of insider trading and failure to disclose information (Zey 1993). The Bre-X scandal in Canada (after it was discovered in May 1997 that samples documenting the "world's richest gold find," in Busang, Indonesia, were salted) led to regulation tightening at the Ontario Securities Commission and the Toronto Stock Exchange, but the brokers who touted the stock and then sold out before it collapsed have not yet been sanctioned or held accountable.

7. Ironically the financial scandal of the preceding decade, the most financially costly corporate crime before Enron, the U.S. Savings and Loan crisis, was also enabled by deregulation. In the early 1980s, laws restricting owners and managers of Savings and Loan companies ("thrifts") to stable, "blue chip" stocks were repealed, as were requirements that thrift owners and managers maintain a minimum percentage of assets as capital reserves (a cushion against investment losses). "Hot deals" (land flips, nominee loans, and reciprocal lending), "looting" (diverting investments to executive salaries, bonuses, yachts, etc.), and falsified records proliferated. By the late '80s, 284 thrifts had failed, overall losses exceeded $500 billion, $12,420,065 per institution, an estimated $5,000 per household. Eerily, given today's scandals, every major accounting firm in the United States but one was implicated (Zey 1993; *New York Times* June 10, 1990; *Observer* April 8, 1990; Calavita, Pontell, and Tillman 1997).

8. On May 25, 2006, Enron CEOs Kenneth Lay and Jeff Skilling were convicted by a jury in Houston Texas of multiple counts of fraud. Sentencing will take place September 11, 2006. Lay died before his sentencing, and his conviction was vacated by the judge. Skilling was sentenced to twenty-four years and four months in prison and a $45 million fine. His case is under appeal and he is serving his sentence in a minimum security prison.

9. Michael Watson, head of enforcement at the OSC, argued before the Senate Banking Committee that this wording would make successful prosecution impossible, forcing the Crown to prove suspects knew the information was not publicly disclosed, and sought to take advantage of this fact. He recommended "trading with knowledge of" inside information instead. However no wording changes were made.

10. By spring 2002 an investigation was continuing into the Royal Bank of Canada (Canada's largest bank) and its pension fund managers at RT Capital Management, accused of artificially boosting a stock price by running a number of late-day trades through the Toronto Stock Exchange.

11. Of course employees bear some responsibility for workplace accident and injury. Workers, like other human beings, smoke tobacco and abuse legal and illegal drugs. They may be careless or stupid. Machismo subcultures — real men take risks, wimps wear safety helmets and whine about coal dust — prevent safety consciousness (Glasbeek and Tucker 1992).

12. Again, one must be careful with overgeneralizing. Self-regulation has not produced universal disasters everywhere, and state regulation has not been universally destroyed. In the chemical and nuclear industries, for example, a combination of disasters, lawsuits, and high insurance costs, following accidents in chemical plants such as Bhopal in 1984 and nuclear disasters such as Chernobyl in the (former) Soviet Union and Three Mile Island in the United States, drove up insurance and liability costs for manufacturers. Public fear drove politicians to enact new regulations in some countries. This combination has apparently produced higher safety standards within these industries (Pearce and Tombs 1998).

13. For the purpose of this chapter, we will also refer to *Bill C-45* as the *Westray Bill*.

14. Access to information is also a casualty, and the real figures may be lower still. The Canadian Institute for Environmental Law and Policy states that fines totalled only $955,000.

15. Not only that, a 1999 decision by the Supreme Court of Canada allows companies to treat

"virtually all fines and penalties," from health and safety to environmental, as business expenses and deduct them as a business cost (Boyd 2003).

REFERENCES

Association of Workers' Compensation Boards of Canada. 2006. "Fatalities by Province." Accessed through "Dying for a Job," CBC News online. April 22. Available at <http://www.cbc.ca/news/background/workplace-safety/dyingforajob.html> accessed July 2007.

Baldanza, A., D. New, and B. Facey. 1995. *Competition and Marketing Law Bulletin, The Bulletin of the Competition and Marketing Law Group.* Toronto: Fasken Campbell Godfrey.

Barcott, Bruce, 2004. "Changing the Rules." *New York Times Magazine* April 4: 39-45.

Becker, G. 1958. "Competition and Democracy." *Journal of Law and Economics* 1, (October).

_____. 1985. *Human Capital.* Chicago: University of Chicago Press.

Bliss, M. 1974. *A Living Profit: Studies in the Social History of Canadian Business.* Toronto: McClelland and Stewart.

Boyd, David, 2003. "Thanks to a Tax Loophole, Corporate Crime Does Pay." *Globe and Mail,* March 23: B2.

Braithwaite, John, 2005. *Markets in Vice, Markets in Virtue.* Annadale, Australia: Federation Press.

Calavita, K., H. Pontell, and R. Tillman. 1997. *Big Money Crime.* Berkeley: University of California Press.

Canada. 1995. *It's About Our Health: Towards Pollution Prevention.* Report of the House of Commons Standing Committee on the Environmental and Sustainable Development. Ottawa: House of Commons #81. Ottawa: Environment Canada.

_____. 1997. *Annual Report of the Director of Investigation and Research, Competition Act* (for the year ending March 31, 1996). Ottawa: Industry Canada.

_____. 1998. *Annual Report of the Director of Investigation and Research, Competition Act* (for the year ending March 31, 1997). Ottawa: Industry Canada.

_____. 1999. *Annual Report of the Director of Investigation and Research, Competition Bureau.* Available at http://strategis.ic.gc.ca

_____. 2000. *Juristat, Crime Statistics 1999.* Ottawa: Canadian Centre for Justice Statistics.

Canada, Bureau of Competition Policy. 1989. *Competition Policy in Canada: The First Hundred Years.* Ottawa: Consumer and Corporate Affairs.

Carson, W. 1970. "White Collar Crime and the Enforcement of Factory Legislation." *British Journal of Criminology* 10: 383–98.

_____. 1980. "The Institutionalization of Ambiguity: Early British Factory Acts." In G. Geis and E. Stotland (eds.), *White Collar Theory and Research.* Beverly Hills: Sage.

CBC News online. 2006. "Dying for a Job." April 22. Available at <http://www.cbc.ca/news/background/workplace-safety/dyingforajob.html> accessed July 2007.

Cohen, M. 1989. "Corporate Crime and Punishment: A Study of Social Harm and Sentencing Practice in the Federal Courts." *American Criminal Law Review* 26, Winter: 605–60.

_____. 1991. "Corporate Crime and Punishment: An Update on Sentencing Practice in the Federal Courts, 1988–90." *Boston University Law Review* 71 (March): 247–80.

Condon, M. 1992. "Following Up on Interests: The Private Agreement Exemption in Ontario Securities Law." *Journal of Human Justice* 3 (2): 76–92.

Doern, G.B. 1995a. *Fairer Play: Canadian Competition Policy Institutions in a Global Market.* Toronto: C.D. Howe Institute, Policy Study #25.

_____. 1995b. "Sectoral Green Politics: Environmental Regulation and the Canadian Pulp and Paper Industry." *Environmental Politics* 4: 219–42.

_____. 1996. "Comparative Competition Policy: Boundaries and Levels of Political Analysis." In G.B. Doern and S. Wilks (eds.), *Comparative Competition Policy: National Institutions in a Global Market.* Oxford: Clarendon: 5–40.

Doern, G.B., and T. Conway. 1994. *The Greening of Canada: Federal Institutions and Decisions.* Toronto: University of Toronto Press.

Doern, G.B., and S. Wilks (eds.). 1998a. *Comparative Competition Policy: National Institutions in a Global Market.* Oxford: Clarendon.

_____. 1998b. "Conclusions: International Convergence and National Contrasts." In G.B. Doern and S. Wilks (eds.), *Comparative Competition Policy: National Institutions in a Global Market.* Oxford: Clarendon.

Fudge J., and B. Cossman, 2002. "Introduction: Privatization, Law and the Challenge to Feminism." In B. Cossman and J. Fudge (eds.), *Privatization, Law, and the Challenge to Feminism.* Toronto: University of Toronto Press.

Fishman, T. 1998. "Up in Smoke." *Harper's Magazine* December: 37–46.

Friedman, M. 1962. *Capitalism and Freedom.* Chicago: University of Chicago Press.

Gallon, G. 1996. "Ontario Government Backsliding on Environment." *Canadian Environmental Business Letter: The Gallon Report* 11 (46).

Galloway, Gloria. 2006. "Health Groups do Slow Burn over Tobacco Case." *Globe and Mail* April 14: A4.

Glasbeek, H. 2002. *Wealth by Stealth.* Toronto: Between the Lines.

Glasbeek, H., and E. Tucker. 1992. "The Westray Story: Death by Consensus." Unpublished paper. Toronto: York University.

Institute of Management Accountants. 2004. "The Sarbanes-Oxley Act and the Evolution of Corporate Governance." *CPA Journal.* Available at <http://www.nysscpa.org/cpajournal/2004/504/perspectives/nv5.htm> accessed July 2007.

Jackall, R. 1988. *Moral Mazes: The World of Corporate Managers.* New York: Oxford University Press.

Leiss, W., D. Van Nijnatten, E. Darier, and H. Mitchell. 1996. *Lessons Learned from ARET: A Qualitative Survey of Perceptions of Stakeholders.* Working Paper Series 96-4, Environmental Policy Unit, School of Policy Studies, Queen's University, Kingston.

Mackay R., and M. Smith. 2004. "Bill C-13: An Act to Amend the Criminal Code." (Capital Markets Fraud and Evidence-Gathering.) Ottawa: Parliamentary Research Branch, Legislative summary, LS-468E.

McBarnet, Doreen. 2004. "After Enron: Governing the Corporation, Mapping the Loci of Power in Corporate Governance Design." In J. O'Brien (ed.), *Governing the Corporation: Regulation and Corporate Governance in an Age of Scandal and Global Markets.* London: J. Wiley.

McClam, Erin. 2005. "Eight Former KPMG Executives Indicted." *Globe and Mail* August 30: B9.

McMullan, J., and S. Hinze. 1999. "The Press, Ideology and Corporate Crime." In C. McCormick (ed.), *The Westray Chronicles: A Case Study in Corporate Crime.* Halifax: Fernwood Publishing.

Naylor, R.T. 2000. "Economic and Organized Crime: Challenges for Criminal Justice." *Strategic Issues* Series RPO2-12e. Ottawa: Department of Justice, Research and Statistics Division.

Nikiforuk, A. 1997. *The Nasty Game: The Failure of Environmental Assessment in Canada.* Toronto: Walter and Duncan Gordon Foundation.

Pearce, F., and S. Tombs. 1998. *Toxic Capitalism: Corporate Crime and the Chemical Industry.* Aldershot: Ashgate/Dartmouth.

Perry, Ann. 2003. "Firm to Pay $5M over False Claims." *Toronto Star,* March 3: A4.

Posner, R. 1976. *Antitrust Law* Chicago: University of Chicago Press.

_____. 1977. *Economic Analysis of Law.* Second edition. New York: Little Brown.

Puri, P. 2001. "Sentencing the Criminal Corporation." *Osgoode Hall Law Journal* Summer/Fall, 39 (2/3): 612–53.

Rebovich, D., J. Layne, J. Jiandani, and Scott Hage. 2000. "The National Public Survey on White Collar Crime." National White Collar Crime Centre Training and Research Institute. Available at <www.prisonpolicy.org/scans/nw3c/research_monograph.pdf> accessed July 2007.

Rhodes D., and P. Paton. 2002. "Lawyers, Ethics and Enron." *Stanford Journal of Law, Business and Finance* 8, 1 (Autumn): 9–38.

Rosoff, S., H. Pontell, and R. Tillman. 2004. *Profit Without Honor: White-Collar Crime and the*

Looting of America. Third edition. New Jersey: Prentice Hall.

Schrecker, T. 1989. "The Political Context and Content of Environmental Law." In T. Caputo, M. Kennedy, C. Reasons, and G. Brannigan (eds.), *Law and Society: A Critical Perspective.* Toronto: Harcourt Brace Jovanovich.

_____. 2000. "Using Science in Environmental Policy: Can Canada Do Better?" In E. Parson (ed.), *Governing the Environment: Persistent Challenges, Uncertain Innovations.* Toronto: University of Toronto Press.

Simpson, S. 1989. "Corporate America." *Social Forces* 65: 493–563.

Snider, L. 1978. "Corporate Crime in Canada: A Preliminary Report." *Canadian Journal of Criminology* 20: 142–68.

_____. 1991. "The Regulatory Dance: Understanding Reform Processes in Corporate Crime." *International Journal of Sociology of Law* 19: 209–36.

_____. 1993. *Bad Business: Corporate Crime in Canada.* Scarborough: ITP Nelson.

_____. 1997. "Nouvelle Donne Legislative et Causes de la Criminalite 'Corporative.'" *Criminologie* XXX (1): 9–34.

_____. 2004. "Resisting Neo-Liberalism: The Poisoned Water Disaster in Walkerton, Ontario." *Social and Legal Studies* 5 (2): 27–47.

_____. 2005. "The Criminological Lens: Understanding Criminal Law and Corporate Governance." In J. O'Brien (ed.), *Governing the Corporation: Regulation and Corporate Governance in an Age of Scandal and Global Markets.* London: J. Wiley.

Stanbury, W. 1977. *Business Interests and the Reform of Canadian Competition Policy 1971–75.* Toronto: Carswell/Methuen.

_____. 1986–87. "The New Competition Act and Competition Tribunal Act: Not with a Bang but a Whimper?" *Canadian Business Law Journal* 12: 2–42.

Statistics Canada. 2004. *Income Distributions by Size in Canada.* Ottawa: Ministry of Supply and Services.

Sykes G., and D. Matza. 1957. "Techniques of Neutralization: A Theory of Delinquency." *American Sociological Review* 22 (December).

Tombs, Steve. 1996. "Injury, Death and the Deregulation Fetish: The Politics of Occupational Safety Regulation in United Kingdom Manufacturing Industries." *International Journal of Health Services* 26 (2): 309–29.

_____. 2004. "Workplace Injury and Death: Social Harm and the Illusions of Law." In Paddy Hillyard, Christina Pantazis, Dave Gordon, and Steve Tombs (eds.), *Beyond Criminology? Taking Harm Seriously.* London: Pluto Press.

Tucker, E. 1995. "And Defeat Goes On: An Assessment of 'Third-Wave' Health and Safety Regulation." In F. Pearce and L. Snider (eds.), *Corporate Crime: Contemporary Debates.* Toronto: University of Toronto Press.

Walters, V., W. Lewchuk, J. Richardson, L. Moran, T. Haines, and D. Verma. 1995. "Judgements of Legitimacy Regarding Occupational Health and Safety." In F. Pearce and L. Snider (eds.), *Corporate Crime: Contemporary Debates.* Toronto: University of Toronto Press.

Wong, Jan. 2006. "A Maid's Life: Cleaning Houses for a Living." *Globe and Mail,* April 1: M1, 5–6.

Zey, M. 1993. *Banking on Fraud: Drexel, Junk Bonds and Buyouts.* New York: Aldine de Gruyter.

12

Welfare Fraudsters and Tax Evaders
The State's Selective Invocation of Criminality

Janet Mosher

KEY FACTS

> Dramatic reforms to social assistance were introduced in several Canadian jurisdictions in the 1990s in the wake of the federal government's revocation of the Canada Assistance Plan.

> Fighting welfare fraud was one of three central goals informing the welfare reforms introduced in Ontario in 1997.

> In 2001–02 there were 38,452 fraud investigations, but only 393 convictions, representing 0.1 percent of the welfare caseload.

> A review of the tax violation convictions for Ontario posted on the Canadian Revenue Agency website <www.cra-arc.gc.ca/newsroom/convictions/on/menu-e.html> shows that of approximately sixty-five convictions between January and June 2006, only three involved jail sentences.

> Over a two-year period, some 26,214 calls were made to Ontario's welfare fraud hotline and of these, 136 were referred to the police for further investigation and 36 prosecutions were commenced.

> Effective April 1, 2000, Ontario introduced a lifetime ban on receipt of social assistance benefits for those convicted of welfare fraud; the ban was repealed in December 2003 in settlement of litigation challenging its constitutionality.

> Sixty-eight percent of Canadians agree that, "Given the opportunity, most people would hide income or overstate an expense or deduction to avoid paying tax."

> Current policy is not to prosecute tax evasion by indictment unless the amount evaded is greater than $250,000 and at least one other aggravating factor exists. The break point for indictment for welfare fraud is $5,000.

Sources: Ontario, Ministry of Community and Social Services 2004; Canada Revenue Agency 2005.

A comparison between welfare "fraud" and tax "evasion," as their respective labels might well imply, reveals striking differences in attributions of blameworthiness, in the scope and intrusiveness of surveillance strategies, in the processing of suspected violations, and in sentencing patterns. Taxpayers who defraud the public purse, largely men with significant assets, are regarded indulgently, while welfare recipients who defraud that same purse, more likely to be women and invariably poor, are harshly condemned.

These differences have long existed, but have become more exaggerated in the past two decades with the rise of neo-liberalism and its attendant insistence upon individual responsibility and self-sufficiency.

> Taxpayers who defraud the public purse, largely men with significant assets, are regarded indulgently, while welfare recipients who defraud that same purse, more likely to be women and invariably poor, are harshly condemned.

The focus on individualism inherent in neo-liberalism casts tax evaders as only mildly transgressing taxpayers. Tax evaders benefit from the positive attributes commonly ascribed to the "taxpayer": employed, entrepreneurial, independent, hard-working, self-reliant and a contributor to society, in short, a good neo-liberal citizen. From this perspective, tax evaders invite not scrutiny of their actions, and punishment for their transgressions, but understanding, forgiveness, and in the minds of some, even respect. By contrast, welfare recipients, positioned as the very antithesis of the taxpayer (obscuring the fact that they too pay taxes), are represented as lazy, lacking a work ethic, dependent, wanting something for nothing, and not to be trusted. According to this stereotype, all welfare recipients are regarded suspiciously, as potential criminals poised to defraud the state. To contain the threat posed by this class of undeserving, "failed" neo-liberal citizens, sweeping surveillance measures and harsh treatment seem not only reasonable, but essential.

The comparison between welfare fraud and tax evasion illustrates some of critical criminology's main concerns. The increasingly intrusive and punitive regime that governs welfare recipients, by contrast to the relatively lax and forgiving treatment given taxpayers, and the sharp variations in the invocation of criminal law and criminal processes to deal with those who defraud the public purse (through welfare fraud or tax evasion), reveal the socially constructed and contingent nature of criminal miscon-

> Tax evaders benefit from the positive attributes commonly ascribed to the "taxpayer": employed, entrepreneurial, independent, hard-working, self-reliant and a contributor, in short, a good neo-liberal citizen.

duct. The comparison also shows how criminal law is engaged in a political project: the state's selective invocation of criminal law in relation to frauds upon the public purse serves to create and maintain categories of deserving and undeserving citizens that in turn, reproduce the norms of neo-liberalism. Welfare recipients, as a class, are punished because they are not the self-reliant, independent citizens required by neo-liberalism. They are defined as criminals not because of what they have done, but rather because of who they are. Tax evaders, being good neo-liberal citizens, largely escape attributions of criminality and criminal justice processing.

Welfare Fraud: The Construction of a Problem

Welfare fraud, approached in purely legalistic terms, is governed by section 380 of Canada's Criminal Code.[1] As with other criminal offences, fraud has two components: the *actus reus* (the guilty act) and the *mens rea* (the guilty mind). The *actus reus* of fraud contains two elements: the prohibited act (of "deceit, falsehood or other fraudulent means"); and deprivation that is caused by the prohibited act. While "deceit, falsehood and fraudulent means" are three separate heads, the courts have held that the real core of the offence of fraud is dishonesty (Ewart 1986). Whether an act is appropriately characterized as dishonest is to be determined not by reference to the accused's subjective mental state (whether the accused subjectively believed the act in question to be dishonest) but by whether a reasonable person would stigmatize the act in question as dishonest. The Supreme Court of Canada, in *R. v. Olan*, noted that while "dishonesty" was difficult to define with precision, it connotes an underhanded design, is discreditable, and perhaps unscrupulous.

The *mens rea* of fraud also contains two elements: subjective knowledge of the prohibited act (the act which, based upon a reasonableness standard, is appropriately stigmatized as dishonest); and subjective knowledge that the prohibited act could have as a consequence the deprivation of another. With regard to the second of these elements, the accused must have a subjective awareness that undertaking the prohibited act (of deceit, falsehood or other dishonest means) could cause deprivation. In his dissenting judgment in *R. v. Theroux*, Mr. Justice Sopinka (with whom then Chief Justice Lamer concurred), while agreeing with the majority, took care to point out that it is important to distinguish between the conclusion that an accused's belief that his act is honest will not prevail if objectively the act is dishonest and his belief in facts that would deprive the act of its dishonest character. This distinction is a crucial one, yet while it is dutifully made in the tax context, it is regularly ignored in the context of welfare.

The case of *R. v. Maldonado* illustrates the importance of the distinction. Mr. Maldonado was in receipt of General Welfare Assistance, the precursor to what is now "Ontario Works" (ow). He had been told that he must report any change in income to social services. When his wife obtained part-time employment, it was dutifully reported. But when he began attending school and obtained a student loan he did not report it. When the government learned that Mr. Maldonado had received of loan, he was charged with fraud. His evidence was that he had not considered a loan to be income, since it had to be repaid, so he had never even contemplated that it needed to be reported. He did not know that the Ontario Works Regulations defined "income" to include loans. Nor did he know that had it been so reported, his benefits would have been reduced. Based on Supreme Court jurisprudence, it will not matter if Mr. Maldonado subjectively believed his actions to be honest. The question is can his actions be appropriately stigmatized as dishonest — not merely negligent, but as an underhanded design or as unscrupulous? Or to invoke Mr. Justice Sopinka's query, is there a belief by the accused in a set of facts (here, that a loan is not income and need not be reported) that would deprive the act of its dishonest character? When one considers Mr. Maldonado's state of mind, while he had knowledge of the prohibited act (the non-disclosure of the loan), his belief that a loan was not income and hence not reportable deprived the act of its dishonest character. Moreover, given his belief in this set of facts, he lacked the subjective knowledge that the non-reporting could have as a consequence the deprivation of another. Mr. Justice Weagant, the trial judge hearing Mr. Maldonado's case, concluded the trial by stating the following:

> Not only do I have a doubt that Mr. Maldonado did not have the subjective knowledge of the possibility of deprivation, I am quite sure he did not... I would not be surprised if Mr. Maldonado, even if given a copy of the Regulations to read for himself, were unable to glean the true meaning of "income" or "change of circumstances." The Regulations are extremely complicated and difficult to read... my own experience of wading through the Regulations leads me to believe their inaccessibility plays a major role in the scenario under consideration. The Regulations governing the question of entitlement are fiendishly difficult to understand... the sense or structure of the policy which might help a person

on welfare to determine when he or she is breaking the law, is not apparent on the face of the Regulation. (*R. v. Maldonado*: para. 40)

Problematically, however, within the welfare system one rarely sees the result in *Maldonado*, and even within the criminal justice system *Maldonado* may be more the exception than the norm. Rather, a welfare recipient's lack of knowledge of the complex, voluminous, and "fiendishly difficult" requirements of welfare law and regulations is routinely, and wrongly, assumed to be irrelevant to the question of whether fraud has been committed. More commonly, the mere fact that a recipient has not disclosed information that welfare authorities later say ought to have been disclosed brings an allegation of fraud. But the invocation of the language of fraud to capture conduct that falls outside the domain of the criminal law proper is more sweeping still and, as detailed below, the state has been an active participant in that expansive construction.

> A welfare recipient's lack of knowledge of the complex, voluminous, and "fiendishly difficult" requirements of welfare law and regulations is routinely assumed irrelevant to whether fraud has been committed.

In the case of Ontario, welfare fraud occupied a central position in the social assistance reforms introduced in the mid-1990s; indeed, the government expressly identified "fighting" welfare fraud as one of the three goals of welfare reform. Welfare fraud had been, and continues to be, successfully constructed as a social problem spinning out of control and requiring increasingly intrusive and punitive measures to curb its proliferation. As Patrick Parnaby (2003) argues, claims-makers, in seeking to convince the public that a problem or condition is real and urgent, will attempt to ground the problem through the use of official statistics and/or through claims alleging the widespread nature of the condition. Certainly, those claiming the problem of welfare fraud, such as conservative policy-makers and interest groups, used both these methods. In constructing welfare fraud as a significant problem, rhetorical claims about its magnitude and harms abounded. The invocation by the state of explicitly criminal terms — "fraud," "cheats," "liars," "theft," "zero tolerance," and "crackdowns" — aided in the construction of the problem as a criminal menace, and thus all the more serious and threatening. Welfare-fraud "cheat sheets," posted on the government's website, and accounts of complex frauds involving multiple fabricated identities appearing in local media further contributed to the sense of serious criminality.

> It is the government's use of "official statistics" that provides the most revealing window into the construction of the problem of welfare fraud.

But it is the government's use of "official statistics" that provides the most revealing window into the construction of the problem of welfare fraud. Capitalizing upon the lack of definitional clarity and precision as to just what constitutes welfare fraud, the "official statistics" widely circulated by the government included all errors giving rise to an overpayment (but tellingly not an underpayment) of welfare benefits. An error giving rise to an overpayment could occur in a situation such as Mr. Maldonado's, where the failure to report "income" arises not because the intent exists to defraud the state, but rather due to the lack of knowledge of the regulations defining loans as income.

The government's *Welfare Fraud Control Report 2001–2002* exemplifies this collapsing of fraud and error (Ontario, Ministry of Community, Family and Children's Services 2003). The report is permeated with the language of "fraud"; reference is made to the Welfare-fraud Hotline, to the fraud control database to track fraud investigations, to "anti-fraud measures [that] help catch welfare cheats and deter others from thinking about cheating" and to welfare fraud as a crime that the government is cracking down on through the introduction of a zero-tolerance policy. The report claims that, "over $49 million was identified in social assistance payments that people were not entitled to receive and an estimated $12 million in avoided future costs." Given the general thrust of the report and its title, the message conveyed is that these dollars are directly attributable to welfare fraud. But a close examination reveals a different picture; in 2001–02 there were 38,452 fraud investigations, resulting in only 393 convictions for welfare fraud (representing approximately 0.1 percent of the caseload) and 12,816 cases where assistance was reduced or terminated as a result of the ministry reassessing the recipient's case. In more than 12,000 cases fraud had not been established; no crime had been proven, and any dollars saved were not the result of fraud detection. While some of the 12,000 cases may represent a modest number of instances where prosecution was not recommended even though there existed a strong case to support a conviction for fraud, the vast majority are likely to be instances where an administrative rule had been broken, but without the requisite intent to constitute criminal fraud — in other words as a result of client misunderstanding, oversight or error. But the report, by collapsing all errors into fraud and through its use of terms such as "cheats," "cracking down on crime," and "zero tolerance," portrays a picture of criminal fraud as rampant and, correspondingly, of recipients as actual or potential criminals.

It is important to appreciate how complex the welfare system is (Matthews 2004). Governed by some 800 rules that determine eligibility, it has variously been described as "Kafkaesque" and "fiendishly difficult" to comprehend (R .v. *Maldonado* 1998). Many of the rules are counter-intuitive, others incomprehensible, and it is extremely difficult to access accurate and timely information about the governing rules. Commonly, recipients find themselves in situations in which they stand accused of "fraud" where they had no idea that the rule they had allegedly violated existed at all: that a loan or a cash advance is treated as income and has to be reported (and will be deducted dollar for dollar); that gifts and, in some parts of the province, leftovers from meals are also treated as income and reportable; or that details about intimate relationships are expected to be disclosed (and just what level of detail is far from clear). Given the number of rules, their complexity and their impenetrability, it is hardly surprising that inadvertent rule violations are an endemic feature of the welfare system. The routine categorization of such rule violations as criminal fraud — not only in the annual *Welfare Fraud Control Reports*, but by those on the frontlines in the administration of the system — is the sleight of hand that has rendered welfare fraud a serious problem and welfare recipients a dangerous class.

> Commonly, recipients accused of "fraud" had no idea that the allegedly violated rule existed: that a loan or cash advance is treated as income and must be reported; that gifts are also reportable.

The approach taken in the *Welfare Fraud Control Reports* reflects that advocated in *Reducing Fraud and Waste in Income Security Programs in Canada,* a report prepared for the Fraser Institute, arguing against the desirability of carefully delineating criminal and non-criminal conduct when assessing overpayments to welfare recipients.

> There is no clear-cut delineations [sic] of fraud and error in the sense that the dividing line, where error crosses into fraud, is based on the psychological construct of *intent*. And fraud is a legal term which applies when *intent* can be proven

> in a court of law. There are many cases investigated in which the investigator is sure that fraud occurred, however the strict rules of evidence may prevent the case being proven in court. This category could be referred to as "program abuse"... All of the categories of error and fraud overlap, and it is often a matter of convenience or legal requirements which determine how a particular case is labelled [sic]... "client error" is often the administrator's way of saying that intent to defraud could not be easily proven in court. (MacDonald, MacDonald, and Blair 1995: 7–8)

This analysis presupposes that client error is inevitably fraud; the rules of evidence just get in the way of proving it, or it would be "inconvenient" to do so. This view is, however, completely incompatible with what is known about how the system and recipients of benefits interface. As noted above, the complexity of the system and the difficulties of adequately communicating the rules make client error — and indeed significant system error — unavoidable (Matthews 2004). Moreover, the analysis simply disregards the importance of the construct that lies at the heart of criminal liability; the guilty mind. If all rule breaches, irrespective of intent, are characterized as "fraud," every recipient who breaches a rule — whether through inadvertence, lack of knowledge/information, mental or cognitive disability, or misunderstanding — is tainted with the moral brush of criminality. But in the effort to eliminate waste (itself a problematic notion), characterizing that waste as the result of criminal fraud rather than recipient and administrative error helps to construct a more serious social problem requiring aggressive, harsh, and punitive responses. It also, of course, renders all welfare recipients less deserving of public support, and thus helps to facilitate the state's retreat from the provision of support to its citizens and a corresponding reinvigoration of the enforcement of private obligations.

Invasive Strategies for Detecting Welfare "Fraudsters"

To respond to the serious problem that welfare fraud was constructed to be, a broad array of measures was introduced in the mid-1990s. In turn, the extent, breadth, and severity of these measures reinforced the constructed view of the severity of the fraud problem. A significant development in the arsenal of measures to combat welfare fraud was the introduction of first "enhanced verification" and, later, "consolidated verification procedures" (CVP). In the CVP environment, priority-ranking factors, based upon an assumed risk of fraud, are used to determine when a review by social assistance workers will be conducted on a recipient file. High-risk factors include high accommodation costs (equal to or greater than 80 percent of the participant's net revenue — a common experience for those on OW) and receipt of social assistance for more than thirty-six months. Medium-risk factors include another person residing at the participant's address, a Social Insurance Number that begins with a nine or is blank (a nine indicates a person without citizenship or permanent residence status), accommodation costs amounting to 75 to 79 percent of the payment, and the participant having received social assistance for twenty-four to thirty-five months.

The amount of information required to be provided at the time of applying for assistance and during regular or risk-determined reviews is sweeping, as is the scope of the consent to the collection and release of information that must be signed as a precondition to receiving benefits. The extensive and ongoing reporting requirements, together with a host of information-sharing agreements negotiated with a range of provincial and federal departments, permit the ministry to gather and share vast amounts of information about social assistance recipients.

The Welfare Snitch Line

The public is charged with a responsibility — a civic duty — to engage in the project of spying on welfare recipients. As noted above, the public is told that welfare fraud is rampant, that people not genuinely in need are taking money from the pockets of the hard-working taxpayer. One way to discharge this civic duty is to call a toll-free welfare-fraud hotline (6,527 people did in 2001–02, down from 9,348 in 2000–01). Introducing the welfare-fraud hotline on October 2, 1995, then-minister of community and social services David Tsubouchi proclaimed in the House that, "Welfare fraud is a problem that hurts the most vulnerable people in our society. Every cent that is paid to the wrong person through fraud is help taken from the needy." He noted that experience had shown hotlines to be an effective device to ensure this does not happen, projected savings of $25 million per year, and invited the people of Ontario to call 1-800-394-STOP to help "stop fraud and to protect the system for people who really need help" (Ontario Legislative Assembly, *Hansard* October 2, 1995).

> The public is charged with a responsibility — a civic duty — to engage in the project of surveilling and scrutinizing welfare recipients.

As the number of calls to the snitch line suggest (not including calls made directly to local OW or Ontario Disability Support Program (ODSP) offices), recipients' lives are scrutinized intensely by non-state agents. Present or current abusive boyfriends or spouses, landlords, and neighbours have all taken up the government's invitation to participate in the surveillance project (Mosher and Hermer 2005). No doubt, class, gender, and race stereotypes play into who calls to report what about whom. So, for example, class and race stereotypes of racialized women portray them as bad and potentially dangerous, as likely criminals. Dominant stereotypes caricature Aboriginal people as "living off the system," too lazy to get a job, and single mothers — especially those with children by more than one father — as promiscuous, having children to increase welfare dollars, and likely to be hiding men in their homes. Under the gaze of surveillance by concerned citizens who harbour these stereotypes, virtually any racialized woman, any single mother, or any Aboriginal person is a person suspected of fraud and ought to be investigated. The sweep and impact of surveillance by non-state actors is therefore likely to impact differently on particular groups of recipients — racialized peoples, women, and, most pervasively, racialized women.

In addition, the snitch line is not uncommonly used for purposes completely extraneous to preventing or detecting fraud. Abusive men make false reports to further their power and control over women; landlords make false reports to facilitate the eviction of a tenant; and vindictive neighbours or other acquaintances make false or misleading reports simply out of spite (Mosher, Evans, and Little 2004, Mosher and Hermer 2005).

Fraud Investigations

Allegations of fraud — of which there are strikingly large numbers (over 35,000 in 2001–02 and over 52,000 in 2000–01) — are investigated by Eligibility Review Officers (EROs). The *Ontario Works Act, 1997 (OWA)* and regulations thereto expanded the powers available to EROs to undertake their investigations of welfare fraud. EROs have the power to enter any place other than a dwelling if there are reasonable grounds to believe evidence relevant to eligibility may be found there, as well as the power to demand to see records. They can also require "information or material from a person who is the subject of an investigation… or from any person who the officer has reason to believe can provide information or material relevant to the investigation" (O. Reg.134/98, s.65). These powers are reinforced by subsection 79(3) of the Act, which makes it an offence to obstruct or knowingly give false information to a person engaged in an investigation.

In the course of their investigations, EROs will often seek information from landlords, neighbours, teachers, and others who may know something of the circumstances of the recipient under investigation; as well, they often meet with the person being investigated, and they have the authority to demand to see records. *Charter* cautions are not routinely provided during these meetings and evidence gathered in this manner is regularly used against recipients in criminal prosecutions. Certainly one characterization of these meetings is that they are solely for the purpose of determining eligibility and are thus integrally connected to enforcing a regulatory regime. But a competing and compelling characterization is that they often take the form of *de facto* criminal investigations and, as such, require *Charter* warnings and limitations on the use of evidence so gathered. While the issue of when a regulatory investigation becomes a *de facto* criminal investigation has received significant attention in the income-tax context, it has received very little critical interrogation in the welfare context (*R. v. Jarvis*, 2002). This is disconcerting because it appears to be not at all uncommon for police and Crown attorneys to rely upon nothing but the investigations undertaken by EROs in the prosecution of persons accused of welfare fraud. Given the number of fraud investigations and given the statutory power of EROs to compel information, there is a very good argument that *Charter* rights of recipients are regularly being violated.

A related concern is that recipients under investigation who are called in for a meeting with an ERO frequently do not fully understand the import of the interview, nor that the statements given may subsequently be used against them in a fraud prosecution. Moreover, fearing a possible criminal charge, and within a broad context where the language of "fraud" is pervasive and recipients are constantly dehumanized, those accused (even inferentially) of fraud agree all too readily to administrative sanctions such as paying back supposed "overpayments" or having their benefits terminated altogether (Mosher and Hermer 2005). Recipients are also understandably reluctant to complain about mistreatment during investigations. They are in a position of extreme vulnerability in their interactions with agents of the administrative regime, who can cut them off benefits, assess overpayments, and refer matters to the police. Rocking the boat almost always promises to be more trouble than it is worth.

Harsh Penalties for Conviction: The Lifetime Ban and Incarceration

Perhaps the most punitive measures introduced in the new welfare-fraud control regime were the additional penalties upon conviction. The government first introduced a three-month ban on receipt of welfare for a first conviction, six months for subsequent convictions, and later a lifetime ban (for crimes committed after April 1, 2000). Thus, upon conviction for welfare fraud, one was automatically banned for life from receiving social assistance. The constitutionality of the lifetime ban was under challenge when the Liberal government announced its repeal in December 2003, while at the same time introducing a revised policy directive making referral of cases by welfare administrators to the police mandatory in all cases where there is sufficient evidence to suspect intent to commit fraud (*R. v. Broomer* 2002; Ontario, Ministry of Community and Social Services 2004). Although both the OWA and the *Ontario Disability Support Program Act, 1997 (ODSPA)* contain offence provisions that prohibit knowingly obtaining assistance to which one is not entitled, these provisions are never resorted to. Rather, it is the policy of the ministry to deal with such matters as criminal, rather than as provincial, offences.

> Recipients describe being on welfare as "living under a microscope" or "having one's life gone through with a fine-tooth comb."

Recipients variously describe the experience of being on welfare as "living under a microscope" or "having one's life gone through with a fine-tooth comb," where virtually everything you do is everyone's business (Mosher and Hermer 2005). The climate around recipients' interactions with the system is permeated with suspicion and hostility, and constant fear is part of their everyday reality: fear of not being able to meet the basic needs of their children; fear of losing custody; fear of declining health; fear — especially for their children — of the impacts of social ostracism, stigmatization, and discrimination; and fear of breaching a rule or of someone calling the snitch line and making them the target of a hostile investigation. Front-line workers sometimes encourage this latter fear. Recipients report being told by their workers that they know they must be up to something because it is just not possible to survive on their welfare cheques, and it will only be a matter of time before they figure out exactly what they are up to. As Herd and Mitchell describe,

> the new system is more concerned with surveillance and deterrence, than it is with assisting people to find employment… What is new is the intensity of surveillance and the technologies employed, the importation of private sector methods and standardized business practices… Overall the mood of the focus groups was that the new system was inspiring a greater degree of suspicion and hostility… more concerned with constant surveillance and treating "everybody like they're cheating the system." (Herd and Mitchell 2002: 8–9, 33)

Sentencing: "The Most Despicable Form of Theft"

Significantly, conviction for welfare fraud has long attracted disproportionately harsh punishments (Mosher and Hermer 2005; Martin 1992). The paramountcy of general deterrence and the characterization of welfare fraud as a serious crime involving a breach of trust have supported a *de facto* presumption of imprisonment as the appropriate sentence. *R. v. Thurrotte*, a 1971 decision of the Ontario Court of Appeal, has long been regarded as a leading case on this matter. In *Thurrotte* the court observed that,

> The paramountcy of general deterrence and the characterization of welfare fraud as a serious crime involving a breach of trust have supported a presumption of imprisonment as the appropriate sentence.

> although this case is pitiful in many respects, this court is unanimously of the opinion that the paramount consideration in determining the sentence is the element of deterrence. Welfare authorities have enough difficulties without having to put up with persons who set out to defraud them. This is one such instance,

and others who are similarly minded must be warned that these offences will not be treated lightly.

The trial court had ordered five months imprisonment for a fraud of $1,700 and the Court of Appeal affirmed that anywhere up to five months would be an appropriate sentence. Subsequent cases have confirmed that absent unusual or exceptional mitigating circumstances, a period of incarceration is warranted.

Of the fifty cases reviewed by Dianne Martin in the early 1990s, a jail sentence was ordered in 80 percent (Martin 1992). A recent review of fifty-eight welfare-fraud sentencing decisions covering the period 1989–2002, revealed that custodial sentences were ordered in thirty-three cases, conditional sentences in fifteen, suspended sentences in eight, a conditional discharge in one, and a fine in another. Given that before a conditional sentence may be imposed the sentencing judge must find a period of incarceration to be warranted, when combined with jail terms imposed, incarceration was found to be warranted in 83 percent of cases, a rate almost identical to Martin's finding. In thirty of the cases sentences also included a restitution or compensation order and in thirteen, community service ranging from 100 to 300 hours was an additional component (Mosher & Hermer 2005). The severity of the sentences imposed in welfare-fraud cases is dramatically out of step with sentences for infractions that occur in other administrative regimes and with other Criminal Code offences. For a first offence of theft under $5,000 (the break point for summary and indictable theft) an accused without a criminal record is several steps away from a custodial sentence. Yet a first offender accused of welfare fraud is at serious risk of incarceration.

Justificatory Framework

Several common tropes invoked by Crown counsel and judges provide the justification to support imprisonment as the "appropriate" sentence in cases of welfare fraud. These expressions of moralistic outrage are pervasive in both political and public discourse. One of the most common devices is for the court to personalize the state; judges are at pains to point out that a crime has been committed not against some faceless, amorphous entity but against every citizen of the community. Commonly, welfare fraud is described as, "depriving all citizens of the province" or as a "crime against every member of the community" (*R. v. McIsaac, R. v. Gallagher, R. v. Reid*). It is rendered a crime of colossal proportions; unlike a simple theft from a single individual, the pocketbooks of every citizen have been pinched.

Commonly, judges also scold the accused for having taken from those genuinely in need, inferring that the accused is herself not genuinely in need and obscuring the reality that in the overwhelming majority of these cases, need and desperation motivated the actions in issue. This trope also commonly blames recipients who "abuse" the welfare system for the difficult circumstances of others on welfare. Judges frequently observe, though incorrectly, that every extra penny the accused has received causes a corresponding diminution of money available for those "genuinely in need." In this manner, it is the accused who is blamed for the hardship experienced by other welfare recipients. The accused, and others who "abuse" the system, are also held responsible for the erosion of public support for welfare programs. Recipients who "abuse" the system by stealing from those "genuinely in need" are blamed for eroding taxpayers' willingness to fund the system. Consider for example the judicial discourse in the case of *R. v. McGillivray*. Mr. Justice Daniel sentenced the accused to six months' incarceration and one year of probation for a fraud of $23,263. The accused had not disclosed her common-law relationship with a man whose only income was a student loan and from whom she received no financial benefit (note that the court does not query whether on the facts the state had been deprived, an essential — and one would have thought contested — issue in this case). Although the court found that by all accounts the accused "was an emotionally abused, battered wife who is very much manipulated by her boyfriend," the judge went on to characterize her actions as criminal insofar as her living arrangements as a social assistance recipient were concerned. Justice Daniel, in characterizing the accused, quoted favourably from another case in which welfare fraud was described as the following:

> the most despicable form of theft. There is only a certain amount of money available for people in need. And as the fund is abused by people who are not entitled to it, there is less money to go around, and others who possibly need more help simply don't receive it…. So theft of this nature is, when you analyze it, really a theft from the poorest people of the community. And that is one of the major reasons that this type of offence must be treated very, very seriously by the Courts.

Judges are also given to characterizing welfare fraud as a violation of trust, and thus a serious matter (and an aggravating factor relevant to sentencing). It is important to interrogate this idea of a violation of trust. One way of understanding the nature of the trust at issue is that the welfare system, as judges are prone to point out, depends upon self-reporting. (While this is true in one sense it obscures the enormous amount of active surveillance that happens as detailed earlier.) The system's functioning and integrity are portrayed as depending on recipients' candour and honesty, and in this sense recipients are being trusted to make full disclosure. But one also has a sense that the nature of the trust and of the violation at issue may well be something quite different. Cases in which the offence in question is characterized as a violation of trust are frequently marked by a tone of self-righteousness and outrage that the accused has taken advantage of the taxpayer, whose largesse and compassion have not been dutifully respected and gratefully appreciated.

Both explicitly in their remarks, and more commonly implicit in their failure to acknowledge the circumstances of those who commit these "crimes," judges project a particular view about the welfare state: that it provides a finely woven web of protection, ensuring that no one goes without adequate shelter or food. These assumptions about the extent of welfare assistance are profoundly out of step with the realities of life on welfare. Recipients struggle to survive on benefit levels that reflect often as little as 30 to 40 percent (in one province as low as 19 percent, one as high as 73 percent) of Statistics Canada low income cut-offs, the most widely accepted poverty line (National Council of Welfare 2006). Most recipients struggle to survive without adequate food, shelter, or clothing, often depleting their monthly benefits to secure accommodation. But the mistaken assumption that the welfare state provides adequately for all lends itself to a characterization of those who are accused of fraud as greedy, rather than needy, and of the taxpayer as righteously indignant that his generosity is being exploited. Thus, the strongly articulated sense of a violation of trust seems to flow more directly from a view that taxpayer generosity and largesse has been exploited, than from welfare recipients' failure to make full disclosure within a system whose integrity depends on the candour of its beneficiaries.

Conditional Sentences

A significant development in sentencing was the introduction of the conditional sentence in 1996, making "house arrest" an option to incarceration in a custodial facility. While conditional sentences may at first blush appear to ease the harshness of sentencing in welfare-fraud cases, upon further examination it is not at all clear that this has been the effect. Without doubting the gravity of being in prison, it is imperative to consider the impact of a conditional sentence upon a low-income person. The difficulties created by conditional sentences are emphasized by the troubling circumstances of the death of Kimberly Rogers. Ms Rogers had been sentenced to house arrest for six months upon her conviction for welfare fraud for not disclosing student loans she had received while on welfare, loans that she knew she was obliged to disclose to social services (*R. v. Rogers*). At the time of her conviction, a three-month ban on receipt of benefits was in effect for those convicted of welfare fraud (this preceded the lifetime ban). Ms Rogers, eight months pregnant, died in her apartment during a heat wave in August 2001. Confinement to one's home, if that home is overheated (as in the case of Ms Rogers), underheated, infested with cockroaches or rodents, overcrowded, covered in mildew, or shares any of the characteristic features of much low-income housing, will have harmful effects on both physical and mental health. So too, trying to acquire the other material necessities of life often requires much more time for a low-income person than for someone with adequate financial means. For many, getting food means visiting multiple food banks and/or other charities and/or shopping at several stores (to find the best buy), rather than at one supermarket. Similarly, acquiring clothing and other necessities is often time-consuming and complicated. Trying to find these necessities often requires long absences from home; the three hours, one day per week during which Ms Rogers was permitted to leave her home was inadequate. Ms Rogers, even after her lawyers were successful in having the three-month ban lifted pending a constitutional challenge, still had only eighteen dollars per month to live on once her rent was paid.

Another problematic feature of conditional sentences is compliance with the terms attached, and the risk of breach thereof (where breach will land one in prison). For example, reporting obligations is difficult for persons without access to phones or adequate transportation. So too, community service orders that commonly accompany conditional sentences can create enormous compliance problems. It is not at all unusual to see 150 to 250 hours of community service ordered. Performing this service often requires transportation and/or childcare, which the recipient cannot afford. Problematically, it seems that often judges share the view of former Premier Mike Harris, who observed, when introducing the Ontario Works legislation, that those on social assistance were being paid to "sit home and do nothing" (Ontario Legislative Assembly, *Hansard* 1995). Judges often fail to understand how time consuming living in poverty is in fact, and the tremendous work required to meet basic needs from day to day (Swift and Birmingham 2000).

Also implicit in judicial decisions is the view that low-income people only "take" from their communities: this is a further mischaracterization of the lives of most low-income people. Many are actively involved in their communities as volunteers, as well as rearing and caring for children. The view of welfare recipients as "takers," not "contributors" pervades many sentencing cases. Disturbingly, in *R. v. Rogers* the characterization of Kimberly Rogers as a "taker" was used by the sentencing judge to justify a conditional sentence rather than a jail term; indeed it is clear from his decision that he understood that for Ms Rogers a conditional sentence would be more punitive than jail. In sentencing Kimberly Rogers, Mr. Justice Rodgers admonished her in the following terms: "This is how serious the matter is, Ms Rogers. There is a jail term that is going to be involved, it just happens to be a jail term that will be served in your home, and not at the expense of the community. You have taken enough from the community." Jail would have provided adequate food and shelter for Kimberly Rogers; house arrest did not. In Mr. Justice Rodgers' view, Kimberly Rogers was so dehumanized that even jail was too good for her; she was to fund her own incarceration and to do so without access to any welfare benefits.

Restitution orders also create incredible burdens for low-income people. Many of those convicted of welfare fraud are receiving social assistance at the time of sentencing. Their benefits will be reduced by 5 to 10 percent to collect the monies owing as a result of the overpayment. Given that existing benefit levels are already below what is required for subsistence, taking more money away means further reducing people's ability to meet basic needs, which will damage their physical and mental health. Moreover, because in most instances it was need that led to the "crime" in the first place, further decreasing recipients' income serves to tighten the knot of the moral double bind they are forced to confront. Complete candour about money or food received from friends or family, or small amounts of earned income, may prevent allegations of fraud, but full disclosure commonly results in a dollar-for-dollar deduction from the welfare cheque, leaving recipients unable to meet their basic needs and those of their children.

Thus, in many of the reported cases decision-makers do not try to understand the realities of life on welfare; rather they construct, demean, and devalue the "other," as all that they are not. While some aspects of the life of the accused may be described in the decision, that context is quickly discarded as irrelevant, rather than mitigating. So too, the accused's circumstances, while considered "pitiful," are often seen as their own fault — ignoring the ways in which social structures, institutions, and ideologies construct and limit their choices. This juxtaposition of the welfare recipient and the taxpayer, and the values and attributes ascribed to each, underlies the starkly different treatment of welfare fraud and tax evasion.

Income Tax Evasion

While income-tax evasion will usually meet the Criminal Code test for fraud, unlike welfare fraud, it is invariably dealt with under the provisions of the *Income Tax Act* (ITA). The ITA creates an offence of income-tax evasion, defined pursuant to subs. 239(1)(d) as the "wilful evasion or attempt to evade compliance with the Act or payment of taxes imposed by the Act." While the offence has been characterized by the Supreme Court of Canada as criminal in nature and as such requiring full *mens rea* for conviction, the terminology of "evasion" and the avoidance of explicitly criminal terms softens the image of the tax evader and renders the harms of tax evasion less obvious and troublesome. While crime is something the public is encouraged to be outraged about, tax evasion is not.

Like the welfare system, proper functioning of the income-tax system is largely dependent upon the candour of taxpayers in the full and honest disclosure of income. While many taxpayers' taxes are deducted at source, leaving little room for hiding income, it is often those with larger incomes and/or who are self-employed who have the greatest opportunities to evade taxes (Giles and Tedds 2002; CCRA 2005). The precise amount of income not disclosed to the Canada Customs Revenue Agency (CCRA), either as a result of taxpayer error (similar to welfare, the rules governing tax are extremely complex, and errors are likely to be common) or due to wilful evasion, is unknown and estimates vary significantly. Reporting on the lacklustre performance of the CCRA in addressing the underground economy (a significant source of wilful evasion) the Auditor General's Report of 1999 estimated that the underground economy constituted 4.2 to 4.5 percent of gross domestic product (GDP). Assuming a rate of 4.5 percent, in 1997 this amounted to $38 billion, and a loss of tax revenues of $12 billion (Auditor General 1999a). Giles and Tedds' estimate is much higher; 15 or 16 percent of GDP, totalling almost $44 billion in lost tax revenues in 1995 alone (Giles and Tedds 2002). By contrast, the Ontario government estimated for 2001–02 that $49 million was paid to those not entitled to receive the funds, an estimate that notwithstanding government rhetoric, includes all overpayments, only a tiny percentage of which are attributable to fraud. Projected as a national figure, the amount lost to welfare fraud would still be dramatically less than that lost to tax evasion.

Lorne Sossin cites survey data for 1994–95 that show 50 to 60 percent of respondents had avoided taxes (Sossin 1999). In a telephone survey undertaken by Varma and Doob (1998), 18.4 percent of respondents admitted evading tax on one or more measures. While attitudes regarding evasion are not directly correlated with actual behaviour, data from the 2002–03 CCRA tax compliance survey of 2,732 Canadians found that 15 percent believed it was okay to cheat on taxes and many others believed tax cheating to be justifiable in certain situations (e.g., paying cash to avoid taxes) and minimally harmful (CCRA 2003). The 2004 survey found that 68 percent of respondents agreed that, "Given the opportunity, most people would hide income or overstate an expense or deduction to avoid paying tax" and three out of four agreed that, "The CCRA would not know about income received in cash unless you declare it" (CCRA 2005).

The auditor general has noted that "academic studies have shown that many people view even wilful non-compliance with income-tax laws as a victimless and not particularly serious crime. To some extent, this public attitude has shaped the way tax administration operates in Canada, as evidenced by low rates of enforcement coverage and the relatively lenient treatment of tax evaders" (Auditor General 1990). The converse may be equally true: low rates of enforcement and lenient treatment may shape public attitudes regarding compliance. The low rates of enforcement are reflected in prosecution and conviction statistics: nationwide in 2004–05 there were 250 convictions for tax evasion or fraud (there were also convictions for non-filing and for failing to register for GST/HST) (CCRA 2005).

> The line between tax "avoidance" and tax "evasion" is blurry, making it easy to regard tax evasion not as criminal conduct but as minor technical breach by a hard-working, contributing citizen.

The widespread evasion of taxes is rationalized by a range of claims: the system is too complex; tax administration is unreasonable; no real harm comes of it/there is no victim; the tax burden is too heavy; government mismanages its spending of tax dollars; others are doing it; there is little risk of being caught; and penalties are minimal (Auditor General 1999b, Sossin 1999, Brooks 1998). In addition, the line between tax "avoidance" — which is not merely condoned but celebrated and heavily supported through the professional assistance of lawyers, accountants, and other experts — and tax "evasion" is a blurry one, making it easy to regard tax evasion not as criminal conduct but as a minor technical breach by a hard-working, contributing citizen. Moreover, the norms and values of neo-liberalism — individualism, self-reliance, entrepreneurial spirit, and material consumption — cut against the values underpinning a collective and redistributive taxation system, and help to valorize tax avoidance. This is evident in the rationalized non-compliance described above, but even more so in the active encouragement to disregard tax obligations espoused by some. Consider, for example, Pierre Lemieux's editorial in the *Globe and Mail*, arguing that tax evasion is a response to tax invasion. In his characterization, the underground economy represents a "peaceful tax revolt… a useful restraint on Leviathan, and a benefit to all taxpayers" (Lemieux 1994).

Monitoring Compliance

Surveillance and detection methods employed to catch tax "evaders" are dramatically different from those used against welfare "fraudsters." Under the ITA the audit is the primary tool used to detect failure to comply with the Act (Van Der Hout et al. 2000, CCRA 1987). The CCRA's 2004–05 report to Parliament notes that there were 24.4 million individual tax filers and 318,337 reviews, examinations, and audits (it is not clear whether this is of all returns or only individual returns, but it seems to be the former). By contrast, virtually every social assistant recipient is under the equivalent of a constant audit, given informational reporting demands within the CVP (consolidated verification procedures) environment. The Social Assistance Review Committee's (SARC) observation in 1988 that the *Income Tax Act* operates in a different and less intrusive way than the social assistance system is even more apt today, given the dramatic increase in surveillance and scrutiny under the social assistance system without corresponding changes on the income-tax side (Social Assistance Review Committee 1988). Importantly, within both the social assistance and tax systems, various investigative and monitoring tools are justified by citing the need to maintain public confidence in the integrity of the respective systems, both of which depend (though to varying degrees) upon self-reporting. However, substantially more extensive scrutiny (and accompanying incursions upon individual privacy) is deemed necessary to maintain confidence in the welfare system than in the tax system.

As well, those with money can draw upon an army of expert resources to protect and guard their privacy as taxpayers. There has been a significant amount of litigation challenging the powers of the CCRA to investigate the taxpayer, especially on the question noted earlier of when a regulatory investigation (audit) becomes a *de facto* criminal investigation. The argument made by Van Der Haut et al. that, "even in a self-assessing system, where fair disclosure is critical, there must be clear limits to and tangible protections for taxpayers, their advisors and other third parties in the course of the audit or investigation, even where that exercise is not criminal in nature" is widely accepted (Van Der Haut et al. 2000: 89). Taxpayers, and those advising them, are encouraged to know the permissible limits of the CCRA's powers to invoke solicitor-client privilege to protect information against disclosure, to realize the potential to sue if an audit is conducted with malice, and to understand the *Charter* remedies available to protect the "target" of an audit (Van Der Haut et al. 2000). The point here is not to suggest that the advice is ill-founded but rather to note just how very different the context is from that of welfare fraud. On the income-tax side, the arguments proceed on the assumption that the taxpayer is a full citizen, worthy of respect, whose interests (privacy, liberty, autonomy) ought to be zealously guarded from incursions by the state. By contrast, the starting assumption for the welfare recipient is that she is undeserving and unworthy of respect; her privacy is scarcely acknowledged, let alone respected (Mosher 2002, MacFarlane 1995). Moreover, no body of accumulated expert resources exists that she or her counsel, should she be lucky enough to have representation, can draw upon.

Advice and guidance are also available to the taxpayer/evader from the CCRA itself, as is a form of immunity from prosecution through its voluntary disclosure program. Pursuant to this program, if a voluntary disclosure (a disclosure made before the client has knowledge of an audit) is made and outstanding taxes (together with interest) are paid, civil and criminal liabilities under the *ITA* will be avoided altogether. If clients or their representatives are uncertain about whether to make a disclosure, they can discuss their situation on a no-name basis with the CCRA. Nothing of this sort exists with the welfare system.

While the CCRA has what may be described as a very low-key snitching program it is not advertised and trumpeted in the manner that Ontario's welfare snitch line has been. Rather, there is a directive, lodged within its website, under the subject of "convictions," that those with information about a suspected violation of any tax law should contact the nearest CCRA tax investigations unit.

If, in the course of an audit, evasion is suspected, the matter can be referred to the "criminal investigations program" (formerly called "special investigations"). The 1994 Report of the Auditor General noted with concern that since 1990 the number of referrals to Special Investigations had decreased by 50 percent — from 1,000 to 500 a year. The 2004–05 report to Parliament affirms 3,898 enforcement actions, including criminal investigations and special enforcement actions (for income obtained from illegal activity) — a number that appears to include all tax filers, not just those filing personal income tax. Contrast this with the number of referrals to Eligibility Review Officers where an allegation of fraud has been made, which in 1997–98 was over 53,000. There are, no doubt, differences in the thresholds used for referral to special/criminal investigations and EROs, but even bearing this in mind, the difference is striking. Indeed the number of fraud investigations by EROs in Ontario approaches the number of audits undertaken by CCRA for the entire country in a given year.

Prosecution under the ITA may be either by summary conviction or indictment. Upon summary conviction, the accused is liable to a mandatory fine of not less than 50 percent and not greater than 200 percent of the amount of the tax that was being evaded, or to a fine and imprisonment for not more than two years. At the discretion of the Attorney General of Canada (with advice from the CCRA), evasion may be prosecuted by indictment. If convicted of an indictable offence, the accused is liable to a mandatory fine of not less than 100 percent and not more than 200 percent of the amount of tax that was sought to be evaded and imprisonment for a term not exceeding five years. Current policy indicates that "it would normally be appropriate to proceed by indictment" where the accused has previously been convicted of tax evasion, has entered a conspiracy to evade tax, or engaged in comparable criminal behaviour, *or* where the tax evaded exceeds $250,000 *and* at least one of several additional circumstances exists, including whether the scheme was sophisticated, whether the accused counselled others to evade taxes, and whether an innocent third party suffered significant losses (Federal Prosecutors Service Deskbook 2006). As the auditor general observed in 1990, when the dollar threshold for prosecution by indictment for tax evasion was $100,000 and the breakpoint for indictment for fraud under the Criminal Code was $1,000 (now $5,000), meaning jail time of up to ten years (now fourteen): "Setting a $100,000 threshold for prosecutions by indictment in tax-evasion cases means that most tax evaders face a much lower chance of being incarcerated than those convicted of other types of frauds" (Auditor General 1990). Moreover, it is important to reiterate that frequently tax evaders avoid prosecution entirely, and the matter is addressed through civil penalties also available under the ITA.

The auditor general's observation regarding the lowered risk of incarceration for tax evaders is certainly borne out by a review of sentencing decisions. While jail time is a possibility, whether prosecuted summarily or by indictment under the ITA (a maximum of two years and five years respectively), a jail term is rarely imposed. The rare punishment of jail time for tax evasion is usually reserved for cases where the accused is, for example, a person who prepares tax returns for others and has facilitated the evasion of taxes by multiple taxpayers (several hundred), or where, in addition to the charge of tax evasion, the accused has also been charged with fraud upon a public-benefits program. Interestingly, in *R. v. Silvestri*, a 2001 decision, the court observed that neither the Crown nor defence counsel were able to point to a case of first offence tax evasion in the range of $50,000 where incarceration was ordered in addition to the fine required by the Act. A review of CCRA convictions for Ontario posted on its website shows that of approximately sixty-five convictions between January and June 2006, only three received jail sentences.

Several authors and the auditor general (on multiple occasions) have commented on the relatively insignificant penalties imposed for tax evasion. Sossin, for example, has argued that tax evasion is treated as a "minor regulatory infraction rather than as a violation of any esteemed social values" (Sossin 1999:1). While the auditor general's office has explicitly refrained from suggesting that the penalties for tax evasion are inadequate, successive auditor generals have invited the government to consider the value judgment reflected by weak enforcement and light penalties and to consider sending a message to Canadians that tax cheating is unacceptable (Auditor General 1999b). Indeed, the repeated advice of successive auditors general has been that tax evasion ought to be considered a serious crime. The 1994 report, for example, observed that, "Tax evasion is a serious criminal offence. It results in a loss of revenue; it shifts the tax burden from dishonest taxpayers to honest taxpayers; and it creates unfair competition between businesses that abide by the law and those that don't" (Auditor General 1994).

Sentencing Tax Evaders

In comparing the judicial decisions on welfare fraud to those for income-tax evasion, two striking differences appear: the attention given to *mens rea* and the discourse invoked to support sentencing outcomes. On the first of these, it appears that in the tax evasion cases — both within the CCRA and throughout the criminal prosecution — the slippage from rule violation to guilt, so pervasive in the welfare system, does not occur. To the contrary, it is accepted as a matter of course that ignorance of the admittedly complex tax rules applicable to the situation in issue will negate *mens rea*. Indeed, even sophisticated businessmen with an advanced grasp of tax law and able to obtain expert assistance have successfully invoked ignorance of the ITA to negate *mens rea*. Consider, for example, the following two cases.

In *R. v. Chusid*, the accused was charged with wilful evasion and the making of false or deceptive statements. Mr. Chusid had failed to disclose a $1 million commission in the year it was received (when it ought to have been disclosed), but did disclose it later (when he knew he was under investigation). The court stressed that mere carelessness or inattention is not enough to establish guilt, rather there must be proof beyond a reasonable doubt that his actions were deliberately undertaken to evade taxes. Likewise, it was not enough that the accused was an experienced businessman, with an advanced grasp of taxation, who should have known of his obligation to report the commission. Additionally, the court noted that he was careless in his bookkeeping and his failure to disclose could have resulted from simple carelessness, thus raising in the judge's mind the benefit of a doubt. Mr. Chusid was acquitted.

In *R. v. McGuigan*, the accused was similarly charged with wilfully evading taxes and making a false or deceptive statement (*R. v. McGuigan* 2002). The case turned on whether Mr. McGuigan honestly believed that the stock options taxable in 1996, and not disclosed by him, were taxable not in 1996 but in 1997 and that he intended to disclose them then. The court noted that the law is complex, the treatment of stock options in this regard perhaps counter-intuitive, and that the law had changed. And while Mr. McGuigan had been the president of a company with sales of $500 million and vice-president of a company with sales of $5 billion, there was, to quote the trial judge, "no evidence of any financial sophistication or knowledge outside his sphere." The court further observed that Mr. McGuigan had recently lost his job and no doubt experienced shock and disorientation as a result: that apart from his actions there was no evidence to infer *mens rea* (e.g., debts, gambling problems, living beyond his means), and that his character evidence provided by witnesses was strong (including that given by a former assistant deputy minister of National Defence). The trial judge concluded, "there was a genuineness in his testimony... something that made me believe him." Mr. McGuigan was acquitted.

As discussed, welfare recipients — those with very limited, if any, access to expert advice and assistance — are commonly imputed with knowledge of the complexity of the rules and regulations surrounding Ontario Works. The complexity of the regulatory regime has meant little in defending against an allegation of welfare fraud, in contrast to the outcome of income-tax cases. It may well be the case that a reasonable doubt is created in the mind of the judge much more readily in the income-tax context than in the welfare context. Perhaps it is easier for judges to imagine how a million-dollar commission might be carelessly missed in reporting taxes, or that losing a prestigious position might be devastating and distracting, than it is for them to understand that one cannot escape from an abusive partner or the destitution of poverty.

> Perhaps, given their social position, judges can better imagine how a million-dollar commission might be carelessly missed in reporting taxes then that one cannot escape from an abusive partner or the destitution of poverty.

The discourse supporting sentence in income-tax evasion cases differs significantly from that heard in welfare cases. While judges will sometimes observe that the income-tax system is dependent upon taxpayer candour and honesty, income-tax evasion is rarely characterized as a breach of trust. Recall that this characterization is extremely common in welfare-fraud cases, and is employed — together with the characterization of the crime as one against the public purse — not only to warrant, but presumptively to require a jail term. The income-tax system is, in fact, more dependent upon candour and honesty than is the welfare system (in large measure because taxpayers are assumed to be honest and welfare recipients are not — a troublesome assumption in light of the data regarding acknowledged evasion). Although evading taxes is also a fraud upon the public purse, the breach of trust rarely generates a presumption of incarceration in tax evasion cases. This difference reinforces the view that the real issue in welfare-fraud cases is the perceived exploitation of the largesse of the hardworking taxpayer.

Consistent with the views regarding tax evasion solicited through compliance surveys, judges tend to regard tax evasion as a victimless crime — not as a crime against every member of the community, nor a crime against those most in need of state support. Finally, one also observes in income-tax cases that the fall from a position of elevated social status is used to justify lighter sentences. While there are exceptions, the accused's high status in the community and his good character and reputation — all somewhat tarnished by the prosecution — are considered relevant to sentencing. The stigma, sometimes personal bankruptcy, and more generally the loss of status, are regarded as dimensions of punishment already inflicted upon the accused. The welfare recipient, by contrast, is unable to invoke these badges of social esteem that are soiled by the criminal prosecution.

Conclusion

The taxpayer, constructed as a homogeneous category, is assumed to be employed, productive, and deserving; should he evade the payment of his taxes, he will enjoy considerable compassion from his fellow citizens who empathize with his desire to hold onto his hard-earned dollars. He can resort to a range of justificatory frameworks to rationalize his small transgression, notwithstanding that its consequence is the diminishing of public resources and the redistribution of the tax burden. The welfare recipient, yet another homogeneous category, is portrayed as the virtual antithesis of the taxpayer: lazy, undisciplined, dependent, and undeserving. Her poverty is cast as of her own making, and her need often misrepresented as greed by those who have infinitely more resources than she. Regarded with intense suspicion she, and others like her, are positioned as a threat to the honest, hard-working taxpayer. The wide public acceptance of tax evasion stands in sharp contrast to public sentiments regarding welfare fraud and welfare recipients. The rationalizations that are regularly invoked to justify tax evasion have no traction in relation to welfare fraud: The amorphous state is transformed into millions of innocent victims; all are expected to know, understand, and comply with the admittedly complex rules; and the inadequacy of benefit levels in no way mitigates the crime. And while much of the conduct of welfare recipients is mischaracterized as "fraudulent" — as criminal in nature — precisely the opposite holds true for taxpayers, whose criminal misconduct is largely ignored, condoned, and excused.

> The wide public acceptance of tax evasion stands in sharp contrast to public sentiments regarding welfare fraud and welfare recipients.

The language of criminality, the imagery of "the criminal," and the deployment of criminal processes and sanctions have been invoked by the state to construct a problem of welfare fraud and to scrutinize, diminish, and punish welfare recipients. By contrast, tax evaders are not regarded as criminals, nor is tax evasion constructed as a serious social problem. Rather, the tax evader is first and foremost a taxpayer; he is a good neo-liberal citizen, worthy of a solicitous response from the state to his minor transgression, should it ever be detected. The very selective invocation of criminality by the state simultaneously draws upon and enlarges the moral worthiness of taxpayers and the moral failings of welfare recipients. In so doing, it entrenches categories of deservedness — categories that valorize competitive individualism and erode collective obligation.

> The language of criminality, the imagery of "the criminal" and the deployment of criminal processes and sanctions have been invoked by the state to scrutinize, diminish, and punish welfare recipients.

DISCUSSION QUESTIONS

1. How should the motivation for engaging in conduct inform our views as to whether or not this conduct is "criminal" in nature? Or should it be a matter relevant to sentencing, or not at all relevant? For example, if a mother defrauds welfare by failing to disclose small amounts of money received from her parents and her motivation in so doing is so that she may feed her children, should this be considered a crime? Or considered relevant to sentencing? Would your views change if you knew that should she fail to adequately feed her children she may be blamed for failing to provide adequately for their needs and possibly lose custody of her children to the state? How would your answers to these questions vary if you were to adopt consensus theories or critical theories?

2. What do we need by "need"? What do we really need: the means necessary to survive, the means to live with dignity, the means to belong? What part should government have in providing for the needs of citizens? Or should society encourage more self-reliance? Does the criminal law have a place in determining whether social responsibility or individualism should be emphasized?

3. Try an experiment. Ask your friends and/or family if they have ever failed to report income to Revenue Canada or paid cash to avoid paying taxes, and ask why they did this? Then try asking about their views regarding welfare fraud and compare the answers.

4. What does this case study reveal about the claim of traditional approaches to criminology that the rules proscribing behaviour are neutral, universal, and unchanging?

5. What alternative approaches to welfare fraud and tax evasion might a critical criminologist argue in favour of?

GLOSSARY OF TERMS

Conditional Sentence: pursuant to section 742.1 of the Criminal Code, where convicted, except where the offence is one punishable by a minimum term of imprisonment, and the court a) imposes a sentence of imprisonment of less than two years and b) is satisfied that serving the sentence in the community would not endanger the safety of the community and would be consistent with the fundamental purpose and principles of sentencing set out in sections 718-718.2, the court may order that the offender serve the sentence in the community subject to complying with the conditions under section 742.3. Most commonly a conditional sentence takes the form of house arrest, with several conditions attached.

Indictable Offences: more serious offences, wherein the maximum penalties will be higher than those for summary conviction offences (see below). The procedures for prosecuting indictable offences are more involved than for summary conviction. Many offences are "hybrid" offences, wherein the Crown elects whether to proceed by indictment or by summary conviction.

Neo-Liberalism: a term used to describe the dominant international political economy in place today. Since the 1970s, international politics and economics have seen the rise of a way of thinking that stresses the shrinking of the public state, with a corresponding emphasis upon the importance of private obligation and self-sufficiency. This theory of government and the state is tied to a belief that open markets, rather than a strong welfare state, will provide the greatest good in society.

Ontario Works: it is governed by the *Ontario Works Act, 1996*. Eligibility depends upon the assessment of the financial needs of the "benefit unit," which includes "spouses" (as defined by the OWA and not pursuant to family law) and dependent children. With few exceptions, all adult beneficiaries are required to engage in work or work readiness activities as a precondition to receiving benefits.

Ontario Disability Support Program: it creates a separate benefit regime, within higher benefits and no work requirements, for persons who are "disabled" as defined by the *Ontario Disability Support Program Act*.

Social Assistance: residual, means-tested government financial assistance programs. In Ontario, Ontario Works and the Ontario Disability Support Program are both forms of social assistance. Social assistance is often commonly referred to as "welfare."

Summary Conviction Offences: generally less serious offences wherein unless a different penalty is specified in the offence section, the maximum sentence is $2,000 and/or six months' imprisonment. The procedures for charging and prosecuting differ from indictable offences.

NOTES

This article draws upon research undertaken by the author and Professor Joe Hermer and funded by the Law Commission of the. Deep gratitude is owed to the Law Commission for its support of this work.

1. If the value is greater than $5,000 the Crown proceeds by way of indictment with the maximum penalty being up to fourteen years of imprisonment; below $5,000 the Crown may elect to proceed by indictment (imprisonment of up to two years) or by summary conviction (fine of up to $2,000 and/or six months imprisonment).

REFERENCES

Auditor General of Canada. 1990. *1990 Report of the Auditor General of Canada.* Ottawa: Office of the Auditor General of Canada.

Auditor General of Canada. 1994. *1994 Report of the Auditor General Canada.* Ottawa: Office of the Auditor General of Canada.

Auditor General of Canada. 1999a. *1999 Report of the Auditor General of Canada* Ottawa: Office of the Auditor General of Canada.

Auditor General of Canada. 1999b. *Opening Statement to the Committee on Public Accounts: Revenue Canada - Underground Economy Initiative.* Available at <http://www.oag-bvg.gc.ca/domino/other.nsf/html/99pa08_e.html> accessed January 24, 2005.

Brooks, Neil. 1998. "The Challenge of Tax Compliance." In C. Evans and A. Greenbaum (eds.), *Tax Administration: Facing the Challenges of the Future.* New South Wales: Prospect Media.

Broomer v. Ontario (A.G.) (June 5, 2002), Toronto 02-CV-229203CM3 (Ont. Sup. Ct.).

CCRA (Canada Customs and Revenue Agency). 2003. *Compliance, Tax Cheating and Social Change in Canada in 2002–03.* Ottawa: Canada Customs and Revenue Agency.

_____. 2005. *CCRA Annual Report to Parliament 2004–05.* Ottawa: Canada Revenue Agency.

Criminal Code of Canada, R.S., 1985, c.C-46.

Ewart, Douglas J. 1986. *Criminal Fraud*. Toronto: Carswell Legal Publications.

Federal Prosecution Service Deskbook, updated to October, 2005. Available at <www.justice. gc.ca/en/dept/pub/fps/fpd/ch19.html/#19_3> accessed July 2007.

Gilles, David E.A., and Lindsay M. Tedds. 2002. *Taxes and the Canadian Underground Economy*. Toronto: Canadian Tax Foundation.

Herd, Dean, and Andrew Mitchell. 2002. *Discouraged, Diverted and Disentitled: Ontario Works' New Service Delivery Model*. Toronto: Community Social Planning Council of Toronto & Ontario Social Safety Network.

Income Tax Act, R.S.C. 1985, c.1 (5th Supp.).

Lemieux, Pierre. 1994. "A Few Words in Support of Tax Evasion." *Globe and Mail*, January 31.

MacDonald, C.A. (Tina), Duncan F. MacDonald, and Sheila Blair. 1995. *Reducing Fraud and Waste in Income Security Programs in Canada*. Edmonton: C.A. MacDonald and Associates.

MacFarlane, Elizabeth. 1995. "No Lock on the Door: Privacy and Social Assistance Recipients." *Appeal* 1:1.

Martin, Dianne L. 1992. "Passing the Buck: Prosecution of Welfare Fraud; Preservation of Stereotypes." *Windsor Year Book of Access to Justice* 12, 52.

Matthews, Deb. 2004. "Report to the Honourable Sandra Pupatello, Minister of Community and Social Services: Review of Employment Assistance Programs in Ontario Works and Ontario Disability Support Program." Toronto: Ministry of Community and Social Services.

Mosher, Janet. 2002. "The Shrinking of the Public and Private Spaces of the Poor." In J. Hermer and J. Mosher (eds.), *Disorderly People: Law and the Politics of Exclusion in Ontario*. Halifax: Fernwood Publishing.

Mosher, Janet, Patricia Evans, and Margaret Little. 2004. *Walking on Eggshells: Abused Women's Experiences of Ontario's Welfare System*. Available at <www.oaith.ca/pdf/Walking_on_Eggshells.pdf> accessed July 28, 2005.

Mosher, Janet, and Joe Hermer. 2005. *Welfare Fraud: The Constitution of Social Assistance as Crime*. Ottawa: Law Commission of Canada.

National Council of Welfare. 2006. *Welfare Incomes 2005*. Ottawa: National Council of Welfare.

Ontario Disability Support Program Act, 1997, S.O. 1997, c. 25, Sch. B.

Ontario, Legislative Assembly. 1995. *Official Report of Debates (Hansard)*, 1st Sess., 36th Leg., September 28.

_____. 1995 *Official Report of Debates (Hansard)*, 1st Sess., 36th Leg., October 2.

Ontario, Ministry of Community, Family and Children's Services. 2003. *Welfare Fraud Control Report 2001–2002*. Toronto: Ministry of Community, Family and Children's Services.

Ontario, Ministry of Community and Social Services. 2004. *Ontario Works: Controlling Fraud (Directive 45.0)*. Toronto: Ministry of Community and Social Services.

Ontario Works Act, 1997, S.O. 1997, c. 25, Sch. A.

Ontario Works Act, 1997, O. Reg. 134/98, amended to O. Reg. 231/04.

Parnaby, Patrick. 2003. "Disaster Through Dirty Windshields Law, Order and Toronto Squeegee Kids." *Canadian Journal of Sociology* 28 (3), 281–307.

R. v. Chusid, [2002] O.J. No. 4644 (Ont. Sup. Ct.) (QL).

R. v. Gallagher, [1996] O.J. No. 4761 (Prov. Div.) (QL).

R. v. Jarvis, [2002] 3 S.C.R. 757.

R. v. Maldonado, [1998] O.J. No. 3209 (Prov. Div.) (QL).

R. v. McGillivray, [1992] A.J. No. 886 (Prov. Ct. Crim. Div.) (QL).

R. v. McGuigan, [2002] O.J. No. 3989 (Ont. Sup. Ct.) (QL).

R. v. McIsaac, [1998] B.C.J. No. 1946 (S.C.) (QL).

R. v. Olan, [1978] 2 S.C.R. 1175.

R. v. Reid, [1995], 137 N.S.R. (2d) 293 (C.A.).

R. v. Rogers, [2001] O.J. No. 5203 (Ct. of Jus.) (QL).

R. v. Silvestri, [2001] O.J. No. 3694 (Ont. Sup. Ct.) (QL)

R. v. Stapley, [1997] O.J. No. 3235 (Gen. Div.) (QL)

R. v. Théroux, [1993] 2 S.C.R. 5.

R. v. Thurrott [1972] 1 Ontario Reports 460.

Social Assistance Review Committee. 1988. *Report of the Social Assistance Review Committee: Transitions.* Toronto: Queen's Printer, 1988.

Sossin, Lorne. 1999. "Welfare State Crime in Canada Revisited: The Politics of Tax Evasion in the 1980s and 1990s." *The Tax Forum* 1 (Autumn).

Swift, Karen, and Michael Birmingham. 2000. "Location, Location, Location: Restructuring and the Everyday Lives of 'Welfare Moms.'" In S. Neysmith (ed.), *Restructuring Caring Labour: Discourse, State Practice and Everyday Life.* Toronto: Oxford.

Van Der Hout, Susan, Robert Goldstein and Angelina Fisher. 2000. "Taxpayer Information: Administration and Enforcement Procedures Under the Income Tax Act (Canada)." *Advocates Quarterly* 23.

Varma, Kimberly N., and Anthony N. Doob. "Deterring Economic Crimes: The Case of Tax Evasion." *Canadian Journal of Criminology* 40 (2).

13

Crime-Making on the Street
A Critical Perspective

Willem de Lint and Christian Pasiak

KEY FACTS

> A peak in the overall crime rate, in terms of Criminal Code offences, was reached in 1991 at just over 10,000 per 100,000 people. Violent crime reached a national peak in 1994 at 1,046/100,000; it fell 9 percent to 965/100,000 by 2002.

> Homicides accounted for about 0.0019 percent of violent crimes in 2002, a rate of 1.85/100,000. Though there were 29 more homicides in 2002 than the year before, the homicide rate still declined by 28 percent between 1992 and 2002.

> Certain types of social harms, such as white-collar crimes like environmental pollution and insider trading, are often filtered out of official records.

> Victimization surveys are currently administered as part of the General Social Survey (GSS) program. The GSS, originating in 1985, conducts telephone surveys, each of which contains a core topic and focuses on exploratory questions and a standard set of socio-demographic questions used for classification.

> Analysis of the content of mass media has found that crime is the fourth largest news category, after sports, general interest, and business. Crime stories focus on individual events, violence, and "street," rather than elite, wrongdoing.

Sources: Sacco and Kennedy 1998; Statistics Canada 2003, 2004.

As social animals we are fixated on order, and nothing captures our interest more than the spectacle of rules being broken and reaffirmed. We are addicted to what Christie (1977) calls "norm-clarification" rituals, or staged dramas confirming the restoration of the *status quo ante*. In this, our fascination today is not far different from our needs in centuries past. Daniel Defoe's *The History and Misfortunes of the Famous Moll Flanders,* written in 1722 and considered by many as one of the first novels in English, treats readers to the moral journey of a poor orphan's experiences, from petty thief to imprisonment and eventual banishment to America as an indentured servant. It demonstrates public fascination with the life of crime.

While today we may sit in front of the TV watching *Cops* or the 6 o'clock news to witness the enforcement of moral order, three centuries ago norm clarification was offered more directly through a variety of "in-your-face" public punishments and executions. In that period, the wayfarer would have entered villages on horseback or carriage greeted by the stench of rotting corpses left in iron cages (known as "bildoes" or "gibbet irons") hung from trees. Inside the town square, hapless petty criminals might have been noticeable languishing in the pillory, a contraption forcing the individual to stand

> As social animals we are fixated on order, and nothing captures our interest more than the spectacle of rules being broken and reaffirmed.

hunched over, head and wrists forced between a hollowed-out vice.

In addition, in the early 1700s, it would have made little sense to speak of changes in crime rates. Crime was essentially viewed as a *moral problem* — perhaps even a result of the work of the devil — and understood in religious, not scientific or actuarial terms. Today crime is understood from a variety of perspectives. There is still the question of moral wrong, but added to this is the *scientific perspective*, including the view that crime is not simply freely chosen, but to some extent determined by various contexts and conditions, including, in the case of Moll Flanders, her chances as a poor orphan living at a time where there was nothing but the occasional charity given to her by others to catch her fall and save her from starvation or prostitution. To this we might add a third general perspective, that crime is a *social construct* in the first place. As this view goes, what causes crime, or even how much crime exists, is not as important as how it is reacted to; the process of reaction is part of the production of a thing *as* crime.

> Crime is a *social construct* the process of reaction is part of the production of a thing *as* crime.

Even such an apparently simple exercise as collecting information on who is committing offences depends upon some decision-making about how to code or register some very contentious concepts. If we want, for example, to know what the relationship between crime and race is, we need to first agree on what both these concepts mean, and anthropologists no longer give any credence to the erroneous claim that there are three or seven or even nine racial designations to cover everyone on the planet.

This highlights a key problem about knowledge. We know things according to categories that we've previously conceived and accepted. We measure crime, but by so doing, not only do we apply scientific concepts to a social fact or phenomenon, we contribute to the very life of that social fact and the validity of its discovery through scientific measurement. As we will see later in this chapter, we could just as easily observe the problem that we encourage to be perceived as "crime" using a prior belief that it is the pathologies of our society that require measurement and accounting, rather than their individualized symptoms.

For instance, given that in modern liberal capitalist societies we are also schooled in the slogans of merit and just reward and the view that venture and risk is necessary to provide incentives and stimulate interests, in a fundamental way our societies uphold contradictory values in which risk promotion and a stable order merit reward and equal chances, and individual interests and communitarian values, are at loggerheads. As we will see, these oppositional values have an impact on what we think we know about the extent and nature of crime. We will see that what we are told through popular media, through reports of surveys on victims, or through police-reports in official crime data is filtered through our values and ideologies.

> What we are told through popular media, through reports of surveys on victims, or through police-reports in official crime data is filtered through our values and ideologies.

Suffice it to say that everything may be contextualized and recontextualized. Given the opportunity, a good lawyer will provide a context for their client's behaviour that will contrast sharply with that of the prosecutor. When we were treated to stories of looting in New Orleans following Hurricane Katrina, the subtext was stratified by our class bias. The portrayal was not: "*Abandoned residents left to fend for themselves forage among abandoned stores.*" Rather, it was: "*Disorder unleashes wicked heart of New Orleans.*" It seems that there were only two extreme positions in reports out of New Orleans in the weeks after Katrina struck, just as there is with crime in general: like Moll Flanders, remaining residents were either overtaken by a "Heart of Darkness" lawlessness or they were subject to uncommon selflessness and humanitarianism. In fact however, the vast majority of human action is prosaic and unremarkable, neither saintly nor wicked. But the unremarkable is by definition un-newsworthy. To underline the point again: we are all here, you included, turning the pages of crime treatments (scholarly or fictional) because we want to know if the hero bests the villain (and his only too-human flaws). We want to know if he takes his reward of the innocent damsel. In our case, the damsel, we would like to think, is "the good" of the social world itself.

In this chapter we will review how crime knowledge is "discovered" or "produced" — or how we know what we think we know. We will find that official reports tell us only part of the story of crime. We will look into victimization surveys and popular accounts and review the biases of collection and reporting. We then turn again to the perspectives we just introduced (medical, penological, and constructive) before making closing observations.

Official Statistics

For the most part, our knowledge of criminal activity is derived from "officially" reported and recorded occurrences of persons charged and sentenced with criminal offences. You may be familiar with the expression "the facts speak for themselves." As we will discuss shortly, this knowledge is filtered in various ways, both in how it arrives and how it is transmitted following its arrival. The following is a brief snapshot of what Statistics Canada offers us with respect to crime in Canada. This data is derived from the Uniform Crime Report (UCR) (Statistics Canada 2003).

- Youth crime and female violent crime are going up while other major crimes have been going down. In 1997–98, 12 percent of all violent crimes were committed by women, but by 2003, this rate climbed to 16 percent. The majority of crimes making up the female contribution to the crime rate were for minor assault. Of all federally sentenced women in 2003, 29 percent were Aboriginal.
- A peak in the overall crime rate was reached in 1991 at just over 10,000 in 100,000. Violent crime reached a national peak in 1994 at 1,046 in 100,000. They were down 9 percent to 965 in 100,000 by 2002.
- Common assaults account for nearly two-thirds of violent crime; sexual assaults are the next most frequently occurring violent crime at 8 percent. Homicides accounted for about .0019 percent of violent crimes in 2002, at a rate of 1.85 in 100,000. Though there were twenty-nine more homicides in 2002 than the year before, the homicide rate still declined 28 percent between 1992 and 2002.
- Property crime declined 27 percent between 1991 and 2002 (and 33 percent between 1992 and 2002). Break and enter crimes have gone down 42 percent between 1992 and 2002. Counterfeiting went up 500 percent in that period.
- Drug crimes rose 42 percent between 1992 and 2002, with cannabis accounting for the largest change (up 80 percent in this ten year period).

When looking over statistical data such as the above highlights from the UCR, we should consider how this data is compiled, the unseen factors that contribute to these final "official" records, and their ability to accurately report the *actual* occurrence of incidents of crime. It is important to recognize that there can be programmatic problems with the Uniform Crime Report records. Here it might be useful for us to invoke the metaphor of the "dark figure of crime," which refers to the portion of criminal activity that goes unreported and/or undetected by official sources. Through the UCR, only crimes that are reported to police, discovered by police, or by someone else who subsequently reports them are included in statistics compiled by this system.

Because most of the complaints made to the police are reported by victims, there is a direct correlation between under-reported crimes and lower official crime rates in those categories. Common examples of under-reported crimes include sexual assault and theft under $5,000. Many people do not consider interpersonal matters or minor disputes to be crimes, regardless of whether or not they would be defined as such according to the Criminal Code. Also, people who distrust authority, those who may be involved in crime *themselves*, illegal immigrants, and others — such as abused spouses who may fear violent retaliation if caught being contacted by the police — are often more reluctant to report victimization through official channels (Haggerty 2000: 29). Conversely, changes in public attitudes about certain types of crimes result in the public's inclination to report certain crimes more readily, for example, concerns with child abuse, and more recently, suspicion of terrorism or undocumented ("illegal") immigrants, the current hot issues in the United States. As we will discuss further in this chapter, public attitudes often coincide with government-backed media campaigns.

It is useful for us to recognize that there is always a portion of reported incidents of crime that are screened out of official record. This concept can be referred to as the "crime filter." Sometimes social harms are reported, but they do not make it through the criminal justice system into official record for various reasons. Charges may be dropped by the victim after their initial report, there may be bureaucratic and/or courtroom technicalities affecting the incident's status as a crime, and the processing of information by criminal justice agencies can play a large role in how the incident will be recorded officially.

Some criminologists have used the metaphor of a funnel to show that at each level of information processing, the chances that an incident will be recorded officially get smaller and smaller (see Winterdyk 2006: 28). Try to envision a funnel's conical shape and the way substances flow through it as the way incidents flow through the criminal justice system. Remember to keep in mind that some information is filtered and does not make its way into official records at all. If you're wondering how our metaphor holds up in light of the fact that most substances are eventually able to make their way through a funnel, let's add another dimension. Picture grains of sand, or pebbles of varying sizes being sifted through the funnel. Now let's say that these represent socio-economic status, and get larger in size as they represent higher levels of social status. Due to a variety of factors discussed further in this chapter, such as the types/nature of acts that are typically criminalized, this might be a more accurate portrayal of how the criminal justice system operates.

To provide a basic example of this funnelling of information, the most common initial point of contact an offender has with the criminal justice system is with the police, and the acting officer's initial decision as to whether or not they will lay a charge affects whether or not the offence will move into the next stage of the system. Should it reach the next stage, it is then up to the courts to decide whether or not the incident will be recognized as a crime officially. Similarly, in cases where physical evidence is involved, it may be up to the discretion of professionals outside the criminal justice system to determine whether or not a case will be further investigated by police (e.g. fire marshals investigate suspected arsons, coroners often determine whether or not circumstances surrounding an individual's death should be ruled foul play, homicide, medical malpractice, etc.)

The "crime funnel" metaphor has alternatively been used on a macro-level to symbolize the much lower number of crimes detected and punished by the criminal justice system than those actually committed, though such a usage tends to imply that crime is an objective occurrence based on the *quality* of certain acts, existing beyond what is proscribed by official channels, which we would argue is *not* the case. We prefer to focus on the "crime funnel," on the effects of numerous direct and indirect social, political, and economic factors that seep into subsequent stages of the crime-reporting process — namely, the reduction of officially reported crimes.

Another element of the crime filtration process involves the relationship between crime and the resources employed in its detection and punishment by the criminal justice system. Critical criminologists sometimes utilize the metaphor of the "crime net" to demonstrate this relationship. Here, agents of the criminal justice system can be seen to operate like fishers. They use "nets" of varying dimensions or with varying sizes of mesh, and the "net" will determine how much crime is caught. This model is useful in understanding how the state can use the criminal justice system to support particular interest groups in society or to legitimize the political and economic arrangements of society.

Related to this concept, and another variable that affects official crime rates, is the way police services record and report the criminal activity that is detected. Calling the police is not necessarily a guarantee that an incident will enter the official record. Police dispatchers may divert matters to another organization if they do not consider it to be a serious criminal matter. It has been suggested that "75 per cent of calls to the police are 'screened, referred, or terminated without being forwarded to officers'" (Haggerty 2000: 30).

> Calling the police is not necessarily a guarantee that an incident will enter the official record; both formal and informal police organizational routines can be seen to affect the crime rate.

Though the Centre for Criminal Justice Statistics works with police agencies on an ongoing basis to minimize variation in the transmission and reporting of data, there are still variations in how police count crime between agencies. Some of the factors that contribute to these variations include changes in the number of police services and police officers, which affects the amount of detected crimes. Enforcement practices also vary between police departments. Community police departments generally tend to create primary targets of specific problems tailored to each community's wants and needs. This tends to affect the degree of vigilance with which certain crimes are enforced, which will be subsequently reflected in crime reports (Schmalleger and Volk 2001: 50).

There is a considerable amount of discretion among officers, who often cast an eye to ultimate organizational consequences when laying charges and documenting events in cases involving personal and institutional preference. The desire to improve a force's statistical profile can inform how particular cases are documented (Haggerty 2000: 30). Therefore, both formal and informal police organizational routines can be seen to affect the crime rate.

There are also certain types of social harms that are more often filtered out of official record, such as white collar crimes (e.g. environmental crimes, insider trading, etc.) that are sometimes dealt with out-of-court in non-criminal tribunals or private administrative bodies (or are not dealt with at all). These are more often administered through regulatory law where criminal intent does not need to be proven, and where it is not necessary to pinpoint a specific individual to hold responsibility for an unlawful act.

As we have shown, both the "dark figure of crime" (unreported crimes) and the "crime filter" (reported crimes that do not make it into official record) threaten the reliability of official data to record the actual incidence of crime. The nature of the filtration process can be symbolized by the "crime funnel" to show how it becomes less likely at each successive level of the information process that a crime will be officially recorded; and the "crime net" shows the relationship to official crime rates in relation to deployment of resources aimed at prosecuting certain crimes, which are often seen to be politically contingent.

There are also methodological concerns with the way the UCR counts crime, especially in incidents that involve multiple offences. The UCR counts only the most serious offence in an incident, determined by maximum sentence length. Therefore, less serious offences tend to be under-reported in the UCR survey. Similarly, for violent crimes, the UCR records the number of incidents in terms of victims (for example, if one individual murders two people, two incidents are reported, whereas if two people murder one individual, only one incident is reported). The exception to this rule is robbery, where one incident can often involve many individuals who could be considered victims. To record them as separate incidents would largely overstate the occurrence of robbery. Therefore, the UCR records for violent crimes, with the exception of robbery, can be seen as a record of the total number of victims reported.

Altering the legal definition of a crime has also been seen to affect the results of UCR data. For example, the types of behaviour that constitute sexual assault have been more clearly defined in recent years to include a wider range of behaviour, from unwanted sexual touching to life-threatening aggravated assault. Amendments to the definition of arson in 1990 to include mischief fires have similarly broadened the scope of this criminal activity. As such, there have been corresponding statistical increases in these categories (Schmalleger and Volk 2001: 50).

The consistency of the definition of a crime also impacts the way incidents are processed and officially recorded. When we discuss child abuse, it is sometimes difficult to draw a line between corporal punishment and physical abuse. If threatening children and acts of indecent exposure were added to the official definition of child abuse, it is estimated that incidents in this category could double (Schmalleger and Volk 2001: 51).

Also, because the UCR receives data from all municipal police forces in Canada, as well as the RCMP, the Ontario Provincial Police, and Quebec's provincial police force, it is unrealistic to expect that all these police services are able to report their data in a uniform manner (Schmalleger and Volk 2001: 49–50). Variances in administrative differences, enforcement practices, public attitudes, and unknown errors in counting procedures can contribute to *unintentional* mistakes made during the data-collection process. This is referred to as "random error." This differs from "systematic error," which is a *predictable* error that occurs during the data-collection process. When enumerators are recording data, it becomes important for them to be aware of certain dependant variables. For example, because property crimes are more often under-reported than serious violent crimes, this creates a larger margin of error for officially recorded property crimes (Winterdyk 2006: 27).

Victimization Survey Data

Victimization survey data can differ considerably from the data gathered in the Uniform Crime Report, largely because the information gathered in victimization surveys is elicited through interviews with members of randomly selected households throughout the country. Because these surveys do not depend on reports of crime to the police, they usually uncover a large portion of crime that would otherwise go unreported. In part due to this factor, and because the information elicited does not pass through the filter of criminal justice agencies, victimization surveys are viewed by many to be a more accurate measure of the actual incidence of crime than the Uniform Crime Report.

> Victimization surveys are viewed by many to be a more accurate measure of the actual incidence of crime than the Uniform Crime Report.

The information collected in these surveys focuses on the nature and extent of criminal victimization in Canada. Victimization surveys are currently administered as part of the General Social Survey (GSS) program. The GSS, originating in 1985, conducts telephone surveys, each of which contains a core topic, and focuses on exploratory questions and a standard set of socio-demographic questions used for classification. The two primary objectives of the GSS are to gather data on social trends in order to monitor temporal changes in the living conditions and well-being of Canadians and to provide immediate information on specific social policy issues of current or emerging interest. Recent cycles have included some qualitative questions that explored opinions and perceptions regarding fear of crime, and knowledge and perceptions of the criminal justice system.

Until 1998, the sample size was approximately 10,000 persons. This was increased in 1999 to 25,000. With a sample of 25,000, results are available at both the national and provincial levels, and also for some special population groups such as disabled persons, visible minorities, and seniors.

Eight types of offences based on Criminal Code definitions are included in the GSS: sexual assault, robbery, physical assault, theft of personal property, breaking and entering, motor vehicle/parts theft, theft of household property and vandalism. Anyone who reports they have been the victim of one of the eight categories of offences in the previous twelve months is asked for detailed information. This includes where the incident occurred; whether the incident was reported to the police; and the level of injury, use or presence of a weapon, and financial loss.

Some highlights from the most recent GSS victimization survey (Statistics Canada 2004) are as follows:

- The rate of violent victimization in Canada was no higher in 2004 than it was five years earlier.
- In 2004 there was no significant change in self-reported rates of violent victimization, namely sexual assault, robbery, or physical assault. However, rates rose by 24 percent for theft of personal property, 42 percent for theft of household property, and 17 percent for vandalism. The only type of offence to show a significant decline was breaking and entering, where rates fell by about one-fifth.
- The risk of self-reported violent victimization was highest among young people aged fifteen to twenty-four, single people, those who frequently participated in evening activities and those who lived in an urban area.

- In general, people living west of the Manitoba-Ontario border were also at higher overall risk of victimization, though there were some exceptions.
- Six in ten Canadians believed that crime was lower in their neighbourhood than elsewhere in Canada. The same proportion of Canadians was of the opinion that crime levels in their neighbourhood were unchanged over the past five years.
- Satisfaction with personal safety has continued to grow since 1993, and was at 94 percent of the Canadian population aged fifteen years and over in 2004. Though the overall figure was high, it was somewhat lower when Canadians were asked to rate their feelings of safety in a variety of situations. For instance, four out of five people (80 percent) indicated that they were not at all worried when home alone at night.
- Canadians living in the Atlantic provinces were generally less fearful of crime. In 2004, 97 percent of residents in Newfoundland and Labrador and 96 percent of residents in Prince Edward Island felt safe walking alone at night, while the same was true for 88 percent of people living in British Columbia and Quebec.
- While fear of crime was generally higher among women than men, the difference has narrowed since 1999. This can be attributed to the fact that women's level of personal safety has improved, while men's overall feelings of safety and safety in particular situations has only marginally increased or remained unchanged.
- Fear of crime tended to be more pronounced for Canadians who believed they lived in a neighbourhood where crime was higher than elsewhere and who thought that neighbourhood crime had increased in the past five years.
- When asked to assess the criminal justice sectors, the majority of Canadians were satisfied with police. As was the case in previous victimization surveys, opinions on the criminal courts, prison, and parole systems were less favourable. Nevertheless, positive assessments of the courts and prisons have generally increased since 1999.
- In 2004, there were inter-provincial differences in satisfaction with the criminal justice sectors. While people in the Western provinces were less likely to give positive assessment, confidence levels in these provinces had not worsened but had either improved or stayed the same, depending on the criminal justice sector and functions.
- Age was also shown to play a role in how Canadians rated the criminal justice sectors. Positive attitudes toward the police generally increased with age, while favourable perceptions of the courts, prison, and parole systems were more common in younger Canadians.

Popular Media

Durkheim (1984) long ago recognized the important function of the stranger and the criminal to what he called "solidarity." Reaction to crime, he argued, was functional in supporting the mores and rules of the collective, so much so that inaction regarding crime or transgression against social norms indicated the absence of, as we might put it today, "the social." Christie (1977) also recognized the value of conflict resolution as a precious commodity. He argued that what had occurred between the time of the village and modern times is the gradual stealing away of this precious resource from the community by officials and experts who then hashed out the conflict in a sterile ritual behind the great stone facades of the court of justice.

In recent times, the mediation of crime is widely recognized. What researchers and commentators have found is that, not only is crime a thing that is *mediated* — or shaped by presentations and representations in various formats, it is also a thing that has been presented and re-presented according to certain well-defined scripts. These scripts are not only a function of our cultural prejudices or expectations, but also of the way that the cultural industries have come to create capital out of our appetite for conflict resolution and for a morality play or drama in which good triumphs over evil.

Much if not most of what people perceive of crime — including its extensiveness and character — is mediated through the news or entertainment frames and formats of the cultural industry (Skogan and Maxfield 1981). By format, what is meant is that each kind of media has a certain style of presentation. A situation comedy, for instance, has a regular cast of characters who are dealing with a humorous situation. A frame is the restrictiveness of each kind of media format in terms of what kind of issues and content is appropriate. A news journal frame (*60 Minutes*) has a slightly more probing and critical aspect than a tabloid entertainment frame (*Entertainment Tonight*).

> Much, if not most of what people perceive of crime — including its extensiveness and character — is mediated through the news or entertainment frames and formats of the cultural industry.

Mass media may be broken down in terms of content, platforms, and distribution. The top news and entertainment mass media will be dominant in two or all three of these categories. The top chains in terms of gross news product also have licenses from the CRTC (or in the U.S., the FCC) to distribute this product and own vehicles for broadcast or publication. News and story editors, chosen and following the directions of publishers or producers, are key gatekeepers — keeping, for instance, movies about 9/11 under wraps until the "timing is right" or deciding not to publish a news story in which George W. Bush is referred to as a "war criminal."

The concentration of media ownership into a handful of mega-corporations (Viacom, etc.) over the past ten to fifteen years has reduced the number and ranges of dissident voices that can be heard by the average "consumer" of mass-media product. This is partly because investors like a predictable return on investment and company executives do not like to spurn political and capital elites by presenting counter-ideological narratives. Newspapers and broadcasters have dedicated police and crime reporters, and a repertoire of half a dozen or so dramatic treatments with which to work up the regular dosage of human misery, frailty, and incompetence. Police reports are a staple news source and have the added value of being considered reliable, given that they are the product of authorized officials.

This, however, does not fully explain the tremendous appetite for crime stories — a phenomenon that is obvious to anyone who turns on the TV or picks up a newspaper. A full explanation cannot be provided here, but it is noteworthy that our appetite for watching conflict and its resolution can now be experienced from the armchair behind the television or computer screen. As Christie would say, our retreat from the village has been matched by a new voyeurism. As Durkheim would say, we have come to lust after the profane, perhaps because the temple is now that of misery, frailty, and incompetence; a temple to which we turn to make our lives at once more and less meaningful.

Whatever the cause, we are "buying" crime like never before. Analysis of the content of mass media has found that crime is the fourth largest news category, after sports, general interest, and business (Kennedy and Sacco 1998: 26–27). In addition, crime stories focus on individual events, violence, and "street," rather than elite, wrongdoing (Ibid 27).

This is largely because newsworthiness, or judgments about whether a story belongs within the frame of the front page, is based on whether or not the report is timely, has a shock or recognition value (any unexpected event, particularly in familiar places) and concerns people who are deemed worthy (prominent, innocent). Mass murders and serial killings fit into this frame easily, and a familiar dramatic narrative (disorder into order) is expected by the reader or viewer and easy to reconstruct. Not so familiar or exciting, even if it involves worthy or prominent people, is the complicated case of the Enron accounting fraud or the illegal use of tax monies investigated in the Inquiry of Justice John Gormley.

On the entertainment side of the ledger, a variety of formats pander to our appetites. Crime-based reality TV continues to be a mainstay of contemporary prime-time viewing. Shows like *Cops* and *Dallas SWAT* are popular for their depiction of police as responsible and considerate (*Cops*), but tough and deliberate (*Dallas SWAT*), and victims and villains alike as poor, minority, and uneducated. *Cops* and *World's Wildest Police Videos*, as Prosise and Johnson (2004) find, serve to justify controversial police practices, including racial profiling. Michael Moore once sent up the street crime emphasis of this genre by suiting up as a superhero fighting fraud and corruption. The skit dramatized the distance between the arid exploits of corporate or white-collar operations and the downward intrigue of the drug sting.

Popular television crime and justice dramatizations both follow and push fashionable opinion. *Da Vinci's Inquest* features a mix of complex characters, including a crooked cop, prostitute informants, a criminal mayor, a wizened coroner, and a duo of underworld enforcers. The subtle message presented is that the upper world of careerist criminal justice officials is as ethically compromised as the underworld of prostitutes, drug addicts, and their stalkers. The show *24* captures current fascination with counter-intelligence, and has the main character regularly mocking interviewees' pleas for lawyers and rights. *24* affirms the exceptional politics of post-9/11 in which heroes, and even presidents, must regularly and deliberately kill even innocent life as a means to a greater end (stopping the terrorists).

> There is an important interplay between news story selection, popular opinion, and crime policy.

There is an important interplay between news story selection, popular opinion, and crime policy. As Gusfield (1980), Hall et al. (1978), and Fishman (1980) have each shown the interplay between a media crime wave and policy change is intermediated by opportunistic political motivations. In Great Britain, Hall et al. explored how a "mugging" crime wave was, despite a lack of rise in "objective" robbery statistics to back up the case, spearheaded by broadsheet opinion leaders.

The murder of Vancouver teen Reena Virk in Victoria, B.C., in 1997 is a case in point. She was from an extended family that had emigrated from India but were Jehovah's Witnesses, making them a minority within a minority. She also had a difficult home life, and had been placed in foster care following allegations that she had been sexually abused by a member of her extended family. This compromised her peer bonding, and she was regularly taunted and bullied by her schoolmates. According to testimony at the murder trial, on the day she was killed, she was invited to a party on a bridge that was regularly used as a gathering place, and once there she was punched and kicked by some teens as others watched. The beating ended and she was able to walk away, but was subsequently set upon by two of the youths, one of whom held her head underwater until she drowned. Shortly after this story filled the newspapers, background stories also appeared on the extent of youth bullying and violence, particularly emphasizing its crisis proportions.

One story, published May 10, 1998 in the Ottawa Citizen, was entitled "Violent Girls New Crime Wave." It said that

> Violent acts by young girls — brought sharply home by this week's murder trials in the deaths of Calgary's Isabel Cho, 19, and Victoria's Reena Virk, 14 — have become the fastest-growing category of crime in Canada. The number of teen-age girls charged with violent crimes has tripled since 1986, according to the Canadian Centre for Justice Statistics. In all, 5,191 female youths aged 12 to 17 were charged with violent crimes — including murder and assault — in 1996, compared with 1,728 in 1986, centre figures show. Meanwhile, the number of boys 12 to 17 charged with violent crimes over the same decade doubled to 16,620 from 7,547. "It's not at crisis levels but it is serious," said Sibylle Artz, a Victoria-based expert on violence and teenage girls. "It's serious because people are getting killed."

Just three days later, on May 13, Minister of Justice Anne McClelland stated that the government would introduce new legislation to replace the *Young Offenders Act*.

The interplay between media, social movements, and political change is not a one-way street. In 2003, the largest mass protests in history were staged against the U.S. invasion of Iraq. Similar protests have been staged against "Washington consensus" organizations including the IMF and the World Bank, as well as economic and political forums like the G-8 and the World Economic Forum. These have sought to draw attention to the criminal actions of multinational oil, arms manufacturers and pharmaceuticals, and the depredation on the third world carried out under the auspices of globalization. What is important to note is that these expressions of popular opinion were facilitated by so-called alternative media via the internet. As Chomsky has pointed out, despite the vigorous public relations work carried out on behalf of a predatory corporate-state ideology (e.g., Iraq, war on crime, war on terrorism, vilification of the poor, handouts to the rich), public opinion even in the United States is still more "Left" than the corporate media (Chomsky 2005). This is confirmed by studies that have found that what people read or view in popular media does not have a great impact on their feelings of personal safety (Doob and MacDonald 1979).

Using Caution with Statistics and Empirical-Based Knowledge

The prominence of state-based empirical knowledge about the "crime problem" can be directly related to the dominance of the state in the execution of the control function. As Johnston (1992) has shown, in the experience of Britain, the state has only been dominant for a relatively brief time, specifically during the rise of the welfare state. What is meant by this is that as the administrative state emerged to, in effect, take care of the whole population of citizens, it developed a large array of measuring devices so that it could know citizens well enough to utilize the power of people or, on the other hand, to minimize the social and economic costs of disruption. In Canada, it was in the mid-1800s when the state really began to exercise this kind of knowledge of control. The development of the census, full-time paid police, municipal services, a criminal code, etc., came mostly during the latter half of the 1800s.

Once the usefulness of knowing things by the numbers became clear, there was almost no end to the reorganization of society through expert knowledge of populations.

For example, in 1920 in Ontario, there was a Royal Commission on the Feebleminded, which heard testimony from psychiatrists and other experts on the extent of what was discovered (by the use of the new IQ testing) to be a large number of school-age and adult citizens who were deemed not fully competent. The recommendation considered was institutionalization for this quantifiable (through testing) set of people. This exercise, it should be noted, was consistent with a quite powerful eugenics movement in Canada, by which fear of immigrants, racial prejudice, and social Darwinism stimulated draconian social control response; as well, widespread anti-communism encouraged drawing up which watch lists of labour activists and others to facilitate quick internment. These examples are meant to show that the state's use of empirical knowledge was growing and sometimes outpaced the political and cultural context.

In the 1960s (about which more will follow later) the depth and breadth of social control by state knowledge of populations (and individuals) became politically contentious. Mostly, this was a result of a rising consciousness about civil rights and about the state's capacity to act unjustly both externally (Vietnam) and internally (putting down student protests). In keeping with the anti-establishmentarian view of many academics and students, not to mention the *avant-garde* as a whole, there was a rising acceptance of interpretational types of sociological analysis, such as ethnomethodology and phenomenology. Whether or not the ascendance of interpretational analysis should be regarded as a symptom or a pivotal force that drove criticism of then-dominant empirical research, it is evident that debates over fundamental methodology and epistemology have long proliferated within the field of criminology. Critiques of official statistics prompted rebuttals, further critiques, and calls for "broader reflections about the power of the state and the institutions that produce these numbers" (Haggerty 2000: 25).

> The utility and the accuracy of representation that can be made possible through empirical data continue to be points of contention in contemporary debates about crime rates.

The utility and the accuracy of representation that can be made possible through empirical data continue to be points of contention in contemporary debates about crime rates. Early arguments of pundits from interpretational sociologies often revolved around the "referentiality" of official statistics. Referentiality signifies the degree to which statistics correspond with the actual events they purport to describe (Haggerty 2000: 25–26). Kitsuse and Cicourel, in an influential early critique, emphasized the schism between the social processes that produce *deviant behaviour* and the organizational activity that produces *rates of deviant behaviour*. In essence, there is a host of intermediary factors within rate-producing agencies that influence the production of crime rates (Haggerty 2000: 26). Cicourel argued in subsequent work that a major factor that accounts for variability in statistics is the background assumptions and tacit knowledge of rate-producing agents, exemplified in his study of social organizations of criminal justice agencies that influence day-to-day labelling and processing of youths, which ultimately affect juvenile delinquency rates (Haggerty 2000: 26–27). This paints a picture of discretionary labelling practices that vary from individual to individual within criminal-justice organizations, especially when classifying some behaviours as deviant while ignoring others. In cases where the law cannot be strictly applied, these practices are mediated through interpretation and tacit knowledge of officials (Haggerty 2000: 27).

While a number of studies at this time drew similar conclusions about the role of personal factors and institutional routines that vary between time, nation, culture, and geography in determining classificatory outcomes, others responded to the phenomenological challenge by defending the enterprise of empirical research in general, offering that the proper scientific response is to attempt to discern the degree of error the aforementioned variations introduce into each data-collecting regime. For example, Barry Hindess criticized Cicourel and Douglas' suggestion that sociologists should turn their attention to research that seeks to provide accurate descriptions of real-world events on the grounds that, if background expectancies shape how individuals record statistical data, these same assumptions would also structure sociologists' observations through their own tacit knowledge, which operates to transform the world of objects into intelligible phenomena (Haggerty 2000: 27–28).

As an alternative to abandoning empirical enterprises altogether, Hindess proposed that attention be paid to conceptual and technical instruments in the production of official statistics. Conceptual instruments refer to the systems of categories that govern the assignment of cases into classes, whereby technical instruments are the actual surveys or recording devices used by enumerators. Hindess argued that technical instruments are the primary source that builds an enumerator's background expectancies, rather than the seemingly infinite possibilities available through Cicourel's position (Haggerty 2000: 28).

Since these early debates, other authors have called attention to the degree to which theories and interests underlie the process of data collection. More recent studies encourage that attention be paid to the institutional processes of the state's statistical agencies, and their employees, as their interests and actions also shape the production of official statistics. We should note that the range of non-crime factors taken into account as potentially influencing crime rates has expanded considerably since the 1960s (Haggerty 2000: 29).

Social Problems According to Three Models: Medical, Penological, and Risk

When we hear of a problem, we often also hear alongside it how it is to be addressed. Without a sociological or historical understanding of "issues" or "social problems" we are likely to accept both description and script: that is to say, we are likely to think of an event we are confronted with (generally though media) according to the frame and formats we are given.

It would seem that given the term criminology (or "study of crime," in its most basic etymology), we would observe a social problem as a crime problem. In other words, given that you have already arrived here with a criminology text in your hands, it would seem to be going backwards to now hear that criminologists are not at all on the same page: that the "problem" or "issue" that you suspect to be "crime" may be considered something else. Yet for as long as criminology has existed this has been exactly the state of affairs for this discipline. Especially at its leading edge, criminology refuses the simple prescription that criminology is the study of crime.

This can be seen, as we suggested, both by reviewing the historical development of "social problems" and by

> Without a sociological or historical understanding of "issues" or "social problems," we are likely to think of an event we are confronted with (generally though media) according to the frame and formats we are given.

> Especially at its leading edge, criminology refuses the simple prescription that criminology is the study of crime.

showing how competitive disciplines vie to explain the same phenomenon according to their individual viewpoints.

> Behaviour that offended a social majority needed not only to be condemned but somehow explained.

With respect to historical development, criminology emerged in the eighteenth century because behaviour that offended a social majority needed not only to be condemned but somehow explained. Particularly where acts appeared to be irrational, it was necessary to come up with an account that could show why and when the proper social response should be condemnatory instead of remedial. With the Enlightenment came the need to posit, and in positing, establish the default view that people are essentially rational actors who may be held accountable, and that the proper response of an enlightened society to perceived wrongdoing is to respond in parsimonious but predictable terms.

In addition to being "juridical subjects" (or persons constrained and enabled by law) and rational actors (or people constrained and enabled by reason), human beings are understood as the products of genetics, environmental conditions, social chances, family upbringing, etc. For the emerging discipline of criminology, this meant that biology, chemistry, and also family and peer group and even social class may influence a person, increasing or decreasing his or her chances of entering into a life of crime, beyond any deliberate choice he or she might make.

> The treatment paradigm emerged with the notion that scientific measurement and analysis could determine what and where the pathology lies and also what the best course of medicine should be.

Out of this view that people may be shaped by a host of conditions came the view that the best response was to treat the "pathologies." The treatment paradigm emerged with the notion that scientific measurement and analysis could determine what and where the pathology lies and also what the best course of medicine should be.

Unfortunately, the treatment model is at loggerheads with aspects of the notion of the juridical subject and rational actor. Particularly, it was felt that treating people against their will offended subject's rights. Consequently, after its emergence in the late nineteenth century and rise throughout the first half of the twentieth, early biological positivism and the individual treatment model began to falter in the 1960s, when a deinstitutionalization movement took hold and many psychiatric patients could also no longer be coerced into care. The idea that offenders could be rehabilitated and that prison was a good place to compel that rehabilitation also suffered a decisive setback in the early 1970s when not only was it argued that coercion of treatment was questionable from a moral point of view, but also that it was of limited or no utility in changing recidivism rates.

Here it is necessary to point out that much discussion of treatment already takes it as a given that criminal justice officials have little right to intervene except where someone is determined to be guilty of a criminal offence. This restriction quickly predetermines the scope of the resolution. That scope is limited to the rights-bearing individual. One cannot, for instance, cordon off a whole town because there are too many social problems in it requiring the expenditure of too many precious resources. Yet, this suggests the limitation of the treatment model and distinguishes it from a medical model, particularly epidemiology, where for instance the spread of infectious disease is prevented through surveillance and early warning systems. It is also noteworthy that the "medical model" has itself been adapting to include more holistic reference to the relationship between the body, disease, environment, treatment conditions, etc. Evidence-based medicine has influenced problem-solving policing, for example, as in when the RCMP under its CAPRA model placed the police constable in a diagnostic and preventive, rather than just reactive position.

Given the travails of the treatment model, in retrospect it is not surprising that a return to a more parsimonious view of intervention emerged. "Just deserts," or the idea that it is important that offenders are held accountable for their crimes, became popular in the late 1970s and 1980s, when the victim also returned to prominence as a forgotten actor in the "square of crime." Also gaining popularity was the idea that if offenders could not be treated, at least they could be prevented from doing further harm. Offenders could be incapacitated, and this, at least during the time of their incarceration or other incapacitation, could protect society. During the 1980s and into the 1990s, the idea that societal resources should be expended differentially on the individual offender in the service of his or her recuperation or restoration was supplanted in large part with the idea that it is the non-offending population that ought to be protected.

This brings us to the most recent views of how social problems or issues are constructed by criminologists. We say "constructed" because in contrast to the views of positive science and variants of rational-actor theories, emerging also in the 1960s was a more radical position that crime is not much more *than* a social construction. Howard Becker famously put that crime is behaviour that people so label. A whole school of criminologists looked not at the individual criminal but at the interaction between individuals and social institutions, which resulted in the differential designation of the criminal label. This group of analysts was more concerned with process because it sought to dig underneath the label to the practices by which the label could be affixed. This tied to a host of critical views about how and why certain individuals and groups are more prone to the "outsider" status. This line of thought reached a boiling point when radical and critical analysts were dismissing the right of the poor and disenfranchised to use the criminal label to improve blighted neighbourhoods and communities. Realist criminology was born in the 1980s out of the recognition that it might be arrogant and elitist to dismiss the victims of crime with a focus mainly on the offender.

We noted earlier that how a problem is framed is dependent on where the person doing the framing is standing. From a position of psychology, crime becomes an effect of some unresolved pathology or mental disease or psychological trauma. From the standpoint of the urban geographer, crime is a problem of zoning, environmental design, people flows, etc. From a multidisciplinary and integrative standpoint the answer may require both working up the various hypotheses into constructs and contributing variables and reconciling or cross-weighting the orienting standpoints or meta-theories.

Risk Assessment Model

Consistent with neo-liberal trends in governing and the shift from a welfare state governed through Keynesian techniques of demand management (Braithwaite 2000: 222) and transformative measures to a decentralized regulatory state that, as Nikolas Rose has surmised, is more concerned with "steering than rowing" (Rose 2000: 332), new ways of thinking about and understanding crime and crime control have developed, filtered through the globalizing logic of risk assessment. Malcolm Feeley and Jonathan Simon have suggested that a "new penology" is taking shape, where an emphasis on crime control and prevention is driven through managerialism, regulating levels of deviance, mapping out distributions of conduct across populations, and reshaping the social and physical habitat of target populations to minimize criminal conduct and to maximize the efficiency of the population as a whole (Rose 2000: 331–32).

> The governing mentalities behind these new methods of crime control are no longer concerned with rehabilitation and treatment, or any ultimate goals of integrating offenders back into the larger social body.

The governing mentalities behind these new methods of crime control are no longer concerned with rehabilitation and treatment, or any ultimate goals of integrating offenders back into the larger social body. When it comes to the individual offender, his or her reasons for criminal involvement are of little, if any, significance (Barak 1998: 283). An example of this shift could be shown through the language of changing campaigns, such as the transition from the "War on Poverty" to the "War on Crime."

Some view this "new penology" as strictly punitive, with an emphasis on incapacitation, deterrence, and retribution, efficiently targeting and managing "high-rate offenders" or "career criminals" (Barak 1998, 282–83) — those who are unable or unwilling to manage their own risk (Rose 2000: 331). Others view current changes as part of an emerging style of thought that is informed by risk, whereby the primary goal is to predict future undesired events and make their avoidance central to decision-making processes, allotting resources and administrating individuals, institutions, and expertise toward this task. Viewed in this light, risk classifications have become the means by which many professionals, especially in the criminal justice field, think, act, and justify their actions (Rose 2000: 332).

Conclusion

In this chapter we have seen that we can get at the crime picture by comparing the "data" of a variety of sources (official sources, media, and victimization surveys). To this we could also have added self-reports. Had we done so, we would have discovered that the difference in incidence of crime among the working class and upper middle class as reported by the youth themselves is much less than the difference indicated by official statistics.

The point of this exercise is twofold. One lesson is that crime is a social construct. This is to say that what passes as crime is a product of many people, agencies, and belief systems that combine to create the crime fact. This is in some ways a difficult point to accept. When you see a youth sneakily taking a wallet from someone's coat unaware of your gaze, you may be unprepared to accept that what you are seeing is not a crime. But it may be that a father has asked his son to play a trick on his wife by showing up her carelessness of leaving her wallet vulnerable to such predation. Officially, a crime depends upon a court determination, and that in turn depends on reporting, prosecution, and conviction based on legal thresholds including *mens rea* and *actus reus*. No one person can determine, even if she or he witnesses it, the presence of a crime.

This brings us to the other lesson, which is that the social construct of crime is not done in conditions of equality. Not everyone has an equal chance of being labelled "criminal." Not every act which we've officially repudiated with a criminal designation is equally likely to be officially acted upon. And above all, not everything morally outrageous or offensive is equally likely to be outlawed as criminal. The construction of crime is accomplished in a particular social, economic, and political setting. Crime

> The social construct of crime is not done in conditions of equality; it is accomplished in a particular social, economic and political setting; crime is stratified by power relations.

is stratified by power relations.

Let's go even further than this point and add a twist: Crime is *inescapably* stratified in power relations. We may not be happy with the picture of crime offered by official statistics. We may also take exception to that offered by mediated presentations and representations. We may agree that many variables including ethnic origin, class, and literacy will act to marginalize some while saving others from a criminal label. However, the operation of such variables is only *intermediate*.

This is to say that even were these particular bases for discrimination eliminated, the power to exclude and to be protected from exclusion will still be differentially available to the powerful. Going back to Durkheim, every society requires some bases in which to differentiate behaviour so that order can be produced. Without rewards and punishments (even if the latter is only the withholding of rewards) that are connected in some way to the preservation of the social body, no "society" in any meaningful sense is possible. This means that some will have accumulated more rewards than others and can invest them in protection from vulnerability to non-discriminating social sanction. Put another way, the very structure of society provides for differentiation between people based on the accumulation of rewards, which is then parlayed into differential protection from sanction or penalty.

DISCUSSION QUESTIONS

1. Drawing on a variety of media outlets (e.g., TV, newspapers, magazines, internet), think of some current events that could be viewed as examples of "norm-clarification" rituals, and describe how you think their coverage contributes toward the restoration of a *status quo ante*. What might be some underlying factors to motivate or influence the type of coverage you described (e.g. social, political, economic, religious, etc.)? Explain.

2. Compare and contrast the way crime was viewed in the 1700s to some of the different ways crime is viewed today, as discussed in the chapter. Explain how a critical perspective (such as the one offered throughout most of the chapter) might actually be able to point out some *similarities* in the rationale behind some of these views.

3. How can the way that crime is actually defined affect the outcome of Uniform Crime Report stats for those crimes, and the *overall* crime rate? What other factors (besides crime definition) could affect the accuracy of Uniform Crime Reports?

4. Discuss some of the differences between the collection methods of the Uniform Crime Report (UCR) and General Social Survey (GSS) and explain why many see data gathered through the GSS (e.g., victimization surveys) as more accurate representations of the "actual" incidence of crime in Canada.

GLOSSARY OF TERMS

Actuarial Science: mathematical and statistical methods used to calculate risk, traditionally associated with the insurance industry, though recently becoming popularized within criminal justice and securities agencies, especially in the United States.

Actuarial Justice: a term often employed when actuarial methods are used to calculate risk for data such as offender recidivism and potential terrorist threats, based on categories of age, race, sex, nationality, religion, ethnicity, etc. These methods have received criticism for pre-conceiving that not all suspects have an equal chance of being found innocent/guilty based on how they are sorted into "trouble" (e.g., ethnic group) categories, potentially skewing data on the assumption that human agency plays less a factor in criminality than certain combinations of "risky" categories.

Crime Filter: broad term used to show that a portion of reported incidents of crime are screened out of official record as a result of bureaucratic/structural/external/political elements that reduce the number of cases that actually go to trial, and thus get "officially" reported.

Crime Funnel: metaphor used to show that at each level of information processing, the chances that an incident will be recorded officially get smaller and smaller.

Crime Net: symbolizes the relationship between crime and the resources employed in its detection and punishment by the criminal justice system.

Crime Rate: denotes the ratio of crimes committed to the population of a given area per year (in Canada, usually converted into units per 100,000). For example, Statistics Canada reported the homicide rate in 2004 as 1.9:100,000 so there were, on average, 1.9 homicides per 100,000 individuals in 2004 (the rate would have been derived from raw data, such as 570 *actual* homicides out of a population of 30 million).

Dark Figure of Crime: the portion of criminal activity that goes unreported and/or undetected by official sources.

General Social Survey (GSS): includes data collected through telephone surveys, each containing a core topic, and focusing on exploratory questions and a standard set of socio-demographic questions used for classification. These have included qualitative data that highlight perceptions of fear of crime, the criminal justice system, etc. Victimization surveys are part of the GSS.

Juridical Subjects: persons constrained and enabled by law.

Just Deserts: the idea that it is important that offenders are held accountable for their crimes.

Mediation of Crime: recognition that crime is shaped by presentations and representations in various formats. It is also a thing that has been presented and re-presented according to certain well-defined scripts.

New Penology: an emphasis on crime control and prevention driven through managerialism, regulating levels of deviance, mapping out distributions of conduct across populations, and reshaping the social and physical habitat of target populations to minimize criminal conduct to maximize the efficiency of the population as a whole.

Norm-Clarification Rituals: staged dramas enacted as a means to confirm the restoration of the *status quo ante*. They take on the performative function of re-establishing norms.

Random Error: *unintentional* mistakes made during the data collection process as a result of variances in administrative differences, enforcement practices, public attitudes, and unknown errors in counting procedures.

Rational Actors: people constrained and enabled by reason.

Referentiality: the degree to which statistics correspond with the actual events they purport to describe.

Solidarity: introduced by Emile Durkheim, a concept that highlights the function of the stranger and the criminal, where *reaction* to crime is functional in supporting the mores and rules of the collective. This is such to the extent that *inaction* regarding crime, or transgression against social norms, indicates the absence of "the social."

Status Quo Ante: a state of affairs that previously existed.

Systematic Error: *predictable* errors that occur during the data collection process, for example, whereby enumerators are aware that certain types of crimes are under-reported, thus skewing the data in those categories.

Victimization Survey: focuses on the nature and extent of criminal victimization in Canada elicited through interviews with members of randomly selected households throughout the country.

SUGGESTED READINGS

Hacking, Ian. 2002. "Making Up People." *Historical Ontology*. Cambridge: Harvard University Press.
Haggerty, Kevin. 2000. *Making Crime Count*. Toronto: University of Toronto Press.
Smart, Carol. 1989. *Feminism and the Power of Law*. New York: Routledge.
Henry, S., and D. Milovanovich. 1996. *Constitutive Criminology: Beyond Postmodernism*. Newbury Park, CA: Sage Publications.

REFERENCES

Barak, G. 1998. *Integrating Criminologies*. Toronto: Allyn and Bacon.
Brathwaite, J. 2000. "The New Regulatory State and the Transformation of Criminology." *British Journal of Criminology* 40, 2 (spring): 222–38
Chomsky, N. 2005. 2005. "Imperial Presidency." *Canadian Dimension* 39 (1) (January/February)
Christie, N. 1977. "Conflict as Property." *British Journal of Criminology* 17, 1: 1–15.
Doob, T., and B. McDonald. 1979. Television Viewing and Fear of Victimization: Is the Relationship Causal? *Journal of Personality and Social Psychology* 37, 2: 170–79.
Durkheim, E. 1984. *The Division of Labor in Society*. New York: Free Press. [Original work published: *De la division du travail social*, Paris, 1893.]
Fishman, M. 1980. *Manufacturing the News*. Austin: University of Texas Press.
Gusfield, J. 1980. *The Culture of Public Problems: Drinking, Driving and the Symbolic Order*. Chicago: University of Chicago Press.
Haggerty, K. 2000. *Making Crime Count*. Toronto: University of Toronto Press.
Hall, S., S. Critcher, T. Jefferson, T. Clarke, and B. Roberts. 1978. *Policing the Crisis: "Mugging," the State and Law and Order*. London: MacMillan.
Johnston, L. 1992. *The Rebirth of Private Policing*. London: Routledge.
Kennedy, L., and V. Sacco. 1998. *Crime Victims in Context*. New York: Roxbury.
O'Neil, P. 1998. "Tougher Young Offender Law Promised." *Calgary Herald*. Feb 17: A4.
Prosise, T., and A. Johnson. 2004. "Law Enforcement and Crime on *Cops* and *World's Wildest Police Videos*: Anecdotal Form and the Justification of Racial Profiling." *Western Journal of Communication* 68, 1: 72–91.
Rose, N. 2000. *Powers of Freedom: Reframing Political Thought*. United Kingdom: Cambridge

University Press.

Sacco, V., and L. Kennedy. 1998. *Crime Victims in Context*. New York: Roxbury.

Schmalleger, F., and R. Volk. 2001. *Canadian Criminology Today*. Toronto: Pearson.

Skogan, W., and M. Maxfield. 1981. *Coping with Crime: Individual and Neighborhood Reactions*. Beverley Hills: Sage

Statistics Canada. 2003. "The Daily: Crime Statistics." Thursday, July 24. Available at <www.statcan.ca/Daily/English/030724/d030724a.htm> accessed July 2007.

_____. 2004. "General Social Survey on Victimization, Cycle 18: An Overview of Findings." Ottawa.

Winterdyk, J. 2006. *Canadian Criminology*. Second edition. Toronto: Pearson.

14 Aren't Women Violent, Too?
The Gendered Nature of Violence

Elizabeth Comack,
Vanessa Chopyk and Linda Wood

KEY FACTS

> Law historically gave men the authority to use force against their wives. Until 1983 it was legal in Canada for a husband to rape his wife; Britain did not change its laws until 1992.

> Fifty-one percent of Canadian women have experienced at least one incident of physical or sexual assault since the age of 16.

> Among the 478 solved homicides in 2005, four out of five victims knew their killer; half (49 percent) of the victims were killed by an acquaintance; one-third (33 percent) by a family member; 18 percent were killed by a stranger.

> In 2001, 29 percent of all homicide victims were women, and over half (52 percent) of these women were murdered by someone to whom they had been married or who they dated. For men, the figure is 8 percent.

> Women are three times more likely to be injured than male victims of spousal violence, five times more likely to need medical attention, five times more likely to be hospitalized, three times more likely to need time off to deal with the consequences of the violence and twice as likely to suffer repeated assaults.

> Aboriginal people are three times more likely than non-Aboriginal people to be victims of violent crime, specifically, sexual assault, robbery, and physical assault.

Sources: CAEFS 2006; Dauvergne and Li 2005; Statistics Canada 2006.

Even though acts of violence make up only a small proportion of the offences dealt with by the criminal justice system, they figure prominently in public perceptions and fears of crime. Indeed, in recent years public concerns over the level of violence in our communities have intensified. These concerns have typically been met with calls for the police and judiciary to "get tougher" on violent crime. The "tough" proposals usually include increased surveillance and monitoring of public spaces, stricter law enforcement practices, and harsher prison sentences for violent offenders, all of which amount to an expansion of criminal justice intervention into people's lives.

Our perceptions and responses to violent crime raise political and empirical questions of importance to criminology, among which is the question of whether or not incidences of violence are connected to issues of gender. In short, we might ask, *is violence gendered?* If we understand gender as meaning those characteristics or traits normally associated with being either male or female in our society, then to ask if violence is "gendered" is to inquire into whether the

> Our perceptions and responses to violent crime raise political and empirical questions important to criminology, including whether or not violence is connected to issues of gender.

manifestations of violence — its particular patterns or contexts — are tied to social or cultural distinctions attributed to men and/or women. More specifically, what are the social relationships in which men's and women's violence occurs? What is the gender dynamic within these relationships? When men and women use violence, do they differ in the tactics employed?

Three Positions on Gender and Violence

Violence Is What Men Do to Other Men

Traditionally, criminologists did not even ask such questions when they examined violent crime. Like other academic disciplines, criminology has been a male-centred enterprise. Despite the use of generic language (defendants, criminals, deviants, offenders), criminology has concerned itself about what men do. Researchers more or less assumed that violence was equated with the behaviour of males; it was something that men — especially lower-class men — did to other men. The official crime statistics reinforced this assumption. In any given year, men make up the vast majority of adults charged with violent offences. In 2003, for instance, 83 percent of adults charged with crimes against the person were male (Statistics Canada 2004). Victim surveys, in which respondents were asked to self-report their experiences of victimization, indicated as well that young males were most at risk of violent crimes such as assaults and robberies (Hindelang, Gottfredson, and Garofalo 1978; Gottfredson and Hindelang 1981; Sacco and Johnson 1990). Even the law assumed that violence was something that emerged in encounters between men. The law on self-defence, for example, was historically premised on the paradigmatic case of the "one-time barroom brawl" involving two males of equal size and strength engaged in an altercation (Comack 1993).

Mainstream criminology's focus on males as both offenders and victims produced a number of theories to account for the observed patterns of violent crime. From as far back as Frederic Thrasher's 1927 work on gangs through to the 1950s theorists such as Albert Cohen and Walter Miller to more recent formulations (such as Rice and Goldman 1994), criminologists have concentrated on how male violence and aggression are tied to values that emerge in lower-class subcultures. Cohen (1955), for instance, understood the "malicious, non-utilitarian and negativistic" behaviour of lower-class boys as the result of a "reaction formation" that emerged from the boys' failure to succeed according to the middle-class value system. Miller (1958) explained lower-class males' adherence to "focal concerns" like "toughness," "smartness," "fate," and "autonomy" as men's way of demonstrating their manhood in lower-class communities where female-dominated households were the norm. In a similar fashion, Marvin Wolfgang (1958) saw homicides as resulting from a masculine defence of honour and reputation: "Quick resort to physical combat as a measure of daring, courage or defense of status appears to be a cultural expectation, especially for lower class males" (Wolfgang, quoted in Polk 1994: 89). While such explanations have been subject to critical appraisal over the years, they continue to occupy an important place in the canon of the discipline and are usually featured prominently in most criminology textbooks.

Male Violence against Women

The relationship between gender and violence only came under close scrutiny with the emergence of the feminist movement in the 1970s. Feminists used a range of social and political activities to publicize and work towards changing the subordinate position of women as a group in Canadian society. One of these activities was the formation of consciousness-raising groups, which aimed to bring women together to talk about their experiences. As women began to share their stories, it became evident that many of them had encountered both physical and sexual violence at the hands of men. When feminists initiated support and services for women victimized by male violence (in the form of shelters for abused women and rape crisis centres), the enormity of the problem became even more apparent. The growing awareness of the nature and extent of male violence against women, coupled with an increasing recognition of the deficiencies in law and legal practice, led to calls for government intervention in the form of increased funding for social services and legislative reforms. As a result of these initiatives, laws dealing with sexual assault underwent a series of reforms over the following decades (Busby 2006; Comack and Balfour 2004: ch 5). Wife assault, once thought to be a private trouble between a husband and wife — and therefore "not the law's business" — was transformed into a public issue meriting a criminal justice response.

> The relationship between gender and violence only came under close scrutiny with the emergence of the feminist movement in the 1970s.

In addition to their social and political activities, feminists also challenged the invisibility of women in academic disciplines, including criminology. Victim surveys, for instance, were criticized for their gender bias, because both the construction and carrying out of these surveys precluded their ability to accurately and reliably measure women's experiences of victimization (Johnson 1996). Feminists, therefore, called for research that would better address the issue of male violence against women. As a result an enormous body of work was produced in this area (for example, Brownmiller 1975; Clark and Lewis 1977; MacKinnon 1983; Stanko 1985; and Dobash and Dobash 1992). One of the most comprehensive studies was released by Statistics Canada in 1993. Using definitions of abuse that conformed to criminal law, this national survey found that one-half (51 percent) of Canadian women had experienced at least one incident of physical or sexual violence since the age of sixteen. One in four women had experienced physical or sexual violence at the hands of a male partner (Statistics Canada 1993; Johnson 1996). Findings such as these have reinforced the feminist claim that male violence against women is widespread and pervasive.

Feminists succeeded not only in raising the issue of gender and violence, but also in politicizing it. While a variety of feminist frameworks and perspectives have been put forth, all of them share in common the belief that patriarchy — a system of male domination — pervades Canadian society. Patriarchy is understood as both a structure and an ideology that privileges men over women. In this respect male violence against women is one manifestation of patriarchy, of the power that men exercise over women. In feminist terms, then, violence is "gendered" because it is something that men do to women.

But Women Are Violent, Too

In drawing attention to the gendered nature of violence, feminists focused their attention on how women are victimized by male violence. In other words, they cast men as the "offenders" and women as the "victims." In recent years this typification has been challenged. For instance, in her book, *When She Was Bad: Violent Women and the Myth of Innocence*, journalist Patricia Pearson (1997) argues not only that "women are violent, too" but also that their violence can be just as "nasty" as men's. Following on the footsteps of the 1950s criminologist Otto Pollak, Pearson (1997: 20–21) suggests that women's violence is more masked and underhanded than men's violence: women kill their babies, arrange for their husbands' murders, beat up on their lovers, and commit serial murders in hospitals and boarding houses. Nevertheless, argues Pearson (1997: 61), when their crimes are discovered women are more likely to receive lenient treatment from a chivalrous criminal justice system.

Pearson draws support for her analysis from studies that utilize the Conflict Tactics Scale (CTS) to measure abuse in intimate relationships. Developed by U.S. researcher Murray Straus (1979), the scale is a quantitative instrument that consists of eighteen items and measures three different ways of handling interpersonal conflict in intimate relationships: reasoning, verbal aggression, and physical violence. The scale categorizes items on a continuum from least to most severe (for example, "discussed an issue calmly" and "cried" to "threw something," "hit with a fist," and "used a knife or a gun"). Respondents in a survey are asked how frequently they perpetrated each act in the course of conflicts or disagreements with their partners within the past year, and how frequently they had been on the receiving end. These self-reports of perpetration and victimization are then used to construct estimates of the rate of violence used by male and female partners. Most researchers who have employed the CTS have found equivalent rates for women and men on both minor and severe types of violence (Straus and Gelles 1986; Steinmetz 1981; Brinkerhoff and Lupri 1988; Kennedy and Dutton 1989). Such findings have led to the conclusion that there is a sexual symmetry in intimate violence; that is, that women are just as violent as men.

> Most researchers who have employed the CTS have found equivalent rates for women and men in terms of both minor and severe types of violence.

Despite its popularity, the CTS has not been without its critics (for example, DeKeseredy and MacLean 1998; DeKeseredy and Hinch 1991; Dobash et al. 1992; Schwartz and DeKeseredy 1993; Johnson 1996). Writers have noted that the CTS is an incomplete measure of intimate violence because:

- it measures only incidents of violence and thus ignores the social context of the violence (such as whether a woman is acting in self-defence);
- it situates items only in the context of settling quarrels or disputes and thus misses assaults that "come out of the blue" or are motivated by the desire to control another person;
- it relies on self-reports of violence and may thereby underestimate the incidence of violence by males (who, it has been found, are more likely to under-report);
- it fails to make adequate distinctions between the severity of different forms of violence (for example, "tried to hit with something" is defined as "severe" while "slapped" is defined as "minor"); and
- it does not capture the outcome of the violence (for example, the degree of injury incurred by the participants).

Pearson (1997: 121) argues that these methodological concerns amount to unwarranted attacks by battered women's supporters who are invested in a gender dichotomy of "men as evil" and "women as good." Similar to Pearson, Donna Laframboise (1999: A1), in a *National Post* article titled "Women Are Men's Equals in Violence," tells us that "a good deal of what we've been told about domestic abuse over the last 25 years is wrong" and that studies conducted by "researchers without a political axe to grind" are more trustworthy, valid, and objective than three decades of feminist-inspired work.

Essentially, then, what writers like Pearson and Laframboise are arguing is that women are "men's equals" in violence — that violence is gendered only to the extent that women and men differ in the methods they use and the vocabularies of motive that accompany their actions. The problem, they say, is that under the sway of feminist politics we have failed to acknowledge that women, like men, possess a "will to power"; there are "dimensions of power that have nothing to do with formal structures of patriarchy" (Pearson 1997: 32, 243); and to ignore women's violence is to promote a "culture of victimhood" that denies women's agency and responsibility.

The issue of gender and violence is reflected, then, in three different positions: the first understands the problem of violence in terms of men's violence against other (especially lower-class) men; the second focuses on men's violence against women and locates it within the context of the patriarchal nature of society; and the third focuses on women's violence (especially against men in intimate relationships) and makes the claim that women are "men's equals" in violence. What are we to make of these different positions? Is one more accurate than the others, or is there a kernel of truth in each account? Are the three positions founded on incompatible assumptions, or is there a ground for compromise and synthesis?

Perhaps a starting point for resolving these questions is to recall our earlier statement that how we understand and respond to violence raises important political and empirical questions. Indeed, the political nature of the issue is reflected in the three positions outlined: given its failure to attend to gender issues, mainstream criminology has taken a seemingly "apolitical" stance (albeit, as we will see later, with political implications); the feminist movement's endeavour to draw attention to male violence against women has been motivated by the political goal of ending women's inequality; and the claims advanced by journalists like Pearson and Laframboise carry a distinctly "anti-feminist" political tone. But the positions also raise significant empirical questions, especially in considering the kinds of data that we bring to bear on the issue of gender and violence. Given the methodological concerns apparent in the use of the CTS, perhaps it is time we look to other data sources to address the issue of whether women are "men's equals" in violence. One untapped data source is Police Incident Reports (PIRs).

Police Incident Reports

Criminologists have long recognized that official sources of information on crime are limited by their nature and scope. For instance, the actual number of crimes that occur in a given area is larger than the number reported to police, and more are recorded in police reports than end up in court and prison records. As well, given the purpose of most official documents on crime — to establish the presence of legally relevant factors that would define an act or event as a criminal matter — the predominant standpoint or interpretation reflected in the accounts may well differ from the participants' explanation.

Nevertheless, PIRs do offer a number of advantages as a source of information on violent crime. Since the police are the point of entry into the criminal justice system, police records will be more inclusive than those maintained by the courts or correctional agencies. While many crimes (especially less serious ones, such as property offences) are not reported to police, events involving violence have a greater likelihood of police intervention and will thus be included in their records. Also significant is that with the transformation of intimate violence from a private trouble to a public issue, police policies and practices have been revised to focus more attention on domestic violence. As a result, mandatory charging and zero-tolerance policies have opened a door into the private sphere of the home, making violence between partners much more visible. With this increased police attention has come more documentation of what goes on when violence occurs between intimates.

To the extent that Police Incident Reports now include documentation on domestic violence, they also hold a number of advantages over the Conflict Tactics Scale for measuring women's and men's violence. For one, while CTS research relies on respondents' self-reports of perpetration and victimization, PIRs are based on a variety of information sources, including statements from complainants, accused, and bystanders or witnesses. Since they draw from a number of accounts, PIRs offer a potentially richer source of information about the nature of women's and men's violence than do self-reports (Sacco and Kennedy 1998: 223). Also, because PIRs record events on a case-by-case basis and are normally collected closer in time to the actual event, they do not encounter the problems of recall inherent in CTS research, in which respondents are asked to describe events that occurred over the previous twelve months.

While CTS research approaches the issue of intimate violence from the vantage point of "settling disputes" in marital relationships, PIRs are governed by the requirement to establish evidence (physical or otherwise) that a criminal act has occurred. Consequently, police officers include fairly detailed accounts in their reports of "who did what to whom." These descriptions provide a record of the specific violence tactics used by each of the participants in an event. Criminal law also distinguishes between violent offences on the basis of their "seriousness" (for example, assault, assault with a weapon, assault causing bodily harm, and aggravated assault). Accordingly, one important measure of seriousness is the harm or injury that results from an incident. This factor makes PIRs a good source of information for measuring the degree of injury incurred by the participants in a violent event — a variable missing in CTS research.

A final benefit of PIRs, especially for our purposes, is that they allow for a more all-encompassing picture of women's and men's violence. Rather than focusing solely on violence between intimates, we can broaden the investigation to explore the various social contexts in which women's and men's violence occurs, and to consider the similarities and differences between those contexts.

The Social Contexts and Patterns of Violence

For our purposes, Winnipeg offers a prime location for exploring women's and men's violence, and we will consider data drawn from PIRs held by the Winnipeg Police Service to sort out the connections between gender and violence. According to official crime statistics, the rate of violent crime in Winnipeg is one of the highest of the nine major Canadian cities. In 2004, for instance, Winnipeg's homicide rate (4.9 per 100,000 population) and robbery rate (229 per 100,000 population) were the highest in the country (Statistics Canada 2005). Women make up a larger proportion of adults charged with violent offences in Winnipeg compared with results from the country as a whole.[1] Winnipeg has also been the site of a number of criminal justice initiatives pertaining to domestic violence.

In response to a national initiative in 1983, the Manitoba attorney general issued a formal directive whereby police were to place charges in all reported cases of assault when reasonable and probable grounds existed that an offence had occurred. This was to be done regardless of the relationship between the victim and the accused. Previously it had been left to victims to initiate complaints. The net effect of this mandatory charging policy was to increase the number of arrests involving abusive partners.[2] A Family Violence Court was established in Winnipeg in September 1990,[3] and in response to a Domestic Violence Review (Pedlar 1991) the Winnipeg Police Service introduced a zero-tolerance policy in July 1993. Under this more rigorous protocol, police are mandated to lay charges any time complaints have been made, regardless of the presence (or absence) of corroborating evidence. The decision is then left up to the Crown attorney as to whether the case will proceed to court.

When we examine police records of violent crime, one factor rings clear: even in an era of zero tolerance, men are far more likely to appear as accused persons than women. Of the 23,090 violent crime charges laid in Winnipeg between 1991 and 1995, only 15 percent of persons charged were women. The quantitative difference between men's and women's violence is obvious. But what about qualitative differences?

> When we examine police records of violent crime, one factor rings clear: even in an era of zero tolerance, men are far more likely to appear as accused persons than women.

To explore qualitative differences between women's and men's violence, we gathered data from Winnipeg Police Incident Reports on cases of women and men charged with violent offences (assault, robbery, sexual offences, attempted murder, homicide) over a five-year period (1991–95). A random sample of women (stratified by offence type) generated 501 cases or 15 percent of those charged. For comparative purposes we drew a sample of men (stratified by offence type) charged over the same period, yielding 501 cases or 2.5 percent of those charged. We collected information on the social characteristics of the accused, the social setting or location in which the violent event occurred, and the relationship between the accused and the complainant or victim. Because we were interested in the forms and severity of the violence used by women and men, we coded each PIR according to the violence tactics employed during the course of the event[4] as well as the resulting injuries.

Stranger Violence: The "Mean Streets" of Manitoba?

Fuelled by sensationalized front-page headlines like "The Mean Streets of Manitoba" (*Winnipeg Free Press* July 23, 1998: A1), the public's perception of crime has been largely built upon fears of encountering violence in the street late at night. These fears easily conjure up images of "dark strangers" lurking in doorways and back alleys, waiting to do us harm.

While violence against strangers does appear in the police reports, it is far less prevalent than newspaper headlines and the public perception would have us believe. In our sample, only 16 percent (159) of offences involved violence between individuals not known to one another. While one-third of these events occurred in streets and laneways, an equal number took place in commercial establishments such as gas stations and stores.

Stranger violence was almost as likely to happen during the daytime (29 percent) as in the evening (32 percent) or late at night (39 percent). As well, the prevalent image of the "dark stranger" is one that doesn't quite hold up, because the majority of the men charged with violence against strangers were white. While it is now widely acknowledged, for example, that Aboriginal people are overrepresented in the crime statistics relative to their numbers in the general population, they are more likely to be charged with violence against members of their own communities, especially intimate partners and other family members.

Mainstream criminology has traditionally understood violence as something that men do to other men. In the case of violence against strangers, this image is at least partly justified. The men accused who engaged in stranger violence were most likely to do so in groups with other men, and most of their complainants (72 percent) were also male. But men are not the only ones to be charged with violence against strangers. Women also engage in stranger violence, but when they do they are most likely to participate alongside men in mixed-sex groups, and their victims are as likely to be female as male. For both women and men accused, the violence used against strangers is most likely to involve tactics like "pushing, shoving, grabbing or pulling" (32 percent for women versus 33 percent for men) and "property damage or theft" (49 percent for women versus 44 percent for men).

Even though stranger violence conjures up our greatest fears for our physical safety, it is actually the form of violent event that has the least frequency of injuries to complainants. In events involving strangers the complainants received no injuries in one-third of the cases, and of those injured the majority of injuries were of a "minor" nature (cuts, scratches, bruises, and the like). Perhaps one of the main reasons why stranger violence results in fewer and less serious injuries to the victims is the motive behind many of these incidents: 37 percent of the charges laid by police in stranger events were for robbery. This suggests that perpetrators of stranger violence are not so much intent on inflicting injury or harm as they are on stealing property (whether money, Nike sports jackets, or, in several cases cited in the reports, cases of beer).

Violent Encounters between Friends and/or Acquaintances

Contrary to the public perception of violent crime, we are more likely to encounter violence from friends and/or acquaintances than we are from strangers. Of the 1,217 complainants cited in the Police Incident Reports, the accused and the complainant were known to each other 78 percent of the time. Rather than stranger violence committed on the "mean streets," most violent events occurred in private dwellings between individuals known to one another. Violence against friends and/or acquaintances accounted for 21 percent (207) of the cases we studied in the Police Incident Reports. These events differed from stranger violence in a number of significant ways.

> Contrary to the public perception of violent crime, we are more likely to encounter violence from friends and/or acquaintances than we are from strangers.

As in stranger violence, the men accused were most likely to assault other men, but with an important exception: 23 percent of the charges against men in the friend/acquaintance category were for sexual assaults against females. (By comparison, sexual assaults represented only 4 percent of the charges in the stranger events.) As in the violence against strangers, the women accused were most likely to be involved with both male and female co-accused. However, their violence was most often directed against female friends and/or acquaintances.

Whereas stranger violence was most likely to involve the features of "pushing, shoving, grabbing or pulling" and "property damage or theft," violence between friends and/or acquaintances takes on a more serious tone. In addition to being "pushed, shoved, grabbed or pulled" (30 percent for women versus 36 percent for men), complainants in events involving friends and/or acquaintances were more likely to be "repeatedly punched or beaten" by both men and women accused (30 percent for women versus 36 percent for men). Yet there were also gender differences reflected in the violence tactics used against friends and/or acquaintances. Women accused were four times more likely than men to "pinch, bite, scratch, or poke" (17 percent versus 4 percent), eight times more likely to engage in "hair pulling or cutting" (33 percent versus 4 percent), and twice as likely as men to "kick or knee" (41 percent versus 21 percent). Men were twice as likely to "utter threats" (32 percent versus 16 percent). Men were also far more likely to engage in "sexual assaults" (25 percent versus 3 percent) and "sitting on or restraining" (25 percent versus 6 percent) — violence tactics that reflect men's use of sexual violence when the complainant is female.

The resulting injuries also show that the violence against friends and/or acquaintances is more serious in those cases than it is in cases of stranger violence. Whereas 68 percent of the cases involving stranger violence reported injuries, 91 percent of the complainants in friends/acquaintances events sustained injuries. While the majority (60 percent) of women's complainants incurred minor injuries, 60 percent of men's complainants received moderate and major injuries (such as broken bones, lacerations, lost teeth, or internal injuries). Corresponding with the harm inflicted during the violent event, women and men who engaged in violence against friends and/or acquaintances were also likely to face more serious criminal charges: 29 percent of women accused and 25 percent of men accused were charged with either assault causing bodily harm or aggravated assault.[5]

Women's capacity for violence is clearly evident in these data. What is also apparent is that men's violence against women (especially in the form of sexual assaults) is a matter of concern. These two findings become even more evident when we examine the violence that occurs within the family setting.

Violent Encounters with Family Members

Excluding, for the time being, violence between intimate partners, incidences of violence occurring between other family members — children, parents, siblings, extended family members, and in-laws — represented only 9 percent (89) of the cases we examined. But events involving these other family members did make up a greater proportion of women accused's charges than they did for men accused (14 percent for women versus 4 percent for men). Children were the most likely victims for both women and men accused (representing 41 percent and 48 percent of women's and men's complainants, respectively). Siblings — especially sisters — were the second most likely victims for women accused, and extended family members or in-laws for men.

While men's violence in the other relationships examined is mainly directed at other men, their violence against other family members is primarily directed at females. Even though men's victims are most often female children and relatives, they do not appear to shy away from using more severe violence tactics: the men accused not only "push, pull, shove or grab" their complainants (38 percent of the cases), but also "sit on or restrain" (29 percent), "beat or repeatedly punch" (24 percent), and "slam bodies or head into something" (24 percent). Also significant is the prevalence of sexual violence: in 38 percent of the cases involving violence against other family members, the men accused sexually assaulted their complainants.

Whereas men's violence in the family setting is primarily intergendered, women's violence is more likely to be intragendered or directed at other females. While the women accused were five times more likely than men to engage in "hair pulling or cutting" (25 percent for women versus 5 percent for men) and to "pinch, bite or scratch" their complainants (21 percent for women versus 5 percent for men), they were just as likely as men to "push, pull, shove or grab" (35 percent for both) and "beat or repeatedly punch" (27 percent for both) other family members. To this extent, women's violence against other family members appears to be similar to the incidences involving friends and/or acquaintances.

Encounters between Intimate Partners: Equals in Violence?

While we have seen notable differences in the social dynamics involved in men's and women's violence, the fact that women use violence tactics, sometimes with similar frequency as men, might be taken as evidence that they are "men's equals" in violence. Nevertheless, we do not yet have the complete picture. Indeed, over half (53 percent) of the cases in the Police Incident Reports involve violence between intimate partners (husbands and wives, boyfriends and girlfriends, common-law partners, and gay and lesbian partners).[6] What remains to be seen, then, is whether women are "men's equals" when it comes to partner violence.

That violence between intimates has attained the status of a criminal matter is clearly reflected in the Police Incident Reports. In our study, partner violence made up 49 percent (243) of the cases involving women accused and 57 percent (285) of those involving men accused. Save for three cases involving gay or lesbian partners, violence between partners was intergendered (male/female; female/male).

Studies that utilize the CTS have concluded that a sexual symmetry exists in intimate violence: men are as likely as women to be victims of abuse, and women are as likely as men to be perpetrators of both minor and serious acts of violence. A different picture emerges, however, when we examine four indicators found in the police reports: 1) the violence tactics used by men and women accused; 2) the use of violence by complainants; 3) the degree of injury or harm inflicted; and 4) "who called the police?"

1. Violence Tactics Used by Men and Women Accused

One of the ways of determining if violence is gendered is to gauge whether there are statistically significant differences in men's and women's use of violence tactics. Men and women who engaged in stranger violence were most likely to push, pull, or grab complainants and to engage in property damage or theft. There were no statistically significant differences in the violence tactics used by men and women in stranger events. In events involving friends and/or acquaintances, gender differences in violence tactics became more evident: of the violence tactics used by women and men accused, six showed statistically significant differences. In events involving other family members, only two violence tactics — "sitting on or restraining" (6 percent versus 29 percent) and "sexual acts" (7 percent versus 38 percent) — were statistically significant.

But when we examine the violence tactics used by men and women accused in events involving partners, gender differences become much more acute: statistically significant differences existed in nine different items (see Table 14-1). Men accused were almost twice as likely as women to "push/pull/grab" (52 percent versus 28 percent). When combined with tactics such as "sitting on or restraining," "slamming body or head into something," and "strangling or choking," the picture that emerges is one of men using their physical strength or force against their female partners.[7] Women are almost six times more likely than men to "pinch/bite/scratch/poke." They are also more likely to "hit with or throw something" and to "stab or slash." The picture that emerges is one of women — lacking the physical strength or force of their male partners — resorting to the use of objects or weapons during the course of a violent event.

Indeed, women accused were more likely than men to use weapons in their encounters with intimate partners (42 percent for women versus 28 percent for men) (see Table

Table 14-1: Violence Tactics Used by the Accused in Partner Events

Type of Violence	Women Accused	+	Men Accused	+
Property damage/theft	23	9.5%	51	18%
Uttering threats/threaten with a weapon	33	4%	63	22%
Push/pull/grab/shake/elbow/ wrestle	68	28%	147	52%
Pinch/bite/scratch/poke	67	28%	14	5%
Pull or cut hair	40	16.5%	47	16.5%
Hit with/threw something	79	32.5%	51	18%
Slapping	54	22%	67	23.5%
Kicking/kneeing	47	19%	57	20%
Sitting on/restraining	4	2%	43	15%
Punched	55	23%	72	25%
Beat (repeated punching)	44	18%	62	22%
Slamming body or head into something	6	2.5%	75	26%
Sexual acts	0		11	4%
Strangling/choking	6	2.5%	39	14%
Stabbing/slashing	21	9%	6	2%
Shooting	0		1	.4%
Other	0		12	4%
No. of violence tactics	547		818	
No. of accused	243 (2.3 per person)		285 (2.9 per person)	

+ Percentages add up to more than 100 due to multiple responses.

14-2). The weapon of choice for many women appears to be beer bottles and other "sharp objects" such as knives or scissors. These objects accounted for 66 percent of the weapons used by women in partner events (versus 51 percent for men). Men accused used firearms in three of the cases, and they were twice as likely as women to use "blunt objects" such as bats, wooden boards, hammers, or metal pipes (19 percent for men versus 9 percent for women).

What is especially interesting in these findings is the considerable range of "other" articles (accounting for 43 percent versus 40 percent of the weapons used) cited in the police reports. "Other objects" included bathroom plungers, telephones, wooden spoons, ashtrays, coffee pots, dishes, books, hair brushes, TV remote controls, running shoes, pizza boxes, clothes baskets, and hair gel bottles — a list suggesting that virtually any object readily accessible in a domestic setting might be seized upon to be used during the course of a violent event and thus subsequently come to be defined as a "weapon" in Police Incident Reports.[8] As long as CTS researchers collapse all of these objects into one category, "tried to hit with something" (which is defined as "severe" according to the scale) the statistics for use of a weapon will include both a man who wields an iron bar or a hammer and a woman who throws a laundry basket or a bottle of hair gel at her partner.

2. Use of Violence by Complainants

While women and men accused differ in their use of violence tactics in their encounters with intimate partners, what of the use of violence by their complainants? CTS researchers have described the violence that occurs between men and women in intimate relationships as "mutual combat." When we examined the use of violence by complainants in partner events, however, we found that the female partners of men accused used violence in only 23 percent of the cases. In contrast, the male partners of women accused used violence in 65 percent of the cases.

The violence tactics used by male and female complainants tend to mirror the gendered differences we saw for male and female accused. In other words, male complainants, like male accused, are most likely to engage in "pushing, shoving or grabbing" (53 percent versus 30 percent), "sitting on or restraining" (17 percent versus 0 percent) and "slamming body or head into something" (17 percent versus 3 percent). Women complainants, like

Table 14-2: Weapons Used by Accused in Partner Events

Type of Weapon	Women Accused	+	Men Accused	+
Firearm	0		3	4%
Beer bottle	28	27%	13	16%
Sharp object	40	39%	28	35%
Blunt object	9	9%	15	19%
Other weapon	44	43%	32	40%
Total no. of accused using weapons	103 (42% of accused)		80 (28% of accused)	

+ Percentages add up to more than 100 due to multiple responses.

women accused, are more likely to "pinch, bite or scratch" (18 percent versus 5 percent) and "hit with or throw something" (29 percent versus 10 percent).[9] Such findings challenge the depiction of violence in intimate relationships as "mutual combat."

3. The Degree of Injury or Harm Inflicted

One of the factors missing in CTS research is "outcome," in particular, the nature and extent of the injuries incurred by participants in a violent encounter. In our study, 73 percent of women's complainants and 78 percent of men's complainants were injured during the course of the event. The majority of the injuries (54 percent for women's complainants versus 64 percent for men's complainants) were classified as "minor" in nature, involving cuts, bruises, sprains, black eyes, bleeding noses, and hair loss. But when we investigated whether the accused person incurred injury, we found that almost one-half (48 percent) of the women accused — as opposed to only 7 percent of the men accused — were injured during the course of the event. While the majority of these injuries were of a "minor" nature, this finding adds weight to the conclusion that violent events between women and men are not symmetrical.

4. Who Called the Police?

One of the variables often included in Police Incident Reports is "who made initial contact with the police?" In incidents involving partners, the complainants called the police in 77 percent of the cases involving a male accused (versus 40 percent for women accused) (see Table 14-3). In contrast, the accused woman herself called the police in 35 percent of the cases involving a female accused (versus only 5 percent for male accused).

> Investigating more fully the violence that occurs between intimate partners, we find that — contrary to CTS research — while women are certainly capable of violence, they are not "men's equals."

If calls to the police are interpreted as a form of "help-seeking behaviour" on the part of someone in trouble, this finding would suggest that in more than one-third of the cases involving a woman accused, she was the one who perceived the need for police intervention. Nevertheless, she also ended up being charged with a criminal offence.

More rigorous policies and protocols that mandate police to lay charges in cases of domestic violence have provided us with a previously unavailable window into the domestic sphere. Through this window we are now able to investigate more fully the

Table 14-3: Who Made Initial Contact with the Police in Partner Events?

	Women Accused		Men Accused	
Complainant	89	39.7%	220	77.2%
Accused	68	30.4%	13	4.6%
Both	10	4.5%	1	.4%
Witness/Bystander	42	19%	46	16.1%
Police Happened By	15	6.7%	5	1.8%
Total	224 *	100%	285	100%

*There are 19 missing cases.

nature of the violence that occurs between intimate partners. When we do, we find that — contrary to CTS research — while women are certainly capable of violence, they are not "men's equals." In combination, the four indicators — the violence tactics used by women and men accused, the use of violence by complainants, the degree of harm or injury inflicted, and who made the initial call to the police — suggest that partner violence is asymmetrical.

Making Sense of Gender and Violence

Police Incident Reports, then, provide us with an understanding of the patterns of violence and the social contexts in which violence occurs. In the process we have been able to identify some of the gender dynamics involved when violence occurs in social relationships. The three positions outlined at the beginning of this chapter each have their merits in terms of making sense of the picture of violence that emerges from police reports on violent

> To say that violence is "political" is to say that it has to do not only with the power to exercise force but also the power that accompanies an individual's social standing or position.

crime. Nevertheless, each position also has its gaps or inconsistencies. For one thing, we still need to consider how the current controversies over the connections between gender and violence can be addressed by working from a standpoint that views violence as an inherently political act.

To say that violence is "political" is to say that it has to do with power — not just the power to exercise force over or against another person, but also the power that accompanies an individual's social standing or position within the social structure of society. To this extent, individuals who use violence make choices, but those choices are conditioned or contoured by their social location — in particular, by their race and class as well as their gender. For instance, Aboriginal people are overrepresented in police reports on violent crime relative to their numbers in the general population. Almost one-half (48 percent) of the individuals who appeared in the reports we examined were of Aboriginal origin. The majority of this violence occurred in relationships with intimate partners, family members, and friends or acquaintances. To begin to understand why violence has become so endemic in many Aboriginal communities means acknowledging the deep scars created by colonization. Economic hardship, the impact of the residential school system, and other features of colonial rule have contributed to the dislocation and marginalization of countless Aboriginal people. Such conditions readily produce frustration, anger, and despair. When combined with limited options, the conditions easily result in violence against friends and loved ones.

Recognizing that people's choices are limited or constrained is one important part of the violence equation. Understanding the cultural messages that influence those choices is another. One of the benefits of mainstream criminology's approach to gender and violence is that it draws attention to how elements of culture contribute to the violence that men inflict in their confrontations with other men. Yet this approach is limited in its focus on violence as a phenomenon of lower-class subcultures. To understand violence more fully, we need to broaden our gaze to include the wider cultural messages in our society that encourage and condone men's violence — and we don't have to look very far. Whether it be Tom Cruise battling it out with his nemesis (while his love interest looks on) in the latest *Mission Impossible* movie, "The Rock" going up against "The Undertaker" in a WWF bout, or video games like *Soldier of Fortune*, where the players can eviscerate, decapitate, dismember, and burn their victims, the messages are clear: violence is normative. To the extent that these messages are directed largely at boys and young men, we should not be surprised when those boys and men begin to act out such masculine scripts in their own lives. Indeed, police reports are replete with cases of young men "taking it outside" at the local bar to settle their differences with friends or acquaintances (see also Comack and Balfour 2004: ch 3).

James Messerschmidt (1997) applies the concept of "hegemonic masculinity" to indicate how culturally idealized forms of masculinity become dominant in society. One point he emphasizes is that masculinity may be acted out differently depending upon the social situations of the participants. In this respect, professional and managerial men are not immune to cultural messages that normalize violence. For instance, risk-taking is widely documented as a masculine practice, and in boardrooms this tendency can translate into management decisions that cost lives (see Snider 2006). Messerschmidt provides an analysis of the decision to launch the *Challenger* space shuttle, which subsequently exploded. He argues that the decision of managers to overrule the engineers' judgment that the launch was unsafe was tied to the ways in which masculinity played out in the decision-making process. The end result was the deaths of all seven crewmembers on board the *Challenger*.

Lower-class individuals are most likely to appear in police reports on violent crime. Of the 1,002 cases we examined, 54 percent of the accused relied on welfare payments to make ends meet; only 27 percent were employed at the time of arrest. Because Messer-schmidt's analysis encourages us to think about how masculinity and violence play out in different social contexts, it is also an important reminder that our conceptions of "crime" are heavily loaded towards behaviours more commonly associated with the lower class. We need to be careful, therefore, not to be lulled into thinking that only those acts that appear in police reports constitute the complete range of violence occurring in society.

Feminists have been attuned to the ways in which violence is political, seeing it as a manifestation of men's power over women. Patriarchy is used as the template for under-standing the unequal power and resources available to men and women. In the process, however, feminists have tended to rely on the dualistic notion of "men as offenders" and "women as victims." This dualism, by and large, rests on an essentialist understanding of men's and women's inherent natures. Derived from the radical feminist theorizing of the 1970s, such a formulation asserts not only that men and women are different, but also that the difference is rooted in biology. Men are by nature assertive, aggressive, and competitive. Women are by nature nurturing, caring, and sensitive. While this formula-tion may have made sense in the face of the revelations of the overwhelming reality of the violence that women encounter at the hands of men, such one-dimensional construc-tions have the effect of denying agency: men are seen as captives of their hormones and chromosomes and women are the passive recipients of abuse.

Writers such as Patricia Pearson are to be credited for pointing to the "culture of victimhood" that is produced when feminists rest their understandings on such dualistic constructions. But in her endeavour to call attention to women's capacity for violence, Pearson goes to the other extreme. Her efforts to downplay the impact of patriarchal structures on women's lives and experiences do not avoid the fall into essentialism. Women who engage in violence are cast as scheming, underhanded manipulators who use violence "to defend their aspirations, their identity and their place on the stage" (Pearson 1997: 20). In many respects, she replaces the "men as evil" image that she so roundly criticizes feminists for with a "woman as evil" imagery. Like Eve in the Garden of Eden, women are not to be trusted.

Once we locate violence as political, the act of recognizing the inequalities that exist between men and women in our society becomes an important component in making sense of the gendered nature of violence. As reflected in the police reports, male violence against women — in the form of sexual violence against family members and friends/acquaintances and violence against intimate partners — is a significant matter of concern. Nevertheless, while the concept of patriarchy allows us to understand some of the pervasive patterns of male violence in society, we should not conclude that women are without power or agency. Indeed, there is no reason to believe that women are not influenced by the cultural messages that permeate our society — especially when those messages herald violence as a means of "getting your way." So long as violence is held up as a resource to be used when someone is confronted with problems and conflicts in life, we should not be surprised when women act out violently — be it against their children, their sisters, their female friends and acquaintances, or their abusive partners.

> We need to question whether "getting tough" on crime will provide the solution to violence.

Violence is not just political in terms of the power to commit aggressive acts. It also involves the power to alleviate or respond to violence. In this respect, we need to question whether "getting tough" on crime will provide the solution to violence. For instance, "get tough" policies like zero tolerance have brought more men — and women — into the criminal justice system on charges of violent crime. Whereas partner violence represented 43 percent of all men's violent charges in 1991, by 1995 it represented 64 percent. An even more significant change occurred for women. In 1991, 23 percent of women accused's charges were for partner violence. By 1995, the number had more than doubled: 58 percent of all violent crime charges against women involved partner violence. Most of the charges involving partner violence — 80 percent of those laid against women accused and 51 percent of those laid against men accused — were subsequently stayed by the Crown. While the underlying intent of the more rigorous charging protocol was to assist victims of domestic violence (who are predominantly women), zero tolerance has opened the way for "double-charging" (whereby both partners are charged with an offence when police are called in). Both the accused and the complainant were charged in 55 percent of the cases involving women accused and in 10 percent of those involving men. Stays of proceedings were even higher in those cases where double-charging occurred (88 percent versus 70 percent respectively).

Findings such as these raise serious questions about the use of a zero-tolerance policy for responding to partner violence. At the very least, we need to examine the merits of a protocol that removes all discretion from police in deciding whether or not criminal charges are warranted in a particular case. At the same time, we need to ensure that individuals are receiving the help they require when they need it. One promising recommendation came from a public inquiry that followed the murder/suicide of a Winnipeg couple (Schulman 1997): to establish a unit of specially trained police officers who would work in tandem with an auxiliary team of social service providers to offer crisis intervention to people at risk when relationships turn violent. Such an approach would ensure individuals' physical safety without overextending the reach of the criminal justice system into people's lives.

One of the main findings to emerge from police reports is that criminal violence is most likely to occur between individuals known to one another. For instance, friends and/or acquaintances are more at risk of violent encounters than are strangers, and more likely to incur injuries as a result. This finding suggests that rather than "getting tough" on crime, we should be strengthening our communities by providing people with access to the ways and means of resolving their troubles in non-violent ways.

DISCUSSION QUESTIONS

1. Why has the public perception and fear of crime centred on images of stranger violence — that is, on violence as occurring out on the streets, late at night, and at the hands of "dark strangers"?

2. What are the benefits and problems encountered in using different data sources (i.e., the Conflict Tactics Scale and Police Incident Reports) to study violence?

3. What are the prospects and pitfalls encountered in using mandatory charging and zero-tolerance policies to respond to domestic violence?

4. Given the social contexts and social relationships in which men's and women's violence occurs, what strategies would you advocate to reduce the levels of violence in your community?

GLOSSARY OF TERMS

Conflict Tactics Scale: a quantitative instrument that is used to study the incidence and frequency of interpersonal conflict in intimate relationships.

Feminism: a social and political movement aimed at ending the subordination of women in society. Within the academy, feminist work has produced a variety of theories and perspectives that tend to share

in common the belief that patriarchy or a system of male domination characterizes contemporary societies.

Gendered Violence: a term used to refer to the ways in which violence in society, its patterns or contexts, are tied to social or cultural distinctions attributed to men and women.

SUGGESTED READINGS

Comack, Elizabeth, and Gillian Balfour. 2004. *The Power to Criminalize: Violence, Inequality and the Law.* Halifax: Fernwood Publishing.

Johnson, Holly. 1996. *Dangerous Domains: Violence against Women in Canada.* Toronto: ITP Nelson.

McGillivray, Anne, and Brenda Comaskey. 1999. *Black Eyes All the Time: Intimate Violence, Aboriginal Women, and the Justice System.* Toronto: University of Toronto Press.

McKenna, Katherine, and June Larkin (eds.). 2002. *Violence Against Women: New Canadian Perspectives.* Toronto: Inanna Publications and Education Inc.

Price, Lisa. 2005. *Feminist Frameworks: Building Theory of Violence Against Women.* Halifax: Fernwood Publishing.

NOTES

The research on which this chapter is based was made possible by a grant from the Social Sciences and Humanities Research Council (SSHRC). The study would also not have been possible without the support of the Winnipeg Police Service. In particular, Inspector Ken Biener, Sergeant Murray Kull, and Ms. Normal Danylyshen were instrumental in facilitating our access to the data. We would also like to thank Wayne Antony, Carolyn Brooks, Glen Lewis, Bernard Schissel, and the anonymous reviewers for their generous support.

1. In 1996 women made up 18 percent of those charged with violence offences in Winnipeg compared with 12.5 percent for Canada as a whole (Canadian Centre for Justice Statistics 1996).
2. For instance, the number of cases of spousal assault in which charges were laid in the City of Winnipeg went from 629 in 1983 to 1,137 in 1989, an 80 percent increase in six years (Ursel 1998a).
3. In the following years the number of cases passing through the court increased dramatically: from 1,800 in 1990–91 to 2,660 in 1991–92, 3,646 in 1992–93 and 4,140 in 1993–94 (Ursel 1998b: 75).
4. This coding produced a list of seventeen different violence tactics, which ranged in seriousness from "uttering threats" to "shooting."
5. In contrast, only 16 percent of women and men involved in stranger violence were charged with these offences.
6. Since violence does not always end once a relationship is terminated (indeed, it sometimes escalates), we include in this category both individuals currently in a relationship and former or ex-partners. For the sake of brevity, we use the term "partner" to refer to all of these relationships.
7. The greater use of physical force by male accused is reflected in the charges laid by police: men were twice as likely as women to be charged with assault causing bodily harm (19 percent versus 10 percent).
8. One consequence of the more frequent use of "weapons" on the part of women accused is that when police are called to intervene, women are more likely than men to be charged with the (more serious) offence of assault with a weapon; 32 percent of women's violence charges in the partner category involved assault with a weapon compared with only 11 percent of men's charges.
9. The gender differences for each of these violence tactics were statistically significant.

REFERENCES

Brinkerhoff, Merlin, and Eugen Lupri. 1988. "Interspousal Violence." *Canadian Journal of Sociology* 13 (4).

Brownmiller, Susan. 1975. *Against Our Will: Men, Women and Rape.* New York: Simon and Schuster.

Busby, Karen. 2006. "'Not a Victim Until a Conviction is Entered': Sexual Violence Prosecutions and Legal 'Truth.'" In E. Comack (ed.), *Locating Law: Race/Class/Gender/Sexuality Connections.* Second edition. Halifax: Fernwood Publishing.

Canadian Association of Elizabeth Fry Societies (CAEFS). 2006. "Violence Against Women and Children Fact Sheet." Available at <www.elizabethfry.ca> accessed March 17, 2006.

Canadian Centre for Justice Statistics. 1996. *Uniform Crime Reporting Survey.* Ottawa.

Clark, Lorenne, and Debra Lewis. 1977. *Rape: The Price of Coercive Sexuality.* Toronto: Women's Press.

Cohen, Albert. 1955. *Delinquent Boys: The Culture of the Gang.* Glencoe: Free Press.

Comack, Elizabeth. 1993. *Feminist Engagement with the Law: The Legal Recognition of the 'Battered Woman Syndrome.'* The C.R.I.A.W. Papers No. 31. Ottawa: Canadian Research Institute for the Advancement of Women.

Comack, Elizabeth, and Gillian Balfour. 2004. *The Power to Criminalize: Violence, Inequality and the Law.* Halifax: Fernwood Publishing.

Dauvergne, Mia, and Geoffrey Li. 2005. "Homicide in Canada, 2005." *Juristat* 26, 6.

DeKeseredy, Walter, and Ronald Hinch. 1991. *Woman Abuse: Sociological Perspectives.* Toronto: Thompson Educational Publishers.

DeKeseredy, Walter S., and Brian MacLean. 1998. "'But Women Do It Too': The Contexts and Nature of Female-to-Male Violence in Canadian Heterosexual Dating Relationships." In Kevin Bonnycastle and George Rigakos (eds.), *Unsettling Truths: Battered Women, Policy, Politics, and Contemporary Research in Canada.* Vancouver: Collective Press.

Dobash, R. Emerson, and Russell P. Dobash. 1992. . *Women, Violence and Social Change.* London: Routledge.

Dobash, Russell P., R. Emerson Dobash, Margo Wilson, and Martin Daly. 1992. "The Myth of Sexual Symmetry in Marital Violence." *Social Problems* 39 (1): 71–91.

Gottfredson, Michael R., and M.J. Hindelang 1981. "Sociological Aspects of Criminal Victimization." *Annual Review of Sociology* 7: 107–28.

Hindelang, M.J., M.R. Gottfredson, and J. Garofalo. 1978. *Victims of Personal Crime: An Empirical Foundation for a Theory of Personal Violence.* Cambridge: Ballinger Publishing.

Johnson, Holly. 1996. *Dangerous Domains: Violence Against Women in Canada.* Toronto: ITP Nelson.

Kennedy, Leslie, and Donald Dutton. 1989. "The Incidence of Wife Assault in Alberta." *Canadian Journal of Behavioural Science* 21.

Laframboise, Donna. 1999. "Men and Women are Equals in Violence." *National Post* July 10.

MacKinnon, Catharine. 1983. "Feminism, Marxism, Method, and the State: Toward Feminist Jurisprudence." *Signs* 8.

Messerschmidt, James. 1997. *Crime as Structure Action: Gender, Race, Class, and Crime in the Making.* Thousand Oaks, CA: Sage Publications.

Miller, Walter B. 1958. "Lower Class Culture as a Generating Milieu of Gang Delinquency." *Journal of Social Issues* 14.

Pearson, Patricia. 1997. *When She Was Bad: Violent Women and the Myth of Innocence.* Toronto: Random.

Pedlar, Dorothy. 1991. *The Domestic Violence Review into the Administration of Justice in Manitoba.* Winnipeg: Manitoba Department of Justice.

Polk, Kenneth. 1994. *When Men Kill.* Cambridge: Cambridge University Press.

Rice, T.W., and C.R. Goldman. 1994. "Another Look at the Subculture of Violence Thesis: Who Murders Whom under What Circumstances?" *Sociological Spectrum* 14.

Sacco, Vincent F., and Holly Johnson. 1990. *Patterns of Criminal Victimization in Canada.* Ottawa: Minister of Supply and Services.

Sacco, Vincent F., and Leslie W. Kennedy. 1998. *The Criminal Event: An Introduction to Criminology.* Second edition. Toronto: Nelson Canada.

Schulman, Mr. Justice Perry W. 1997. *A Study of Domestic Violence and the Justice System in Manitoba.* Winnipeg: Report of the Commission of Inquiry into the Deaths of Rhonda and Roy Lavoie.

Schwartz, Martin, and Walter DeKeseredy. 1993. "The Return of the 'Battered Husband Syndrome' Through the Typification of Women as Violent." *Crime, Law and Social Change* 20.

Snider, Laureen. 1999. "Relocating Law: Making Corporate Crime Disappear." In Elizabeth Comack (ed.), *Locating Law: Race/Class/Gender/Sexuality Connections.* Halifax: Fernwood Publishing.

Stanko, Elizabeth. 1985. *Intimate Intrusions: Women's Experiences of Male Violence.* London: Unwin Hyman.

Statistics Canada. 1993. "The Violence Against Women Survey." *The Daily.* November 18.

Statistics Canada. 2004. *Canadian Crime Statistics 2003.* Ottawa: Canadian Centre for Justice Statistics. Catalogue no. 85-205.

Statistics Canada. 2005. "Crime Statistics." *The Daily.* Thursday, July 21. Available at <http://www.statcan.ca/Daily/English/050721a.htm> accessed on August 8, 2006.

Statistics Canada. 2006. "Aboriginal People as Victims and Offenders." *The Daily*, June 6.

Steinmetz, Suzanne. 1981. "A Cross-cultural Comparison of Marital Abuse." *Journal of Sociology and Social Welfare* 8.

Straus, Murray A. 1979. "Measuring Intrafamily Conflict and Violence: The Conflict Tactics (CT) Scales." *Journal of Marriage and the Family* 41, 1.

Straus, Murray A., and Richard J. Gelles. 1986. "Societal Changes and Change in Family Violence from 1975 to 1985 as Revealed by Two National Surveys." *Journal of Marriage and the Family* 48 (August).

Thrasher, F.M. 1927. *The Gang.* Chicago: University of Chicago Press.

Ursel, Jane. 1998a. "Eliminating Violence Against Women: Reform or Co-optation in State Institutions." In L. Samuelson and W. Antony (eds.), *Power and Resistance: Critical Thinking About Canadian Social Issues.* Second edition. Halifax: Fernwood Publishing.

Ursel, E. Jane. 1998b. "Mandatory Charging: The Manitoba Model." In Kevin Bonnycastle and George Rigakos (eds.), *Unsettling Truths: Battered Women, Policy, Politics, and Contemporary Research in Canada.* Vancouver: Collective Press.

Wolfgang, Marvin E. 1958. *Patterns of Criminal Homicide.* New York: John Wiley and Sons.

Part V

The Contemporary Shape
and Form of Punishment

Consensus and traditional approaches in criminology have provided the philosophical framework for our society's justice policies; they try to explain why individuals break laws and what society should do about it. A general assumption of the consensus paradigm in criminology is that inequality among individuals with regards to the distribution of honours, status, and goods is based on fair competition and legitimate entitlement. In other words, if you are poor, generally that is where you belong according to your abilities. Furthermore, if you commit crimes that are the result of your poverty or your marginalization, you are ultimately responsible. Thus, the classical theory of crime control focuses on deterring the "rational individual" away from committing crime by supporting the allotment of punishment that "fits" the crime committed. Much of our social and judicial system is based on this method of crime control. Concomitantly, the criminal justice system assumes that we can achieve fairness and justice by treating all people equally under the eyes of the law.

The chapters in Part V discuss key problems in traditional law and order approaches and therefore also demonstrate critical criminological concerns with consensus criminology. In such a consensus belief system, punishment deters potential criminals from engaging in deviant behaviour by making sure they fear the consequences of their actions. Simply put, if you punish enough, you will deter crime and bad behaviour. Indeed, a raging political debate, especially during elections, centres around whether we have made prisons "so attractive and so comfortable" that they are no longer an effective deterrent. Right-wing ideologues often suggest that we need to strip prisons bare — take away televisions, gymnasiums, or smoking privileges, for instance — so that prisoners, and those contemplating crime, will truly understand how their actions lead not just to confinement but also to a lack of comfort and a basic deprivation — in other words, punishment. This argument does have a kind of behaviourist logic, but we also know, in general, that if you strip people of the things that make their lives bearable, you contribute in the end to their inability to live as responsible citizens.

Donald Morin's personal account of prison here debunks the conservative law-and-order position that prisons are too comfortable; his work, among other first-hand accounts of prison life, shows that prison, to the contrary, is a dangerous, lonely, and unforgiving place. The liberal extensions of consensus theory include rehabilitation as part of the role of prisons, and the original prisons in Canada and the United States were indeed envisioned as places of moral, spiritual, psychological, and social rehabilitation.

351

Imprisonment could take an incorrigible criminal, and, through hard work and solitude, reconstruct that person as a productive citizen. That rhetoric is still a big part of the justification for prisons, as the official term "corrections" implies. But years of research have shown that the conventional prison experience creates criminality rather than reduces it. Morin's chapter reveals that the psychological and physical violence of prison life diminishes rather than repairs inmates.

Part V further develops the basic themes of critical criminology: that the distribution of goods, riches, and honours is unequal across society, and that inequality is further located in class, race, gender, age, and physical ability; that institutions within society, including the law, criminal justice, and the media, work in the interest of elite classes, those with power and influence; and that by treating unequals equally before the law, our system of "justice" contributes to the further production of inequalities. As the system works, the idea of "equality before the law" only hides the substantive inequalities of our social structure, thereby adding to the oppression of people under capitalism.

The conventional discourse of law and order, based on using punishment to instill conformity, not only fails to reduce crime but also contributes to factors that cause more crime. Critics have repeatedly described the criminal justice system as an expensive mess, "wasting scarce resources and tragically, needlessly wasting lives" (Stuart 1993). David Cayley (1998: 4) states, "The product of imprisonment is a person who will require more imprisonment in the future." The authors in Part V explore the contemporary form of criminal justice and explain the damaging impact of "punishment" as well as the reasons that Canadians (and Americans) continue to embrace a failing criminal justice system. Taken as a whole, they argue that prison and policing control a part of the population that is feared and condemned, not for their criminality, but for their disadvantaged position in the political-economic hierarchy. The behaviours that are most often criminalized and controlled have their roots in the social inequalities of class, race, gender, age, and geography.

Carolyn Brooks's chapter, "The Politics of Imprisonment," examines the link between contemporary forms of punishment and current economic and social conditions. She explores the increase in poverty, homelessness, and inequality that goes hand in hand with increasing globalization. Alongside growing inequalities we are witnessing a trend away from social welfare provisions towards social repression and the increase of policing and prisons — including measures such as Three Strikes legislation, chain gangs, and building maxi-maxi and high security prisons. Prison populations are increasing at a time when crime is declining. Brooks draws on Gramsci's notion of hegemony and Nils Christie's discussion of the prison industrial complex, to describe the ideological, structural, and economic function of incarceration. By putting mostly poor and marginalized people in prison and taking up neo-liberal policies that are individualistic in their approaches to rehabilitation or punishment, the state and the justice system leave the impression that the members of a certain class of people are immoral or criminal. The media also reinforce individual or familial explanations of crime and suffering. Judicial condemnation of the poor tells us that the poor are "morally defective" and avoids any consideration of how their crimes and their poverty could be symptomatic of socio-economic inequality. Brooks concludes that the so-called "dangerous classes" are "threatening" because they have the potential for revealing the fundamental injustices within the global economy.

Carl James's chapter, "'Armed and Dangerous!' Racializing Suspects, Suspecting Race," focuses mainly on the issue of race and policing. He questions how we have, in Canada, constructed young Black men as "troublemakers and potential lawbreakers" and how this discourse informs the behaviour of citizens and police. He begins by telling the story of the shooting of a Black man, Hugh Dawson, in Toronto. The police version of the crime, contradicted by eyewitness accounts, was never challenged. James describes the "racist interpretive framework" that informs citizens and even police, making them fear Black men as sources of violence and danger, and discusses how convictions of Black men are often rearranged to fit this racist framework. Police argue that they need to know the criminal elements in society and that this knowledge is based on empirical evidence indicating that certain races are more involved in crime than others; the police contend that they are not targeting racial groups. James counters police rationalizations by discussing the mystification of multiculturalism, the role of the media in criminalization and the setting of agendas, and the absence of an alternative discourse that could challenge racist assumptions and policing practices.

In her chapter "Women in Prison in Canada," Helen Boritch reveals how corrections in Canada are not equipped to be a solution for women in conflict with the law — how women prisoners are faced with a system ill-equipped to deal with their personal problems. She shows that most women in prison have experienced violence either personally or indirectly through poverty or substance abuse, and that they have more in common with non-offending women than they do with male prisoners. She discusses as well the commonalities amongst women prisoners and the detrimental impact of prison life on the women and their families. Her discussion of *Creating Choices,* and the reforms for women within federal penal institutions, shows that although these were intended to create central facilities that would increase choices and empower federally sentenced women, many of the long-standing problems of female incarceration remain unsolved. Concluding with a discussion on the current state's of women's corrections, she argues that although csc (2006) claims to have addressed problems embedded in *Creating Choices* noted by the Arbour report and CHRC, a decade of reform has not addressed central problems "including over-classification, inadequate programs and services, and harsh, punitive, and illegal treatment of women prisoners." Prisons, in general, fail because they do not respond to the economic, political, and social conditions that underpin women's "crime."

Donald Morin's chapter, "Doing Time," reflects on his personal experiences as a prisoner inside the Canadian system. He also shares the story of his friend Ivan. Given the blatant overrepresentation of Aboriginal people in prison, Morin's account is powerful and telling. The road to prison is often marked by "trouble at home, foster home placements, and academic problems" as well as juvenile centres, provincial jails, and finally the federal penitentiary. Morin writes of how he lost trust and hope through the hostile environment of foster care homes and prison: "Foster homes can make you suffer and experience a loss of identity — which may parallel the experience of prison." Survival in prison is based on a prisoner's ability to compartmentalize his emotions and alter his worldview; this psychological adjustment for the inside makes survival outside of prison difficult. Ironically, prison can, in some instances, become a preferred place — at least relative to the outside. "It's easy when you're in jail... I mean they take care of you, they put a roof over your head, they feed you three times a day, they even got drugs all over the place if you want to get high." His words indirectly link the historical genocide and racism experienced by First Nations people to their subsequent involvement in crime and unfair treatment in our justice system. By putting a name and face on the reality of crime and prison life, Morin clearly shows that, rather than being a solution to crime, incarceration can, in fact, create even more prisoners.

15

The Politics of Imprisonment

Carolyn Brooks

KEY FACTS

> In 1996 the richest 10 percent of the population in Canada made 314 times more than the poorest 10 percent. Between 1990 and 2003 the income of the richest 10 percent increased by 14.6 percent.

> In the United States in 2004, the poorest 60 percent of families received 26.8 percent of the total income, whereas the richest 20 percent made 50.1 percent.

> According to the United Nations *Human Development Report*: "It would take the combined wealth of 2.3 billion of the globe's poorest individuals to equal the combined wealth of the globe's 358 richest... these super-rich 358 people control almost half of the world's wealth."

> Correctional services expenditures for 2004/2005 totalled $2.8 billion, a 2 percent increase from 2003/2004. Custodial services accounts for 71 percent of the total. Community supervision accounts for 14 percent and parole accounts for 2 percent.

> There were approximately 152,600 adults under custodial or community supervision (on any given day) in Canada in 2004/2005.

> U.S. prison population growth for one year is eight times larger than the entire population of prisoners in Denmark, Norway, Finland, and Sweden combined.

> One of the first prosecutions under the "Three Strikes" legislation was of a twenty-seven-year-old San Diego man subject to 25 years to life in prison for stealing a piece of pizza. His two previous felonies were for robbery and attempted robbery.

Sources: Comack 1999; Reiman 2007; UNDP 1997; Besserer and Tufts 2006; Beattie 2006; Christie 2000; Reuben 1995.

> *Another wrong is still greater than having no money, and that is to take money from those who have it. The global market's prisons bulge with the perpetrators of this double, unforgivable sin. White-collar criminals are not such a problem... They still fit into the market ethic as people with money wanting more money... But those who have no money and take it from others who have it have no redeeming trait in the market morality. Such miscreants are duly incarcerated, and if need be, killed.*
> —John McMurtry 1998: 161–62

Today, prisons and the "corrections" system continue to be seen as the ultimate answer to crime. Of the $11 billion a year that Canada spends on its criminal justice system, over $2 billion goes to "corrections," over $1 billion to courts and legal aid ($1,039 and $512 million, respectively), and approximately half goes to providing police services ($6,801 billion) (Statistics Canada 2002). The costs of the prison system are high:

the average cost for one prisoner is $110,000 a year (maximum security), $71,640 (medium security) and $74,431 (minimum security). For women, the average cost of incarcerating an inmate is $150,867 (for multi-level security) (CSC 2005). Housing a federal prisoner requires an expenditure of $121 a day (Roberts 2000), and in recent years prison populations have been growing by 4 percent annually.

The average annual cost for one prisoner is $110,000 (maximum security), $71,640 (medium security) and $74,431 (minimum security). For women, the average cost is $150,867 (multi-level security) (CSC 2006).

Despite the already high costs, many Canadians and Americans continue to demand increasingly severe penalties for criminal violations and increased expenditures on criminal justice, mainly because they believe this spending will help keep them safe from harm. Yet the spheres of corrections and public safety are not necessarily connected. For example, only 3 to 5 percent of the people who commit offences against the law end up with prison sentences of any length (Statistics Canada, cited in Roberts 2000). In the case of sexual assault, for example, of 350,000 officially reported offences in 1991, only 2,000 sentences were imposed (Roberts and Grossman 1994, cited in Roberts 2000). Similar research suggests that the court system penalizes almost 1 percent of wife assaults (see, for example, Roberts 2000). Most research has found no correlation between increases in punishment and decreases in the rate of crime (Morris and Rothman 1995, cited in Cayley 1998; Reiman 2004). Indeed, incarceration, it would seem, functions only to ostracize and stigmatize offenders. "The product of imprisonment," David Cayley (1998: 4) notes, "is a person who will require more imprisonment in the future." Reiman (2004: 3) adds, "Indeed, by humiliating and brutalizing prisoners we can be seen to increase their potential for aggressive violence."

Critical criminology analyzes why prison continues to be used and promoted, despite its apparent lack of success in solving problems of crime, by understanding the intricate links between crime, corrections, and the global economy. Given the demands of the much-touted economic globalization, companies are now more than ever concerned with being "competitive" and creating wealth for shareholders, and not with promoting the well-being of workers and their communities. As part of this scheme, Canadians are experiencing the dismantling of social programs and ultimately of the welfare state. On the flip side, we continue to spend tax dollars on more policing and new and improved prisons. The system highlights the crimes of the poor and attributes the issues of crime and poverty to problems of individual failure or pathology. In this political-economic context, policing and prison become one means of containing a certain part of the population — people who are feared and condemned not for their criminality but for their low position in the political-economic hierarchy. Prison becomes, at least in part, a means of housing people extraneous to the needs of capitalism. Globalization has created a new class of people who can be defined as "redundant": "a new underclass of disposable people" (Bauman 1995b: 74).

Canadians are experiencing the dismantling of social programs and ultimately of the welfare state. On the flip side, we continue to spend tax dollars on more policing and new and improved prisons.

The emphasis on imprisoning these "redundant" people illustrates another aspect of the global economy: the process of ideological hegemony, defined as the manipulation of the ideas, knowledge, and values of the working-class population in a way that makes existing social institutions and relationships — the status quo — appear to be legitimate, even though they work only in the best interests of capitalists. Theorist Chantal Mouffe

(1979, quoted in Bottomore et al. 1983: 202) points out:

> What a dominant, hegemonic ideology can do is to provide a more coherent and systematic worldview, which not only influences the mass of the population but serves a principle of organization of social institutions... It organizes action through the way it is embodied in social relations, institutions and practices, and informs all individual and collective activities.

Although the criminal justice system fails to meet its stated objectives, it gains tremendous support because it serves the function of legitimating global capitalism and corporate restructuring while hiding the effects of growing poverty, the increased division between the rich and the poor, and racism. The crime-control system continues to be a hegemonic and ideological political tool that deflects attention from our shattered communities. The message conveyed by the judicial condemnation of the poor is that the poor are "morally defective" and that their crimes and their poverty are not symptomatic of socio-economic inequality. In effect, the so-called "dangerous classes" are threatening because they have the potential to reveal the fundamental injustices within the global economy.

Critical studies from a variety of viewpoints have explained the role of imprisonment as a part of hegemony and social control, and as being essential to the functioning of capitalism: These include the earlier works of Thomas Mathiesen and Ian Taylor (see chapter 3), more current writing by John McMurtry, Jeffrey Reiman, Nils Christie and Zygmunt Bauman, and, perhaps more poignantly, the words of infamous prisoners who fought for freedom from "the larger social prison around them" (McMurtry 2000: 180) — statements by Mahatma Gandhi, Nelson Mandela, Antonio Gramsci, Angela Davis, and George Jackson. It is to the critical analysis of the prison that we now turn — providing some detail first on "corrections" in the United States and Canada. I deal first with the rise in harsh and emotive punishment, and discuss briefly the competing resurfacing of intellectual support for rehabilitation, communitarian, and restorative justice (discussed in more detail in chapters 20 and 21). Current rhetoric in the United States and Canada favours militaristic, harsh, deterrence-based models of exclusion (Garland 2001; Christie 2000; Moore and Hannah-Moffat 2002), yet jurisdictions throughout the world are also adopting (although marginally) communitarian models (chapters 18 and 19). This chapter aims to understand the rise and impact of current apparatus of crime control using critical criminological theory to contextualize it within new forms of our global society.

Imprisonment and Social Control

We want them to have self-worth...
so we destroy their self-worth.
We want them to be responsible...
so we take away all responsibility.

We want them to be part of our community...
so we isolate them from our community.
We want them to be positive and constructive...
so we degrade them and make them useless.

We want them to be trustworthy...
so we put them where there is no trust.
We want them to be non-violent...
so we put them where there is violence all around them.
We want them to quit hanging around 'losers'...
so we put all the 'losers' in the province under one roof.
We want them to quit exploiting us...
so we put them where they exploit each other.
We want them to take control of their lives, own their own problems
And quit being a parasite...
so we make them totally dependent on us.
    — Dennis Challeen, speaking about prison (quoted in Morris 2000)

"Get Tough/No Frills": The United States and Prison Growth

In the post-war penal system, the prison was viewed as a problematic institution that was counter-productive, failing to meet its own correctionalist goals, and reporting high levels of recidivism (Garland 2001). The aim of much government work was to expand other penalties such as probation, community supervision, and fines. The last twenty-five years, however, has seen this tendency reversed, especially in the U.S. and the U.K. (Garland 2001; Christie 2000). Part of this is the increased use of the prison. Garland (2001: 14) states:

> In the last few decades, the prison has been reinvented as a means of inca-pacitative restraint, supposedly targeted upon violent offenders and dangerous recidivists, but also affecting masses of more minor offenders. Probation and parole have de-emphasized their social work functions and give renewed weight to their risk-monitoring functions.

Increased incarceration is reflected in the statistics. The United States increased its prison population by 500 percent between 1973 and 1997 (Garland 2001), and prison terms got longer (Garland 2001; Christie 2000). In 1983 the enormous growth of the prison population in the U.S. was discussed in *Correctional Magazine*:

> "Fantastic... enormous... terrifying," were the words chosen by Norval Morris of the University of Chicago Law School to describe last year's increase in the U.S. prison population... "It's an astonishing increase," says Alfred Blumstein of Carnegie-Mellon University in Pittsburgh. "We don't have the resources to confine these people and the cost is going up. There's got to be an explosion." (cited in Christie 2000: 92)

In 1983 the prison population was 643,371 (274 per 100,000) — frightening at that time. Yet, by 1998, it had tripled (Christie 2000: 93). State-to-state results also show increases. California, for example, grew from 80/100,000 in 1977 to 483/100,000 — 158,742 prison-ers. Interestingly, the solution in California was found in building mega-prisons.

Conditions inside U.S. prisons reflect militaristic and punitive trends. Human Rights Watch, for example, reported that prisoners were being sentenced twice in maxi-maxi prisons — first by courts and second by prison administrations that impose harsh, isolating conditions (Christie 2000). Inmates in a number of federal and state prisons can be held in cell confinement twenty-three hours a day with no visits. The *Los Angeles Times* described Pelican Bay:

> Pelican Bay is entirely automated and designed so that inmates have virtually no face-to-face contact with guards or other inmates. For 22 hours a day, inmates are confined to their windowless cells, built of solid blocks of concrete and stainless steel so that they won't have access to materials they could fashion into weapons. They don't work in prison industries; they don't have access to recreation; they don't mingle with other inmates. They aren't even allowed to smoke... the SHU (Secure Housing Unit) has its own infirmary... inmates can spend years without stepping outside the unit. (May 1990; cited in Christie 2001: 101)

Other examples are just as glaring. Florida State Prison at Starke, for example, has a windowless Q-Wing where inmates are not allowed to go outside (and some inmates have been held here for up to seven years). Closely managed inmates may be deprived of any form of exercise and not allowed outside for years at a time (Christie 2000: 102). Oklahoma reports similar conditions: the *Sunday Oklahoma* reported that the inmates in high-max secure conditions could potentially be moved into a cell house where they would never be outside again (Feb., 1991; cited in Christie 2001: 101).

Pelican Bay was found to be in violation of the U.S. Constitution by Judge Henderson, who wrote that "dry words on paper cannot adequately capture the senseless suffering and sometimes wretched misery (of the inmates)" (cited in Cayley 1998: 53). His accounts included prisoners who were assaulted: heads bashed into floors and against walls while they were shackled, kicked, teeth and jaws fractured and knocked out, bodies burned and limbs broken. Conditions at Pelican Bay and several other high-tech/security prisons in America are criticized in United Nations human rights reports as "inhuman and degrading" (Cayley 1998: 53).

> Current rhetoric details prison as a place where people go to be punished. This is in contrast to the post-war image of the "prison as punishment."

Current rhetoric describes prison as a place where people go to be punished (Garland 2001; Christie 2000; Simon 2001). This is in contrast to the post-war image of the "prison as punishment." The rhetoric is one of cruelty, indicative of a trend towards inflicting pain and vengeance — destroying bodies and lives. Simon writes that "a disturbing and prominent feature of this penality of cruelty is a satisfaction at the suffering implied by or imposed by punishments upon criminals, as well as emotions of anger and desire for vengeance-taking violence" (2001: 126). The agenda within corrections was previously concerned with humane measures of rehabilitation but is now about efficiency and fiscal accountability (Garland 2001). These conditions are exacerbated by the concept of Three Strikes and You're Out, and by the pressure of chain gangs and other backwards measures. The demand for politicians to get tough has revived strategies and conditions used prior to the recognition of prisoners' civil rights in the 1970s. Mississippi, for example, reintroduced caning, and "ordered that convicts once again wear striped uniforms — red and white for maximum-security offenders, black and white for medium, green and white for minimum — with the word 'convict' written on the back" (Mississippi Legislature 1998). Grants for post-secondary education were cut by the crime bill of 1994. In some jurisdictions, prisoners have been required to pay for being incarcerated: "In 1996, a Missouri circuit court judge ruled that Daryl Gilyard, who is serving a life sentence without parole, must reimburse the state for the cost of his imprisonment, beginning with a back payment of $97,724.61" (Cayley 1998: 47).

Arizona, Alabama and Florida have reinstated chain gangs and the shackling of uniformed convicts with leg irons and chains when on work detail. The philosophy behind chain gangs and their reintroduction in U.S. prisons proposes to remove any privilege from sentenced offenders as a measure of deterrence. They are not to receive any education, programming, benefits, or special privilege, hoping to eradicate the concept of entitlement to anything. Critics insist that this will deliver deeply dangerous and unreformed men who require more imprisonment in the future.

Three Strikes and You're Out is also a decidedly punitive measure. Three Strikes legislation introduced by President Bill Clinton in 1994 under the *Violent Crime Control and Law Enforcement Act* authorized mandatory life imprisonment for anyone convicted on two previous separate occasions for two serious violent felonies. Revised statutes under accountability laws lessened the requirements for the life penalty: in California a criminal convicted of a property crime or burglary may receive life imprisonment for the third burglary conviction. The following examples speak for themselves concerning the harshness of this approach:

> A drunken parolee who broke into an Orange County restaurant and stuffed his pockets with chocolate chip cookies was sentenced yesterday to 25 years to life under California's three strikes law... [California] Superior Court judge said she had no alternative after Kevin Weber, 32, was convicted of second-degree commercial burglary. Mr. Weber's first two strikes stemmed from separate burglaries in 1989 at a Huntington Beach apartment, which earned him two years after he pulled a gun on a surprised tenant. (*Globe and Mail* 1995)

> One of the first... three strike prosecutions was of a twenty-seven-year-old San Diego man subject to life in prison for stealing a piece of pizza because he previously had pleaded guilty to two felonies — robbery and attempted robbery.... The first prosecution of a woman under the law was for a $20 cocaine purchase she allegedly made nearly fourteen years after her second strike. (Reuben 1995)

The unconstitutional nature of the three strikes legislation is extremely controversial, meting out unusually cruel jail terms for non-violent crimes. The Campaign for an Effective Crime Policy (CECP) has revealed that 85 percent of the offences under this new law are non-violent (1995; cited in Cayley 1998). Some of the effects of Three Strikes are devastating — vast overcrowding in prison facilities; evidence of further violence (often against police) when cornered and at risk of a twenty-five-year-to-life sentence; and extremely high costs.

Getting Tough in Canada

We will never build glorified country clubs to house Ontario's inmates.
—Ontario Minister of Corrections Rob Sampson 2000

Canadians similarly demand more severe and longer prison terms for criminal violations. Prisons are 15 percent over their official capacity today, with many prisoners sharing a cell meant for a single person. Reports from Canada's correctional investigator assert that overcrowding within Canadian prisons defies decency and is against international convention (cited in Cayley 1998). Trends in incarceration are not supported by increased crime. In fact, in Canada (as well as the United States), crime has gone down for a number of years while the number of prisons increases (*Globe and Mail* 2006). Despite the declining crime rate, the Canadian prison system has been expanding, apparently at the expense of social systems such as education, health care, and the social welfare of individuals.

> Despite the declining crime rate, the Canadian prison system in general has been expanding since the early '80s at the expense of social systems that people need, such as education and health care.

The new Conservative crime bill in Canada demonstrates political support for increased incarceration. The Harper crime bill would impose escalating sentences for a variety of offences, including firearms offences such as smuggling and trafficking, robbery with a stolen weapon, first-time weapons offences and second-time and multiple offenders. The plan is also to eliminate house arrest for a number of offences and to implement minimum mandatory sentences. Justice Minister Vic Toews said in the House of Commons: "If criminals are to be held to account, they must face a punishment that matches the severity of their crime" (*Globe and Mail*, May 5, 2006). The Conservative government's plan is to spend "untold millions on new prison spaces, while scrapping proposed public day-care spots" (*Macleans* 2006). Anthony Doob, a criminologist at the University of Toronto, told the *Globe and Mail* these measures are "not going to make me and you any safer... this has nothing to do with making our streets safer and everything to do with politics" (May 5, 2006). Doob argued that filling prisons does not tackle crime problems and furthermore takes away money that could prevent crime. There is "no evidence to support the suggestion that heavier sentencing works as a deterrent against violent crime" (*Globe and Mail*, May 5, 2006), especially if the United States is the example.

> The Conservative government's plan is to spend "untold millions on new prison spaces while scrapping proposed public day-care spots" (*Macleans* 2006).

Law-and-order politics in Ontario is comparable to that of the U.S., drawing on the same themes of punitiveness, victim centredness, exclusion and enhanced control, and calling for increased use of prisons, restrictions on parole-release, austere prisons, super max prisons, and boot camps (Moore and Hannah-Moffat 2002). Current rhetoric in Ontario rejects rehabilitation, community corrections, and culture and gender sensitivity, in opting for a return to inexpensive accountability deterrence with its harsh militaristic models. The decarceration practices called for in the 1980s in Ontario have been halted in favour of a harsher, punitive agenda denouncing "club fed." Envisioned and implemented by the Ontario Correctional Renewal Project (OCRP) are privatized correctional facilities and "super-jails" with electronic surveillance, minimal staff, and reduced parole.

The super-max facilities in Ontario are witnessing the same patterns seen in the U.S. The super-max in Youngstown, Ohio, for example, was plagued with homicides, high-profile escapes, and violations of the rights of prisoners, with investigations linking these events directly to the facility's size and private status (Office of the Corrections Trustee, cited in Moore and Hannah-Moffat 2002: 111). Even the senator of Ohio warned then-premier Mike Harris against the private mega-prison building.

Ontario's punitive approach, introduced in 1996, reflects a no-frills philosophy: safety, security, and efficiency. The Adult Infrastructure Renewal Project (AIRP) reflects this plan, closing about twenty correctional institutions and detention centres and building two new 1,500-bed mega-jails of a panoptic design, allowing for minimal staff and maximum surveillance. Access to rehabilitative programming is limited and those incarcerated are rendered unknowable because of the high volume of offenders. Liberal Premier McGuinty has now promised to build additional prisons, including the controversial Super Jail for young offenders. The planned facility will be built in Brampton and will cost $81.1 million (Kingston's *Progressive Independent Community Newspaper* 2006).

The province's detention centres also observe the no-frills mandate. The government slashed virtually all programs, life skills, education, and social work from these prisons in 1997. Inmates are locked in their cells for twenty-three hours per day with no recreation time other than the legislated twenty minutes that they are entitled to. The guards report that the severity and frequency of prison violence have increased as a direct result of the implementation of these changes in July 2000 (Moore and Hannah-Moffat 2002). Penal practices throughout Ontario reflect the U.S. trends:

> Prisoners are now expected to bear the cost of their own incarceration through prisoners work programs in which they are taught skills of questionable value, such as how to pick up trash on the highway. Upon entry to prison, inmates have their heads shaved and are stripped of even minor personal effects such as jewelry. In the new order, these practices are intended to build self-esteem. For the inevitable prison violence that will ensue, a zero-tolerance policy has been adopted. (Moore and Hannah-Moffat 2002: 116).

Although incarceration is increasing in Canada, especially among Aboriginal peoples, alternative measures such as restorative justice (for more complete details on restorative justice see chapters 20 and 21) have also been embraced. The federal government began to demonstrate a concern with the rise in prison populations with the report of the Sentencing and Corrections Review Group in 1995. The main commitment to devising alternatives to incarceration was the conditional sentencing provisions within the Criminal Code. Section 742.1 of the Criminal Code allowed offenders to serve sentences of two years or less in the community, as long as safety was not a concern. Quebec and New Brunswick also announced decarceration policies, which are in marked contrast to Ontario's cheaper and more isolating conditions. Robert Perreault, in a report released in April 1996, aimed to close six or more of the prisons within the province to reduce their populations by at least 13 percent. The government of Quebec suggests that by substituting prevention and conflict resolution for repression, it will save $16 million a year and decrease imprisonment by 7.5 percent annually. There is a hope for a reduction of 25 percent in the provincial jails in New Brunswick (Cayley 1998).

The Priority of Public Sentiment over Professional Judgment and Penological Experts

Whoever speaks on behalf of victims speaks on behalf of us all — or so declares the new political wisdom of high crime societies.
— Garland 2001.

There is very little evidence to suggest that reintroducing maxi-maxi and super-maxi prisons, chain gangs, increased incarceration, or legislation such as Three Strikes reduces the incidence of crime or helps to rehabilitate offenders. Ironically, there is much research that shows the opposite is true: Harsh law-and-order penalties and draconian measures increase crime (see, for example, Morris 2000; Clarke 2000; McMurtry 2000; Mathiesen 1974, 1990; Reiman 2001; Cayley 1998; Comack 1996). Yet most Americans and many Canadians support these get-tough policies (Cayley 1998; Hermer and Mosher 2002; Christie 2000; Reiman 2004). "Punishment — in the sense of expressive punishment, conveying public sentiment — is once again a respectable, openly embraced penal purpose and has come to affect not just high-end sentences for the most heinous offences but even juvenile justice and community penalties" (Garland 2001: 9). The language of the condemnation of the offender is purporting to express the sentiment of the public, and this public discourse informs political platforms and becomes policy. Public sentiment takes priority over professional and expert opinion. Thus draconian measures are indicative of a public that fears crime and strategies that are soft on crime (Garland 2001; Moore and Hannah-Moffat 2002). Alongside punitive measures are public panics, fear, and victim-centredness. The general public seeks gratifying unity though punishment and condemnation of deviance and criminality, often under the guise of sentiment towards the victims, victims' families, and the fearful public.

Feeding public sentiment is a return to the focus on victims — their protection, memory, fears, and voices heard — which often means harsh treatment of offenders in the name of protecting and honouring victims' suffering: "The interests and feelings of victims — actual victims, victims' families, potential victims, the projected figure of 'the victim' — are now routinely invoked in support of measures of punitive segregation" (Garland 2001: 11). Routinely, when political figures announce new laws, crime victims or family members will accompany them. Laws are often named for the victims, such as Megan's law or Jenna's law. Victims represent the public, and victimization is seen as indicative of a society whose risk of crime is very high: "Publicized images of actual victims serve as the personalized, real-life, it-could-be-you metonym for a problem of security that has become a defining feature of contemporary culture" (Garland 2001: 11). This concept of victimization can be used as a powerful political tool, which feeds politics of harsh law-and-order, instilling passions that are collective against a common enemy. Schissel (1997: 29) reminds us:

> Victimization is used as a discursive mechanism... textual and pictorial depictions of victims' experiences are intended to evoke very primal and passionate responses to crime and our own and others' potential victimization. The vicarious victims' experience frames our understanding of the criminal event and creates empathy not only for the victim but also for advocates of law and order.

Another prominent theme within Western cultures and in criminological literature is the fear of crime. Most statistical research shows that the fear is unfounded: Crime is feared to be escalating at times when there is either no change or a decrease in rates (Schissel 2006; Garland 2001). The media dramatizes crime, conjuring up images of folk devils — unruly, pathological, nihilistic career criminals who require harsher law-and-order measures. Media images are false, hateful, and stereotypical yet inform the public, which in turn provides politicians with justification for tough law-and-order campaigns.

Misinformed policy comes from ill-informed public sentiment. Garland (2001:

10–11) eloquently articulates the situation: "The background effect of policy is now more frequently a collective anger and a righteous demand for retribution rather than a commitment to a just, socially engineered solution." Policy on crime and its control is no longer informed by experts and professionals, but has a prominent part in electoral campaigns. Criminological knowledge and research is replaced with the voice of "common sense":

> New initiatives are announced in political settings — the U.S. part convention, the British part conference, the televised interview — and are encapsulated in sound-bite statements: "Prison works," "Three-strikes and you're out," "Truth in sentencing," "No frills prisons," "Adult time for adult crime," "Zero-tolerance," "Tough on crime, tough on the causes of crime." (Pillsbury, cited in Garland 2001: 13)

As mentioned, while there is a celebration of emotive, deterrent-based forms of crime control, there is also growing intellectual and practical support for rehabilitation and measures of restorative and communitarian justice. To get a sense of the multiplicity of competing discourses on crime control and prevention, see chapters 19 and 20.

Our critique of retributive justice is levelled on ideological and ethical grounds by critical criminologists who detail the fit between criminal justice reform and global conditions. Industrialized countries in recent years have been changing state policy regarding criminal justice and welfare provisions. Critical criminologists have defined this shift as moving from the welfare state towards the repressive state (White 2002; Clarke 2000; McMurtry 2000). This position suggests that the retributive (and the restorative) justice tag support this political agenda. The role of the government is no longer to ensure the well-being of the population through full employment and social welfare. Instead, that role has shifted towards creating a favourable environment for transnational investment (Clarke 1997; Dobbin 1998). Governments are cutting funding for the poor, privatizing social services, and spending more money on criminal justice (White 2002; Clarke 2000). It is within this social context that I will contextualize restitutive justice.

Globalization, Postmodernity, and the New Underclass

Despite the complexity of neo-liberal globalization (see, for example, O'Loughlin, Staeheli, and Greenberg 2004), trends are said to be instructive (Routledge 2006; Anderson and Cavanagh 2000; Dobbin 2003). The size and power of transnational corporations are difficult for most of us to even imagine. Fifty-one of the largest one hundred economies in the world are transnational corporations: Wal-Mart, with a gross revenue greater than the Gross Domestic Product (GDP) of 161 countries, is the twelfth largest economy in the world (Anderson and Cavanagh 2000); on paper Ford is larger than South Africa; General Motors surpasses Denmark; Toyota is bigger than Norway. The poorest four-fifths of humanity has less economic worth than the top two hundred corporations: "the combined annual revenues of the largest two hundred transnational corporations are greater than those of 182 countries that contain 80 percent of the world's population" (Ellwood 2001, cited in Routledge 2006). The World Bank reported that the poorest 57 percent of the world's population had an income equal to the richest 1 percent (cited in Routledge 2006).

Even though the top two hundred transnational corporations account for about 30 percent of the world's GDP, these corporations only employ half to three-quarters of 1 percent of the worldwide workforce (Dobbin 1998), and more and more people everywhere are losing steady or decent employment. The losses are a result of "restructuring" within the global market: mergers, downsizing, takeovers, and the shifting of production to countries with the lowest costs. The Canadian Labour Congress has estimated that rather than creating jobs, which free trade promised to do, the Canada–U.S. Free Trade Agreement cost Canada nearly sixty thousand jobs within a year of implementation (Bronson 1993). Anderson and Cavanagh (2000:1) argue that the CEOs benefit financially from cuts in jobs:

> A total of 59 of the Global Top 200 are U.S. firms. Of these, 9 laid off at least 3,000 workers in 1995; AT&T, Boeing, Lockheed-Martin, BellSouth, Kmart, Chase Manhattan, GTE, Mobil, and Texaco. Even worse, the CEOs of these 9 made millions of dollars in the increased value of their stock options after announcing the layoffs. Indeed, on the day that the CEOs of these 9 firms announced the layoffs, the value of the stock options of their 9 CEOs rose $25,218,819.

Despite economic growth, downsizing means that newly created jobs are low-paying, insecure, and part-time. More and more people are employed in casual labour or part-time work:

> People are now asking: What happened to full-time employment?... We are being told by many business people and politicians that [casual labour] will allow Canadians to use their entrepreneurial skills to improve the economy, to get rid of the deficit and so on. Euphemisms such as "contingent" and "non-standard" labour are used to describe the phenomenon. And, like the euphemisms of "collateral damage" (murder of civilians) and "friendly fire" (being accidentally killed by one's own troops) used in recent imperialist wars, these new terms are intended to hide real human suffering. (Broad 2000: 5)

The rising power of transnational corporations works in tandem with the declining role of the state. In the global economy, governments no longer seem willing to ensure full employment and social well-being. Instead, the primary function of the state is to create an environment favourable to transnational investment (O'Loughlin et al. 2004; Dobbin 2003; Clarke 1997). The economic strategy, as promoted, for example, by the Business Council on National Issues, becomes creating jobs to support the needs of the business community. By following this strategy, both provincial and federal governments accommodate the demands of big business to the detriment of the social and economic rights of citizens, which means downsizing the public sector, deregulating corporate wrongdoing and crime (see chapter 10), and slashing social spending and corporate taxes (see, for example, Dobbin 2003).

Zygmunt Bauman (1995a) examines the changing role of the state and how the co-ordinating society has become the responsibility of the market. He calls this new social terrain "postmodernity." In previous so-called modern societies, all citizens were promised a part in economic life. Certainly, at times some people were economically idle and as such were considered part of a "reserve army." After World War II, most people were protected through the welfare state and secure in the knowledge that their labour would eventually be needed again. In contrast, the state under global capitalism maintains no primary obligation to the unemployed or to the workforce in general. As the head of the International Labour Organization remarked, "Anyone who thinks that everyone on earth is going to get a job is no longer just an optimist, but actually mad" (quoted in Cayley 1998: 75).

In his discussion of how, under global capitalism, the organization of social life has become the responsibility of the market, not of citizens or the state, Bauman (1995) argues that citizens follow rules because of the seductive allure of consumerism. To survive, to flourish in this market-dominated world, people must be able to obtain commodities. This disciplined world is regulated by competition, envy, and self-interest and based on the principle of endless production and consumerism (Pettigrew 1996). Globalization is thus fed by the non-human and abstract rather than by life experiences, human emotions, and need. In theory, if we don't like what the state does we can democratically force governments to show concern. But as Pierre Pettigrew said as minister for international co-operation in 1996, at a conference on African development: "If we don't like what the market does, we can't repeal its laws.... if we storm the bunker of globalization, we won't find a madman there or a clique of conspirators — just an empty space" (quoted in Cayley 1998: 78).

Accompanying these trends is the dismantling of our welfare state and the abrogation of the social rights of Canadians. One of the greatest fallacies promoted in recent years by governments and corporations is that government debt and deficits are created by overspending on social programs. A 1991 Statistics Canada study found that only 2 percent of the debt was due to spending on social programs and that 94 percent of the debt "was a result of high interest rates and tax breaks to the rich and corporations" (*Prairie Dog News*, February 1996). Dobbin (2003) notes:

> The actions of the Canadian government caused the so-called deficit. The problem is that there was never a public debate about exactly which actions of the government caused it. The overwhelming message of the deficit warriors was that we were paying a price for our attachment to social programs. However, as many studies revealed at the time and since, this wasn't the case. The crisis, if there was one, was initially a crisis of falling revenue, which was then exacerbated by compound interest.

Still, the Business Council on National Issues successfully lobbied governments to cut back on social spending, and those cuts have had significant effects on poverty and unemployment.

Paul Martin was described as the prime minister who defeated the deficit. Murray Dobbin (2003), however, argues that Martin redefined the role of government in the lives of Canadians, especially in terms of social spending. By 1996–1997, boasted Martin, "we will have reduced program spending from $120 billion in 1993–4 to under $108 billion. Relative to the size of our economy, program spending will be lower in 1996–7 than at any time since 1951" (budget speech, February 27, 1995, <www.fin.gc.ca/budget95/>, cited in Dobbin 2003: 3). The recent history of unemployment insurance helps demonstrate how Canadian governments are abandoning those in need. Before four sets of reforms to the unemployment insurance program (now Employment Insurance), Canada was offering assistance to 87 percent of the unemployed. By 1996 (and to this day), less than 40 percent of unemployed Canadians were eligible for benefits, which were also being paid out in lower amounts than before. Interestingly, cuts in spending caused a budget surplus. Rather than restoring the social programs that were cut, Martin implemented larger tax breaks for Canada than ever before, with most of the benefit going to corporations: "seventy-seven per cent of the personal income tax cuts went to those earning over $65,000 per year — the richest 8 percent of the population" (Dobbin 2003: 4).

Today, the UN says there is an emergency for Canada's poor:

> Welfare benefits in most provinces have dropped in value in the past 10 years and often amount to less than half of basic living costs, a UN watchdog group charged yesterday. The Employment Insurance program needs to be more accessible, minimum wages don't meet basic needs, and homelessness and inadequate housing amount to a "national emergency," says the UN body's report from Geneva. (UN Committee on Economic, Social and Cultural Rights; cited in *Toronto Star* 2006).

The UN report was a sharp criticism of Canadian poverty and social programs. Minimum wage in every Canadian province was considered insufficient to allow workers a decent standard of living. The report stated that social assistance rates "bear no resemblance" (*Toronto Star* 2006) to the cost of living in Canada.

Cuts in social programs have both an ideological and economic basis. The welfare state was initially seen as a route to freedom: Through social support, the state could increase the health of the population and therefore eventually make welfare largely unnecessary. The safety net allowed people to take more risks because, as Bauman (1995a) states, "They can exert themselves because there is always this safety provision if they fail" (quoted in Cayley 1998: 78). Under globalization this idea of a safety net for those who have "unluckily fallen" has shifted to a perception that those who collect have given way to a "permanent crippling dependency." The idea of collective responsibility towards all citizens has thus been replaced with the idea of individual responsibility. The clamour for tax cuts speaks to a similar ideological belief in personal rather than collective responsibility.

> Employment Insurance must be more accessible, minimum wages don't meet basic needs, and homelessness and inadequate housing represent a "national emergency," says the UN Committee on Economic, Social and Cultural Rights (*Toronto Star* 2006).

With globalization, corporate downsizing, and the restructuring and dismantling of the social welfare state, class inequalities have grown. The census data and CCSD analysis show increasing numbers of Canadians living in poverty — from 4.39 million in 1990 to 4.9 million in 2003 (NAPO 2006). The number of children living in poverty has similarly increased. One child in six in Canada lives in poverty, or 1.2 million — an increase of 20 percent since 1989 (NAPO 2006). The disparity between the rich and the poor has also increased in the last few decades. For example, in 1971 the richest 10 percent of Canadian families made 21 times the income of the poorest 10 percent. In 1996 the richest 10 percent made 314 times more than the poorest 10 percent (Comack 1999a: 14). Income inequality continues to grow. Between 1990 and 2003, the income of the richest 10 percent increased by 14.6 percent and that of the poorest by less than 1 percent (NAPO 2006). In the United States some 37 million men, women, and children live below the poverty line, with countless people unable to afford proper diets, education, and health care (Reiman 2007). In 2004, the poorest 60 percent of families received 26.8 percent of the total income, whereas the richest 20 percent made 50.1 percent (Reiman 2007). "This means that the richest 5 percent — less than

> In 2003, 4.9 million people In Canada were living in poverty (NAPO 2006).

4 million families — have more money to divide among themselves than the 30.4 million families who make up the bottom 40 percent" (Reiman 2007: 189). The National Anti-Poverty Organization, citing the United Nations *Human Development Report*, puts the disparity of wealth on a global level in a way that demonstrates the magnitude of the inequities: "It would take the combined wealth of 2.3 billion of the globe's poorest individuals to equal the

> In the United States some 32.3 million men, women, and children live below the poverty line, with countless people unable to afford proper diets, education, and health care (Reiman 2004).

combined wealth of the globe's 358 richest... that means these super-rich 358 people control almost half of the world's wealth" (UNDP 1997).

A shift in thinking towards neo-liberal ideas accompanies the institutional changes of globalization (White 2002; Clarke 2000). This means that citizens are viewed as autonomous individuals, responsible for their own actions and fate. Economic opportunity is recast as individual responsibility, not connected to social structural conditions. This reinforces cutbacks in welfare provisions and further polarizes rich and poor, to which the state must respond (White 2002).

With more poverty and homelessness, laws and other policies have the potential to unite people against a common enemy. The critical criminological position is that the attempt by the state to contain the most desperate and most vulnerable sections of the population (which includes Indigenous people), has led it to embrace law and order as well as "reconfigure police-community relations (through zero-tolerance approaches and community policing initiatives), to expand surveillance and intervention into working-class communal life (through crime prevention and community safety projects), and to reinforce state authority (through tougher sentencing legislation)" (White 2002: 388). Debates over restorative justice are also part of this struggle, which is political (see Rob White, chapter 20).

Condemning the Marginalized: Crime and Punishment

Imprisonment thrives as a "psychological safety valve" in the unstable order of the market (Cayley 1998: 80). The global market sets the tone of personal responsibility and therefore has the dual effect of providing a person's chance for advancement and the possibility of failure (Bauman 1995a). In the global economy, with its inducement to greed, desire, and competition, citizens become "unfulfiled consumers" whose desires are never satisfied. This new global market is a "war of all against all," raising a strong possibility, in the end, of chaos or anarchy. While some people thrive in this new social/market organization, others must fail: they are defined as "redundant" or "imperfect consumers," people "who are of no visible utility... from the point of view of the circulation of commodities" (Bauman 1995, quoted in Cayley 1998: 76). These redundant people come to be defined as disorderly because they do not — cannot — follow the rules of the consumerist marketplace society. Indeed, the unemployed and the poor threaten the internal functioning of consumerism and market society; they are reminders of failure. A critique of the criminal justice system and the prison as an essential part of hegemony, hiding capitalist inequalities and reinforcing the poor as "criminal," is developed by critical criminological authors such as Christie 2001; Davis 2005; Reiman 2001, 2004; Clarke 2000; and Bauman 1995a, who argue that an ideological function of the prison is to blame individuals for acts that are stimulated by capitalism's economic and social inequality, without asking whether society upheld its obligations towards the social rights of individuals.

What we call "crime" may not be the most dangerous or the most anti-social behaviour. The critical criminological position is that crime is a social creation, satisfying the needs of the market economy. This means that actions of corporations and the well-off are often not criminalized even when they may pose a

> Imprisonment thrives as a "psychological safety valve" in the unstable order of the market (Cayley 1998: 80).

grave threat to our social well-being (Snider 1999; West and Morris 2000; Reiman 2004), whereas the "redundant" or "disposable" people — the underemployed, unemployed, and poor — become the "dangerous class" (West and Morris 2000; Clarke 2000; Martin 2002; Reiman 2004). The criminal reminds the consumer personality of what might come about if self-regulation is not kept in check: "This explains not just the fantastic rise in imprisonment but also the widespread preoccupation with crime. This preoccupation is expressed in a political concern that has grown out of any proportion to actual registered crime, and in a taste for movies, television programs, and journalistic media that place the same disproportionate emphasis on deviance" (Bauman 1995, quoted in Cayley 1998: 80).

> What we call "crime" may not be the most dangerous or the most anti-social behaviour. The critical criminological position is that "crime" is a social creation, satisfying the needs of the market economy.

Disorderliness begets fear, which in turn feeds a public appetite for imprisoning the disorderly. As global capitalism progresses, more and more poor and disenfranchised people are labelled criminal and imprisoned. They become, as Bauman puts it, "the enemies who have laid siege to [society's] walls," the system's "own inner demons." They are "moulded into an alien body; into a tangible enemy one can fight against, and even swear to conquer" (Bauman 1995, quoted in Cayley 1998: 76). In labelling the addict or the woman working in the sex trade, for instance, as "criminal," society forgoes the obligation of dealing with the underlying social inequalities that lead people into these desperate living conditions. Rather than addressing the roots of increasing homelessness, poverty, and numbers of marginalized people, society uses the criminal justice system to squash the human manifestations of the problem. As anti-poverty activist John Clarke (2000: 82) puts it, the "balance between reluctant social provision and repression is being tilted" in favour of the latter. In its "social regulation of the poor," the state cuts back on income and housing programs and provides more and more police patrols, courtrooms, and prison cells. For example, in 1999, 255 schools were shut down in Ontario, 1,700 needed repair, and funding for both immigration and housing decreased — yet funding for prisons was up 17 percent (Hanson 2006). Approximately two-thirds of the prisoners in Canada, or 80 percent of inmates in provincial facilities and 20 to 30 percent of federal prisoners, are incarcerated for offences deemed non-violent (Statistics Canada 2006).

The homelessness problem in the larger cities, for instance, has led to more and more people sleeping in parks and begging on city streets. As homelessness becomes more and more visible in Canada, it interferes with commercial and residential development. The National Coalition on Housing and Homelessness (cited in CCPA 2006) show us that more than two million Canadians "are still in desperate need of decent, affordable housing [yet] the federal government is poised to take billions of housing dollars out of housing." To solve these problems, residents and business people pressure politicians to act against the homeless. This

> As anti-poverty activist John Clarke (2000: 82) puts it, the "balance between reluctant social provision and repression is being tilted" in favour of the latter.

problem escalates as housing is renovated and built for the more affluent while social housing initiatives decline, the victim of policies that see low-income housing as an unnecessary expense. Criminalizing the poor becomes a way of cleansing the city, making it a supposedly safe and attractive environment for affluent people (Clarke 2000).

> "Acts of survival like petty drug dealing or prostitution are focused on but the real agenda is the 'social cleansing' of the homeless" (Clarke 2000: 82).

This drive against the dispossessed and marginalized is often disguised as an anti-crime movement: "Acts of survival like petty drug dealing or prostitution are focused on but the real agenda is the 'social cleansing' of the homeless" (Clarke 2000: 82). In Ontario, for instance, the *Ontario Safe Streets Act*, passed by the Conservative government in 2000, makes it illegal to squeegee and to panhandle — acts most likely involving the homeless and poor. Public safety is the official reason for this new act, as Ontario Attorney General Jim Flaherty proclaimed to a news conference: "*The Safe Streets Act* responds to the real life concerns the people of Ontario have about these activities that compromise our safety in our communities... People must be able to carry out their daily activities without fear, without feeling afraid" (*Star-Phoenix* Feb. 1, 2000: B7). But the Safe Streets legislation is in essence not about safety but about economic distress, unemployment, and homelessness. Similarly, the City of Toronto has developed "community action policing," giving police permission to persecute the poor and homeless. Aggressive panhandlers and squeegee kids can receive a fine of up to $500, with the possibility of incarceration is they don't pay. There are an estimated 25,000 homeless people in Toronto. These initiatives are ensuring that many of the homeless and poor will end up behind bars.

Justice system statistics also provide a different picture (than the news media) of just what is embodied by this "dangerous class." The average length of a prison sentence in Canada is thirty days (Statistics Canada, updated 2006); one-quarter of admissions to custody are for two weeks or less; and 50 percent of those sentenced to jail get less than thirty days (Roberts 2000). In 2003, some 30 percent of people convicted in court received fines, not jail sentences; 38 percent of convictions resulted in incarceration. It would seem, then, that our courts see most offenders as being of no great danger to society. Federal penitentiary time or sentences of two years or longer account for less than 3 percent of all sentences (Roberts 2000). In 2003, the offence of theft under $5,000 was the most frequently heard type of case in adult courts in Canada (Statistics Canada 2006). Violent crimes accounted for 11.8 percent of the cases heard. Assaults (from level 1 to level 3) account for 9.1 percent of the 11.8 percent of violent crimes. The offences that would be considered most "dangerous" — abduction, sexual abuse, attempted murder, robbery, and homicide — represented less than 1 percent of all of cases heard. Homicides accounted for .02 percent of the 11.8 percent, and attempted murder accounted for .023 percent (Statistics Canada 2006).

> In 2003, the offence of theft under 5,000 was the most frequently heard type of case in adult courts in Canada (Statistics Canada 2006).

Most crimes committed by women are property related (see chapter 17). The second highest proportion of crimes charged against women involved morality offences. Women are typically charged with offences such as "being drunk in a public place, drinking under age, purchasing liquor under the legal age." When women face drug-related charges, many of the cases (46 percent) involve possession of or trafficking in cannabis (Boritch 1997: 17). Another element in the picture of the "dangerous classes" is the racial skew in prisons. Aboriginal people make up 16 percent of the Canadian inmate population, but only 3 percent of the Canadian population. (See chapter 8 for more details on Aboriginal overrepresentation in the criminal justice system.)

> The offences that would be considered most "dangerous" — abduction, sexual abuse, attempted murder, robbery, and homicide — represented less than 1 percent of all of cases heard. (Statistics Canada 2006).

The statistics not only demonstrate that most prisoner/offenders are not particularly dangerous, but also raise questions about the very definition of "crime." The typical prisoner is poor, male, probably Aboriginal or Black, undereducated, and unemployed. The idea of a typical criminal becomes attached to a stereotype. Although we condemn offenders for not upholding their obligations to society and fulfiling their responsibilities as good citizens, we fail to ask whether society has upheld its responsibility to the offenders (Reiman 2004; 2007). This prevailing approach denies the reality that the acts of the poor are most often not nearly as dangerous as, for instance, the everyday activities of many corporations — activities that are often praised or acknowledged as simply being "good business." Even worse, in recent years corporate lobbies and neo-liberal governments have pushed to deregulate corporate activity, to dismantle government protection of environmental and human life (see chapter 11).

Law-and-order politics is a key strategy in trying to forge alliances between the rich and the poor. The themes of criminal responsibility and dangerous social groups are ideological tools that try to manage the most vulnerable social classes. The criminal justice system functions as a powerful tool to manipulate the majority of the population into believing that it is the poor and marginalized that must be feared as the dangerous class (Reiman 2001; Clarke 2000). Critical criminology attempts to penetrate the ideologies that mask capitalist exploitation, in order to "deflect attention away from capitalist society's real interests, naked oppressions and structural inequalities" (Pavlich 2000: 51). Harsh, militaristic, punitive law and order, and maxi-maxi and super-maxi prisons, reinforce the imagery of the criminal as dangerous and (dichotomously) different from the "respectable, conforming" population (Moore and Hannah-Moffat 2002; Garland 2001; Reiman 2004).

> We condemn offenders for not upholding their obligations to society and fulfiling their responsibilities to be good citizens, but we fail to ask whether the society has upheld its responsibility to the offenders (Reiman 2004).

Nils Christie (2001) and Angela Y. Davis (2005) add a powerful critique of the prison industrial complex and demonstrate how these prisons are an integral part of a system that uses people to generate massive profits. The most vulnerable people are the "raw material" for the prison industrial complex; imprisoning the poor and racial minorities is a complex political act, depoliticizing inequalities and yielding vast profits. This is evident in the pain market of the penal system — profits are generated from the building of prisons, the privatization push, and the technological push. This latter point is well articulated in Christie's description of advertisements for prison building and equipment for prisons.

Bell Construction says:

> The Pros on Cons... for more than 20 years we've been building. Building a reputation. Building a client list, and building correctional facilities. That's all we do, we build... and we do it well. Twenty-five correctional facilities worth $300 million have given us the experience, and now our clients call us the "pros."

Point Blank Armour says:

> Some inmates would love to stab, slash, pound, punch and burn you. But they won't get past your STAR Special Tactical Anti-Riot vest. (cited in Christie 2001: 113–14)

Christie (2001) and Davis (2005) write that the expansion of the U.S. prison system is not abating, has powerful ideological appeal, and is relying on racism as the foundation for profits. The people who live in super-max prisons (or any prison) are seen as society's problems. Yet they are often members of racial minorities who cannot find work. The war against crime is a war that strengthens control by the state over those who are "the least useful" part of the population — those who illustrate that the social fabric is not as it should be.

Conclusion

The criminal justice system might seem to be unfair and ineffective, but it does not fail the status quo, and it successfully accomplishes what the more elite groups see as being in their best interests (Reiman 2004; 2007). Those who have the power to change the system benefit from it and don't have the desire to change it. Those without power suffer the costs of the failure of the criminal justice system. Reiman (2004; 2007) argues that the current criminal justice system is the best possible model for the creation of crime. What we have is a profound system for causing more crime: labelling someone as an "offender"; expecting criminal tendencies; failing to deal with the issues in society that may create criminogenic conditions; lowering self-esteem; criminalizing victimless and consensual acts; lumping disenfranchised individuals together in demeaning conditions; and creating a breeding ground for dangerous criminal behaviour. We continue to use this costly, obviously ineffective, criminal justice system because it enhances and legitimates the global economy and market, despite the human devastation created in the process.

> Labelling someone as an "offender," expecting criminal tendencies, lowering self-esteem, criminalizing victimless and consensual acts, and lumping disenfranchised individuals together in demeaning conditions creates a breeding ground for dangerous criminal behaviour.

In asking us to consider the benefits provided for the wealthy and powerful, Reiman (2007: 183) points to the ideological message that results from criminalizing the actions of the poor and marginalized: "The ultimate sanctions of criminal justice dramatically sanctify the present social and economic order, and the poverty of criminals makes poverty itself an individual moral crime!" Those from the middle and upper classes can easily justify the large disparities in wealth as they come to believe that the poor are at fault for their plight. "Thus by focusing on individual responsibility for crime, the criminal justice system effectively acquits the existing social order of any charge of injustice!" (Reiman 2004: 166). Public demands for more equality and an equal distribution of wealth are not part of the current political agenda. Morality and fairness do not appear to be part of the social justice picture in Canada:

> If we acknowledge the degree to which our economic and social institutions themselves breed poverty, we would have to recognize our own responsibilities toward the poor. If we can convince ourselves that the poor are poor because

of their own shortcomings, particularly moral shortcomings like incontinence and indolence, then we need acknowledge no such responsibility to the poor. Indeed, we can go further and pat ourselves on the back for our generosity in handing out the little that we do — it is my view that this conception of the poor is subtly conveyed by the way our criminal justice system functions. (Reiman 2007: 182–83)

As Reiman (2004, 2007) points out, we know too much about the causes of poverty to assume that the rich are rich only because of skills and motivation, or that the poor are poor because of laziness or incompetence. The global market is based on self-interest — creating never-satisfied consumers wanting more material goods and penalizing those who have little. Free-enterprise philosophy is based on the assumption that everyone has the potential to succeed as long as they possess the required skills and motivation. But with the restructuring of the market and decreased social programs, we are nowhere near offering everyone an equal opportunity for education or income, or addressing the cycle of poverty and racism. We may not, in clear conscience, argue that income distribution is representative of what people deserve or have earned. That we have adopted a false ideology becomes abundantly clear when we consider the workings of law, crime, criminal justice, and incarceration.

Clearly, social justice initiatives must resist simple criminal justice strategies and the urge to separate the problem of crime from other social problems such as poverty, homelessness, abuse, and racism. We can begin not only with restorative measures that address the immediate needs of the convicted or incarcerated person, but also by working on community development. To work towards real justice means building strong social movements to counter the effect of globalization, deregulation of corporate wrongdoing, and the criminalization of the poor. The development of a counter-hegemony that will work towards a democratization of criminal justice, law, media, and the state requires active citizen groups demanding human rights: to drink pure water, to enjoy clean air, and not to be subject to toxins at work. It requires people who will enjoy fair wages, safe working environments; access to education and full employment; to adequate, decent, affordable housing; to good nutrition; and to truly safe communities. As Reiman (2007: 211) spells it out:

> Every step toward reducing poverty and its debilitating effects, toward criminalization of the dangerous acts of the affluent and vigorous prosecution of "white-collar" crime, toward decriminalization of "illicit drugs" and "victimless crimes"... every step toward creating a correctional system that promotes human dignity, toward giving ex-offenders a real opportunity to go straight, toward making the exercise of power by police officers, prosecutors and judges more reasonable and more just, toward giving all individuals accused of crime equal access to high-quality legal expertise in their defence; and every step toward establishing economic and social justice is a step that moves us from a system of *criminal* justice to a system of criminal *justice*. The refusal to take those steps is a move in the opposite direction.

DISCUSSION QUESTIONS

1. How does the prison industrial complex help to demonstrate a changing mindset from rehabilitation of prisoners to profit maximization within corrections?

2. Do you agree/disagree with the Safe Streets legislation in Ontario? Taking up the approach of a critical criminologist, explain how this legislation may not be there for the reasons it is said to be there.

3. What is the role of the get-tough, no-frills approach to prison in the current economy?

4. John Clarke argues: "As global capitalism progresses, more and more of the poor, homeless and disenfranchised are imprisoned and labelled 'criminal.'" Explain this statement with reference to his position against the recent safe-streets legislation (which addressed squeegee kids and aggressive panhandling).

5. Marxist criminologists argue that it is a function of the prison to "divert attention from the really dangerous acts that are committed by those in power." Explain this statement, showing how the criminal justice system and prison industrial complex broadcast an ideological message that supports prevailing social and economic inequalities.

GLOSSARY OF TERMS

Criminalized: the act of making someone or something "criminal."

Discrimination: practices that deny particular groups and their members access to societal rewards.

Disenfranchised: to be deprived of a right, privilege, or power to which others are entitled.

Hierarchy: a group of persons organized in a system of class or rank, based on social and economic standing.

Institutional Racism: racial practices that are discriminatory and built into social structures such as the criminal justice system, media, and political and economic systems.

Ideology: refers to the set of socially constructed ideas that people share about the world. Because these ideas are socially constructed (created through interaction of individuals and within institutions), ideology also refers to the possibility that these ideas can be false. With regards to crime and criminality, for example, the media may report on crime in a way that is stereotypical and does not adequately reflect the reality.

Ideological Hegemony: a concept developed first in Antonio Gramsci's *Prison Notebooks* (1971). It is defined as the manipulation of the ideas, knowledge, and values of the working-class population in a way that makes existing social institutions and relationships — the status quo — appear to be legitimate, even though they work in the best interests of capitalists. In other words, ideological hegemony is known as the universalization of capitalist-class ideas, representing a basis of consent from the social order that is created and recreated through the web of social institutions, relations, and ideas.

Ostracize: to apply a form of rejection or exclusion from society — by general consensus.

Prison Industrial Complex: This involves organizations whose business is correctional facilities — construction companies, companies supplying surveillance technology, and others. The critical position is that these companies are concerned with making more money rather than with rehabilitating criminals or reducing criminal activity. Also, prisons often provide free or cheap labour, along with union positions for correctional workers, all contributing to profits from prison systems. Some argue that the prison industrial complex is a state of mind, replacing ideas of safety with a drive towards high profits.

Postmodernity: the culture coming after modernity and defined as a time of intense change; often chaotic, fragmented, and ambiguous.

Stereotypes: exaggerated and oversimplified images pertaining to the characteristics of certain social categories.

Stigmatize: to mark an individual with some form of disgrace that takes away from the character or reputation of that person; an indication that something is not "normal" about the person.

SUGGESTED READINGS

Blombert, Thomas G., and Stanley Cohen. 2003. *Punishment and Social Control.* New York: Aldine De Gruyter.

Christie, Nils. 2001. *Crime Control as Industry: Towards Gulags, Western Style.* Third edition. New York: Routledge.

Davis, Angela Y. 2005. *Abolition, Democracy; Beyond Prison, Torture and Empire.* Toronto: Seven Stories Press.

Garland, E. 2001. The Culture of Control: Crime and Social Order in Contemporary Society. Chicago: Oxford University Press.

Reiman, Jeffrey. 2007. *The Rich Get Richer and the Poor Get Prison: Ideology, Class and Criminal Justice.* Boston: Allyn and Bacon.

REFERENCES

Anderson, Sarah, and John Cavanagh. 2000. "Top 200: The Rise of Global Corporate Power." *Global Policy Forum.* Available at <www.global policy.org/socecon/tncs/top200.htm> accessed July 2006.

Bauman, Zygmunt. 1992. *Intimations of Post-Modernity.* London: Routledge.

_____. 1995a. *Life in Fragments: Essays in Post-Modern Morality.* Oxford: Blackwell.

_____. 1995b. "From Welfare State into Prison." Unpublished paper for the International Conference on Prison Growth, Oslo, April, 1995.

_____. 2000. *Modernity and the Holocaust.* Ithaca, NY: Cornell UP.

Beattie, K. 2006. "Adult Correctional Services in Canada, 2004/2005." *Juristat* 26, 5.

Besserer, S., and J. Tufts. 2006. "Justice Spending in Canada." *Juristat* 19, 12.

Boritch, Helen. 1997. *Fallen Women.* Toronto: ITP Nelson.

Bottomore, Tom, Laurence Harris, V.G. Kernan, and Ralph Miliband (eds.). 1983. *A Dictionary of Marxist Thought.* Cambridge, MA: Harvard University Press.

Broad, Dave. 2000. *Hollow Work, Hollow Society? Globalization and the Casual Labour Problem in Canada.* Halifax: Fernwood Publishing.

Bronson, Harold. 1993. "Economic Concentration and Corporate Power." In Peter Li and B. Singh Bolaria (eds.), *Contemporary Sociology: Critical Perspectives.* Toronto: Copp Clark Pitman.

Callinicos, A. 2003. *An Anti-Capitalist Manifesto.* Cambridge: Polity Press.

Canadian Centre for Policy Alternatives. 2006. *Alternative Federal Budget – Minority Report.* Available at <http://policyalternatives.ca/documents/National_Office_Pubs/2006/AFB_Minority_Report.pdf> accessed July 2007.

Cayley, David. 1998. *The Expanding Prison: The Crisis in Crime and Punishment and the Search for Alternatives.* Toronto: House of Anansi.

Christie, N. 1977. "Conflicts as Property." *The British Journal of Criminology* January.

_____. 1993. *Crime Control as Industry.* New York: Routledge.

_____. 2000. *Crime Control as Industry.* New York: Routledge.

Clarke, John. 2000. "Serve the Rich and Punish the Poor." In Gordon West and Ruth Morris (eds.), *The Case for Penal Abolition.* Toronto: Canadian Scholars Press.

Clarke, Tony. 1997. *The Silent Coup: Confronting the Big Business Takeover of Canada.* Toronto: Canadian Centre for Policy Alternatives.

Comack, Elizabeth. 1996*. Women in Trouble.* Halifax: Fernwood Publishing.

_____ (ed.). 1999. *Locating Law: Race/Class/Gender Connections.* Halifax: Fernwood Publishing.

CSC (Correctional Service of Canada). 2005. *Basic Facts about the Correctional Service of Canada.* Available at <http://www.csc-scc.gc.ca/text/pblct/basicfacts/BasicFacts_e.shtml> accessed July 2007.

Davis, Angela Y. 2005. *Abolition, Democracy; Beyond Prison, Torture and Empire.* Toronto: Seven Stories Press.

Dobbin, Murray. 1998. *The Myth of the Good Corporate Citizen: Democracy Under the Rule of Big Business.* Toronto: Stoddart.

_____. 2003. *Paul Martin: CEO For Canada?* Toronto: James Lorimer.

Ellwood, W. 2001. *The Non-Nonsense Guide to Globalization.* London: Verso.

Garland, E. 2001. *The Culture of Control: Crime and Social Order in Contemporary Society.* Chicago: Oxford University Press.

Globe and Mail. 2006. "Crime bill sets mandatory minimum sentences." May 5.

_____. 1995. "What's the Real Cost of Punishment?" March 31.

Gramsci, Antonio. 1971. *Selections from the Prison Notebooks.* New York: International Publications.

Hanson, Ann. 2006. "Brampton Prison Blues." *Independent Voice*, 1 XV (2), March. Damian T. Lloyd, editor. Kingston, ON: PIC Press.

Hermer, Joe, and Janet Mosher. 2002. *Disorderly People: Law and the Politics of Exclusion in Ontario.* Halifax: Fernwood Publishing.

Jackson, George. 1970. *Soledad Brother: The Prison Letters of George Jackson. Introduction by Jean Genet.* New York: Coward-McCann.

Kingston's *Progressive Independent Community Newspaper.* 2006. "Brampton Prison Blues: New Jail for Youth to be Built While Other Facilities are Closed." March.

Macleans. 2006. "Tory Plan Will Create Jail Spaces at Expense of Day-Care Spaces, Critics Say." May 4.

Martin, Dianne. 2002. "Demonizing Youth, Marketing Fear: The New Politics of Crime." In Joe Hermer and Janet Mosher (eds.), *Disorderly People: Law and the Politics of Exclusion in Ontario.* Halifax: Fernwood Publishing.

Mathiesen, Thomas. 1974. *The Politics of Abolition: Essays in Political Action Theory.* London: Martin Robertson.

_____. 1990. *Prison on Trial.* London: Sage Publications.

McMurtry, John. 1998. *Unequal Freedoms, The Global Market as an Ethical System.* Toronto: Garamond Press.

_____. 2000. "Caging the Poor: The Case Against the Prison System." In Gordon West and Ruth Morris (eds.), *The Case for Penal Abolition.* Toronto: Canadian Scholars Press.

Moore, Dawn, and Kelly Hannah-Moffat. 2002. "Correctional Renewal Without the Frills: The Politics of "Get-Tough" Punishment in Ontario." In Joe Hermer and Janet Mosher (eds.), *Disorderly People: Law and the Politics of Exclusion in Ontario.* Halifax: Fernwood Publishing.

Morris, Norval, and David Rothman. 1995. *The Oxford History of the Prison.* New York: Oxford University Press.

Morris, Ruth. 2000. *Stories of Transformative Justice.* Toronto: Canadian Scholars' Press.

Mouffe, C. (ed.). 1979. *Gramsci and Marxist Thought.* London and Boston: Routledge and Kegan Paul.

NAPO (National Anti-Poverty Organization). 2006. "Media Advisory. Canada Fails to Meet Economic and Social Rights Obligations, United Nations Told." April 28. Available at <www.napo-onap.ca/en/news.php> accessed July 2007.

O'Loughlin, John, Lynn Staeheli and Edward Greenberg (eds.). 2004. *Globalization and Its Outcomes.* New York: Guildford Press.

Ontario Ministry of Correctional Services (OMCS). 2000. "Modernization of Jails Puts Public Safety First." Press Release. In Elizabethtown Township. May 5.

Pavlich, George. 2000. *Critique and Radical Discourses on Crime.* Burlington, Great Britain: Dartmouth Publishing.

Pepinsky, Hal. 2000. "Empathy Works, Obedience Doesn't." In Gordon West and Ruth Morris (eds.), *The Case for Penal Abolition.* Toronto: Canadian Scholars Press.

Pettigrew, Pierre. 1996. Notes from speech to a conference on "Accelerating Rural Development in Africa." Airlie, Virginia, Sept. 23.

Reed, Micheline, and Julian Roberts. 2000. "Correctional Trends, 199697." In Julian Roberts (ed.), *Criminal Justice in Canada: A Reader.* Toronto: Harcourt Brace and Company.

Reiman, Jeffrey. 2001. *The Rich Get Richer and the Poor Get Prison: Ideology, Class and Criminal Justice.* Boston: Allyn and Bacon.

_____. 2004. *The Rich Get Richer and the Poor Get Prison: Ideology, Class and Criminal Justice.* Seventh Edition. Boston: Allyn and Bacon.

_____. 2007. *The Rich Get Richer and the Poor Get Prison: Ideology, Class and Criminal Justice.* Eighth Edition. Boston: Allyn and Bacon.

Reuben, Richard C. 1995. "Get-Tough Stance Draws Fiscal Criticism." *American Bar Association Journal* Jan.

Roberts, Julian. 2000. *Criminal Justice in Canada: A Reader.* Toronto: Harcourt Brace and Company.

Routledge, Paul. 2006. "Book Review: *Globalization and Its Outcomes.*" *Growth and Change* 37: 331.

Schissel, Bernard. 1997. *Blaming Children: Youth Crime, Moral Panics and the Politics of Hate.* Halifax: Fernwood Publishing.

_____. 2006. *Still Blaming Children: Youth Conduct and the Politics of Child Hating.* Black Point, NS: Fernwood Publishing.

Simon, J. 2001. "Entitlement to Cruelty: The End of Welfare and the Punitive Mentality in the United States." In K. Stenson and R. Sullivan (eds.), *Crime, Risk and Justice.* Cullompton, U.K.: Willan Publishing.

Snider, Laureen. 1999. "Relocating Law: Making Corporate Crime Disappear." In Elizabeth Comack (ed.). *Locating Law: Race/Class/Gender Connections.* Halifax: Fernwood Publishing.

Star Phoenix. 2000. Feb. 1, B7. "Squeegee Kids No Longer Welcome on Ontario Streets." February 1.

Statistics Canada. 2002. "Justice Spending in Canada, 2000–2001." *The Daily.* Ottawa: Statistics Canada. Available at <http://www.statcan.ca/english/freepub/85-002-XIE/0110285-002-XIE.pdf> accessed July 2007.

_____. 2006. CANSIM, "Sentenced cases and outcomes in adult criminal court (Median length of prison sentence)." 252-0021 and Catalogue no. 85-002-X. Last modified: 2006-04-21.

Toronto Star. 2006. UN: Canada's Poor Face 'Emergency': UN Group Says Social Programs Lacking, Sharply Critical on Rights of Aboriginals." May 23.

UNDP (United Nations Development Program). 1999. *Human Development Report.* Toronto:

Oxford University Press.

West, W. Gordon, and Ruth Morris (eds.). 2000. *The Case For Penal Abolition.* Toronto: Canadian Scholars' Press.

White, R. 2002. "Restorative Justice and Social Inequality." In B. Schissel and C. Brooks (eds.), *Marginality and Condemnation: An Introduction to Critical Criminology.* Halifax: Fernwood Publishing.

16   "Armed and Dangerous"/ "Known to Police"
Racializing Suspects

Carl E. James

KEY FACTS

> According to the census, some 396,130 of the people living in the Toronto area in 2001, nearly 9 percent, identified as African, Black, and Caribbean (Ornstein 2006). People of Jamaican origin alone were 116,180, nearly 3 percent of the population and just over 40 percent of individuals (278,285) who claimed to be of Caribbean origin.

> Immigration laws have been historically used to limit and control the immigration of Black and other minority groups to Canada.

> A *Toronto Star* study (October 2002) reports that Black drivers were twice as likely as White drivers to be arrested for simple drug possession (something that could only be uncovered following a traffic stop), taken to police station, and detained pending bail hearing.

> There is a tendency to attribute increase in crimes to immigrants, particularly family class immigrants.

> Subsection 70 (5) of the *Immigration Act* makes it possible for permanent residents of Canada who have served a prison term of ten years or more and who, in the opinion of the minister of immigration, "constitute a danger to the public" to be arrested and deported.

> A federal court judge said of a twenty-two-year-old Guyanese immigrant who had lived in Canada since he was eleven years old, and at the time was being deported, "An individual who has spent all of his youth and early adulthood in Canada... can appropriately be described as a product of his environment in Canada rather than of the environment of his early life."

Sources: Rankin et al. 2002a and 2002b; *National Post* 1999a.

[Identity constructions] are very real. People live by them, after all — and nowadays, increasingly, they die from them. You can't get more real than that.
—David Halperin 1995

On Easter Sunday in 1997 an unarmed man, Hugh Dawson, was shot dead in his car in "a hail of 11 Metro police bullets" after being stopped by police at a traffic light. Dawson had apparently been under surveillance after having sold a police "agent" $600 worth of crack cocaine (*Toronto Star* June 27, 1997: A7). A front-page *Toronto Star* story (April 4, 1997) reported, "Eyewitness accounts suggest Hugh Dawson died amid police gunfire on Easter Sunday after a chain of events that began when the officer used a gun to break a car window, discharging the firearm" in the process. Glass from the car window presumably hit one officer who, along with his six other colleagues at the scene, thought it was a bullet and consequently opened fire. The chief of police gave reporters the official version of events: "A violent struggle ensued when the suspect attempted to seize an officer's firearm. This led to two officers discharging their firearms" (*Toronto Star* April 4, 1997: A24).

In June, a single police officer was charged with manslaughter in the Dawson case. At that time, with reference to eyewitness accounts, Philip Mascoll and Rosie DiManno (*Toronto Star* June 27, 1997: A7) reported that during the incident two police officers had used "a nightstick and the barrel of a shotgun to strike Dawson in the face." The blood from the wound, the reporters suggested, most likely blinded Dawson so that he was unable to see what was happening. The report continued,

> The bullet hit Dawson in the left arm, sources said, and he reared back, throwing up his arms — whether in reflex or surrender is unclear. It was then that [the police officer] allegedly pulled the trigger of his semi-automatic 10 times. All the shots hit Dawson in the torso and powder residue indicates all were fired from within one-third of a metre of his body, it is alleged. Gun experts point out that the Glock is not an automatic pistol that will keep firing once the trigger is held down. "It is a semi-automatic pistol... You will have to pull the trigger each time to discharge a round." All the spent cartridge casings were inside the car, indicating that none of the shots had come from outside the vehicle. The car was smothered with residue from the spent gunpower. Dawson's fingerprints were not found on [the officer's] gun.

Both the newspaper reports of eyewitnesses and the material evidence contradicted police accounts of the shooting. Pondering the evidence, one *Toronto Star* editorial stated what could be considered as the obvious:

> We may yet hear that Hugh George Dawson was a drug dealer, terrible citizen and a known bad guy to Metro police. Or that he was a lovable Scarborough father of two. Either way, did he deserve to die at the hands of the police?... So we have a troubling but familiar circumstance: another police shooting, another death, and the officers involved refusing to speak to the Special Investigations Unit (SIU) that investigates all police shootings. And citizens are left to ponder whether justice is being meted out in a fair and even-handed way, or if police are properly trained to handle the volatile situations they encounter. Why couldn't seven well-armed officers arrest an unarmed suspect without resorting to deadly force?... Police have a difficult job... But how long must we remain blind to the obvious — there's something fatally wrong with the way police are trained to handle citizens who run afoul of the law, especially citizens of colour. (*Toronto Star* April 2, 1997: A16)

The incident was not Dawson's first encounter with the police. Several years earlier he had been charged and acquitted of "a drug offense by officers from the same squad" (*Toronto Star* April 2, 1997: A7). This earlier incident, hence being known to police, plus the fact that this thirty-year-old Black Jamaican was not a permanent resident of Canada — it was reported that he often visited, spending three to four months each time, and was in the process of being sponsored by an uncle as a landed immigrant — was likely part of "the record" that influenced not only the squad's actions that day but also the public "indifference" (Benjamin 2002) to the shooting.

The police version of the events that day, despite being contradicted by eyewitness reports, went largely unchallenged, and Torontonians, for the most part, remained silent about yet another shooting of a Black man. Perhaps this is not so surprising in a society that constructs young Black men as troublemakers and potential lawbreakers. Indeed, in this light, the reactions of police officers and citizens can be seen as a reflection of the perceptions that are held of young Black men. My subject here is the construction of the prevailing perceptions of Black people as suspects, immigrants, and Jamaicans, and my goal is to raise questions about the extent to which such perceptions inform police and citizens' behaviours.

Racialization and the Law in a "Raceless State"

In her dissection of Rodney King's beating by Los Angeles police officers in 1992, Judith Butler (1993: 15) argues that within a "racist interpretive framework," King's beating represents a reading of "the black body" as a "source of danger, the threat of violence, and... an intention to injure" (see also Fanon 1967). Given this racial schema, citizens, even police officers, tend to feel "endangered" and "vulnerable," with the need to be protected. Hence, insofar as "police are structurally placed to protect whiteness against violence," writes Butler (1993: 18), the violence of the police "cannot be read as violence; because the black male body... is the site and the source of danger, a threat, the police effort to subdue this body, even if in advance, is justified regardless of the circumstances. Or rather, the conviction of that justification rearranges and orders the circumstances to fit that conclusion." Accordingly, eyewitness accounts or "readings" of the "visual evidence" will be scrutinized in such a way that it will be difficult to establish "the truth" about police brutality, for "when the visual is fully schematized by racism, the 'visual evidence' to which one refers will always and only refute the conclusions based upon it; for it is possible within this racist episteme that no black person can seek recourse to the visible as the sure ground of evidence... The visual field is not neutral to the question of race; it is itself a racial formation, an episteme, hegemonic and forceful" (Butler 1993: 17).

This paradigm of cultural democracy holds that in Canada race does not determine how groups or individuals are treated; hence, minority and/or immigrant people can expect to live free of racism and discrimination.

In the Canadian context of multiculturalism (in contrast to the U.S. melting pot or assimilationist paradigm), the black body is read for what it signals — part of the cultural diversity of Canadian society, a diversity based on race, nationality, and ethnicity and which the Canadian government, through the federal multicultural policy/act, purports to acknowledge and enhance (James 2003: 208). This paradigm of cultural democracy holds that in Canada race does not determine how groups or individuals are perceived and treated; hence, minority and/or immigrant people can expect to have lives devoid of racism and discrimination. But, as critics (e.g., Day 2000; Clarke 1998; James 2003; Razack 1999; Walcott 1997) point out, this discourse of diversity preserves the dominance and categorization of British and French ethnic group members as "Canadians" — people who are phenotypically white — while placing all other Canadians in the "Other ethnic group" category (see Royal Commission on Bilingualism and Biculturalism 1970).[1] These

"Other Canadians" are represented in the multiculturalism discourse as homogeneous, with likeness or sameness based on largely physical characteristics used to ascribe "cultural group" membership to them. Constructed as "different," they are perceived as "people with a 'heritage' from elsewhere, whose 'foreign' cultural values and practices are conceived as static and based on their past experiences in other countries" (James 1998: 4). Further, their "foreign bodies" signal that they are non-English, non-French-speaking with "accents," and hence neither "look nor sound Canadian" (James 2003: 210).

Essentially, Canada's multicultural discourse, this "sincere fiction," as Anita Sheth (2000) terms it, represents Canada's historical claim to being what David Goldberg (2000) calls a "raceless state." This is a state, unlike the United States, in which race is not considered to be a problem or an issue, because we have rendered invisible the physical characteristics of bodies — in other words, Canada is a "colour-blind" society. But, as Goldberg (2000) argues, this claim to racelessness masks the historical conditions that account for the contemporary issues and problems related to racism, and it simultaneously contributes to the silencing of voices about racism. Further, it makes claims of experiences with racism and discrimination not merely a private or individual matter, but a non-existent matter. While this approach to the body politic does not end racism, it seeks to avoid charges of racism.

To the extent that Canada presents itself as a raceless state or colour-blind society, police attitudes and actions towards racial minorities will not be perceived as being founded on race, but on attempts to be proactive, to maintain law and order, and to "serve and protect" the "citizens" (often those who by their skin colour are perceived as "Canadians") from the troublemakers and "misfits" (those perceived to be the likely criminal element) of society. That the targets of police gaze and surveillance tend to be people of colour and in many cases Black (Harcourt 2003; Henry and Tator 2006; Tator and Henry 2006; Tanovich 2006; Wortley 2002; Wortley and Kellough 1998), is not, in the colour-blind discourse, to be interpreted as a case of "racial profiling" but rather as an attempt on the part of the police to be pre-emptive — to deal with a potential criminal situation before a crime takes place or before it becomes serious.[2] In the process of carrying out their duties, police officers understand that they must protect themselves and their colleagues from any eventuality, which includes, most importantly, the possibility of being shot. Because hesitating to shoot could cost police officers and/or their colleagues their lives, it is in their best interests to "know" the potential criminal elements of society and act accordingly. This idea of "recognizing" or "knowing" the potential criminal elements of society, police officers say, has more to do with understanding who is typically committing crimes than with targeting particular groups in society.

> Canada presents itself as a colour-blind society, so police attitudes are not considered racism but attempts to "serve and protect."

This idea was expressed to me on many occasions in my work with police officers (facilitating workshops and sitting on police-community committees) and in teaching students in the law and security and corrections programs at a college in Southern Ontario. As one police aspirant in a law and security class reflected in an essay, "We argued and argued over the matter of the Black community and the police. My argument, and I think I can speak for at least one-quarter of the class, was that Black people tend to be more involved in crime. From statistics or police documents I can draw this conclusion" (James 2003: 211). This viewpoint is quite significant, especially when we consider, and as the students also admitted, that most of the people whom police tend to associate with are white.

The attitudes and actions of police officers and citizens reflect the complex web of individual and systemic racism in our society. Racism refers to the hegemonic ideology and discourses rooted in the inequalities of society that operate in allocating racial groups to particular categories and class sites. The resulting norms, values, and ideas found in the society serve to justify the inferiority and superiority of groups based on socially selected physical characteristics or race (James 2003: 136). By individual racism, I refer to negative attitudes held by an individual, attitudes premised on an ideology of race — a social construct. Systemic racism is evident in the rules, policies, and regulations of an organization that promote the differential treatment of groups in society. These regulations, as James Dobbins and Judith Skillings (1991: 42) state, "are used to maintain social control and the status quo in favour of the dominant group." The reciprocal relationship between individual and systemic racism is apparent in organizational policies and practices that individuals develop and implement; these people, because of their training and allegiance to the organization (or society), understand that they must adhere to certain norms (including the role relationships) and sanctions, hence maintaining the social order of things (James 2003: 137).

> Racism refers to the hegemonic ideology and discourses rooted in the inequalities of society that operate in allocating racial groups to particular categories and class sites.

The perception of Black people as being more likely to be involved in crimes depends in part on how they are socially constructed in society. Contrary to the notion of the colour-blind multicultural state, there is, then, in Canada, a significance to race, and a conceptualization of race, which would suggest that not even the law and by extension its enforcers are "impartial, neutral, and objective" (Comack 1999: 56; see also Aylward 1999; Kobayashi 1990; Mirchandani and Chan 2002; Razack 1999).[3] Audrey Kobayashi (1990: 449) argues that the law plays a role in the racialization of some Canadians "through direct action, interpretation, silence and complicity. The law has been wielded as an instrument to create a common sense justification of racial differences, to reinforce common sense notions already deeply embedded within a cultural system of values." In this regard, any examination of individuals' experiences and encounters with the Canadian justice/legal system (including Canada immigration) must necessarily take into account "the experiences and standpoints of racialized groups" (Comack 1999: 56). As Comack (1999: 61) argues: "To single out this need to incorporate race and racism within our investigation of the law-society relation is not to suggest that racial oppression (in all its various forms) is the only or primary form of oppression in society. But it does raise the question of how we are to understand the connections between race, class, and gender." However, as scholars indicate, race, class, and gender do not only provide the basis for how we experience and are positioned in society, but are also factors that mediate experiences with racism — experiences resulting from a person's location on the hierarchical structure based on race, class, and gender (Satzewich 1998: 43). Insofar as these factors help us to understand "the multiple meanings and expressions of racism" (Satzewich 1998: 43), they should not be "compartmentalized" or considered "additives" (Comack 1999), but rather seen as interlocking factors always functioning in relation to each other and simultaneously informing the perceptions, interactions, and experiences of every encounter.

Accordingly, in the case of Hugh Dawson the police "takedown" and fatal shooting represent the intersection of race with both gender (in this case, male) and with assumed citizenship, immigrant status, and nationality (here, Jamaican)[4] to inform police (and citizens') perceptions and actions (see also Jiwani 2002). Within this racial imaginary schema, Dawson was not just another suspect; he was construed as a potentially dangerous man, an agent of violence whose criminal activities had to be stopped or prevented from escalating. Having earlier sold a police agent crack cocaine, Dawson had presumably provided evidence that he was a "drug dealer" and a suspect whose perceived violence would be released in any encounter with police; hence it was necessary for police to be proactive and take pre-emptive action to restrain him in whatever way possible. In this schema police actions are likely to be perceived as "reasonable" and "justifiable" because not only are the officers dealing with a "known" criminal, but they are in a position of having to act in "self-defence," particularly in a situation where, as the police chief claimed, "the suspect attempted to seize an officer's firearm." Within this context, then, Dawson's gesture of "throwing up his arms" was read "not as self-protection but as the incipient moment of a physical threat" (Butler 1993: 16). Beating up Dawson and eventually shooting him might be considered a matter of the police firing before Dawson did, thus preventing him from releasing his violence.

> As law-enforcement officers, and often as the first representatives of the state that individuals encounter in legal or justice matters, the police play a critical role in people's lives.

As law-enforcement officers, and often as the first or most visible representatives of the state that individuals encounter in legal or justice matters, the police play a critical role within the social and political hierarchy of the state and in people's lives. In their administration of the law as part of state power, police exercise discretion not only in their interpretation of the law, but also in the decisions they make regarding what laws to apply, how to apply them, and to whom. Given this level of influence and discretion, it is conceivable that police will at times abuse their powers and sometimes dispense punishment under the guise of justice. Because the police are "the most visible embodiment of the dominant group's power" (Henry and Tator 2006: 152), and given the general perceptions, attitudes, and behaviour towards particular groups of citizens, any examination of the policing of Canada's racial-minority communities has to include consideration of how the society at large views those communities. As Henry and Tator (2006: 152) put it: "The attitudes of the police are a reflection not only of the current social views of the people of colour, but also of the historical attitudes of the White majority."

Policing Blackness

Historically, Black young men have been represented in Canadian society as potential criminals who should be feared. This stigmatizing of Black people as a "problem group" that through criminal activities is likely to threaten the social order, safety, and security of citizens not only racializes but also criminalizes them, turning them into a "group" that is "always under suspicion"[5] especially if or when they are known to police. This suspicion is evident in the ways in which Blacks have been treated historically and contemporarily by immigration officers who seek to limit or control their entry into Canada (Barnes 2002; Benjamin 2002; James 1997; Shepard 1997), and by police officers who monitor their actions to pre-empt and/or deter criminal activities (Chigbo 1992; Henry 1994; Tator and Henry 2006; Tanovich 2006; Wortley 2002). In their study of high-school students in Toronto, George Dei et al. (1995: 51–52) quote one young woman as saying, "When you're a Black male... you don't have to do anything... You could be a good student, you could be a good father or whatever, [but] when you're on the street, you're a criminal... a drug dealer." With reference to the problem of stereotyping and the lack of any positive image of Black people, one high-school student commented, "Police assume all Black people are the same" (Frater 1991: 68). So, as Scot Wortley (2001) found, "Social class and age do not appear to insulate black people from involuntary contact with criminal justice personnel" in the same way that those features do for whites and Asians.

> The close scrutiny of groups seen as potential lawbreakers — racial profiling — contributes to overpolicing and raises the likelihood of evidence being produced that justifies police actions.

That police are doing their jobs in trying to limit or pre-empt criminal activities when they closely scrutinize Black people seems to be an inadequate justification, especially when we take into account that such scrutiny, coupled with the perception of Black people as security risks or potential lawbreakers — the practice of racial profiling — contributes to overpolicing of the group and raises the likelihood of evidence being produced that justifies police actions in the first place — the self-fulfilling prophecy. As Brogden, Jefferson and Walklate (1988: 112) point out, "Once a group has been statistically identified as criminal, and satisfies other criteria such as low status and relative powerlessness, the resulting police 'overattention' begins to produce the sort of results that justify the original overattention." Wortley (2001: 21) suggests: "If black people are systematically stopped, questioned and searched more frequently than other people, they are also more likely to be detected and arrested for breaking the law than people from other racial backgrounds who *engage in exactly the same behaviour*" (see also Harcourt 2003). Since Dawson, on the basis of race, matched a police profile of the likely drug dealer, he was more likely to be observed, hence increasing his likelihood of encountering the police agent to whom he attempted to sell drugs. Given the police "war on drugs" (Henry 1994; Wortley 2002), Dawson was a prime target for a takedown.

Significantly, the shooting of Dawson occurred some three years after the murders of Georgina (Vivi) Leimonis in April 1994 (at the Just Desserts café in downtown Toronto; see chapter 5) and police constable Todd Baylis in June 1994 (in a Toronto public-housing area). The shootings of both Leimonis, a young white female, and Baylis, a young white officer, and the subsequent community discourses about the young Black Jamaican men who murdered them also added to the race profile of the criminals in Toronto.[6] These incidents, just three years earlier, in which the life of an "innocent" Canadian (not an immigrant) woman was taken, as well as the life of one of "their own," probably helped to inform police actions towards Black males, and in particular towards the situation involving Dawson.

Evidently, many police surveillance activities — including stops, searches, and undercover sting operations — take place on the streets, which, according to Henry and Tator (2006: 163), "is exalted as a *raison d'être* of policing, and the 'street' experience is asserted to be the foundation of police knowledge." With this knowledge, and with the perception of the street as "white" property that must be policed and protected from potential lawbreakers, the street, then, as racialized space, remains the exclusive domain of the police. Hence, users of the street, especially drivers, are susceptible to police examination and scrutiny, particularly when they might be regarded as violating the cultural norms of the street — by trespassing, disturbing the peace, or speeding. It is on the streets that they will be always under suspicion or perceived as, according to a number of Black youths, being "up to no good" (James 1998; see also Zatz and Krecker 2003). When I researched the experiences of Black youths' encounters with police on the street, a number of respondents, particularly the males, reported that they "were often stopped, questioned, searched and harassed by police... and they were often perceived to be working class, immigrants and/or refugees" (James 1998: 171). They said it was not their clothes, jewellery, or hairstyles that contributed to the treatment they received from the police; rather, as one respondent put it, "It's your colour, your colour, and it's your colour" (James 1998: 166).

From most accounts, race is a major determinant of an individual's chances of being stopped and questioned by police, whether that individual is driving or walking (Henry 1994; James 1998; Wortley 2002). In the context of the street, racial identity takes on particular meanings that inform discriminatory judgments by police officers. The decisions to stop, question, and search Black individuals, and to claim that these individuals "look like" or "match the description" of a crime suspect are not merely a matter of "all Blacks look alike," but a reflection of the racialized ways in which police carry out "routine checks" of people they imagine to be potential lawbreakers (James 1997, 1998; Neugebauer-Visano 1996). The evidence shows that police see Black youth as "bad people" who are likely "to steal and kill people." One youth in the study I conducted recalled how after a robbery in the area he was driving in, "the cop pulled me over and all of a sudden a whole swarm of cops came. It was eight cops. I was with three guys. The cops said that we fit the description of the robbers, who were five in number but we fit the description of three. They surrounded us and asked us to lie on the ground and they had their guns out" (James 1998: 167; see also Chigbo 1992). Essentially, in their attempts to manage the street and apprehend lawbreakers through stopping, questioning, and surveillance activities, police are likely to mistreat individuals, particularly members of stigmatized minority groups (Henry and Tator 2006). Within this context, then, Dawson, like any other young Black male on the streets, was vulnerable to police actions. Furthermore, he was not only "driving while Black" or "walking while Black" but also engaged in illegal activities on the streets — which made him a sure target of a police takedown. Still, it was not only race that accounted for the treatment of Dawson, but also the perception of him as an immigrant.

Policing the Gates

In her article "Making Canada White: Law and the Policing of Bodies of Colour," Sherene Razack (1999: 160) writes that the "1990s inaugurated a new era of policing the border, one in which a variety of legislative initiatives were introduced to regulate more tightly the flow of immigrants and refugees to Canada." In these new initiatives, the racialized figure of "the criminal attempting to cross our borders" was a central feature of the type of individuals to be monitored, managed, and kept out of the country. "More than ever," Razack (1999: 160) continues, "immigration truly was framed as being about who we can trust. Included in this category of those who cannot be trusted are people of colour already in the country. They too can be good or bad; thus the policing of the border requires as well the policing of bodies of colour already inside it." This policing of bodies of colour, and Black bodies in particular, is evident in how they are stigmatized and marked, not only to be questioned by police about their activities, but also about their status as Canadian.

Indeed, police officers are part of the network of state representatives who are expected to enforce the discriminatory immigration policies that favour wealthy, white, well-educated, English-speaking or French-speaking Europeans. As Lisa Jakubowski (1999: 115) notes, with reference to *Immigration Bill C-86* and the *Not Just Numbers* document, "In both documents, standard criteria may be universally applicable to all people, but not all people have equal opportunity to meet the standard. The contents show an interplay among class, ethnicity and race that creates a preferential category of immigrants, one that the majority of Canadians will be comfortable with." The preferred immigrant is also one who enters Canada through the independent class (scoring high on the point system) as opposed to the family class (typically, parents, fiancée, and children under eighteen). For while use of the independent class enables the state to retain "discretionary control" and effectively manage who gets in, use of the family class increases the "probability that Canada would receive too many less developed, undesirable, economically unsuitable, less assimilable people who would disrupt the existing fabric of Canadian society" (Jakubowski 1999: 118; see also Jakubowski 1997). Little wonder therefore that police, as well as immigration and customs officers, would most often fix their gaze on, and scrutinize more closely, racial-minority immigrants whom they assume to be likely family-class immigrants or even illegal immigrants.

Both Razack and Jakubowski remind us of Canadians' concern with having law-abiding immigrants and not "bad" ones who would be disruptive to the social system. Not surprisingly, and given the racial bias of immigration policies and practices, "bad" immigrants are most often portrayed as being "people of colour." In the federal election of 2000, for instance, a Canadian Alliance candidate referred to what she termed the "Asian invasion" — that is, the recent group of Chinese migrants who had arrived by boat off the coast of Vancouver seeking refugee status in Canada. The South Winnipeg candidate, Betty Granger, said these people "were not the best clientele you would want for this country" (*Toronto Star* Nov. 19, 2000). As Kiran Mirchandani and Wendy Chan (2002: 15) point out:

> Cloaked in the rhetoric of public interest and concerns about maintaining social stability and order, the Chinese migrants seeking a better life in North America were labelled as "undesirable, cheaters, and illegitimate claimants" by both media and state institutions... By tagging the label of criminal unto the migrants, the government could gain legitimacy for their response, which involved their imprisonment and eventual deportation. Not only was their approach characterised by racist overtones, but framing the problem as a threat to public order and safety effectively stifled any opposition to the management of the issue.

Criminalizing migrants by identifying them as a threat to public order has functioned as an effective strategy for restricting entry to Canada. If such people do manage to get in, they can be controlled while here, and eventually deported when they are deemed to be "a danger to the public." Immigration legislation provides immigration officials and police alike with the legal means by which they can maintain the necessary controls over individuals. *Bill C-44* of the *Immigration Act*, enacted in 1995 is a relevant reference here. Subsection 70 (5) of the Act makes it possible for permanent residents of Canada who have served a prison term of ten years or more and, in the opinion of the minister of immigration, "constitute a danger to the public" to be arrested and deported (see Barnes 2002; Henry and Bjornson 1999). The legislation was first tabled by the federal government in June 1994, some three months after the shooting of Vivi Leimonis and around the time of the shooting of Todd Baylis. That both incidents involved Black immigrant youth (two of whom were here illegally and had been deported) of Caribbean backgrounds was not lost on the public, media, and government. As Frances Henry and Marnie Bjornson (1999: 97) demonstrate in their analysis of the Leimonis case in the print media, "moral panic around issues of immigration and deportation" was generated and created widespread support for the government's immigration legislation — which seemingly was also designed to address the belief of "an unprecedented clear majority of Canadians" that "immigration levels were too high."[7] These public sentiments served to influence the parliamentary debates of what the media dubbed the "Just Dessert Bill," prompting both those for and against it to focus on the "policing of immigration." As Henry and Bjornson (1999: 97) also observed, the impact of the bill "on the Black community in general and the Jamaican community in particular" was "excessive."[8]

With front-page images such as that of "two fuzzy, freeze-frame video photos juxtaposed with a photo of Georgina Leimonis, under a headline which describes the attack as 'urban terrorism,'"[9] newspapers reinforced the idea of the dangerous young Black immigrant male. Supported by these media images, the Toronto police chief claimed that "urban terrorism" was "appearing increasingly in the Metro area after leaving big U.S. cities like Miami and Detroit" (Henry and Bjornson 1999: 67–68). This fear of terrorism — especially since 9/11 — combined with the concern over the international trafficking of illegal drugs, continues to cause immigration officials much consternation, especially in cases in which Canadians do not want to give the impression that the country has an easy entry policy or is too liberal with immigrants. Accordingly, Martha Nixon (2000), assistant deputy minister of operations, Citizenship and Immigration Canada (in a panel presentation entitled "Managing Gateways: The Moral Challenges of a Liberal Democracy"), commented, "There are large numbers of people who want to come to, or live in, Canada and the U.S. who are not legally admissible and who will attempt illegal entry, sometimes for the sole purpose of reaching the other country. Some of these people may be seen as dangerous — reflective of the trends which see an increase in international terrorism and transnational crime." She continues, "We have to protect ourselves from genuine threats posed by the illegal entry of migrants."

The takedown of Dawson, then, happened in this context of ongoing debates over immigration — and it took place only two years after the passing of the "danger to the public" Bill. The subsequent debates about ridding Canada of "criminals" — the "drug dealers and traffickers" and "urban terrorists" — conceivably provided compelling reasons that encouraged the active policing of immigrants, particularly those from "non-traditional" parts of the world, who were not to be trusted if we were to ensure the safety of Canadians. But such ideas did not apply to all the immigrants from non-traditional areas, nor did they refer to Caribbean and Black immigrants generally; coming from Jamaica — specifically — was a significant factor in the construction of the "criminal element." That Dawson was not only a Black male but also Jamaican was a key to the police actions — signalling clearly that crimes are not only racialized but also "Jamaicanized."

The "Jamaicanization" of Crime

According to the census, some 396,130, nearly 9 percent, of the people living in the Toronto area in 2001 identified as African, Black, and Caribbean (Ornstein 2006). People of Jamaican origin alone were 116,180, nearly 3 percent of the population and just over 40 percent of individuals (278,285) who claimed to be of Caribbean origin, making them by far the largest individual group of Black/African or Caribbean origin (see also James and Lloyd in press). Logically, then, Torontonians are more likely to encounter Jamaicans than other Black people in daily activities in the city. Given that Jamaicans make up a significant proportion of the Black population means their presence and influence will be considerable and/or noticeable. Still, this prominence does not justify the perception held by police and others that most Black Torontonians, especially those with "dreadlocks" and who speak "Jamaican patois," are immigrants from Jamaica, or that the males are "drug dealers and gangsters." Yet many Canadians seemingly continue to hold this point of view. As one youth in the study I conducted remarked, "Even if you are not Jamaican, if you're Black, [you are] considered Jamaican." The youth I talked to insisted that the police deal with them on this basis (James 1998: 168).

> Given that Jamaicans make up a significant proportion of the Black Toronto population, their presence and influence will be considerable and/or noticeable.

Henry (1994: 219) writes that the media play a crucial role in racializing and criminalizing members of the Black community by choosing to write stories of Black people in "highly dramatic and evocative language" that "plant images and ideas in the minds of readers." Henry points to a series of *Globe and Mail* articles on Jamaica published in July 1992 as "One primary example of this phenomenon." The first article, "Island Crime Wave Spills Over: Criminal Subculture Exported to Canada," begins with a description of life in a Kingston slum, painting a picture of a city and a people plagued by violence — a man injured by "a bullet wound in the neck," a "robber rapist terrorizing neighbourhood" — and, hence, having to be policed, not by regular police officers, but by plainclothes cops from the intelligence unit. One "Western diplomat" is quoted as saying that Jamaica's crime rate was among the world's highest: "I've never seen violence to this extent — to kill for no apparent reason" (Henry 1994: 218–19). To demonstrate that "this criminal subculture has been exported" from Jamaica and "is evident in the streets of Toronto," the newspaper quotes "named and unnamed Toronto police sources" as saying:

> Black crime is no myth, it is a reality "which manifests itself in arrest records" and is proof that a "volatile group of young Jamaican males has altered Toronto's criminal landscape... in an explosion of guns and crack cocaine."... It ends by offering another "expert's" opinion that Jamaicans are aggressive and violence-prone because they are the descendants of the most rebellious slaves who were offloaded in Jamaica more than two centuries ago (Henry 1994: 220).[10]

Newspaper reports (including the *Globe and Mail* series) and police officers have at times conveyed the notion that much of the criminal activities are carried out by Jamaican "posses" that operate in U.S. and Canadian cities (see Gunst 1995).[11]

Adding to these media and police images of Jamaica and Jamaicans, are the police arrests over the years of a number of young Black Jamaican men for murder, drug trafficking, and being in the country illegally.[12] Such images may help to convince Canadians that indeed our immigration policy is too liberal, that it enables too many people to enter the country, and that Jamaican immigrants, especially the "riff raffs who migrate" (Henry 1994: 220), are responsible for the escalation in criminal activities in the city. To this we could also add the experiences of deplaning from Jamaican flights and seeing police officers and their drug-sniffing dog at the door of the plane, and recount the number of times we have heard about planes from Jamaica being impounded and searched for drugs. Such occurrences are less often heard of or noted with regard to planes coming from other destinations. This "racial profiling" of Jamaicans at the airport is corroborated by a survey of passengers returning from Jamaica on Air Canada fights in 1998. That survey revealed: "More than half — 56 percent — of the Blacks on eight flights surveyed were searched by customs officials, while only 10 percent of the whites were searched. In fact, more than two in three whites were simply waved through, without even being questioned" (*Toronto Star* Nov. 29, 1998: A1, A9).

Further, the number of deportations to Jamaica contributes to the perception of Jamaicans as unwanted members of the society. Actually, Department of Immigrant figures for 1995 to 2000 indicate that about 50 percent of Caribbean people deported from the Ontario Region were sent to Jamaica (1995/6, 493/996; 1996/7, 409/806; 1997/8, 437/682; 1998/9, 332/638; 1999/2000, 285/556). In more recent years (from 2000–2005), between 30 and 40 percent of Caribbean deportations have been to Jamaica. It is important to put these figures into context, taking into account that Jamaica has the largest English-speaking Caribbean population and that it is to the United States that the majority of Canada's deportees (by inference, U.S citizens) are sent. For instance, in 2005, Canada deported 2,185 people to the United States (1,153 were from Ontario). Nevertheless, according to Annmarie Barnes (2002: 194), Jamaicans, usually deported on the basis of drug-related charges, "have borne the brunt of the punitive effects of *Bill C-44*, and since 1995, represented an overwhelming majority of persons declared a danger to Canadian society, and subsequently deported from Canada."

While many of the deportees were born in Jamaica (as well as in other Caribbean islands) but grew up in Canada (having immigrated here with their parents before high school), their behaviours are often considered to be largely a product of their "island heritage." The three young men accused in the murder of Leimonis provide a good example of this tendency. Under the *Toronto Star* (Dec. 8, 1999) headline, "Their Fair Day in Court: Born in Jamaica, the Three Men Accused of the Death of Georgina Leimonis Were a Product of Canada," the reporter, Philip Mascoll, challenges the widespread notion that the accused were Jamaicans and argues that the accused must be recognized as Canadians. Mascoll, who identifies himself as "a Jamaican, and a Canadian citizen," points out that although the three men were born in Jamaica, their experience was in essence Canadian:

> [They] grew up in west Toronto, in an Ontario housing project, and went to Canadian schools. They ate McDonald's, not mangoes; Swiss chalet, not soursop. None of the trio has ever been back to Jamaica. It would be a challenge for any of them to find the bus stop at Norman Manley Airport in Kingston, let alone the places in the Jamaican countryside in which they were born.

Indeed, as a federal court judge said of a twenty-two-year-old Guyanese immigrant who had lived in Canada since he was eleven years old, and at the time was being deported, "An individual who has spent all of his youth and early adulthood in Canada … can appropriately be described as a product of his environment in Canada rather than of the environment of his early life" (*National Post* Dec. 30, 1999: 2).

That Jamaicans tend to be perceived as being unable to escape their socialization in "the environment" of their early lives is, to an extent, reflective of the Canadian understanding of "difference" when it comes to race and nationality. In Canada, race is not viewed so much as a social construct but as the national, physical, and biological features of a people, or "an ascribed characteristic on which difference is based" (Comack 1999:

56). The interlocking features that identify individuals as Jamaicans (as constructed by some Canadian viewers) also determine their "mental and emotional capacities," and position them at the lower level of the racial and social hierarchy of Canadian society, "based on their supposedly innate features and capacities" (Comack 1999: 56). Furthermore, in a society dominated by Anglo-Celtic culture, which is viewed as the norm, the perceived "innate culture of Jamaicans" is seen as an element that makes them different and less capable of integrating into the society compared to other immigrant groups. (The perception is sustained when in February 2003 the Toronto chief of police Julian Fantino went to Jamaica to learn how to deal with issues of violence and crime in Toronto). This approach ascribes the problems of Jamaicans in Canadian society not merely to inequalities, racism, and discrimination, but to their inability to fit into Canada because of their cultural values and norms. The problem for Dawson, therefore, was not only that his black skin communicated to the police that he did not "fit" the profile of a "Canadian," but also that as a Jamaican, given the "violent culture" from which he had come and the early socialization from which he could not escape, he should be considered "armed and dangerous."

Responses in a Racially Contested Terrain

The fatal shooting of Dawson in 1997 brought to thirteen the number of Black males (nine in their early thirties or less) who had been shot and killed by police in the Toronto area since 1978. In addition, five people (including one young female) had been injured, in some cases paralyzed, by police bullets (see James 1998: 157; Commission on Systemic Racism 1995: 378). The record of police shootings should be of concern to all Canadians, particularly in a society that prides itself on its commitment to cultural freedom and equality as enshrined in the *Multicultural Act*. This concern should be reflected in citizens' actions, such as widespread protests, calling upon government and politicians to take measures to ensure that such incidents cease, and criticizing and denouncing the news media for their sensational treatment of the issues, which only perpetuates an "Us–Them" discourse. This response was certainly not the case in the shooting of Dawson. We might have expected the eyewitness accounts in particular to inspire or convince the general public that something was dreadfully wrong. But Torontonians seemed to have simply accepted the shooting as merely another incident involving a Black man (Benjamin 2002). Perhaps the media, with their news reporting, and the governments and politicians, with their legislation, have influenced Canadians to the degree that they are convinced that the police acted reasonably given the situation.

The Commission on Systemic Racism in the Ontario Criminal Justice System (1995: 377) reports that much of the outcry about police shootings has come from members of the Black community, who are convinced "that the police are quicker to use their gun against black people and that the shootings are unduly harsh responses to the incidents under investigation" (see also Quamina 1996: 149–55). Contrary to the notion of Canada as a colour-blind and just society, for the Black community the shootings reinforced their belief in the "destructive force of systemic racism" in Canada, which makes them all "vulnerable to police violence" (Commission on Systemic Racism 1995: 377). In this racially contested terrain, how Black people read and in turn responded to the shooting of Dawson is informed by their belief in their own vulnerability. As such, their response will be different from those for whom Canada remains an open, free, and colour-blind society, and for whom Dawson's actions and presence in Canada reflect the media and police images of Black Jamaican males. For these Canadians, Dawson represents a "danger to the public" — a view that has been "culled, cultivated, regulated — indeed policed" (Butler 1993: 16) by the media and immigration legislation before and after the shooting. Related to this view, the "evidence" as based on eyewitness accounts and the eleven bullets lodged in Dawson's body were not enough to elicit public outcries or actions. For as Butler (1993: 16) asserts, "This is not a simple seeing, an act of direct perception, but the racial production of the visible, the workings of racial constraints on what it means to 'see.'" The variation in the eyewitness and police accounts has "to be read not only as instruction in racist modes of seeing but as a repeated and ritualistic production of blackness" and Jamaicanness. In other words, as Butler (1993: 20) submits, "It is necessary to read not only the 'event' of violence, but for the racist schema that orchestrates and interprets the event, which splits the violent intention off from the body who wields it and attributes it to the body who receives it." Presumably, this reading of the "evidence" is what accounts for the failure of the court system to convict a police officer for the shootings in Toronto.[13]

As Henry and Bjornson (1999: 17) point out, since most people do not experience crime directly, their information about it and how they understand it usually come from the media. While we cannot accurately determine the extent to which media reporting influences attitudes, there is evidence that the media "re-enforce attitudes already held by members of the community," and that they do this through what is referred to as "agenda setting" — focusing on particular topics while ignoring others (Henry and Bjornson 1999: 17–18).[14] This perspective is evident in the media's treatment of the Leimonis and Baylis murders and issues of immigration. By the time of Dawson's shooting, the "moral panic" generated by the media over those murders three years earlier (Henry and Bjornson 1999) had so polarized the Toronto communities that it was left mainly to members of the Black community to call for justice, government intervention, and independent investigation into police shootings (see Benjamin 2002; Quamina 1996). Akua Benjamin (2002) contends that the discourse of the media around police shootings has "demonized and criminalized Blacks and exonerated white police officers" contributing to the "acceptance" of shootings by police "as justifiable homicide" — acts that are "mainly engendered by Blacks themselves" and as such are "mainly a Black problem."

This notion of "a Black problem" was part of the discussion in Toronto in 2005 when Torontonians, particularly members of the Black community, struggled over how to put a stop to the shootings that were occurring mostly among Black youth. And when fifteen-year-old Jane Creba was fatally shot on Boxing Day in busy downtown Toronto, allegedly by a bullet from a group of young men, many of them Black, who were "involved in a shooting spree," it was said that "Toronto had lost its innocence." Interestingly, it was only then that Torontonians and Canadians in generally, including our politicians of all levels and parties, appeared to have paid attention to the gun-related homicides that were occurring in Toronto, which by then had numbered 52 of 78 homicides. Before then, on November 19, eighteen-year-old Amon Beckles was shot and killed on the steps of a Toronto church while attending the funeral of his seventeen-year-old friend, Jamal Hemmings who also died of gun shot wounds. Earlier that year (April 2005), Livvette Moore, a widow (her husband had died of cancer a year earlier) and mother of four children between the ages of five and ten years, was shot and killed at a "Jamaica themed" club in the west end of Toronto while celebrating a friend's birthday party. She was Toronto's eighteenth homicide. The shootings of these two Black Torontonians did not bring out any significant outcry or protest by Torontonians or politicians. In this respect, Black Torontonians asked: was it because Beckles was known to police (which he was), and Moore was in the wrong place at the wrong time — a club where such problems might be expected?

Critics have claimed that over time, the media and police practices toward issues pertaining to Blacks have become so normalized that the general public seem to have come to believe that Black victims are responsible for their outcomes (even their own deaths) and the conditions in which they find themselves; consequently, concerns that would lead to collective action, including protest, are never taken up (Benjamin 2002; Mirchandani and Chan 2002; Tanovich 2006). Moreover, it is possible this lack of action, or the "indifference" shown to the shootings (in the case of Dawson, by most Torontonians") relates to the failure to convict a police officer for the shootings. In this regard, individuals might come to assume that any action taken by them would be inconsequential and unproductive. In the absence of widespread public outcry the status quo remains, and Dawson's shooting, like the others, continues to be part of the discourse of the racialization, criminalization, and Jamaicanization of Blacks, and as such serves as evidence for why Black people need to be managed, subjugated, regulated, and policed, both as they enter Canada and after they are here.

However, in recent years, with the publication of the *Toronto Star* series of articles, "Singled Out," and rulings by judges in Ontario and Quebec and by the Human Rights Commission of Nova Scotia the issue of racial profiling being recognized as more than something that exists in the imagination of Blacks, Aboriginals, and other minorities. Using some six years (1996–2002) of police data pertaining to incidents in which individuals were ticked and/or arrested for an offence, the *Toronto Star* (October 2002) findings revealed that Blacks were disproportionately stopped and charged with such things as failing to update their driver's licences. Specifically, almost 34 percent of Black drivers were charged with such offences while they make up about 8 percent of the city's population. Also, Black, compared to white, drivers were twice as likely to be arrested for simple drug possession (something that could only be uncovered following a traffic stop), taken to a police station and detained pending bail hearing (see also Henry and Tator 2006; Tanovich 2006). Nevertheless, there are cases in which judges have ruled that racial profiling indeed operates in the way police officers deal with Black men.

The case against former Toronto raptor basketball player, Dee Brown is particularly significant, not only because it was dismissed but for what the judge said in his ruling. Kirk Makin reported in the *Globe and Mail* (January 30, 2002) that Justice Brian Trafford of the Ontario Superior Court rebuked the lower court trial judge for prejudging the case and impeding the defence attempts to prove Mr. Brown, a Black American, was a victim of racial profiling (A1). The profile, according to Brown's defence counsel, was based on the stereotypical view that Black men in big cars (Brown was driving a Ford Expedition) must be criminals. The earlier judge called the counsel's allegations of racial profiling by police "distasteful" and "really quite nasty, malicious accusations based on… nothing" (A1). On the contrary, as Makin writes, Justice Trafford noted that there was a great deal of evidence that racial factors were at play when Mr. Brown was stopped on November 1, 1999" (A1). The judge also asserted that "racism is part of our culture and justice system… This is a sensitive issue to a multicultural community such as Toronto;" and he acknowledged that the action of the earlier judge "calls into question not only the personal integrity of the trial judge but the entire administration of justice." The courts, he said, "should be held to the highest standards of impartiality" (A9).

Similarly, in "completely clearing" a young Black man, Kevin Khan, of a drug charge recently, Ontario Superior Court judge, Anne Molloy, ruled that the two Toronto police officers involved in the case had no reasonable grounds for stopping Khan in the first place. The judge wrote that the officer singled out the accused and decided to search his car "because he was a Black male driving an expensive Mercedes" (*Globe and Mail*, September 17, 2004: A1). And in 2003, in a case involving an eighteen-year-old Black male, Quinn Borde, charged with firing a gun into the air while being chased by a gang and pistol-whipping a rival later, the Ontario Court of Appeal ruled unanimously that when sentencing a defendant, it is appropriate for courts to take into account the role that systemic racism might have played in the defendant's action. Justice Marc Rosenberg noted, "Systemic racism and the background factors faced by black youths in Toronto are important matters" hence "might be taken into account in imposing sentence" (*Globe and Mail*, February 13, 2003: Al). In Quebec, Justice Juanita Westmoreland-Traoré reached the same conclusion in the case against young Alexer Campbell. Campbell was charged in spring 2004 "for breach of recognizance" after police officers, claiming that he behaved suspiciously, stopped him when he exited a taxi in downtown Montreal and was walking. (He ran when the police stopped him). One of the officers remembered Campbell from a previous arrest and that he had a curfew of 10 p.m., and upon searching him they found a small quantity of marijuana. Justice Westmoreland-Traoré reasoned that the police officers "had singled out Campbell... because he was Black and likely fit their stereotypical profile of a drug dealer," and as for his actions, she noted that in "the context of a minority person, his reflex to move away from the police does not necessarily infer that he had committed an offence" (Tanovich 2006: 49).

> Justice Brian Trafford of the Ontario Superior Court: "racism is part of our culture and justice system."

In Nova Scotia, the Human Rights Commission Board of Inquiry chaired by Dalhousie law professor Philip Girard, like the judges in Ontario and Quebec, concluded that a Halifax police officer acted differentially in stopping Kirk Johnson (the complainant) and his friend, Fraser, on Easter Sunday in 1998.[15] And while the officer claimed that he "couldn't see the race of the driver" before he pulled him over, the Board wrote that the officer was indeed "*aware of the race of the occupants of the car*," for as Fraser told the Board, the "officer had looked into their vehicle as he passed them on the highway and then braked to let Fraser pass." The officer had testified that "he was initially attracted to the vehicle because it was a 'nice sports car [1993 black Ford Mustang] with tinted windows and with a Texas licence'" (Tanovich 2006: 39–40). In such a context, there is little wonder that Black young people in Halifax, Toronto, and Calgary would report that getting stopped in public places by police, being arrested, and being harassed or treated rudely by police would bring them much stress. Specifically, in research that investigated the relationship between racism and the health of African Canadians in the three cities, we found that being arrested was thought to be most stressful, especially among the young people in Toronto and Calgary (see Appendix).[16]

In citing the relationship between police actions and systemic racism, as exemplified through racial profiling/ stereotyping, judges and human rights commissioners (including the Ontario Human Rights Commission 2003) underscore the fact that racism is not merely a case of police officers independently perceiving young minority men as likely troublemakers and lawbreakers

> Racism is not merely a case of police officers independently seeing young minority men as likely law-breakers; these perceptions are also informed by policies and practices found within institutions.

who need to be targeted by the police (Ericson and Haggerty 1997; James 1998; Tanovich 2006; Wortley and Tanner 2004), but that these perceptions are informed by a system of policies and corresponding practices which are to be found within institutions. Furthermore, in this era of the fight against drugs, violence, and terrorism, and in the absence of alternative training, law-enforce-

> The street is not neutral space; it takes on the racial characteristics of those with the power to define its use and determine what activities may be carried out there.

ment personnel will continue to employ strategies that will enable them to recognize and police potential lawbreakers — a matter of profiling. And when we add the real and/or imagined terrorism threats — especially since the bombings in Madrid, Spain (2004) and London, England (2005), the fires in Paris, France (2005), the arrest of eighteen (initially seventeen) young Muslim men in the Greater Toronto area on "terrorism related offences" (June 2006), and the alleged planned bombings of commercial aircrafts flying from London, England to the United States (August 2006) — the relationship between law-enforcers and racialized Canadians will continue to be ambivalent, distrustful, and tension-ridden. However, we can hope that the rulings of some Ontario and Quebec judges mean that judges, as Justice Trafford asserted in the case of Dee Brown, "will be careful to maintain public confidence in the fairness and impartiality of the trial process."

DISCUSSION QUESTIONS

1. Discuss the social construction of race in Canada, noting how race operates in the identification of who is Canadian.

2. To what extent have the media, police action, and government legislation (e.g., immigration) influenced Canadians' perceptions of Black people and Jamaicans in particular?

3. What role have immigration policies and legislation historically played in the social construction of people we tend to consider "outsiders"?

4. What images do you or people you know have of Jamaicans? What are some of the factors that have contributed to the construction of these images? Are these images different from or similar to those held of people from other Caribbean islands?

5. Is there a relationship between an increase in crime rate and increase in immigration? Discuss, fully noting the conditions that might account for such a relationship.

GLOSSARY OF TERMS

Jamaicanization: the tendency to classify individuals on the basis of Black skin colour, language, accent, and/or particular behaviour practices (such as illegal activities) as being from Jamaica. Doing so is based sometimes on the assumption or knowledge that individuals are from the Carib-

bean, in which case no attention is given to the ethnic and racial diversity of people living in or coming from that region.

Multiculturalism: the policy and corresponding practices in Canada, as informed by the Multicultural Policy (1971) and the *Canadian Multicultural Act* (1988), whereby we seek to accommodate the diverse ethnic cultures of people living here. As the *Multicultural Act* states: "The Constitution of Canada... recognizes the importance of preserving and enhancing the multicultural heritage of Canadians... [and] the government of Canada recognizes the diversity of Canadians as regards race, national or ethnic origin, colour and religion as a fundamental characteristic of Canadian society and is committed to a policy of multiculturalism designed to preserve and enhance the multicultural heritage of Canadians while working to achieve the equality of all Canadians in the economic, social, cultural and political life of Canada."

Permanent Residents: according to the *Immigration Act,* refers to immigrants and refugees living permanently in Canada. Individuals qualify or gain the right to live permanently in Canada by being sponsored by relatives (parents, children); or nominated by a husband, wife, or fiancée who are permanent Canadian residents or citizens, eighteen years or older. Sponsors are expected to provide maintenance for up to ten years. There is also an independent category of immigrants who qualify for residency by scoring a minimum of seventy points out of a possible hundred based on age, level of education, job skills, occupational demand, knowledge of English or French, "personal suitability" (a capacity to adapt to Canada, typically determined by the immigration officer), and security and health considerations. Among those in this category are people who come as investors and entrepreneurs with large sums of money and whose intent is to operate businesses and employ more than one Canadian.

Racial Identity: the socially constructed identification, categorization, or labelling of individuals by race, typically defined in terms of skin colour (black, white, red, yellow, brown) and other physical attributes. Race is understood to be an arbitrary and therefore problematic term that is employed in the classification of human beings. Ethnicity, the arbitrary and subjective categorization of individuals by their ancestral roots (Italian, Irish, British, African, for example), is often used interchangeably with race. Racial identity differs according to context and history. For example, the Irish were once referred to as a different race of people; today we refer to them as racially white.

Racial Profiling: the practice of identifying individuals on the basis of race, colour of skin, and accent as being more likely to engage in particular kinds of activities; typically, illegal activities. In the case of Black people in Canada (compared to the United States, where the practice also takes place and from where the term originates) this process of racial profiling also includes the classification of Black people as immigrants (or illegal immigrants) from the Caribbean, usually Jamaica.

Refugees: people who enter Canada seeking to live here permanently. Canada must first recognize the country of which claimants are citizens as refugee-producing countries; this is with reference to the United Nations Convention, which holds that people should be granted refugee status in a country if they do not have a country of nationality, and/or by reason of a well-founded fear of persecution based on such things as race, religion, nationality, or membership in a particular social or political group; or, because of political opinion, they are unable to safely live in their country.

Street as a Racialized Space: the notion of the street as a culturally defined space in which only particular kinds of activities can take place. Those activities are considered to be legal or legitimate, and are informed by the cultural norms, values, and practices of the dominant racial/cultural group of the society. In this regard, there is an association between the race of people who make legitimate use of the streets and those who do not. The street thus becomes not a neutral space, but one which takes on the racial characteristics of those with the power to define its use and give permission to the activities which may be carried out by those seen as making appropriate or legitimate use of it.

SUGGESTED READINGS

Aylward, Carol A. 1999. *Canadian Critical Race Theory: Racism and the Law*. Halifax: Fernwood Publishing.

Gill, Peter. 2000. *Rounding Up the Usual Suspects? Developments in Contemporary Law Enforcement Intelligence*. Aldershot, UK: Ashgate Publishing.

Harris, David A. 2002. *Profiles in Injustice: Why Racial Profiling Cannot Work*. New York: New Press.

Hawkins, Darnell F., Samuel L. Myers, and Randolph N. Stone. 2003. *Crime Control and Social Justice: The Delicate Balance*. Westport, CT: Greenwood Press.

James, Carl E. 2003. *Seeing Ourselves: Exploring Race, Ethnicity and Culture*. Toronto: Thompson Educational Publishing.

Satzewich, Vic (ed.). 1998. *Racism and Social Inequality in Canada: Concepts, Controversies and Strategies of Resistance*. Toronto: Thompson Educational Publishing.

Tanovich, David. 2006. *The Colour of Justice: Policing Race in Canada*. Toronto: Irwin Law.

Tator, Carol, and Frances Henry. 2006. *Racial Profiling in Canada: Challenging the Myth of a Few Bad Apples*. Toronto: University of Toronto Press.

NOTES

1. In his essay, "White Like Canada," George Elliott Clarke (1998: 100–101) states, "Canadian identity, such as it is, defines itself primarily in opposition to the United States. Canadians are nice, Americans are trigger-happy… Canada celebrates a gorgeous 'mosaic' of peoples permitted to maintain their ethnic particularities. The most significant difference between Canada and the U.S. is, finally, that America has a race problem. In Canada, the party line goes, there are no racists save those who watch too much American television."

2. Immigration and custom officers are likely to have the same attitudes, perceptions, and practices as the police, thus operating with similar race profiles (see the *Toronto Star* (February 15, 2005: A15) in which Tonda MacCharles examines federal politicians claims and denial of racial profiling. While Public Safety Minister, Anne McLellan claimed, "We do not racially profile, that would be a firing offence," Senator Mobina Jaffer responded by saying, "I don't accept that at all… The police, CSIS, they all racially profile. I have documents that show it."

3. In her discussion of Canadian critical race theory, Aylward (1999: 40) states: "In the United States, most observers would acknowledge that racism exists; the controversy is over the role that law plays in its maintenance and perpetuation. In Canada, it is hard even to reach this issue because of pervasive denial of the very existence of racism in Canadian society."

4. I am raising here the question of nationality and citizenship, since we can assume that there would be no way of police ascertaining that Dawson was not a citizen of Canada unless they had asked. If they asked, we would have to wonder about the basis for such a question. Caribbean people have long complained about police attributing nationality based on skin colour and accent. We would have to wonder about the police officer's qualification to connect accent

to nationality. Of course, errors will be made, especially when Caribbean people, and youth in particular, even without having been to Jamaica, adopt what they consider or construct as a "Jamaican accent" as a way of claiming or asserting their identity or "Caribbeanness."

5. A participant in the *Toronto Star* 1985 "Minority Report" about the experiences of Black people with the police made this comment (Ward 1985: 6; see also Chigbo 1992). The comment captures the sentiments of many members of the community who believe that Black people are more likely to be stopped, questioned, and searched by the police and customs and immigration officers (see Wortley's [2001] essay "Under Suspicion: Race and Criminal Justice Surveillance in Canada," in which he makes the point that "race is a 'master status' that continues to draw all blacks into the 'web of suspicion'" [p. 25]).

6. Of the Leimonis case, Foster (1996) writes, the murdered woman "became a representative of all the ills black men can inflict on white women." Citizens and police alike acted as though the colour of the three Black male suspects was "the most important aspect of this robbery and murder" (p. 206). Foster goes on to say that the police and media portrayed the suspect as "lawless, a drug dealer, fatherless, a street hustler and someone who should have been kicked out of the country long ago" (p. 209).

7. This assertion was that of Michael Valpy as quoted in the *Globe and Mail* (cited in Henry and Bjornson 1999: 97). Henry et al. (2000: 177) also quotes Cannon as saying, "A majority of Canadians told a polling company that the immigration quotas were too high, that the refugee determination process was too easy, and that the immigration appeal process was obviously designed to permit dangerous felons to kill Canadians." But as one reviewer of this chapter points out, such polls also find that most Canadians do not actually know what immigration levels are, or what the refugee process involves, or that homicide victims are almost always killed by friends, family, or other individuals they tend to know intimately.

8. In light of such an immigration bill, we saw the Canadian government take such drastic measures as chartering a plane to take deportees to Guyana (considered to be their "home"). Some of those deportees had been living in Canada since childhood (see "Guyana Doesn't Want Dumped Deportees," *National Post* Dec. 23, 1999: 3).

9. This image appeared on the front page of the April 7, 1994, edition of the *Toronto Star* (in Henry and Bjornson 1999: 67–68). This representation could be added to Betty Granger's reference to urban terrorism, specifically her comment about the "problems of immigrants in Toronto who support 'Tamil terrorists'" (*Toronto Star* Nov. 19, 2000).

10. The comments by Gwyn Morgan, CEO of Encana Corporation, is instructive. He was nominated by Prime Minister Harper less than four months after making these comments to head a new Public Appointments Commission. In his speech to The Fraser Institute in December 2005, in which he attempted to explain the violence among some racial groups in Canada, Morgan stated that there is a "run-away violence driven mainly by Jamaican immigrants in Toronto, or the all too frequent violence between Asian and other ethnic gangs right here in Calgary… Immigrant groups blame 'poverty' or 'police discrimination' or 'lack of opportunity.' Once again these are symptoms not the root cause." The "root cause," Morgan explains, is the "vast majority of violent, lawless immigrants come from countries where the culture is dominated by violence and lawlessness… Why do we expect different behaviour in Toronto, Ontario than in Kingston, Jamaica?" (Morgan 2005: 11).

11. Newspaper reports refer to the "posses" as "Jamaican organized crime groups" and "criminal gangs" (Henry 1994: 65, 204). Originally the posses were loosely organized groups of mostly men engaged in political activities. In more recent times they have become much more organized, and with groups in the United States and Canada connecting with Jamaica, they have been engaging in criminal activities. Members of the "gangs" tend to be described as coming from poverty "ghetto" backgrounds (see Gunst 1995).

12. In their report on the racialization of crime in the print media, Henry and Bjornson (1999: 85) note that the columnists and editors of the various newspapers all contribute substantively to an image of Black young men as "drug-crazed, gun-toting barbarians" who engage in "American-style criminal activities."

13. This idea of reading/interpretation of the "evidence" is further captured in the case of Ama-
    dou Diallo, a twenty-two-year-old Ghanaian-American who was hit nineteen times from the
    forty-one bullets fired at him by four New York police officers in February 1999. Despite the
    "evidence" and the protests, all four officers were acquitted (Stolen Lives Project 1999).
14. Henry and Bjornson (1999: 18) also make the point that crime is usually presented by the
    media "as an individual act," thus shifting attention "from the socio-structural and economic
    factors which actually cause a lot of the criminal activity."
15. Johnson complained that he was stopped by the Halifax police some "twenty-eight times"
    between 1993 and 1995. On this occasion, he was stopped and ticketed, and his car was
    towed.
16. The five-year CIHR-funded research project is composed of Wanda Thomas Bernard as team
    leader with David Este, Carl James, Akua Benjamin, Carol Amaratunga, and Bethan Lloyd.
    It seeks to examine the experiences of a cross-section of the Halifax, Toronto, and Calgary
    Black communities in terms of racism and violence, noting the impact of both on individual,
    family, and community health and well-being. For more information visit the website <www.
    dal.ca/rvh>. Research assistant Oyin Shyllon constructed the tables used here.

Appendix

A Brief Description of the Sample

Of the 900 participants in the RVH sample, 408 were young adults between the ages
of eighteen and thirty-four. Not all of the participants had prior experience with law
enforcement or the legal system, so the questions that were raised were not applicable
to all of them.

The Young Participants (18–34 years)

In general, we observed that the most stressful experience for survey participants involved
being arrested, while the least stressful involved experiences with probation or parole.
Being harassed or treated rudely by the police was the second most stressful experience
for participants.

Participants also indicated a greater amount of stress associated with concerns with
family member's experiences with the law enforcement or legal system when compared
with the stress they experience themselves from their own encounters with the law enforcement or legal system.

All Three Sites — Halifax, Toronto, and Calgary

Participants in all three cities indicated that their most stressful experience involved
being arrested. Interestingly, the level of stress was higher for residents of Toronto and
Calgary.

In Halifax the second most stressful experience involved getting stopped in public
places by the police. In Toronto it was experiences with probation or parole, while in
Calgary it was being harassed or treated rudely by the police.

The least stressful experience varied from city to city. In Halifax and Calgary, this
involved experiences with probation or parole. In Toronto, this involved experiences
with the court system.

Table 16-1: To What Extent Have the Following Been Stressful?

	Level of Stress Experienced			# of Respondents
	A Bit/ Somewhat	Pretty Big	Major/ Biggest	
Getting stopped in public places by the police	39%	26%	34%	151
Being arrested	29%	13%	59%	68
Being harassed or treated rudely by the police	36%	25%	39%	160
Experiences in the court system	46%	20%	34%	98
Experiences with probation or parole	60%	12%	28%	25

Table 16-2: How Stressful Have Experiences with Law Enforcement or Legal System Been for You?

	A Little Stressful	Somewhat Stressful	Very Stressful	Extremely Stressful	# of Respondents
Overall, while living in Canada	36%	28%	24%	12%	210
Over the last three years	39%	28%	21%	11%	183
When you think of your family member's experiences	32%	28%	20%	21%	225

All Three Sites — Halifax, Toronto, and Calgary

Participants in Halifax and Calgary indicated a greater amount of stress associated with concerns with family members' experiences with the law-enforcement or legal system when compared with the stress they experience themselves from their own encounters with the law-enforcement or legal system. Also, participants who had experiences in the last three years (2001–2004) in these two cities found them to be slightly less stressful than the experiences over time of all participants.

Participants in Toronto indicated a greater amount of stress associated with their personal experiences with law-enforcement or the legal system when compared with the concerns they have for their family members.

Table 16-3: To What Extent Have the Following Been Stressful?

	Halifax				Toronto				Calgary			
	A bit/Somewhat	Pretty Big	Major/Biggest	Total	A bit/Somewhat	Pretty Big	Major/Biggest	Total	A bit/Somewhat	Pretty Big	Major/Biggest	Total
Getting stopped in public places by the police	39%	32%	29%	56	30%	23%	46%	43	46%	23%	31%	52
Being arrested	35%	19%	47%	26	27%	8%	65%	26	25%	6%	69%	16
Being harassed or treated rudely by the police	39%	37%	25%	57	29%	25%	46%	52	39%	12%	49%	51
Experiences in the court system	48%	30%	21%	33	54%	10%	36%	39	31%	23%	46%	26
Experiences with probation or parole	78%	11%	11%	9	29%	14%	57%	7	67%	11%	22%	9

Table 16-4: How Stressful Have Experiences with Law Enforcement or Legal System Been for You?

	Halifax			Toronto			Calgary		
Context	A little	Somewhat/Very/Extremely	Total	A little	Somewhat/Very/Extremely	Total	A little	Somewhat/Very/Extremely	Total
Overall, while living in Canada	38%	62%	76	26%	74%	66	43%	57%	68
Over the last three years	41%	59%	69	26%	74%	54	50%	50%	60
When you think of your family member's experiences	31%	69%	89	30%	70%	60	33%	67%	76

REFERENCES

Aylward, Carol A. 1999. *Canadian Critical Race Theory: Racism and the Law.* Halifax: Fernwood Publishing

Barnes, Annmarie. 2002. "The Dangerous Duality: The 'Net Effect' of Immigration and Deportation on Jamaicans in Canada." In W. Chan and K. Mirchandani (eds.), *Crimes of Colour: Racialization and the Criminal Justice System in Canada.* Peterborough, ON: Broadview Press.

Benjamin, Agua 2002. "The Social and Legal Banishment of Anti-Racism: A Black Perspective." In W. Chan and K. Mirchandani (eds.), *Crimes of Colour: Racialization and the Criminal Justice System in Canada.* Peterborough, ON: Broadview Press.

Bernard Harcourt. 2003. "The Shaping of Chance: Actuarial Models and Criminal Profiling at the Turn of the 21st Century." *University of Chicago Law Review* 70 (105).

Brodgen, M., T. Jefferson, and S. Walklate 1988. *Introducing Policework.* London: Irwin Press.

Butler, Judith. 1993. "Endangered/Endangering: Schematic Racism and White Paranoia." In R. Gooding-Williams (ed.), *Reading Rodney King, Reading Urban Uprising.* London: Routledge.

Comack, Elizabeth. 1999. "Theoretical Excursions." In E. Comack (ed.), *Locating Law: Race, Class, Gender Connections.* Halifax: Fernwood Publishing.

Commission on Systemic Racism in the Ontario Criminal Justice System 1995. *Report of the Commission on Systemic Racism in the Ontario Criminal Justice System.* Toronto: Queen's Printer for Ontario.

Chigbo, O. 1992. "Boyz 'n The Law: Black Youth, White Authority and the Search for Solutions." *Toronto Life* August 25–27, 44–49.

Clarke, George Elliott. 1998. "White Like Canada." *Transition* 73.

Day, Richard 2000. *Multiculturalism and the History of Canadian Diversity.* Toronto: University of Toronto Press.

Dei, George S., L. Holmes, J. Muzzuca, E. McIssac, and R. Campbell. 1995. *Drop Out or Push Out? The Dynamics of Black Students Disengagement from School.* Toronto: Department of Sociology, Ontario Institute for Studies in Education.

Dobbins James E., and Judith H. Skillings. 1991. "The Utility of Race Labelling in Understanding Cultural Identity: A Conceptual Tool for the Social Science Practitioner." *Journal of Counselling and Development* 70, 1: 37–44.

Ericson, Richard V., and Kevin D. Haggerty. 1997. *Policing the Risk Society.* Toronto: University of Toronto Press.

Fanon, Franz. 1967. *Black Skins, White Masks.* New York: Grove Press

Foster, Cecil. 1996. *A Place Called Heaven: The Meaning of Being Black in Canada.* Toronto: Harper Collins.

Frater, T. 1991. "Just My Opinion." *Racism and Education. Our Schools/Our Selves* 3, 3.

Gill, Peter. 2000. *Rounding Up the Usual Suspects? Developments in Contemporary Law Enforcement Intelligence.* Aldershot, UK: Ashgate Publishing.

Globe and Mail. 2002. "Verdict against ex-Raptor quashed." (Kirk Makin). January 30: A1, A9.

_____. 2003. "Court grants blacks special sentencing." February 13: A1, A7.

_____. 2004. "Judge lashes police for racial profiling." September 17: A1, A7.

Goldberg, David. 2000. "Raceless States." Keynote address at the "End Racism! Activism for the 21st Century." Vancouver. November.

Gunst, Laurie. 1995. *Born fi Dead: A Journey through the Jamaican Posse Underground.* New York: Henry Holt and Company.

Halperin, David M. 1995. *Saint Foucault.* London: Oxford University Press.

Harcourt, Bernard E. 2003. "The Shaping of Chance: Actuarial Models and Criminal Profiling at the Turn of the Twenty-First Century." *University of Chicago Law Review* 70 (1): 105–28.

Harris, David A. 2002. *Profiles in Injustice: Why Racial Profiling Cannot Work.* New York: New Press.

Henry, Frances. 1994. *The Caribbean Diaspora in Toronto: Learning to Live with Racism.* Toronto: University of Toronto Press.

Henry, Frances, and Marnie Bjornson. 1999. *The Racialization of Crime in Toronto's Print Media: A Research Project*. Toronto: School of Journalism, Ryerson Polytechnic University.

Henry, Frances, and Carol Tator. 2006. *The Colour of Democracy: Racism in Canadian Society*. Toronto: Nelson, Thomson Ltd.

Henry, Francis, Carol Tator, Winston Mattis, and Tim Rees. 2000. *The Colour of Democracy: Racism in Canadian Society*. Toronto: Harcourt Brace.

Jakubowski, Lisa Marie. 1997. *Immigration and the Legalization of Racism*. Halifax: Fernwood Publishing.

_____. 1999. "Managing Canadian Immigration: Racism, Ethnic Selectivity, and the Law." In E. Comack (ed.), *Locating Law: Race, Class, Gender Connections*. Halifax: Fernwood Publishing.

James, Carl E. 1997. "The Distorted Images of African Canadians: Impact, Implications and Responses." In C. Green (ed.), *Globalization and Survival in the Black Diaspora: The New Urban Challenge*. Albany, NY: State University of New York Press.

_____. 1998. "'Up to no good': Black on the Streets and Encountering Police." In V. Satzewich (ed.), *Racism and Social Inequality in Canada: Concepts, Controversies and Strategies of Resistance*. Toronto: Thompson Educational Publishing.

_____. 2003. *Seeing Ourselves: Exploring Race, Ethnicity and Culture*. Toronto: Thompson Educational Publishing.

James, Carl E., and Bethan Lloyd. (in press). "Differentiating the 'Other'/Disaggregating 'Black': On the Diversity of African Canadian Communities." In D. Zinga (ed.), *Navigating Multiculturalism, Negotiating Change*. London: Cambridge Scholars Press.

Jiwani, Yasmin. 2002. "The Criminalization of 'Race,' the Racialization of Crime." In Wendy Chan and Kiran Mirchandani, (eds.), *Crimes of Colour: Racialization and the Criminal Justice System in Canada*. Peterborough: Broadview Press.

Kobayashi, Audrey. 1990. "Racism and the Law." *Urban Geography* 5, 5: 447–73.

Morgan, Gwyn. 2005. "Getting Beyond the Symptoms to Root Causes... What Politicians Are Afraid to Say." T.P. Boyle Founder's Lecture, The Fraser Institute, December 7.

Mirchandani, Kiran, and Wendy Chan. 2002. "From Race and Crime to Racialization and Criminalization." In W. Chan and K. Mirchandani (eds.), *Crimes of Colour: Racialization and the Criminal Justice System in Canada*. Peterborough, ON: Broadview Press.

National Post. 1999a. "Deportee Identified as Product of his Environment." December 30.

_____. 1999b. "Guyana Doesn't Want Dumped Deportees." December 23: 3.

Neugebauer-Visano, Robin. 1996. "Kids, Cops and Colour: The Social Organization of Police-Minority Youth Relations." In G. O'Bireck (ed.), *Not a Kid Anymore: Canadian Youth, Crime and Subcultures*. Toronto: Nelson Canada.

Nixon, Martha. 2000. "Managing Gateways: The Moral Challenges of a Liberal Democracy." Panel presentation at the Fifth International Metropolis Conference. Vancouver, November.

Ontario Human Rights Commission. 2003. *Paying the Price: The Cost of Racial Profiling*. Toronto: Ontario Human Rights Commission.

Ornstein, Michael. 2006. *Ethno-Racial Groups in Toronto, 1971–2001: A Demographic and Socioeconomic Profile*. Toronto: Institute for Social Research, York University. Available at <http://atwork.settlement.org/sys/atwork_library_detail.asp?doc_id=1004044> accessed July 2007.

Quamina, Odida T. 1996. *All Things Considered: Can We Live Together*. Toronto: Exile Editions.

Rankin, Jim, Jennifer Quinn, Michelle Shephard, Scott Simmie and John Duncanson. 2002a. "Singled Out: An Investigation into Race and Crime." *Toronto Star*, October 19: A1.

_____. 2002b. "Police Target Black Drivers." *Toronto Star*, October 20: A1.

Razack, Sherene H. 1999. "Making Canada White: Law and the Policing of Bodies of Colour in the 1990s." *Journal of Law and Society* 14, 1: 159–84.

Royal Commission on Bilingualism and Biculturalism. 1970. *The Contributions of the Other Ethnic Groups*, Book 1V. Ottawa: Queen's Printer.

Satzewich, Vic. 1998. "Race, Racism and Racialization: Contested Concepts." In V. Satzewich (ed.), *Racism and Social Inequality in Canada: Concepts, Controversies and Strategies of Resistance*. Toronto: Thompson Educational Publishing.

Shepard, R. Bruce 1997. *Deemed Unsuitable: Blacks Form Oklahoma Move to the Canadian Prairies.* Toronto: Umbrella Press.

Sheth, Anita. 2000. "'Sincere Fictions': An Analysis of News-Claims of Non-White Immigrants in the Canadian Press." Paper presented at the "End Racism! Activism for the 21st Century." Vancouver, November.

Stolen Lives Project. 1999. *Stolen Lives: Killed by Law Enforcement.* New York: October 22nd Coalition to Stop Police Brutality, Repression, and the Criminalization of a Generation.

Tanovich, David M. 2006. *The Colour of Justice: Policing Race in Canada.* Toronto: Irwin Law.

Tator, Carol, and Frances Henry. 2006. *Racial Profiling in Canada: Challenging the Myth of a Few Bad Apples.* Toronto: University of Toronto Press.

Toronto Star. 1997. "Metro officer is charged in fatal shooting." (Philip Mascoll and Rosie DiManno). June 27: A1.

_____. 1997. "Story behind police shooting." (Philip Mascoll). April 4: A1.

_____. 1997. "Police at fatal shooting scene hold 2 meetings, sources say." (Philip Mascoll). April 2: A7.

_____. 1998. "Black Passengers Targetted in Pearson Searches." (Royson James). November 29: A1.

_____. 1999. "Their fair day in court: Born in Jamaica, the three men accused in the death of Georgina Leimonis were a product of Canada." (Philip Mascoll). December 8: A1.

_____. 2000. "Candidate says sorry in race row." (Tonda MacCharles). November 19, A8.

_____. 2002. "There is no racism: We do not do racial profiling." October 19: A14.

_____. 2005. "McLellan defends reach, scope of anti-terror law." (Tonda MacCharles). February 15" A15.

Ward, Mary 1985. *Minority Report. Toronto Star.*

Wortley, Scott. 2002. "Under Suspicion: Race and Criminal Justice Surveillance in Canada". In W. Chan and K. Mirchandani (eds.), *Crimes of Colour: Racialization and the Criminal Justice System in Canada.* Peterborough, ON: Broadview Press.

Wortley, Scott, and Gail Kellough. 1998. "The 'Probable' Offender: Police and Crown Discretion and the Over-Representation of Black People in the Ontario Criminal Justice System." Paper presented at the International Conference on Criminology and Criminal Justice in the Caribbean. Barbados. October.

Wortley, S., and J. Turner. 2004. "Social Groups or Criminal Organizations: The Extent and Nature of Youth Gangs in Toronto." In J. Phillips and B. Kidd (eds.), *From Enforcement and Prevention to Civic Engagement: Research Colloquium on Community Safety.* Toronto: Centre of Criminology, University of Toronto.

Walcott, Rinaldo 1997. *Black Like Who? Writing Black Canada.* Toronto Insomniac Press

Zatz, Marjorie, and Krecker, Richard. 2003. "Anti-Gang Initiatives as Racialized Policy." In D. Hawkins, S. Myers and R. Stone (eds.), *Crime Control and Social Justice: The Delicate Balance.* Westport, CT: Greenwood Press.

17 Women in Prison in Canada

Helen Boritch

KEY FACTS

> Women in conflict with the law typically are from marginalized economic situations and are charged with property offences.

> The problem of overrepresentation of Aboriginal peoples is even more severe for Aboriginal women. Aboriginal women make up 28 percent of the female penitentiary population. Aboriginal men make up 18 percent of the male penitentiary population.

> It costs (on average) $150,000 per year to imprison a woman in a federal prison. This can be more than $250,000 per year for women in isolated confinement.

> Corrections logged 264 women admissions to administrative segregation in federal custody in 2002–2003, when the official number of women serving time was 376. Eighty-three of these admissions to segregation were for longer than ten consecutive days.

> Women are the fastest growing prisoner population worldwide. In the United States, the number of women prisoners has grown from 5,600 in 1970 to 161,200 in 2001.

> In 2004, federally sentenced women accounted for 3 percent of federal inmates.

> Marlene Moore committed suicide behind the walls of the Prison for Women at Kingston (P4W) in 1988. CAEFS (the Canadian Association of Elizabeth Fry Societies) attributed lack of therapeutic support within P4W as contributing to her death. Marlene had a history of self-injurious behaviour, which is common amongst the female prisoners.

Sources: Balfour 2006; CAEFS 2007.

One must resist the temptation to trivialize the infringement of prisoners' rights as either an insignificant infringement of rights, or as an infringement of rights of people who do not deserve better. When a right has been granted by law, it is no less important that such right be respected because the person entitled to it is a prisoner.
—Commission of Inquiry into Certain Events at the Prison for Women in Kingston, (Arbour 1996: 183)

The history of Canada's treatment of women prisoners reveals a sad legacy of harsh, cruel, and discriminatory treatment. In a prison system designed, managed, and operated for and by men, the plight of women prisoners has always been especially bleak. Since the early part of the nineteenth century, when prisons became the dominant means of punishing criminals, women have suffered some of the worst deprivations and abuses of incarceration — both because of their small numbers relative to men and because traditional stereotypes of women and women offenders have defined correctional policies and practices. Women prisoners have been housed in inferior and inadequate accommodations under regimes stressing the domestic role of women in society, and they have been denied many of the programs and services available to their male counterparts (Cooper 1993; Shaw 1994). Ignored by correctional authorities whose concerns centred on the larger male prison population, women have been physically locked away from society, isolated from family, friends, and children, rarely allowed to be heard, and even more rarely thought of by the public. The secrecy typically associated with prison regimes has made women in jail all but invisible.

Although numerous government reports, task forces, and commissions for well over a century have documented the many injustices and inequities faced by women prisoners, little of substance was done to improve conditions in women's prisons until very recently. In particular, the 1990 report of the Task Force on Federally Sentenced Women (TFFSW), *Creating Choices*, promised to reverse the long history of bureaucratic apathy and usher in a new and progressive era in women's corrections. This report, which advocated a radically different, woman-centred model of corrections, has been the catalyst for broad-ranging transformations in federal imprisonment of women. In the years since the publication of *Creating Choices*, however, significant events have raised questions about the limitations of attempts to restructure women's prisons in ways that are consistent with feminist principles.

Profiles of Women Prisoners in Canada

Incarceration Numbers and Trends

In Canada offenders sentenced to two years or more serve their time in federal institutions, while those sentenced to less than two years are housed in provincial/territorial facilities. In the present, as in the past, women represent a small proportion of adult offenders in the Canadian criminal justice and correctional systems. In 2003, for example, women accounted for 19 percent of adults charged with criminal offences and about 10 percent of all adult admissions to federal and provincial/territorial prisons (Wallace 2004: 25; Statistics Canada 2005a: 1). Federal prisoners represent a minority of all prisoners in Canada and a very small proportion of the female prison population. In 2005 women accounted for only 5% of new admissions to federal custody, and as of 2006, only 3.2 percent or 401 of 12,648 prisoners incarcerated in federal prisons were women (Correctional Service of Canada [CSC] 2006: 12; Public Safety and Emergency Preparedness Canada [PSEPC] 2005: 43). Typically, the Prairie region has the highest proportion of federally incarcerated women, followed by Ontario, although the Atlantic and Quebec populations have been increasing over the last several years (CSC 2005a: 7). Women comprise a larger proportion of the provincial/territorial inmate population; in 2003-04, women accounted for 10 percent, or approximately 8,100, of admissions to provincial/territorial prisons (Statistics Canada 2005b: 6).

Among the provinces and territories, there was substantial variation in the proportions of female admissions, ranging from 13 percent in Alberta to 0 percent in Nunavut (Beattie 2005: 14).

Canada has seen a significant increase in the punishment and incarceration of women over the past few decades.

As in other countries such as the United States, England,

and New Zealand (Chesney-Lind and Pasko 2004; Cook and Davies 1999), Canada has seen a significant increase in the punishment and incarceration of women over the past few decades. Although the overall crime rate has been declining since 1991, and the incarceration rate and number of men sentenced to prison has declined since 1994–95, the proportion and number of women charged with criminal offences and sentenced to prison has steadily increased, especially in the provincial/territorial system. For example, from 1978–79 to 2003–04 the proportion of women sentenced to provincial/territorial prisons increased from 5 percent to 10 percent of all admissions, and the number of women in these prisons rose from 4,550 to approximately 8,100. The proportion and number of women admitted to federal custody has fluctuated over the past decade but overall has increased from 3.2 percent in 1994-5 to 5 percent in 2005, representing an increase from 151 to 229 admissions (Beattie 2005: 5; CSC 2002a: 5; PSEPC 2005: 2; Thomas 2000: 5).

Offence Profiles of Women Prisoners

Research on the characteristics of offenders reveals long-standing and significant differences in the offender profiles of female and male prisoners in Canadian correctional facilities (CSC 2002b, 2005, 2005b; Finn et al. 1999; Trevethan 2000). Despite recurrent media claims that women are becoming more violent and serious offenders, when compared to male prisoners women continue to be incarcerated for less serious offences, and their criminal histories are less extensive and involve less serious crimes. More specifically, women in provincial/territorial facilities are much less likely than men to have been convicted of crimes against the person (28 percent versus 34 percent) (Finn et al. 1999: 4). These women are most often incarcerated for property crimes, such as theft (12 percent) and fraud (10 percent), and drug-related offences (13 percent). Similarly, a smaller proportion of women than men imprisoned in federal facilities had been convicted of violent offences (75 percent versus 84 percent), and more women than men were incarcerated for drug offences (20 percent versus 12 percent) (CSC 2005b: 12).

In provincial/territorial prisons, one-half (50 percent) of women (compared with 36 percent of male inmates) have never been convicted or have had only one prior adult conviction (Finn et al. 1999: 5). At the federal level in 1996, a much larger proportion of women than men were serving their first federal sentence (69 percent versus 49 percent); by 2002 the proportion of first-time federally sentenced women had increased to 82 percent (Sinclair and Boe 2002: 3). Moreover, the recidivism rate for federally sentenced women is approximately 22 percent, compared with 59 percent for men (Canadian Association of Elizabeth Fry Societies of Canada [CAEFS] 2005a: 4). These differences are reflected in the generally shorter sentences imposed on women. In 2003–04, almost three-quarters (72.8 percent) of women and just over half of men (55.4 percent) who were incarcerated upon conviction received a sentence of one month or less; 93.8 percent of women and 87.7 percent of men were sentenced to six months or less; and 1.4 percent of women and 2.8 percent of men received sentences of one to two years. Only 2.1 percent of women, compared with 4.0 percent of men, received a federal sentence of two years or more (PSEPC 2005: 15). Of the federally sentenced inmates, a larger proportion of women than men (37 percent versus 23 percent) are serving under three years, while men are more likely to be serving sentences of ten years or more (38 percent versus 22 percent; CSC 2005b: 12). It is also noteworthy that the proportion of women serving sentences of five years or more is decreasing, while the proportion of women serving from two to five years has increased (Sinclair and Boe 2002: 3). Consequently, most of the recent increases in the number of women in federal custody represent short sentences.

A disproportionate number of men and women in both federal and provincial/territorial prisons are Aboriginal; in 2003–04 Aboriginals accounted for 3 percent of the adult Canadian population but made up 21 percent of provincial/territorial admissions and 18 percent of federal admissions (Beattie 2005: 4). Even more disturbing, Aboriginal women have been overrepresented even more than Aboriginal men at all levels of the correctional system for some time and their numbers are increasing. Among admissions to provincial/territorial prisons in 2003–04, Aboriginal women represented 30.4 percent of female admissions while Aboriginal men represented 19.8 percent of male admissions (Beattie 2005: 15). There has also been a significant federal-level increase in the proportion of Aboriginal women prisoners. In 1981, Aboriginal women comprised 18 percent of women in federal custody; by 2004 this figure had grown to 28 percent while Aboriginal men constituted 18 percent of male federal inmates (Sinclair and Boe 2002: 2; CSC 2005a: 5, 2005b: 11). Aboriginal women also have different offender profiles from non-Aboriginal women prisoners: they are much more likely to be incarcerated for violent offences and to have served more than one federal prison sentence (CSC 2005a; Belcourt, Nouwens, and Lefebvre 1993).

> Aboriginal women have long been overrepresented at all levels of the correctional system and their numbers are increasing.

Social Histories of Women Prisoners

Research consistently reveals that the lives of most women prisoners are characterized by disadvantage and reflect the subordinate status of women in society (Boritch 1997). As a group, women prisoners are socially and economically marginalized and often have been victimized by family members and intimates. The experiences of abuse, poverty, and substance abuse are their most common pathways to crime. Research also demonstrates that among female prisoners, Aboriginal women are more disadvantaged than non-Aboriginal women because they have also endured the formidable lifelong burden of racism and oppression (CAEFS 2005a; Monture-Angus 2002). While men in prison also tend to come from disadvantaged backgrounds, a number of important differences in the personal histories of male and female prisoners combine to make the life experiences of women generally worse. Consequently, women in prison present different circumstances and needs than their male counterparts, and attempts to design effective, gender-responsive programs must necessarily address the specific and unique needs of women.

> Attempts to design effective, gender-responsive programs must necessarily address the specific and unique needs of women.

Female prisoners in Canada are young; 43 percent are between twenty-five and thirty-four years of age and most are single (Finn et al. 1999; CSC 2002a). Amongst federal female inmates, the average age of admission is younger for Aboriginal offenders and the proportion of women over twenty-five has steadily increased, from 75 percent in 1981 to 85 percent in 2002 (Sinclair and Boe 2002: 2). The majority of federal and provincial/territorial prisoners (76 percent and 55 percent respectively) have less than Grade 12 education and were unemployed at the time of incarceration (80 percent and 64 percent, respectively). Aboriginal women have even more disadvantaged education and employment histories than non-Aboriginal women (CAEFS 2005a; Trevethan 2000: 5). In addition, women prisoners are further economically marginalized and distinguished from male prisoners given that at least two-thirds of them are mothers, two-thirds of whom are single mothers (CAEFS 2005a: 4).

Female prisoners, more than women in the general population or male prisoners, also tend to have complex histories of substance abuse and trauma. Some 70 to 80 percent of women in prison have a serious problem with drugs or alcohol, and this substance abuse is associated in some way with their offences. Substance-abuse problems are even more prevalent among Aboriginal female offenders (Shaw 1994; CSC 2002a). While many male prisoners have similar problems, female federal prisoners are twice as likely as male federal prisoners to report at least moderate drug abuse (Loucks and Zamble 1994). As a result of their higher rates of substance abuse, the HIV infection rate is significantly higher among women prisoners than male prisoners (4.7 percent versus 1.75 percent), as are reported rates of hepatitis C infection (41.2 percent versus 23.2 percent) (CAEFS 2006b).

> Female federal prisoners are twice as likely as their male counterparts to report at least moderate drug abuse.

The mental health issues faced by female prisoners are considerable and tend to be different from those of their male counterparts. For many women prisoners, substance abuse stems from attempts to deal with the pain caused by abusive families and battering relationships (Bloom 1999). Research repeatedly finds that most women prisoners have experienced abuse in childhood, adulthood, or both. *Creating Choices* found that 78 percent of federally sentenced women were physically abused and 53 percent were sexually abused. The figures for Aboriginal women are even higher: 90 percent have experienced physical abuse and 61 percent have been victims of sexual abuse. Elizabeth Comack's 1996 study of women in Manitoba's women's prison found that 78 percent had histories of physical and sexual abuse. Such victimization makes women prisoners more likely than men to have histories of psychiatric disorders, self-destructive behaviours such as slashing and cutting, and previous suicide attempts (CAEFS 2006a; Daigle, Alaire, and Lefebvre 1999; Shaw 1994). In 2004–05, 40 percent of federal female offenders had previously been hospitalized for psychiatric reasons compared with only 17 percent of male offenders (PSEPC 2005: 55).

> Women prisoners are more likely than men to enter prison with histories of psychiatric disorders, self-destructive behaviours such as slashing and cutting, and previous suicide attempts.

While these statistics paint a dismal portrait of the life experiences of most women prisoners, individual stories tell us much more vividly of women who have endured fractured childhoods of neglect, abandonment, and abuse and gone on to struggle with often unimaginably painful and violent circumstances. The tragic life and violent death of Marlene Moore, who committed suicide at the Prison for Women in 1988 at the age of thirty-one, provides one such story (Kershaw and Lasovich 1991). Sexually abused as a child and deemed incorrigible by her parents, Moore began her institutional life at the age of thirteen, when her mother surrendered her to the juvenile corrections system. In prison she expressed her pain and anguish through repeated self-mutilation; by the time of her death she had slashed herself as many as a thousand times, disfiguring nearly every reachable part of her body. Similarly, in her interviews with fourteen women prisoners, Evelyn Sommers (1995) found that central to their lawbreaking experiences was the absence in their lives of positive, supportive, empathic relationships — deficits that they tried to overcome, often in self-destructive ways. As children and adults many of them endured separations from important people in their lives as the result of divorce, death, and abandonment, and some experienced the loss of self as a result of physical or sexual abuse. In the face of these emotional losses, women often turned to drugs or alcohol as a way of obliterating their pain and connecting with others. The story of Yvonne Johnson, serving a life sentence for murder, chronicles a life marked by poverty, abuse, violence, racism, misogyny, and oppression (Wiebe and Johnson 1998). Yet her story is an eloquent testament to the triumph of a courageous spirit against enormous odds. As is the case with many women prisoners, surviving such life experiences is nothing less than a miracle.

Creating Choices and the Transformation of Federal Corrections for Women

The Prison for Women

God be merciful and let me die in my sleep. But not here.
— Yvonne Johnson, inmate at Prison for Women, 1991–95 (Wiebe and Johnson 1998: 326)

Creating Choices is the most important in a long succession of government and private-sector reports documenting the abysmal conditions of federally sentenced women. Although Canada has more than forty men's prisons with varying security levels, until the mid-1990s there was only one prison for women, the Prison for Women in Kingston, Ontario, known as P4W. Before the construction of that prison in 1934, women sentenced to long terms were housed in the Kingston Penitentiary, built in 1835. Viewed as an inconvenience by prison management, and with no special accommodation for them, women were initially confined to a small attic space and subsequently managed and moved around in whatever ways seemed to be least disruptive to the larger male population (Cooper 1993; Faith 1993).

In this environment women prisoners endured abominable, filthy living conditions, suffering from infestations of rodents and insects, inadequate nutrition, and disease (Faith 1993). Public concerns about the brutal treatment of women (and children) at the penitentiary led to the appointment of an investigative royal commission in 1848 (Beattie 1977). The Brown Commission documented a range of abuses of females inmates, from cruel and excessive discipline to starvation and sexual abuse by guards, and recommended the establishment of a separate facility for women prisoners. In 1875 Ontario provincial authorities constructed the Andrew Mercer Reformatory in Toronto as a separate prison for women serving sentences of less than two years. But it was not until 1934 that the Prison for Women was finally constructed just across the road from the Kingston Penitentiary.

The Kingston Prison for Women was a forbidding structure that reproduced the architecture, structure, organization, and maximum-security conditions of the men's penitentiary. Described as a dark, dismal, and forbidding edifice built of "stones cut high and straight and thick as irrefutable sin," the prison consisted of a "dysfunctional labyrinth of claustrophobic and inadequate spaces" with two-tier ranges of cage-like cells (Wiebe and Johnson 1998: 7; Arbour 1996: 9). Because it was the only federal prison for women, prisoners from all over the country, many of them thousands of miles away from homes and families, were incarcerated under maximum-security conditions, regardless of their actual security classification. This geographic dislocation was partially ameliorated in the 1970s when federal-provincial exchange-of-service agreements allowed about half of all federally sentenced women to serve their sentences in provincial institutions so that they could remain closer to home (Faith 1993). These transfers were not equally available to all women, though, and in addition provincial prisons could not meet the needs of all federal prisoners. They were designed for short-term prisoners and offered fewer vocational and educational programs, recreational facilities, and counselling services. Moreover, provincial prisons were stressful and demoralizing for many federally sentenced women inmates because they were housed with women serving minimal sentences under less restrictive conditions (Hannah-Moffat 1991; Law Society of British Columbia 1992; TFFSW 1990).

After the establishment of the Prison for Women, numerous government reports attempted to resolve the dilemmas associated with one centralized facility housing a small and diverse population: geographic dislocation, inferior services and programs, and overclassification in terms of security of women prisoners. Only four years after the prison opened, the Archambault Commission recommended that the prison be closed and that women be allowed to serve their sentences in their home provinces (Cooper 1993). Some forty years later, in 1977, the MacGuigan Report condemned the prison as "unfit for bears, much less women" (TFFSW 1990: 30). In all, more than a dozen government reports have identified essentially the same problems, and all but one recommended that the prison be closed.

Regional Facilities for Women

Creating Choices largely reiterated the many problems cited in previous investigations of P4W: It was overly secure; it was erroneously built on a model of male corrections that ignored women's special needs; it unnecessarily subjected women to geographic dislocation and separation from families; it had inadequate programs and services; it ignored the special needs of prisoners serving life sentences and those of francophone and Aboriginal women; and it lacked community. The report recommended that the P4W be closed and replaced by four regional correctional facilities and a healing lodge for Aboriginal women.

What sets this report apart from its predecessors is its explicit feminist philosophy, its emphasis on the lower-security and reoffending risks posed by women inmates compared with men, its particular recognition of the unique problems of Aboriginal women, and its coincidence with a political, social, and legal climate receptive to major transformations in women's federal imprisonment. Based largely on extensive interviews with women prisoners, the Task Force on Federally Sentenced Women (1990) stressed that women inside prison have more in common with women outside prison than they do with male prisoners, and that significant reform must recognize and accommodate differences and diversity in the life experiences of women prisoners. In particular, the TFFSW advocated a new woman-centred, holistic approach to women's prisons, an approach based on the core feminist principles of empowering women: providing more appropriate choices in programs and community facilities; treating women with respect and dignity; providing a physically and emotionally supportive environment; and shared responsibility for women's welfare by correctional workers and members of the community. It stressed the need for physical environments that are conducive to reintegration, interactive with the community, and reflective of the low security risk of most federally sentenced women. Further, it urged that programs and services be implemented in regional facilities, including accommodations for prisoners' children, which would be responsive to women's needs and encourage the development of self-esteem and self-sufficiency.

By 1990 many factors had converged to intensify pressure on the government to initiate major reforms in federal women's imprisonment; these included the increasing strength of the feminist movement, the enactment of the Canadian Charter of Rights and Freedoms, and an increased awareness of the special problems of Aboriginal women prisoners (Adelberg and Currie 1993; Hannah-Moffat 1995; Shaw 1993). Feminist efforts to increase awareness of women's inequality in society in terms of poverty, racism, and violence against women had contributed to a general understanding that most imprisoned women were not primarily violent, dangerous offenders, but rather "high needs, low risk" women (Hayman 2000: 43). As well, the suicides of eight women (five of them Aboriginal) between 1989 and 1991 were an indictment of the sordid and desperate conditions at P4W. In particular, the suicide of Marlene Moore, the first woman to be declared a "dangerous offender," became a major impetus for the government to make a clear commitment to comprehensively address the needs of federally sentenced women and to the creation of the TFFSW (Kershaw and Lasovich 1991).

Beginning in the 1980s, feminist social reformers increasingly, and successfully, began using litigation to improve the treatment of women prisoners and to demand the same vocational and educational programs, and physical and mental health services that were available to male prisoners (Hannah-Moffat 1994). In 1981 the Canadian Human Rights Commission declared that "federal female offenders were discriminated against on the basis of sex and that in virtually all programs and facility areas, the treatment of federal women inmates was inferior to that of men" (Hannah-Moffat 1991: 189). In 1990, in *R. v. Daniels*, the Saskatchewan Court of Queen's Bench agreed with a federal prisoner that her right to life and security under the charter would be violated if she were incarcerated at P4W, because the high risk of death by suicide there was "unacceptable in a free and democratic society" (Arbour 1996: 246).

It was in this political climate that the federal government accepted the recommendations of *Creating Choices*, and the solicitor general announced that the Prison for Women would be closed and new regional facilities constructed. Between 1995 and 1997 new prisons, each designed to house from thirty to seventy women in a community-living environment as recommended in *Creating Choices*, were opened: Nova in Truro, N.S. (Atlantic regional facility), Grand Valley Institution for Women (GVI) in Kitchener, Ont. (Ontario regional facility), Joliette Institution in Joliette, Que. (Quebec regional facility), and Edmonton Institution for Women (EIW) in Edmonton, Alta. (Prairie regional facility). In addition, the Okimaw Ohci Healing Lodge for Aboriginal women was built on the Nekaneet Reserve in Saskatchewan. The Burnaby Correctional Centre for Women (BCCW), a provincial prison already housing federal female prisoners under an exchange-of-service agreement, became the Pacific regional facility. In 2004, BCCW was closed and federal female offenders in the Pacific region were moved to the newly opened Fraser Valley Institution (FVI) in Abbotsford, B.C. As well, Isabel McNeill House, in Kingston, Ontario, which was established in 1990 as a minimum-security facility for women offenders, was retained.

The First Decade in Review

Creating Choices was undoubtedly a groundbreaking report, and together with the opening of the regional facilities signalled the start of a new era in corrections for women serving federal sentences. However, events of the 1990s that occurred during the implementation process heightened concerns that the task force's original vision was being eroded beyond all recognition (Faith 1999; Hannah-Moffat and Shaw 2000). Among these concerns was the exclusion of agencies outside government, particularly the Canadian Association of Elizabeth Fry Societies (CAEFS), from crucial decisions such as the location of the new prisons and the appointment of wardens. Referring to budgetary constraints, the government failed to provide the funds to set in place some of the key components of the TFFSW report, such as the development of community services and the day-care centre and gymnasium at the Healing Lodge. In the past decade there have been major changes in the regional facilities, moving them further away from fulfiling the promise of *Creating Choices* and confirming that "the path to achieving a women-centred correctional system would be longer and more difficult than the Task Force had contemplated" (Canadian Human Rights Commission [CHRC] 2004: 1).

> The physical design of the regional facilities has been drastically altered to enhance security.

Of particular significance is that the physical design of the regional facilities has been drastically altered to enhance security. Originally the planners intended that the new prisons would replace the fortress-like living conditions of the Prison for Women with cottage-style houses, each designed to promote wellness by providing "natural light, fresh air, colour, space and privacy" (TFFSW 1990). Each facility would accommodate all federally sentenced women in that region, and the overall security model would reflect the generally low-risk and low security needs of the majority of prisoners. The emphasis would be on "dynamic security," reflected in a high level of staff-prisoner interaction and staff support, rather than by traditional physical security measures (fences, locks, high-tech surveillance) or traditional discipline (segregation) (Shaw 1993).

The model advocated by *Creating Choices* was based on a view of women prisoners as having been first and foremost victims of violence and abuse. This model was singularly flawed because it failed to acknowledge the existence of, or to make provisions for, women who were violent, had serious psychiatric problems, or were otherwise deemed high-risk. As a result, the new regional facilities opened without adequate provisions for these women. When problems arose, correctional authorities quickly fell back on traditional punitive methods for dealing with those women deemed to be "violent, disturbed, or problematic" (Hayman 2000; Shaw 2000).

From the beginning there was public concern and anger about the perceived risks of situating female prisons within residential communities, especially in the wake of the revelations surrounding the arrests and trials of Paul Bernardo and Karla Homolka. Public perceptions of women prisoners as being violent and dangerous were further fuelled by trouble at the newly opened Edmonton Institution for Women in 1996: Seven prisoners escaped and one inmate murdered another. In response, the Edmonton Institution was virtually closed in order to make security upgrades (Watson 2004). In the end, all of the women classified as maximum-security and those deemed high risk because of serious psychiatric problems were returned to higher security facilities. Some of the women continued to be housed at the Prison for Women, while others were moved to small units constructed in men's maximum-security institutions.

As a consequence, visible security measures (alarm fences, cameras) were enhanced, and all the regional facilities expanded the number of secure accommodations for maximum-security prisoners. In 1999, after several years of research and deliberation, the Correctional Service of Canada (CSC) announced the Intensive Intervention Strategy, an accommodation and management plan aimed at better addressing the needs of women classified as maximum-security prisoners and those with mental health problems who were classified as minimum- and medium-security inmates (Correctional Service of Canada 2002a; 2006). The strategy entailed building secure units for maximum-security women at the regional facilities as well as the construction of a Structured Living Environment house at each of the regional facilities for the lower-security women with mental health problems. All women in the regional facilities were now subject to increased security measures — paying the price for the actions of a few. While CSC pressed budgetary cuts of key aspects of the model of the regional facilities envisioned in *Creating Choices*, hundreds of thousands of dollars were spent to implement the tougher security measures in the regional facilities, as well as to create the units to house women deemed high risk in maximum-security men's penitentiaries.

The Prison for Women, originally scheduled for closure in 1994, remained open, serving as a "dumping ground" for maximum-security women, almost half of whom were Aboriginal (Faith 1999: 114). These women continued to be housed in a destructive environment where suicide, attempted suicide, and self-mutilation had long been routine, inescapable aspects of everyday life (Horii 2000; Marron 1996). In 1995 conditions at P4W came to national attention through a videotape shown on television that documented abuses against eight women in segregation cells (Faith 1999; Marron 1996). After several days of unrest, during which prisoners attacked guards, lit fires, and threw human waste, the warden called in a male riot squad, the Institutional Emergency Response Team (IERT), which shackled and strip-searched the women. The inmates were subjected to body-cavity searches, kept in segregation for many months, and denied access to lawyers and basic necessities. CSC responded immediately with the rapid completion in 1995 of a new, higher-security segregation unit in the prison at a cost of $750,000 (Horii 2000: 112).

While the commissioner of corrections publicly defended the actions of the emergency response team, public outcry over the televised images of women being stripped and degraded by the baton-wielding male emergency team prompted an official inquiry chaired by Madam Justice Louise Arbour. In her report Justice Arbour (1996) wrote a scathing indictment of the abusive and illegal treatment of the women inmates, and the inaccurate and misleading account of its actions presented by CSC. The revelations in the report led to the resignation of the head of CSC. The report enumerated a long list of policy recommendations to prevent future violations of female prisoners' rights dealing with such issues as security classification; cross-gender staffing (male front-line staff in female prisons); use of force; Aboriginal women; segregation; accountability; and the prisoner grievance process. In particular, the Arbour Report stressed the need for an independent body to monitor CSC's treatment of female prisoners and to ensure that CSC did not violate prisoners' rights under the law. Although the Arbour Report led CSC to commission several major reviews of segregation, cross-gender monitoring, and policy in women's facilities over the years, only one of the report's recommendations, the appointment of a deputy commissioner for women to examine complaints of violations by

> The Arbour Report (1996) documented widespread abusive and illegal treatment of women prisoners.

women prisoners, was acted upon quickly; that appointment appears to have been largely a token gesture, since the commissioner holds no seniority or separate authority over the implementation of the federal women's prisons and community programs (CAEFS 2000).

Although the Prison for Women was officially closed on July 6, 2000, the opening of new regional facilities has not resulted in the effective women-centred correctional policies and practices for women anticipated by *Creating Choices* and reaffirmed in the Arbour Report. The failure of CSC to implement key recommendations of the Arbour Report has been well documented in subsequent reports, most recently that of the Canadian Human Rights Commission (CHRC 2004). In its broad-ranging report, entitled *Protecting Their Rights: A Systematic Review of Human Rights In Correctional Services for Federally Sentenced Women*, the commission reiterated many of the findings of the Arbour Report and made nineteen far-reaching recommendations to alleviate various sources of discrimination and violation of female prisoners' human rights. In particular, the report criticized the current risk/needs-assessment and security-classification processes designed for men and unable to "identify, reflect or accommodate the needs, capacities and circumstances of federally sentenced women or members of racialized groups" and which make "explicit distinctions on the basis of mental and physical disability" (CHRC 2004: 28). All new federal inmates go through an initial assessment to develop a profile of their dynamic risk/need factors (factors that led an individual to crime and that can be addressed through programming rated as low, medium, or high) and a security classification (based on the custody rating scale — CRS), which assesses an offender's probability of escape, risk to public safety, and need for supervision) ranked as minimum, medium, or maximum. The commission report documents the many negative consequences to women resulting from a discriminatory and invalid security classification process. Of greatest concern is that Aboriginal women and women with cognitive disabilities are systematically discriminated against by being misclassified and placed under higher security than necessary, thereby denying them many programming and release opportunities and making them more likely to be kept in segregated, isolated living conditions.

> The CHRC Report (2004) stated that Aboriginal women and women with cognitive disabilities are systematically discriminated against.

The commission was also highly critical of the negative impact on women, especially Aboriginal offenders, of the blanket policy in effect since 2001 that requires that federally sentenced offenders serving a life sentence for first- or second-degree murder be classified as maximum-security for at least the first two years of federal incarceration, even though the CSC acknowledges that not all of them constitute the same risk and need. In the opinion of the commission, the policy violated both the *Corrections and Conditional Release Act* and the *Canadian Human Rights Act* since it added to the court-imposed sentence a retributive element not rationally related to the legitimate purpose of assessing risk. The commission therefore recommended that the policy be rescinded immediately in favour of a fair and balanced individual assessment (CHRC 2004: 31–33). And, consistent with many previous reports, the commission once again calls for independent monitoring and accountability mechanisms to ensure CSC's adherence to principles of justice fairness and the rule of law.

The CSC's response to the CHRC report released in February 2005 (CSC 2005c) provides a bureaucratic action plan to further review, study, and implement many of CHRC's recommendations. However, in the view of CAEFS (2006b) as well as the ombudsman for federal offenders, the Office of the Correctional Investigator (OCI), (2005a, 2005b), CSC's response, largely skirts the substance and intent of the recommendations and continues to fail in its obligation to implement appropriate and timely changes. Although a risk/ needs assessment and security classification process appropriate to women offenders was identified as problematic by the TFFSW in 1990, and their finding was reaffirmed in numerous subsequent reports, the CSC timeframe for implementation of a new initial classification tool is not scheduled until 2008–09. Moreover, in the face of long-standing criticism and the significant recent empirical research attesting to the lack of validity and discriminatory nature of the current classification tools (Webster and Doob 2004), it is somewhat paradoxical that CSC continues to claim that the existing custody rating scale (CRS), which will be used in the interim, is valid for women offenders (CSC 2005c: 5, 2006: 27).

Since the publication and implementation of *Creating Choices,* Canada has received widespread acclaim for its progressive, even radical, "women-centred" policies; other countries have used it as an inspiration in designing their own female correctional facilities. While there has been some progress towards achieving a correctional system that recognizes and meets women's needs and is more respectful of their human and legal rights, it is clear that the need for fundamental changes is ongoing and urgent.

Current Realities of Women's Experiences of Imprisonment

By law they must keep our bodies alive in here, but what will we be when we're released? The human need for kindness, grace — it's impossible in prison.
—Yvonne Johnson, at Prison for Women (Wiebe and Johnson 1998: 326)

I don't think women should be incarcerated. Seriously. I see too much destruction. I see these women losing their children permanently. I see homes falling apart. I see women go to pieces.
— Prisoner at Portage Provincial Prison, Manitoba (Comack 1996: 133)

Prisons are run as small totalitarian societies; prisoners are systematically robbed of their personal identities, and rules govern virtually every detail of life (Faith 1993). As such, pain is an inevitable feature of the experience. Nonetheless, the pain of imprisonment is different for women than men and has a more severe impact on them. When the many problems that women bring into prison are combined with the long-standing lack of programs and services to deal with these problems, the experience of prison is, not surprisingly, worse for women than men. Women tend to identify certain factors as primary sources of emotional distress: unnecessarily rigid and arbitrary rule enforcement; negative inmate-staff interactions; the use of segregation; and especially the loss of children (Owen 1999: 87).

Women in prison are more strictly supervised than men are, and they tend to be charged for more trivial misbehaviour and much less serious violence than men (Bloom 1999; Shaw 2000). These conditions reflect traditional gender stereotypes that require more rigid and formal rule compliance by women. From the establishment of separate women's prisons in the nineteenth century, women have tended to be treated as recalcitrant children in need of strict supervision, with severe restrictions placed on their autonomy (Rafter 1990; Strange 1986). This pattern of patriarchal control has continued into the present. As one prisoner noted in *Creating Choices*, "You come in here as an adult and you leave as a child" (TFFSW 1990: 8). A provincial prisoner notes that prison is a "game" in which the rules are to "go along with everything" (Comack 2000: 120).

Inmate-staff relations form the cornerstone of women's experiences in prison. Women prisoners consistently report on negative staff interactions — disrespectful and undignified treatment; subjection to arbitrary rules; favouritism, discrimination, and intimidation; insensitivity to their life experiences. They are left feeling frustrated, uncertain, and worthless (Comack 1996; Gironella 1999; McDonagh 1999; TFFSW 1990). Despite the emphasis in *Creating Choices* on establishing empowering prison environments that would promote women's self-esteem, the inevitable reality is that the power imbalances between prisoners and staff, as well as limited training in women-centred approaches for front-line staff, make this ideal unattainable. Currently, women-centred training consists of a ten-day program with refresher training every two years (CSC 2006: 20). Women interviewed at the Edmonton Institution for Women point to the problems associated with inexperienced and unprofessional primary workers who are uncertain about the new women-centred model, apply rules inconsistently, and often have little knowledge about the rules, provisions, and policies of CSC. In the words of one prisoner, "Person to person, staff to staff, shift change to shift change, everybody interprets the rules and regulations of this institution the way they want to, for whatever their purposes" (Gironella 1999: 58).

> Inmate-staff relations form the cornerstone of women's experiences in prison.

Power imbalances between prisoners and staff are a key cause of the ineffectiveness and inefficiencies of the current internal grievance process available to federally sentenced women. Women prisoners often perceive staff members as being mutually supportive in opposing offender attempts to contest staff decisions or conduct; as being able and willing to take reprisals against inmates who lodge complaints against staff; as being unable to review and resolve complaints in a considered, objective fashion; and as being unwilling to manage complaint systems to make them effective and to provide accountability for improper review of complaints (OCI 2004: 26–27). Moreover, women in prison report being advised to consider how grievances might affect their family visits, their release planning process, their security classification, and other aspects of their progress through the correctional setting. For these reasons, women are very reluctant to make complaints against staff; Aboriginal women and women with mental health needs are those least likely to access the current redress system (CAEFS 2006b: 13). Although the CHRC report is only the latest of many to recommend an independent external redress body to ensure appropriate, fair, and timely resolution to inmate grievances, this recommendation has not been accepted or implemented to date.

The deployment of a male riot squad at the Prison for Women in 1994 served to underscore the broader issue of the role of male correctional staff in women's prisons. Given that the majority of female prisoners have been victims of physical or sexual abuse, and because of concerns to preserve women's privacy and to protect them from sexual harassment, coercion, or assault, TFFSW took the position that men should not be employed as primary workers in the new prisons. However, the staffing model envisioned in *Creating Choices* was seriously altered when CSC decided to open up front-line staff positions to men in the regional facilities. Currently, all of the regional facilities, with the exception of the Healing Lodge, have male front-line staff that constitutes 18.5 percent of all primary workers (CSC 2006: 19).

To minimize the potential negative impact of male staff on female inmates, CSC implemented a protocol which, among other things, prohibits male workers from access to women's living quarters when they are most likely to be showering and dressing, and mandates that night rounds be done by two guards, only one of whom can be male. A Cross-Gender Monitor appointed by CSC in 1998 to monitor implementation of the protocol found extensive violations of the protocol, and her final report of 2001 recommended that men not be employed as front-line primary care workers (CHRC 2004: 42). More recent interviews with women inmates confirm that the protocol is not always followed (CHRC 2004: 42). It is difficult to know how many incidents of sexual or other harassment by male guards occur since fear of reprisal and lack of faith in the current grievance system keeps many women offenders from making official complaints about inappropriate behaviour by guards (CHRC 2004; OCI 2004). While the CHRC noted that many women prisoners are supportive of the presence of male staff and recommended that CSC take steps to ensure that the protocol regarding male staff be strictly respected, the Canadian Association of Elizabeth Fry Societies (2005b) and the Office of the Correctional Investigator (OCI 2005a) continue to oppose the use of men as front-line staff in women's prisons.

Women consistently report the use of segregation, or "the hole," used to isolate prisoners from the general inmate population, as one of the harshest aspects of prison conditions (Comack 1996; Martel 1999). Research suggests that women experience segregation as rejection, abandonment, invisibility, and a denial of their existence and are more deeply affected by the punishment than men are (CHRC 2004: 45). Under the law, segregation is only supposed to be used when there is no other reasonable alternative and when there are reasonable grounds to believe that an inmate may jeopardize the safety of the prison, herself, or the general inmate population. However, in 2002–03, among a population of 376 women, there were 265 admissions to administrative segregation, of which 83 (31 percent) lasted for longer than ten days (CSC 2005a: 29, 32). Of particular concern is that Aboriginal women appear to be singled out for segregation more than other inmates. While Aboriginal women constituted 28 percent of all federally incarcerated women in 2003, they accounted for 35.5 percent of involuntary admissions to segregation (CSC 2005a: 29). In its report, the CHRC (2004: 45) noted that as of March 31, 2003, one Aboriginal woman had been in segregation for 587 days. The commission further stated that segregation "does not further women's rehabilitation and it often jeopardizes a woman's safety and mental health by exacerbating her distress" (CHRC 2004: 45). As Joane Martel (1999) documents in her study of women's experiences of segregation in prison, the process is about coping with loneliness, deprivation, ruptured relationships, enforced idleness, and apprehensions about mental deterioration. As a general rule, women reported living in more severe conditions when segregated in provincial prisons than in federal institutions, although federal institutions themselves showed significant differences in conditions of segregation. In all prisons, women's descriptions of their experiences were uniformly similar, emphasizing the cruelty of segregation and the anxiety and fear associated with being "caged." "Emily," for example, describes segregation as "extreme mental torture and a gradual creation of unfeeling, uncaring dehumanization" (Martel 1999: 98).

The CHRC report, once again echoing the recommendation of the Arbour and other reports over the years, called for implementation of independent adjudication for decisions related to involuntary segregation. CSC's action plan on the report did not accept this recommendation, committing only to examining alternatives to segregation and to establishing a pilot project at Edmonton Institution for Women to review and report back in 2008 on cases of all women in long-term segregation (CSC 2005c, 2006).

None of the many pains of imprisonment compares with the separation of women from their children. Much more than is the case for men, women prisoners suffer the stress of worrying about the care and placement of their children, the risk of losing them to child welfare authorities, and prison policies and rules that make it difficult to see them (Faith 1993; Labrecque 1995; Martin 1997; Wine 1992). Over the years, federal and provincial corrections officials have made isolated efforts to facilitate women's relationships with their children, but such programs continue to be limited and inadequate. At the provincial level, the Burnaby Correctional Centre in British Columbia and the Portage Correctional Institution in Manitoba have had infant live-in programs that allowed babies to stay with their mothers. Due to overcrowding and other problems, neither of these programs is now operational. Similarly, the initial recommendation in *Creating Choices*, reaffirmed in CSC's latest program strategy for federal women offenders (Fortin 2004) that children be allowed to live with their mothers is not being fulfiled. Although regional women's facilities are required to offer the Mother-Child Program to eligible inmates, this requirement is based on long-term accommodation availability; there is currently only one child living with its mother.

Health is another serious issue. The OCI (2004: 20–34) reports that from 2002 to 2004, it received complaints from eighty-nine federally sentenced women about lack of access to and quality of health care provided by the institution. Women interviewed in a provincial prison reported a range of minor and major health problems and identified access to better health care as the most important non-criminogenic need (Monster and Miccuci 2005). Women are also much more likely than men to suffer from various mental health problems and to report depression and suicide attempts (CHRC 2004; CSC 2003; Loucks and Zamble 1994; Daigle, Alaire, and Lefebvre 1999). More than two-thirds (71 percent) of the women in maximum-security had attempted suicide compared with 21 percent of maximum-security males (CHRC 2004: 39). Other problems such as high-anxiety levels, eating disorders, and self-injury are also more prevalent among women prisoners (Shaw 1994). The range and severity of these problems are greatest for Aboriginal women and women serving the longest sentences, although a Quebec study found that provincially sentenced women reported significantly more suicide attempts than federally incarcerated women (Wichmann, Serin, and Abracen 2002; Daigle, Alaire, and Lefebvre 1999).

One manifestation of the desperation experienced by women in prison is the frequency of self-injurious behaviour. The use of sharp-edged objects as a means of self-mutilation has been a long-standing problem in women's prisons. Research suggests a link between self-injurious behaviour and prior sexual abuse, and indicates that "slashing" offers women temporary relief and distraction from the emotional pain, tension, and anger of imprisonment (Wichmann, Serin, and Abracen 2002; Kershaw and Lasovich 1991; Hoffman and Law 1995; Shaw 1994). The punitive response of segregating women who injure themselves or attempt suicide only tends to increase their desperation (Faith 1993; Shaw 2000). Another common response is to prescribe psychotropic drugs of various kinds (tranquillizers, antidepressants, sleeping pills). Drugs have long been used as a means of controlling female prisoners, and, as is the case in the general population, such medications are much more likely to be prescribed to women than men (PSEPC 2005; Dobash, Dobash, and Gutteridge 1986; Hattem 1994).

The realities of the prison environment, together with more women being admitted to federal prisons, severely limits all programming. Women prisoners repeatedly told the CHRC that many programs are not offered at all institutions and there are long waiting lists for some programs (CHRC 2004: 50). The Office of the Correctional Investigator (OCI 2004: 9–11, 2005b: 16) consistently receives complaints from federal female prisoners about correctional plans that are not completed within the mandated timeframes; long waiting lists for core programming and for employment programs; lack of access to long-term individualized psychological counselling; and few opportunities for acquiring meaningful and marketable employment skills in prisons. Many women have to waive their right to a parole hearing because inadequate programming means they have been unable to fulfil their correctional plan.

Programming to address women prisoners' emotional and mental-health problems is particularly inadequate. The recent suicides (and subsequent inquests) of an inmate at the provincial prison in Thunder Bay and another at the "special living environment" (i.e., mental health unit) of

> The Office of the Correctional Investigator receives *daily* phone calls from women prisoners struggling with mental health issues.

the Grand Valley Institute underscore the problem (CAEFS 2005b). The OCI (2004: 22) reports that it receives *daily* phone calls from women struggling to deal with their serious mental health issues while in prison. Current correctional mental health programs are seen to fall far short of women-centred concepts designed to empower and support women and instead perpetuate traditional practices focused on regulation and control. Shoshana Pollack (2005: 72) argues that women prisoners are subject to excessive psychiatric labelling, and the resulting treatment constructs women prisoners as disorderly and disordered, and in need of "taming." Kathleen Kendall (2000) points out that most of the counselling offered to women in prison is centred on helping them cope with the emotional distress of their confinement and does not address the roots of their problems. Generally, women tend to find prison programs of limited benefit because they primarily reflect authorities' concerns with making prisoners more "manageable" within the prison environment rather than preparing women for their release and reintegration in society (Horii 2000).

In the new regional prisons, the programming strategy ostensibly designed to give women opportunities for "empowerment" and "meaningful choices" in a "supportive environment" has penalized women for failing to meet institutional expectations concerning "rehabilitation." While the system rewards women who participate in programs such as substance abuse, parenting skills, and vocational and educational training by granting them lower security classifications, women who refuse to attend these programs may find themselves labelled as "risky" and subject to higher classifications (Hannah-Moffat 1999). Women at the Edmonton Institution for Women cited their lack of choice and control over program selection as a major concern. As one woman stated:

> They offer you a program and your name's on the list to go and you go because if you don't go there'll be an impact right there, you know, it's against you. Whether you think you need it or not. And because they design a wonderful Correction Plan for you, that you have very little input into. It's what they perceive your problems to be. (Gironella 1999: 42)

As the CHRC (2004: 50–51) documents, the systematic flaws in how programming needs are identified and poor access to programming have unique implications for

Aboriginal federally sentenced women. The increasing numbers of Aboriginal federally sentenced women, and their multi-faceted problems, underscores the urgency for programming designed to meet their special needs. Although the CSC has recently created some new programs specifically for Aboriginal women offenders (Fortin 2004: 21), it has not fulfiled its promise of more than a decade ago to create a separate but parallel program strategy for Aboriginal offenders. Women prisoners interviewed by the CHRC (2004: 51) indicated that women who were not located at the Healing Lodge had very limited access to Aboriginal programming. Moreover, the original vision of Aboriginal culture and spirituality defining the management, services, and programs offered to women in the lodge has been eroded by security concerns and the implementation of standard prison programming (Hayman 2000; Monture-Angus 2000, 2002). Aboriginal women with maximum-security classifications are not allowed to reside at the Healing Lodge; few senior staff positions at the lodge are consistently held by Aboriginal people and most of the programming is the same as in all regional facilities — inadequate (Monture-Angus 2002: 18–20).

> Systematic flaws in how programming needs are identified and poor access to programming have unique implications for Aboriginal federally sentenced women.

The current reality of women's experiences in prison underscore the incompatibility of realizing concepts such as rehabilitation, empowerment, and meaningful choices in the context of a system still dominated by traditional concerns with punishment, security, and discipline.

Current Issues in Women's Prisons

Provincial/Territorial Prisons

Since most recent research and reform efforts have been directed at federally incarcerated prisoners, comparatively little attention has been directed at improving conditions for the larger numbers of women incarcerated in provincial/ territorial prisons. These women continue to experience discrimination and to have poorer programs and services than male prisoners and federally sentenced women.

> Little attention has been directed at improving conditions for women in provincial/territorial prisons, compared to those for federally sentenced women.

Because there are relatively few women in provincial/territorial prisons and they are scattered across a wide range of facilities and serving short sentences, it is impossible to offer worthwhile vocational and educational programs or counselling. Provincial prisons are overcrowded and in some facilities — the Thunder Bay Jail, for example — women are rarely able to access any services or programming (CAEFS 2005b). Overarching these problems, one of the most significant barriers to meeting women's needs is the requirement that staff work within the framework of power and control, which leaves many women prisoners feeling that they cannot trust staff (Comack 1996).

In Manitoba, severe overcrowding at the Portage women's prison, built in 1893, has led to worsened living conditions, cancellation of many programs, and overworked and harried staff. The Manitoba government has announced that a new jail will open in 2009 and possibly house federally sentenced women as well. Due to government cut-backs, the Burnaby Correctional Centre for Women (BCCW), which housed both provincially and federally sentenced inmates, was closed in 2004 and the women moved to other prisons. Federally sentenced women went to the new Fraser Valley Institution in Abbotsford, B.C., while provincially sentenced women were moved to the Alouette Correctional Centre for Women in Maple Ridge, B.C., which was previously a men's medium-security prison. Maximum-security provincial or federal prisoners were transferred to the Surrey Pre-trial Centre, a high-security men's facility, which outraged prisoners' advocacy groups and partly led to the investigation and 2004 report of the Canadian Human Rights Commission. The closure of BCCW was intended as a cost-saving strategy, but the end result is that the number of women incarcerated is likely to increase as the total available prison beds for women in B.C. has doubled from 150 to 300 (Prisonjustice.ca 2004).

Federal Prisons

The current state of women's corrections must be viewed within the context of the vision for change initiated by *Creating Choices* in 1990. The central theme of the report — that women's correctional needs are profoundly different from men's and that the correctional system must be gender-sensitive — led to major changes in the treatment of federally sentenced women. The Arbour Report, which criticized CSC's disturbing lack of commitment to the ideals of justice, provided further impetus for reform and a set of eighty-seven specific recommendations designed to ensure that future correctional practices would meet the needs of women offenders. In its status report on women's corrections since the release of the Arbour Report, CSC (2006) claims to have taken decisive action on virtually all the recommendations of the Arbour Report over the past decade. Nonetheless, recent reports and commissions continue to document the failure of CSC to implement the key recommendations of the Arbour Report (CHRC 2004; OCI 2005b; CAEFS 2006b). A decade of reform efforts have not ameliorated some of the central problems in women's prisons, including overclassification, inadequate programs and services, and harsh, punitive, and illegal treatment of women prisoners. Some of the problems faced by women in prison are due to inherent flaws in the model of women's corrections, described in *Creating Choices*, such as the failure to address the issue of violent women. Others are related to the implementation process of *Creating Choices*, which saw feminist ideals undermined in response to public concerns, and to institutional dynamics and the requirements of CSC. These events raise broader questions about the formidable obstacles facing feminists attempting to achieve fundamental changes in the context of traditional prison structures.

> A decade of reform efforts has not ameliorated some of the central problems in women's prisons.

The CHRC (2004) report stated that the process of transforming women's corrections in order to achieve a truly women-centred correctional system must begin with security classification, which is the foundation of the correctional system. The classification and assessment of federally sentenced offenders have a critical impact on decisions about where women are incarcerated, how they are managed and supervised, what kind of programming is available to them, and the conditions under which they are released. In particular, the commission (2004: 71) argued that the "generally lower-risk profile of most federally sentenced women has been acknowledged for many years, but it has not yet been fully reflected in correctional services relating to their custody and supervision." The problems associated with current security classification practices that systematically misclassify women are part of a broader phenomenon in modern penal policy. In particular, the postmodern prison has increasingly embraced a model that relies on the actuarial techniques of risk assessment to manage prison populations (Hannah-Moffat 1999). Crime is regarded as a threat to public safety that can be minimized through the presumably objective and scientific calculations developed to determine a prisoner's "risk score" and to assign a security classification. As applied, however, the concept of

> The generally lower-risk profile of federally sentenced women is not reflected in correctional services custody and supervision practices.

risk is gendered and discriminatory because it is not designed to assess women, and the bar used to label offenders as "risky" or "dangerous" is lower for women than for men; for example, the classification of Lisa Neve as a "dangerous offender" in 1994 (overturned in 1999). Her most serious crime, aggravated assault, fell far short of the typical offences of murder, serial sexual assaults, and pedophilia for which men have been designated as dangerous offenders. As of March 2006, 40 women (10 percent of federally incarcerated inmates) are classified as maximum-security and the maximum-security units are full in all but the newly opened Fraser Valley prison (CSC 2006: 12; CAEFS 2006b: 11).

Over the last fifteen years, the perception of women prisoners has shifted from "high need, low risk" to "high need, high risk." The much-publicized events of April 1994 at the Kingston Prison for Women, together with escapes, murder, and assaults on guards at the regional facilities in Truro and Edmonton, have contributed to exaggerated perceptions of the dangerousness of women prisoners. In addition, the risk-management classification scheme utilized for federally sentenced women has had the effect of emphasizing the criminogenic character of women's needs — so much so that the distinction between need and risk has been virtually obliterated (Hannah-Moffat 1999). The characteristics previously considered problems to be addressed therapeutically — such as a history of abuse, self-injury, or mental-health problems — have been redefined as risk factors and used to justify increased security classifications. As a result, women with mental health issues, cognitive limitations, and substance abuse dependency are dispro-

> Aboriginal women and women with mental health issues, cognitive limitations, and substance abuse dependency are disproportionately classified as maximum security.

portionately classified as maximum-security (CHRC 2004: 28).

The concept of risk is not only gendered, but also racialized. As we have seen, a disproportionately high percentage of Aboriginal women are classified as maximum-security. As of 2003, Aboriginal women accounted for 29 percent of women incarcerated and fully 46 percent of women classified as maximum-security (CHRC 2004: 28). One of the most adverse effects of a maximum-security rating for Aboriginal women is that they are not permitted to live at the Healing Lodge, which CSC classifies as a medium-security facility. Although *Creating Choices* clearly intended that all federally sentenced Aboriginal women would have the option of serving their sentences at the Healing Lodge, many of those who might benefit most from that possibility will never have the opportunity. More generally, as access to programming and services in secure units is problematic, the overclassification of women offenders, particularly Aboriginal women, limits their ability to reintegrate successfully into the community (OCI 2005b).

At the other end of the continuum is the plight of the 34 percent of inmates (136 women) designated as minimum-security (CSC 2006: 12). There is only one minimum-security facility for federally sentenced women, the Isabel McNeill Minimum Security House in Kingston, which can accommodate only thirteen women. However, women are reluctant to transfer there because of the ongoing threat of its closure, and as of April

2006 it housed only five women (CSC 2006: 11). All other women classified as minimum-security reside within the more restrictive environment of regional women's prisons, which are supposedly medium-security facilities. The lack of minimum-security facilities for federally sentenced prisoners prevents them from being housed in the least restrictive conditions possible as mandated by law — another case of gender discrimination in the correctional system. While minimum-security women in regional facilities live with physical barriers such as fences, razor wire, and cameras, their male counterparts tend to be housed in a number of minimum-security prisons across Canada that do not even have fences (CHRC 2004: 47).

Feminism and Prison Reform

Creating Choices is probably one of the most powerful things that has ever been written by so many women, but it's still only a piece of paper. And sometimes I look at it and think it's not worth the paper it's written on.
— Prisoner, Edmonton Institution for Women (Gironella 1999: 35)

Given the realities of women's imprisonment in Canada, it is understandable that many of those directly or indirectly involved in conceiving and implementing *Creating Choices* are disillusioned with the prospects of achieving significant reforms in women's corrections. However, history teaches us that the various problems encountered over the years by feminists attempting to change a male-dominated correctional system are neither new nor unique. Feminists' reform attempts have always been fraught with the inherent dangers of reinforcing the very structures, ideologies, and practices that serve to perpetuate existing prison conditions and the expansion of prisons. The institutional dynamics of prison regimes, notoriously resistant to change, exert a seemingly irresistible pressure to revert to traditional, established, and familiar correctional policies and practices. Moreover, history serves to temper our expectations that the establishment of new women's prisons will put an end to harsh and cruel punishment. After all, separate women's prisons, including the Prison for Women, were once seen as solutions that promised to initiate a new era in the treatment of women prisoners.

Although the woman-centred philosophy of *Creating Choices* was hailed as revolutionary and innovative, feminist involvement in prison reform has deep historical roots. For well over a century, feminists have been trying to implement gender-specific prison reform strategies based on a core commitment to the principles of equality and justice for women prisoners. The feminist approach has also undergone considerable change over time, especially with the emergence of new ideas on the meaning of equality and woman-centred reforms (Boritch 1997; CHRC 2004; Hannah-Moffat 1994, 2001). The acceptance of feminist principles in itself does not yield a clear, specific, or unanimous vision for social change, because feminist ideology can include many different approaches to prison reform.

Initial feminist involvement with prison reform in the nineteenth century embraced the ideology of "separate spheres," which accepted the belief that a woman's primary role was that of wife and mother (Cott 1987). The "first-wave" feminists advocated the establishment of separate prisons for women, in which rehabilitation rather than punishment would be the primary goal. They argued for the necessity of developing policies that recognized that women prisoners had very different needs from men. In Canada, their efforts led to the 1875 establishment of the first separate prison for women, the Mercer Reformatory in Toronto (Strange 1986). From a contemporary perspective, it is easy to lose sight of the monumental achievement that a separate prison, founded on prevailing feminist ideals and managed and staffed by women, represented for the times. These early feminists, with their focus on the notion of "maternal care," laid the groundwork for a correctional model that stressed gender-specific programs delivered in a supportive environment. Ultimately, the Mercer Reformatory, like other women's reformatories throughout North America in the nineteenth century (Rafter 1990), failed to live up to these ideals. They became primarily places of punishment, largely because of the conventional and complacent attitudes of successive male bureaucrats who lacked the insight to comprehend what feminists were trying to achieve (Oliver 1994).

By the 1960s feminist reform efforts became increasingly influenced by the idea of "formal equality," which stresses equal rights and equal treatment for male and female prisoners. In this symmetrical model of gender relations, the focus is to remove practices and policies based on the ideology of separate spheres and so-called natural differences between men and women (Daly 1989, 1990). "Second-wave feminists" involved in these reform efforts sought to further the objective of equality by publicizing conditions in women's prisons and revealing how correctional practices and policies discriminated against female offenders. In addition, by the 1980s reformers increasingly used the courts to push for implementation of equal-rights legislation and to abolish the unequal treatment of female prisoners.

By the late 1980s many feminists had come to see that the traditional equality doctrine was restrictive and had failed to achieve important objectives as a reform strategy. In response, they began to advocate a concept of "substantive equality," an "asymmetrical" model of gender relations that stressed differences between men and women as well as diversity among women in terms of their experiences, life circumstances, and vantage points (Daly 1990; Hannah-Moffat 1994). According to this view, attempts at achieving formal legal equality for women do not provide substantive equality and can even result in a general worsening of women's situations. The implication is that there can be no absolutes as to what constitutes equality or justice for women, because each woman has her own unique situational context, including life experiences, race, culture, and class. Correctional policies, therefore, must accommodate the different needs and experiences of women as a group, while being sensitive to the specific needs of each individual woman.

As its title suggests, *Creating Choices* elaborated a philosophy and a woman-centred reform agenda that emphasizes the concept of substantive equality and gives priority to gender over all other factors. So, while it stressed the diversity of women's experiences and needs, the report also gave particular emphasis to the idea that women prisoners share basically the same problems encountered by other women in a society characterized by inequality and in which women constitute a subordinate class. As Hannah-Moffat (2001) points out, this emphasis on shared gender-based oppression tends to minimize the heterogeneity that characterizes women's lives and the ways in which women's experiences are differentiated, depending on factors such as race, class, sexual orientation, employment, status, education, and motherhood. In addition, the fact of their involuntary confinement remains a crucial difference between women prisoners and all other women. Consequently, overemphasizing common disempowerment of women serves to trivialize women's experiences as prisoners. Moreover, it leads to the erroneous belief that prison conditions for women will necessarily improve if prisons are staffed and managed by women, even if the wider institutional framework and dynamics of prison regimes go unchallenged.

One of the dangers of feminist involvement in prison reform has always been that by "working within the system," feminists are necessarily caught in the vicious cycle of reinforcing and expanding the notion of incarceration. Such efforts, most recently reflected in *Creating Choices*, fail to challenge the notion of incarceration as an appropriate response to the crimes of most female offenders; consequently, they ignore possible alternatives to imprisonment. Because it is assumed that a women-centred approach can be achieved in a prison setting, the model legitimizes the incarceration of women. As Karlene Faith (1993: 145) predicted more than a decade ago, the building of five new regional prisons cannot be seen as an advance over the existence of one centralized prison, because when "those beds are filled, advocates of carceral 'solutions' will propose the construction of yet more women's facilities." The numbers of women incarcerated indeed continues to increase, and the regional facilities have been overcrowded almost from the time they opened. The long-term objective should instead be to reduce the failures, costs, and inequities associated with women's prisons by reducing the use of prisons. Such an undertaking obviously requires a radical change in correctional thinking — a change that would move beyond a "system-improvement" approach towards a serious consideration and implementation of non-carceral alternatives for women offenders.

> One of the dangers of feminist involvement in prison reform is reinforcing and expanding the notion of incarceration.

It would be unfair and erroneous to suggest that reform efforts within the institutional framework cannot improve prison conditions for women, or that this objective should not be vigorously pursued. Certainly, the physical design of the regional prisons today is a significant improvement over the oppressive Prison for Women, and undoubtedly some federally sentenced women have benefited from the restructuring of women's prisons over the past decade. But in general women's prisons have not reduced female criminality; rather, they have largely exacerbated the pre-existing problems of women offenders.

Women prisoners remain faced with a system ill-designed and ill-equipped to deal either with the problems that brought them into prison or those they encounter while there. Prisons do not deter women whose lives are characterized by inequality, poverty, and abuse, and the prison environment is wholly incompatible with rehabilitation. Prisons necessarily fail because they do not, and cannot, address the broader structural social, economic, and political forces that lead women to commit crimes. These are complex issues that can only be dealt with adequately outside the prison system. To expect prisons as they are — oriented towards concerns with security and punishment — to deal with the failings of society's institutions, and the resulting long-standing and diverse problems of women prisoners, is an unrealistic dream.

DISCUSSION QUESTIONS

1. What factors led to the appointment of the Task Force on Federally Sentenced Women to investigate and report on prison conditions for female federal prisoners?

2. What are the critical differences between the TFFSW report *Creating Choices* and the many government reports that preceded it?

3. What are some of the philosophical and practical problems related to the new regional facilities for federally sentenced women? Is it possible for these problems to be resolved?

4. What are some of the strengths and weaknesses of the woman-centred, holistic approach advocated in *Creating Choices?*

5. Should women prisoners be allowed to keep their children with them in prison?

6. Should the policy imposing an automatic two-year maximum-security classification on all offenders serving life sentences be continued?

7. What are some of the key problems in women's corrections documented in the 1996 Arbour Report and the 2004 Canadian Human Rights Commission Report? Why are many of the same problems repeatedly identified?

8. Should a wholly separate correctional system for Aboriginal women offenders be implemented?

9. What are the most important issues that need to be addressed in future reform efforts in women's corrections?

GLOSSARY OF TERMS

Aboriginal Healing Lodge: the Okimaw Ohci Aboriginal Healing Lodge, on the Nekaneet Reserve in Saskatchewan, is one of the five regional facilities built as a result of the recommendation of *Creating Choices: The Task Force Report on Federally Sentenced Women.* The original vision of this Healing Lodge was that Aboriginal culture and spirituality would define the management and programs for Aboriginal federally sentenced women. The Healing Lodge now faces concerns that security and prison standards are eroding the initial vision.

Creating Choices: Report of the Task Force on Federally Sentenced Women: the most important government report detailing the abysmal conditions for federally sentenced women in Canada. This report detailed conditions inside the Prison for Women at Kingston (P4W), such as the lack of proper educational, recreational, and therapeutic programs; geographic dislocation (leaving so many women serving time in an institution far away from family and supportive communities); overclassification in terms of security of women prisoners; the lack of programming for First Nations Women; and self-injurious behaviours and suicides inside the prison. What sets this report apart is the feminist philosophy and the recognition of unique problems of Aboriginal women.

Commission of Inquiry into Certain Events at the Prison for Women in Kingston by Madam Justice Louise Arbour (the Arbour Report): An investigation commissioned to investigate conditions at the Prison for Women at Kingston following a brief but violent confrontation between correctional staff and six inmates. The report documented extensive violations of law and policy in the treatment of women prisoners that extended to all levels of the correctional bureaucracy and made eighty-seven specific recommendations for reforming women's corrections.

Dynamic Security: created through enhancing the support, relationships, and interactions between staff and inmates; as opposed to traditional physical security, which is represented in the form of fences, high-tech surveillance, and discipline.

Federally Sentenced Women: female offenders sentenced for two years or more who serve time in federal institutions.

Protecting Their Rights: A Systematic Review of Human Rights in Correctional Services for Federally Sentenced Women (Canadian Human Rights Commission 2004): The most recent far-reaching investigation of the treatment of federally sentenced women. The report documents extensive instances of discrimination and the violation of human rights of federally sentenced women with respect to issues such as overclassification, segregation, and programming. Particularly affected are Aboriginal women and women with mental health issues. It makes nineteen broad-ranging recommendations to alleviate the systematic discrimination experienced by federally sentenced women.

Regional Facilities: after the Prison for Women at Kingston (P4W) was closed, it was replaced by four regional correctional facilities and the Healing Lodge for Aboriginal women. These facilities, all opened between 1995 and 1997 and designed for thirty to seventy women, were intended to operate on a woman-centred philosophy of empowerment, dynamic security, and a holistic model of healing.

Segregation: a practice used to isolate prisoners from the general inmate population for a variety of reasons, from disciplinary practices and punishment to safety and administrative segregation.

Self-Injurious Behaviour: examples of incarcerated women using sharp-edged objects as a means of self-mutilation — slashing; eating disorders, and suicide.

Woman-Centred Philosophy: an approach that addresses the needs of women and recognizes the link between women in conflict with the law and issues involving the status of women and showing that women in prison have more in common with other women than with men in prison.

SUGGESTED READINGS

Boritch, Helen. 1997. *Fallen Women: Female Crime and Criminal Justice in Canada*. Scarborough, ON: ITP Nelson.

Faith, Karlene. 1993. *Unruly Women: The Politics of Confinement and Resistance*. Vancouver: Press Gang.

Hannah-Moffat, Kelly. 2001. *Punishment in Disguise: Penal Governance and Federal Imprisonment of Women in Canada*. Toronto: University of Toronto Press.

Hannah-Moffat, Kelly, and Margaret Shaw (eds.). 2000. *An Ideal Prison? Critical Essays on Women's Imprisonment in Canada*. Halifax: Fernwood Publishing.

REFERENCES

Adelberg, Ellen, and Claudia Currie. 1993. *In Conflict with the Law: Women and the Canadian Justice System*. Vancouver: Press Gang Publishers.

Arbour, The Honourable Louise. 1996. *Commission of Inquiry into Certain Events at the Prison for Women in Kingston*. Ottawa: Public Works and Government Services Canada.

Balfour, G. 2006. "Introduction." In G. Balfour and E. Comack. (eds.), *Criminalizing Women: Gender and (In)Justice in Neoliberal Times.* Halifax: Fernwood Publishing.

Beattie, John M. 1977. *Attitudes Towards Crime and Punishment in Upper Canada, 1830–1850: A Documentary Study.* Toronto: Centre of Criminology, University of Toronto.

Beattie, Karen. 2005. "Adult Correctional Services in Canada, 2003/04." *Juristat* 25, 8, Canadian Centre for Justice Statistics.

Belcourt, R., T. Nouwens, and L. Lefebvre. 1993. "Examining the Unexamined: Recidivism among Female Offenders." *Forum on Corrections Research* 5, 3.

Bloom, Barbara. 1999. "Gender-Responsive Programming for Women Offenders: Guiding Principles and Practices." *Forum on Corrections Research* 11, 3.

Boritch, Helen. 1997. *Fallen Women: Female Crime and Criminal Justice in Canada.* Scarborough, ON: ITP Nelson.

CAEFS (Canadian Association of Elizabeth Fry Societies). 2000. "Recent Issues Impacting Women's Imprisonment in Canada." Available at <http://www.elizabethfry.ca/Icopa.htm> accessed July 2007.

_____. 2005a. "Fact Sheet." Available at <http://www.elizabethfry.ca/eweek05/factsht.htm> accessed April 14, 2006.

_____. 2005b. "CAEFS' 2005 Annual Report." Available at <http://www.elizabethfry.ca/areport/2004-05/english/ed.pdf> accessed April 15, 2006.

_____. 2006a. "Health and Mental Health." Available at <http://www.elizabethfry.ca/week06/pdf/methlth.pdf> accessed May 1, 2006.

_____. 2006b. "10th Anniversary of the Arbour commission Report." Available at <http://www.elizabethfry.ca/arbr10e.pdf> accessed May 9, 2006.

_____. 2007. "Human and Fiscal Costs of Prison." Fact sheets. Available at <http://www.elizabethfry.ca/eweek07/pdf/costs.pdf > accessed July 2007.

Chesney-Lind, Meda, and Lisa Pasko. 2004. "Sentencing Women to Prison: Equality Without Justice." In M. Chesney-Lind and L. Pasko (eds.), *The Female Offender: Girls, Women and Crime.* Thousand Oaks, CA: Sage Publications.

CHRC (Canadian Human Rights Commission). 2004. *Protecting Their Rights: A Systematic Review of Human Rights in Correctional Services for Federally Sentenced Women.* Ottawa.

Comack, Elizabeth. 1996. *Women in Trouble: Connecting Women's Law Violations to Their Histories of Abuse.* Halifax: Fernwood Publishing.

_____. 2000. "The Prisoning of Women: Meeting Women's Needs." In K. Hannah-Moffat and M. Shaw (eds.), *An Ideal Prison? Critical Essays on Women's Imprisonment in Canada.* Halifax: Fernwood Publishing.

Cook, Sandy, and Susanne Davies (eds.). 1999. *Harsh Punishment: International Experiences of Women's Imprisonment.* Boston: Northeastern University Press.

Cooper, Sheila. 1993. "The Evolution of the Federal Women's Prison." In E. Adelberg and C. Currie (eds.), *In Conflict with the Law: Women and the Canadian Justice System.* Vancouver: Press Gang.

Cott, Nancy F. 1987. *The Grounding of Modern Feminism.* New Haven: Yale University Press.

CSC (Correctional Service Canada). 2002a. *Regional Women's Facilities Operational Plan.* Office of the Deputy Commissioner for Women. Available at <http://www.csc-scc.gc.ca/text/prgrm/fsw/fsw12/region_women_facilt.fsw12_e.shtml> accessed April 13, 2006.

_____. 2002b. *The Transformation of Federal Corrections for Women.* Available at <http://www.csc-scc.gc.ca/text/pblct/choix/index_e.shtml> accessed April 13, 2006.

_____. 2003. *Secure Unit Operational Plan: Intensive Intervention.* Office of the Deputy Commissioner for Women. Available at <http://www.csc-scc.gc.ca/text/prgrm/fsw/secureunitop/secure-unitop-2003_e.shtml> accessed April 13, 2006.

_____. 2005a. *Women Offender Statistical Overview 2003.* Available at <http://www.csc-scc.gc.ca/text/prgrm/fsw/wos14/statisticaloverview_wos14_eshtml> accessed March 28, 2006.

_____. 2005b. *Basic Facts About the Correctional Service of Canada.* Available at <http://www.csc-scc.gc.ca/text/pb/ct/basicfacts/basicfacts_e.pdf> accessed May 1, 2006.

_____. 2005c. *csc Action Plan in Response to the Report of the Canadian Human Rights Commission*. Available at <http://www.csc-gc.ca/text/prgrm/fsw/gender4/CHRC_response_shtml> accessed April 13, 2006.

_____. 2006. *Ten-Year Status Report on Women's Corrections 1996–2006*. Available at <http://www.csc-gc.ca/text/prgrm/fsw/wos24/tenyearstatusreport_e.pdf> accessed May 2, 2006.

Daigle, Marc, Mylene Alaire, and Patrick Lefebvre. 1999. "The Problem of Suicide Among Female Prisoners." *Forum on Corrections Research* 11, 3.

Daly, Kathleen. 1989. "Criminal Justice Ideologies and Practices in Different Voices: Some Feminist Questions about Justice." *International Journal of Sociology of Law* 17, 1.

_____. 1990. "Reflections on Feminist Legal Thought." *Social Justice* 17, 3.

Dobash, Russell P., R. Emerson Dobash, and Sue Gutteridge. 1986. *The Imprisonment of Women*. New York: Basil Blackwell.

Faith, Karlene. 1993. *Unruly Women: The Politics of Confinement and Resistance*. Vancouver: Press Gang.

_____. 1999. "Transformative Justice versus Re-entrenched Correctionalism: The Canadian Experience." In S. Cook and S. Davies (eds.), *Harsh Punishment: International Experiences of Women's Imprisonment*. Boston: Northeastern University Press.

Finn, Anne, Shelley Trevethan, Gisele Carriere, and Melanie Kowalski. 1999. "Female Inmates, Aboriginal Inmates, and Inmates Serving Life Sentences: A One Day Snapshot." *Juristat* 19, 5.

Fortin, Doris. 2004. *Program Strategy for Women Offenders*. Programs for Women Offenders. Correctional Services of Canada. Ottawa.

Gironella, Fiona D. 1999. "Creating Choices or Redefining Control? Prisoners from the Edmonton Institution for Women Share their Standpoint." Unpublished research project. Edmonton: University of Alberta

Hannah-Moffat, Kelly. 1991. "Creating Choices or Repeating History: Canadian Female Offenders and Correctional Reform." *Social Justice* 18, 3.

_____. 1994. "Unintended Consequences of Feminism and Prison Reform." *Forum on Corrections Research* 6, 1.

_____. 1995. "Feminine Fortresses: Woman-Centered Prisons?" *The Prison Journal* 75, 2.

_____. 1999. "Moral Agent or Actuarial Subject: Risk and Canadian Women's Imprisonment." *Theoretical Criminology* 3, 1.

_____. 2001. *Punishment in Disguise: Penal Governance and Federal Imprisonment of Women in Canada*. Toronto: University of Toronto Press.

Hannah-Moffat, Kelly, and Margaret Shaw (eds.). 2000. *An Ideal Prison? Critical Essays on Women's Imprisonment in Canada*. Halifax: Fernwood Publishing.

Hattem, Tina. 1994. "The Realities of Life Imprisonment for Women Convicted of Murder." *Forum on Corrections Research* 6, 1.

Hayman, Stephanie. 2000. "Prison Reform and Incorporation: Lessons From Britain and Canada." In Kelly Hannah-Moffat and Margaret Shaw (eds.), *An Ideal Prison? Critical Essays on Women's Imprisonment in Canada*. Halifax: Fernwood Publishing.

Hoffman, L.E., and M.A. Law. 1995. *Federally Sentenced Women on Conditional Release: Survey of Community Supervisors*. Ottawa: Federally Sentenced Women Program, Correctional Service of Canada.

Horii, Gayle K. 2000. "Processing Humans." In Kelly Hannah-Moffat and Margaret Shaw (eds.), *An Ideal Prison? Critical Essays on Women's Imprisonment in Canada*. Halifax: Fernwood Publishing.

Kendall, Kathleen. 2000. "Psy-Ence Fiction: Inventing the Mentally-Disordered Female Prisoner." In Kelly Hannah-Moffat and Margaret Shaw (eds.), *An Ideal Prison? Critical Essays on Women's Imprisonment in Canada*. Halifax: Fernwood Publishing.

Kershaw, Anne, and Mary Lasovich. 1991. *Rock-a-Bye Baby: A Death Behind Bars*. Toronto: McClelland and Stewart.

Labrecque. R. 1995. *Study of the Mother-Child Program*. Ottawa: Federally Sentenced Women Program, Correctional Services of Canada.

Law Society of British Columbia. 1992. *Gender Inequality in the Justice System*. Vancouver: Law Society of British Columbia.

Loucks, Alex, and Edward Zamble. 1994. "Some Comparisons of Male and Female Serious Offenders." *Forum on Corrections Research* 6, 1.

Marron, Kevin. 1996. *The Slammer: The Crisis in Canada's Prison System*. Toronto: Doubleday Canada.

Martel, Joane. 1999. *Solitude and Cold Storage: Women's Journeys of Endurance in Segregation*. Edmonton: Elizabeth Fry Society of Edmonton.

Martin, M. 1997. "Connected Mothers: A Follow-up Study of Incarcerated Women and Their Children." *Women and Criminal Justice* 8, 1.

McDonagh, Donna. 1999. "Maximum Security Women: 'Not Letting the Time Do You.'" *Forum on Corrections Research* 11, 3.

Monster, Miranda, and Anthony Micucci. 2005. "Meeting Rehabilitative Needs at a Canadian Women's Correctional Centre." *The Prison Journal* 85, 2 (June).

Monture-Angus, Patricia. 2000. "Aboriginal Women and Correctional Practice: Reflections on the Task Force on Federally Sentenced Women." In Kelly Hannah-Moffat and Margaret Shaw (eds.), *An Ideal Prison? Critical Essays on Women's Imprisonment in Canada*. Halifax: Fernwood Publishing.

_____. 2002. "The Lived Experience of Discrimination: Aboriginal Women Who are Federally Sentenced." Available at <http://www.elizabethfry.ca/submissn/aborigin/aborigin.pdf> accessed May 13, 2006.

OCI (Office of the Correctional Investigator). 2004. "Correctional Investigator's Response to the Canadian Human Rights Commission's Consultation Paper for the Special Report on the Situation of Federally Sentenced Women." Available at <http://www.oci-bec-gc.ca/reports/OCIResponse_CHRC_e.asp> accessed April 15, 2006.

_____. 2005a. "Correctional Investigator's Analysis of CSC Action Plan in Response to the Report of the Canadian Human Rights commission (2003)." Available at <http://www.oci-bec.gc.ca/reports/Response_CSCAP_e.asp> accessed April 15, 2006.

_____. 2005b. "Annual Report of the Correctional Investigator 2004–2005." Available at <http://www.oci-bec.gc.ca/reports/AR200405_download_e.asp> accessed May 1, 2006.

Oliver, Peter. 1994. "'To Govern by Kindness': The First Two Decades of the Mercer Reformatory for Women." In Jim Phillips, Tina Loo, and Susan Lewthwaite (eds.), *Essays in the History of Canadian Law*, Vol. V. Toronto: Osgoode Society.

Owen, Barbara. 1999. "Women and Imprisonment in the United States: The Gendered Consequences of the U.S. Imprisonment Binge." In Sandy Cook and Susanne Davies (eds.)., *Harsh Punishment: International Experiences of Women's Imprisonment*. Boston; Northeastern University Press.

Pollack, Shoshana. 2005. "Taming the Shrew: Regulating Prisoners Through Women-Centered Mental Health Programming." *Critical Criminology* 13, 1.

PrisonJustice.ca. 2004. "BCCW Closed and Women Moved to New Prisons." Available at <http://www.prisonjustice.ca/starkravenarticles/sr100404_4.html> accessed March 23, 2006.

Public Safety and Emergency Preparedness Canada. 2005. *Corrections and Conditional Release: Statistical Overview*. Ottawa: Public Works and Government Services Canada.

Rafter, Nicole H. 1990. *Partial Justice*, Second edition. New Brunswick, NJ: Northeastern University Press.

Shaw, Margaret. 1993. "Reforming Federal Women's Imprisonment." In Ellen Adelberg and Claudia Currie (eds.), *In Conflict with the Law: Women and the Canadian Justice System*. Vancouver: Press Gang.

_____. 1994. "Women in Prison: A Literature Review." *Forum on Corrections Research* 6, 1.

_____. 2000. "Women, Violence and Disorder in Prisons." In Kelly Hannah-Moffat and Margaret Shaw (eds.), *An Ideal Prison? Critical Essays on Women's Imprisonment in Canada*. Halifax: Fernwood Publishing.

Sinclair, Roberta Lynn, and Roger Boe. 2002. *Canadian Federal Women Offender Profiles: Trends from 1981 to 2002*. Correctional Service of Canada. Available at <http://www.csc-scc.gc.ca/text/rsrch/reports/r131/r131_e.shtml> accessed April 1, 2006.

Sommers, Evelyn K. 1995. *Voices From Within: Women Who Have Broken the Law*. Toronto: University of Toronto Press.

Statistics Canada. 2005a. "Adult Correctional Services, Admissions to Provincial, Territorial and Federal Programs." Available at <http://www.40.statcan.ca/l01/cst01/legal30b.htm> accessed April 13, 2006.

_____. 2005b. "The Daily: Adult Correctional Services." Available at <http://www.statcan.ca/Daily/English/051216/d051216b.htm> accessed February 21, 2006.

Strange, Carolyn. 1986. "Unlocking the Doors on Women's Prison." *Resources for Feminist Research* 14, 4.

Task Force on Federally Sentenced Women. 1990. *Report of the Task Force on Federally Sentenced Women — Creating Choices*. Ottawa: Ministry of the Solicitor General.

Thomas, Jennifer. 2000. "Adult Correctional Services in Canada, 1998–99." *Juristat* 20, 3, Canadian Centre for Justice Statistics.

Trevethan, Shelley. 2000. "An Examination of Female Inmates in Canada: Characteristics and Treatment." Correctional Services Canada. Ottawa. Available at <http://www.aic.gov.au/conferences/womencorrections/trevetha.pdf> accessed May 14, 2006.

Wallace, Marnie. 2004. "Crime Statistics in Canada, 2003." *Juristat* 24, 6, Canadian Centre for Justice Statistics.

Watson, Lisa. 2004. "Managing Maximum Security Women in Federal Corrections 1989–2004." *Forum on Corrections Research* 16, 1.

Webster, Cheryl M., and Anthony N. Doob. 2004. "Classification Without Validity or Equity: An Empirical Examination of the Custody Rating Scale for Federally Sentenced Women Offenders in Canada." *Canadian Journal of Criminology and Criminal Justice* 46, 4.

Wichmann, Cherami, Ralph Serin, and Jeffrey Abracen. 2002. *Women Offenders Who Engage in Self-harm: A Comparative Investigation*. Correctional Services of Canada. Available at <http://www.csc-scc.gc.ca/text/rsrch/reports/r123/r123_e.shtml> accessed April 22, 2006.

Wiebe, Rudy, and Yvonne Johnson. 1998. *Stolen Life: The Journey of a Cree Woman*. Toronto: Alfred A. Knopf Canada.

Wine, S. 1992. "A Motherhood Issue: The Impact of Criminal Justice System Involvement on Women and their Children." Report prepared for Corrections Branch, Ministry of the Solicitpr General of Canada. Ottawa: Supply and Services Canada.

18 Doing Time

Donald Morin

KEY FACTS

> The majority of Aboriginal prisoners, as compared to non-Aboriginal prisoners, started serving time at a young age. They have been convicted of violent offences or property crime, were represented exclusively by legal aid counsel, and suffer from alcohol and substance abuse.

> Of the 3,850 admissions into Saskatchewan's provincial jails in 1998–99, 76 percent were Aboriginal. In the federal system, Aboriginal men account for 16 percent of admissions.

> Forty-two percent of victims of violent crime in Prince Albert and Regina were Aboriginal, even though Aboriginals constitute only 10 percent of the population in these two cities.

> A high percentage of men doing time have experienced violence in the homes of their biological parents, their communities, foster homes, residential schools, or prisons.

> A study of 556 Aboriginal people (50 percent of the Aboriginal inmates in the federal system in the summer of 1996) identified 88.2 percent of them as needing help with substance abuse.

> The Native Brotherhood has its roots in Saskatchewan in the early 1960s. As an umbrella group for Aboriginal prisoners, it lobbies governments on behalf of Aboriginal prisoners, and facilitates cultural and social events for Aboriginal prisoners.

Sources: Johnson 1997; Waldram 1997.

As I work on the introduction to this chapter I stumble about to find the right words. Am I writing about offenders, Aboriginal prisoners, convicts? The words are important because they have the power to label and, as such, they are very much political. After reading Gayle Horii (2000: 108), who argues, "Prisoner is the only correct term to describe a person locked into a cage or cell within a facility not of one's choice and whose quality of existence therein depends upon the keepers," I decide to use her definition. This is a quick synopsis of the prison world that I experienced. I want to introduce you to this world.

While I touch upon provincial prisons, the focus is on the federal prison system. In provincial and federal prisons on the Prairies there are many Aboriginal men serving time. It is a place that many others know only through movies, and it is a society where wrong can be right, right can be wrong, right is right, and wrong is wrong but not all the time.

The men in prison are from isolated reserves, small towns, and larger urban centres. Each has had his own unique experiences and events in life, yet there are a lot of commonalities. The majority of Aboriginal prisoners, as compared to non-Aboriginal prisoners, started serving time at a young age. They have been convicted of violent offences or property crime, were represented exclusively by legal aid counsel (appointed by the courts when the offenders cannot afford a lawyer), and suffer from alcohol and substance abuse. You will find siblings, fathers and sons, nephews and cousins, and four to five people from the same community, and increasingly it is an intergenerational issue.

I speak for no one but I try to convey how it is to do time in the Canadian prison system. As a First Nations person I am sensitive to the reality that history is not apolitical or linear; human history is about how power determines what happens to people and how gains and losses for groups of people fluctuate over time. As such, there are many factors that contribute to imprisonment.

> In prison you will find siblings, fathers and sons, nephews and cousins, and four to five people from the same community, and increasingly it is an intergenerational issue.

My account is based on personal reflections but it includes an interview with my friend Ivan, who also served time inside prison. There is movement back and forth between periods of our lives as well as between prison and the street. We are both cognizant of the future, because all people who are healing work towards the future. Ivan is a forty-one-year-old Métis originally from a community in Northern Saskatchewan. He is a father and partner, and is employed in the area of justice. I am a thirty-five-year-old Cree from Northern Saskatchewan, a father and partner, and am enrolled in sociology at the University of Saskatchewan.

Road to Prison

The prison road — juvenile centres, provincial jails, and then the federal penitentiary — while not altogether predictable, has some connections to trouble at home, foster home placements, and academic problems. Looking back I can see the path that I travelled to prison, which began in my early preteen years. I never did well academically, experienced emotional turmoil, was always angry and resentful, hated authority, and always got into "small" trouble.

Ivan's childhood is similarly characterized by foster care, trouble at home, juvenile jail, and the adult system:

> My parents died when I was young, when I was very young, and I ended up in foster homes and uhh... as a teen I was trying to find my family and came to Saskatoon to see my dad and... because of that I ran away from foster homes... and ended up under the... what's called the *Juvenile Delinquents Act* and ended up in Kilborn Hall... from there graduated to jail.

"Bridging the Cultural Divide," a survey of Aboriginal prisoners at the Saskatchewan Penitentiary, "discovered that more than 95 percent had been in either a foster home or a group home" (RCAP 1996: 129). I also want to acknowledge, however, that not everyone who lived in a foster home was abused, nor did all those who suffered abuse get into trouble or go to prison. But, arguably, their quality of life was affected.

For many of us who lived in foster homes, we quickly learned that we could not trust nor count on others to help. James Waldram, in *The Way of the Pipe* (1997: 51), quotes an Aboriginal prisoner whose reality also reflects our feelings: "I remember when I was first going into foster homes and what not, like they'd cut our hair and they'd tell us or accuse us of being culturally deprived and stuff like that. That was a common thing, they were there to teach us. If you didn't listen, you'd get a strap or you'd get this or that." The same thought patterns differ little in prison, where you expect little help.

The hostile environment of foster care, later replicated in prison, sets a pattern that teaches you much about violence and the power of violence. Mark S. Fliesher (Sacco and Kennedy 1998: 255) identifies a "defensive worldview" of offenders that consists of six traits, rejecting our lived reality:

- a feeling of vulnerability and need to protect oneself
- a need to maintain social distance
- a belief that no one can be trusted
- a willingness to use violence and intimidation to repel others
- an attraction to similarly defensive people
- an expectation that no one will provide aid.

The tools that I used as a child to cope with circumstances beyond my control, I believe, planted the seeds of criminality in my particular experience. I spoke no English, only Cree, but was forced to learn English under acts of violence and threats. My immediate and foster siblings were constantly degraded and abused. The quality of life that we experienced and were subjected to would not enhance anyone's self-esteem. Ironically, if you persist in crime long enough you gain a measure of confidence in yourself that you may not have had before. Foster homes can make you suffer and experience a loss of identity — which may parallel the experience of prison.

Crime as Power and Habit

Childhood rage and powerlessness may eventually turn into anger, which is expressed through various means, including crime. As Judith Lewis-Herman said, "Abused children are survivors... anger, resentment, and hate are engendered" (quoted in Waldram 1997: 45). As a child, I believed I could do what I wanted to. No one was going to stop me. I believe crime stems from many unresolved issues. One is about asserting a kind of control that you did not have as a child. The coping and surviving skills of living in a hostile environment were later reinforced on the street and in prison. A person builds up defensive walls, and those walls are extended in the prison culture where you learn to "do your own time" or mind your own business.

On the street and in prison, dope and money are forms of power, a gun in your hand is power, as is a reputation on the inside or the outside as being a person not to "fuck with." Crime can be a means of losing control and yet being in control. Ivan states:

> Yeah, especially when you think about guns and violence, violence is a real form of control, a real form of... I'm in control... guns it's a real power issue because you have a gun in your hand... you feel totally powerful... I know you feel totally in control.

Doing time and committing crime are "bad habits," and both, like all chronic habits, can be hard to break. I remember in my mid-twenties when I thought I would grow old in prison and how depressed that I felt. A person feels helpless with no hope for a better future.

Being in prison in my late teens and early twenties was not a deterrent; it never stopped me at all from wanting to continue in that lifestyle. It was a game I found exciting and fun, and this frame of reference came to dominate my way of thinking and actions. It is my belief that many people who commit crimes have a higher threshold for risk-taking. As a result I did things knowing there was a possibility of getting caught, but that was not a major concern. I was driven by a calculated greed for materialistic goods. Ivan initially drifted into crime on the street at the age of sixteen to survive:

> Crime at least in my case was a basis of survival... you know... you don't have a job or don't have any real skills... so you get into stealing or uhh... robberies or whatever the case is... I think at the initial stage it wasn't for... searching for anything... it was basically trying to survive.

I, however, gravitated towards crime, pro-criminal associates, and the street life in my late teen years and into my twenties when I was not doing time. I resented rules, authority, and structure. I was not addicted to hard drugs and, in fact, have only tried them once in my life. Ironically, being imprisoned at a young age may have prevented me from engaging in large-scale experimentation and subsequent addiction.

You can walk into any adult provincial prison or a federal prison in the Prairie region and you will see a large number of Aboriginal people like yourself doing time. Of the 3,850 admissions into Saskatchewan's provincial jails in 1998–99, 76 percent were Aboriginal (O'Brien 2000: 5). In the federal system, Aboriginal men account for 16 percent of admissions (CSC 1989–99). After a few bits, your network of friends and acquaintances widens due to transfers between prisons. As a result, jail becomes less hostile and intimidating. Furthermore, the negative impact of childhood trauma and the resulting identity problems leave you open to influences that fill the vacuum of unmet needs. In certain ways prison and the friends that you make there fill a vacuum and so does crime, particularly if you have had little positive experience and guidance from the adults in your life. Ivan talks about his loss of identity and culture:

> When my parents died I only spoke Cree, I didn't speak English... and within six years I couldn't speak Cree anymore, my Cree was totally lost, I was back to speaking English so that... I think that, I think when I began to look for my family and began to hang around with my family, my brothers and sisters, and I spent a lot of time in two worlds.

Friendship networks share a common bond that focuses on talk of past scores and talking and planning future scores. These are often the main points of conversation, morning to midnight, inside the walls. You listen to others and how they did this or that and say to yourself, I would do it this way; so you learn vicariously. A person does a lot of scheming and dreaming about crime or scores. While most teenagers were experiencing high school, first loves, or jobs, I was in prison planning future scores when I got out. So did Ivan:

> You listen to how others did this or that; so you learn vicariously. A person does a lot of scheming and dreaming about crime or scores.

> and I was in the same boat... lot of people were... were experiencing high school... were experiencing all these growing pains... I was in jail experiencing growing pains in terms of making plans for my next robbery, making plans for my next... to make it big in crime... in the same way someone would make plans to make it big in education by going to university I was making plans to make it big from

pulling "B&Es" or stealing cars... I was going to do an armed robbery and I was going to make a lot of money.

From my personal experiences I can see an obvious escalation in terms of the crimes that you commit, starting from nuisance crimes such as vandalism, to break and enters, then armed robberies and other profit-motivated crimes such as drug trafficking. Prison contributes to the escalation, as "success" is defined by the type of scores that you do. You learn this cultural norm by observing the status that some are accorded inside compared to others. Ivan's words are also telling here:

> You become very calculating in your means of survival and meet people in their greed, right? Who have done that for a very long time and gained some status from being armed robbers, from being connected... to those career criminals to people who have been involved in crime all their lives... and you want that status too... you want to have people to look up to you.

You hit the street and your worldview tells you to take care of number one and that people who are successful manipulate their way to the top by any means. I believed this to be true for a long time. If I wanted something it was only through crime that I got it or would get it. My thinking was very self-centred, individualistic, and focused on the here and now. This type of thinking affects your whole way of thought and is even reflected, to an extent, in your personal relationships.

> The street teaches you to take care of number one. If I wanted something it was only through crime that I got it. My thinking was very focused on the here and now.

The success that you have in that world, either in prison or on the street, operates at the internal and external levels: how you view yourself and your status or rep(utation) (not so much to the larger public but to your peers). You are mindful of status even when you are on the street as you hear others and even yourself referring to somebody as "solid" or being a "good money-maker."

Absolute conformity to non-criminal norms is damaging to the self, especially for prisoners. To leave crime is to lose your contact with your circle of friends, acquaintances, and a comfort zone in which your self-efficacy or level of confidence is high. It is both a physical and a mental process:

> You want people to look up to you and that becomes a means... an end result of your thinking... I'm going to be up there someday... I'm going to be recognized for all these armed robberies that I did... for all this craziness I did... you know... it's about reputation, it's uhh about gaining a... foothold on that status in prison... in the community of criminals.

Prison

I basically grew up in prison from the age of sixteen until I was thirty-three years old, mostly in the federal system along with provincial sentences and periodic breaks on the street. Doing time has taken me across Canada from Alberta to Quebec and into seven federal institutions ranging from super-maximum to minimum security and three provincial prisons.

When you first start doing time at a young age you are scared and excited, not knowing what is going to happen. To a large extent it is a game that wears off as the days, weeks, months, years pass you by. You learn the ins and outs of prison; out of necessity, as this is where you will live until you are released. This process dictates how you react to situations. See no evil, speak no evil, and hear no evil are the basic tenets that you learn quickly when you start doing time, are on the street, or as you work your way up through the system. A process of emotional detachment occurs where you learn to block out things that will affect you emotionally and will affect the quality of your time. The outcome is that detachment translates into a coldness that you may or may not be aware of, whether it is in prison or on the street.

Prison is about conformity and to stand out is to go against the reality of the day-to-day existence. I remember laughing with friends, and a staff member asking me whether I was intoxicated because I was laughing. I can recall watching a fight that happened because one person sat on another person's chair in the dining room. In both cases it was a losing proposition to argue for or against. John Lowman (1986: 255) writes, "While it is clear that some inmates are more socially predisposed than others to the inmate code, all inmates are exposed to the discipline of that code. No one can avoid the impact of the logic of inmate social realities in the course of living out the day-to-day routines of prison life."

> No one can avoid the impact of inmate social realities in the course of living out the day-to-day routines of prison life.

Change or the desire to change is also very much situational, in that a person can sit on the fence and move on or off it depending on the circumstance. One day you want to go straight, then the next you are content to remain where you are. The social norms of prison life and routine shape your worldview slowly so that eventually you do not even have to physically look the other way not to see. It is a small world where you are moulded and sculpted by years on the range and in the yard. Ivan states:

> Entering a new prison you subtly check everything out, who is who and what is what… you're not in a healthy position when you're in there in most cases… that thought came when I got out… well, I got really thinking about what I am doing… because you know I need to be able to reconcile myself to be able to think as they think out here and, you're right, you can't think like that in jail because there is a definite hierarchy and I'm used to being on top of the hierarchy… you know where I was… they call them "wheels"… and I was part of the wheel culture in there and you don't want to lose your status in there because that just opens you up to abuse and everything else that occurs in there and that's part of the "con code."

A person develops a keen sense of intuition, or at least a belief that you have one. An argument can be made that previous experiences on the street and in prison with like-minded people have conditioned you to be aware of both facial and body language. In prison, to walk by someone and to stare openly at them or to bump them is tantamount to a challenge. I can remember my anger at university when people would bump into me in the tunnel on campus, but with thousands of students going to and from class, this was a normal occurrence. In the small world of prison, an issue such as a bump very often becomes magnified, because you may own little except the "respect" you have earned, command and must maintain.

In some parts of the prison, and around certain people compared to others, you maintain a certain vigilance. I remember when I was first transferred to Edmonton Institution from the Special Handling Unit at Saskatchewan Penitentiary, I was watching television in the common room in a certain way where I could watch the door, television, and the room, so that my back was not exposed. One day I got into a show and forgot about everything and I can still remember the shock that I felt when I realized how careless I had become.

In the old prisons such as Laval (now a museum) or Saskatchewan Penitentiary, I could touch opposite cell walls with the fingertips on both hands — arms spread wide. The newer prisons such as Drumheller or Edmonton are larger and afford more privacy. Your cell can be a sanctuary or a place of infinite boredom. In that little piece of prison was a place that you could make your own. Mementos of the outside world dot your cell, plus artwork from fellow prisoners or pictures out of magazines. Some cells are super clean to the point of being sterile, with no pictures or photos in the cell, almost lifeless.

At night or during lock-up, you put on your headphones or the television, write letters, read, do your hobby or pace back and forth wondering what people are doing out there. Of course often your mind is on what was happening on the range, at your work placement, or in the population. When the range is quiet and the lights are out, except for the lamps in the cells casting their shadows on the wall from between the bars, you think or try not to think. You lie on your bed with your mind racing until you fall asleep and dream about the past or the future until you awaken and start another day, with many more to come. Sometimes you awaken with the cell wall a few inches from your face, trying to remember for a few brief seconds where you are. Then you do and go back to sleep.

One of the realities is that to do easier time a person needs to get into a good routine; this seems to be a natural occurrence in prison. For some it means weights after work or hooking up with friends and doing laps, or just relaxing on the range/cell block. There are days when breaking your routine is simple and others when breaking that routine can throw your day out of whack. Time can go by quickly but there are days and weeks when it seems to drag. The daily routine is often quite boring, contrary to the prison movies that portray prison as nonstop action. Time speeds up and slows down. Hans Toch (1992: 28) writes:

> William James told us that during periods that are devoid of highlights our time clock slows down, but that in memory such periods of time seem to speed up. Both facts work against prison inmates. If time is psychologically longer than the chronological sentence of the inmate, his punishment exceeds its prescription. And if time in prison seems short in retrospect, the deterrent effect of imprisonment is reduced.

Based on my own experience, I believe that statement contains some truth, in that a person tends to forget all the times they "shook-it-rough" and remembers only the good times. You can recall the friends that you left behind, the laughter, camaraderie, but can forget the long boring days and the hard times. As your release date draws near and as you get "short," you focus on the street with your emotions going back and forth between anxiety and elation. The mind is racing, thinking about what you are going to do, who you will see first, or where you are going to go. For myself, the world always tended to look so new, just like the first snowfall of the year when a fine blanket covers the ground and it all looks so clean.

David Cayley, in *The Expanding Prison* (1998: 111), argues, "Prison becomes a habit that's hard to break. It removes from people who are poor at making decisions the need to make any decisions at all. In prison you don't even open the door for yourself." I remember more than a few times coming up to the gate, yelling "key-up" across the dome floor without checking the gate. After a few minutes a guard would walk over with a smirk on his face and pull open the gate — which was not locked! Prison is like that, in that you do not realize that you hold the key to freedom within yourself; doing time and the routine of thinking have blinded you to the fact.

> Prison becomes a habit that's hard to break. It frees people from the need to make any decisions at all. In prison you don't even open the door for yourself.

The physical and mental distance from loved ones and the world means that to keep sane you try to stay busy and avoid thinking. Time will come to a standstill when you think too much, as your mind races with a jumble of thoughts. There would be days and weeks when I completely forgot about life on the outside.

Keeping yourself busy is not necessarily negative; it can include working on proposals to host events, doing hobby work, or playing sports. I participated regularly in the Native Brotherhood, which the prison called the Native Awareness Group. The prison administration deemed the name "Native Brotherhood" to be too much like a revolutionary group or a gang; but we still referred to it as the Brotherhood. Yet the process of "keeping busy" could and can result in a narrowing of your world, and to make time go faster you go deeper into that world. Ivan talked about the "institutionalization" process:

> I think what that does... it tells me... that you know... people get used to being in jail and that they're more comfortable in jail and I always like to... when I felt better was when I was there where... when I got out it was just a race... you know... and I didn't have a real or say have marketable skills but when I was in prison I could go to school, I could be involved in programming or I could be involved in a lot of things and I became more comfortable with that... environment than I was with the outside and that's a big issue... is you become institutionalized, you start to recognize that's your place and once you start to do that you lose sight of not only yourself but the outside.

The fine balance is that it does not help you to dwell on your sentence or to lose sight of the outside world. Yet the reality is that a long prison sentence does mean that many inmates do lose contact with loved ones and close friends (see also Griffiths and Cunningham 2000: 234). This is true as well when prison "bits" are spliced together with brief periods of freedom like a week or a few months.

The prison environment limits your contact to a restricted range of people that rarely varies through the weeks, months, and even years. This is particularly true for penitentiaries, where the population remains fairly stable, whereas the provincial prisons have a high turnover rate of men being admitted and leaving. This conditioning process and lack of social and human stimuli carry implications for when you are released, because most situations you will encounter outside are totally new and you lack the ability to deal with them. The difficulties include, for example, cooking meals, shopping for clothes or groceries, filling out job applications and rental forms, applying for a social insurance number, opening a bank account, and helping your partner/spouse with the children. Institutionalization means an inability to cope with a new environment, because your mind and living skills are influenced by your old environment. I believe this is a two-way process, in that when you meet prison staff on the street they don't know what to do and most of them will avoid you. This may be due to security reasons, to a certain extent, but I believe it is also due to the prison staff also having become "institutionalized" to see you as a case file, number, and inmate. Of course, not all staff are alike.

Friends and Acquaintances

In the course of doing time you meet all types of people. Some of them become good friends and some you have only a courtesy acquaintance with. Some you do not even talk to at all, and others enter your circle located somewhere between your friends and courtesy acquaintances. Acquaintances are individuals whom you may hang around with or deal with on certain matters but usually not on a steady basis, so that the motives for being together are superficial. Ivan notes, "That's part of the 'con code'... you don't accept people for what they are, you accept people for what they can do for you or what you can do for them." Proximity does not necessarily equate into a friendship, because there is a mental and emotional distancing with acquaintances, unlike those you consider your friends or brothers (see also Cooley 1992). Conversely, you can live beside someone for years and never really get to know them, beyond niceties.

Doing time is very much a mental process, and honing your mind is as important as keeping physically active, because your mental state dictates how your time goes. Loyalty to your friends is important because they are the men you rely on in times of crisis. Ivan notes how discrimination within jails and within the justice system engenders feelings of race-based loyalty: "That's a fundamental principle in jail in that we are all Indian people, we are all in the same boat, the court doesn't care whether you are Métis, whether you're an Indian or non-status... they want to give ten years because you are an Indian."

The Trauma of Violence

Post-traumatic stress disorder (PTSD) is recognized "as a legitimate diagnosis for a constellation of psychological and psychical symptoms related to traumatic life events" (Waldram 1997: 43). PTSD also reflects a collective history. Patricia Monture-Angus (2000: 367) writes, "criminal justice... experts minimize the historic relations between Aboriginal people and the state as a source of [current] problems." A high percentage of men doing time have experienced violence in the homes of their biological parents, their communities, foster homes, residential schools, or prisons. The violence has been continuous and sustained. The impact of trauma and the legacy of colonization manifest themselves in brown-on-brown violence in Aboriginal communities: "A police study, released January 2000, notes that 42% of victims of violent crime in Prince Albert and Regina were Aboriginal, even though Aboriginals constitute only 10% of the population in these two cities" (National Crime Prevention 2000). In Saskatoon, a study showed that Aboriginal people were victims in 60 percent of the city's murders, even though they only made up 7.5 percent of the population. In Saskatchewan as a whole, where Aboriginal people make up 17 percent of the population, they ended up being victims in 56 percent of the homicides (Perreaux 1999: A1). The question remains, then, how does prison stem from and contribute to the collective trauma of Aboriginal people? The answer lies, in part, with prison as a psychological barrier to emotional growth.

Prison can be described as an emotional deep-freeze, where your growth as a person stops or slows to a glacial crawl. You age chronologically, but not necessarily emotionally, spiritually, and mentally, just as overstimulation of the senses can cause us to shut ourselves down. In that sense, as Rupert Ross (1992: 94) puts it: "We adopt a guarded stance towards life rather than an open one, and we become less than we could be." Understimulation can also result in the shutting down of emotions. After all, as a closed environment meant to keep certain people in and the public out, prison offers few opportunities to grow. When it comes to the institutionalization of Aboriginal people, prisons have inherited the role of residential schools.

> When it comes to the institutionalization of Aboriginal people, prisons have inherited the role of residential schools.

Prison can be an intimidating place to live day in and day out, so you must have a strong mind and a lot of heart. If healing is predicated on being open, then survival is based on being closed, guarded, and vigilant. Survival inside physically and mentally dictates that you maintain a measure of distance from those around you. It takes courage to discuss issues that you as a person have yet to acknowledge to yourself, never mind to men whom you may barely know. Communication does not happen quickly, and if you are unable to relate to others, often this is seen by prison staff as being uncooperative. This difficulty can hurt your security rating, parole application, and passes, and it can have other negative consequences.

Violence has to an extent become normalized, and the bleak environment of prison can negate healing. I have for a large part of my life hated and resented authority figures both on the street and in prison. My institutional record clearly illustrates this feature, with a long list of disciplinary charges as well as Criminal Code charges. One could argue that the hatred that I and others feel is applicable to all Aboriginal prisoners, who are keenly aware of the racism in Canadian society and within the justice system now and in the past. The trauma is lived at the micro/personal and macro/political levels. John Lederman (1999: 76) states, "Poverty, depression, substance abuse, exploitation, anger, and violence are connected to a sense of powerlessness and hopelessness and are all part of the Native justice problem."

Another way of understanding the impact of trauma is to examine the rate of alcohol and substance abuse among Aboriginal prisoners. I have always believed that addiction is about untreated pain at the deepest inner level or soul of the person. A study of 556 Aboriginal people (50 percent of the Aboriginal inmates in the federal system in the summer of 1996), identified 88.2 percent of them as needing help with substance abuse. The second highest need was personal and emotional: roughly eight out of ten, or 82.4 percent (Chase Johnston 1997). It is very much a symbiotic relationship. Ivan states:

> I think that this is absolutely true... if you look at the issues that people have in prison... be they sexual abuse, abandonment... they all show themselves in our addictions... they all show themselves in our predilections to alcohol, to drugs to... any kind of high, anything that takes you away from the reality and that... becomes second nature to you.

Family

Family is important. Family members are often the only contact with the outside world that a person in jail has. The letters, phone calls, and visits are very important. Marcel, an inmate I got to know, wrote in a letter to me, "It is real nice for yourself and her to stay in touch" and that he was grateful that "people out there" were letting him know they had "not forgotten about us." Seeing a letter on your bars, hearing your name called on the floor when you open your cell door, can be uplifting; you open the letter like unwrapping a present, and you reopen it over and over.

> Family members are often the only contact that a person in jail has with the outside world.

On visiting days you anxiously wait or "hang-on-the-gate" for your visit(ors) to show, trying not to reveal your disappointment if they are unable to attend. Yet as I write this and look back at that period of my life, I realize that my siblings were not foremost on my mind when I was trying to make money; in other words, I was selfish. Ivan relates how being in prison can have an impact on loved ones:

> I've been living with [my partner] for the past eleven years but since then I've done probably five years in prison and, uhh, you know she's… my kids are directly affected in terms of when I'm in jail, they get apprehended and they end up in foster homes and that's real hard on them and that's hard on [my partner] because she is unable to… and then she told me… you know… that when I'm in there it's like her doing time because she has to visit me every week, she's gotta bring the kids every week to visit me, she's gotta wait for my phone calls, you know, when you're in jail… with the phones in jail… you're constantly waiting to phone home and she's constantly waiting for me to phone home… she's got no life, her whole life is sitting around the phone waiting for Ivan to call home and that's hard… I know it's hard because she's expressed that it's real hard.

Often visits are moments of sanity when you can escape the routine of prison if only for a few hours. You experience the outside through your visitors, and you discuss issues that brothers and sisters, sons and parents, and spouses can only talk about.

A man is lucky if his family remains in contact, especially if his sentence is long or if he is from another region. In the words of a white-collar offender: "Most who enter prison lose their family… cannot see a future… receive no mail, visits, and have no one to call" (Griffiths and Cunningham 2000: 240). I was lucky in that during my years of doing time, my sisters and I kept in touch via letters, phone calls, and visits.

> It is a serious error to conclude that the problem of overrepresentation is borne by our men. These men are brothers, fathers, husbands, and sons of Aboriginal women.

Poverty is another factor for partners who must provide for their children and maintain the household when their spouses/partners are imprisoned. Monture-Angus (2000a: 372) writes: "It is a serious error to conclude that the problem of overrepresentation is borne by our men. These men are brothers, fathers, husbands, and sons of Aboriginal women." Ivan states:

> When I'm out I work and I support my family and that is… you know it is difficult for her to… to cope when I'm not out because she has to deal with four

kids, she has to deal uhh... going from being independent and having money to being on welfare.

It is particularly stressful when a family member, close relative, or a friend goes through a crisis or when a death occurs. Ivan told me about a time, a couple of years earlier, when he was in prison and his daughter had an accident, bumped her head on the coffee table, and his partner had to take her to the hospital. "It was so frustrating because she wasn't able to get emergency help without going next door or whatever or relying on an ambulance and that made things more serious than they really were." Having a partner in prison "magnifies everything" he says, for those at home.

While the prison authorities may allow an escorted pass in the case of a personal tragedy, the favour depends on the security rating, length of sentence and time served, institutional record, type of conviction, and level of institutional support. If you are stuck in prison during a time of family crisis you cannot do anything but feel extremely helpless; you need a strong heart and mind and close friends or someone you can talk to. I was lucky and never experienced a death in my family, but I have witnessed the torture that men go through during this time of their lives.

Prison Culture and the Aboriginal Community

When you leave prison you take back into the community the attitudes, values, and cognitive maps that you learned and used in prison. The result is that certain segments of the Aboriginal community and youth are being influenced by prison culture. The two worlds do not exist in isolation from each other, in that men are being released daily or weekly on warrant expiry, parole, or mandatory supervision. One only has to look at how prison culture has influenced the music genre of rap; the baggy denim wear favoured by rappers has its roots within the prisons of the United States. Eric Schlosser (1998: 77), in *The Prison-Industrial Complex,* writes, "Many of the customs, slang and tattoos long associated with prison gangs have become fashionable among young people. In cities throughout America, the culture of the prison is rapidly becoming the culture of the streets."

For certain segments of Aboriginal society, doing time has become intergenerational and normal, almost a rite of passage. Ivan notes:

> All the people that were in young offender with me... juvenile delinquents, were in prison with me, it was just sort of... it was a natural accepted growing stage... you know... yes, I knew a lot of people in there, a lot of family was in there already, my brothers, a lot of relatives.

As such, the philosophy of "respect" and "doing your own time" has infiltrated Aboriginal communities, some segments more than others and especially those located in urban centres. The process of socialization means that family members, especially in the new generation, are experiencing the role-modelling process of an adult caregiver's incarceration. It is a natural process whereby you internalize some of the philosophy of the adults within your circle of life, both the positive and negative, and use that as a basis of your own choices as you mature. Many factors come into play that push and pull us into various avenues that may or may not be good for us as individuals and as a society. For example, an attitude of "doing your own time" means that on the outside you may tend not to get involved in the lives of others and run the risk of either becoming (or at least being perceived as) a person who does not care for others or is not a community-minded person.

When you are released from prison, unless you dealt with the problems that contributed to your imprisonment, and even if you have made an honest serious attempt to do so, the odds are that you will go back into what can be called a "high-risk" environment. It is a combination of high-risk situations and being high-risk yourself — not functioning on a healthy balanced level. That is why it is almost impossible to maintain positive growth in prison, no matter how much of an impact a certain program may have on you, because each day you are thrust back into the same environment. It is like being an island of change in a sea of conformity, and if you do not have positive coping mechanisms you are in serious trouble. This can apply when you get released and must return to the same conditions.

To survive on the outside, you draw upon your stock of knowledge and use it within the community at large. This prison knowledge may seem perfectly normal. This normality operates on the basis of attitudes, values, and beliefs that may or may have not originated in prison but were certainly accepted as normal inside. This is the rule rather than the exception. The problem for Aboriginal prisoners, in this regard, is that if you adopt prison-based values and behaviours that are counterproductive on the outside (like "doing your own time"), you will find it particularly difficult to depend on traditional communities for guidance and support. The values that produce cohesion and a sense of community no longer reside within the offender. You have become an outsider, and your risk for reoffending is great.

Jobs

The "nine-to-five" routine was never appealing to me, because I believed that only "square-johns" got jobs. Having a job meant drudgery, following rules, and having a boss. If you have a problem with authority and are living what at times is a chaotic lifestyle, a nine-to-five job has little appeal, and is probably impractical.

The idea of having a career only entered my world in the last few years, because it is tied in or is congruent with a change in philosophy in terms of my personal life, family life, and community life; thus, it is now part of my circle. A significant factor in recidivism is the lack of decent employment and its partner, which is the lack of marketable job skills. A lack of job skills combined with a criminal record and few references closes more doors than it opens. Except for fire-fighting in my early teens and the odd labour job, I have no employment history

This record highlights the perils of living in an unhealthy and unbalanced socio-economic environment. Most often the social network in deprived areas may be severely strained as a result of problems such as high unemployment, which in turn limits a person's opportunities of employment via word of mouth or by reference to an employer by a friend or neighbour. Further, when you do start to search for employment, it is hard to explain the large gaps on your resumé (if you have one). Ivan notes:

> When you're in jail... you know you don't have any living skills let alone marketable job skills and you need to... you need to pick up skills as a person in the community because people don't... they don't hire you for... because you

look good... they hire you because you can do a job and in jail you don't learn anything like that.

As well, it can be hard to make concrete plans for employment prior to release. You probably don't have the contacts or even the money to call long distance. Finally, a lack of education hinders most men.

A process of de-skilling occurs inside prison in that a lot of work placements there (such as mopping the range for three years) are not readily transferable to the outside job market. There are few employable trades that you can actively learn inside that will result in employment upon release. The repetitive nature of work in prisons means that only rarely can a person broaden his work skills. The focus on security hinders job skills as the majority of men are restricted at work to a narrow range of duties and mobility. The type of work placement available depends on the security level of the job, security level of the prison, your own security level, and a waiting list. This means that if you are in a maximum-security institution, there are fewer job placements than in medium- or minimum-security prisons. At the provincial level, the high turnover rate due to short sentences means you receive little job training.

Importantly, social skills are vital to live a healthy balanced life but are also a vital asset for employers and today's economy. The closed insular world of prison rarely allows for interaction with people of varying circumstances and interests, so your "recipes" as such are very limited. Basically, prison routine does not allow real social experience. As Ivan notes, you often do not learn the proper life skills that you need to know, and often what you have learned or your stock of knowledge is not useful: "When you're in jail you have no social skills at all, you don't need social skills in there... the only skills... are to be able to be tough and to be able to defend yourself, and those are not skills readily saleable in the community."

> There are few trades that you can learn inside that will lead to employment. When you're in jail you have no social skills at all, you don't need social skills in there.

Acquiring job search skills is a process that involves numerous steps, and the essential step is to be proactive. Prison breeds dependency in that you do not learn practical living skills such as negotiating with potential employers, people who are requesting identification; these skills are not taught in prison to any extent. You are in a Catch-22 situation in that employers look to work history in deciding who does and does not get a job. Yet you need someone to give you that first job, and this is especially problematic for those released from prison.

Change and Growth

Change is a small incremental step towards a moment of epiphany. From my own perspective and experience, people change only when they want to and believe that they are capable of doing so. Ivan talks about change:

> Yeah, I think that change occurs when you recognize... that yeah I can contribute... yeah I can... I'm a good person, recognizing that... and it's slow, it doesn't happen overnight... I mean it took us twenty-five to thirty years to get to the stage that we are at and it took a lot of abuse, a lot of loneliness, and a lot of fear and a lot of hurt to get us as dysfunctional as we are... and... functional in a survival sense but dysfunctional in a... uhh... social sense, and you know that's

important to recognize this because you have those survival skills within prison and... within the street or on the street that... those are good skills to have for that community but into the larger community and into a community which is healthy you need to be able to do things that they do which is... learn to be able to get along with people, learn how to work and not to... to have some social skills, and you know these are skills that you learn, everything that you learned as a prisoner you can unlearn and you can learn those skills that you learned as a prisoner in the community to be able to work better in the community.

There must be a recognition of the need for change and a belief in one's capacity to change. For many years my immediate and extended family would tell me to go back to school. At the time I refused to listen. My state of consciousness and spirit were not at the right level and I continued to get into trouble and continued to return to prison. Change must originate from what we would call the spiritual, and it is in your heart from which growth as a person emanates. I remember, at a conference that I attended at the Drumheller Penitentiary, talking to an Aboriginal man who spoke about change with his hand on his heart. He said that was where true change originated. He pointed to his head and said how change, if intellectualized, does not work and that this was not where true change comes from. I agree, because for many years I thought about change but never internalized change. Gregory Cajete (2000: 72), writing on the philosophy of Native science, says "Native science attempts to understand the nature or the essence of things. This does not mean that Native science excludes rational thought, but rather that it includes heart and being with rational perception to move beyond the surface understanding of a thing to a relationship that includes all aspects of one's self."

The belief in personal capabilities is not to suggest that change is solitary, but, rather, to say that the need to change lives within the individual. But people have to take advantage of available help in a proactive manner. Prison and its structures can and do breed dependency in that they undermine belief in yourself and in others. For example, when a guy is being released people will often jokingly bet on how long he will last before he comes back. On the surface the comments are passed off as a joke, yet they illustrate the degree of cynicism that exists. You learn little about self-responsibility and contributing to the community at large, because you have little opportunity in prison to do so. Lowman (1986: 253) argues:

> The most important aspect of the conventions of inmate social order is that it individualizes the experience of prison. Although the code affirms resistance to authority, it tends to deny communal organized resistance by stressing toughness, the virtues of self-reliance, and minding one's own business ("doing your own time").

This may be one of the reasons why the Native Brotherhoods, in particular prisons in Western Canada, have always been under attack and scrutiny. The Native Brotherhood has its roots in Saskatchewan in the early 1960s (Gladue 1999: 16). As an umbrella group for Aboriginal prisoners, it lobbies for Aboriginal prisoners and facilitates cultural and social events. It was in prison where I first started to get in touch with myself as a First Nation person through attending meetings, volunteering at events, going to sweats, and talking with the elders. I cannot stress the benefits that I received from the Native Brotherhood and the elders; they were a vessel of change that I was fortunate to gain access to while I was in prison.

At the time I needed a situation that was personal and questioned long-held attitudes and values. It was during and after my arrest by the Emergency Response Team and my subsequent incarceration that I knew that I wanted and needed to change my way of living. My relationship with my daughter was instrumental in bringing about a desire to change. I was sitting in a visiting room and witnessed how another person's addiction was hurting the people around him, especially the children in his life. I suddenly realized how, if I continued to live the life I was caught up in, I would necessarily damage my daughter's state of care and well-being and her future. At that moment I finally reached a level of consciousness and could understood how I, through selling drugs, was depriving children not just of food and clothing but also of their parents, love, and opportunities in life. I was serving a sentence for "possession of cocaine for the purpose of trafficking." In this respect, I too was contributing to the overrepresentation of Aboriginal men and women in the justice system by exploiting their addictions, which would most likely result in their arrests. This chain of thought led to a life-changing experience. Ivan notes:

> you recognize you're not doing it to you… you're doing it to somebody else now, when I was a kid it was always doing it to me but not anymore… you didn't have to look at the reality of someone else's pain but when it's your family, when it's your children, you have to look at that, recognize it for what is… that's a signal that you need to change.

The process of healing, regardless of who you are, is predicated on it being an active process and on seeing pain as a stepping stone towards recognizing that healing and change come from within and ripples out. Ivan and his work with people experiencing trouble in their lives exemplify this process:

> I help a lot of people off the street, and I help people coming into [our office]. They need somebody to advocate with social services, somebody to advocate with justice, somebody to advocate for them in court, write a letter, uhh, be supportive of them, that's what I do and I enjoy it because it's giving back to where I come from.

Most individuals in society who think about committing an illegal act quickly banish the thought and rarely act because the short- and long-term consequences are too great. The scales are tipped when they realize they have a lot more to lose than they could ever gain. It helps when they also have a reasonable amount of life experience on which they can base their choices. Ivan notes:

> It's easy when you're in jail, they… I mean they take care of you, they put a roof over your head, they feed you three times a day, they even got drugs all over the place if you want to get high and kick back, and it's when you recognize that it is not where you need to be, you need to be out helping your family, and I've had a couple of those moments of clarity as I call them, its stark reality… hits you and you go "holy shit" what am I doing?

To survive in prison on a mental and physical level you learn to compartmentalize your emotions, and this division of the senses predominates your worldview on the street. It can best be described by the term "jagged worldview," which Leroy Little Bear applies to the effects of colonization on Aboriginal people. This "jagged worldview" may work for you in prison or when you are living the street life, but it is not congruent with healing or with living a balanced life in the community. Yet it is a difficult way of being to escape from, especially when "prison life" was the only stable structure that you stood upon for many years. As you mature and mistakes

> To survive in prison you learn to compartmentalize your emotions, and this division of the senses predominates your worldview on the street.

become lessons, and as you interact and share stories with others, you learn more about yourself; and thus bit by bit that "jagged worldview" gets less jagged.

DISCUSSION QUESTIONS

1. Donald Morin asserts that there may be a link between foster home placements, academic problems, juvenile centres, provincial prisons, and federal penitentiaries. How does he demonstrate this link?

2. What are the common life situations shared by many Aboriginal prisoners that may be linked to their crimes and subsequent imprisonment?

3. How have prisons inherited the role of residential schools in terms of the institutionalization of Aboriginal people?

4. Describe how Donald Morin's chapter is an example of postmodern criminology, and discuss the value of this postmodern approach. How does the presentation of biographies contribute to a better understanding of crime, racism, and social control in Canadian society?

5. Detail the experiences of prison and the social norms of prison life that Donald Morin describes. What effect do these norms have on changing or sculpting a new worldview for the prisoner?

6. Morin states, "As you mature and mistakes become lessons, and as you interact and share stories with others, you learn more about yourself; thus bit by bit that 'jagged worldview' gets less jagged." Taking this statement into account, discuss the process involved in healing.

7. How does the experience of prison contribute to the collective trauma of Aboriginal people?

GLOSSARY OF TERMS

Convict Code: a code designed to increase the solidarity of inmates and imploring prisoners to demonstrate strength while they confront the deprivation that is part of their confinement; it often means that inmates do not exploit each other and assume an oppositional stance to the correctional authorities within the prison.

Escorted or Unescorted Absences: granted to prison inmates for humanitarian, medical, or rehabilitative purposes.

Legal Aid Agencies: provide legal representation as well as referral and information, covering criminal law and some aspects of civil law. Legal aid is designed to assist the most needy citizens and is therefore available only if the accused qualifies and meets certain financial requirements. With regards to criminal cases, legal aid is provided for summary conviction offences and all indictable offences where there is a reasonable chance that the accused may either lose their livelihood or go to jail.

Parole: a conditional release for inmates to serve a portion of their sentence under supervision within the community.

Recidivism: when offenders who have been released into the community return back to the institutions either because of the commission of a new offence or due to a violation of their mandatory supervision or parole.

Security Levels: the Correctional Service of Canada uses three broad classifications of security for inmates, depending on the security risk: minimum security — inmates are not likely candidates to escape and are not deemed as being harmful within the community if they did escape; medium security — inmates are likely to escape if the opportunity arises but will not cause serious harm in the community if they do escape; and maximum security — inmates are likely to attempt to escape and likely to cause serious harm in the community if such an escape occurs.

SUGGESTED READINGS

Cayley, David. 1998. *The Expanding Prison.* Toronto: House of Anansi Press.

Horii, Gayle K. 2000. "Processing Humans." In Kelly Hannah-Moffat and Margaret Shaw (eds.), *An Ideal Prison? Critical Essays on Women's Imprisonment in Canada.* Halifax: Fernwood Publishing.

Murphy, P.J., and Lloyd Johnson. 1997. *Life 25: Interviews with Prisoners Serving Life Sentences.* Vancouver: New Star Books.

Monture-Angus, Patricia. 2000. "Aboriginal Overrepresentation in Canadian Criminal Justice." In David Long and Olive Patricia Dickason (eds.), *Visions of the Heart: Canadian Aboriginal Issues.* Second edition. Toronto: Harcourt Canada.

Royal Commission on Aboriginal Peoples. 1996. *Bridging the Cultural Divide.* Ottawa: Canada Communication Group Publishing.

Waldram, James. 1997. *The Way of the Pipe.* Peterborough, ON: Broadview Press.

REFERENCES

Cajete, Gregory. 2000. Native *Science: Natural Laws of Interdependence* Santa Fe: Clear Light Publishers.

Cayley, David. 1998. *The Expanding Prison.* Toronto: House of Anansi Press.

Cooley, Dennis. 1992. "Prison Victimization and the Informal Rules of Social Control." Forum on Corrections Research, 4. Available at <http://www.csc-scc.gc.ca/text/pblct/forum/e043/043l_e.pdf> accessed July 2007.

csc (Correctional Service of Canada), Aboriginal Issues Branch. 1998–1999. *Activity Year End Report.* Ottawa.

Gladue, Yvonne Irene. 1999. "Penitentiary Holds Workshops on Health And Healing." *Alberta Sweetgrass.*

Griffiths, Curt T., and Alison Cunningham. 2000. *Canadian Corrections.* Scarborough: Nelson Thomson Learning.

Horri, Gayle K. 2000. "Processing Humans." In Kelly Hannah-Moffat and Margaret Shaw (eds.), *An Ideal Prison? Critical Essays on Women's Imprisonment in Canada* Halifax: Fernwood

Publishing.

Johnson, Chase. 1997. *Aboriginal Offender Survey: Case Files and interview Sample.* Chase Johnston Consulting. Ottawa: Research Branch, Correctional Service of Canada.

Lederman, John. 1999. "Trauma and Healing in Aboriginal Families and Communities." *Native Social Work Journal* 2, 1.

Little Bear, Leroy. 2000. "Jagged Worldviews Colliding." In Marie Battiste (ed.), *Reclaiming Indigenous Voice and Vision.* Vancouver: UBC Press.

Lowman, John. 1986. "Images of Discipline in Prison." In Neil Boyd (ed.), *The Social Dimensions of Law.* Toronto: Prentice Hall.

Monture-Angus, Patricia. 2000. "Aboriginal Overrepresentation in Canadian Criminal Justice." In David Long and Olive Patricia Dickason (eds.), *Visions of the Heart: Canadian Aboriginal Issues,* Second edition. Toronto: Harcourt Canada.

National Crime Prevention Centre, Department of Justice. 2000. "Aboriginal Canadians: Violence, Victimization, and Prevention." Ottawa, ON.

O'Brien, Mike. 2000. "New Inmates Likely Aboriginal." Prince Albert: *Prince Albert Daily Herald,* Friday, June 2.

Perreaux, Leslie. 1999. "Mean streets take a toll." Saskatoon *Star Phoenix.* February 27.

RCAP (Royal Commission on Aboriginal Peoples). 1996. *Bridging the Cultural Divide.* Ottawa: Canada Communication Group Publishing.

Ross, Rupert. 1992. *Dancing with a Ghost: Exploring Indian Reality.* Markham, ON: Reed Books Canada.

Sacco, Vincent F., and Leslie W. Kennedy. 1998. *The Criminal Event,* Second edition. Scarborough: International Thomson Publishing.

Schlosser, Eric. 1998. "The Prison Industrial Complex." *Atlantic Monthly* 282, 6 (December).

Toch, Hans. 1992. *Living in Prison.* Washington, DC: American Psychological Association, APA Books.

Waldram, James. 1997. *The Way of the Pipe.* Peterborough, ON: Broadview Press.

Part VI

Changing Responses to Crime

U nderstanding crime is not easy. As the preceding parts of this book demonstrate, the issues, debates, and problems in the sphere of crime and justice are complex. The construction of responses to crime and anti-social behaviour can be even more perplexing — to the point where it seems that nothing works. Yet we remain optimistic; and critical criminology, in its ability to situate crime and justice within our stratified political economy, is the source of our optimism.

The diversity of solutions to the "crime problem" is striking, ranging from a rise in retributive vigilantism (the so-called "get tough" approach to crime) to a growing movement for treatment, rehabilitation, and restorative measures. The diversity is, in part, a reflection of the various streams of criminological theory, which provide advice for the creation of policy as well as abstract explanations of criminal and anti-social behaviour. The policy debates within criminology centre on at least three key questions. What are the "new" responses to crime, and what potential do these measures have to deal with the crime problem? What policy responses best address the problems of crime within our communities? Can criminal justice responses address issues of social injustice?

The readings in Part VI elaborate on critical criminological approaches that run counter to the injustices and inadequacies of the discourse and practice of conservative, consensus-based justice and punishment. Consensus theories, in general, define crime as a violation of the law or norms within society; the policies for dealing with crime focus on punishment, rehabilitation, or treatment for individual offenders. Consensus theories that are based on deterrence advocate punishment that "fits the crime" — an approach that supports traditional criminal justice systems, relying heavily on individual punishments in the form of incarceration, fines, and fine options. Canada, a country that relies on deterrence, ranks third in the world in incarceration rates for adults (Mihorean and Lipinski 1992). Approximately 90 percent of the offenders convicted for robbery in Canada are sentenced to a prison term (Roberts 2000).

The new response to crime within this deterrence approach is retributive vigilantism. "Get tough" policies — such as three-strikes-and-you're-out legislation, chain gangs, and boot camps — rely on harsh, terror-inducing punitive measures to deal with crime. Three-Strikes legislation, for example, introduced by U.S. President Bill Clinton in 1994 under the *Violent Crime Control and Law Enforcement Act*, authorizes mandatory life imprisonment for anyone convicted on two previous separate occasions for two serious violent felonies. (Significantly, the classical and neo-classical schools of criminology, although supporting the deterrence philosophy inherent in "Three-Strikes" policies, considers that legislation excessive for the crime.) In California a criminal convicted of a property crime or burglary can receive life imprisonment for the third burglary conviction. Similarly, chain gangs — reintroduced in the United States and advocated in Alberta — remove many of a sentenced offender's privileges. Prisoners in chain gangs are not to receive any education, programming, benefits, or privileges. Chain-gang justice addresses the widespread notion that prison life is too lenient. Boot camps, similarly, are a means of replacing correctional institutions with military-style life — high activity, discipline, and self-discipline.

Ironically, these conservative law-and-order approaches are criticized by other consensus theories — in part because most serious analysis has always shown that imprisonment is ineffective at reducing crime. Indeed, studies and experience both show that prison is criminogenic: A prison warehouses individuals and returns them to society more damaged than before they entered. In response to this finding certain consensus theories advocate policies that increase social bonding to decrease crime. Interventions, including individual and family counselling, are meant to develop social unity and the sense of right and wrong in youth. The approach also supports education and work projects designed to foster conformity through involvement in conventional activities, as well as community outreach vans that supply food, warmth, and counselling for street people (working in the sex trade, involved in drugs and drug-related activities, or youth who have run away from home or migrated from rural areas to the city). The outreach vans and workers, for example, work to develop bonds with the street people, helping them to eventually discover more self-worth and a connection to alternative lifestyles.

Functionalist-based consensus theories, similarly, propose measures to reduce social disintegration and deregulation and to reverse the dismantling of the state-sponsored social safety net. Policy initiatives aim to redistribute resources to broaden access to occupational and educational means of success. Such theories support training prisoners for jobs that will, in turn, help them to become functioning citizens. Importantly, however, functionalist theories also support imprisonment as a way of reinforcing ethical and moral principles. Prison supposedly serves as a reminder to all of society of what is considered normal and what is deviant, and about the consequences of deviant actions.

Even interactionist theories, which generally tend to de-emphasize the punitive responses of most other consensus theories, blame the least powerful for social ills, especially crime. The premise of interactionist theories is that people come to define themselves — who they are, what kind of person they are — in interaction with others. For crime policy, this understanding implies that offenders need to be placed in contexts that will enhance their self-image and power. From an interactionist perspective, the traditional criminal justice system works to disintegrate the offender through the process of negative labelling and social control. John Braithwaite offers, in response, the process of reintegrative shaming, which he argues can be self-empowering: offenders are given the opportunity to make amends within their communities. Sentencing circles and family group conferences are, similarly, strategies aimed at giving offenders an interpersonal context in which they can take responsibility for their actions and restore the damage they have done. They are both personally empowering activities. Unfortunately, such policies still rest upon the orthodox assumption that people who do bad things are solely responsible for their deviance.

The consensus approaches — as well as the more liberal interactionist approaches — rarely question what is defined as "criminal." They persist in locating the problem of crime — rather than the problem of justice — within the individual rather than in the structure of inequality in society. They are based on the philosophical assumption that individuals have free will and freedom of choice to be rich or poor or to commit crimes.

All consensus approaches, even those advocating less punitive responses such as reintegrative shaming, see the solution to crime in the transformation of individual behaviour. All such theories, then, accept, rather categorically, that economic opportunity and morality are personal matters, and as such not linked to social structure. They advocate, as a consequence, policies such as individual access to education, outreach van services, and counselling. They do not advocate the transformation of the prevailing social structure, and without that crucial step the crimes of inequality — the exploitation of labour by capital, discrimination against minorities, subjugation of women — will persist.

Critical criminology includes the optimism of less punitive crime policies yet critiques their adoption, arguing that they choose to ignore the existence of crime and deviance as social definitions created in the interests of elite groups and ruling classes. What gets defined as "crime" and who gets processed through the criminal justice system are the results of social and political acts. This critical perspective demonstrates that many actions deemed criminal (typically, actions of the marginalized) are relatively less socially and economically damaging than many of the actions of the elite and corporations, which are often less regulated or, if regulated, more lightly punished for the offence. As such, a critical approach argues for diverse proposals that advocate social change as well as non-punitive responses to the problems of crime and (in)justice. All of the critical criminological perspectives reject "tougher" laws and incarceration and advocate instead for structural and cultural changes: abolishing all prisons in favour of restorative justice; complete structural transformations; redefining what we define as "crime"; and challenging institutions, such as the media and law, that frame public understandings of crime.

For example, neo-Marxist criminology (instrumentalism and structuralist Marxism) argues that the criminal justice system hides the real workings of oppression. At every stage — from the definition of crime through the discriminatory practices of the courts and sentencing procedures to incarceration — the system excludes the rich. Because the justice system focuses on criminalization, punishment, and imprisonment, it deflects attention from the inequalities of the social system by scapegoating the poor and impoverished — often racial minorities — as the cause of social problems. The phenomenon of globalization has been accompanied by increasing joblessness, poverty, homelessness, environmental destruction, and cutbacks in the social programs that would help, at least partially, to mitigate these problems. The response has been to put more of the poor behind bars. In essence, the state has responded to the growing numbers of marginalized people by using the criminal justice system, which means an increase in harsh law-and-order approaches, including imprisonment and vigilantism, which means, in turn, that criminal justice is increasingly expensive.

All of the critical criminological approaches, from neo-Marxism to prison abolitionism, are critical of these extreme measures and of ideological power as a mechanism that blames the poor for social problems. The fundamental critique is that the state, through the criminal justice system, asks whether individual people have upheld their responsibilities to society, and not whether society has upheld its responsibility to individual citizens.

The policy implications of critical criminological approaches are by no means simple and straightforward. Such approaches agree with non-punitive measures to deal with the problem of crime, but they fear that support for these measures may perpetuate the conventional definitions of crime as the actions of mainly the poor and racial minorities. Critical criminologists also fear that proposed reforms will only reinforce the notion that crime is about individuals doing bad things and that the only solutions rest with changing the individual, not the social structure. For example, the approaches of peacemaking, abolitionism, left realism, and postmodernism all advocate reducing or eliminating imprisonment, as a means of empowering the disadvantaged and rebuilding communities. Prison reduction is to be accompanied by restorative measures such as sentencing circles and family group conferencing, along with a call for the eventual elimination of structural inequalities. Some critical criminological discourse (often found in the structuralist or instrumentalist Marxist research) argues that restorative measures are only a band-aid solution and do nothing to redress inequality. More importantly, they argue that solutions such as restorative justice continue to focus on working-class crime and crimes related to marginalized people and, consequently, reinforce the ideology that the "poor are more criminal."

The chapters in this final section demonstrate the diversity, overlap, and complexity of the practical implications of mainstream and critical criminology. Carolyn Brooks and Bernard Schissel's chapter, "The Application of Criminological Theory to Contemporary 'Crime' Issues," applies both consensus and critical paradigms towards an analysis of gang involvement and prostitution. Consensus-based theories are more popular in public policy decision-making and with the voting public. Deterrence theories and modern classical theories, for example support criminal justice measures and incarceration, including imprisoning youth involved in gangs and exploited through the sex trade. More progressive programs are also drawn from consensus theories such as strain theory, social control, and subcultural theory — which aim to rebuild social and economic support for street involved youth. Programs such as *Urban Aboriginal Youth: An Action Plan for Change* provide recreational, educational, and cultural support for youth involved in gangs. *Operation Help* aims to help young women and women leave the sex trade by increasing societal and cultural supports. Feminist, critical, and postmodern theories also challenge retributive forms of justice and advocate for socially engineered solutions. For some critical theorists this means advocating for restorative social-justice solutions. Others advocate for transformative justice and address the civil rights of vulnerable people. For the sex trade and gang involvement, this means asking why those most marginalized are also the most condemned. Critical theorists draw attention to the privilege of class, race, and gender, and criticize restorative and restitutive measures of justice for not doing so.

Rob White's chapter, "Restorative Justice and Social Inequality," provides cautious support for the promise of restorative justice. He explores a variety of restorative approaches — some focusing on rebuilding relationships between victims and offenders, others trying to reinstate community harmony and redress structural inequality. He discusses programs that lay false claim to the label of restorative, and he considers the process of co-optation of the restorative model by the mainstream criminal justice system. For example, Australia's conferencing circles are called restorative although the end result is to shame offenders rather than establish peace. Although restorative justice emphasizes community involvement, in recent years governments have cut welfare for the poor, privatized social services, and spent more money on law enforcement and prison — all programs that damage the community. As a result, restorative programs continue to deal with crime after it has been committed, thus reinforcing mainstream criminal justice. Restorative justice continues to focus on street crime and target working-class young people — mostly ethnic minorities. By being co-opted, restorative justice has become, in essence, a form of neo-liberal policy in which crime remains a property of the individual and not part of social and structural inequality. Hence, such programs tend to divert the attention of agencies of social control away from the powerful and towards the poor.

With a cautious optimism, White argues that restorative social justice will prevail only if initiatives to raise political and social consciousness, and to assist in mobilizing a divided public around themes of democracy and collective welfare, develop and flourish. If the dialogues of restorative justice address issues such as globalization, downsizing, corporate wrongdoing and racist policing practices, its alternative approaches may well offer the potential of responding to injustice and alleviating human suffering.

Healy's chapter, "A Letter from Saskatoon Youth Court," is both emotive and practical, informed as it is by his many years in youth court as a legal aid lawyer. Healy maintains that we could eradicate youth crime by applying the principles of restorative justice and offering what youth in conflict with the law actually need and want — not to lose hope, and to control their lives and become respected community members. This may be, he adds, as simple as education and the support of a tutor, a little money, and some love. He argues that we know too well that the youth who fill our detention centres are uneducated and have often been victimized by families, schools, and communities; yet our response is to further victimize them through the criminal justice system. Imprisoning these kids — which we do at an alarming rate — is not just unethical but also impractical. It is an expensive form of ensuring that those who have been hurt and abused and who have suffered poverty will lose even more hope. The promise lies instead in how communities treat the poorest and the weakest among us.

The chapters in Part VI all offer hope for substantive restorative alternatives to the injustices in our criminal justice system. But still we would caution that criminal justice measures are never enough when the roots of structural injustice — poverty, racism, classism, sexism — remain in place. Although White's concerns are cogent and must be taken seriously, Healy's personal letter provides a concluding sense of passion and optimism with his reminder of the role that all of us play in the continuing struggle to realize social and criminal justice.

19

The Application of Criminological Theory to Contemporary "Crime" Issues

Carolyn Brooks and Bernard Schissel

KEY FACTS

> It is estimated that one million children are sexually exploited every year through the sex trade.

> Youth with poor economic resources are at higher risk of both perpetrating and being victimized by physical violence

> Only a small minority of young people commit acts of violence.

> Most research agrees that youth become street involved and exploited through the sex trade because of an unstable home life and a child welfare system unable to help them.

> Canadian research indicates a growth in young men exploited through the sex trade.

> Youth of Aboriginal ancestry are vastly overrepresented in the youth sex trade.

> An attitude survey done by Save the Children Canada, found that 47 percent of Canadians claim youth are in the sex trade by their own choice.

> Youth in the sex trade and who are sexually exploited are more likely to be and continue to be charged with prostitution-related offences than their sex trade customers and pimps.

> Sentences for the youth in the sex trade tend to be harsher than sentences for adults who sexually exploit them in the sex trade.

> "Operation Help," a Saskatoon initiative, uses a non-traditional inter-agency approach focusing on alternative measures and positive supports to encourage street involved youth towards lifestyle change. It has proven to be an effective in helping youth exit the sex trade.

Sources: Gorkoff and Runner 2003; Public Health Agency of Canada 2005; Caputo, Weiler, and Kelly 1994a, 1994b; Busby 2003.

Our current criminal justice system is primarily retributive, focusing on who did the crime and what is the best punishment. These inquiries avoid questions such as who has been hurt and how can they heal (Morris 2000). Kearney Healey and Rob White describe, in chapters 20 and 21, how many people advocate moving away from retributive justice towards a restorative form of justice that includes a focus on healing. In this chapter, we suggest that restorative justice may not be enough. Restorative justice continues to define certain acts as right and others as wrong and often omits the history and the social structure that cause crime. Transformative justice demands that we examine each criminal "event" by recognizing the complex web of societal structures and distributive/social injustices (Morris 2000).

Perceptions about "crime" are shaped by different sources — including law, media, and criminology (addressed throughout the book). This gives rise to diverse visions of how best to address crime. In the present chapter, we demonstrate the richness of criminological theories and their link to crime policy and social policy. We discuss two contemporary crime issues: youth gangs and the sex trade. We review various consensus theories first, to illustrate how different theoretical models advance both the theoretical and applied knowledge of criminality. We see quite clearly, with respect to knowledge utilization and transfer, that certain paradigms of explanation — primarily consensus-based — are more popular in public policy decision-making and are certainly more popular with the voting public. We conclude with an assessment of critical criminology and call for socially transformative justice, not criminal justice.

The Consensus Paradigm

There are multiple criminological theories under the rubric of consensus criminology that attempt to explain why youth become involved in gangs and the sex trade. The consensus paradigm contains both micro- and macro-level analyses that focus on the social structure as well as the individual. In terms of youth gangs, structure-based theories like Social Control (Hirschi 1969; Vigil and Yun 1990), Strain/Anomie (Bartollas 2005; Fagan 1989; Ebensen and Huizinga 1993), and Social Disorganization (Sullivan 1989) frame the general-consensus paradigm of crime and combine elements of social structure and individual choice. In terms of the sex trade, commonly applied consensus-based theories include the pathological model (Lombroso and Ferrero 1895; Glueck and Glueck 1934; Benjamin and Masters 1964), the criminal subculture model (Gray 1973; Jarvinen 1993), and an orthodox functionalist model and economic model (Kinsey, Pomeroy, and Martin 1948; Verlare and Warlick 1973).

Applying Consensus Models: Understanding Youth Gangs

A good deal of sensationalism occurs in the west regarding public sentiment, political discourse, and youth gangs. Arguably, the media sensationalizes the "gang problem," especially the involvement of ethnic minorities in gang activity, crimes, and violence. Media sources also often report the difficulty in attempting to explain the problem of gang activity, saying that "theories of youth violence could fill a newspaper: family breakdown and poor parenting, poverty, violence in the home, the Internet, the decline of religion and morality, video games, the proliferation of guns, lenient laws and weak sentences, a lack of discipline in schools, and on and on" (*Toronto Sun*, Dec. 2004). Unfortunately, much of the talk about the causes of youth crime is misinformed, although, interestingly, it draws upon many of the beliefs about crime that we see in consensus theories in criminology. The demand for retribution and punishment is very much a part of the reasoning behind many of the orthodox theories that we describe — theories that presume crime can be dealt with by focusing our efforts on the individual offender.

The discussions we engage in here are based on the need to understand how criminological theories from the consensus model explain youth gangs, and how such theories inform public policy. As we see, most formal justice policy is based on a rather traditional view of criminogenesis, which we label generically as consensus criminology.

Strain Theory

Strain theory emphasizes cultural norms of "success," and links illegal and gang activity with the unequal distribution of the means to obtain this success. Bartollas (2005), for example, argues that with a decline in opportunity for minority youth, more youth are using drug trafficking within gangs as economic opportunity. Fagan (1989), Esbensen and Huizinga (1993) add that drug use is becoming more widespread and normative as an economic response to lack of legitimate opportunity. Quite clearly, this line of thinking resonates very well with researchers and policy-makers who are interested in the "economies of crime," but only at the street level. The preoccupation is with the inner workings of crime "syndicates." There is little focus on either the unfairness of the disadvantage under which many people live or the associated reality that crime at the organizational, upper-class level is much more economically and socially damaging than anything that occurs at the street level (Snider chapter 11 in this volume; Moore and Mills 2001; Reiman 2007). Many of the "research-based" studies that take a strain-theory emphasis are actually quite progressive, as they focus on the machinery of troubled communities and relate it to the embeddedness of disadvantage and blocked opportunity (cf Hagan and McCarthy [1998], for example). However, strain theory-based work does not tend to frame lack of opportunity in a large political-economic, structural context that consistently disadvantages a section of the population, often identified by race and ethnicity (a step that we will see is taken by critical criminology) (cf. Wilson 1996).

Social Disorganization Theory

In a similar vein to strain theory, social-disorganization theory suggests crime varies according to area, neighbourhoods and community characteristics. Such ecological theories hearken back to the work of Shaw and McKay in Chicago in the 1930s, in which they mapped cities and were able to identify areas that had persistent high crime rates. They extended their argument to suggest that certain areas, such as the inner-city core, were characterized by social disorganization, and as such produced generations of delinquents that passed on their deviancy from one generation to another. Sullivan (1989), for example, in his ethnographic, ecological study of neighbourhoods and gangs, characterizes criminogenic communities as having low socio-economic status, high poverty rates, low labour-force participation, and high unemployment.

Sullivan's (1989) work and others like it has a great deal of influence with policy-makers and the public (although it is somewhat less prominent in the academic literature than in the past). As we think about stereotypes of typical gang activity, our imaginations turn to the "dangerous inner city." In practice, the stereotypes are imaginary, as police presence is dominant in poor, non-white urban areas, and civic officials focus on the inner city in developing crime policies (James 2002; Tator and Henry 2006).

Social Control Theory

Social control theory links gang involvement to weakened social bonds with family, school, or other social institutions (Hirschi 1969; Vigil and Yun 1990). When bonds are broken, youths seek bonds with other groups, using gangs as one of the ways to meet their needs. For example, the lived reality for many young offenders is characterized by lack of success in schools and dysfunctional families. The easy conclusion from these empirical realities is a link between delinquency and lack of "bonding" to conventional institutions like family and education. And many youth-gang members are school dropouts and are so disaffected from their families that they search for security and nurturance in a gang family. The logic of the connection seems reasonable. However, as is typical of many orthodox theories, the causal logic is not always clearly explored. For example, schools may discriminate against students who have non-traditional abilities and learning styles; families who live on the margins of society may not have the resources to be functional families; and gangs may be non-criminal and still fulfil valuable socio-economic functions.

Deterrence Theory

At the heart of social control theories is the classical criminological assumption that adolescent criminal behaviour is largely rational and that criminal actions can be prevented through discouraging crime. Deterrence theory assumes that adolescents will tend not to commit crime if the penalties for doing so outweigh the benefits of engaging in crime. In effect, our judicial and penal systems are based on two presumptions of deterrence — that punishment will deter the individual from committing another act of deviance (specific deterrence) and that the act of punishment will deter individuals in the general population from committing a premeditated criminal act (general deterrence). In general, although rehabilitation is the official mandate of our justice system, punishment as a deterrent to crime is really the cornerstone of our system of justice and corrections.

> Our judicial and penal systems are based on deterrence — that punishment will deter the individual from committing another act of deviance and that punishment will deter individuals from committing a premeditated criminal act.

If we believe that deterrence works, then our approach to youth gangs would be to "get tough" and increase punishments. This is, in fact, a common strategy for dealing with young people, especially in the last few decades, during which political movements have used tough crime policies to score points with the voting public. The justice system response to youth gang panic in North America is to get tough on youth by increasing surveillance and punishment. For example, Canada's *Youth Criminal Justice Act* has provisions for longer and tougher sentences for repeat offenders (Tustin and Lutes 2007), plus there is a push for tougher sentences for youth involved in gang activities. In America, there is strong support for legislation such as the *Gang Deterrence and Community Protection Act* of 2005 (H.R. 1279), which creates new gang offences and transfers youth to adult prisons and courts. This act also favours new mandatory minimum sentences and will expand the death penalty.

Such deterrence-based responses are very popular with the general public, as there appears to be a fundamental belief that punishment stops criminal behaviour. Get-tough policies always seem to allow politicians to score political points, even in light of more evidence that punishing young people is not only ethically suspect and dangerous to the young person (Schiraldi and Zeidenberg 1997), but also counterproductive in reducing crime (Green and Healy 2003). As mentioned previously, deterrence has proven largely ineffective for many types of criminal behaviour, especially serious crime.

Forensics

Lastly, consensus theories lend themselves to a broad and very popular approach to youth crime which, for want of a better term, is simply entitled Forensics. Forensic investigations focus on detecting the criminal before s/he acts, or on ensuring an offender is detected and caught. The forensic paradigm is based on crime as emanating primarily from the individual. The power of this particular ideological explanation of "immorality" has incredible resonance with the general public, given the popularity and proliferation of television shows like CSI.

The public policy extension of forensics as applied to young offenders is to find ways to detect their delinquency before the fact — sometimes referred to as pre-delinquency. For example, the Level of Supervision Inventory (LSI), a risk assessment tool used in one form or another in Canada and other countries, is a mechanism for determining whether a young person will break the law, and, if so, the degree, type, and level of intervention that the young person should be given. Fundamentally, the measurement instrument assesses criminal history, education/employment, family/marital issues, leisure/recreation issues, companions, substance abuse, pro-criminal attitude/orientation and anti-social patterns (Girard and Wormith 2004). The scientific premise of such tools is that they are diagnostic mechanisms for detecting criminal potential, and for that they are efficient.

> The public policy extension of forensics as applied to young offenders is to find ways to detect their delinquency before the fact — sometimes referred to as pre-delinquency.

The problem with such forensic tools is that the logical underpinning is tautological — using criminality to predict criminality, risk to predict risk. The LSI can predict criminality, but so can any common-sense judgment made by a youth worker who understands the life of a marginalized or dispossessed youth. The power of the instrument is that it has the credibility of science, especially empirically based science, to condemn the already condemned. As with all forensic types of investigation, however, such detection instruments focus on deficiencies and are never able to focus on potential. They are scientific methods that confirm only the bad things in a person's life, an orientation that should be contradictory to philosophies of care and healing.

Applying Consensus Models: Understanding Sex Trade Involvement

A sizable body of theorizing on prostitution has included many of the general theories that we discussed in the earlier section on gangs. The goal of this section is to demonstrate how consensus perspectives explain prostitution. This is in contrast to a richer, more evolved, more nuanced, and less condemnatory understanding of the sex trade, evident in some critical feminist theories.

The Pathological Model

The first level of inquiry on prostitution is the pathological model, which attributes the cause of prostitution to individual pathology or abnormalities.

> The physical and moral characteristics of the delinquent belong equally to the prostitute... both phenomena spring from idleness, misery and especially alcoholism... both are connected likewise with certain organic and hereditary tendencies. (Lombroso and Ferrero 1895: 186)

This model essentially creates the label of "prostitute" and defines women in the sex trade as being different from other women. (Phoenix 1999: 37) Lombroso and Ferrero (1895) saw prostitution as the equivalent to male forms of criminalization. They argued that women who were prostitutes exhibit more degenerative qualities than other female offenders (monstrosity, degeneracy, insanity, epilepsy). They believed that women were less evolved generally than men because of their maternal functions, which produced a "retardation" of evolution. While they conceded that social conditions such as poverty and population density encouraged women's involvement in prostitution, the main factor cause, they argued, was evolutionary degeneracy (cited in Phoenix 1999).

> Lombroso and Ferrero (1895) argued that women who were prostitutes exhibit more degenerative qualities than other female offenders (monstrosity, degeneracy, insanity, epilepsy).

Several decades later, Sheldon and Eleanor Glueck in *Five Hundred Delinquent Women* (1934) claimed that female prostitution resulted from "feeblemindedness," which was the result of parents' low mentality, broken homes, and unintelligent disciplinary practices. This, they argued, was the unfortunate psychological atmosphere that contributed to the development of women with psychopathic personalities who could not survive in legitimate ways.

Benjamin and Masters (1964), although working years later, similarly saw some prostitutes as "compulsive," with deep neurotic needs that compelled them into prostitution. These behaviour were attributed to the violence and trauma they experienced.[1]

Although these models focused on the individual pathology of "prostitutes," they also allowed for feminist and other critical work by hinting at violence, trauma, poverty, and other social factors that limit women's choices. Pathological theorizing, however, failed to break free from a problematic essentialism that prostitutes are fundamentally abnormal and in need of "correction."

The Subcultural Model

> We are dealing with a class of people whose behaviour standards are utterly different from our own… a beating-up is of far less significance to the girl herself than others who hear about it imagine. (Wilkinson 1955: 122, cited in Phoenix 1999: 47)

The subcultural model examines the subculture of prostitution (Wilkinson 1955; Gray 1973; Jarvinen 1993), identifying the extent to which women are segregated from legitimate relationships and therefore seek out alternative social connections that make prostitution inevitable. This theoretical model, which focuses on the cultural context in which prostitution occurs, is often intertwined with more micro-level, interactionist models that study the interpersonal dynamics of prostitution, including relationship formation (Gray 1973; Salomon 1989). Such research focuses on the macro-level structural conditions that determine prostitution, such as "rootlessness, drifting, and belongingness that lead some women to become involved in sex work" (Wilkinson 1955). Other studies describe the life of the "typical prostitute" at an interpersonal level.

Wilkinson's 1955 work *Women in the Streets*, for example, saw women in the sex trade as like other women in their need for social bonding, family, and friends while also being different, mostly because of the nature of these bonds (cited in Phoenix 1999). The bonds and connections that are acceptable by society's standards were not available to prostitutes, either because of a deficiency or because of a circumstance (such as giving birth to an illegitimate child). The women thus developed alternative bonds and normative structures. These relationships were often characterized by violence and coercion, not acceptable to society but normal to the women in the sex trade as they established their own "livable culture."[2]

Subcultural analysis allows room to explore the similarities and differences between sex trade workers and other women. Phoenix (1999) describes two other important theoretical spaces opened up from the subcultural analysis: reference to different "types of prostitutes" and the examination of "social" causes for entrance to and effects of prostitution. Wilkinson, for example, asked

> Wilkinson's *Women in the Streets* (1955) saw women in the sex trade as similar to other women, especially regarding their needs for family and friends, while being different, mostly because of the nature of these bonds.

questions regarding prostitutes' perceptions of their engagement in prostitution, as well as their identity and the ways that similar experiences for women (such as violence against them) may be experienced differently by women involved in the sex trade. However, Wilkinson also argued that not all women who experience dislocation and participation in deviant subcultures become involved in prostitution. She explains this by discussing an individual pathology of a "disorganized personality" (Wilkinson 1955: 54–55, cited in Phoenix 1999: 50) to women who enter prostitution.[3]

In general, subcultural and related interactionist models, while interesting in an anthropological way, fail to consider the economic and social structures that frame the lives of many marginalized women and essentially prohibit them from alternatives to prostitution. The subcultural orientation also ignores the issue of human rights and the fundamental need to be safe and secure as is illustrated by the international prostitutes' rights movement that lobbies for prostitutes' rights as an antidote to discrimination against women in desperate life circumstances.

The Economic Model and Orthodox Functionalism: A Variation of Strain Theory

> You want to get across that we are ordinary women. (Sally in McLeod 1982, cited in Phoenix 1999: 57)

The economic model has a natural parallel with strain theory explanations for youth gangs. In a previous section, we illustrated how strain theory focuses on gang activity as a viable economic alternative to living on the margins of society; one could make the same claim for prostitution. The essence of the economic model is that women engage in prostitution because their labour market chances are limited and that their "career" choices are driven by poverty (Roberts 1992; Romensko and Miller 1989; Overall 1992, cited in Phoenix 1999). Women engage in prostitution because of a lack of other opportunities and/or because prostitution tends to be economically more beneficial than many economic options available. As Phoenix (1999) tells us, this model emphasizes prostitutes' similarities to other women in poverty and shifts away from a consensus, orthodox view of prostitution to a more critical position that accounts for economic inequality and gender discrimination.

McLeod (1982, cited in Phoenix 1999), for example, examines prostitution as a profession, like other labour choices for women in the context of patriarchal capitalism. Women suffer economic, social, and political oppression as well as disenfranchisement. Prostitution, therefore, is a rational choice as a means to survive economically. Women's individual choices are made within a gendered

> This is the essence of the economic model; that women engage in prostitution because their labour market chances are limited and that their "career" choices are driven by poverty.

division of labour and their relatively low status in capitalist economies; prostitution, in effect, is a rational response to living on the margins of society.

Like prostitutes, married women often "barter sex for goods" (McLeod 1982: 28, cited in Phoenix 1999: 55). Emotional detachment during sexual encounters is a "part of a women's sexual repertoire in a day to day way" (McLeod 1982: 38, cited in Phoenix 1999: 55). Violence against women is also an experience that all women share and a manifestation of their position in society; spousal violence, in this paradigm, is no different than client perpetrated violence in the sex trade.

In the end, the economic model helps us understand the connections between poverty and "deviance."[4] However, such analyses share an essentialist quality with consensus theories of crime, not for assuming a biological or psychological pathology, but rather for assuming that men and women are fixed categories with shared social locations. Phoenix states that "the difficulty that arises from this essentialism is that it prohibits questions and theorizing about (1) the differences between prostitutes and other women, (2) the differences between groups of prostitutes (for example, black prostitutes, 'high-class call girls' and so on), and (3) how and under what conditions prostitutes can gain control over their own work and lives" (1999: 58). In many ways, the economic model, however critical, sees the world of prostitution as a fixed reality, simple and understandable in terms of male and female sex. It is, on the other hand, a natural bridge to conflict/critical feminist theories on prostitution that take us beyond the world of sex into the realm of gender construction and socio-economic exploitation. The explanations in the following section are based on the presumption that economic and patriarchal power are the mechanisms through which women and children (and some men) are commodified and exploited for their sexuality.

The Critical Paradigm

From critical perspectives, macro structures such as colonialism, global capitalism, and patriarchy are part of an abstract set of principles that help us understand gang activity and the sex trade — and ultimately help us frame social justice policies that should reduce criminal injustice. These macro structures condition and limit choices individuals make as they go about their daily lives. Relevant critical theories are critical Marxist criminology, critical feminism, postmodernism, and critical race theory. In relation to the sex trade, most of the work has included different versions of feminism. Although there are some primarily Marxist works on prostitution, the most relevant critical work that has existed for decades is decidedly feminist — and too extensive for a complete review (Smart 1978, 1989, 1992; Edwards 1987, 1988a, 1988b; Boritch 1997; Fedec 2002; Phoenix 1999). In this section, we apply Marxist criminology and critical race theory to gang involvement and the sex trade (together). Feminism and postmodernism are applied to the issues separately — showing the diversity of these theories.

Applying Critical Criminology: Understanding Youth Gangs and Sex Trade Involvement

Recent critical Marxist theories argue that gangs and prostitution are quite a normal response to living marginally in the wider society. Communities and their families form multiple marginalities brought on by inequality in the larger society (cf. Sheldon, Tracy, and Brown 2001; Gorkoff and Runner 2003). Involvement in both marginalizations results from inequality (social, economic, and racial) brought about by unequal distribution of power stemming from current economic structures (cf. Sheldon, Tracy, and Brown 2001). A number of critical authors link growing inequalities, globalization, and crime (cf. Brooks 2002; White 2002; Martin 2002; Gorkoff and Runner 2003).

> Recent critical Marxist-based theories argue that gangs and prostitution are a normal response to living apart from the wider society, communities, and their families.

The growing inequalities in Canadian society that result in part from globalization are accompanied by a downsizing of social programs and are justified by neo-liberal and neo-conservative ideologies that blame individuals for their own poverty and justify racist exclusion.[5] Statistics on the poverty of children, for example, are discouraging — especially as child poverty is arguably a precursor to social problems such as prostitution, crime, and gang involvement:

> As a particularly discouraging measure of how lax Canadian society has become in dealing with a primary, if not the primary, cause of youth crime, statistics on child poverty are not encouraging. In a report entitled "Child Poverty in Canada: Report Card 2000," the group Campaign 2000 recalled and restated a resolution of the House of Commons in 1989 to seek to achieve the goal of eliminating poverty among Canadian children by 2000. This report found that goal to be elusive, observing in the year 2000, that one in five children in Canada still lives in poverty — an increase of 402,000 since 1989. (Green and Healey 2003)

Neo-liberal governmental policies are largely based on economic principles of fiscal restraint; they often attack government spending on social programs and education, and promote a shrinking in the social safety net (White 2002). The deregulation of rents, the downsizing of social programs, and the abolition of many social-housing projects contribute to increased homelessness and visible poverty (Martin 2002). Young people suffer much of the effect, and especially Aboriginal youth. Disadvantaged children, especially those who have suffered deprivation and neglect, have historically been provided for, somewhat, as wards of the state. Kids older than fourteen, however, have had fewer options — and since the mid-90s they have not been eligible for student welfare.[6] As well, alternative educational programs to help children stay in school have been cut. As Martin (2002: 94) argues:

> Marxist political economy theories show the cutbacks in social spending guarantee that certain youth have nowhere to go but on the street, especially when funding changes to education are combined with current zero tolerance to school violence.

> School funding formulas [mean that] dropouts become a liability who only receive funding based on students enrolled... sometimes leads to the death of flexible, part time programs that have kept some at least tenuously attached to the educational system.

Even the Department of Justice (1998) argues that this lack of social-service support forces kids into crime, gangs and prostitution.

Marxist theories of political economy show that dramatic cutbacks in social spending guarantee that certain youth have nowhere to belong except on the street, especially when funding changes to education, for example, are combined with current zero-tolerance policies that ensure the expulsion of any student who engages in violence (cf. Martin 2002; Gorkoff and Waters 2003). The critical criminology response would be to attack the bases of inequality, institute social programs that distribute wealth and opportunity, and ensure that the fundamental institutions in society, like law, education, and politics, give privilege to the poor as well as the wealthy. If gangs and prostitution are a logical response to economic and social deprivation, then programs to reduce that deprivation are also logical.

Critical Feminism

The critical perspective of socialist feminism teaches that power differentials exist in race, class, age, and gender. The sex trade is built on the subordinate status of women and children. Fedec (2002: 256), for example, writes:

> since women and children, in general, occupy subordinate economic positions in patriarchal, capitalist societies, the hierarchical structure of society defines and creates a certain type of criminality for women and children, often based on imputed sexual morality. For most prostitutes, then, selling sex is a survival mechanism.

Socialist feminism examines the structures of class and gender inequalities and examines how class discrimination, racism, and sexism influence the choices of women to enter what is essentially street exploitation. This type of theory also debunks the idea that women and youth enter into the sex trade by choice. Lowman (1987: 111, cited in Gorkoff and Runner 2003: 21) writes:

> Once we transcend a phenomenal level of analysis to consider the context of a youth's choice to sell sexual services, it becomes obvious that the choice must be located in the "wider origins of the deviant act," particularly the marginal position of youth in the labour force, and patriarchal power structures both inside and outside the family.

Broad socio-structural factors, including poverty, marginalization, racism, and violence determine that some women are more vulnerable than others to choosing the sex trade and to being exploited by pimps and johns. When young women are in a situation of poverty, it is difficult to survive, and sometimes that means involvement in activities that the society defines as illegal.

> Broad socio-structural factors, including poverty, marginalization, racism, and violence determine that some women are more vulnerable than others to choosing the sex trade and to being exploited by pimps and johns.

It is important to remember that social problems such as poverty, violence against women, lack of helping agencies, and lack of employment for youth are the result, not of individual choice, but of macro-level societal structures including socio-economic inequality that give rise to ideologies and practices that devalue women, engender violence against them, and marginalize them because of their race and ethnicity — and condemn them for their sexuality (especially homosexuality).

Indeed… some individuals such as gay and lesbian youth, Aboriginal and migrant/immigrant girls, and the poor are in positions where they are more vulnerable to choosing sex-trade work simply because of these characteristics. Homophobia, racism and cultural genocide, and lack of opportunities for the poor, impact on children's decisions to run away and seek approval from other sources. (Jiwani 1998, cited in Gorkoff and Runner 2003: 21)

As for gang involvement, critical feminist theory focuses on masculinity and violence as a social construct embedded in patriarchal culture. Male violence results in part from a society that constructs masculinity around themes of domination and violence, reinforced through the celebration of male violence in war, sports, and popular culture (Robinson 1998; Messner and Sabo 1994; McBride 1995). Gender, as a result, is a social construct: girls and boys adapt to a social script based on patriarchal norms of what constitutes masculine and feminine.

The myth of the "real man" is one from which boys learn that the dominant culture expects them to be tough and strong — cultural norms that feed dangerous stereotypes that encourage violence among young men (Katz 1999; Robinson 1998; Messner and Sabo 1994; McBride 1995). Importantly, masculine constructs affect racial minorities more severely. A quote from the powerful film *Tough Guise*, says of urban Black males that "social and economic structures deny them success… one thing that has not been taken is their ability to pose as tough guys so they can get respect… masculinity is a pose of culture… men become real men through power and through control."

> Male violence results, in part, from a society which constructs masculinity around themes of domination and violence — reinforced through the celebration of male violence in war, sports, and popular culture.

From this perspective, we can see the "maleness" of gangs as a typical "gendered" response to marginality. Gangs are not very different from sports teams or the military, in which violence and domination are the norm (Dunning 1999; Miedzian 1991). In effect, the gang is a typical gendered response to being excluded from mainstream society, and the violent and gendered nature of gangs has a template in the larger patriarchal world. A logical social policy response from this perspective would be to attack sources of economic and gender inequality. As with all the critical theories, the focus of social policy would include social-support programs for young people living on the margins of society, with awareness that girls and boys live in different worlds of security and vulnerability.

Critical Race Theory

Critical race theory attributes Aboriginal people's involvement in gangs and the sex trade, in part, of overt and institutional racism and economic exploitation, yet youth are defined in the law, media, and many government reports as a racialized "other," who is outside "normal society" and is identified by race. The material consequences of racism and economic exploitation are vulnerability to poverty, social alienation, racism, high suicide rates (estimated to be five to six times higher for Aboriginal youth), and criminal activity (Assembly of First Nations Proceedings, June 2002). Such high rates of social pathology (including gang and sex-trade involvement) disturb the public, which rarely hears the argument that such pathologies originate within a political and social context. Statistics in the media and in government reports seldom have coinciding theoretical and political analyses of why certain groups and communities have more social problems than others. Crime statistics that "prove" that members of visible minorities are more "criminal" than white citizens rarely have accompanying narratives that explain how racism, class discrimination, and sexism foster criminal involvement.

In critical race theory, the public's construction of the "identity" of the racialized other is a precursor to racial discrimination. The belief system that attributes crime to individuals of a certain race results because the pubic sees social problems like gang involvement and sexual exploitation as the result of bad people doing bad things. Furthermore, the harm that racism does to people is rarely considered in the justice system's decisions about guilt and punishment (Hudson 2006; Comack and Balfour 2004). In general, the language of media, politics, and public policy normalizes whiteness and reinforces racist assumptions. Aboriginal people are stereotyped as people with social pathologies. Stories of gang involvement focus almost exclusively on incidents, not on the individual, familial, social, and political realities that lead some Aboriginal youth to join gangs.

The criminal justice system/government/public-policy role in the construction of normalized racism is of fundamental concern in a critical race-theory paradigm. From this perspective racial minorities suffer bigotry and social injustice in part because structural racism (especially institutional racism) is hard to identify, whereas the racist leanings of a jury, for example, are relatively obvious. "Critical race theorists have demonstrated that law is structurally racist: the racialization of crime, criminalization of race, and/or the discriminatory sentencing and lack of serious legal response to attacks on the persons and property of minority citizens, are structural" (Schur 2002, cited in Hudson 2006).

When critical criminology and critical race theory talk about gangs and the sex trade, they often describe some of the most vulnerable people in society, many of whom have become the "raw material" for media stories. The fact is that societies mostly fail to address marginalization in employment, socio-economics, schooling, housing, neighbourhoods, and gendered violence. Instead, the various mechanisms of social control and political influence focus on youth as "gang members" and "criminals" and by using strategies of traditional criminal justice (or even strategies of restorative community approaches) to control youth, they contribute to the false ideology of Aboriginal and disenfranchised youths as primarily bad, dangerous, or violent. In the language of the law, media, and government, the visible minority person is talked about as a racialized "other," someone who is different from the "average." As someone who is not average, the visible minority person and his or her community become the focus of intervention when logically and morally, the focus should be on the racist structure of modern society.

In the end, critical race theorists focus on race as a social construction and on how society comes to make moral estimations of people based on their perceived primordial characteristics. We know that racial minorities and poor youth are overrepresented in gangs and in custodial institutions. These realities demand that we reflect on why there is a war on youth rather than a war on social disenfranchisement and structural disadvantage. Perhaps we focus on prostitution and gang involvement as individual "criminal activities" because it soothes the conscience of the middle class?

Postmodernism and Critical Criminology

Discourse Analysis and Gangs

One of the issues that framed the previous discussion on critical race theory was the connection between living on the margins of the society and the way that crime is constructed in the media. One branch of postmodern theory looks at how we come to speak and think about issues in a particular, rather rigid way and how people who "produce" knowledge have a great deal of ideological power (see chapter 3, especially the discussions on Foucault). Discourse analysis, as a methodology for studying images and beliefs, is based on uncovering the hidden messages in public discourse.

> Extensive and sensational reporting on events and headlines such as "Gang Attacks Becoming More Violent" (*Petaluma Argus-Courier* 2006) or "The Immigrant Gang Plague" (City Journal 2005) raise fear based on exaggerated stereotypes.

For youth gangs, the focus is on how youth are portrayed in all sorts of public venues, including TV, newspapers, political talk, and how those portraits lead to inequality and injustice. The concern is how stereotypes of badness and criminality become equated with racial, ethnic, gender, class, and age traits. Media portraits of youth-gang members are often fraught with fear-invoking statements and images of minority group members.

Sensational reporting of exceptional events — e.g., "Gang Attacks Becoming More Violent" (*Petaluma Argus Courier* 2006); "The Immigrant Gang Plague" (*City Journal* 2005) — are commonplace and raise public fear. Furthermore, law enforcement, government, and some academic agencies extend the biased discourse by focusing on statistics, events, and media reports that often ignore the context within which gang involvement arises and are based on ambiguous, unclear definitions of what a gang actually is (Sullivan 2005). The Criminal Intelligence Services Saskatchewan (2005) highlights gang activity, especially among Aboriginal youth, as a serious problem and estimates 1,315 young gang members — more per capita than anywhere else in Canada. The agency argues that Native gang activity is "associated with violent crimes, drug trafficking, prostitution, and cross-border smuggling," and there is heightened concern about Aboriginal youth as "prime recruits" (CISS 2005). The public in Saskatchewan hears of youth gangs identified as the Crips, Junior Mixed Blood, Indian Mafia Crips, and North Central Rough Riderz.

One of the ways that such a narrow, rather infantile form of public discourse maintains its legitimacy is by drawing upon the "knowledge of experts." A *Toronto Sun* article of December 12, 2004, quotes a psychologist and researcher at Central Toronto Youth Services as saying that "kids are fed a steady diet of aggression in all forms of popular culture... if you need scripts to teach you how to act out violently, they're everywhere." Similarly, the Canadian Press (December 7, 2003) cites the testimony of Corrado (a criminologist), who "speculated": "I've argued it might reflect the cultural norms of the last 15, 20 years, where video games and movies and music, even television, portray a level of violence that is really extraordinary." Discourse analysis seeks to unpack the overt and covert messages in public commentary that distort the ways we view others, especially those who live on the margins of society.

This type of research, which focuses on public discourse, is critical in that it tends to concentrate on how people with knowledge, or with the ability to produce and disseminate knowledge, use that power to their advantage. So, for example, we might ask whether newspaper moguls have a particular vested interest in attaching images of crime to the young and the poor in order to divert attention from crimes of the wealthy. Or we might investigate how public discourse draws on the work of medical/forensic experts to talk about crime only as a "phenomenon of the individual" rather than a product of class, race, and gender structures. From this perspective, the prevailing method of talking about goodness and badness, within a context of street crime and official justice, is seen as a way of ascribing immorality to the least privileged in the society, and the "gang talk" that we discuss above is typical of how public discourse condemns the already condemned.

Standpoint Feminism and Agency Theory

In discussing gangs, then, the focus is on discourse (involving the control of language and knowledge) and how such control profoundly affects how society comes to define, understand, and control deviant behaviour. In this section, we explore another dimension of postmodernism that focuses on how the reality of individuals' lives, especially marginalized individuals, is much deeper than the "objective" view of the outside observer (the researcher, the policy-maker, the journalist). Researchers within this tradition focus less on social structure and more on the agency (or choices) of the individuals (sometimes referred to as agency theory). Standpoint feminism is a typical variation of agency theory that tries to better understand the sex trade by studying the narrative experiences of women in combination with structural analysis of sexual identity and gender conformity.

The standpoint feminist perspective, as a form of postmodernism, has the potential to see the multiple lives of individuals involved in the sex trade and to create a forum in which women's voices can be heard. O'Neill (2001) relates that by studying women's voices, we acknowledge and communicate their hope, struggle, humour and pain. Furthermore, we gain insight into the subculture of prostitution, including the relationships of prostitutes to men as partners, pimps, and clients, and insights into how people come to identify themselves and others as sexualized beings. In the end, the body of knowledge that emanates from this perspective is formidable and rather rare, and helps us understand profoundly the complex world of prostitution.

For standpoint theorists (similar in many ways to socialist and Marxist theorists), prostitution must first be studied within the current socio-economic context, which includes globalization and a growing gap between the rich and poor (Comack 1999; White 2002). To study prostitution in context, we need to understand the increasing social, sexual, and cultural inequalities related to income, education, health, and welfare. Any attempt to comprehend the nature of prostitution must involve the reality of poverty and its relation to gender and masculinity — that poverty is becoming feminized. We need to discuss state activities such as criminal and civil law that tend to maintain or exacerbate the oppression of women working within the sex trade. Further, we need to realize that women's and children's bodies and sexualities are commodified through advertising, journalism, and pornography. This last point reinforces the importance of discourse to postmodern analyses that we discussed in the previous section on gangs.

The most important insight that a critical standpoint feminist perspective brings to the study of prostitution is that marginalized women and children are empowered by having their voices heard. This simple methodological reality is so important because it tells us not only that marginalized people are acted upon by oppressive forces, but also that they make choices. In essence, they have human agency. Thus, a standpoint feminist position combines experiences of women in the sex trade (a woman-centred position) with an understanding of the sexual, social, and economic inequalities and changing forms of government under which the women and children must survive. The social policy implications of this are profound: the stories of women and children (including voices of privileged women and children) help us commit to social policies that are based on reducing structural inequities while remembering individuals' varying needs and wants.

That said, we must also remember that the knowledge of people exploited in the sex trade is "necessarily partial" and incomplete because it is shaped by history, culture, and social context. Comack (1999) argues that we must acknowledge how social categories such as race, gender, and class exist and impact people's lives. The acknowledgement of these structures does not negate the importance of everyday social interactions or social agency. Rather, the choices that sex workers make may be shaped and influenced by their social position.

Transformative Justice Initiatives and Critical Perspectives: Rethinking Strategies of Justice for Youth Gangs and for Prostitution

The brief discussion in the last section of this chapter is extremely important to the overall critical theme of this book. We show here that a conflict or critical world view is more than "tilting at windmills," that it can shape progressive, "transformative" social policy. The basic premise is that current attempts to address the sexual exploitation of youth and/or women in the sex trade or measures to alleviate involvement in gangs are, basically, Band-Aid solutions that rarely affect the fundamental problems of social inequality, marginalization, and exploitation built into the social structure. A critical orientation, at a general level, focuses not only on individuals in prostitution, or youth in gangs, but also on the structural and material conditions that give rise to the sex trade and to an individual's "choice" to be involved in illegal gang activities. This is the essence of transformative policy, and it is substantially different from the existing, orthodox justice system.

Within criminology, theories such as deterrence theory and modern classical theories support tougher measures and continued incarceration. We now have legislation designed to imprison youth who are involved in youth gangs, and we continue to imprison women and youth involved in prostitution. On the other hand, we have devised innovative measures to help youth exit the sex trade (such as the *Protection of Children in Prostitution Act*), but they too continue to permit the arrest and detainment of young women and men on the streets, as does the Canadian Youth Gang strategy, which is lobbying for tougher sentences for gang-involved youth.

More progressive programs, drawn from consensus theories such as subcultural theory, strain theory, and economic theory, may focus on rehabilitation and restorative initiatives by supporting measures that rebuild social supports and economic opportunities. For example, in Saskatoon, Saskatchewan, the program entitled Urban Aboriginal Youth: An Action Plan for Change hopes to reduce the social isolation of youths involved in gangs by improving education, recreation, readiness for the labour market, and providing more community, family, and cultural supports. Also in Saskatoon, a program entitled Operation Help employs a multi-agency approach to help women and young women leave the sex trade. Operation Help aims to provide immediate support from a variety of agencies that can help individuals change their lifestyle. Importantly, programs such as this seem socially relevant and progressive, but they still lack the power to fundamentally alter the society in a way that reduces inequality and exploitation.

> Like most other crime and justice paradigms, restorative justice may undermine, or at least overshadow, other types of political struggle that are aimed at poverty and abuse of human rights.

In dealing with problems of gangs and prostitution, traditional rehabilitation (corrections) or retribution (punishment) approaches are not only costly, not only fail to prevent recidivism, not only damage offenders' life chances, and not only fail to deter crime, but they also largely ignore the needs of victims (White 2002; Cunneen and White 1995). Restorative justice, as an alternative, emphasizes repairing harm, rebuilding relationships, reintegrating offenders into the society, and establishing social inclusion. The drawback of restorative justice, however, is that by focusing on street crime, by targeting lower-class people, and by defining "crime" as an individual action, social policy tends to ignore structural inequality; consequently, it may serve to reinforce the ideology that is the cornerstone of the criminal justice system, a system that punishes and imprisons (Walgrave and Bazemore 1999). The heart of restorative justice is similar in philosophy to harsh measures of social control — to control crime we need to change the offender and not the communities or structural conditions of inequality (White 2000).

Restorative justice is therefore not really a radical shift but a policy shift to deal with working- and lower-class people. As such, it does not involve substantial change; it fails to include consciousness-raising or political mobilization, and it ignores questions of social injustice and inequality (as discussed by Rob White in chapter 20). Like most other crime and justice paradigms, restorative justice may undermine, or at least overshadow, other types of political struggle that are aimed at poverty and abuse of human rights. In the end, even for restorative justice the real problem is crime and not class divisions and global inequalities.

For gang involvement and the sex trade, what this means is that although community supports, alternative educational programs, and employment opportunities are important, the need for a fundamental "civil rights" change remains unanswered. We are still left with a system that privileges people on the bases of race, gender, and class. The overrepresentation of racial minorities and the poor in youth gangs, in youth custody, and in the sex trade is a clear indication that privilege exists. Transformative justice demands an answer to justice-based wars on youth on the street and women and children in the sex trade. Critical advocates for transformative justice define these troubles

> Transformative justice is about civil rights of vulnerable people who have become the "raw material" for offender facilities and media stories, and who have been criminalized for their race, class, and gender.

as the result of social disenfranchisement rather than "deviance." Transformative justice is about the civil rights of vulnerable people who have become the "raw material" for offender facilities and media stories, and who have been criminalized for their race, class, or gender. The fundamental problems are poor or no employment, socio-economic inequality, poor and ineffective schooling, poor housing, unlivable neighbourhoods, and gendered violence (all which contribute to choices to become street-involved). Social control institutions, by focusing on deviance and crime rather than structure, contribute to the false ideology that people break the law because they are immoral or amoral. This masks the reality of colonization, racism, and discrimination, and keeps such fundamental structural issues off the political radar screen. To go beyond orthodox justice requires that the social control institutions come to understand that the decision to engage in sex work or gang involvement goes beyond issues of victimization into issues of social and economic marginalization. To date, the strategies to eradicate youth involvement in the sex trade or gang involvement have not addressed a social-change perspective; they are only temporary solutions and most certainly are not transformative.

Conclusion

We have explored the social phenomena of gangs and prostitution to give you a sense of how two very different issues of crime and justice can be seen from various theoretical perspectives. We have not been able to discuss all the possible theories but have tried to show how the general paradigms of consensus and critical criminology are quite different in their understandings of deviance and crime, although in some ways quite complementary.

In the end, most social and justice (crime-control) policies are based on a consensus-theory view of the world that the moral guidelines of the society are correct and "consensual" and that violations must be dealt with. Critical criminology provides a challenge to this view. In his critique of retributive justice and imprisonment, Garland (2001: 10–11), for example, proposes that "the background effect of policy is now more frequently a collective anger and a righteous demand for retribution rather than a commitment to a just, socially engineered solution." Critical theorists advocate for transformative social policy, which strikes at the heart of privilege of class, race, and gender and critiques restitutive and restorative programs for not doing so.

> Critical criminology asks why those most marginalized are also the most condemned.

The prevalence of racial minorities and poor people in youth gangs, in youth custody, and in the sex trade demands an answer as to why there is a war on marginalized people rather than a war against social disenfranchisement and inequality. Critical criminology asks why those most marginalized are also the most condemned.

DISCUSSION QUESTIONS

1. Develop a presentation in favour of the Canadian Youth Gang Strategy and harsh measures against gang involved youth. Now switch roles and advocate against this position. Include a discussion on which criminological theory best influences each of your presentations.

2. Critical and consensus theories are quite different in their understanding of crime, yet also quite complementary. Please explain.

3. Define the key differences between retributive, restorative, and transformative justice. Which of these crime control strategies does critical criminology propose to be the most effective and why?

4. Levels of explanation in criminology concerning gang and sex-trade involvement range from biological pathologies, to understanding gendered prescriptions (masculinities and femininities), to problems of structural inequalities. Which perspective or combination of perspectives resonates best with your understanding of these issues? Explain.

5. Critical criminology asks why those most marginalized are also the most condemned. Explain this theoretical question, drawing on central themes developed throughout this book.

GLOSSARY OF TERMS

Social Disorganization Theory: has its origin in ecological studies and refers to the failure of social organizations and institutions (including schools, policing, real estate, and more) in certain neighbourhoods and communities to maintain public order. Modern social disorganization theorists have introduced the terms "collective efficacy" and "social capital" to criminology, demonstrating the community's ability to maintain order and the informal networks that assist in this process.

Social Control Theory: focuses on formal and informal control mechanisms (external to the individual) that regulate human conformity/compliance to society's rules, including morals, beliefs, families, school, and more. Social control theory may be macrosocial, focusing on formal control systems including legal, economic, educational, and government institutions, or microsocial, focusing on informal controls that help individuals conform.

Deterrence Theory: shifts attention to the criminal act and asks what can/should be done to prevent this or make this less attractive to the individual. The aim is to develop crime policies that persuade individuals not to engage in criminal activity. Strategies include legal deterrents such as mandatory sentencing, Three Strikes laws, and the death penalty.

Forensic Science: is defined as the application of science to legal questions. This may include scientific searches for physical traces, indicated as useful to establish an association between a suspect and a victim or the scene of a crime.

Institutional Racism: refers to the systematic practices and policies within organizations/institutions that disadvantage certain racial and ethnic groups. Examples include systematic profiling of certain races by law-enforcment and security workers as well as steroetyped representations and mis/representations of racial groups in the media.

Discourse Analysis: is a deconstructive interpretation of text or reality (which is itself socially constructed text, in postmodern theories). Discourse analysis does not provide absolute answers but examines conditions and assumptions behind a socially constructed reality. It aims to make assumptions and epistemologies explicit and therefore to gain a "higher," more comprehensive view.

Postmodernism: says we must reject the search for universal truth and knowledge. These theories point out that dominant discourses reflect the interests of the powerful and tend to silence alternative views and voices. In criminological analysis, these alternative voices are most often the marginalized and those labelled "criminal."

Postmodern Feminism: rejects claims of scientific objectivity and truths. The analytical central task is to unpack gender thereby revealing the reality of womens' lives by collaborating with women in research and documenting their oral histories.

Standpoint Feminism: begins with women's own perspectives. This perspective draws on common themes and experiences in women's lives to develop a way of making sense as they are situated in the structures of patriarchy, colonialism, and capitalism.

Transformative Justice: is a philosophical approach concerned with root causes of social and criminal problems. Criminal offences are treated as transformative opportunities to deal with societal inequalities, community problems such as poverty, housing, employment, and more.

Marginalized/Marginality: refers to groups of people who are treated differently or unequally. Marginalization is a form of collective discrimination, in which certain groups are excluded and ostracized by the wider society.

Condemnation: refers to prounouncing blame or condemning as wrong. This may include judicial condemning.

SELECTED READINGS

Bartollas, Clemens. 2007. *Juvenile Delinquency*, Seventh edition. Boston: Allyn and Bacon.

Green, Ross Gordon, and Kearney Healey. 2003. *Tough on Kids: Rethinking Approaches to Youth Justice*. Saskatoon: Purich Publishing.

Gorkoff, Kelly, and Jane Runners. 2003. *Being Heard: The Experiences of Young Women in Prostitution*. Halifax: Fernwood Publishing and RESOLVE.

Martin, Dianne. 2002. "Demonizing Youth, Marketing Fear: The New Politics of Crime." In Joe Hermer and Janet Mosher (eds.), *Disorderly People: Law and the Politics of Exclusion in Ontario*. Halifax: Fernwood Publishing.

Schissel, Bernard. 2007. *STILL Blaming Children: Youth Conduct and the Politics of Child Hating*. Halifax: Fernwood Publishing.

Tatar, Carol, and Frances Henry. 200 . *Racial Profiling in Canada: Challenging the Myth of a Few Bad Apples*. Toronto: University of Toronto Press.

NOTES

1. However, Benjamin's and Masters's position is actually a dual explanation: "compulsive prostitutes possess an individual psychological abnormality that predisposes them to involvement in prostitution, whilst voluntary prostitutes engage in prostitution because of the poverty they have experienced and the social environment in which they grew up" (cited in Phoenix 1999: 40)

2. Also interesting are those who combine approaches. Jarvinen (1993), for example, blends a subcultural, interactionist, and feminist approach in her study, which explores social relationships between prostitutes, pimps, and clients as well as the control experienced by the women during their career as prostitutes. She argues that the factors that bind women to their subculture include interpersonal relationships and socializing with men (pimps and others) and other prostitutes. The feminist part of this work argues, however, that subcultures are male and work to reinforce the interests of clients and pimps, primarily men. Her work is based on her reading of other subcultural studies of prostitution, which are very structural-functionalist in nature. They are based on studying and defining fixed categories of subcultures. Davis's (1971) study, for example, suggests there are three main categories of subcultures to which prostitutes belong: hustler (women structure their lives around prostitution and live in an environment that includes drugs and alcohol); dual-world culture (conventional jobs and families are combined with the sex trade); and criminal (criminal activity, such as theft and drug offences, are combined with prostitution). Jarvinen's work is an attempt to reduce the conservative nature of strict subcultural studies by studying the patriarchal structures under which women develop subcultural attachments.

3. The idea of attributing a psychological pathology to explain deviant behaviour was dominant in literature on criminality during the time of Wilkinson's writings (Phoenix 1999).
4. A sexist ideology embedded within the legal system reinforces a stigma against women engaged in prostitution. For McLeod (1982) this state-sanctioned oppressive practice affects all women, as it is derived from and reinforces the prevailing sexist assumptions regarding female sexuality.
5. The extent to which the division between the rich and poor is increasing is clear in a report on poverty that said the average net wealth for families at the bottom 20 percent of the income scale fell more than 51 percent, while the top 20 percent increased by 43 percent.
6. Student welfare meant (until the mid 1990s) that youth fourteen and older could apply for a form of social assistance — if they remained in school they had rent and food covered. Conservatives lobbied and won, arguing that this would encourage kids to move away from home.

REFERENCES

Assembly of First Nations. 2002. "Assembly of First Nations Proceedings." June 11. Available at <www.turtleisland.org/news/absenyouth2.htm> accessed Feb. 1, 2006.

Bartollas, Clemens. 2005. *Juvenile Delinquency.* Addison-Wesley.

_____. 2007. *Juvenile Delinquency,* Seventh edition. Boston: Allyn and Bacon.

Benjamin, H., and R. Masters. 1964. *Prostitution and Morality: A Definitive Report on the Prostitute in Contemporary Society and an Analysis of the Causes and Effects of the Suppression of Prostitution.* London: Souvenir Press.

Boritch, Helen. 1997. *Fallen Women: Female Crime and Criminal Justice in Canada.* Scarborough, ON: ITP Nelson.

Brooks, Carolyn. 2002. "Globalization and a New Underclass of 'Disposable People.'" In B. Schissel and C. Brooks (eds.), *Marginality and Condemnation: An Introduction to Critical Criminology.* Halifax: Fernwood Publishing.

Canadian Press. 2003. "Viciousness of Youth Attacks Increases While Numbers Remain Static." December 7. Violent Crime Statistics, Canada. Available at <http://www.fradical.com/Violent_crime_statistics_Canada.htm> accessed February 20, 2006.

Caputo, T., R. Weiler, and K. Kelly. 1994a. *Phase II of the Runaways and Street Youth Project: The Ottawa Case Study.* Ottawa: Department of Supply and Services Canada.

_____. 1994b. *Phase II of the Runaways and Street Youth Project: The Saskatoon Case Study.* Ottawa: Department of Supply and Services Canada.

CISS (Criminal Intelligence Service Saskatchewan). 2005. "2005 Intelligence Trends: Aboriginal-based Gangs in Saskatchewan." Available at <http://ciss.sasktelwebhosting.com/PDF/Public-gang-report.pdf> accessed July 2007.

City Journal. 2005. "The Immigrant Gang Plague." Summer. Available at <www.city-journal.org/html/14_3_immigrant_gang.html> accessed February 20, 2006.

Comack, Elizabeth (ed.). 1999. *Locating Law: Race/Class/Gender Connections.* Halifax: Fernwood Publishing.

_____. 2004. *The Power to Criminalize: Violence, Inequality, and the Law.* Halifax: Fernwood Publishing.

Comack, Elizabeth, and Gillian Balfour. 2000. "The Prisoning of Women: Meeting Women's Needs?" In K. Hannah-Moffat and M. Shaw (eds.), *An Ideal Prison? Critical Essays on Women's Imprisonment in Canada.* Halifax: Fernwood Publishing.

Cunneen, C., and R. White. 1995. *Juvenile Justice: An Australian Perspective.* Melbourne: Oxford University Press.

Department of Justice, Canada. 1989. "Street Prostitution: Assessing the Impact of the Law: Synthesis Report." Ottawa, ON: Research Section, Department of Justice.

Dunning, Eric. 1999. *Sport Matters: Sociological Studies of Sport, Violence, and Civilization.* London: New York: Routledge.

Edwards, W. (ed.). 1987. *Gender, Sex anode the Law.* London: Croom Helm.

_____. 1988a. "Policing Street Prostitution: The Street Offences Squad in London." *Police Journal* 61 (3), 209–19.

_____. 1988b. "Prostitution, Policing, Employment and the Welfare of Young Women." Report prepared for the Nuffield Foundation.

Esbensen, Finn-aage, and D. Huizinga. 1993. "Gangs, Drugs, and Delinquency in a Survey of Urban Youth." *Criminology* 31: 565–89.

Fagan, J. 1989. "The Social Organization of Drug Use and Drug Dealing Among Urban Gangs." *Criminology* 27: 663–67.

Fasilio, R., and S. Leckie. 1993. "Canadian Media Coverage of Gangs: A Content Analysis." Research Report No. 1993-14. Solicitor General of Canada. Ottawa: Ontario.

Fedec, Kari. 2002. "Women and Children in Canada's Sex Trade: The Discriminatory Policing of the Marginalized." In B. Schissel and C. Brooks (eds.), *Marginality and Condemnation: An Introduction to Critical Criminology.* Halifax: Fernwood Publishing.

Garland, David. 2001. *The Culture of Control: Crime and Social Order in Contemporary Society.* Chicago: University of Chicago Press.

Girard, Lina, and Steve Wormith. 2004 "The Predictive Validity of the Level of Service Inventory — Ontario Revision on General and Violent Recidivism Among Various Offender Groups." *Criminal Justice and Behaviour* 31, 2: 150–81.

Glueck, Sheldon, and Eleanor Glueck. 1934. *Five Hundred Delinquent Women.* New York: Knopf.

Gordon, R.M. 2000. "Criminal Business Organizations, Street Gangs and 'Wanna-Be' Groups: A Vancouver Perspective." *Canadian Journal of Criminology* 42, 1: 39–60.

Gorkoff, Kelly, and Jane Runner (eds.). 2003. *Being Heard: The Experiences of Young Women in Prostitution.* Halifax: Fernwood Publishing and RESOLVE.

Gorkoff, Kelly, and Meghan Waters. 2003. "Balancing Safety, Respect and Choice in Programs for Young Women Involved in Prostitution." In Kelly Gorkoff and Jane Runners (eds.). *Being Heard: The Experiences of Young Women in Prostitution.* Halifax: Fernwood Publishing and RESOLVE.

Gray, D. 1973. "'Turning Out': A Study of Teenage Prostitution." *Urban Life and Culture* 4: 401–25.

Green, Ross Gordon, and Kearney Healey. 2003. *Tough on Kids: Rethinking Approaches to Youth Justice.* Saskatoon: Purich Publishing.

H.R. 1279 [109]: "Gang Deterrence and Community Protection Act of 2005." Legislation: 109 U.S. Congress (2005-2006). GovTrack.US. Available at <www.govtrack.us/congress/bill.xpd?bill=h109-1279> accessed July 3, 2007.

Hagan, John, and Bill McCarthy. 1998. *Mean Streets: Youth Crime and Homelessness.* Cambridge: Cambridge University Press.

Hirshi, T. 1969. *Causes of Delinquency.* Berkeley: University of California Press.

Hudson, Barbara. 2006. "Beyond White Man's Justice: Race, Gender and Justice in Late Modernity." *Theoretical Criminology* 10, 1: 29–47.

James, Carl. 2002. "Armed and Dangerous: Racializing Suspects, Suspecting Race." In B. Schissel and C. Brooks (eds.), *Marginality and Condemnation: An Introduction to Critical Criminology.* Halifax: Fernwood Publishing.

Jarvinen, M. 1993. *Of Vice and Women: Shades of Prostitution.* Scandinavian Studies in Prostitution. Oslo: Scandinavian University Press.

Katz, Jackson. 1999. *Tough Guise: Violence, Media, and the Crisis in Masculinity.* Media Education Foundation.

Kinsey, A.C., W.B. Pomeroy, and C.E. Martin. 1948. *Sexual Behaviour in the Human Male.* London: W.B. Saunders.

Lombroso, Cesare, and William Ferrero. 1895. *The Female Offender.* New York: Philosophical Library.

Lowman, John. 1987. "Taking Young Prostitutes Seriously." *Canadian Review of Sociology and Anthropology* 24, 1.

Martin, Dianne. 2002. "Demonizing Youth, Marketing Fear: The New Politics of Crime." In Joe Hermer and Janet Mosher (eds.), *Disorderly People: Law and the Politics of Exclusion in Ontario.* Halifax: Fernwood Publishing.

McBride, J. 1995. *War, Battering, and Other Sports: The Gulf Between American Men and Women.* Atlantic Highlands, NJ: Humanities Press.

McLeod, E. 1982. *Women Working: Prostitution Now.* London: Croom Helm.

Messner, M., and D. Sabo. 1994. *Sex, Violence and Power in Sports: Rethinking Masculinity.* Freedom, CA: Crossing Press.

Miedzian, Miriam 1991. *Boys will be Boys: Breaking the Links Between Masculinity and Violence.* Toronto: Doubleday.

Morris, R. 2000. *Stories of Transformative Justice.* Toronto: Canadian Scholars Press.

O'Neill, Maggie. 2001. *Prostitution and Feminism: Towards a Politics of Feeling.* Cambridge: Polity Press.

Overall, C. 1992. "What's Wrong with Prostitution? Evaluating Sex Work." *Signs: Journal of Women in Culture and Society* 17, 41: 705–24.

Petaluma Argus Courier. 2006. "Gang attacks becoming more violent." February 15. Available at <www.arguscourier.com/news/news/gangactivity060215.html> accessed August 2007.

Phoenix, Joanna. 1999. *Making Sense of Prostitution.* London: MacMillan Press.

Public Health Agency of Canada, National Clearinghouse on Family Violence. 2005. "Youth and Violence." Available at <http://www.phac-aspc.gc.ca/ncfv-cnivf/familyviolence/html/nfnt-syjviolence_e.html> accessed July 2007.

Reiman, Jeffrey. 2007. *The Rich Get Richer and the Poor Get Prison: Ideology, Class and Criminal Justice.* Eighth edition. Boston: Pearson.

Roberts, N. 1992. *Whores in History.* London: Harper Collins.

Robinson, L. 1998. *Crossing the Line: Violence and Sexual Assault in Canada's National Sport.* Toronto: McClelland and Stewart.

Salomon, E. 1989. "The Homosexual Escort Agency: Deviance Disavowal." *British Journal of Sociology* 40, 1–21.

Schiraldi, V., and J. Zeidenberg. 1997. *The Risks Juveniles Face When They are Incarcerated With Adults.* Washington, DC: The Justice Policy Institute.

Schissel, Bernard. 2006. *STILL Blaming Children:* Youth Conduct and the Politics of Child Hating. Halifax: Fernwood Publishing.

Schur, Richard. 2002. "Critical Race Theory and the Limits of Auto/Biography: Reading Patricia Williams's The Alchemy of Race and Rights Through/Against Postcolonial Theory." *Biography* 25, 3 (Summer).

Sheldon, Randall G., Sharon K. Tracy, and William B. Brown. 2001. *Youth Gangs in American Society,* Second edition. Belmont, CA: Wadsworth and Thompson Learning.

Smart, C. 1978. *Women, Crime and Criminology.* London: Macmillan.

_____. 1989. *Feminism and the Power of Law.* London: Routledge.

_____. 1992. *Regulating Womanhood: Historical Essays on Marriage, Motherhood and Sexuality.* London: Routledge.

Sullivan, Mercer L. 1989. *Getting Paid: Youth Crime and Work in the Inner City.* Ithaca, NY: Cornell University Press.

_____. 2005. "Maybe We Shouldn't Study "Gangs": Does Reification Obscure Youth Violence?" *Journal of Contemporary Criminal Justice* 21, 2: 170–90.

Tator, Carol, and Frances Henry. 2006. *Racial Profiling in Canada: Challenging the Myth of a Few Bad Apples.* Toronto: University of Toronto Press.

Toronto Sun. 2004. "Violent Youth Crime Rising." December 12. In Violent Crime Statistics—Canada. Available at <http://www.fradical.com/Violent_crime_statistics_Canada.htm> accessed February 20th, 2006.

Tustin, Lee, and Robert E. Lutes. 2007. *Guide to the Youth Criminal Justice Act,* 2007 edition.

Butterworths Canada Ltd.

Vigil, J.D., and S.C. Yun. 1990. "Vietnamese Youth Gangs in Southern California." In C. Ronald Huff (ed.), *Gangs in America*. Newbury Park, CA: Sage.

Walgrave, L., and G. Bazemore. 1999. *Restorative Juvenile Justice: Repairing the Harm of Youth Crime*. Monsey, NY: Criminal Justice Press.

White, R. 2000. "Social Justice, Community Building and Restorative Strategies." *Contemporary Justice Review* 3, 1.

_____. 2002. "Restorative Justice and Social Inequality." In B. Schissel and C. Brooks (eds.), *Marginality and Condemnation: An Introduction to Critical Criminology*. Halifax: Fernwood Publishing.

Wilkinson, R. 1955. *Women of the Streets: A Sociological Study of the Common Prostitute*. London: British Social and Biology Council.

Wilson, William Julius. 1996. *When Work Disappears: The World of the New Urban Poor*. New York: Random House.

20

Restorative Justice, Inequality, and Social Change

Rob White

KEY FACTS

> Studies reveal that victims tend to be satisfied with the restorative justice process and that the restorative justice process helps victims of violent crime deal with their anger.

> Victims are divided in their willingness to meet with offenders. Reasons cited for rejecting such meetings included fear (13 percent), no interest (16 percent), and refusal in principle (33 percent).

> Research shows that victims tend to participate in restorative programs in order to confront the offender about the impact of their crime, help the offender, learn more about the offender, and seek reparation.

> Hollow Water, an Aboriginal community, introduced a holistic healing circle program, using restorative methods to keep community members out of prison and in their communities. The Hollow Water community believes that incarceration leads to increased violence, whereas community support towards healing leads to healthier people and communities. Their recidivism rates have declined.

> Too often restorative justice programs are, in practice, an extension of the criminal justice process, dealing with and punishing offenders rather than restoring communities.

Source: Wemmers and Canuto 2002.

A round the world today many jurisdictions have embraced the idea of "restorative justice," particularly in relation to juvenile justice (Braithwaite 1999; Bazemore and Walgrave 1999a). It is an approach to criminal justice that deals with offenders by working to repair harm; the reparation process involves victims and communities as well as offenders.

The practice of restorative justice has many and varied origins. Culturally, it has been linked to indigenous methods of dispute resolution that emphasize "whole of community" approaches to criminal and deviant behaviour, as in the case of the Maori people in New Zealand and Aboriginal peoples in Canada (see, for example, Maxwell and Morris 1994; Stuart 1997). The approach is also tied to particular religions and religious prescripts among certain groups, such as the Mennonites (see Zehr 1990) or, more broadly, the Canadian Church Council on Justice and Corrections (1996), which see acts of social transgression as disrupting the basic harmony and peace of communities. The point of intervention is to restore peace and the boundaries of good behaviour. The restorative justice approach is also associated with particular political ideals and theoretical models, especially that of "republican justice" (see Braithwaite and Pettit 1990). Republican justice, for example, emphasizes personal dominion, conceptualized as "republican liberty," which carries an expectation that institutions of civil society and the state will guarantee maximum freedom, now and into the future, for offenders, victims, and community members. Across these cultural, spiritual, and political domains there is broad agreement that "justice" should be about the direct incorporation of all those harmed by crime and incivility in a positive process of reconciliation and reparation.

To understand restorative justice we need to consider its dynamics and nature in relation to the dominant models of criminal justice in most advanced industrialized countries — and especially in relation to the retributive justice model and the varying ways in which punishment, welfare, and restitution have developed. We need also to consider how restorative justice deals with matters of working-class criminality, especially in the contemporary social and political context. This in turn means exploring the main features of restorative justice as it has been implemented in various countries and addressing the limitations and potential of the approach.

Retributive and Restorative Justice

When discussing broad system orientations and imperatives, critics often make a distinction between retributive and restorative justice (see, for example, Zehr 1990; Bazemore and Umbreit 1995). They often cast retributive justice as being backward-looking and grounded in the past and portray restorative justice as progressive and looking to the future. One perspective is guided by notions of blame, guilt, individual responsibility, and punishment for past harms, and the other is informed by concepts such as repairing harm, social restoration, community harmony, and problem-solving. A retributive system of justice is essentially punitive in nature, with the key focus on using punishment as a means of deterring future crime and providing "just deserts" for any harms committed. A restorative approach is concerned with promoting harmonious relationships by means of restitution, reparation, and reconciliation involving offenders, victims, and the wider community.

> A restorative approach is concerned with promoting harmonious relationships by means of restitution, reparation, and reconciliation involving offenders, victims, and the wider community.

In abstract terms, we can draw clear differences between a system of justice based primarily upon the concept of retribution and one based upon restoration. Most of the literature dealing with restorative justice recognizes this distinction (see, for example, Bazemore and Umbreit 1995; Zehr 1990). But the restorative justice literature in itself also carries different analytical emphases. Some writers place greater importance on community than do others; some put victims at the centre of the criminal justice process; and others pay most attention to how best to respond to offenders (Bazemore 1997; Church Council on Justice and Corrections 1996). Different approaches emphasize different objectives, including victim restoration, shaming and denouncing offenders, citizen involvement, and community empowerment (Bazemore 1997).

Restorative justice thus shows a range of specific models and institutional approaches (see Bazemore 1997; Braithwaite 1999; Bilchik 1998). These different approaches include:

- *Victim–offender mediation and dialogue* — involving victim restoration, along with active victim involvement, protection of the victim, and meeting of victim needs.

Under the guidance of a trained mediator, victims and offenders meet in a safe and structured setting to discuss the nature of the harm committed. Offenders are held directly accountable for their behaviour and must provide assistance to victims in an agreed upon manner.

- *Family group conferencing* — values victim restoration and includes a denunciation, through reintegrative shaming, of the offender's actions. The approach encourages participation by community members (including and especially the friends and family of the victims and offenders) in a meeting, which has the purpose of revealing and discussing the impact of the crime on the various parties. The group decides, as a whole, how the offender can repair the harm done.
- *Circle sentencing (sentencing circles or peacemaking circles)* — emphasizes citizen involvement and sharing of power, and community empowerment. The approach involves the creation of a respectful space (literally, a circle of concerned people) in which consensus decisions can be made on an appropriate disposition or outcome that addresses the concerns of all parties. The circles place an emphasis on speaking from the heart, allowing participants to find the best way of assisting in healing all the parties involved, and preventing future occurrences.
- *Reparative probation* — has as its main concern victim restoration and community empowerment, with offenders undertaking tasks that directly benefit victims and communities. The young person works in the community to perform personal services for victims and/or community services. Often the community services are oriented towards enhancing conditions for disadvantaged or less fortunate people within particular communities.
- *Balanced restorative* — provides victims with the opportunities, as well as the necessary services, for involvement and input, and gives offenders the opportunity to increase their skills and capacities with connections forged between different community members. It includes an assessment of the offender from the point of view of ensuring community safety, allows for offender accountability for their actions, and works to enhance the competency of the offender while that person is in the criminal justice system.

Some restorative justice approaches have a moral application, as in the case of reintegrative shaming, where the aim is to cast shame on the offence while offering forgiveness to the offender (Braithwaite 1989). Other approaches involve a strategic assessment of offenders and events; in the balanced restorative approach, for instance, the aim is to design interventions that best address issues of offender accountability, competency, and community safety (Bazemore 1991; Bilchik 1998). Some approaches focus almost exclusively on meeting victim needs, usually via some method of restitution or compensation involving the offender; others place emphasis on widespread community engagement in dealing with the underlying problems and issues that have manifested themselves in the specific offence.

Some advocates of the approach see restorative justice as being, essentially, a form of diversion from the formal criminal justice system; others see it as a potential alternative to that system (see Bazemore and Walgrave 1999b). Whatever the specific differences, the common thread of restorative justice appears to be the spirit within which justice is undertaken. The intent and outcomes of the process are primarily aimed at repairing the harm caused by a crime, which means working to heal the victims, offenders, and communities involved (Bazemore and Walgrave 1999b; Zehr and Mika 1998).

Some writers argue that retribution and restoration, while basically different, are not mutually exclusive. For example, "punishment" can occur within a restorative framework as well as within a retributive system (Daly and Immarigeon 1998; Daly 2000, 2002). Typically, though, the kind of punishment delivered as part of a restorative process is the discomfort or deeply felt need to respond associated with face-to-face meetings with victims — which is not the same thing as the more abstract "punishment" that informs the basic makeup of the conventional criminal justice system. The restorative form of punishment is direct, particularistic, and experiential; much depends upon the character of the specific of-fender. The retributive form is conceptual, universal, and institutional; it shapes the social organization of the criminal justice system. For the offender, the experience of punishment in the restorative approach depends upon the person's emotional state, personality, connection with the victim, and so on. For the institution, punishment is an impersonal ideal that is tied to the basic logic of a system; the system's objectives may include such elements as "just deserts" and deterrence. Thus, we need to distinguish between punishment as a principle or objective of a system (i.e., retribution), and punishment as an experience of young people (e.g., feeling ashamed in a conference). In regards to the latter, the feeling of "being punished" does not necessarily derive from the express intent of the intervention (which, under restorative justice, is to repair the harm) — although it may be a by-product of the process.

> The restorative form of punishment is direct, particularistic, and experiential; much depends upon the offender's character. The retributive form is conceptual, universal, and institutional; it shapes the social organization of the criminal justice system.

In practice, most criminal justice systems today are hybrid systems: they incorporate elements that, at least on the surface, appear to be drawn from very different, and even opposing, approaches to dealing with offenders. For example, recent years have seen criminal justice systems paying much greater attention to victims (through the use of victim impact statements and the provision of victim support services), and placing more emphasis on restitution (through sentencing legislation that includes offender recompense to victims). They might utilize community-based options (through the use of community service orders or youth camps) or encourage greater offender involvement in repairing harm (as in the case of the mandatory use of apologies). The mixing and matching of many diverse sanctions and institutional options reflect the historical tensions between "justice" and "welfare" approaches to criminal justice, as well as the more recent integration of specific restorative measures into the system.

Still, criminal justice, particularly for adults, has remained dominated by "just deserts" sentencing practices, reflecting the classical approach to crime and punishment that presumes individual rationality and responsibility for one's own actions (see White and Haines 2004). This has been reinforced over the last decade or so by the trend toward increased emphasis on "individualization" and "responsibilization" in regards to social policy and service provision (O'Malley 1996; Beck and Beck-Gernsheim 2001). Young people, as well as adults, are demanded to be accountable and responsible for their fate, including any breaches of criminal law and social order (White and Wyn 2004; Muncie 2002).

The administration of criminal justice has also been influenced by "actuarial" models of risk assessment, in which the primary goal of incarceration is not so much punishment per se as the incapacitation of people deemed to be dangerous to the public (Feeley and Simon 1994). For young people in Canada, the renewed concern with risk and risk management is reflected in personal assessment tools such as the Youth Level Service Case Management Inventory. These kind of instruments are used to evaluate individual factors that together are used to predict the risk of offending. Such tools basically substitute individual biographies for the historical dynamics of societies. In other words, certain characteristics — such as being unemployed, and failure to complete schooling - are represented as failings of individuals rather than the outcome of inequality, discrimination, and disadvantage. This, too, bolsters the notion that "deviancy" is basically a matter of individual predilection, choice or deficit.

Institutional responses to criminality (and, indeed, to "risk" itself) have also been influenced by perspectives that emphasize the need for rehabilitation, treatment, and concerted efforts to reform the offender. Here the focus has been less on the offence than on the biological, psychological, and social pathologies that have influenced offender behaviour and that must be corrected through work on the individual (White and Haines 2004). The response, therefore, is to emphasize the importance of, for instance, drug rehabilitation, group therapy, case management of individual offenders, and education and training programs. The notion of diverting young offenders away from courts and away from detention is important to this approach insofar as the individual needs of young people are seen to be best met in community-based programs and activities.

The restorative justice approach constitutes another add-on to systems that have come to include, usually in an ad hoc manner and to varying degrees, elements associated with both "just deserts" and pathology understandings of crime and criminality. The historical development of criminal justice systems has essentially been marked by the simultaneous incorporation of apparently contradictory sentencing principles (for example, retribution versus rehabilitation) and conflicting institutional responses (for example, punishment versus treatment). The result of this hybridization is that in many different jurisdictions criminal justice officials have adopted what appear to be very similar measures. Whether they speak of "community service," "individual responsibility," or "juvenile conferences," the use of the same language implies sameness in application. But the superficial similarities in form belie the substantive differences in content. Lode Walgrave (1999: 40), for example, describes "community service" as yet another form of retributive forced labour:

> Some practices use community service as a punishment. The objective is not to restore a harm by fulfilling a compensating service, but to inflict suffering by imposing an unpleasant and even degrading task. The offender must feel pain, in order to be deterred from reoffending and to satisfy the victim's feelings of revenge.

Community service can also, of course, be associated with rehabilitation objectives, or with restorative-justice objectives. The specific content of the practice, therefore, can vary according to the philosophical framework informing its implementation.

The Case for Restorative Justice

Theoretically, restorative justice promises a more constructive, positive approach to criminal justice than do the retributive or traditional rehabilitation approaches. At a systemic level, punitive responses have proven to be costly. They also tend to damage offenders' life chances, do little to prevent recidivism, and fail to act as a general deterrent. They do not take into account specific offender circumstances and how these circumstances shape offending behaviour; and they do not address the fundamental causes of crime.

For its part, rehabilitative treatment has been criticized for its lack of attention to victim needs, for viewing offenders as inherently deficient, for the patronizing attitudes of some medical staff and social workers towards their clients, and for making inadequate transitional arrangements between treatment and non-treatment phases (Cunneen and White 2002; Walgrave 1999). The approach has also shown inconsistencies in the treatment of offenders. Some young people, for example, are subjected to long periods of treatment (including incarceration) if they do not to seem be responding to the assistance provided. Others experience only short periods of treatment if they show the right signs and demonstrate a positive response to the expert intervention.

> Restorative justice emphasizes reintegrative and developmental principles. It offers hope of enhanced opportunities for victims, offenders, and their immediate communities.

Restorative justice, with its emphasis on repairing harm, emphasizes reintegrative and developmental principles. It offers the hope that opportunities will be enhanced for victims, offenders, and their immediate communities, with the direct participation of all concerned in this process. The most detailed and sophisticated example of restorative justice is probably the balanced restorative approach (Bilchik 1998), although considerable institutional resources have also been put into juvenile conferencing, especially in New Zealand and Australia (Morris and Maxwell 2003; Braithwaite 1999; Daly 2000). The benefits of restorative justice can be seen in terms of its emphasis on active agency (that is, young people doing things for themselves), cost-effectiveness (compared with detention or imprisonment), victim recognition and engagement (often through face-to-face meetings with offenders), and community benefit (through participation and community service).

> The benefits of restorative justice include its emphasis on active agency (that is, young people doing things for themselves), cost-effectiveness (compared with detention or imprisonment), victim recognition and engagement, and community benefit.

Compared with previous theoretical approaches to offending, restorative justice does appear to offer a practically effective, philosophically attractive, and financially prudent method of doing justice. Rather than being based on the idea of punishment, it is oriented towards peacemaking; rather than being reliant upon experts and officials, it is socially inclusive; rather than being a response to violation of laws, it attempts to provide a symbolic and practical solution to actual harms; and rather than being peripheral to the processes of criminal justice, victims and community, as well as offenders, are central to resolving issues of harm.

The introduction of restorative justice approaches and methods has varied enormously across governmental jurisdictions (Hudson et al. 1996; Braithwaite 1999; Bazemore and Walgrave 1999a). In most cases, governments have adopted the approach either as a diversionary measure (primarily used at the front end of the traditional criminal justice system) or as a specific response applicable or appropriate only for particular types of offenders. For example, in Australia most serious and repeat juvenile offenders are not invited to take part in juvenile conferences. As a result, due to their early and repeated contacts with the criminal justice system, Indigenous youth are less likely than non-Indigenous youth to be referred to conferences (Cunneen 1997; Harding and Maller 1997), and they are more likely to be taken to court and less likely to be cautioned than their non-Indigenous counterparts (Chan 2005).

The popularity of restorative justice notions among practitioners is reflected in words such as "diversion," "conferencing," and "repairing harm," terms that have now become familiar and ingrained parts of the everyday language of contemporary juvenile justice. Far from being a revolution in thought and practice, however, restorative justice — as a newly institutionalized form of juvenile justice intervention — has largely fit into existing regimes rather than departing from them. How and why this is the case is worthy of close consideration. For critical criminologists, putting things into social context and asking the hard questions is one way of exposing the limitations of restorative justice as it has generally been implemented. It also helps us to identify radically different ways in which we might engage with and enact the principles of restorative justice.

> Far from being a revolution in thought and practice, restorative justice has largely fit into existing regimes rather than departing from them.

At the level of sentiment and utopian vision, restorative justice does have a powerful emotional appeal. This has drawn the critical attention of those who question its basic propositions about justice, its reliance on "good news" stories and its apparent optimism that even the most heinous of crimes can be dealt with in a restorative manner (Acorn 2004). Even supporters of the broad thrust of restorative justice have asked questions about the prominent myths that feature in advocates' stories and claims (Daly 2002). What is being done to whom, why, and with what consequences, remain central questions for skeptic and supporter alike.

The Politics of Reform

Certainly, the political struggle over basic principles of criminal justice — the contest between "retributive" and "restorative" justice — is a worthy one and it does open the door to a more profound critique of inequality and social injustice. This is partly recognized by those who argue that "we need to engage with other forms of social movement politics besides the social movements for restorative justice to tackle seriously the economic institutions" that are at the root of problems such as unemployment, homelessness, educational disadvantage, sexism, and racism (Braithwaite 1999: 93). The problem with this position, however, it that it winds up diminishing these overarching social and economic concerns, since it is argued that these concerns warrant action in different political spheres and that they are not the core business of restorative justice as such. As a consequence, this kind of argument thereby fails to fully acknowledge how restorative practices in the here and now can and do reinforce important aspects of the contemporary criminal justice system. For, partly due to the diversity of opinion, values, and models under the restorative-justice tag, there has been a tendency for specific forms of restorative justice to be implemented in a manner that actively reproduces the dominant forms of social control.

For example, the restorative tool of juvenile conferencing may be used solely for first-time offenders and/or trivial offences — as a means of diversion at the "soft" end of the juvenile justice spectrum — and it therefore acts as a filter that reinforces the logic and necessity of the "hard" end of the system (the "real justice" of retribution and punishment). The restorative approach thus may well help to legitimate the retributive approach, rather than constitute a challenge to it. Similarly, diverse jurisdictions — from the legislative to the administrative and operational — show substantial variations in the introduction of restorative justice. In almost all cases restorative justice has been blended into existing institutional patterns and become, as such, part of the continuing hybridization of criminal justice. The very manner of this blending makes a major difference in terms of the system's orientation.

While the retributive, rehabilitative, and restorative models of intervention have their differences, and much debate occurs over those differences, from a social justice perspective they nevertheless also have much in common. Most restorative-justice interventions, for example, make a good fit with other prevailing systems of criminal justice (and related discourses of law and order), precisely because:

- the focus tends to be on "street crime," and hence it dovetails with hegemonic conceptions of "real crime" that omit from serious consideration crimes of the powerful;
- the main targets are working-class young people, which matches the social profile of the "criminal classes" as ideologically constructed; although for logistical (for example, language), technical (for example, nature of offence) and historical (for example, longstanding antagonisms with the police) reasons, Indigenous and ethnic minority young people may be underrepresented in such forums;
- there is an emphasis on making offenders "accountable" for their actions, which is another way of saying that individual choice and responsibility are at the heart of criminality;
- the concept of crime is premised upon the empirical relationship between individual actors, and hence the focus is shifted away from the social nature of criminality, while concentrating "blame" within the individual;
- the idea of social harm is conceptualized in immediate, direct, and individualistic terms and, as such, ignores the broader social processes underpinning, and patterns of, both offending and victimization;
- the emphasis on repairing harm tends to be restricted to the immediate violations and immediate victim concerns, thereby ignoring communal objectives and collective needs in framing reparation processes;
- the heart of the matter remains that of changing the offender, albeit with their involvement, rather than transforming communities and building progressive social alliances that might alter the conditions under which offending takes place.

The "political challenge" of restorative justice too often basically becomes, then, a policy dispute, a disagreement over the terms under which the criminal justice system deals with working-class offenders. For if the agenda does not include social transformation, political mobilization, and consciousness-raising, then what is "radical" about an approach that attempts to make peace within communities and families but leaves untouched the hard questions of social injustice and social inequality? This dilemma is one that Indigenous people know well (see Blagg 1997, 1998).

Differences in perspective over the purposes of restorative justice are manifest in analyses that make distinctions between "restorative justice" and "community justice" (Crawford and Clear 2001), between "restorative justice" and "restorative social justice" (White 2003), and between "governmentalist" and "communitarian" types of restorative justice programs (Woolford and Ratner 2003). In each case, the point of distinction lies in the containment of restorative justice within criminal justice rationales and mandates, or its expansion

> The heart of the matter is changing the offender rather than building progressive social alliances that might alter the conditions under which offending takes place.

to include matters of social justice and transformative potentials. To take an example, most discussions of restorative justice tend to concentrate on specific cases within existing criminal justice systems, and to evaluate practice in relation to traditional criminal justice objectives (such as reducing juvenile reoffending). Conversely, "community empowerment," which connotes a desire to intervene and transform community relations, does not feature strongly in some of the more popular restorative-justice models, such as juvenile conferencing (see Bazemore 1997).

Even when advocates of the approach do raise issues of social justice, they find difficulties translating these problems into practical program and policy prescriptions within the confines of existing state apparatuses. Often, when advocates of change buy into program-based, policy-oriented approaches to issues of crime, they will also buy into the logic of crime control rather than struggles for social justice. The approach assumes the existence of a particular "crime problem" to be dealt with, thereby accepting that working to find the best way to manage working-class offenders, for instance, is the primary object of analysis and action.

Responding to juvenile crime through restorative justice does not necessarily have to be premised upon controlling working-class youth, but there are dangers in any intervention that targets specific types of offenders, and specific types of offences, if these in turn are socially constructed by the dominant ideologies and institutional regimes. Intervention in the lives of working-class young people can offer a range of developmental and political possibilities. In this case the rationale for positive interventions must be clearly distinguished from the logic of "crime control" that emphasizes working-class deviancy in lieu of approaches that emphasize social empowerment and community development objectives.

It is from the grassroots up that significant change is most likely to occur when it comes to realizing the possibilities offered by restorative justice. For example, in Edmonton, the Youth Restorative Action Project (YRAP) has emerged in counterpoint to the usual adult-dominated, highly controlled and ultimately conservative operationalization of juvenile conferencing (Hogeveen 2006). Starting from the premise that "community" also includes young people themselves, the YRAP has challenged both the participatory elements of standard restorative-justice forums (by engaging youth in the decision-making processes directly) and the purposive elements of standard restorative-justice forums (by mobilizing discussions and resources around social justice issues). In their first case, for instance, the YRAP dealt with an incident involving a racially provoked knife attack by an Asian youth. The case was sent to the YRAP for sentencing recommendations, a process that involved participation by a committee of racially diverse young people, some of whom had experienced racism in the past. This particular "conference" was held in a creative space for young people (a place of art and music activities). While understanding the sense of victimhood on the part of the offender, the YRAP group made it clear that violence was not justified. They then probed the young offender about how he could have more positively handled the situation. In the end, the "sanction" agreed upon was that the offender produce a statement on the negative elements of racism, through an audio or visual project using the local recording facilities. The result was a hip-hop song — penned, produced. and performed by the young offender (Hogeveen 2006: 60–61). Such creativity in dealing with offending behaviour, and explicit acknowledgement of the social context within which offences are committed, stemmed from the experiences of the young members of YRAP as *young people*. Furthermore, a commitment to social justice — arising from first hand experience of marginalization and social inequality — ensures that they are emboldened to act without the cultural and bureaucratic baggage of conventional justice systems.

There is a sense in which the basic principles and practices of restorative justice can be thought of as prefiguring the changes required for creating a just and equal society (see Walgrave and Bazemore 1999). Any response intended to fix the crime problem will necessarily be limited insofar as it does not address the class (and racist) nature of law and order politics. An appreciation of the class politics ingrained in the law-and-order debate opens the door to transitional interventions, which are expressly meant to challenge and place pressure on existing institutions and thereby to raise political consciousness. Such interventions can also assist communities in mobilizing around themes of democracy, public accountability, and collective interests. But for this to occur, we need to see restorative justice not as an answer to the crime problem but as a means of subverting the existing system. The key challenge, therefore, is how to engage in "restorative social justice" (White 2003) through the twin processes of subversion and transitional activity.

Theoretically, and in selective practical circumstances, restorative justice may prove effective in providing offenders with greater developmental possibilities and in ensuring greater victim and community satisfaction and engagement in criminal justice matters. At an experiential level, it offers constructive and positive outcomes and possibilities for individuals brought into contact with the criminal justice system — especially compared with retributive and rehabilitation approaches.

But at the same time such interventions still do not address systemic problems of justice, for several reasons. They tend to deal predominantly with offenders from working-class backgrounds (including Indigenous and ethnic minority people), thus reflecting the class biases in definitions of social harm and crime, and basing responses on these biases. In so doing, they reinforce the ideological role of law and order discourse in forging a conservative cross-class consensus about the nature of social problems. The reinforcement of this discourse also unwittingly enhances the legitimacy of coercive state intervention in the lives of working-class people.

From a class perspective, therefore, restorative justice also effectively reinforces mainstream approaches to crime, thereby undercutting alternative forms of class struggle directed at addressing poverty, state violence, and systemic abuse of human rights. At a social-structural level, it confirms the role of "crime" as the central problem, neglecting or avoiding entirely the roles of class division and social inequality. As indicated above, however, restorative justice also opens up space for consideration of wider social justice considerations, space that needs to be capitalized on if structural issues are to be addressed.

Strategic Directions: Challenging the Logic of the System

If restorative justice is to address structural issues of social inequality, its advocates or practitioners will need to consider a number of strategic matters related to political campaigns and offender interventions.

Political Campaigns around Crime and Justice

- *Shifting the focus:* constituting restorative justice as a project explicitly informed by notions of social justice, and involving political struggles to extend democratic participation, redistribute communal resources, and enhance social rights. Politically, the emphasis should be on notions of solidarity and collective problems rather than individualism and individual responsibility.

- *Making demands for social justice as opposed to criminal justice:* politicizing criminal justice by contrasting the goal of jobs, not jail; by offering compensation to disadvantaged and oppressed communities rather than incarcerating their members; by exposing criminal justice responses to poverty and marginalization and contrasting those mainstream approaches with proactive social development measures. Noneconomic crimes involving violence, racist vilification, and, for instance, attacks on gay men and lesbians represent the alienations, frustration, and cultural dislocations of a socially divided society, and they demand political responses and campaigns.

- *Recasting "crime" problems:* contrasting the extensive harms of capitalist criminality with the lesser offences of working-class criminality. Key demands can include the decriminalization of most street offences and a minimalist intervention in dealing with members of working-class communities, especially young people (given that the most serious juvenile crimes are committed by a small minority of young people). Communities can also be mobilized to deal with issues of corporate malpractice and exploitation.

- *Supporting the principle of self-determination:* backing the cause of self-determination in the case of Indigenous people, as well as pushing for greater public participation in addressing issues of communal health and well-being. Key demands can include social compensation for inadequate housing, high levels of unemployment, poor health and educational services, and inadequate welfare supports, coupled with greater direct say in the provision and management of services. The demands also include greater control over, and public accountability in relation to, police services and private security guards.

Offender Interventions

- *Promoting community notions of harm:* viewing "harm" as a community phenomenon requiring community input, with clear conceptions of class, gender, Indigenous, and ethnic minority needs and interests. The repairing of harm needs to be reconceptualized as a social, rather than individual, goal and as a process that entails state-provided resources as well as input from specific individuals and groups.

- *Providing victim compensation:* establishing programs to help communities deal with past wrongdoings and present disadvantages; while individual victims of crime require compensation and reassurance from the community as a whole, this process does not necessarily need to focus directly on a specific offender.

- *Implementing selective targeting:* devoting intensive resources, facilities, and staffing to the most alienated, marginalized sections of the offender population as a means of compensating for class-based and racially linked inequalities and social oppression; emphasizing the development of basic social and educational competencies as a human right.

- *Establishing public accountability:* using existing forums to generate discussion and action around issues such as police powers, state sanctioned forms of violence, and the quality of public institutions. Restorative justice forums can be used as opportunities for making issues of institutional abuse and neglect, and resource disparities, matters of substantive concern.

> The issue centres not on trying to solve the problem of crime, which is exacerbated under conditions of widening social divisions, but in seeking transitional pathways towards a new society.

If restorative justice strategies are to go beyond the management and containment imperatives of the present system, they must challenge, in many different ways, the logic of that system. After all, one of the hallmarks of the development of mainstream criminal justice has been a capacity for allowing for a degree of innovative change and experimentation, as well as a diversity of approaches — so long as the foundations of the system are not undermined. In the end, any challenge to the basic inequalities of the system must be based on the forging of cross-class alliances; and restorative justice is one area in which such an alliance may be possible. But those alliances have to be constructed not on any assumptions of "crime" but on the basis of social justice ideals. The issue centres not on trying to solve the problem of crime, which is exacerbated under conditions of widening social divisions, but in seeking transitional pathways towards a new society, which necessarily involves struggles around the social divisions of the old society.

Conclusion

The coercive power of the state frames the manner in which restorative justice is applied with respect to street crime: the full weight of state violence is brought to bear upon working-class people and specific minority groups who transgress the law or who are perceived to be "deviant." They are arrested, have severe restrictions placed upon their liberty, and are made to comply with a wide range of behavioural norms and reparation tasks. For many of these offenders, the question of what is being restored will continue to be a challenge for them as well as for their families and communities. Poverty, social disorganization, oppressive social conditions, and profound marginalization and alienation are hardly conducive to a peaceful existence and communal wellbeing.

In theoretical terms, the restorative justice approach does contain the seeds for a creative and constructive response to the injustices of life as suffered by most working-class offenders. At the least, it implies a recognition that families and communities have an important role to play in trying to grapple with the causal reasons for personal offending. In one sense, while the state is the instigator of the action taken against an offender, it is the community that is given a greater scope to deal with the concrete issues surrounding victim needs, offender circumstances, and particular social contexts. In managing conflict and

> Poverty, social disorganization, oppressive social conditions, and profound marginalization and alienation are hardly conducive to a peaceful existence and communal well-being.

resolving immediate social problems, responsibility can thereby be shifted from the state in its more formal and coercive forms to friends, families, and community members. Within this context of dialogue and negotiation, personal and communal change is possible to the extent that clear social objectives become an essential part of restorative justice. Ultimately the efforts could include tackling issues of corporate wrongdoing (as manifest in specific issues such as plant closures, environmental pollution, and preventable workplace deaths), and the oppressive role of the state (as manifest in differential policing, abuse of rights, and racist targeting of alleged offender groups, for instance). Useful and appropriate responses to social harm can also apply to conventional forms of street crime.

For instance, attempts to deal with specific instances of personal violence, group conflicts, and property damage need not ignore the collective nature of much youth offending (with the influence of peer-group behaviour), or the context of such offending (the availability of neighbourhood resources, or unemployment). If street violence is the problem, why not recruit young people who best know the streets to take part in making them safe? The "troublemakers" can also be the "peacemakers." Shortly after the Los Angeles riots in the early 1990s, for example, the Bloods and the Crips (perhaps the most notorious youth gangs in the United States) prepared a joint proposal for rejuvenating their neighbourhoods. Among the recommendations was the idea of creating a community-based buddy system that would involve former gang members, who would receive training and then work side by side with the L.A. police to help make the local neighbourhoods safe and secure (Lusane 1992). That case illustrates the possibility of involving even the most violent and alienated young people in building creative and alternative ways of expressing solidarity and co-operation. It also demonstrates a consciousness of the importance of building strong community bonds and expanding local social infrastructures as a means of addressing the conditions that give rise to individual and group offending as well as conflict with authority figures such as the police.

> Young offenders can become part of an inclusive strategy designed to forge a sense of common purpose, communal security, and local neighbourhood democracy.

Young offenders can become part of an inclusive strategy designed to forge a sense of common purpose, communal security, and local neighbourhood democracy. Restorative social justice is precisely about the integration of class agendas and social action in a manner that involves collectivities, not simply individuals. Community action can and ought to be built around pertinent social justice-based themes, such as employment, environmental issues, and oppressive policing practices. Therein lies the hope, and the potential, of restorative social justice.

DISCUSSION QUESTIONS

1. What are the main differences between retributive, rehabilitative, and restorative approaches to criminal justice?

2. What are the different practical ways in which restorative justice can be expressed?

3. Which groups are the main targets of criminal justice intervention, and why is this the case?

4. How is "law-and-order" ideology and practice linked to social inequality?

5. What are some ways of linking community-building and a restorative justice response to juvenile offending?

GLOSSARY OF TERMS

Balanced Restorative: a form of intervention in which victims are afforded services and opportunities for involvement and input, and where there is an assessment of the offender from the point of view of ensuring community safety, allowing for offender accountability for their actions, and enhancing the competency development of the offender while they are in the criminal justice system.

Circle Sentencing or Peacemaking Circles: a form of intervention that involves forming a circle of concerned people so that consensus decisions can be made on an appropriate disposition or outcome that addresses the concerns of all parties.

Family Group Conferencing: a form of intervention in which affected community members are encouraged to participate, including and especially the friends and family of the victims and offenders, as well as justice officials, in order to discuss how the crime has affected the various parties, and to decide, as a group, how the harm may be repaired by the offender.

Law-and-Order Politics: a political orientation in which it is assumed that crime is getting worse, that dangerous people and groups are totally to blame for the crime problem, that street crime is out of control, and that the state must get tough on crime through extensive use of coercive policing and harsh punishments.

Rehabilitative Approach: an approach to criminal justice that places great emphasis on the background and circumstances of the offender; crime is seen in terms of factors or forces beyond the immediate control of the offender, and responses to crime are based upon doing something for offenders by attending to their welfare, medical, and educational needs.

Restorative Justice: an approach to criminal matters that places great emphasis on the social nature of harm; crime is seen in terms of the violation of people and relationships, and responses to harm involve something being done by offenders, and by victims and the community, that will promote repair, reconciliation, and reassurance.

Retributive Justice: an approach to criminal justice that places great emphasis on the offence; crime is seen in terms of the personal choices and responsibility of individuals, and responses to crime involve doing something to the offender in the form of punishment and the meting out of just deserts.

Social Justice: a political agenda focused on the extension of democratic participation and public accountability, the redistribution of societal resources as a means of dealing with poverty and inequality, and the enhancement of social rights to health, welfare, employment, a safe and clean environment, and education.

Victim–Offender Mediation: a form of intervention in which victims and offenders meet in a safe and structured setting to discuss the nature of the harm committed, under the guidance of a trained mediator, and where the offender is to provide assistance to the victim in an agreed upon manner.

SUGGESTED READINGS

Braithwaite, J. 1999. "Restorative Justice: Assessing Optimistic and Pessimistic Accounts." In M. Tonry (ed.), *Crime and Justice: A Review of Research*, Volume 25. Chicago: University of Chicago Press.

Crawford, A., and T. Clear. 2001. "Community Justice: Transforming Communities through Restorative Justice?" In G. Bazemore and M. Schift (eds.), *Restorative Community Justice*. Cincinnati: Anderson Publishing.

Daly, K. 2002. "Restorative Justice: The Real Story." *Punishment and Society* 4, 1: 55–79.

Hogeveen, B. 2006. "Unsettling Youth Justice and Cultural Norms: The Youth Restorative Action Project." *Journal of Youth Studies* 9, 1: 47–66.

Walgrave, L. 1999. "Community Service as a Cornerstone of a Systemic Restorative Response to (Juvenile) Crime." In G. Bazemore and L. Walgrave (eds.), *Restorative Juvenile Justice: Repairing the Harm of Youth Crime*. Monsey, NY: Criminal Justice Press.

White, R. 2003. "Communities, Conferences and Restorative Social Justice." *Criminal Justice* 3, 2: 139–60.

Woolford, A., and R. Ratner. 2003. "Nomadic Justice? Restorative Justice on the Margins of Law." *Social Justice* 30, 1: 177–94.

REFERENCES

Acorn, A. 2004. *Compulsory Compassion: A Critique of Restorative Justice*. Vancouver: UBC Press.

Bazemore, G. 1991. "Beyond Punishment, Surveillance and Traditional Treatment: Themes for a New Mission in U.S. Juvenile Justice." In J. Hackler (ed.), *Official Responses to Problem Juveniles: Some International Reflections*. Onati, Spain: Onati International Institute for the Sociology of Law.

_____. 1997. "The 'Community' in Community Justice: Issues, Themes, and Questions for the new Neighbourhood Sanctioning Models." *The Justice System Journal* 19, 2: 193–227.

Bazemore, G., and M. Umbreit. 1995. "Rethinking the Sanctioning Function in Juvenile Court: Retributive or Restorative Responses to Youth Crime." *Crime & Delinquency* 41, 3: 296–316.

Bazemore, G., and L. Walgrave (eds.). 1999a. *Restorative Juvenile Justice: Repairing the Harm of Youth Crime*. Monsey, NY: Criminal Justice Press.

Bazemore, G., and L. Walgrave. 1999b. "Restorative Juvenile Justice: In Search of Fundamentals and an Outline for Systemic Reform." In G. Bazemore and L. Walgrave (eds.), *Restorative Juvenile Justice: Repairing the Harm of Youth Crime*. Monsey, NY: Criminal Justice Press.

Beck, U., and E. Beck-Gernsheim. 2001. *Individualization*. London: Sage.

Bilchik, S. 1998. *Guide for Implementing the Balanced and Restorative Justice Model*. Washington, DC: Office of Juvenile Justice and Delinquency Prevention.

Blagg, H. 1997. "A Just Measure of Shame?" *The British Journal of Criminology* 37, 4: 481–501.

_____. 1998. "Restorative Visions and Restorative Justice Practices: Conferencing, Ceremony and Reconciliation in Australia." *Current Issues in Criminal Justice* 10, 1: 5–14.

Braithwaite, J. 1989. *Crime, Shame and Reintegration*. Cambridge: Cambridge University Press.

_____. 1999. "Restorative Justice: Assessing Optimistic and Pessimistic Accounts." In M. Tonry (ed.), *Crime and Justice: A Review of Research*, Volume 25. Chicago: University of Chicago Press.

Braithwaite, J., and P. Pettit. 1990. *Not Just Desserts: A Republican Theory of Criminal Justice*. Oxford: Clarendon Press.

Chan, J. (ed.). 2005. *Reshaping Juvenile Justice: The NSW Young Offenders Act 1997*. Sydney: Sydney Institute of Criminology, University of Sydney.

Church Council on Justice and Corrections. 1996. *Satisfying Justice: Safe Community Options that Attempt to Repair Harm from Crime and Reduce the Use or Length of Imprisonment*. Ottawa: Church Council on Justice and Corrections.

Crawford, A., and T. Clear. 2001. "Community Justice: Transforming Communities through Restorative Justice?" In G. Bazemore and M. Schift (eds.), *Restorative Community Justice*. Cincinnati: Anderson Publishing.

Cunneen, C. 1997. "Community Conferencing and the Fiction of Indigenous Control." *The Australian and New Zealand Journal of Criminology* 30, 3: 292–312.

Cunneen, C., and R. White. 2002. *Juvenile Justice: Youth and Crime in Australia*. Melbourne: Oxford University Press.

Daly, K. 2000. "Restorative Justice in Diverse and Unequal Societies." *Law in Context* 17, 1: 167–90.

_____. 2002. "Restorative Justice: the Real Story." *Punishment and Society* 4, 1: 55–79.

Daly, K., and R. Immarigeon. 1998. "The Past, Present and Future of Restorative Justice: Some Critical Reflections." *Contemporary Justice Review* 1, 1: 22–45.

Feeley, M., and J. Simon. 1994. "Actuarial Justice: The Emerging New Criminal Law." In D. Nelken (ed.), *The Futures of Criminology*. London: Sage.

Harding, R., and R. Maller. 1997. "An Improved Methodology for Analyzing Age-Arrest Profiles: Application to a Western Australian Offender Population." *Journal of Quantitative Criminology* 13, 4: 349–72.

Hogeveen, B. 2006 "Unsettling Youth Justice and Cultural Norms: The Youth Restorative Action Project." *Journal of Youth Studies* 9, 1: 47–66.

Hudson, J., A. Morris, G. Maxwell, and B. Galaway (eds.). 1996. *Family Group Conferences: Perspectives on Policy and Practice*. Sydney: Federation Press.

Lusane, C. 1992. "Gang-banging and Budget-writing." *Crossroads* June 5.

Maxwell, G., and A Morris. 1994. "The New Zealand Model of Family Group Conferences." In C. Alder and J. Wundersiz (eds.), *Family Conferencing and Juvenile Justice*. Canberra: Australian Institute of Criminology.

Morris, A., and G. Maxwell. 2003. "Restorative Justice in New Zealand." In A. von Hirsch, J. Roberts, A. Bottoms, K. Roach, and M. Schiff (eds.), *Restorative Justice and Criminal Justice: Competing or Reconcilable Paradigms?* Oxford: Hart.

Muncie, J. 2002. "Policy Transfers and What Works: Some Reflections on Comparative Youth Justice." *Youth Justice* 1, 3: 27–35.

O'Malley, P. 1996. "Post-Social Criminologies: Some Implications of Current Political Trends for Criminological Theory and Practice." *Current Issues in Criminal Justice* 8, 1: 26–38.

Stuart, B. 1997. *Building Community Justice Partnerships: Community Peacemaking Circles*. Ottawa: Aboriginal Justice Section, Department of Justice of Canada.

Walgrave, L. 1999. "Community Service as a Cornerstone of a Systemic Restorative Response to (Juvenile) Crime." In G. Bazemore and L. Walgrave (eds.), *Restorative Juvenile Justice: Repairing the Harm of Youth Crime*. Monsey, NY: Criminal Justice Press.

Walgrave, L., and G. Bazemore. 1999. "Reflections on the Future of Restorative Justice for Juveniles." In G. Bazemore and L. Walgrave (eds.), *Restorative Juvenile Justice: Repairing the Harm of Youth Crime*. Monsey, NY: Criminal Justice Press.

Wemmers, Jo-Anne and Marisa Canuto. 2002. "Victims' Experiences with Expectations and Perceptions of Restorative Justice: A Critical Review of the Literature." Ottawa: Policy Centre for Victim Issues; Research and Statistics Division. Department of Justice Canada, March.

White, R. 2003. "Communities, Conferences and Restorative Social Justice." *Criminal Justice* 3, 2: 139–60.

White, R., and F. Haines. 2004. *Crime and Criminology*, Third edition. Melbourne: Oxford University Press.

White, R., and J. Wyn. 2004. *Youth and Society*. Melbourne: Oxford University Press.

Woolford, A., and R. Ratner. 2003. "Nomadic Justice? Restorative Justice on the Margins of Law." *Social Justice* 30, 1: 177–94.

Zehr, H. 1990. *Changing Lens: A New Focus for Crime and Justice*. Scottdale, PA: Herald Press.

Zehr, H., and H. Mika. 1998. "Fundamental Concepts of Restorative Justice." *Contemporary Justice Review* 1, 1: 47–56.

21

A Letter from Saskatoon Youth Court

Kearney Healy

KEY FACTS

> Unemployment among youth worldwide is rising and at an all time high.

> Regina Police Chief Cal Johnson stated that the living conditions of Aboriginal people in Regina (poverty, substance abuse, unemployment, and dysfunction within families) are directly connected to Regina's position as the leader for break and enter offences.

> Seventy-five percent of youth in prison have some form of disability (Green and Healy 2003).

> Chief Judge Barry Stuart of the Yukon Territorial Court states that at least half of the youth in custody are mentally challenged from fetal alcohol effects and early life trauma, and that the dangers of incarcerating these youth "cannot be overstated."

> Massachusetts Department of Youth Services closed down maximum-security facilities for youth inmates in 1969 and introduced community homes, prevention programs, and education and work opportunities. The recidivism rates for youth dropped dramatically.

> Family Group Conferencing was introduced in New Zealand in 1989 in response to high incarceration rates. Between 1989 and 1995 the number of youth incarcerated dropped by 80 percent, with no rise in detected youth offending.

> Youth offenders who are steered away from custody and complete conditions within restorative circles are "rarely seen by the justice system again."

Sources: Schissel 2006; Green and Healy 2003; Mallea 1999.

Dear fellow students of our society:

I am writing this letter, after many years of daily observation, to tell you that in Saskatoon it seems the Emperor is naked. Punishment does not end youth crime. It may actually increase it.

Maybe these things are only true of Saskatoon, and other communities are different. Perhaps in other communities punishment diminishes crime. Let me tell you about youth in Saskatoon, and you judge if this applies to your community.

We all know that virtually everyone commits crimes at some point in their lives. As I write this I'm in youth court. Perhaps I'm using a pen provided by my employer, and if I'm using it outside my employment without permission, that would be theft under Canada's Criminal Code. If I am doing that and it can be proved beyond a reasonable doubt, I can be found guilty. If I am guilty and you are careless about my guilt, perhaps you are guilty of possession of stolen property, because without the ink I can't argue these ideas.

So what is the difference between ourselves (those who think about our civilization and seek out others who are serious about understanding our civilization) and those who are punished for their crimes? Generally, the ordinary person in Saskatoon, when presented with this question, will try to describe crime either in terms of someone like themselves (When I was young, or when we were young, my father would...) or someone very unlike themselves (I don't understand how a person could get to that point where they could...). These seem like reasonable starting points, so perhaps we could look at youth crime and our response from these two perspectives.

> Generally the ordinary person in Saskatoon, when presented with this question, will try to describe crime either in terms of someone like themselves or someone very unlike themselves.

Let's look at ourselves. Since we have all committed at least one crime in the past, let's, for the moment, call ourselves criminals. While no doubt a few among us might have been charged and convicted of a criminal offence, most of us weren't caught. Surely, as thinkers serious about our civilization and as honest, fearless students, we can see there is essentially no difference between us in this regard. (Unless, of course, we still believe that punishment for crime improves us, which means we must admit that those of us who were caught and punished for our crimes are better people than we who were not caught.)

> While no doubt a few among us might have been charged and convicted of a criminal offence, most of us weren't caught.

So the question becomes the difference between us and those in prison, and there is no doubt that there are important differences. Average Saskatoonians would object that the crimes they committed were minor, related to specific circumstances, and youthful excesses, and in any case they never (or rarely) break the law anymore because they don't like to hurt people, or they value our community, or for some other moral reason. Many theorists would argue with all these points, but could we, for the sake of our exploration, accept that the average Saskatoonian is mostly right, and let the theorists, who need to leave us at this point, go?

The average Saskatoonian would argue that if there were no chance of getting caught, well, then they would commit lots more crimes. There's a difference, of course, between being caught and being punished, but the essence of the objection should be examined, at least, to understand ourselves. I assume that you are like me: I object to the notion that all that stops me from crime is that I'll be punished. In fact, I constantly try to change my behaviour so that my eccentricities are less painful for others, and so that whatever I have to offer others is made available to them, whether it's pounding nails to help house those without a home or going to meetings to try to develop a community strategy to end homelessness. These are parts of the same reason we don't commit crimes that would injure our community. You too probably feel this way, or I suspect you wouldn't be reading this far.

Let's assume we are different from the average Saskatoonian because our interests are in this field as opposed to, say, curling, or snowmobiling, or gardening, whatever. Ah, but that's the problem, you may say. Just because you can gather together a group of people who are driven, for whatever personal reasons, to consider society and crime; and just because generally people like us do like to modify our behaviours so that our relationships, from familial to social, constantly move forward to greater harmony, that doesn't mean everyone else feels that way. Well, I don't know about your community, but in Saskatoon volunteerism is a way of life across all cultural barriers. Charities are very alive and well. The spirit of co-operation is strong. Curlers, snowmobilers, and gardeners also work towards a more peaceful community.

So, once again, why don't we commit more crimes? Surely punishment is more likely to be the deterrent than the reliance on something so ephemeral and uncertain as… as… alms-giving? But is punishment the disincentive? I know it's our habit to think so, and I rely on habits to organize my life. My biggest victories are creating more effective habits. I would guess that you do that too. I read detective fiction, which has as its implicit belief that criminals will always get caught (Wile E. Coyote never gets the Road Runner, Tom never catches Jerry) because the criminals are not very smart (like Wile E. Coyote, like Tom, they never learn from their mistakes). Youth crime in Saskatoon fits into the Wile E. Coyote category. It's amazing how poorly thought out it is.

Are we unable to learn from our mistakes?

But let us ask ourselves, does this describe us? Are we unable to learn from our mistakes? Is the average Saskatoonian able to learn from his or her mistakes? Surely that does not describe us. Surely we would be quite capable of committing crimes to our benefit, safe in the knowledge that it's as likely that we would be struck by lightning as that we would be caught. Crime is such a broad category that perhaps some of us are still committing crimes now, and we feel quite safe. If we examine the closed-custody facilities and the jails of Saskatoon and find mainly the poorly educated and almost never the reasonably well-educated, resourceful, well-adjusted, thinking person, then we know that some force other than punishment keeps us criminals at bay. Since we could outthink and outplan those who would catch us (and some of us possibly still do), then there must be something else that determines our actions. Crime can include my use of this pen, but we are quite capable of stretching our tale.

Just a minute, you might say — what force? Could we hold that question until we look at the second half of the average Saskatoonian's defence of the theorists who may have already put this down? The average Saskatoonian said, "I don't understand how someone could do something so terrible." Note the need to underscore the difference that implies a divide, a gap, in social or moral understanding. Let us criminals take a walk down to the closed-custody facility for youth in Saskatoon, called Kilburn Hall. We won't be staying long, not overnight, probably not even for a meal. That's the first thing we should notice. We're not going to live there. In Saskatoon, the next thing you'd notice is that all those who have to stay are very young (this is a youth facility) and that they are almost all of Aboriginal descent. Some days, many days, they all are of Aboriginal descent.

We find only the poorly educated and almost never the reasonably well-educated, resourceful, well-adjusted, thinking person, then we know that some force other than punishment keeps us criminals at bay.

Many people in Saskatoon, nurses in hospitals, for example, will tell you that they can predict the children who will have trouble in school and are likely to end up in youth facilities. Others, like schoolteachers of the early grades will tell you that they have similar powers. They probably do. When you speak to these children about their early childhoods, or when you speak to those involved in their early lives, you are struck by the trauma you'll find. You'll hear of children alone, children abused, children huddled while violence rages around them, constant moving, constant racism, constant failing in school.

Indeed, if you speak to the guards either here at the facility or in the lock-up behind youth court, many of them will say it's the parents who belong in jail, not these kids. That, of course, is the age-old chicken-and-egg problem, not the least of which is the fourteen-year-old in closed custody who is pregnant and wants to keep her baby. That this is true is no revelation; other pages in this book speak eloquently of these facts. The purpose of this letter is to say that in Saskatoon, in this closed facility, in Kilburn, the

Emperor Punishment has no clothes.

So I'm noticing that you are looking a little shaken by these kids. That's okay. Everyone feels bad. What's that? You say if they quit committing crimes their lives could get better. The person next to you argues that this place is *better* for a lot of these kids. Maybe you're both sort of right, maybe a little wrong. Let's stop for a moment and ask why our community picks this place, jail, as an answer to crime. But, someone says, don't crime and punishment go together? Everybody says so. Why, just the other day Saskatoon's newspaper quoted Osama bin Laden; he wanted the Danish cartoonists turned over to him for "trial and punishment." Clearly most people agree that crime and punishment belong together. Who needs to look behind that formula? Wouldn't we be better off without trials and lawyers so that punishment became more automatic? Maybe we could have mandatory sentences to make sure criminals got enough punishment.

Enough punishment to do what? Well, the theory is that people are kind of like bookkeepers. A person sits in their office or some quiet place and calculate something like this. If I commit such-and-such a crime, the chances of getting caught are x, the benefit to me of committing a crime is y, and the benefit of getting caught is z, so clearly x plus z is less than y, so I benefit in doing crime. Solution? Make x, your chance of being caught, and more importantly z, the cost of crime, more expensive; i.e., harsher punishment. And what's the gold standard in punishment? Jail, of course. It is sometimes called the economic model of crime response. All you do is make crime too painful (i.e., expensive) for there to be any benefit.

So you know the theory, but you still feel bad for these kids. You wonder why: I think it is because you have a good heart and you suspect that these kids don't have such a clear balance sheet. They've already experienced so much pain from babyhood on. Maybe, you think, it's time to work on the happy, successful side of the balance sheet. Well you're not alone in thinking like that.

This facility's workers over a period of time took a bold step. They questioned every youth in the facility as to his or her position in school. They discovered that not one child in Saskatoon's closed-custody facility had been in school when they were arrested. Furthermore, they discovered that before being arrested these children, or youth, if you will, had not been in school for an average of two years. The average age was approximately fifteen.

You'll notice that the conversations among the young people will often veer to their family's failures (a good disclosure, think the guards and therapists), the bad teachers, bad neighbours, strangers, abusive common-law partners to their mothers. They're encouraged to get it out. Alone they come to the obvious conclusion: they can only rely on each other day after day. And who is to say they're wrong?

We can leave youth jail now — oh, just a minute! Here's worker who is doing a risk assessment on these youth. Risk assessments, in Saskatchewan, are examinations of such things as a kids' contact with police, their school experience, their family, how they spend their leisure time, who their friends are and what contact their friends have with criminal justice, whether they have an alcohol or drug problem, whether their attitudes and opinions are consistent with those of people who commit crimes. Some of you may think that marginalized kids would do badly on these scores, partly because of lack of money and a stable residence. I agree, but the worker explains to us that research shows that the children of the very rich seem to commit as many crimes per capita as do the children of the very poor but that their tests don't reflect poverty and racism. You have a question. How many children of the very rich are here in this youth jail? None. When was the last time such a youth was here? No one can remember. How many of these youth are children of the very poor? Almost all. Would it be fair to guess that maybe the worse criminals, the children of the very rich, are dealt with in a different way? A way that involves improving their life circumstances? Not in a financial way, perhaps, but in the sense that they are taught how to see the connection between their personal success and their community's success?

So what does this mean? Remember the average Saskatoonian said, "I don't know how someone could do something like that." And clearly many Saskatoonians, and you too no doubt see a direction here and that an objection—or better yet, an observation — is in order. It is correct to say that there are children who grow up in similar circumstances who don't commit terrible and hurtful acts, and therefore can this background ever be an excuse? I suppose it's possible, but after twenty years I can't say that any situation comes to mind. So it's rarely an excuse. The average Saskatoonian comes to my aid and says that they can see, though, that this helps to explain what's going on: a fair comment, so let's follow down that path and see where it takes us.

One wonders why these children/youth are not in school (nor do they show great educational improvement when they graduate to the adult criminal justice system; jails and prisons are notorious for the low educational levels of their inmates). Isn't a necessary function of our society to educate? If all our children (or even many of our children) decided not to go to school anymore, ever, wouldn't that be a crisis? Is it not true that my responsibility to my children, to my city, to my civilization, ends with making education available for my fourteen-year-old child? I work with my partner to make sure my child goes to school. Given the opportunity to miss school on any given day, how many of our children would opt out? And if given the opportunity day after day, how long would it take before they would start to fall behind? Then what? Stay home? I am not talking about the failures of some parents here. I'm saying as a civilization, as a citizen of Saskatoon, we have the responsibility to see to this education; it's in our best interests to do so.

So why are these youth in Kilburn not in school? And what does that have to do with punishment for crimes (or the price of tea in China, for that matter)? Remember that we've been asked, "How could someone get like that?" How could someone get to the point where at fifteen years of age they've given up on entering the job market? Hands up all of you who think that in the twenty-first century, Grade 7, 8, 9, or 10 is enough education to ensure a reasonable and comfortable living. And guess what? Not one hand went up in Kilburn Hall. Not one guard, not one youth, raised their hand.

In Saskatoon I'm asked by teachers to speak to their children about the YCJA. I ask: How many of you can imagine yourselves at, say, thirty years old, deciding that you'd like to buy a new car. I know it's better that you walk, or rollerblade, or skateboard, bike, or bus it, but you decide, for whatever reason, that you'd like to buy a new car. You've decided you'll get a job, if you don't already have one, or if you already have a job you'll be careful with spending and you'll try and save at least a down payment. You then go to the car lot, pick one out, get a loan for the rest, and drive away when you're finished. Right? In middle-class classrooms, everyone says yes. The kids in Kilburn, they all say no.

We're talking about why punishment doesn't work here. We're talking about why it may, and probably does, make it worse. You see, the children/youth in Kilburn don't believe that they have a future in the mainstream society; their only future is with each other. And they don't want to be a Wile E. Coyote or a Tom, oh no, and so their future depends on ever more effective criminality. And so, you see, the difference between us criminals and those criminals is that they are marginalized and have no hope of ending their marginalization. While we, lucky people that we are, are becoming, on the whole, ever less marginalized and as time passes ever more effective at looking after ourselves within our community.

I know all that, says the average Saskatoonian, and I must say it took you a long time to get there, but so what? Crimes must be punished, or else there'll be more. We can't reward criminal behaviour; that'll only encourage more. We must discourage it. Ah yes, but what discourages crime? Is it the fear of punishment that keeps us from staying awake all night with a gun, waiting for the graffiti artist who painted our building or who painted some other building, you know, just to scare him or her? Really, the chance of getting caught can be extremely small.

No, it's many reasons. Moral reasons are very important, but for a moment let's look at another reason. Who really wants to change their life that much? In this extreme example you have to get a gun and bullets so that it can't be traced back to you. Even the research in how to do such a thing can't be traced back to you.

> Who really wants to change their life that much?

Let's recap—everyone commits crimes, so we can't divide ourselves simply on that basis. We aren't deterred from crime because of punishment alone, because we are quite capable of committing crimes and never being caught. We don't commit crimes because we want to live a better life tomorrow than today, if at all possible. Youth who are in custody for their crimes are different from the rest of us in that not only do they normally come from terrible circumstances, but they've also given up on their future, as evidenced by not going to school. So what are the punishment fans not telling us?

I would suggest, then, to my ordinary Saskatoon friend that the answer seems clear. I would say that each young person who is in custody for her or his crimes is there because of a path, so to speak, that they are on. That path is one of growing discouragement; the people there are losing hope. They are losing hope that they will be able to control their lives and get the benefits of being a well-accepted member of our society. The answer, then, I would suggest, includes, as a basic, whatever attention is necessary to show these young people how to succeed at being respected members of our community on terms acceptable to the youth.

> The answer, then, I would suggest, includes, as a basic, whatever attention is necessary to show these young people how to succeed at being respected members of our community on terms acceptable to the youth.

That's utopian, and it's not clear, my friend says. It's expensive, it's impossible, and it takes criminals and rewards them, for crying out loud. Besides, it's likely to cause more crime because it treats criminals too well.

Let's look at the last objection first. As a parent, when I struggle with my children I use the technique of catching them when they're good. That is, I try to keep separate their mistakes (bad behaviour, if you will) and their successes. The youth who hurt others need to know that they have hurt others. They need to be encouraged to react in a positive way to the harm they have caused. It is always the moral position to correct the harms we inflict. It is meant to be an expression of dignity to acknowledge mistakes and to attempt to correct them. The tailors who persuaded the emperor to try these fine new clothes have tried to convince us that the acceptance of guilt is to allow ourselves to be degraded. You must sentence me to the maximum possible sentence, said Mahatma Gandhi to his judge, because I am unrepentant and I believe in an independent India. In effect, Gandhi reversed the process. Unless they could recognize their mistake (in denying India its freedom) and correct it, they must degrade him, but Gandhi turned their attempt at degradation into a moral victory. These kids need moral victories: look at their histories.

The response to crime is one thing; the response to marginalized youth is another. The response to crime, while it must be a separate process, must never allow itself to interfere with the process of persuading, in this case marginalized youth, not to hurt others — or to prevent crime, if you wish to put it that way. The presence in Kilburn Hall of almost always marginalized youth tells us we have failed. We accepted the tailors' arguments; we responded to the crime; we did not care to use our enormous intellectual, financial, and community resources to reduce further harmful behaviour. In effect, we put these youth into an environment where hopelessness becomes more real. We created more crime.

Taking youth out of hopelessness and to a state of enthusiasm for their future reduces crime. Many would say, though, that post-industrial capitalism requires a constant supply of inexpensive labour and that unemployment is a part of its structure. With the decline in the power of states as a result of the globalization of market economies, arguably marginalization of significant portions of the workforce is inevitable. That in some regions unemployment is coincidental with race is unfortunate and certainly not an intended result. Wow. How can someone in Saskatoon keep all that in mind?

In Saskatoon we estimate that there are about one thousand children from Grade 1 to Grade 11, inclusive, who aren't in school. They've given up. We've tried to estimate some of the costs of these children remaining so marginalized that their chances of successful employment diminish year by year. Let's start with a couple of crimes — home break-ins and car thefts. Now, as luck would have it, my office does the defence work for almost all those charged with these offences (the police solve about 10 to 11 percent of all the break-and-enters in Saskatoon residences). We studied the relationship between school, and B&Es and car theft. We found that virtually every one of these crimes was committed by groups of youth, and that these groups were either dominated by or consisted entirely of children who had lost their connection to school.

Of the one thousand children out of school in Saskatoon, there are some in a smaller group who do B&Es and car thefts; estimates vary from as few as fifty or eighty to as many as three hundred. A conversation with the appropriate people in the insurance industry reveals that it costs city insurance offices about $5 million to cover B&Es and car thefts committed by this small number. The custody facilities (remember they're mainly for youth who haven't been in school for two years) cost about $4 million per year in Saskatoon, or $4,000 for every youth out of school.

The provincial government gives grants to the school boards of $5,000 per youth in school. If you have one thousand youth not in school that equals $5 million not sent by the province of Saskatchewan to my city of Saskatoon. These youth, not being in school, will soon be adults not working or needing social assistance. Assuming social assistance costs of over $800 per month, or about $10,000 per year for each person, and multiply that by one thousand — it's about $10 million per year when they become adults and parents.

Youth not in school become adults not working, which means adults not purchasing from local businesses, not paying taxes, not making Saskatoon an attractive place to do business. In Saskatoon, for example, if we were to achieve a level of Aboriginal incomes from employment equal to ordinary Saskatoonian incomes, the benefit would be around $250 million per year. But as the Linn Commission on Aboriginal Justice noted, an Aboriginal male youth is more likely to go to jail than to graduate from high school. We could also look at the health costs, the value of housing, the tourism potential, whatever—the value of ending marginalization would be enormous. All that's assuming a completely amoral attitude.

Sure, sure, says my gentle Saskatoonian opponent, but before we try it here shouldn't we look elsewhere? It is being tried elsewhere, and it is succeeding. Great Britain, for example, embarked on an experiment in September 1999. The country provided special funds to each family of a child disconnected from school to figure out unique ways of ensuring reconnection. A few months later, in March 2000, it cancelled the experiment. It was clear it worked, and so it made it permanent and expanded it and cited crime reduction as one of the benefits. The Ford Foundation Quantum Opportunities Project enlisted, at random, twenty-five children from high-crime neighbourhoods in five different U.S. cities. The foundation provided them with caring, compassionate, and consistent tutors and paid them to do community work at the rate of $1 per hour (later raised to $2 per hour) from 1989 to 1994. In addition to all the other benefits that a society can expect from a better-educated youth, the arrest rate for these youth was 70 percent less than it was for others in their neighbourhood.

In Regina, a brief but brilliant experiment, the most difficult of all, involved the most marginalized youth. The youth had to go to school every day from Monday to Thursday. On Friday they became a part of a job co-op. They had a contract to valet government cars to places where the vehicles could be washed, vacuumed, given an oil change, and so on. The youth had among them amassed some five thousand convictions before they entered the experiment (indeed, most of them had an "escape lawful custody" included in their convictions). During the life of the experiment the youth committed six new offences. Somehow, the dreamer who began it, Denis Losie, persuaded them to begin a pension plan. Then the program ended. We could walk around Saskatoon. I could show you these same kids working on art, or on computers, or on their drama skills, or on repairing bicycles, or on their paddling strokes and their wilderness skills, or on their bank accounts, in schools, in homes, in groups — youth who have a community of growth, hope, and dignity are abandoning crime shamelessly.

So what I want to tell you is that we're working too hard, we're running too fast. What it is, is that we're running on a barrel—you know, the faster we run, the faster the barrel spins. What's really happening is we're taking frustrated, isolated youth with little hope and treating them to more isolation, more frustration, and giving them reasons for hopelessness. What if traditional justice and restorative justice, if punishment and rehabilitation, if shame and reintegration, if crime control and due process were all only parts of the puzzle? What if our youth criminal justice system has a basic structural flaw? Like a building or bridge that looks just great but once every couple of decades, the wrong combination of weather events, the wrong storm, comes along and the building or bridge collapses.

In Saskatoon, in Saskatchewan, we incarcerate more youth (mostly Aboriginal) per capita than anywhere else in North America. This should be enough to cause us to re-examine our assumptions. But our demographic future is that our population will increasingly be young and Aboriginal. More and more of our population will be made up of marginalized youth (as well as adults who were marginalized as youth and are still marginalized). Remember Judge Linn's note that an Aboriginal male youth in Saskatchewan had statistically a better chance of going to jail than graduating from high school.

What if the structural defect in our thinking is trying to divide the well-being of marginalized youth charged with

> We're running on a barrel — you know, the faster we run, the faster the barrel spins. What's really happening is we're taking frustrated, isolated youth with little hope and giving them reasons for hopelessness.

a crime and our social well-being? What if the structural defect is in the habit of thinking that being tough on crime means being tough on those charged? What if, with marginalized youth, being tough on them is encouraging crime? What if equality before the law is a fraud, because with marginalized youth it controverts (in the interest of being hard on offenders) their right to equality within our society? What if the addition of the concept that leading youth out of marginalization is the most effective tool for crime reduction? The price of maintaining our small slice of paradise is how we treat the weakest and poorest among us.

> What if the structural defect in our thinking is trying to divide the well-being of marginalized youth charged with a crime and our social well-being?

Not likely in my community, you say. All right, in Saskatoon we have youth committing robberies. They steal hats, sweaters, and other clothes. We have thefts, often children stealing clothes, maybe junk food snacks, sometimes fruit. Forget cars; youth are wearing other people's clothes. In Saskatoon youth are dying at an alarming rate, at least my clients are. They're sick — sometimes almost every other client has kidney disease, liver disease, Hep C, HIV or diabetes.

Every indicator we have to measure happiness, such as health, an okay place to live, friends and family doing well, having the possessions you need, having enough money to look after yourself, and, most importantly, having some sense that your life can be better—these young people we call criminals don't have it.

The study of crime has been taken over by the emperor's sycophants. They ask us to examine details, pieces of the puzzle. They say don't look up. They say don't ask why, after hundreds of years of crime and punishment, we haven't moved forward. Why must we get into our most pretentious clothes, hold ourselves a little more tensely, and pontificate that it's more complicated than connecting youth with caring, compassionate, and consistent tutors who are dedicated to making their lives better? How dare we dodge the question by saying that this is too complicated, that it requires too great a reorientation of too many government agencies, too many businesses, too big a change for lawyers, police, and judges? How dare we take refuge in hopelessness and then condemn those who live in hopelessness?

So thank you for hearing me out. I know that you're a busy person who is worried about much more than just youth crime and what it means. I hope this letter finds you in good health and that all your families, friends, and loved ones are all happy and healthy. I hope that you enjoy your studies and that you have great success. I am sure that people who know you expect great things from you and, while you'll be your own person, they will have great pride in your accomplishments. Someday you'll look back and you'll see that you made contributions to our community that give you a sense of real accomplishment. I hope your children, if you have any, grow strong and full of hope for their futures. But most of all I hope that one day we'll meet and we can laugh about the darker days, when the emperor had no clothes.

Sincerely,

Kearney Healy

DISCUSSION QUESTIONS

1. If you were to set out to create a society, what role would you give to criminal law?

2. If a society is structured so that almost all people born to a certain race (or races)

or a certain class will never be able to enjoy the full benefits of that society, can the criminal law be based on equality?

3. Assume that one of the primary purposes of criminal law is the prevention of serious harm. However, not all cases of serious harm or even death are considered to be criminal. This is true even when the deaths and injuries are caused by human interaction, even when a decision is made knowing that it could well result in deaths. How would you decide when an act is criminal and when it must be permitted?

4. In your life, do you find that the threat of punishment governs your ordinary choices? Do you think businesses should use punishment more often with their employees and customers?

5. When Erik Nielsen was the deputy prime minister (to Brian Mulroney), he was asked to examine the federal civil service to find ways of making it more efficient. He reported that, with business, the least effective method of changing behaviour in a positive way was punishment. If that is true for business, do you think that punishment is more effective with children who are poor, subjected to racism, or who come from broken homes?

GLOSSARY OF TERMS

YOA/YCJA: in Canada, youth between twelve and eighteen years old are charged as youth in the YOA. In April 2003, the *Young Offenders Act* was replaced by the *Youth Criminal Justice Act*. One of the goals of the YCJA is to reduce "the over reliance on incarceration for non-violent young persons" (from the Preamble to the YCJA).

SUGGESTED READINGS

"The Effects of Punishment on Recidivism." 2002. Public Safety and Emergency Preparedness Canada. Available at <http://publicsafety.gc.ca/res/cor/sum/cprs200205_1-en.asp> accessed July 2007.

Gabor, Thomas. *Everybody Does It!* Toronto: University of Toronto Press.

Holman, Barry, and Jason Ziedenberg. "Dangers of Detention: The Impact of Incarcerating Youth in Detention and Other Secure Facilities." Justice Policy Institute Report. Available at <http://www.justicepolicy.org/reports_jl/11-28-06_dangers/dangers_of_detention_report.pdf> accessed July 2007.

REFERENCES

Green, R.G., and K. Healy. 2003. *Tough on Kids: Rethinking Approaches to Youth Justice*. Saskatoon: Purich Publishing.

Mallea, Paula. 1999. *Getting Tough on Kids: Young Offenders and the "Law and Order Agenda."* Winnipeg: Canadian Centre for Policy Alternatives-Manitoba.

Schissel, Bernard. 2006. *Still Blaming Children: Youth Conduct and the Politics of Child Hating*. Halifax: Fernwood Publishing.

Index